A

COMMENTARY

ON THE

EPISTLE TO THE ROMANS.

BY

MOSES STUART,

LATE PROFESSOR OF SACRED LITERATURE IN THE THEOLOGICAL SEMINARY
AT ANDOVER.

EDITED AND REVISED
BY
R. D. C. ROBBINS,
PROFESSOR IN MIDDLEBURY COLLEGE.

FOURTH EDITION.

Eugene, Oregon

Wipf and Stock Publishers
199 W 8th Ave, Suite 3
Eugene, OR 97401

A Commentary on the Epistle to the Romans
By Stuart, Moses
ISBN: 1-57910-611-0
Publication date 3/9/2001
Previously published by Andover, 1862

PREFACE.

In the Preface to the second edition of this work, Professor Stuart says: "Since the publication of the first edition of this Commentary, several works have appeared, some of which are adapted to afford aid of no inconsiderable importance. New editions of Usteri's *Creed of Paul* (Lehrbegriff Pauli), with the commentaries on the Epistle to the Romans by Beneke, Glockler, Ruckert, and Reiche, have been published in Germany; and, in our own country, the Rev. A. Barnes, of Philadelphia, has also published a brief but very comprehensive and valuable work on the same epistle. All of these, with the exception of Ruckert, which has not come to hand, have been consulted by me in preparing the present edition. The work of Reiche (in two octavos) is exceedingly copious. I have been aided in some respects by his *Philology*; for his *theology* is any thing but consistent and evangelical. His book in various respects is an able one; but his method is confused, and his manner often tedious. Yet no commentator on this epistle should now choose to dispense with the use of him. I thank him sincerely for the valuable hints that he has given me, of which I have omitted no opportunity to avail myself.

The works of Beneke and Glockler are short. The first holds to the preexistence of human souls, and accounts for the present degradation of men, on the ground of sin in a previous state; the second appears to be a moderate Pantheist of the recent school, and not unfrequently exhibits a portion of their mysticism. Yet both of these writers are in the main sensible men, and appear to possess serious and evangelical feelings. I have obtained some hints from each, which I consider as of value.

From Usteri's new edition I have also taken some hints. From Mr. Barnes's work I have also derived aid; and especially have I been often cheered on my way, by finding the result of his investigations to tally so well with my own. I have altered and I hope amended, so many passages in this edition, that to specify them all is out of question. I have bestowed on it scarcely less labor than the first writing cost me. On many places, indeed I may say on all, which I have not materially altered, I have bestowed much study in order to satisfy myself that they should remain unchanged.

For myself, I am so far from being satisfied with my first efforts, that they only serve to stimulate me to new labors of investigation, in order more fully to ascertain whether they will abide a thorough scrutiny. Experience has taught me, that first views on subjects so difficult as some of those which the Epistle to the Romans discusses, are not always the safest. If there be any whose first impressions are always and only right, and who find no reason to alter and amend, they will not sympathize with these remarks; but others who, like myself, are obliged to investigate a second time, and review and amend, will enter fully into the meaning of what I say."

In the preparation of the present edition, use has been made of most of the commentaries which have appeared, for the first time, or in new improved editions, since the publication of the second edition, some of which are of much value. Ruckert, Meyer, Alford, Olshausen, De Wette, and Philippi, all have their excellences, and are occasionally referred to, especially in the foot-notes. I have, however, been careful to introduce nothing into the body of the Commentary that is at variance with the Theological or Exegetical views of Prof. Stuart. Whenever I have been led to a different view of any passage, I have either indicated it in the notes, or simply satisfied myself with giving the view of the author as it appeared in the previous edition. I have endeavored to keep in mind that my province was that of an editor merely. Besides, the desire to reduce the size of the work has prevented me from making as many additions as I should otherwise have been inclined to do.

It seemed desirable to change the Introduction more than the body of the Commentary. A considerable part of that has accordingly been re-written. Condensation, with occasional verbal alterations, has been my main object throughout the body of the work. Some of the Excursus, especially the V., have been abridged more freely, as the subjects there discussed were subsequently more fully developed by Prof. Stuart in Articles in the Biblical Repository and elsewhere.

R. D. C. ROBBINS.

MIDDLEBURY COLL., July 30, 1858.

PREFACE TO THE FIRST EDITION.

I PUBLISH to the world the result of my labors upon the Epistle to the Romans with unfeigned diffidence, and with a trembling sense of the responsibility which I incur by so doing. This epistle has been the grand arena, If I may so express myself, on which theological combatants have been contending ever since the third century, and perhaps still earlier. The turn which the apostle James has given to his discussion respecting justification, makes it probable that even in his time there were some who abused the words of Paul, in his Epistle to the Romans, concerning the doctrine of "justification by faith without the deeds of law." If so, then it would seem that there has been no period since this epistle was written, in which its meaning has not been more or less a subject of contest.

How could this be otherwise, since it discusses the highest and most difficult of all the doctrines which pertain to the Christian system? Men must be more alike in their early education, their illumination, their habits of reasoning, and their theological convictions, than they have hitherto been, and they must love God and each other better than they have ever yet done, not to differ in their interpretation of the Epistle to the Romans. It strikes at the root of all human pride and vain-glory; it aims even a deadly blow. And where a passionate attachment to these is rankling in the breast, how is it possible that this epistle should meet with a welcome reception, and the authority of its simple and obvious meaning be admitted? Even where the remains of such an attachment are still lurking within, and only now and then developing themselves, because the heart is in some measure unsanctified, there we cannot expect to find an unprejudiced interpretation of the writing in question. An epistle which is, as it were, the very *Confession of Faith* that a true Christian is to make, must needs receive an interpretation more or less forced, on the part of all who are influenced by pride, by passion, by prejudice, by ill-directed early instruction, or by ignorance.

For these reasons, an interpreter of this epistle must expect opposition at the present day, let his views be what they may. Be he Calvinist, Arminian, Pelagian, Antinomian, Socinian, or of any other sect, it is in vain for him to think of escape. Paul is a writer too formidable to be acknowledged as an opponent. Hence, when he is interpreted so that the views of one party in any particular point seem to be favored, other parties are very apt to unite in condemning the interpretation. Nothing will satisfy them but to have such a writer explained as siding with them. Alas, then, for the interpreter! While he meets, perhaps, with the approbation of a few, he must of course expect the vehement dissent of many. He must make up his mind, therefore, before he publishes, to bear with all this, and to bear with it patiently and firmly; or else he had better abstain from publishing. It may appear to him as a very undesirable remuneration for painful and long-protracted labors; but it is one which others have been obliged to receive, and which he also must expect. The only offset for all the pains which this may occasion him, must be the hope that his labors after all may do some good; and that, if they do not themselves on the whole directly advance the cause of truth, they may at least be the means of exciting others to make inquiries, which will result in the accomplishment of such an end.

For myself, I do not profess to be free from all prejudices of education and all attachment to system, in such a degree as to make it certain that my views may not sometimes be affected by them. Nor do I profess to be so illuminated in respect to divine things, and so skilled in the original language and criticism of the New Testament, as to be certain that all my conclusions respecting the meaning of the epistle before us are correct. *Homo sum, et nihil humani a me alienum puto.* When, therefore, I speak in the *indicative* mood, and say that this means thus and so, the reader will not understand that anything more is intended, than that this is true in my opinion. To be always dealing in the *conditional* mood, and filling one's pages with, *if, perhaps, probably, possibly, may it not, can it not, etc., etc.*, would be intolerable in such a writing as a commentary. Besides, it would represent the author himself as in a perpetual state of doubt or uncertainty. This I cannot truly say of myself. My convictions, for the most part, have become definite and full in respect to far the greater portion of the Epistle to the Romans. To represent them otherwise, would be to misrepresent them.

But this does not imply that I am insensible to the weakness of human nature, or to my exposedness to err. If I have any knowledge of my own heart, it is very far from such insensibility. After all, however, a man who is liable to err, may form opinions, and may be satisfied that they are correct. This all men do, and must do; and all which can be properly demanded of them is, that they should hold themselves open to conviction, whenever adequate reasons are offered to convince them of their errors.

In this position, I trust and believe, do I hold myself, as to the opinions advanced in the interpretations that follow. I can say truly, that there are no opinions advanced here, which have been hastily taken up. I have been long engaged in the exposition of the Epistle to the Romans, and have studied it much more than any other part of the Bible. I have taken an extensive range in consulting commentators ancient and modern, as well as exegesis contained in theological essays and systems. This, however, I mention for one purpose, and one only, viz., to show that I have not come lightly to the responsible task of writing and publishing a commentary on the epistle under consideration; and that the opinions, therefore, which are advanced in it, are not the offspring of mere education or hasty conjecture.

PREFACE TO THE FIRST EDITION. VII

Dissent, and probably contradiction, are almost of course to be expected. I may be permitted, however, respectfully to solicit those who may see fit to publish anything of this nature, that they would investigate thoroughly, before they condemn, what I have said. When they have so done, I shall value their opinion, however it may differ from my own. Aiming, as I trust I do, at the development of truth, I shall rejoice to find any of my errors corrected (for errors, no doubt, there are in my work); and, if the correction be made in the spirit of love and Christian friendship, so much the more acceptable will it be. If it be made in a different spirit, and is still a real correction, I would fain hope for magnanimity enough to say: *Fas est ab hoste doceri.*

From some of those who have never deeply studied the Epistle to the Romans, and who have a traditional and systematic exegesis which answers their purposes in an *a priori* way, I may probably expect, in regard to some things, vehement and unqualified dissent. Such, however, can hardly assert the right of demanding that my views should be accommodated to theirs; since we proceed in our respective interpretations, on grounds so exceedingly diverse. I hope, therefore, that such will excuse me from any obligation to contend with their exegesis.

To those who may differ from me, after thorough research, I can only say: "The field is open; as open for you as for me. You have the same right to publish your thoughts to the world, as I have to publish mine; and as good a right to defend your views, as I have to proffer mine. The result of doing this, if done with deep, attentive, protracted consideration, and in the spirit of kindness, cannot be otherwise than favorable to the interests of truth. I may not live to vindicate my own views where just, or to abandon the errors of which you might convince me; but others will live, who will do the one or the other for me, should it become necessary. The truth, at last, must and will prevail."

I confess, frankly, that I do not expect for this book the favor of such as are truly *sectarians*. I have written it, so far as in my power, without any regard to sect or name. Doubtless my efforts have been imperfect; but so far as in me lay, the one only and simple inquiry with me has been: What did Paul mean to teach? What Calvin, or Augustine, or Edwards, or Arminius, or Grotius, or any other theologian or commentator has taught or said, has been with me only secondary and subordinate. No one is farther from disrespect to the great and good than myself; but when explaining the Bible, to call no man *master*, and to bow to no system as such, are sacred principles with me. If I have not always adhered to them, it results from my imperfection; not from any conscious and allowed design. Of course, all *party* men in theology will probably find some things in the following pages with which they will not agree. How can it be otherwise? I have, to the utmost of my power, left their systems out of sight, and made it my constant and only effort, to follow simply the way in which the apostle seems to lead me. Such a course will be estimated differently from what it now is, when less attachment to system and party in theology, and more of simple-hearted love of truth, just as it stands in the Scripture, shall prevail in the churches.

My views of Rom. v. 12—19, of vii. 5—25, and of viii. 28, seq., will, no doubt, be controverted. I have anticipated this; for who can help knowing that these passages have, for time immemorial, been the great πρόσκομμα καὶ σκάνδαλον of theology? To hazard an interpretation here, and not to accompany it with reasons, would be justly deemed presumptuous. To give reasons, demands at least the appearance of *theologizing.* Whatever of this exists in the Commentary or the Excursus, is, I may say, involuntary on my part. It is inserted only to guard against being misunderstood, or else to support the interpretation which I have given. In order to do this, it is now and then necessary to show that a different interpretation is replete with difficulties, some of which are insurmountable.

Those who are disposed to find fault with what they may call my *theological* discussions,—brief and few as they are,—would probably not make any objections to such discussions, had the result of them been accordant with their own views, or with those of the authors whom they highly esteem. But how can I be under obligation to make wishes of this nature a rule to guide my interpretations, or my explanation and defence of them? I know of no precept in theory, nor any obligation from usage, which hinders an interpreter from reasoning upon the doctrines which the Scriptures appear to teach, or which they have been represented as teaching. How can it be one's duty not to guard against the misrepresentation of his own views in respect to the meaning of Scripture, and not to defend those views by producing the arguments which appear to justify them?

Whatever the following pages contain, either of truth or error, they have been written under no ordinary sense of responsibility. The epistle itself must needs create such a feeling in the breast of every reflecting man, who undertakes to comment upon it; and, in addition to this, I have been repeatedly interrupted in my labors by my state of health; and this under circumstances that rendered it not improbable, that I should not live to see the completion of my work. The day of my account cannot be far distant; and in view of it, can I publish to the world what I do not seriously regard as being true? Can party purposes have any strong attractions for a man in such a condition? I hope and trust I can say, that the tribunal before which this and all other works are to be finally judged, appears to me a matter of immeasurably higher interest than all the praise or blame which men can bestow.

May that omniscient and merciful Being, the God of love and truth, forgive whatever of error may be in this book; and accept and bless to the good of his church, whatever of truth is explained or defended!

I should be ungrateful if I should omit to mention my special obligations to some of the interpreters, who have labored to explain the Epistle to the Romans. Calvin, Grotius, J. A. Turretin, Flatt, and Tholuck have been my favorite authors; although I have by no means confined my reading to these. Most of all am I indebted to the excellent book of Tholuck on this epistle. I have often relied on him in my statements with respect to the opinions of other commentators whom I had not at hand. I am indebted to him, also, for various classical quotations and allusions, and also for not a few valuable philological remarks, as well as views of the reasoning and argumentation of the apostle. He has my most unfeigned thanks for all the aid which his excellent work has afforded me.

Throughout, I have adopted and expressed no views or opinions without study; and none upon the *authority* of others. Those who read the following pages will perceive, I apprehend, that while I have not neglected the study of other writers, I have not omitted to study and think for myself. In this way only can any advance be hoped for in the all-important work of interpreting the Bible.   *   *   *

M. STUART.

THEOLOGICAL SEMINARY ANDOVER,
Sept. 1832.

INTRODUCTION

TO

THE EPISTLE TO THE ROMANS.

§ 1. *First Planting of the Church at Rome.*

THE origin of the church at Rome is involved in obscurity. Neither the time at which, nor the persons by whom it was founded can now be definitely and certainly designated. The testimony of the Clementine Homilies, (Clem. Recogn. 1, 6,) that during the life-time of Christ, the truths of the gospel had been disseminated, and had taken root at Rome, may be true, but is very improbable. Neither is there more substantial foundation for the belief of the Catholic Church, that Peter was the founder of this church, and first bishop of the imperial city. Eusebius, it is true, places his arrival there in the second year of Claudius, (Chron. ad ann. 2 Claud.,) and Clement of Alexandria says that he went there at that time to confront Simon Magus, (Euseb. Hist. Eccl. ii. 14,) and Jerome adds (De Script. Eccl.,) that he was bishop there 25 years. Isidore of Spain combines all these traditions: Hic postquam Antiochenam ecclesiam fundavit, sub Claudio Cæsare contra Simonem Magum Romam pergit, ibique practicans evangelium xxv. annis ejusdem tenuit pontificatum.

" But these *traditionary* statements," as Davidson says,* "have neither the impress of credibility nor truth," and besides are plainly refuted by the following considerations: In Acts xii. 3, 4, we find an account of the imprisonment of Peter by Herod Agrippa, in the last year of this king's reign (comp. v. 23); and this year synchronizes with the *fourth* year of Claudius. Of course Peter was at Jerusalem, not at Rome, *after* the period when Jerome and Eusebius affirm that he went to Rome and resided there. We find Peter at Jerusalem in the *ninth* (some say eleventh) year of Claudius; he being present at the council there, Acts xv. 6, seq. Nothing is said in the book of Acts, or in the New Testament, respecting Peter's visiting Rome; and if he had done so, before the time at which the history in the book of Acts terminates, we can hardly suppose so important an occurrence would have escaped the notice of Luke. Paul came as a prisoner to Rome,

* Bib Introd. II 159.

in the 7th year of Nero's reign, *i. e.*, A. D. 60 (but some say in 61, 62 or 63); on which occasion there is no mention, and there seems to have been among the Jews of that city no knowledge of Peter, Acts xxviii. 17, seq. The arrangement made between the Apostles when at Jerusalem (Acts xv.), fourteen years after Paul's conversion, A. D. 54, as a result of previous labors (Gal. ii. 7, seq.), that James, *Cephas*, and John should go to the circumcision, and Paul and Barnabas to the Gentiles (Gal. ii. 9), would prevent him from going soon to Rome, which Paul plainly claimed as within his sphere of labors, Rom. i. 5, 6, 13 et saep. This agreement was doubtless adhered to until the imprisonment of Paul rendered a deviation from it desirable, for Lactantius, contemporary with Eusebius, plainly implies that Peter did not visit Rome until the reign of Nero. De Mort. Persecut.: Cumque jam Nero imperarat, Petrus Romam advenit et editis quibusdam miraculis, etc.

Several of Paul's Epistles, too, were doubtless written at Rome, as that to Philemon, the Colossians, Ephesians, Philippians, and the 2d to Timothy. In these, other persons are mentioned as fellow-laborers, and sometimes as his only aids in the work of his mission, as Coloss. iv. 10, 11; Philip. ii. 20, iv. 11; and their salutations recorded, whilst no allusion is made to Peter. And besides, the apostle expressly indicates in Rom. xv. 20, seq, 2 Cor. xv. 14, seq., that he avoided building on another's foundation, and with this feeling, he would not have written to them as he did, and especially would not have spoken of coming to them in person to impart some spiritual gift.

So clear is this, that some of the best and most impartial scholars among the Catholics themselves do not accede to the general belief of their own church. Feilmoser (in the Tubingen Quarterly Jour. for 1820) shows that he could not have been in Rome earlier than a year before his death. See also Hug, Klee and others.

Still, although it seems clear that Peter cannot be claimed as the founder of the church of Rome, and that he was not there until after the Epistle of Paul was written, yet it is somewhat probable that he was there at some time before the end of Nero's reign. Origen, (in Euseb. Eccl. III. 1); Dionysius of Corinth, (in Euseb. II. 25); Clement of Alexandria, (in Euseb. II. 14, 15, and VI. 15); and Caius, a presbyter, who wrote at Rome at the end of the second, or beginning of the third century, gives testimony to this effect which cannot be impeached. The latter specifies so definitely the place of his martyrdom and burial, etc., that if there had been any mistake or intentional false representation, multitudes could, and would, in all probability, have corrected or opposed his statements. But those who are desirous of examining this question more at length are referred, among other works, to Olshausen's Introduction to Comm. on Romans, p 36, seq, and an article in Stud and Krit. No. 4, 1838; Bleek Stud. No. 4, 1836, p. 1061 seq; Wieseler, Kron. d. Apost. Zeitalt.; Neander's Planting and Training, Book IV. ch. 2; also Baur in Tubingen Zeitschr. No. 4, 1831, and J Ellendorf, translated in Bib. Sac. July, 1858, p. 569, seq, both of whom deny the visit of Peter to Rome; Winer, Real-Lex. Art. *Peter*, who doubts in reference to it.

The question recurs, if Peter had not been at Rome, by whom had

EPISTLE TO THE ROMANS.   XIII

the church there been gathered? It is possible that Andronicus and
Junias, mentioned in 16 : 7, as having been *fellow-prisoners* with Paul,
highly esteemed among the apostles and Christians before himself, or
Rufus, (16 : 13), or others mentioned in chap. 16, first carried the
gospel to Rome, and were instrumental of founding a church there;
still nothing definite is known in reference to it. The most that can
be said with confidence is that the gospel "was introduced into Rome
by Jewish Christians after the remarkable day of Pentecost, and subsequently nurtured in a variety of ways by individuals brought into
the metropolis by different motives, and from many lands." Davidson's Introd. II. p. 165.

That the church at Rome was *early* planted, seems probable from
the fame which it had acquired throughout the Christian world (Rom.
i. 8; xvi. 19), when Paul wrote his epistle. That the persons concerned in the establishment of it were Paul's particular friends and
acquaintances, with whom he had met and conferred, while preaching
in Asia or in Greece, appears very plain from the manner of the salutations in chap. xvi. 3 — 16. In respect to many of its members, as
Aquila and Priscilla, we have a definite knowledge, from Acts xviii.
1 — 3, 18, 26, and from what is said in Rom. xvi. 3, 4. Others are
called the *kinsmen* (συγγενεῖς) of Paul, viz. Andronicus and Junias,
ver. 7; Herodion, ver. 11. Others again are called ἀγαπητοί, συνεργοί,
ἐκλεκτοί, κοπιῶντες ἐν τῷ κυρίῳ, etc. Moreover, the manner in which
Paul addresses the church of Rome, *i. e.* the plain, familiar, authorita-
tive tone of the letter, shows that he considered himself as addressing
those who were in effect his own disciples, or, in other words, such as
had probably been converted to Christianity under the preaching of
his own particular friends and spiritual children. Hence, too, the frequent expressions of strong affection for the church at Rome, and of
strong sympathy with them.

§ 2. *The constituent Parts of the Church at Rome.*

Nothing can be clearer, than that a considerable portion of the
church at Rome consisted of Jewish converts; ii. 17 — iii. 19; iv 1,
12; vii. 1 — 4, and chapters ix. — xi. Nor is there any serious difficulty of a historical nature, in making out the probability of this.
When Pompey overran Judea with a conquering army, about 63 years
before the Christian era, he caused many captive Jews to be sent to
Rome. There they were sold into slavery, as was usual in respect to
captives taken in war. But their persevering and unconquerable
determination to observe the Sabbath, and to practise many of the
Levitical rites and customs, gave their Roman masters so much trouble,
that they chose to liberate them rather than to keep them. As there
was a large body of persons so liberated, the government assigned
them a place opposite Rome, across the Tiber, where they built a
town which was principally inhabited by Jews. Here Philo found
them, just before Paul's time; Legat. ad Caium. p. 1014, ed Frankf.
The reader who wishes for historical vouchers in respect to the number of Jews at Rome, during the apostolic age, may consult Joseph.

Antiq. XVII. 14, XVIII. 5, ed. Cologn. Dio Cassius, XXXVI. p. 37. Suetonii vita Tiberii, cap. 36.

When the first impressions arising from the degradation of captivity and slavery began to wear away, the Roman citizens seem to have looked at the Jewish community with some degree of respect, or at least with not a little of curiosity. Whether it arose from the disgust which delicate females among the Romans felt for the obscene rites of heathenism which they were called to practise or to witness, or whether it sprung from a curiosity which is characteristic of the female sex, the fact was, that in Ovid's time (ob. A. D. 17) some of the most elegant and polished females thronged the Jewish assemblies. The poet therefore advises the young men of the city, if they wished to see a splendid collection of its beauty, to go to the *sabbath-day solemnities of the Syrian Jew.* "Cultaque Judæo septima sacra Syro."

It is not strange, moreover, that some of these should become σεβό-μεναι or proselytes; as Josephus relates of Fulvia, μία τῶν ἐν ἀξιώματι γυναικῶν, *i. e*, a noble woman. By degrees the men also, as was natural, began to frequent the assemblies of those once despised foreigners. Juvenal, at the close of the first century, pours out his contempt and indignation at this in the following bitter words:

> "Quidam sortiti metuentem Sabbata patrem,
> Nil præter nubes, et cœli Numen adorant;
> Nec distare putant humana carne suillam,
> Qua pater abstinuit; mox et præputia ponunt;
> Romanas autem soliti contemnere leges,
> Judaicum ediscunt, et servant, ac metuunt jus,
> Tradidit arcano quodcunque volumine Moses."

Seneca also (fl. A. D. 64), about the time when Paul wrote the Epistle to the Romans, says, in a fragment preserved by Augustine (De Civit. Dei, VII. 11), that "so many Romans had received the Jewish [he means by this the *christian*] religion, that *per omnes jam terras recepta sit, victi victoribus leges dederunt.*" Tacitus, in his Annals, likewise represents the "exitiabilis superstitio" (christian religion) as breaking out again after being repressed, and spreading *non modo per Judæam sed per urbem* [Roman] *etiam*.

When to these testimonies respecting the *Jews* at Rome, we add that of the Epistle before us respecting *Gentile* converts, it is quite certain that the church at Rome was made up of Gentiles as well as Jews. Let the reader compare Rom. i. 16 — 32; ii. 6 — 11; iii. 9 — 19, 29; ix. 24, 30; xi. 13 — 25; xiv. 1 — xv. 13, and no doubt can possibly remain in his mind relative to this point. The general strain of the whole epistle is such, as that it can be best accounted for by the supposition that the church at Rome consisted of both Jews and Gentiles, with their own peculiar interests and feelings.

Much has been written upon the relative number of Jews and Gentiles in the church of Rome. According to Paulus, Neander, Ruckert, De Wette, Olshausen, Tholuck, and others, the Gentile element predominated. They rely upon such passages as those quoted above. On the other hand, Henke, Koppe, Hanlein, Meyer, Baur, Krehl contend for a majority of Jewish Christians. See especially Baur's

Paulus, der Apos. Jesu Christi. But there seems to be nothing decisive on either side, nor is the mere preponderance of numbers a matter of material importance in the exposition of the epistle. Sometimes the one part and sometimes the other is especially addressed. See Davidson's Introd. Vol. II. p. 168 seq.

§ 3. *The Time when, and Place where the Epistle was written.*

The epistle itself furnishes us a kind of stand-point here. It could not have been written before the decree of the emperor Claudius was published, by which the Jews were banished from the city of Rome. In Acts xviii. 2, we have an account of Paul's *first* acquaintance with Aquila and Priscilla, who had *recently* quitted Rome and come to Corinth, because of the decree of Claudius banishing the Jews from the imperial city. Now as Paul salutes these same persons, in Rom. xvi. 3, 4, and speaks of them as having risked great dangers in his behalf, it follows, of course, that his epistle must have been written subsequently to the decree of Claudius; which was probably in A. D. 52, or as some say (improbably however) in A. D. 54.

It would seem also to have been written after the time when the First Epistle to the Corinthians was written, which was during the last visit which Paul made to Ephesus, and near the close of that visit, *i. e.*, about A. D. 56. In Acts xviii. 19, we are told that Paul left Aquila and Priscilla at Ephesus. After this he made another circuit through the churches of Palestine, Syria, and Asia Minor (Acts xviii. 20 — 23), and returned again to Ephesus, xix. 1. There he spent two years or more (xix. 8 — 10); and near the close of this period, in writing to the Corinthians, he sends the salutation of Aquila and Priscilla, who were still at Ephesus, (1 Cor. xvi. 19.) Now as Paul sends a salutation, in his Epistle to the Romans, to Aquila and Priscilla at Rome, it would seem probable that it must have been written after he left Ephesus, and after they had removed from this city to the metropolis of the Roman empire.

Other circumstances concur, to render the matter still more definite. When Paul wrote his epistle, he was on the eve of departure for Jerusalem, whither he was going to carry the contributions of the churches in Macedonia and Achaia, Rom. xv. 25, 26. When he should have accomplished this, he intended to make them a visit at Rome, Rom. xv. 28, 29. In what part of his life, now, do we find the occurrence of these circumstances? Acts xix. 21, compared with Acts xx. 1 —4, gives us a narration of exactly the same thing. Paul, at the close of his last abode at Ephesus, purposing to make a charitable collection in Macedonia and Achaia, first sent on Timothy and Erastus to Macedonia in order to forward it there (Acts xix. 22); afterwards he himself went into Achaia, passing through Macedonia, Acts xx. 1, 2. That he came, on this occasion, to the capital of Achaia, *i. e.* Corinth, there can be no reasonable doubt. Here most probably he abode three months (Acts xx. 3); and then set out on his contemplated journey to Jerusalem, where he was made prisoner, and sent (A D. 59 or 60) to Rome, in order to prosecute his appeal to Cæsar. From a comparison of this account in the Acts, with Rom. xv. 25—29, it follows of course that the Epistle to the Romans must have been written about A. D. 57; although some chronologists put it later. Counting the time which Paul's journey to Jerusalem must have occupied, and adding the two years of his detention as a prisoner at Caesarea (Acts xxiv. 27), and the time necessarily taken up in going to Rome, we must assign to the Epistle to the Romans the date above given, on the supposition that Paul came to Rome (as is most probable) about the beginning of the year 60.

As to the PLACE *where it was written*, there can be no doubt. In xvi. 1, Phebe, a deaconess of the church at Cenchrea, is commended to the Romish church, who probably either had charge of the epistle, or accompanied those who did carry it; and Cenchrea was the port of the city of Corinth, some seven or eight miles from that place. In xvi. 23, Gaius is spoken of as *the host* of Paul; and this Gaius was baptized by Paul at Corinth, 1 Cor. i. 14. Paul speaks also of Erastus, *the chamberlain of the city*, Rom. xvi. 23. The city, then, was a well-known one, *i. e.*, the capital of Achaia ; and moreover, we find this Erastus spoken of in 2 Tim. iv. 20, as abiding at Corinth.

From all these circumstances, we must conclude that the *place* of writing the Epistle to the Romans was Corinth; and that the *time* was that in which Paul made his last visit there, and near the close of it, *i. e.*, about the latter part of A. D. 57.

§ 4. *The Authenticity of the Epistle*

This has been so generally acknowledged, at all times and in all ages since it was written (excepting the last chapters, which have recently been disputed), that it seems to be unnecessary to make any quotations here from the early writers, for the sake of proving it. It is true, indeed, that some early sects, viz , the Ebionites, Encratites, and Cerinthians, rejected it; as appears from Irenæus ad Hæres. I. 26 ; Epiphan. Hæres. XXX.; Hieronym. in Matt. xii. 2. But as this seems to have been purely on *doctrinal* grounds, *i. e.*, because they could not make the sentiments of Paul in this epistle to harmonize with their own views, it follows of course that no weight can be attached to their opinions. The question whether Paul wrote the Epistle so the Romans, is of an *historical*, not of a doctrinal nature.

The reader who is curious to see an exhibition of early testimony respecting this epistle, may find it amply detailed in Lardner's Credibility, and in Schmidii Historia et Vindiciæ Canonis Sac., etc. The circumstantial evidence which evinces its genuineness, he will find admirably exhibited in Paley's Horæ Paulinæ, chap. II.

Those who do not possess the first two of these works, may consult Polycarp, Epist. and Philipp. cap. 6 ; Clemens Rom. Ep. and Cor. cap. 85 ; both in Cotelerii Patres Apostolici. See also Theoph. ad Autolyc. I 20; III. 14, Epist.' Ecc. Vienn. et Lugd. in Euseb. Hist. Ecc. V. 1. Irenæus cont. Hæres. III. 16. § 3. Clem. Alex. Strom. III., p. 457, and I., p. 117, edit. Sylburg. Tertull. adv. Praxeam, cap. 13 ; de Corona, cap. 6. Cypr. Ep. LXIX. It is needless to cite later authors. "The stream of testimony is continuous and unanimous."

§ 5. *The Integrity of the Epistle.*

The integrity of the epistle has often been questioned in modern times, although all the more ancient witnesses of any authority, Fathers of the church, versions and MSS. regard the epistle as a connected whole; for Marcion's rejection of chaps. xv. and xvi. is entirely on doctrinal grounds, if indeed the authority of one who so often perverted other parts of the sacred writings were of any weight.

That chapter xvi. is omitted by Euthalius, in his Elenchus, is of no importance, as he is only enumerating the chapters which were publicly read, and plainly recognizes the existence of the whole epistle elsewhere; and the reference to 16 : 10, as in the *clausula epistolæ*, by Tertullian (adv. Marcion, v. 14), is no proof that this did not belong to the epistle. The arguments against the different parts of the epistle, then, are entirely of an internal nature, the uncertainty of which, at best, is great. Most of the arguments, as will be seen by an examination of their character, are based upon a supposed want of conformity, in the last chapters, to the preceding part of the epistle; as if we should take it upon ourselves to decide in what manner Paul should write, and as if it were not natural that he should turn aside, after he had completed the doctrinal part of the epistle, and give such admonitions, exhortations, and encouragements, as he deemed useful. Is not something like this found elsewhere in his epistles?

Heumann led the way, in these criticisms, by the supposition that there were two distinct epistles combined in what is now called the Epistle to the Romans. The first consisted of chapters i.—xi, with chapter xvi. as a sort of postscript; and the second, of chapters xii.—xv., which was written subsequently to the former, on a reception of unfavorable reports in reference to the conduct of the Roman Christians. Both these were written upon the same parchment, and hence became united as one epistle. In a critical point of view, this hypothesis is of little importance, as it does not properly disprove or even deny the genuineness of any part of the epistle. Still, it is too improbable to need much discussion. I will only add that "the amen (ἀμήν)," as Olshausen says, "is clearly not the close of the epistle, but of the doxology with which St. Paul very appropriately concludes the doctrinal part,"* and chap. xii. is plainly connected by the deductive οὖν, at the beginning, with what precedes.

Semler, in his *Dissert. de dupl. Appendice Ep. Pauli ad Rom.*, advances the supposition "that chap. xv. was not addressed to the Romans, but to those who had charge of Paul's epistle to them (which consisted of chapters i.—xv., with the doxology in xvi. 25—27)" to be communicated by the bearers of the epistle to those Christians who might be met with on the way; and that, in chap. xvi. 1 seq, salutations are sent to some of these persons. But there is not only no proof of this, but, on the contrary, "chap. xv.," says Davidson, Introd. II, p. 195, "cannot be separated from the xiv. without violence. The same subject is *continued* in the first verse of xv. down to the ter-

---

* Introd. to Comm. on Rom., Eng Ed., p 28.

mination." The improbability that these salutations were for persons on the way is easily shown.

For, on this supposition, the first stage of the journey of the letter-carriers was only to Cenchrea, some seven or eight miles from Corinth, to the house of Phebe. But the singularity of Paul's recommendation is, that instead of commending *them* to her hospitality, he commends her to the hospitality of those whom he addresses: συνίστημι δὲ ὑμῖν Φοίβην . . . . . ἵνα αὐτὴν προσδέξησθε, κ. τ. λ. Semler felt the incongruity of this, and referred προσδέξησθε to *receiving into communion*. Did Phebe, then, living within a couple of hours' walk from Corinth, and famous as she was for being a προστάτις πολλῶν (ver. 2), need a written recommendation of Paul, in order that the bearers of his letters might admit her to church communion? But besides this, the word προσδέξησθε, in such a connection, does not admit of such a sense. Comp. Phil. ii. 29, and also (as to general meaning) 3 John v. 6.

Thus much for the outset of this journey. Nor is the progress more fortunate. Aquila and Priscilla are next recommended to the letter-carriers. But the last which we know of them, before the writing of this letter, is that they are at Ephesus, Acts xviii. 18, 19, 26. But Semler provides them with a house at *Corinth;* and this, probably, because it would not be very natural for those who were to travel westward toward Rome, to go some hundreds of miles eastward, *i e.,* to Ephesus, in order to get to the capital of the Roman Empire. But how is the matter helped by this process? What have we now? A letter of introduction (so to speak) from Paul, directing his messengers to greet Priscilla and Aquila on their journey, while these same persons lived in the very town from which they started! Hug has well expressed his views of this matter. After speaking of the first stay of Aquila and Priscilla at Corinth (Acts xviii. 2), and of a second at Ephesus (Acts xviii. 18, 19), he thus proceeds: " Whence now this *third* or *Semlerian* house at Corinth, I know not," Einleit. II. p 397, ed. 3. But, lastly, what are we to do with verses 17—20, on the ground of Semler? Were the bearers of the letter so divided as is there described; and was their obedience (ὑπακοή) so celebrated as is there hinted? Above all, what is to be done with verses 21—24? Would Paul send *written* salutations from those who were with him at Corinth, to the bearers of his epistle who set out from the same place? Did they not confer with Paul himself, and did not his friends as well as himself see and converse with them? And what shall we say to ver. 16, which directs Paul's messengers to *salute one another?*

Schott, too, in his *Isagoge ad Nov. Test.*, recently published, in a note, p. 284 seq , has assigned other, and perhaps better, reasons for rejecting chapter xvi.

(*a*) ' Paul salutes many persons, in xvi. 5—15, as being at Rome, and in a very *familiar* way. How could he, who had never been at Rome (Rom. i. 13), do this ' ?

The answer is, that several of these persons were his own kinsmen; see § 1 above. With all or most of them he had very probably met, in the course of his travels. Intercourse between the metropolis of the Roman Empire and the large towns of the provinces, was very frequent; especially with Corinth, the headquarters of Achaia, and

Ephesus of Asia Minor. And even if Paul had not seen all the persons whom he salutes, what is easier than to suppose that their character and standing were known to him, and therefore he sent them salutations? It is plainly a mistake, to suppose that none but personal acquaintances are saluted in the Pauline epistles.

(*b*) 'But Paul makes no mention of any of the persons here saluted as being at Rome, in his other epistles written there, e. *g*, in his epistles to the Ephesians, Colossians, Philippians, and Philemon.'

The answer is, that in only one of these (that to the Colossians) does he send anything but a mere *general* salutation. Moreover, as all these epistles must have been written some two years and a half, and may have been written some four years later, than the Epistle to the Romans, so the state of that church, exposed as it was continually to increase and decrease, may have greatly altered when he wrote the last-named epistles; or the persons named in his Epistle to the Romans may have gone elsewhere in order to propagate the gospel; or they might have deceased; or it might be that they did not happen to pay him a visit while he was writing the above named epistles, and so a greeting from them was not mentioned. A thing of this nature is so accidentally varied, that we cannot make any conclusions which are valid, either from this appearance or from that.

(*c*) 'Aquila and Priscilla are saluted as being at Rome. In Acts xviii. 19, 26, we find their abode at Ephesus; and in Paul's last stay at Ephesus, when he wrote the First Epistle to the Corinthians, we find them still there, 1 Cor. xvi. 19.'

All this I concede. But since Aquila and Priscilla had, for some time, been obliged to relinquish their abode at Rome, on account of the decree of Claudius, what is more natural than to suppose, that, as soon as might be, they would return to Rome, at least long enough to adjust their affairs there, which it is more than probable had been embarrassed by the decree of banishment?

(*d*) 'But 2 Tim. iv. 19, written at Rome, greets Priscilla and Aquila as residing at Ephesus.'

I grant it. But when was this written? Just before the final martyrdom of Paul (iv. 6—8) *i. e*, probably some ten years after the Epistle to the Romans was written, and also after the persecution by Nero had commenced. What difficulty now in the supposition, that Aquila and Priscilla had fled from Rome when this persecution broke out, and gone back to their former station at Ephesus, where they had spent several years? There Paul salutes them in 2 Tim. iv. 19.

Last, Professor Schott expresses his belief, that chap. xvi. is made up of fragments of some brief epistle of Paul's written at Corinth, and addressed to some church in Asia Minor, and added by mistake, *piece by piece* as it was discovered, to the Epistle to the Romans. Verses 1—16 composed the first fragment; verses 17—20, the second; verses 21—24, the third; verses 25—27, the fourth.

But what a series of conclusions is here made out, without a syllable of historical evidence? Where is the evidence of the lost epistle to an anonymous church in Asia Minor? Where that it was lost excepting a few scattered fragments which "*sensim sensimque deprehendebantur?*" And the conceit of adding all these fragments to the Epistle to the Romans, which already had a good ending with chap. xv.; how should this have ever entered any one's head? Why add them to this epistle, rather than to some of Paul's shorter epistles? And then the persons themselves named in chapter xvi.; what a singular phantasy it must have been in the compiler, to have supposed that, if they belonged to some church in Asia Minor, their names could be tacked on to the epistle written to the church at *Rome!*" How can we admit such gratuitous and improbable hypotheses as these?

Nor can I admit what has frequently been said in respect to chap. xvi, viz, that it is wholly unconnected with the preceding part of the epistle, and may be disjoined from it without injury to it. Thus much is true, indeed, viz., that salutations and expressions of Christian courtesy are not doctrinal discussions nor practical precepts; in a word, the sixteenth chapter, which is principally made up of salutations, must of course be diverse from the preceding part of the epistle. But is it not equally true that chaps. xii.—xv. differ as much from the preceding ones, as chap. xvi. does from all the others? Is it proper, moreover, that Christian salutations should be exchanged, in epistles like that of Paul? This will not be denied. The force of such examples of kindness, and courtesy, and benevolent feeling, is scarcely less than that of direct precept; and in some respects it has evidently the advantage of precept, inasmuch as *practice* speaks louder than theory. Why, then, should the salutatory part of the epistle be thrown away? And would not rejecting it be an injury to the congruity and to the general good effect of the whole?

Nor is it correct to say, that there is not an evident relation and connection of some part of chap. xvi, with what precedes, besides that which has just been mentioned. Let any one diligently consider the contents of verses 17—20, and he will see plainly that they refer to the divisions and erroneous sentiments which are the subject of particular discussion in chaps. xii.—xv. Let him compare xvi. 19 with i. 8, and he will see the same person expressing himself in the same circumstances. In a word, it would be truly wonderful, if the straggling fragments of an epistle, sent to some unknown church in Asia Minor, should fit the place of conclusion to the Epistle to the Romans so well as its present conclusion fits it.

What can we say, moreover, to the τολμηρότερον δὲ ἔγραψα ὑμῖν of xv. 15, if Paul does not refer to the *whole* of the preceding epistle? It would be even ridiculous, on any other ground. And what a singular epistle chaps. xv. and xvi. would make out, consisting almost wholly *salutations!*

Eichhorn (Einleit. in das N. Test.) has advanced a hypothesis still more fanciful, if possible, than that of Semler or Schott. Chap. xvi. 1—20 is, according to him, a letter of recommendation to the *Corinthian* church, which Paul wrote for Phebe, the deaconess mentioned in verses 1, 2. This, after it had been read by them, she obtained again, and carried it along with her to Rome; and because the church there were unwilling that anything from the hand of Paul should perish, they tacked it on upon the epistle of Paul to them, so as to make out a conclusion for it!

Is it worth the pains to refute such criticism? Or rather, can the name of *criticism* be fairly given to such extravagant and incongruous suppositions? One is ready to ask: What sort of a church must it have been, in the metropolis of the world, and whose fame had gone abroad through the whole empire, that could deal thus with Paul's epistles? Why was not the letter of Phebe kept by itself, and published by itself, as well as John's letter to the "elect lady?" But this is only one among the numerous conceits, which are intermingled with the striking and instructive compositions of Eichhorn.

More recently, Baur* has attempted to bring discredit upon the xv. and xvi. chapters of this epistle. His view is that these chapters were added by some one of the Pauline party in the church, at a subsequent date, in order to effect a union of sentiment between those of his own party and the Judaizers at Rome, by softening what might be offensive in the epistle. His arguments have been fully answered by Kling,† Tholuck,‡ Olshausen,§ and De Wette.‖ It is unnecessary here to speak only briefly of those which are more prominent.

The favorable opinion which is given in xv. 14, of the superior piety and Christian knowledge of the Roman Christians is at variance with the object of the writer expressed in i. 11, and also with the general admonitory dogmatic spirit of the epistle. If this be an objection to the authenticity of the last two chapters of Romans, what shall we say of 1 Cor. i. 5, as compared with vi. 5, x. 15, xiv. 20, and passages which might be selected from any other writing of similar object and character.

The allusion to the office of Christ, as related to the Jews as compared with the Gentiles, in xv. 8 seq., is made by Baur an objection to the integrity of the last part of the epistle, as well as the mention of the intended journey to Spain, and the reason for his visit, in xv. 28 seq. But it is unnecessary to do anything more than call the attention of the candid reader to such objections, the main pillars upon which Baur's hypothesis is supported, to bring him to the conclusion that it is "nothing else than the work of a misdirected acuteness, and an unrestrained hypercriticism that will never be able to establish itself."—Olshausen's Introd. p. 31.

In reference to the doxology in chap. xvi. 25—27, there is need of a little more extended examination, as there is considerable variety in the MSS. of the passage, and internal evidence has been adduced, with some apparent plausibility, against it.

It occupies the position which it has in our version, at the end of the epistle, in Codd B. C. D. E. 16, 66, 80, 137, 176; in the Syriac, Erpenian, Arabic, Coptic, Ethiopic, and Vulgate versions, and with these agree the Latin Fathers.

It is placed at the end of the xiv. chapter in Cod. J., and most MSS. written in cursive letters, in most Greek lectionaries, in the Arab.

---

* Tubing. Zeitschr , No. 3, 1836   † Studien und Krit , No 2, 1857, p 297 seq.
‡ Studien u Krit , No 4, 1838, and Introd to Comm , p 30 seq.
§ Comm. Introd , p. 2 seq.   ‖ Comm Introd, 4th ed.

Triglott and Polyglott, in the Sclavonic and most of the Armenian MSS. in Codd. mentioned by Rufinus and in Chrysostom, Theodoret, Damascenus, Theoph. of Antioch, Oecumenius, and Theodulius. It is found in both places in A, 5, 17, 109, and in some Armenian MSS.

This doxology is entirely wanting in F, G (though in the latter there is a space left after xiv. 23), in D, where it is plainly erased by a later hand, and in MSS. spoken of by Jerome and Erasmus.

There can be little room for doubt, after an examination of testimony, that, as far as external evidence goes, this doxology is authentic, *i. e.*, that it belonged to the original writing, and was either at the end of chap xiv. or xvi. or both.

There is, furthermore, a preponderance of external authority for the position at the end of the epistle. It has accordingly been there placed by Erasmus, Stephens, Bengel, Koppe, Boehme, Scholtz, Tischendorf, Hug, Knapp, Lachmann, Hahn, Rückert, De Wette, Philippi, Meyer, Alford, and others. A few, with Griesbach and Matthiae, place it at the end of chap. xiv., but certainly with less weight of external evidence.*

Internal evidence, too, is in favor of the position at the end of chap. xvi. At the end of chap. xiv. it so manifestly interrupts the connection of thought which is so intimate, as indicated both by the ὀφείλομεν δέ of xv. 1, and by a comparison of the course of thought in the first thirteen verses of chap. xv. as compared with the preceding chapter. And besides, the matter at the close of chap. xiv. is not such as would naturally be followed by such a doxology, at least, if we do not, as it plainly cannot be, consider it as the close of the epistle.

The different places of these verses in different MSS. has been variously accounted for. The most probable supposition is, that the position " at the very end of the epistle, contrary to the analogy of all the Pauline letters," and after the benediction in verse 24th, was deemed inappropriate by copyists, and in looking about for a suitable place, they were led to make choice of the end of chap. xiv, by a supposed suitableness of the verb στηρίξαι to the sentiment in that chapter. So Chrysostom says: πάλιν γὰρ ἐκείνων ἔχεται τῶν ἀσθενῶν κ. πρὸς αὐτοὺς τρέπει τὸν λόγον This theory is favored by the fact that many of the authorities for its position at the end of chap. xvi. either leave out the salutation in verse 24, or transfer it to the end of the doxology † Its position in both places may be naturally accounted for by supposing that some transcriber, unable to determine which was the suitable place, retained it in both, whilst a supposed unsuitableness in both caused some few to reject it entirely.

It is not improbable, however, that the division for public reading gave occasion to the position at the end of chap. xiv. If, as is not improbable, the part publicly read ended with chap. xiv., the doxology from chap. xvi. might not unnaturally have been added, as a suitable conclusion, and thus have crept into the MSS. as belonging there.

The supposed arguments from *internal* evidence, *i. e.*, from the lan-

---

* See Meyer, in his Comm., prefatory remarks to chap. xvi, and Gabler Praef ad Griesbach, Opusc , p 24

† See Davidson's Introd II , p. 190; Alford's Comm. upon v. 25—27, also, Olshausen's, Tholuck's, and Meyer's Commentaries

guage and style of the doxology, have been drawn out at length by Reiche, and fully answered by Meyer, Davidson, and others. Indeed, some of his arguments against its genuineness are conclusive in its favor. "It is unsuitable in position," he says, "wants the simplicity of Paul's other doxologies, is bombastic, exaggerated, loaded with unsuitable ideas, obscure, unusual, and even unintelligible in expression," and finally, "it is made up of pieces taken from Paul's writings," *e. g.*, from Rom. ii. 16, Gal. i. 6, Eph. iii. 3, Coll. i. 26, 2 Tim. i. 8, Tit. i. 1, Rom. i 5, 1 Tim. vi. 16, Rom. ii 16, i. 9, Heb. xiii. 20—23.

In answer to this, it is confidently denied that it is *unintelligible* or *bombastic*, and no other argument is necessary than an appeal to the discrimination of the intelligent reader. For the rest it is only necessary to suppose that Paul, after having completed the epistle, in reviewing it, filled with holy fervor at the thought of the magnitude, freeness, and excellence of the salvation for Jew and Gentile, which is the great theme of the epistle, felt constrained to utter the gushing emotions of his soul in words of praise to God. How could words have been more appropriate to the individual, the circumstances of the author, and the position which they were to occupy! Had they been added by a later hand, we should expect them to be conformed to the Apostle's other doxologies, "simple and complete," without solecisms or irregularities. Besides, there is not the difference in the text usually found in spurious passages. Thus Davidson closes his remarks upon the passage as follows: "We cannot doubt that it proceeded from Paul himself. Schott says: '*Its tenor is wholly Pauline;*' so, too, Fritzsche: '*in all Paul's writings, there are no verses more Pauline than these.*' The reasoning of Reiche against them is a burlesque on argumentation. Nor is the flippant mode in which Krehl disposes of the passages likely to advance the same view. His arguments are substantially the same as those of Reiche, and need not therefore be examined He is compelled to admit that the words are Pauline; but takes offence at the construction, etc. * * * But the evidence in favor of the authenticity overpowers all considerations like those urged by Reiche and Krehl. *Subjectivity and misinterpretation of phrases* are insufficient to overthrow the Pauline authorship."—Introd. p. 193, 4.

§ 6. *Language and Style of the Epistle.*

The Epistle to the Romans was doubtless written in the Greek language, in which the apostle was educated, and in which he wrote all his other epistles. The assertion of the Scholiast upon the Peshito version, that it was written in Latin, is of no critical value, standing, as he does, alone, and doubtless was based upon the supposition that a letter to Roman Christians would be written in the Latin language. The claim of Salmero, Harduin, and others, that the Vulgate is the original language of the epistle, needs not a word of confutation, as it is given up by the Catholics themselves. The original MSS. and versions, the style of the epistle (though naturally not free from Hebraisms), also plainly indicate that our Greek text is the original, and not a translation.

Neither is there any objection to this view from the language of the persons addressed. The Jews at Rome, as well as in Palestine and other lands, made use of the Greek language at the time when the epistle was written. They would naturally learn it, both from the Greeks and the Romans themselves, who, many of them, preferred it to their own native tongue. This is clearly shown by the oldest Jewish tombs at Rome, which all have Greek inscriptions.

Of the general use of the Greek among the Romans themselves, there is abundant evidence. Juvenal often ridicules the excessive love of his countrymen for everything Greek. (See for example Sat. VI. 185 seq.) Martial, too, says:

Rusticus es? nescis quid Græco nomine dicar. Spuma vocor nitri Græcus es? ἀφρόνιτρον· and Tacitus, in Dial. de Oratoribus C. 14:

Nunc natus infans delegatur Græculæ ancillæ, etc.

Ovid too (De Arte Amand. L. ii. v. 121), bears witness to the knowledge of Greek in Rome:

Nec levis ingenuas pectus coluisse per artes cura sit, et linguas edidicisse duas.

There are many passages also in other classical writers, as Cicero and Horace, showing the prevalence of the Greek language at Rome, even before the age of the Apostle.

Davidson further adds (Introd. vol. II. p. 187): "Ignatius, Dionysius of Corinth, and Irenæus wrote in Greek to Roman Christians. Justin Martyr, who resided for some time in Rome, addressed his apologies to the Roman emperors in Greek. Of the names of the first twelve bishops of Rome, ten are Greek and only two Latin. Clement wrote in Greek; so, also, Hermas wrote his Ποιμήν, or Shepherd, in the same tongue. * * * The majority of slaves, mechanics, and artisans were of Greek origin; and the Romans addicted to foreign practices were ready to adopt the language of that nation. Hence Greek became the tongue of the more cultivated."

The style of the epistle is such as we might expect from one born at Tarsus, "a city filled with a Greek population, and incorporated with the Roman empire," and educated at Jerusalem, under Gamaliel, the most eminent teacher of the most influential school of the time. It is a strong, manly, Greek style, wanting classical finish, and colored by Aramaean and Hebrew influence. It has the ease of a composition in a tongue with which one has been perfectly familiar from childhood, and yet betrays the influence of close devotion to the Hebrew law and prophets, in their original language.

In general, the style of the Epistle to the Romans is highly vigorous, argumentative, and philosophic, and hence it abounds in abstract terms, and in such particles as γάρ and ὅτι, which introduce a proof, or as ἵνα and ὅπως, or equivalent phrases which denote the end or purpose. γάρ, for instance, is used nearly one hundred and fifty times in this epistle, and frequently in several immediately successive clauses, as in x. 12 seq. Life and spirit is given to the style of this epistle by the frequent use of interrogations and exclamations, as in ii. 4, v. 16, vi. 3, vii. 1, xi. 2, and often elsewhere.

Irregularities of construction are not unfrequent in the Romans. They are such, however, as betray not an ignorance of the Greek language, but a degree of negligence in the use of it. They indicate a spirit fully engrossed by the importance of the theme, and less attentive to the external garb in which the thought is arrayed.

Digressions and parentheses are natural to one who is full of his subject in all its relations, so that utterances press upon him, which break in upon the even and regular flow of a particular train of remark. So, in the very beginning of the epistle, we find that the apostle, after speaking of the "gospel of God," εὐαγγέλιον Θεοῦ, immediately introduces a phrase to indicate the dignity and excellence of that gospel: ὁ προεπηγγείλατο διὰ τῶν προφητῶν . . . . . ἁγίαις. And again the clause τοῦ υἱοῦ αὐτοῦ calls forth the descriptive phrases: Τοῦ γενομένου . . . . . νεκρῶν. So again, in verse 4, after τοῦ κυρίου ἡμῶν, the parenthetical clause διὰ οὗ ἐλάβομεν (ver. 5, 6). See also ii. 11 seq, 5 : 12—18, and other passages. "This singularity," says Paley, "is a species of digression which may properly, I think, be denominated *going off at a word*. It is a turning aside from the subject, upon the occurrence of some particular word, forsaking the train of thought then in hand, and entering upon a parenthetic sentence, in which that word is the prevailing term."

The apostle also exhibits in this epistle the same tact, delicacy, discrimination and tenderness, yet mingled with perfect truthfulness and fidelity, which are conspicuous in his other writings. These characteristics are especially noticeable in the manner of his treatment of his Jewish brethren, many of whose prejudices he is obliged to oppose in this epistle. See, among other passages, ix. 1 seq., x. 1 seq , and we may also notice the manner in which he fortifies a somewhat questionable and disagreeable sentiment, by a reference to the Old Test. Scriptures, whose authority a Jew could not question. See ix. 9 seq., xiv. 11, etc.

There are occasional indications of more elaboration of style, as the use of paranomasia in i. 29, 30, v. 19 seq., specially significant employment of participles, and synonymous words, condensed expressions, etc. But these are probably rather the natural outpourings of an exuberant and highly cultivated nature, than the direct result of study. Upon this whole topic of the style of the Romans, see Davidson's Introd., Vol. II., p. 144 seq.

The general form is that of a letter, with the name of the writer prefixed, as in letters missive of churches, instead of subscribed, and with personal remarks and greetings at the beginning and end, and an occasional direct address in the body of the letter. In all other respects, it has rather the form of an essay than an epistle ; and yet it has not strictly the form of a modern essay. Such a thing was hardly known to the ancients. The author employs a greater freedom in the use and arrangement of materials, but has not less directness of aim and purpose than is exhibited by modern essay writers.

In general value to the Christian and scholar, it is not exceeded if equalled by any other of the epistles of the great apostle. It is inferior, perhaps, in a rhetorical point of view, to the 2d Corinthians, and has less of the emotional, less of the outpouring of the heart than the Epistle to the Ephesians, and some of the other epistles, for its main design is a doctrinal one. It is also a more general discussion of doctrinal points, less limited by the circumstances of the persons addressed, and less polemical than the other epistles, in which doctrines are discussed, as the Galatians; so no one book in the whole sacred canon is perhaps so important to a thorough understanding of the Christian system. Hence Calvin well says: "If a man have attained unto the true understanding of it, he hath a speedy passage made him unto all the most secret treasures of the Scripture."

Olshausen characterizes well a part of the epistle, and the requisites for understanding it, when he says, from the nature of the contents, "It may be understood why it is usually regarded as difficult. Indeed, it may be said that where there is wanting in the reader's own life an experience analogous to that of the apostle, it is utterly unintelligible. Everything in the epistle wears so strongly the impress of the greatest originality, liveliness, and freshness of experience; the apostle casts so sure and clear a glance into the most delicate circumstances of the inward life of the regenerate; he continues, with such genius, to place all that is individual in connection with that which is most general, that the reader who stands on the limited, inferior ground of natural knowledge of the world, must, at one time, become dizzy at the vast prospects into the periods of development of the universe which St. Paul discloses, and, at another, lose sight of these; in order, to look into the, as it were, microscopically exhibited circumstances which the apostle unveils with respect to the most secret processes in the depths of the soul."—Introd., p. 55, 56.

§ 7. *State of Feeling and Opinion in the Church at Rome, when the Epistle was written.*

The Church at Rome manifestly consisted of Jews and Gentiles; see § 2 above. That many of the erroneous views which Paul combats in this epistle, were such as the Hebrews and others, such as the Gentiles, were prone to cherish, there can be no doubt. The national pride of the Jew; his attachment to the Mosaic institutes, and especially to the Levitical rites and distinctions of clean and unclean; his impatience of subordination, in any respect, to Gentiles; his unwillingness to believe that they could be admitted to equal privileges with the Jew, in the kingdom of the Messiah, and particularly without becoming proselytes to the Mosaic religion; his proneness to feel repugnance to the government of heathen magistrates are all plainly alluded to. On the other hand, the Gentiles disregarded the prejudices of the Jews, especially about circumcision, and meats and drinks, and holidays; they were wounded at the claim of superiority which the Jews seemed to make, and doubtless needed all the cautions and precepts, in reference to these points, given in the hortatory part of the epistle.

Whilst, then, it cannot be doubted that there were individual differences of feeling among the Jewish and Gentile members of the Christian community, which would bring them into conflict at times, yet it seems equally certain that these differences were not marked, or such as called for severe reproof, as among the Galatians (see various passages in Paul's Epistle to them). This condition of things is plainly indicated in chap. xvi. 17 seq.: "Now I beseech you brethren, mark (σκοπεῖν) them which cause divisions and offences contrary to the doctrine which ye have learned * * * For your *obedience* is come abroad unto all men. I am glad therefore on your behalf," etc. In the whole discussion of the epistle, and in all the allusions to the proposed visit of the apostle too, there is a freedom from a polemical tone, both of expression and feeling, which to my mind precludes the idea of wrangling and strife among those to whom it was sent. The address to them is not, Oh! foolish Romans, who hath bewitched you? but, "Beloved of God: * * * I thank my God through Jesus Christ for you all. that your faith is spoken of throughout the whole world;" and "I long to see you, that I may impart unto you some spiritual gift, to the end you may be established" (i. 7, 8, 11). Cf. also i. 12, xv. 32, etc. There seems, then, to us, to be nothing in the epistle which is contrary to the belief that it was written without any positive information of differences between Judaizing and Gentile Christians at Rome, but with a strong feeling, derived from observation and experience, that diversities of opinion must exist, which a general discussion of prominent points of doctrine would have a tendency to repress. Still, it would be perhaps too much to say, with Olshausen, that "we find in the Epistle to the Romans a *purely* objective statement of the nature of the Gospel, grounded only on the general opposition between Jews and Gentiles, and not on the more special opposition existing in the church itself, between Judaizing and non-Judaizing Christians."—English Transl., p. 42.

The apostle doubtless meant to establish some great and general principles of Christianity, and also to apply them to the state of the church at Rome. So Luther, Calvin, Melancthon, Bucer, Michaelis, Tholuck, and others, have for substance judged. That Paul intermingles with general truths many things which are local, is almost a matter of course in an epistle to a particular church.

BRIEF ANALYSIS

OF THE

CONTENTS OF THE EPISTLE TO THE ROMANS.

WERE I to select a motto, which would, in a single brief sentence designate the substance of what this epistle contains, it should be taken from the apostle Paul himself:

ΧΡΙΣΤΟΣ ἩΜΙΝ ΔΙΚΑΙΟΣΥΝΗ ΤΕ ΚΑΙ ἉΓΙΑΣΜΟΣ,

CHRIST OUR JUSTIFICATION AND SANCTIFICATION.

The first five chapters exhibit Christ as the author and efficient cause of our justification.

After an appropriate and affectionate introduction (i. 1—16), the apostle proceeds to show, that the Gentiles had universally transgressed the law of God which was written on their hearts, by indulging in a great variety of sins which they knew to be wrong (i. 17—32). He next proceeds to show, that the Jews were still more guilty, inasmuch as they had sinned against more light and more distinguished privileges (ii. 1—3, 19). He now draws the conclusion from these premises, that justification by deeds of law, *i. e.*, on the score of merit or on the ground of perfect obedience, is impossible; for, inasmuch as all men have sinned against the law of God, all are under its condemnation, and therefore grace or mercy only can save them from perishing. This grace is vouchsafed only through Christ, and has been procured by his sufferings and death in behalf of sinners (iii. 20, 31).

The Old Testament also teaches the same doctrine of *gratuitous* justification: and that this should be extended to Gentiles as well as Jews (iv. 1—25).

The happy fruits of such a state of justification — peace with God, support and consolation in the midst of trials and sufferings, a hope which maketh not ashamed, and never can be disappointed — are next described by the writer (v. 1—11). And that it is perfectly proper and becoming on the part of God, to extend those blessings to all, both Jews and Gentiles, is strikingly taught by an exhibition of the fact, that all have been made to share in the evils which flowed from the apostasy of our original progenitors (v. 12—19). Even in those cases where sin has exhibited its greatest power, the grace of the gospel is made to triumph over it (v. 20, 21).

Thus is CHRIST OUR JUSTIFICATION set forth by the apostle. He comes next to exhibit CHRIST OUR SANCTIFICATION. This important topic he introduces, by discussing the objection raised against the doctrine of gratuitous justification, viz., *that it tends to encourage sin.* He shows in the first place, from various considerations, the incongruity and impossibility of this (vi 1—23). He then proceeds to contrast a state of grace and the means and motives to holiness which it furnishes, with a legal state; and to show that in the latter, the sinner has no hope of maintaining a holy character, while in the former he is abundantly furnished with the means of doing it; consequently that a state of grace, so far from encouraging men to sin, affords them the only hope of their being able to subdue and mortify sin (vii. 1—viii, 17).

The apostle then, as he had before done at the close of his discussion respecting justification (v. 1—11), goes on to show the consolation which the gospel affords, under the various troubles of the present life (viii. 18—27); and in the sequel he concludes, as in the former case, with exultation in the certainty of future and eternal glory to all who truly love God (viii. 28—39).

The part of the epistle properly *doctrinal*, concludes with the 8th chapter. Chapter ix. discusses the objection raised against the dealings of God with his creatures, when he makes some of them the distinguished subjects of his mercy, and passes by others. Chap. x. confirms still farther, by various considerations, and particularly by texts cited from the Old Testament, the idea that the Jews who remain in unbelief are and must be cast off; and therefore that this is not a new or strange doctrine. Chap. xi. continues to urge the same subject; but at the close deduces from it the cheering consolation, that even the rejection of the Jews will be made a great blessing to the world, as it will be the occasion of the sending of salvation to the Gentiles. And if their *rejection* be attended with consequences so important, then surely their *reception* again will fill the world with its happy fruits.

The rest of the epistle is *hortatory*, and is adapted specially to warn the church at Rome against several errors, to which, in their circumstances they were peculiarly exposed. First, they are exhorted to lay aside all pride, and envious distinctions, and claims to preference on the ground of office, gifts, etc.; and to conduct themselves in a kind, affectionate, gentle, peaceable manner (xii. 1—21).

Next, they are exhorted to a quiet and orderly demeanor in regard to the civil power, which the Jews were especially prone to contemn (xiii. 1—7). The great law of love is to be regarded and obeyed toward all men, without or within the church (xiii. 8—14).

Thirdly, the Gentile Christians are admonished to respect the scruples of their Jewish brethren on the subject of eating meats offered to idols, and admonished that they have no right to interfere either in this matter or in other things of the like tenor (xiv. 1—xv. 7). On the other hand, the Jews are admonished that their Gentile brethren have equal rights and privileges with themselves, under the gospel dispensation (xv. 8—13).

The writer then expresses his good hopes concerning them all, his kind and tender regard for them, and his purposes in respect to visiting them (xv. 14, seq.).

Lastly, he subjoins the salutation of the various Christians who were with him; cautions them against those who seek to make divisions among them; and concludes with a doxology (xvi.).

Such is the brief sketch of the contents of the epistle before us. It is one, however, which the reader may perhaps not fully understand and appreciate, until he shall have attentively studied the whole; but still, one to which he may recur, in order to satisfy himself in some measure respecting the relation which a particular part has to the whole. To make this satisfaction complete, it is important that he should become well acquainted with the general scope and object of the whole epistle. The details are given in the introductions to the respective parts.

COMMENTARY ON THE ROMANS.

CHAP. I. 1—16.

The introductory part of the Epistle to the Romans, i 1—16, contains (1) A salutation, vers 1—7 (2) A brief declaration of some personal wishes and concerns, vers. 8—16. The apostle, being a stranger in person to the Church at Rome, begins his epistle by exhibiting the nature of his office, as divinely commissioned to preach the Gospel, ver 1; which Gospel had been before announced by the ancient prophets, ver 2, whose subject was Jesus, of the seed of David according to the flesh, but the decreed Son of God, who dispensed the Holy Spirit with power after his resurrection, vers 3, 4. From him, thus constituted *Lord of all*, Paul avers that he had received such grace as made him Christ's devoted follower, and also the office of an apostle to the Gentiles, in order to promote the knowledge of a Saviour among all men, ver 5, and to the Romans, as among these Gentiles, and called to be heirs of the grace of life, he wishes every needed spiritual and temporal blessing, ver. 6.

Having thus indicated his right to speak to them, and given them his salutation, he proceeds to speak of the gratification that the good report of their faith had given him, ver 9, and assures them of his remembrance of them in his prayers, and of his desire to visit them, ver 10; and thus communicate and in return receive spiritual blessings, vers 11, 12 He then reassures the Romans of his long cherished desire to come to them and preach the Gospel, ver 13; since, as apostle of the Gentiles, he was under obligation to preach to *them* everywhere, and did not shrink from the performance of his duty even at Rome, vers. 14, 15; for he was not ashamed of the Gospel, ver 16

(1) *Paul*, Παῦλος, probably a Roman and not a Hebrew name, *i.e.*, *Paulus;* compare the name of the Roman proconsul, Sergius Paulus, Acts xiii. 7, who became a convert to Christianity, through the instrumentality of Paul. The Hebrew name of the apostle was שָׁאוּל, Σαῦλος; and he is first called Παῦλος in Acts xiii. 9, immediately after the mention of Sergius Paulus. Hence many have thought, that Παῦλος is a name which the apostle took in honor of the proconsul. The more natural explanation is, that Παῦλος was a second name of Roman origin, given him in accordance with the custom of the times. While the Jews were subject to the power of the Seleucidæ on the throne of Syria, it was very common among them to adopt a second name of Greek origin; *e. g. Jesus*, Jason; *Jehoiakim*, Alkimos, etc. So under

the Roman power; *Dostai*, Dositheus; *Tarphin*, Tryrpho. A comparison of these will show, that in general the second name bore some resemblance in sound to the first. So Σαῦλος, Παῦλος.

The word δοῦλος means, in itself, *one devoted to the service of another, one who is subject to the will or control of another.* Of course it may import a station or condition which is in itself high or low, honorable or dishonorable, according to the state or rank of the master. A *servant* of a man, *i. e.*, of any common man, is in the strict import of the term, a *slave*. But the *servants of a king* may be courtiers of the highest rank, who count this title a matter of honor. (1) *Servants of God* is an appellation given to the prophets, Moses, Joshua, etc., Rev. x. 7. xi. 18. xv. 3. Deut. xxxiv. 5. Josh. i. 1. Jer. xxv. 4. Amos iii. 7; and in like manner the apostles and primitive preachers of the gospel are called *the Servants of Christ*, Gal. i. 10. Phil. i. 1. Titus i. 1. James i. 1. 2 Peter i. 1. Col. iv. 12. (2) Δοῦλος is also employed as meaning simply or principally *a worshipper* of Christ or of God, *one devoted to his service;* for in such a sense we find the word employed in 1 Peter ii. 16. Eph. vi. 6. Rev. vii. 3. Luke ii. 29. Acts iv. 29. Ps. cxiii. 1, al.

The word δοῦλος here, does not seem to indicate *official* station, like that of the ancient prophets and messengers of God mentioned under No. 1; but is employed in the second sense, to designate the apostle as *one devoted to the service of Christ, one ready to obey him in all things, and to regard the promotion of his interests as the great object of his life.* Interpreted in this way, δοῦλος does not anticipate the meaning of ἀπόστολος. There is rather a *gradation* in the sense. First, Paul is represented as being devoted to the service of Christ, and then as commissioned with a special office in that service; which could not be said of every δοῦλος. So Reiche Glockler, and others.

Jesus Christ, Ἰησοῦ Χριστοῦ, in the Gen. here, shows the relation in which Paul stood to the Saviour, and that the apostle's business or object (as δοῦλος) was to promote the cause of Christ or to forward his work. Ἰησοῦς is the Greek form of the Hebrew name יְהוֹשֻׁעַ or of its later abridgment and substitute יֵשׁוּעַ, *i. e., Saviour,* or *he who will save*. Χριστός is properly a participial *adjective* formed from χρίω, *to anoint*, and means *the anointed one*. It is, like κύριος, which is properly an adjective, usually employed by prefixing the article, as an *appellative*, when applied to the Saviour, and commonly it designates him as *king*, or *possessed of royal dignity*. Kings were appointed to their office, among the Jews; and also high priests. The name *Christ* מָשִׁיחַ, Χριστός, *the Messiah*, may refer then to either of these high offices or dignities; for he is both king and priest for ever. The use of χριστός alone in the Gospels, is hardly to be regarded in the light of a proper *cognomen*, but rather as a mere *attributive* appellation. In the epistles, it is not unfrequently used in the way of a proper *cognomen*.

Κλητός, lit. *called*, but the meaning here is *chosen*, *invited*, viz., chosen to the office of an apostle; see Acts ix. 15, σκεῦος ἐκλογῆς μοί ἐστιν οὗτος, also Acts xxvi. 17, where the κλητός here is expressed by ἐξαιρούμενός σε, *I have taken thee out of*, *I have selected thee from*. In Gal. i. 15, it is more fully expressed by ὁ ἀφορίσας με ἐκ κοιλίας μητρός μου, καὶ καλέσας διὰ τῆς χάριτος αὐτοῦ, *i. e.*, who set me apart or designated me from my earliest years for the apostolic office, and in due time called me to it by his grace; Jer. i. 5. The word κλητός sometimes has the sense merely of *invited*, *bidden*; *e. g.*, Matt. xx. 16, xxii. 14. Yet in the writings of Paul it is not so used, but always in the sense of *efficient calling*, as we say, *i. e.*, it means not only that the person designated has been *invited* or *selected*, but that *he has accepted the invitation*; 1 Cor. i. 1, 2, 24. Rom. i. 6, 7. viii. 28; with which cf. Gal. i. 15. Jude v. 1. Heb. iii. 1. Rom. xi. 29. Eph. iv. 1.

Apostle, Ἀπόστολος may mean a *legate* of any kind, *one sent by another* on any kind of business or message. The word is used in this way, in John xiii. 16. Phil. ii. 25. *A divine messenger* or *prophet* it designates in Luke xi. 49. Eph. iii. 5. Rev. xviii. 20. ii. 2; and in like manner it also signifies *the messengers of Christ* which is the usual meaning of the word throughout the N. Testament. To invest them with this office, an immediate choice by the Saviour in person seems to have been necessary. This is implied in our text; and more plainly still in Gal. i. 1.—Occasionally the *companions* of the apostles, or the *delegates* sent by them, are called *apostles;* so in 2 Cor. viii. 23. Acts xiv. 4, 14. Rom. xvi. 7.

Set apart for the gospel of God, Ἀφωρισμένος . . . . θεοῦ, *i. e.*, chosen or selected in order to preach the gospel of God, viz., that gospel of which God is the author, θεοῦ being *Genitivus auctoris*. The word ἀφωρισμένος *seems to be intended as* epexegetical of κλητός, *i. e.*, it expresses the same idea in different language. Hesychius explains ἀφωρισμένος by ἐκλελεγμένος, *chosen*, διακεκριμένος, *selected*. In the same sense ἀφορίσατε occurs in Acts xiii. 2. See the same sentiment in Gal. i. 15, Jer. i. 5. The meaning is, that God, who foreknows all things, did set him apart, choose, select him for the work of the gospel, even from the earliest period of his life, Gal. i. 15. So it is said of Jeremiah, that he was set apart, selected, for the prophetic office even before he was formed in his mother's womb; by all which expressions is meant, that God who knows all persons and events before they exist or take place, has a definite object in view which he intends to accomplish by them. In classic Greek, the verb ἀφορίζειν is more usually employed in a bad sense *(in malam partem)*, meaning to *exterminate, excommunicate, repudiate*, etc. But in Hellenistic Greek it is more commonly employed *in bonam partem*, as here.

For the gospel, Εἰς εὐαγγέλιον, has the same sense as εἰς τὸ εὐαγγελίσασθαι εὐαγγέλιον, *in order to preach the gospel*. This method of using the Acc. (with the preposition εἰς prefixed) as a *nomen actionis*, is a frequent idiom of Paul's writings, and resembles the use of the Heb. Inf. (with a ב prefixed) as a *nomen actionis*. Εὐαγγέλιον itself is sometimes employed to denote *the preaching of the gospel*; *e. g.*, 1 Cor. iv. 15, ix. 14 — εὐαγγέλιον Θεοῦ Chrysostom understands as meaning *the gospel concerning God*, viewing Θεοῦ as *Genitivus objecti*. But this interpretation is plainly erroneous ; for *the object* is supplied in verse 3, viz. εὐαγγέλιον Θεοῦ .... περὶ τοῦ υἱοῦ αὐτοῦ. Theophylact rightly explains the phrase: ὡς δωρηθὲν παρὰ τοῦ Θεοῦ [the gospel] *as given by God*. For the sentiment that the gospel is of God, and that Christ taught it as received from him, let the reader compare John viii. 28, 38. v. 19, 30. xii. 49. xiv. 10, 24. xvii. 4 — 8.

(2) *Which he formerly, (*or *in former times,) declared (*or *published) by his prophets, in the holy Scriptures*, Ὃ προεπηγγείλατο .... ἁγίαις. In like manner, Paul in his defence before Agrippa says, that he had proclaimed nothing as a preacher of the gospel, which the prophets and Moses had not declared should take place, Acts xxvi. 22. That Christ and all his apostles believed and taught, that the Old Testament abounds in prophecies respecting him, there can be no doubt on the part of any one who attentively reads the New Testament; see Acts x. 43. xviii. 28. 1 Peter i. 10. 2 Peter i. 19.

Even the heathen of the apostle's time had become acquainted with the expectations of the Jews based on their Scriptures, in regard to the appearance of the Messiah. Thus Tacitus speaks of this subject; "Pluribus persuasio inerat, *antiquis sacerdotum literis* contineri, eo ipso tempore forè, ut valesceret Oriens, profectique Judæâ rerum potirentur," Hist. V. 13. In the same manner Suetonius his contemporary expresses himself: "Percrebuerat *Oriente toto vetus et constans opinio*, esse in fatis, ut eo tempore Judæâ profecti rerum potirentur," in Vespas. c. 4. The first promises respecting the Messiah were merely of a general nature, unaccompanied by peculiar and characteristic declarations; *e. g.* Gen. iii. 15. xii. 3. xvii. 4, 5. xlix. 10. In later times, it was foretold that the expected King and Deliverer would be of the progeny of David, 2 Sam. vii. 16. Psalm lxxxix. 35 — 37. In several Psalms, some traits of the life, office, character, and sufferings of this illustrious personage were given; viz. Psalm ii. xvi. xxii. xlv. cx. etc.; still more graphically is the Messiah described in Is. liii.; and individual occurrences in his history are given in later prophets, *e. g.*, Zech. ix. 9. xi. 13, Mal. iii. 1, seq. iv. 2, seq. It has been observed, that Malachi's declaration in the last chapter of his prophecy, is homogeneous with the very first annunciation of the gospel in Mark i. 2. Our English version of προεπηγγείλατο, *promised afore*, does not give the proper meaning of the word.

In the Holy Scriptures, Ἐν γραφαῖς ἁγίαις. The Jews employed either γραφή the singular, or γραφαί the plural, indifferently. The first means the *corpus librorum sacrorum;* the second refers to the same collection, as made up of several particular writings. The epithet ἁγίαι is given to γραφαί, because the Scriptures were regarded as worthy of all reverence, or because they were looked upon as being inspired by τὸ πνεῦμα τὸ ἅγιον.

(3) *Respecting his Son*, Περὶ τοῦ υἱοῦ αὐτοῦ. This clause should be joined, in the readers mind, to εὐαγγέλιον θεοῦ at the close of ver. 1. Verse 2 is a circumstantial declaration, thrown in to enhance the value of the gospel, or its credibility and dignity. Tholuck joins περὶ τοῦ υἱοῦ αὐτοῦ with προεπηγγείλατο; but as the verb itself relates to εὐαγγέλιον θεοῦ, it seems to me more congruous to refer περὶ κ. τ. λ. to the same words.*

Who was born of the seed of David, in respect to the flesh, τοῦ γενομένου . . . . σάρκα. The verse itself is replete with difficulties; and especially so to one who is not familiarly conversant with the character of Paul's style. Tholuck compares the latter to the urgent force of waves, which swell one above another in continual succession. It is an obvious peculiarity of this apostle's style, that he abounds in what are commonly called parentheses. His mind was so glowing and so full of ideas, that the expression of a single word often calls forth, as it were, a burst of thought respecting the import of that word, which hinders him from advancing in the sentence that he had begun, until he has given vent to the feelings thus incidentally occasioned. The expression of these feelings makes here what may be named *parentheses;* although they may not always be designated as such in our printed books. To illustrate what I mean, let us take the examples in the first

---

* It is a matter of little importance as far as the sense is concerned, whether this clause is considered as an adjunct of "the gospel of God" εὐαγγέλιον θεοῦ, or of the nearer clause. "which he formerly announced," ὃ προεπηγγείλατο. Many with Tholuck prefer the latter connection. See Alford's Comm.

paragraph of the epistle before us. When Paul (ver. 1) had named the εὐαγγέλιον θεοῦ which would recall to the minds of his readers the gospel that was then preached by himself and others, he immediately adds, in order to enforce on their minds a becoming idea of the dignity and excellence of this gospel, ὃ προεπηγγείλατο διὰ τῶν προφητῶν αὐτοῦ ἐν γραφαῖς ἁγίαις; after which he resumes his subject. But no sooner has he uttered the words τοῦ υἱοῦ αὐτοῦ, than another burst of thought respecting the exalted personage thus named escapes from him. First, this *Son is* γενομένου .... σάρκα, a descendant of David, the most exalted king who ever occupied the Jewish throne, according to the promises respecting the Messiah, *e. g.*, in 2 Sam. vii. 16, Ps. lxxxix. 35 — 37. Secondly, he is τοῦ ὁρισθέντος .... νεκρῶν, *i. e.*, he is the Son of God clothed, according to decree, with supreme dominion, especially in regard to the bestowment of the Holy Spirit, after his resurrection from the dead. Having thus designated some striking characteristics of the Son of God, he resumes his theme by the words Ἰησοῦ .... ἡμῶν, which are in apposition with τοῦ υἱοῦ αὐτοῦ in ver. 3. The words τοῦ κυρίου ἡμῶν again suggest another train of thought, which the writer stops to utter, viz. δι' οὗ .... Χριστοῦ, after which he resumes his theme and finishes the sentence by πᾶσι τοῖς .... Χριστοῦ, ver. 7. The greater part of this apparently involved sentence, might evidently be included in parentheses; and then the simple sentence would run thus: Παῦλος .... ἀφωρισμένος εἰς εὐαγγέλιον θεοῦ περὶ τοῦ υἱοῦ αὐτοῦ .... Ἰησοῦ Χριστοῦ τοῦ Κυρίου ἡμῶν .... πᾶσι τοῖς οὖσιν κ. τ. λ. (See introduction).

Descended, born, γενομένου; so the word is not unfrequently employed. — Ἐκ σπέρματος, *of the posterity, of the lineage.* — Κατὰ σάρκα, *in respect to human nature* or *his fleshly existence.* Σάρξ denotes literally *flesh, i. e.,* the flesh of a living or animated being, in distinction from that of a dead one, which is κρέας. It denotes *body* also; not in the sense of σῶμα which has reference to the compacting of the whole of the parts into one mass, but *body* as distinguished from mind, the *visible,* as distinguished from the *invisible* part. Hence it is very often used, both in the Old Testament and the New, for our *animal nature,* the *animal man* (so to speak). Frail, perishable man, also, and man with carnal appetites and passions, are often designated by it; as every lexicon will show. As kindred with this, it often means *man as living in his present fleshly and dying* or *transitory state,* in distinction from another and different condition in a future world; so Gal. ii. 20. Phil. i. 22, 21. Heb. v. 7, applied to Christ. 1 Pet. iv. 2. 2 Cor. x. 3. In the passage before us, the *human nature* or *condition* of Christ, as descended from the royal progeny of David, is designated. But why so? Because the promise was made to *David*, that the Messiah should descend from him. Hence the genealogy in Matthew: " The Son of *David*, the Son of Abraham." So the common feeling and views of the Jews decided: " How do they [the Scribes] say, that the Christ is *David's Son?*" So the blind man (Luke xviii. 39) says : "Jesus, thou *Son of David*, have mercy on me." Comp. also Luke i. 27, 32. Matt. xv. 22. xii. 23. xxi. 9, 15. xxii. 41 — 46. John vii. 42. 2 Tim. ii. 8 ; which most abundantly illustrate the views of the Jews and of the apostles. It is not, therefore, merely *a son* of David which is designated by the phrase before us, but *the long expected and hoped for Son* of David, *i. e.*, the promised Messiah.

We must regard this clause, τοῦ γενομένου ἐκ σπέρματος Δαυῒδ κατὰ σάρκα, then, as added to υἱοῦ αὐτοῦ, for the sake of pointing out the fulfilment of the promises of God and the expectations of pious Jews, in regard to the Messiah or Son of God; a thought naturally suggested by what the writer had said before in relation to the declarations in the Scriptures. But lest the reader might argue that *Son of David*, considered as meaning *Messiah*, implied nothing more than one of David's ordinary natural descendants; Paul adds κατὰ σάκρα, *in respect to his human nature;* where σάρξ is plainly employed in the same sense as in John i. 14, ὁ λόγος σάρξ ἐγένετο, *i. e.*, *the Logos became man*, or *took on him a human nature.* But if the Son of God was a mere man, in the view of Paul, how strange it would be for him to say: γενομένου . . . . κατὰ σάρκα; an expression never used respecting any other individual. The application plainly is, that he had some other nature than the *human*. The same distinction is implied in Rom. ix. 5, ἐξ ὧν ὁ Χριστὸς τὸ κατὰ σάρκα. In his other nature, he is there said to be ὁ ἐπὶ πάντων θεός.

Thus we have one special characteristic of the Son of God or of the promised Messiah, viz., that he was, as to his human nature, of the royal progeny of David. Now follows a second, of a more exalted and peculiar kind.

(4) *The decreed Son of God, etc.*, Ὁρισθέντος . . . . νεκρῶν. The word ὁρισθέντος here has often been rendered *decreed, decided, ordained;* so Clavius, Erasmus, Faber, and many others. This accords with the meaning of the word ὁρίζω in Heb. iv. 7. Acts xi. 29. ii. 23. x. 42. xvii. 26, 31. Luke xxii. 22 ; and these are all the instances in which it is used in the New Testament, excepting the case before us. In like manner the oldest Latin interpreters translated *qui prædestinatus est;* as appears from the Latin interpretation of Irenæus, III. 18, 32; from Rufin's version of Origen, and Hilary *De Trinitate*, VII. In the like way, also, some recent interpreters have rendered ὁρισθέντος.

But this sense of the word is alleged, by many critics, not to accord with the design of the writer. In order to prove this, they suppose the passage (by way of illustration) to be construed thus ; '*Ordained* to be the Son of God with power, κατὰ πνεῦμα ἁγιωσύνης, *i. e.*, by the miraculous gifts which the Spirit conferred upon him, or by the miracles which the Spirit enabled him to perform ; ' and then ask, ' How did the miraculous gifts or deeds of Jesus *ordain* him to be the Son of God, or *constitute* him such ? He possessed these gifts, or performed these miracles, because he was the Son of God; he was not made so by the possession of his gifts or the performance of his deeds.' And admitting their grounds of interpreting the rest of the verse, their objection seems to be decisive against the exegesis which they oppose.

Grotius, in order to relieve this difficulty with respect to ὁρισθέντος, construes the passage thus : ' The regal dignity of Jesus, as Son of God, was *predestinated*, or *prefigured*, when he wrought signs and wonders in his incarnate state.' But how *predestinating* can be made to mean *prefiguring*, I am not aware.

Others construe thus : ' Ordained to be the powerful Son of God, in his *pneumatic* condition [or state of exaltation], by his resurrection from the dead.' But in this case we are compelled to ask : How could his resurrection *decree* or *ordain* his exalted state ? It might be the consequence of a decree that he should be exalted ; it was so ; but in what manner the resurrection could *ordain* or *decree* his exaltation, it would be difficult to explain.

The passage has also been interpreted : ' *Constituted* the Son of God *with power*, in his *pneumatic* condition, *after* his resurrection from the dead.' For although he was the Son of God *before* his resurrection, yet he was not the Son of God ἐν δυνάμει, in the sense here meant, until after his ascension to the right hand of the Majesty on high.

Origen, Chrysostom, Cyril, Theodoret, Theophylact, Œcumenius, the Syriac version, and the great majority of modern critics, give the sense: *shown, demonstrated, exhibited, declared,* ὁρισθέντος =δειχθέντος, ἀποφανθέντος, κριθέντος, ὁμολογηθέντος. Of such a meaning for ὁρίζω, it is true, no example can be found in the New Testament, nor in the classics, which seems to be exactly in point. Passow gives no sense of this kind to ὁρίζω, in his lexicon. I find only one example (if indeed this be one) in the instances produced by Elsner, which will stand the test of scrutiny; this is: " A patron of what is just, δικαστὴν ὁρίζομεν γνήσιον, *we call a true judge*, or *we declare to be a judge worthy of the name.*" But even here, the sense of *deciding, determining, defining,* is altogether a good one, and equally good for ὁρίζομεν ; and this agrees with the usual meaning of the word. Still, as ὁρίζω (from ὅρος) means literally to *prescribe the boundaries* or *limits* of any thing, and thus, by defining it, to distinguish it from other things; so the secondary meaning given by Chrysostom, viz. δειχθέντος ἀποφανθέντος, *declared, shown*, is not an unnatural one, although destitute (so far as I can discover) of any actual *usus loquendi* to support it. The lexicon of Zonaras gives the same gloss to the word: ὁρισθέντος = ἀποδειχθέντος, ἀποφανθέντος.

It is a safe rule, not to adopt the meaning of a word which is *not* supported by the *usus loquendi*, when another meaning which *is* supported by it can be given, that will make good sense. And in the case before us it is as good sense to say, that "Christ was *constituted* the Son of God with power, after his resurrection from the dead," as to say, that "Christ was *shown* to be the Son of God with power, after his resurrection from the dead." For after the resurrection, he was advanced to an elevation which, as Messiah, he did not before possess; com. Phil. ii. 9—11. Heb. i. 3. ii. 9. xii. 2. Rev. iii. 21. Matt. xix. 28. Nay one might say, that the more energetic meaning of the word is to be found in *constituted*. As an instance of the like sense, appeal has been made to Acts x. 42, where Christ is said to be ὁ ὡρισμένος ὑπὸ τοῦ θεοῦ κριτὴς ζώντων καὶ νεκρῶν, *the constituted or appointed judge of the living and the dead*. For the like sense of ὁρίζω, appeal is also made to Acts xvii. 31, ὥρισε, sc. κριτήν, *i. e.*, he [God] hath *constituted* or *appointed* him [Christ] the judge, etc., comp. xvii. 26, ὁρίσας . . . . καιροὺς. But of this meaning of ὁρίζω as applicable to Rom. i. 4, I now doubt, although I formerly was disposed to adopt it.

If we should construe the phrase, as some do: "Declared to be the Son of God with power, by the Holy Spirit, on account of (by) his resurrection from the dead;" one might then ask : How could the *resurrection* declare in any special manner, that Christ was the Son of God? Was not Lazarus raised from the dead? Were not others raised from the dead, by Christ, by the apostles, by Elijah, and by the bones of Elisha? And yet was their resurrection proof that they were the sons of God? God did indeed prepare the way for universal dominion to be given to Christ, by raising him from the dead. To the like purpose is the apostle's assertion in Acts xvii. 31. But how an event common to him, to Lazarus, and to many others, could of itself demonstrate him to be the Son of God ἐν δυνάμει, remains to be shown.

The reasons produced by Reiche in his recent commentary, and also by my friend, the Rev. A. Barnes, in his excellent little volume on the Romans, in favor of this interpretation, are not satisfactory to my mind. They both, with many others, understand ἐν δυνάμει, here as *adverbially* employed, and make it to qualify ὁρισθέντος, so that the meaning is *powerfully demonstrated* or *shown*. It cannot be questioned that ἐν δυνάμει might be rendered adverbially, like δυνάτως. But had the apostle meant that ἐν δυνάμει should qualify ὁρισθέντος, all the usual principles of Greek construction and syntax would demand that he should have written, τοῦ ἐν δυνάμει ὁρισθέντος υἱοῦ, the place between the article and the participle being the appropriate one, in order to avoid ambiguity of sense or construction, when a *noun* is thus employed. Then again, no example has been produced, and I must doubt, until I see it, whether any can be produced, of the Greeks applying δύναμις to designate the *force* or *strength* of a logical demonstration made only to the mind. It always, certainly in the New Testament, has reference to the active force or energy of an *agent*, either corporeal or spiritual, when employed in such a way. The Greeks would characterize the *demonstrative* force of *evidence* or *logic*, in a very different way from this. The objections, therefore, in point of grammatical construction and propriety of idiom, seem to me to be conclusive against such an exegesis. And the references by the commentators in question to Col. i. 29, τὴν ἐνέργειαν αὐτοῦ τὴν ἐνεργουμένην ἐν ἐμοὶ ἐν δυνάμει and to Mark ix. 1, ἕως ἂν ἴδωσι τὴν βασιλείαν τοῦ Θεοῦ ἐληλυθυῖαν ἐν δυνάμει, do not give any satisfaction as to their application of ἐν δυνάμει in the case above, because here the δύναμις is that of *agents*, and not that of logic or evidence. *The kingdom of God*, of course means the *persons* who compose it, and ἐν δυνάμει *the efficiency* with which they act, or (at least) with which God himself acts, in building it up.

Nor am I convinced, that the resurrection *powerfully demonstrated* Christ to be the Son of God, by the allegation (in order to remove an apparently formidable difficulty as stated above), that 'in the circumstances of the case, after all the special claims that Jesus had made to be considered as the Messiah, his resurrection was a signal proof that he was the Son of God.' This it would do, however, only in an *indirect* way, and such an inference could be drawn from it only by virtue of reasoning from consequences. It proved only, that the claims of Jesus were allowed to be just and true. How could the power of God the Father, exerted to raise Christ from the dead, prove the divine or exalted nature of the latter? It proved only that God is Almighty, and that he regarded with approbation the claims of Jesus. One of these claims was, that he was the Son of God; but this was only one among many. How then could the whole force of the evidence to be drawn from the resurrection, concentre in this sole point? And when Reiche asserts (p. 119), that "Paul always appeals to the resurrection of Christ as the *princi-*

pal evidence of his divinity," and refers us to Col. xv. 3, 17. Rom. iv. 24. Acts xvii. 23, as proofs of this, one is tempted to ask, what is meant by *evidence?* These passages merely show that Christ was raised from the dead, in order to complete the work of mediation and redemption, and also to be the future judge of the world; nothing more. Nor is it in the nature of things, that resurrection from the dead can prove *Godhead?* Was it the Godhead that died, and was raised again; or was it the *man* Christ Jesus? How could the raising of the man by the Father, then, prove the Godhead of Christ? In whatever light I look at this interpretation, I feel constrained to reject it. Neither Paul nor any other New Testament writer makes the evidences of Christ's divine nature, (or higher nature, if you choose so to name it,) to depend on the resurrection; at least this is done nowhere, unless it be in the passage before us. Would it not be strange that this should stand entirely alone, in respect to such an important point as the interpretation in question makes it?

I understand ὁρισθέντος in its usual (and only defensible) meaning, first stated above, viz. *decreed, appointed, established by decree, determined by decision,* viz. of a superior. I find in this sense of the word a most expressive meaning in reference to Ps. ii. 7, which, I doubt not, the apostle had in his mind; "I will declare *the decree*, (אֲסַפְּרָה אֶל־חֹק); The Lord hath said unto me, Thou art my Son; this day have I begotten thee." Here then is the *decreed, destinated,* or *appointed* Son, to whom Paul refers, the very Messiah promised in one of the most explicit and striking predictions in all the Old Testament; comp. ver. 2, ἐν γραφαῖς ἁγίαις. And what is the *decree* of which the Psalmist speaks? It is, that the Son shall be made universal king, and that his enemies shall be dashed in pieces before him, Ps. ii. 8—12; and all this not in a temporal but *spiritual* sense. What is this now but to be the Son of God ἐν δυνάμει? It has been suggested that there is "no passage where δύναμις means *authority, office,* etc."; but we need only consult Matt. xxvi. 64. Mark xiv. 62. Luke xxii. 69. Luke iv. 36. Acts iv. 7. 1 Cor. v. 4. Rev. xiii. 2, iv. 11. v. 12. vii. 12. xii. 10, in order to correct this impression. It is even employed (by metonymy) for those in office and clothed with power, *e. g.,* 1 Cor. xv. 24. Eph. i. 21; so for angels good or bad, who are high in station, Rom. viii. 38. 1 Pet. iii. 22.

It would be clear enough, then, that we might construe τοῦ ὁρισθέντος υἱοῦ θεοῦ ἐν δυνάμει, as meaning "the Son of God, who by decree is possessed of universal authority or dominion." My only doubt whether ἐν δυνάμει should be so construed here, arises from its junction with the next words.

Κατὰ πνεῦμα ἁγιωσύνης, which, like every other expression in this verse, is contested. Some translate, *by the Holy Spirit;* and some, *by a holy spirit, i. e.,* a divine and miraculous power, which some represent as the miraculous power with which Christ was endowed, and others as that which was shown in raising him from the dead. A third party construe πνεῦμα here, as designating the higher nature or condition of Christ, *i. e.*, his *pneumatic* nature or condition, if I may so express it.

Schleusner, Flatt, Bengel, and others, find in ἁγιωσύνη a meaning designedly different from that of ἁγιότης or ἁγιασμός. Thus Bengel, "ἁγιότης *sanctitas*, ἁγιασμός *sanctificatio*, ἁγιωσύνη *sanctimonia.*" But this seems to be imaginary; for even in Latin, *sanctimonia* and *sanctitas* differ only in form, not in sense. In Greek, as there is no difference between ἀγαθοσύνη and ἀγαθότης, so there appears to be none between ἁγιωσύνη and ἁγιότης. The Seventy use ἁγιωσύνη for עֹז, *strength*, in Ps. xcvi. 6 (xcv. 6); for קדשׁ in Ps. xcvii. 12 (xcvi. 12); and for הוֹד in Ps. cxlv. 5 (cxliv. 5). But as πνεῦμα is here joined with ἁγιωσύνης, I cannot well doubt that the word ἁγιωσύνης is employed in the place of the adjective ἅγιον, (like קדשׁ in הַר קָדְשִׁי, *i. e., my holy mountain.*) So the Gen. case of nouns is employed in almost innumerable instances. If we may conjecture a reason why the apostle here preferred ἁγιωσύνης to ἅγιον, we might say that it was because he wished to avoid the dubious meaning ἅγιον would seem to give to the passage, as the reader might naturally refer such an epithet to the Holy Spirit as an *agent*.

I cannot but regard it as quite certain, that κατὰ πνεῦμα ἁγιωσύνης here, is employed in a similar way with κατὰ σάρκα in the preceding phrase. There κατὰ σάρκα shows *in what respect, in regard to what* Christ was the Son of David. Here κατὰ πνεῦμα ἁγιωσύνης shows *in what respect* the apostle means to set forth Christ as *the decreed Son of God with power*. Not that the mention of one leading particular in which his power was displayed, excludes the possession of other powers by him. So much only is meant, and so much is altogether true and striking, viz. that power in bestowing the πνεῦμα ἁγιωσύνης, *i. e.*, in causing *the new moral creation*, is one of the most conspicuous of all proofs that Jesus is indeed *the decreed Son of God*, who was promised in ancient times, and predicted in the Holy Scriptures, by a declaration and an oath never to be forgotten.

We shall see, in the sequel, more abundant reason for this interpretation. But we must first examine the meaning of the contested phrase ἐκ ἀναστάσεως νεκρῶν. Many have rendered ἐξ *by*. So Chrysostom; who deduces from our verse three proofs which were exhibited in order to show the divine nature of Christ; viz. (1) Ἐν δυνάμει, *i. e.*, the wonderful miracles which Christ wrought. (2) The gift of the Holy Spirit, κατὰ πνεῦμα ἁγιωσύνης. (3) The resurrection. The difficulty with the first and third particulars of his reasoning, is, that in the same manner prophets, apostles, and others may be proved to be divine, for the Saviour says that his disciples will perform "*greater* works than he," after his ascent to the Father; and many others were raised from the dead as well as Jesus. As to the gift of the Spirit, that will be noticed in the sequel. There can indeed be no doubt, that ἐκ (ἐξ) is, so far as this preposition merely is concerned, susceptible of such an interpretation. It is often used in the sense of *propter, ex*, and designates the *causa occasionalis; e. g.*, John iv. 6, "Jesus being wearied ἐκ τῆς ὁδοπορίας," so in Acts xxviii. 3. Rom. v. 16. Rev. viii. 13; or it designates the *causa instrumentalis*, 1 Cor. ix. 14. 2 Cor. vii. 9. Rev. iii. 18. But, on the other hand, that ἐκ signifies *after, since*, in respect to time, is equally clear and certain; *e. g.*, ἐκ κοιλίας μητρός, FROM *the time of one's birth;* Matt. xix. 20, ἐκ νεότητος, FROM *early youth;* Luke viii. 27, ἐκ χρόνων ἱκανῶν, *a long time* SINCE; xxiii. 8, John vi. 64. vi. 66. ix. 1, 32. Acts ix. 33. xv. 21. xxiv. 10. Rev. xvii. 11, ἐκ τῶν ἑπτά ἐστι, AFTER *the seven;* 2 Peter ii. 8.; comp. Sept. in Gen. xxxix. 10. Lev. xxv. 50. Deut. xv. 20.— So in the classics; Arrian Exped. Alex. I. 26. 3. ἐκ νότων σκληρῶν AFTER *vehement south winds.* III. 15. 13. V. 25. 3. Hist. Ind. 33. 5. ἐκ τυσῶνδε κακῶν, AFTER *so many evils.* Xenoph. Res Græcæ, VI. ἐξ ἀρίστου AFTER *dinner.* No doubt can be left, then, that ἐξ ἀναστάσεως νεκρῶν may be rendered, AFTER *the resurrection from the dead*, or SINCE *his resurrection*, etc. So Luther, SINT *der Zeit er auferstanden ist*, SINCE *the time when he arose.*

Ἀναστάσεως νεκρῶν, moreover, is one of those combinations of the Gen. case with a preceding noun which allows great latitude of construction. Here it is equivalent to ἀναστάσεως ἐκ νεκρῶν. Both phrases, viz. ἀνάστασις νεκρῶν and ἀνάστασις ἐκ νεκρῶν, are used by the New Testament writers; *e. g.*, the first, in Matt. xxii. 31. Acts xvii. 32. xxiv. 21. xxvi. 23; and Paul limits himself to this same phraseology, *e. g.*, 1 Cor. xv. 12, 13, 21, 42. Heb. vi. 2; the second, in Luke xx. 35, Acts iv. 2. I can perceive no difference whatever in their meaning. In regard to the latitude in which the Genitive is employed, in order to designate relations which might otherwise be expressed by a preposition, see § 99 of my New Testament Grammar.

The way is perfectly clear, then, to translate AFTER his *resurrection from the dead*, so far as philology is concerned.* Does

* The possibility of referring ἐκ to time cannot be questioned, but most modern critical commentators agree in making it here causal, *by* or *through.* If it refers to time, it should seem to include the *resurrection*, as the point from

the *nature of the case* admit or demand this? It seems to my mind that it does. The manner in which the outpouring of the Spirit is spoken of, as connected with or following the resurrection and consequent glorification of Christ, appears to render this altogether probable, if not certain. Jesus, in promising a copious effusion of the Spirit, says, that "out of the belly [of believers] shall flow rivers of living waters," John vii. 38. The evangelist immediately adds, that "he spake this of the Spirit, which they that believe on him should receive, *for the Holy Ghost was not yet given,* BECAUSE JESUS WAS NOT YET GLORIFIED." In entire accordance with this are the representations of the Saviour, in his last conference with his disciples; "If I go not away, the Comforter will not come unto you," John xvi. 7. This Comforter was to come *after the departure* of Jesus; he was then to abide with the disciples (John xiv. 16); to teach them all things (John xiv. 26); to guide them into all the truth (xvi. 13); to testify of him (xv. 26); and to convince the world of sin, of righteousness, and of judgment (xvi. 8—11). So on the great day of Pentecost (which the apostle would seem to have had in his eye when he wrote our text), Peter says, that the notable outpouring of the Spirit then experienced, was a fulfilment of the prophecy in Joel respecting this event; Acts ii. 14—21. Is. xliv. 3, refers to the like event. In looking at Acts i. 8, it would seem as if the very thing in our text is specifically designated by the words of Christ to his apostles; λήψεσθε δύναμιν ἐπελθόντος τοῦ ὁγίου πνεύματος ἐφ' ὑμᾶς. Here the δύναμις which Christ is to bestow by the sending of the Spirit, is expressly designated; and, as the sequel of the narration shows, it means an extraordinary and hitherto unknown effusion of the Spirit. All the subsequent history of the churches illustrates this. All the extraordinary revivals of religion that followed, were in consequence of the extraordinary outpouring of the Spirit which ensued upon the resurrection and glorification of the Saviour.

The conclusion which I deduce from the whole is, that τοῦ ὁρισθέντος υἱοῦ . . . . νεκρῶν means, that " Christ was the Son of God, agreeably to the decree in the Holy Scriptures, *i. e.*(in Psalm ii. 7) ; and Son of God endowed with power, which he displayed by sending the Spirit in an extraordinary and glorious manner after his resurrection and consequent exaltation." In this simple way, supported by the testimony of the Scriptures as to facts, and its *usus loquendi* as to meaning, would I explain this endlessly controverted verse, respecting which scarcely any two commen-

which the time commences, and as in some sense introductory to, and the cause of subsequent acts and occurrences. *From the time* of the resurrection *onward.*

tators of note wholly agree, and in regard to which, I am now persuaded, that I was in some respects mistaken in the first edition of this commentary. The ground of my mistake was, looking to a distance too great for explanatory facts and principles, when they lay near at hand.*

That the sense now given is far more noble and pregnant with meaning, than the simple declaration that Christ was shown to be the Son of God by his resurrection from the dead, can scarcely fail of being felt by every reader. As now explained, the declaration of the apostle respects one of the highest, most striking, and most glorious of all the proofs that Christ was the true Son of God. It means no less than to assert, that he was and is the author of the *new creation*, of the *making of all things new*, by the peculiar dispensation of his Spirit after his glorification. That glorification was plainly commenced by his *resurrection*. Paul in his address in the synagogue at Antioch in Pisidia (Acts xiii.) explains the resurrection, indeed, as in part a fulfilment of the prediction in the second Psalm respecting the elevation of Jesus as the Son of God. And so it truly was; inasmuch as it was the commencement of his glorification. But the interpretation given above abates nothing from this. It is built on the very supposition, that his resurrection must *precede* the special δύναμις which he exercised, in pouring out the Spirit in an extraordinary manner so as to establish his new spiritual kingdom. In a word, as God at the beginning manifested his power and Godhead by creating the world from nothing, so the Son of God exhibited his

---

* I can hardly avoid thinking that ὁρισθέντος here means *exhibited, manifested*, notwithstanding the strong arguments above adduced for the signification *decreed*, etc., not because I with Olshausen find any doctrinal difficulty in the other signification, but because, in the connection, it seems to me to be much more natural to interpret thus *manifested or set forth with power to be the Son of God*. The fact that ὁρίζω is not found elsewhere with exactly this shade of meaning is not decisive here. From the original significations *bound, limit, define*, etc, the change in this passive form is natural and easy to that of *exhibited, manifested*, since to define a thing is to exhibit to the mind, in its outlines and characteristics, as here, to the minds of men. Then ἐν δυνάμει is naturally interpreted *with power*, and connected with ὁρισθέντος. The position is more emphatic but less definite than if it were between the article and participle. In that case the position would require it to qualify the participle; now it may or may not, as the sense demands. It cannot be questioned that the resurrection of Christ, as apart and distinct from the cases of resurrection previously recorded (e. g. that of Lazarus), is spoken of and considered, by both Paul and other N. Test. writers, to be a proof that he was the "Son of God," "the Messiah," since this resurrection was effected by his own inherent power and strength (John 10. 18), and involves the whole resurrection of man from the dead. See 1 Cor 15 3 sq., esp 20 sq ; 2 Cor. 13 4; Acts 11 36, where ποιεῖν is used, Acts 13 33, etc., and Cf. Calvin, Olshausen, Meyer, Alford, and other commentators.

all-glorious character in the *new creation* effected by the Spirit of holiness, dispensed by him in so peculiar a manner after his glorification. This is the highest evidence we can have of his being indeed *the decreed Son of God*, and Saviour of Sinners. The whole expression, τοῦ ὁρισθέντος υἱοῦ . . . . νεκρῶν, serves to distinguish what Jesus manifested himself to be *after* his resurrection, in distinction from the development he made of himself *before* this period. Before the resurrection "he was anointed with the Holy Ghost and with power" (Acts x. 38); but "the Holy Ghost was not yet given [*i. e.*, bestowed on men,] because Jesus was not yet glorified" (John vii. 38). It is in reference to the *manifestation* of what Jesus was endowed with, and in reference to the decree which respected his spiritual kingdom and reign (Ps. ii.), that the apostle speaks in our text.

With this view of the subject, I cannot (with some expositors) regard κατὰ σάρκα and κατὰ πνεῦμα ἁγιωσύνης as designedly *antithetic* expressions. This indeed they cannot strictly be ; inasmuch as both respect the same person. Nor can I now any longer regard them as a *designed* contradistinction ; for to make out this, we must suppose that the one relates to his *human* person, and the other to his *divine*. It is indeed true, as I formerly maintained, that the *higher* and *glorified* nature of Christ (not simply his *divine* nature), is several times called πνεῦμα, (but not πνεῦμα ἅγιον nor πνεῦμα ἁγιωσύνης). The reader may find instances of this nature in 2 Cor. iii. 17, 18. Heb. ix. 14. 1 Cor. xv. 45. 1 Pet. iii. 18, and perhaps in 1 Tim. iii. 16. It is also true, that "decreed Son of God possessed of power in his glorified state," would be a sense altogether accordant with fact and with the analogy of the Scriptures. But the interpretation given above now seems to me, after much consideration, to be better supported by the context and the intention of the writer; who designs to exhibit Christ as predicted in the Holy Scriptures, first as "the Son of David in respect to his human nature," and then as "the decreed Son of God in respect to the manifestations of his spiritual power in the *new* creation." Consequently, if this view be correct, we must understand κατὰ σάρκα as explaining τοῦ γενομένου, by showing in what respect Christ was descended from David ; and κατὰ πνεῦμα ἁγιωσύνης as explaining in what respect the δύναμις of the decreed Son was peculiarly exercised so as to afford satisfactory evidence of his character and dignity. Not *antithesis*, then, nor even *contra-distinction*, is intended between κατὰ σάρκα and κατὰ πνεῦμα ἁγιωσύνης, but simply the like construction is repeated in order to show a *reference* of the like nature in two cases. Glockler, in his recent, original, and in many respects striking Commentary on the Romans, understands πνεῦμα ἁγιωσύνης in the same way as I have done, but he has missed the scriptural reference to Old Testament prophecy which is contained in τοῦ ὁρισθέντος υἱοῦ. He has therefore applied ἐν δυνάμει to ὁρισθέντος, in the old way, and construes the κατὰ πνεῦμα ἁγιωσύνης as proving the *Godhead* of Christ. *Consequentially*, I should readily admit this; for who that is not *divine*, can dispense the Holy Spirit? But the object of the apostle here is not directly to prove the divine nature of Christ, but to show that he is the decreed and predicted Son of God, whom the Holy Scriptures had taught the Jews to expect.

The phrase υἱοῦ Θεοῦ, which stands connected with all the predicates that have now been explained, is one of high and holy import. If I rightly understand the meaning of it, it designates *the Messiah, the King of Israel, the Lord of all*, in the passage before us. Such was Christ constituted, after his resurrection from the dead, when he ascended to take his place at the right hand of the Majesty on high, was made κληρονομός πάντων, and copiously poured out *the Spirit of holiness*. For a more copious discussion of this important phrase the reader is referred to Excursus I.

The apostle having thus given his views respecting the dignity of Christ, he now resumes the theme mentioned at the beginning of ver. 3, viz. τοῦ υἱοῦ αὐτοῦ, by adding the other usual appellatives of honor and office given to the Son, which are: Ἰησοῦ Χριστοῦ τοῦ κυρίου ἡμῶν. Κύριος is a word of deep interest to Christians. Applied to Christ, it properly denotes him as *supreme Ruler* or *Lord*, specially of his church. Matthew and Mark do not apply this title absolutely to Christ, except after his resurrection, Matt. xxviii. 6. Mark xvi. 19, 20. But Luke, John, and Paul, apply it to him everywhere and often. With Paul the application seems to be in a manner exclusive. God the Father, or God absolutely considered, is named κύριος about *thirty* times, in the Old Testament passages which Paul cites; but elsewhere, with the exception of some four or five instances, Paul gives to Christ *exclusively* the title of κύριος or ὁ κύριος in more than *two hundred and fifteen* instances; see Bibl. Repos. I. 733, seq. The *article* makes no difference in the meaning, inasmuch as the word is a kind of proper name by usage, is employed in like manner as one, and may therefore take or omit the article at the pleasure of the writer. See the Essay on the meaning of the word κύριος, in the Bibl. Repos. as above, where the subject is examined at length.

(5) *By whom we have received grace and the office of an apostle*, Δι' οὗ . . . . ἀποστολήν. Chrysostom, Grotius, and others interpret this as though it meant χάριν τῆς ἀποστολῆς, *the favor or*

privilege of the apostolic office; i. e., they construe the last words as a hendiadys. Augustine says : " *Gratiam* cum omnibus fidelibus accepit—*apostolatum*, non cum omnibus." I prefer to separate the meaning of the words. *Grace*, χάρις, I consider as having reference to the peculiar grace bestowed on Paul, who had been a persecutor ; comp. 1 Cor. xv. 9, 10. Gal. i. 13 — 16. 1 Tim. i. 12 — 16, which seem to make this clear. As to ἀποστολή, *apostleship*, "the office of an apostle," comp. Acts ix. 15. xiii. 2. xxii. 21 ; also the passages just cited above.

On account of the obedience of faith, εἰς ὑπακοὴν πίστεως. Εἰς, followed by an Acc., in almost innumerable instances designates the *object* or *end* for which any thing is, or is done. The idea here is, that the office of an apostle had been given to Paul, '*in order that* (εἰς) he should further or promote obedience to the faith,' *i. e.*, to the gospel; or (as we should here construe πίστεως) *the obedience of faith,* viz. that which springs from *subjective* or *internal* faith. I prefer this latter sense, as being on the whole the most energetic. It seems to me probable, that the apostle meant to designate the *obedience of faith* as contra-distinguished from *legal obedience.**

Among all nations, ἐν πᾶσι τοῖς ἔθνεσι ; ἐν, *among*, a common sense of the word. Ἔθνεσι may be rendered *Gentiles* here, inasmuch as Paul was "the apostle of the Gentiles;" but the expression seems to be more general. He means to say that he received the office of an apostle, in order that the gospel might be preached to all nations, to Gentiles as well as to Jews.

For his name's sake, ὑπὲρ τοῦ ὀνόματος αὐτοῦ, which means *on his account*. But with what is this to be joined? Does the apostle mean to say, that he had received χάριν καὶ ἀποστολήν on his [Christ's] account ; or does he join the latter expression with εἰς ὑπακοὴν πίστεως, and thus designate the following sentiment, viz. that 'obedience springing from Christian faith may be promoted among all nations, so that Christ may be glorified ? '† In this latter way I should prefer to interpret it ; so Tholuck and others.

(6) *Among which* [nations *are ye* Romans], ἐν οἷς ἐστε καὶ ὑμεῖς. The writer means to say ; 'Among those nations are ye,

---

* This is explained perhaps by Acts 6: 21 : "A great company of the priests were obedient to the faith," ὑπήκουον τῇ πίστει. Paul elsewhere joins an objective genitive to ὑπακοήν as in 2 Cor. 10: 5. So Alford says · *The faith*, not = "the Gospel which is to be believed," but the *state of salvation, in which men stand by faith.*

† Perhaps this clause may appropriately be considered as related to the whole preceding part of the verse · we have received grace and apostleship, etc., "in behalf of his name," "for his glory."

who have been won over to obey the Christian faith.' So the sequel: *The called of Jesus Christ*, κλητοὶ Ἰησοῦ Χριστοῦ, *i. e.*, the called who belong to Christ. Κλητός (see on the word under ver. 1) means, by the usage of Paul, not only those to whom the *external* call of the gospel has been addressed, but those who have also been *internally* called; in other words, it designates *effectual* calling. My reason for supposing I. Χριστοῦ here to be a genitive which designates *belonging to*, rather than a *Genitivus agentis* (in which case it would signify *of* or *by Christ*), is, that the usual idiom ascribes *the calling* of sinners to Christ, as effected by the agency of the Father, or of the Holy Spirit. Κλητοὶ I. Χριστοῦ, according to the interpretation now given would mean ' Christians effectually called.' So Tholuck, Reiche, and others.

(7) *To all who are at Rome, beloved of God*, πᾶσι . . . . Θεοῦ; *i. e.*, to all these λέγω, γράφω, I say what follows in the sequel, viz. Χάρις ὑμῖν, etc. The apostle probably meant to include not only the Christians who habitually dwelt in Rome, but also Christians from abroad, of whom there must have been many in that great city. Such was the concourse of Greeks there in Juvenal's time, that he calls it *Græcam urbem*. The apostle may well be supposed to address the whole body of those who joined in Christian worship. Still the language, πᾶσι....ἐν Ῥώμῃ, does not make this supposition certain.

Beloved of God, ἀγαπητοῖς Θεοῦ; an appellation often bestowed on the ancient people of God, or at least implied by what is said concerning them, and which Paul here applies to Christians, the *true Israel* of God. They are the objects of God's love, because they are his children by a new and spiritual birth, because they bear his image, and also because they possess a filial and obedient spirit.

Chosen saints, κλητοῖς ἁγίοις, or *saints effectually called*. So most editions and commentaries unite these words, making κλητοῖς an adjective qualifying ἁγίοις, and so I have translated them. This may be correct, inasmuch as the apostle had just before called them κλητοί I. Χριστοῦ. Thus the two words mean *called* or *chosen to be holy* or *to be consecrated to God, to be devoted to him*. The words however, may be pointed thus, κλητοῖς, ἁγίοις, to *those who are called, who are devoted to Christ*. The sense is substantially the same, whichever way we choose to interpret the words.

As to the appellations ἀγαπητοῖς Θεοῦ, κλητοῖς ἁγίοις, the reader may compare the terms of honor and affection given to God's ancient people, in Exod. xix. 6, Deut. xxxiii. 3, 12. xxxii. 19; with these compare also Col. iii. 12. 1 Pet. ii. 9. 1 Tim. iii. 15. Phil. ii. 15. 1 John iii. 1, 2, 10. v. 1., given to Christians in the New Testament.

May grace be imparted to you! χάρις ὑμῖν, sc. ἔστω. Χάρις denotes every Christian grace and virtue, which the Spirit of God imparts to the followers of Christ; divine favor in the most extensive sense, but specially in the sense of *spiritual blessings.* — Εἰρήνη, like the Heb. שׁלם means *happiness* of every kind, *peace* with God and man, and so a state of quiet and happiness. The same word (שׁלם) is still used among the oriental nations who speak the Shemitish languages, in their formulas of greeting or in expressing their good wishes.

Our Father, πατρὸς ἡμῶν, *i. e.*, the Father of all Christians, of you and me. So Christ has taught his disciples when they approach God in prayer, to say πάτερ ἡμῶν. — Κυρίου, see under ver. 4. One would naturally expect the *article* here, before the monadic nouns Θεοῦ and κυρίου. But nothing is more common than to omit it before such nouns, when frequently employed, and where there is no danger of mistake. See N. Test. Gramm. § 89, 2. *a. b.* More common is it to employ the article before an epexegetical appellative in apposition, like πατρὸς ἡμῶν in the present case. But even here the practice is not uniform; and moreover the article before πατρός in the present case might be dispensed with also, on the ground that ἡμῶν sufficiently marks its definitive nature; N. Test. Gram. § 89. 6, comp. 3.

It should be remarked here that in this prayer or wish Paul seems to take it for granted, that the blessings for which he asks, come as really and truly (not to say as much) from the *Lord Jesus Christ* as from *God our Father.* To the one then he addresses his prayer, as well as to the other.

(8) The apostle now naturally proceeds to the expression of his kind feelings and wishes toward the Church at Rome, in order to prepare the way, to be the more kindly listened to by them. Πρῶτον *in the first place, first of all,* viz. before I speak of other things. It does not here mean *first in point of importance,* but *first in order of time.* — The particle μέν is not here placed *absolutely, i. e.,* without its usual corresponding δέ; for the apostle, after two paragraphs in his usual manner, which begin with γάρ (illustrating and confirming first what he had said in ver. 8, and then what he had said in ver. 10), proceeds to the second part of his declaration in ver. 13, viz. οὐ θέλω δὲ ὑμᾶς, κ. τ. λ. That is, *first,* the apostle thanks God for their faith, etc.; and *secondly,* he is desirous to tell them how much he has longed to pay them a visit, etc. Reiche, following Bretschneider, denies that μέν in ver. 8, and δέ in ver. 13, can stand in relation to each other. But in this he is not supported by the principles of philology. Μέν and δέ stand not only at the head of antithetic and discrepant clauses, but also before those which express a differ-

ence of one thought from another, and so in the room of our *first*, *secondly*, etc. See Passow's Lex. μέν.

My God, τῷ θεῷ μου; the Christian religion which teaches us to say πάτερ ἡμῶν allows us to say θέος μου.—Διὰ Ἰησοῦ Χριστοῦ, *per Christum, auxilio Christi, interventû Christi, i. e.*, through, by or in consequence of, what Christ has done or effected; in other words, *Christo adjuvante, Deo gratias ago respectu vestrûm omnium, ut fides vestra*, etc. The meaning seems to be, that as a Christian, as one on whom Christ has had mercy, and who has now a Christian sympathy for others beloved of Christ, he thanks God for the prosperous state of the Church at Rome. Διὰ I. Χριστοῦ may also be joined with θεῷ μου, and the sense be thus given: 'I thank God, who is my God through what Jesus Christ has done for me; to him I belong as one of his through the intervention of Christ.' So Glockler. Barnes and others construe διὰ I. Χριστοῦ as pointing out the medium through which the thanks of the apostle were offered. This is altogether consonant with the Christian economy; but it does not seem to me to be the most natural sense of the passage.*

On account of you all, ὑπὲρ πάντων ὑμῶν; not *for you, i. e.*, in your room or stead, but because of πίστις ὑμῶν, *your Christian belief, your faith in the gospel.*—Ὅλῳ τῷ κόσμῳ, *i. e.*, through the Roman empire. Κόσμος and οἰκουμένη are frequently used in a *limited* sense, like the ארץ and תבל of the Hebrews. Nothing is more natural than to suppose, that the faith of the Church at Rome might have been widely known or reported, in consequence of that great city being frequented by strangers from all parts of the empire.

(9) *For God is my witness*, μάρτυς γὰρ . . . . θεός. Γὰρ *explicantis et confirmantis; i. e.*, the apostle unfolds and confirms, in the following sentence, the evidence of his strong sympathies with them, and of his gratitude to God on their account. The reason why he here makes the appeal to God seems to be, that, as he was a stranger in person to the Church at Rome, they might otherwise think his expressions to be merely those of common civility.†

Whom I serve in my soul (sincerely) *in the gospel of his Son*, ᾧ λατρεύω . . . . αὐτοῦ. Ἐν τῷ πνεύματί μου I understand as

---

* Such passages as Eph 5· 20· "Giving thanks in the name of the Lord Jesus Christ," and Hebrews 13· 15, favor the latter interpretation. See also Olshausen, Comm in h. l.

† Thus the similar assurances of regard and remembrance in his devotions is made to the Ephesians, Philippians, Colossians, and Thessalonians, but naturally, if we except Phil 1· 8, without the appeal to God as witness. A similar appeal is often, however, made by the apostle; cf. Gal. 1. 20, 2 Cor. 1. 23, etc.

designating *sincerity, i. e., real, internal, spiritual devotedness,* in distinction from what is merely external or apparent; comp. Phil. iii. 3. 2 Tim. i. 3. Eph. vi. 6. Rom. ii. 28, 29.

The phrase: ἐν τῷ εὐαγγελίῳ τοῦ υἱοῦ αὐτοῦ may mean *by the preaching of the gospel which has respect to his Son;* more probably it means, *in the gospel which has respect to his Son,* comp. ver. 2; or it may mean *the gospel of which his Son is the author,* and which he taught me. See, on the various meanings of the Gen. case, New Testament Grammar § 99. That ἐν τῷ εὐαγγελίῳ does not here refer to the *preaching* of the gospel, but to living spiritually according to its precepts, seems rather more probable because of the ἐν τῷ πνεύματί μου which precedes, and which seems to define the kind of service rendered by the apostle. The other sense however, is allowable. *How unceasingly I make remembrance of you,* ὡς ἀδιαλείπτως . . . . ποιοῦμαι. This shows the intense zeal which the apostle cherished for the welfare of the Christian Churches; for if he thus constantly interceded with God for the Church at Rome, which he had never visited, we cannot suppose that he forgot other churches which he had been the instrument of establishing. How different a phase would the Christian Church speedily assume, if all its ministers were now actuated with the same degree of zeal which Paul exhibited! Ποιοῦμαι, *I make to myself.* Midd. voice.

(10) *Always making supplication in my prayers,* πάντοτε . . . . δεόμενος; which is confirming what he had said before, ἀδιαλείπτως μνείαν ὑμῶν ποιοῦμαι, and at the same time pointing out the manner in which he made this remembrance, μνείαν, viz., in his supplications before God. Ἐπί τῶν προσευχῶν μου means, literally, *during my prayers,* or *when I pray.*

[That] *if possible, at some time before long, I may (God willing) make a prosperous journey, and come to pay you a visit,* εἴπως . . . . ὑμᾶς. Εἴπως expresses a degree of uncertainty which hung over the future, in the writer's own mind, *i. e.,* it means *perhaps, if possible, if in some way, if by any means.* Ἤδη, followed by the Future, means *mox, brevi, by and by, soon, before long.* Ποτέ, *aliquando, tandem, at last, at some time, at some future period;* (πότε, with the accent on the *penult,* means *when*). Both the words ἤδη and ποτέ, have often nearly the same meaning when connected with a *future* tense. They may be here rendered thus: ἤδη, *mox, before long;* ποτέ, *at least, at some time,* or *at some future period;* so in the version, where I have given to each word its own particular and appropriate meaning, merely reversing the order, because of our English idiom. Εὐοδωθήσομαι means, *to make a pleasant or prosperous journey.* A journey to Rome, which the apostle so ardently longed to visit, would in itself of course have been a *pleasant* one.—Ἐν τῷ θελήματι τοῦ θεοῦ, *i. e., Deo volente.* Grotius renders the passage very happily: Si forte Dei voluntas felicitatem mihi indulgeat ad vos veniendi.

(11) Γάρ, in this verse, precedes a sentence designed to illustrate and confirm the declaration which Paul had just made, viz., that he felt a deep interest for the Church at Rome, and hoped yet to enjoy the pleasure of visiting them.—Ἵνα τι . . . . . πνευματικόν, *that I may impart to you some spiritual favor or gift;* not some *miraculous gift*, supernatural power, such as the apostles sometimes imparted by the imposition of hands,* but spiritual aid and consolation; cf. xv. 32. In ver. 12, the apostle expresses his expectation of receiving on his part a benefit like to that which he bestows on them. What he expected *from* them, was συμπαρακληθῆναι . . . . . . διὰ τῆς ἐν ἀλλήλοις πίστεως; consequently this was what he expected to do *for* them, viz., to encourage, animate, and strengthen them in their Christian profession and virtues. He speaks of a *spiritual* gift, as characteristic of the graces of the gospel, of which the Spirit is the efficient author, and as differing from common gifts of a worldly nature, often bestowed by friends who pay visits to each other.

So the latter part of our verse: εἰς τὸ στηριχθῆναι ὑμᾶς, *that you may be confirmed*, viz., in the manner stated above. Nor does it follow, that the apostle viewed the Church at Rome as weak in faith, because he says this; unless we say that he was himself weak in faith, because he expects the like advantage of confirmation from his intercourse with them. Faith that is already strong, and Christian virtue that is conspicuous, are capable of becoming still more so; and therefore expressions of this nature are never applied amiss, even to Christians of the highest order. The apostle "did not as yet count himself to have attained" all that elevation of Christian character of which he was capable, and which it was his duty to attain; Phil. iii. 13, seq.

(12) *That is*, τοῦτο δέ ἐστι, *id est*, prefixed to an *epexegesis*, or an ἐπανόρθωσις *(correction)* as the Greeks named explanatory clauses of such a nature as that which now follows. The apostle, lest the meaning of the preceding declaration might be misconstrued, adds (in ver. 12) the more full expression of his sentiment. He does not mean to assert, that the consequence of his visiting Rome would be merely their confirmation in the Christian faith, and so the advantage be all on their side; but he ex-

---

* It is plain that Paul did not value the extraordinary bestowment of the gifts of the Spirit so highly as to make it the business of his life and the subject of his unceasing and earnest prayer, see Olshausen, De Wette, and Alford.

pects himself to be spiritually benefited by such a visit; and this he fully expresses in ver. 12. The remark of Calvin on this passage is very striking and just; " See with what gentleness a pious soul will demean itself! It refuses not to seek confirmation even from mere beginners in knowledge. Nor does the apostle use any dissimulation here; for there is none so poor in the Church of Christ, that he cannot make some addition of importance to our stores. We, unhappily, are hindered by pride from availing ourselves properly of such an advantage." How very different is the spirit and tenor of this remark from that of Erasmus, who calls the expression of the apostle, *pia vafrities et sancta adulatio!*

To be comforted among you by the mutual faith both of you and me, συμπαρακληθῆναι . . . . ἐμοῦ. In Attic Greek, παρακληθῆναι means *to call, to invite, to exhort*. But in Hellenistic Greek, it not only means *to exhort*, but specially to address one in such a way as to administer comfort, encouragement, hope, resolution, etc. I have rendered the word *comfort*, only because I cannot find any English word which will convey the full sense of the original.—Ἐν, *among;* and so, often.—Ἐν ἀλλήλοις, placed between the article and its noun, is of course employed in the manner of an *adjective, i. e.* it means *mutual.*—Ὑμῶν τε καὶ ἐμοῦ seems to be a repetition of the idea conveyed by ἐν ἀλλήλοις. This repetition is intensive, and denotes the strong desire which the apostle entertained, to be understood by the Church at Rome as saying, that he expected good from *them*, as well as hoped that they might receive good from him.

(13) The apostle had already signified his desire to visit Rome. vers. 10, 11, But here he proceeds to show how *definitely* and *frequently* he had cherished such a desire; which gives intensity to the whole representation.

Moreover, I am desirous, brethren, to have you know, that I have often purposed to come to you, οὐ θέλω δὲ . . . . ὑμᾶς. Δέ in this passage I regard as corresponding to μέν in ver. 8, and so making the τὸ δεύτερον or *apodosis* of the apostle's discourse; see the note on ver. 8. Οὐ θέλω ὑμᾶς ἀγνοεῖν is the same in sense as θέλω ὑμᾶς γινώσκειν; but the first form of expression (in a negative way), is what the Greeks call λιτότης, *i. e.*, a softer or milder form of expression than direct affirmation.

I have often purposed, πολλάκις προεθέμην; comp. Acts xix. 21. Rom. xv. 23, 24. It is clear from this and many other like passages, that the apostles were not *uniformly* and *always* guided in *all* their thoughts, desires, and purposes, by an infallible Spirit of inspiration. Had this been the case, how could Paul have *often* purposed that which never came to pass? Those who plead for such a *uniform* inspiration, may seem to be zealous for the honor of the apostles and founders of Christianity; but they do in fact cherish a mistaken zeal. For if we once admit, that the apostles were *uniformly* inspired in *all* which they purposed, said, or did; then we are constrained of course to admit, that men acting under the influence of inspiration, may purpose that which will never come to pass or be done; may say that which is hasty or incorrect, Acts xxiii. 3; or do that which the gospel disapproves, Gal. ii. 13, 14. But if this be once fully admitted, then it would make nothing for the credit due to any man, to affirm that he is *inspired;* for what is that inspiration to be accounted of, which, even during its continuance, does not guard the subject of it from mistake or error? Consequently those who maintain the *uniform* inspiration of the apostles, and yet admit (as they are compelled to do) their errors in purpose, word, and action, do in effect obscure the glory of inspiration, by reducing inspired and uninspired men to the same level.

To my own mind nothing appears more certain than that inspiration in any respect whatever, was not *abiding* and *uniform* with the apostles or any of the primitive Christians. To God's only and well-beloved Son, and to him only, was it given to have the Spirit ἀμετρῶς or οὐ ἐκ μέτρου, John iii. 34. All others on whom was bestowed the precious gift of inspiration, enjoyed it only ἐκ μέτρου. The consequence of this was, that Jesus "knew no sin, neither was guile found in his mouth; but all his followers, whenever they were left without the special and miraculous guidance of the Spirit, committed more or less of sin and error.

This view of the subject frees it from many and most formidable difficulties. It assigns to the Saviour the *pre-eminence* which is justly due. It accounts for the mistakes and errors of his apostles. At the same time, it does not detract in the least degree from the certainty and validity of the sayings and doings of the apostles, when they were under the special influence of the Spirit of God.

But have been hindered until now, καὶ ἐκωλύθην . . . . δεῦρο. — Καί *although* or *but;* Bretschn. Lex. καί, III. " ex Hebraismo, καί est particula adversativa, *sed, vero, at;*" of which he gives many examples. The well-known power of ו to stand before a *disjunctive* clause, throws light on this usage; which is very unfrequent in classic Greek. It cannot be truly said, in cases of this nature, that καί (or ו) properly signifies *but;* yet it may be truly said, that καὶ (ו) connects sentences, or clauses of sentences, whose meaning is *adversative* or *disjunctive.* The *conjunctive office* consists in connecting the sentences, or parts of them; the *disjunctive sense* lies in the nature of the propositions. We may lawfully translate *ad sensum*, in such cases, and so render καί (ו) *but, although*.

That I may have some fruit even among you, as also among other Gentiles, ἵνα τινὰ .... ἔθνεσιν; *i. e.*, that I might see my labors to promote the gospel crowned with success even at Rome, the capital of the world, as well as in all other places where I have preached.* Comp. John xv. 16, iv. 36—38. Phil. i. 11. Col i. 6.

(14) *I am indebted both to Greeks and Barbarians, to the learned and the ignorant,* Ἕλληνσί τε .... εἰμί; *i. e.*, ὀφειλέτης εἰμὶ εὐαγγελίζεσθαι, *I am under obligation to preach the gospel;* comp. 1 Cor. ix. 16. 2 Cor. ii. 6. iv. 5. In classic usage, βάρβαροι means *all who spoke a language foreign to the Greek;* 1 Cor. xiv. 11. Acts xxviii. 2, 4. Of course, the Romans themselves, by this usage, would be named βάρβαροι, and so Philo constantly names them; and Plautus himself calls the Latin language *barbara lingua*, and Italy *barbaria*. But here the question with the apostle seems not to be in respect to language, but only in regard to circumstances and state of knowledge. Ἕλλησι, therefore, appears to be equivalent to σοφοῖς, and βαρβάροις to ἀνοήτοις. Considered in this way, Ἕλλησι καὶ βαρβάροις mean *the polished or unpolished*, or *the learned and ignorant*, (or to use the idiom of the present day) 'the civilized and the savage.' Σοφοῖς τε καὶ ἀνοήτοις should be regarded here as characterizing the *state of knowledge*, rather than the state or measure of the faculties of men thus designated. *Learned and unlearned* is a version *ad sensum*.

Still the two couplets here may be considered as designating, the first, *those who spoke Greek* and *those who did not*, the second, *the learned and the ignorant*, be they of whatever nation they might; and so the whole will simply express with force and by specific language the general idea of obligation to preach to all nations and classes of men without distinction. This is the most simple and natural view of the subject.† Glockler joins Ἕλλησι τε καὶ Βαρβάροις with the preceding ἔθνεσι; invitâ Minervâ.

---

* Calvin well says: "He speaketh of that fruit to the gathering whereof the apostles were sent of the Lord; John 15. 16. Which fruit, albeit he gathereth it not for himself, but for the Lord, yet he calleth it his, because there is nothing more proper unto the godly than that which advanceth the glory of the Lord, whereunto all their felicity is coupled."

† The Apostle here intends, doubtless, to designate by Greeks and Barbarians all the different nations and tribes of the heathen or gentile world, and then by "the learned and unlearned" all the different individuals among them. The first contrast, as Olshausen says, is founded upon a general national distinction, the second upon particular individual differences. Cf. also Alford, De Wette, and others. He does not speak of himself here as

(15) Much difficulty is found in the interpretation of οὕτω here, but without good reason. Surely οὕτω or οὕτως often stands alone, without a preceding καθώς or ὥσπερ, as any one may see by opening a lexicon or concordance. Οὕτω is often employed in this way, in the sense of *similiter, simili modo, eodem modo, in the like way, in such a way, in a similar manner, in the same manner.* Thus in Matt. v. 16. vii. 17. xviii. 14. Mark xiii. 29. xiv. 59. Luke xiv. 33, et sæpe alibi. What hinders now that we should understand it, in the verse before us, in the same way? 'I am under obligation' says the apostle, '*to preach the gospel* [for εὐαγγελίσασθαι is implied in the first clause] to all classes of men.' What then? 'So, *i. e.*, circumstances being thus, I am ready (τὸ κατ' ἐμὲ πρόθυμον) to preach the gospel even to you who are at Rome.' If the reader does not think that the above references go so far as to give to οὕτω the sense here assigned to it, viz., *matters being thus* or *circumstances being thus*, or *I being in this condition*, he may turn to John iv. 6, where it is said: "Jesus being weary on account of his journeying, ἐκαθέζετο οὕτως ἐπὶ τῇ πηγῇ," *he sat down in this condition upon the well*, viz., in a state of weariness. All the attempts that I have seen to give οὕτως any other sense, seem to be in vain. Compare also Rev. iii. 16, "I would thou wert either cold or hot! Οὕτως, *so*," *i. e.*, the matter being thus, "since thou art neither cold nor hot, I will spue thee out of my mouth." In like manner in the text before us; οὕτω, '*the matter being thus*, viz., it being true that I am under obligation to preach to all classes of men, I am ready to preach at Rome;' or, 'since I am bound in my duty to preach to all, *in accordance with this* (οὕτω) I am ready to preach the gospel at Rome.' If καθώς were placed before Ἕλλησι, as Tholuck and others judge it should be, the sentiment would be thus: 'In proportion to my obligation to preach to all men, is my readiness to preach at Rome;' a sentiment which, although doubtless true, does not seem to me to be the one which the apostle means here to convey. It is more simple to understand him as saying: 'Since I am bound to preach to all, in accordance with this obligation I am ready to preach even at Rome (καὶ ὑμῖν), formidable and difficult as the task may seem to be.' Comp. 1 Cor. ix. 16. In this view of οὕτω I find Reiche, in his recent work, fully to agree.

I am ready, τὸ κατ' ἐμὲ πρόθυμον, [lit. there is,] *a readiness in respect to myself.* Or it may be interpreted in this way: 'There is a readiness so far as it respects me,' namely, to the extent of my ability, so far as it depends on me; meaning to intimate, that the actual disposal of the matter is to be wholly committed to God. The adjective τὸ πρόθυμον with the article is here as often used for a noun. Καὶ ὑμῖν has an emphasis in it, *i. e.*, *even to you*, at Rome, the metropolis of the world. In other words : 'I shun not to preach the gospel any where; to the most learned and critical, as well as to the most unlearned and unskilled in judging.' Ἐν, *at;* and so oftentimes before nouns of *place*.

(16) *For I am not ashamed of the gospel of Christ*; Οὐ γὰρ .... Χριστοῦ; a reason or ground of his readiness to preach it, which he had just before asserted ; and therefore it is introduced by γάρ. The apostle Paul gloried in the gospel; in fact, he gloried in nothing else. Although Christ crucified was "to the Jews a stumbling-block, and to the Greeks foolishness," he shunned not to preach it on this account, but was willing, even in presence of the learned and the sophists at Rome, to proclaim the truth as it is in Jesus.

The reading τοῦ Χριστοῦ, is marked by Knapp as wanting an adequate support, and is rejected by Mill, Bengel, Koppe, Griesbach, and Lachmann. In respect to the sense of the passage, its insertion or rejection will make no important difference. If retained τοῦ Χριστοῦ must be construed as *Genitivus objecti*, *i. e.*, the gospel respecting Christ, or of which Christ is the object.

Here ends the first or salutatory part of this epistle. The remainder of verse 16 (with verses 17, 18) constitutes the leading subject or theme of the epistle ; which the writer here as it were formally proposes, and which he in the sequel proceeds to confirm, illustrate, and fortify.

CHAP. I. 16—18.

These three verses contain four propositions, which lie at the basis of all that may be appropriately called the *gospel of Christ*. (1) To gospel truth is imparted a divine energy, in saving the souls of men. (2) Those only can be saved by it, who believe it and put their confidence in it (3) The pardon of sin, or the justification which God will bestow only on sinners who believe in Christ, is revealed from heaven, and proposed to all men for their reception (4) The unbelieving and ungodly will also be the subject of divine indignation and punishment. The apostle does not proceed, formally and in order, to illustrate and establish these propositions ; but now one part of these respective truths, and then another, comes into view, and the whole is fully developed in the course of the epistle.

For it is the power of God, unto the salvation of every one who believes, δύναμις γὰρ .... πιστεύοντι; *i. e.*, it is the efficacious instrument, by which God promotes or accomplishes the salvation of all believers. Δύναμις θεοῦ means, that in and by it God exerts his power, that it is powerful through the energy which he imparts; and so it is called *the power of God*. The γάρ serves to introduce the reason why the apostle is not ashamed of the gospel. It is mighty through God εἰς σωτηρίαν, to salvation, *i. e.*, to the accomplishment or attainment of salvation. Εἰς with the Accusative is, in a multitude of cases, used in the like manner.— Παντὶ τῷ πιστεύοντι, *Dativus commodi:* the gospel brings salvation *to* every believer, or it is the means of imparting it to him.

To the Jew first and also to the Greek, Ἰουδαίῳ .... Ἕλληνι. In proclaiming the gospel, the primitive preachers of it, themselves being *Jews*, were directed first to proclaim the offers of mercy through a Saviour to the Jews, wherever they went, and then to the Gentiles; which was the order usually followed, and to which the clause before us seems to advert. That the πρῶτον here merely relates to the *order* in which the gospel was proposed, and not to any substantial preference of the Jew over the Greek, the sequel of this epistle most abundantly shows. So Chrysostom: τάξεώς ἐστι πρῶτον, *i. e.*, πρῶτον relates merely to *order*.

(17) Δικαιοσύνη γὰρ θεοῦ. Γάρ *illustrantis*, as lexicographers say. In the preceding verse the apostle has said, that the gospel is, through divine power accompanying it, an efficacious instrument of salvation παντὶ τῷ πιστεύοντι, *to every believer*. On this last expression an emphasis is to be laid; inasmuch as the great object of Paul, in the epistle before us, is to show that salvation is *gratuitously* bestowed on the *believer* in Christ, but never conferred in any case on the ground of merit. The design of verse 17 is to suggest, that *faith* or *belief* is the appointed means or *conditio sine qua non* of justification, *i. e.*, of obtaining pardoning mercy from God; that the Old Testament Scriptures confirm this idea; and consequently, that salvation is granted to *believers*, and to them only ; all which goes to illustrate and establish the affirmation in ver. 16. It is in this way that γάρ connects the fine and delicate shades of thought and processes of reasoning, in the Greek language.

The phrase δικαιοσύνη θεοῦ is among the most important which the New Testament contains, and fundamental in the right interpretation of the epistle before us. To obtain a definite and precise view of its meaning, we must in the first place examine the verb δικαιόω, from which come nearly all the shades of meaning that belong to δικαιοσύνη and δικαίωσις, so often employed (especially the former) in the writings of Paul.

The Greek sense of the verb δικαιόω differs, in one respect, from the corresponding Hebrew verb צדק, which (in Kal) means *to be just, to be innocent, to be upright*, and also *to justify one's self, to be justified*, thus having the sense of either a *neuter, reflexive,* or *passive* verb. In the active voice, δικαιόω in Greek has only an *active* sense, and it is used in pretty exact correspondence with the forms צָדַק and הִצְדִּיק (Peal and Hiphil) of the Hebrews, *i. e.*, it means *to declare just, to pronounce just, to justify*, *i. e.*, to treat as just; consequently, as intimately connected with this, *to pardon, to acquit from accusation, to free from the consequences of sin or transgression, to set free from a deserved penalty*. This last class of meanings is the one in which Paul usually employs this word. As a *locus classicus* to vindicate this meaning, we may appeal to Rom. viii. 33, 'Who shall *accuse* the elect of God? It is God ὁ δικαιῶν, *who acquits them*,' viz. of all accusation, or '*who liberates them* from the penal consequences of transgression.' Exactly in the same way is it said, in Prov. xvii. 15, 'He who *justifieth* (מַצְדִּיק) the wicked, and he that condemneth the just, even they both are an abomination to the Lord.' So in Ex. xxiii. 7, 'I will *not justify* (לֹא אַצְדִּיק) the wicked.' In the same manner Is. v. 23 speaks: '*Who justify* the wicked (הִרְשִׁיעַ מַצְדִּיקֵי) for a reward.' In these and all such cases, the meaning *justify* is altogether plain, viz. *to acquit, to free from the penal consequences of guilt, to pronounce just, i. e.*, to absolve from punishment, the direct *opposite* of condemning or subjecting to the consequences of a penalty.

In this sense Paul very often employs the verb; *e. g.*, Rom. v. 1, δικαιωθέντες, *being freed from punishment, being acquitted, being pardoned* . . . . εἰρήνην ἔχομεν πρὸς τὸν θεόν. Rom. v. 9, δικαιωθέντες, *being acquitted, pardoned* . . . . σωθησόμεθα δι' αὐτοῦ ἀπὸ τῆς ὀργῆς, which salvation is the opposite of being subjected to punishment, or of *not* being justified. In Gal. ii. 16, 17, δικαιόω is four times employed in the sense of *absolved, acquitted*, or *treated as just, i. e.*, freed from penalty and admitted to a state of reward. So Gal. iii. 8, 11, 24. v. 4. Tit. iii. 7. In Romans iv. 5, τὸν δικαιοῦντα τὸν ἀσεβῆ is plainly susceptible of no other than the above interpretation; for those who are ungodly, can never be made *innocent* in the strict and literal sense of this word; they can only be *treated as innocent, i. e.*, absolved from the condemnation of the law, pardoned, delivered, from the penalty threatened against sin. That the idea of *pardon*, or *remission of the penalty threatened by the divine law*, is the one substantially conveyed by δικαιόω and δικαιοσύνη, as generally employed in the writings of Paul, is most evident from Romans iv. 6, 7; where the blessedness of the man to whom the Lord imputes δικαιοσύνη, *i. e.*, whom he reckons, counts, treats as δίκαιος, is thus described: "Blessed are they whose *iniquities are forgiven*, and whose *sins are covered;* blessed is the man to whom the Lord *imputes not sin*," *i. e.*, whom he does not treat or punish as a sinner. This passage is a fundamental explanation of the whole subject, so far as the present class of meanings attached to δικαιόω and δικαιοσύνη is concerned.

In the same sense we have the word δικαιόω in Rom. iii. 24, 26, 28, 30. iv. 2, et al. sæpe. So Acts xiii. 38, 39. Luke xviii. 14. Comp. Sept. in Gen. xxxviii. 26, Job xxxii 32. Is. xliii. 26.

The way is now open for an easy and intelligible explanation of the nouns, which stand immediately and etymologically connected with the verb δικαιόω. These are three, viz. δικαιοσύνη, δεκαίωμα, and δικαίωσις, all employed occasionally in the very same sense, viz. that of *justification*, *i. e.*, acquittal, pardon, freeing from condemnation, accepting and treating as righteous. All three of these nouns are employed occasionally by the Seventy in rendering the Hebrew word מִשְׁפָּט; which I mention merely to show that the *usus loquendi* could employ all of them in the same sense; *e. g.*, δικαιοσύνη for מִשְׁפָּט; in Prov. xvi. 11. xvii. 23. Is. lxi. 8. Ezek. xviii. 17, 19, 21, etc.; δικαίωμα for מִשְׁפָּט, Ex. xxi. 1, 9, 31. xxiv. 3, et sæpissime; δικαίωσις for מִשְׁפָּט, Lev. xxiv. 22.

In like manner all three of these nouns are employed in Paul's epistles: *e. g.*, δικαίωμα in the sense of *pardon, justification*, Rom. v. 16, where it stands as the antithesis of κατάκριμα, δικαίωσις in Rom. iv. 25, where it plainly means *justification;* and so in Romans v. 18, where it is the antithesis of κατάκριμα.

But δικαιοσύνη is the *usual* word employed by Paul to designate gospel-justification, *i. e.*, the pardoning of sin, and accepting and treating as righteous. So we find this word plainly employed in Rom. iii. 21, 22 (comp. ver. 24), 25, 26. iv. 11, 13. v. 17, 21, ix. 30, 31. x. 3, 4, 5, 6, 10. 2 Cor. v. 21 (abstract for concrete). Phil. iii. 9. Heb. xi. 7. et alibi sæpe.

Δικαιοσύνη θεοῦ seems then very plainly to have the same meaning here that it has in Rom. iii. 21, and in the other passages just referred to in this epistle, viz. the *justification* or *pardoning mercy* bestowed on sinners who are under the curse of the divine law; or the state or condition of being pardoned, *i. e.*, justified or treated as just. In this sense it is allied to, but is not altogether the same as, the Hebrew צְדָקָה, which often means *kindness*, *benignity, favor, deliverance from evil; e. g.*, Is. xlv. 8, 24, xlvi. 13. xlviii. 18. li. 6, 8. liv. 17. lvi. 1, and often in the Psalms.

The reader must be careful to note, however, the simple idea of *pardon*, unattended by any thing else, *i. e.*, the mere deliverance from punishment is not all which is comprised in the meaning of δικαιόω and δικαιοσύνη. The idea is more fully expressed by *accepting and treating as righteous*. Now, when this is done by a benefactor, he does not stop with the simple remission of punishment, but he bestows happiness in the same manner as though the offender had been altogether obedient. As there are but two stations allotted for the human race, *i. e.*, heaven or hell; so those who are delivered from the latter, must be advanced to the former.

All is now plain. Δικαιοσύνη Θεοῦ is *the justification which God bestows*, or *the justification of which God is the author*; or if any one prefers, he may call it that *state of pardon or acceptance* which is the result of mercy proffered in the gospel and dispensed on account of the atonement made by Christ. That Paul should call it δικαιοσύνη Θεοῦ, was very natural, when he wished to distinguish it from that *righteousness* which the Jews supposed themselves to possess in consequence of *legal* obedience, and which entitled them (in their own view) to divine acceptance. The justification which God allows, or that kind of righteousness which he now admits as a condition of acceptance, is ἐκ πίστεως, οὐκ ἐξ ἔργων, and therefore altogether a matter of *gratuity*, and not of merit or desert. This general view is made altogether clear by comparing Rom. iii. 21—24; and indeed the whole tenor of the discussion in the epistle to the Romans, seems imperiously to demand this sense.*

Having thus explained my own view of the meaning of δικαιοσύνη Θεοῦ, which is for substance the same as that defended by Luther, Wolf, Heumann, Limborch, Flatt, Macknight, Usteri, Reiche, and many others, it may be proper, considering the importance of the subject, briefly to review some of the leading opinions that have been advanced and defended by others.

I. The first class are those who regard δικαιοσύνη Θεοῦ here as designating *an attribute of God*; in which case Θεοῦ is regarded not as *Gen. auctoris*, but as *Gen. possessionis*.

Yet those who hold to such an opinion are by no means agreed in the mode of special explanation. *(a)* Some regard δικαιοσύνη as designating *the perfect holiness and uprightness of the Saviour's character*, which is imputed to believers. So Chemnitz, Hoepfner, Schroeder, and many others.

But how can this δικαιοσύνη in Christ be ἐκ πίστεως, and espe-

---

* This view is substantially that of De Wette, Rückert, Meyer, Neander, Alford, Olshausen, and others, though with some differences in the detail. Olshausen says rather strongly and figuratively: "From the connection with verse 16, which exalts the Gospel as the *power* of God, it is plain that δικαιοσύνη Θεοῦ cannot signify the mere declaring a person righteous, but the real making him righteous," and adds in explanation. Paul "considered the righteousness of all as absolutely realized in Christ. That which in him was perfected once for all, is gradually transmitted to individual men in proportion to the degree of their renewal, and is received by them in faith, and reckoned to their account." De Wette represents this justification as the acquittal from guilt freely given of God and cheerfulness of conscience, attained through faith in God's grace, in Christ.

cially διὰ πίστεως Χριστοῦ? Phil. iii. 9. Is Christ righteous, then, by having faith in himself? And in what part of the Bible are we to find the doctrine, that his righteousness and perfect holiness is actually transferred or imputed to us? In such a case, our pardon would no more be of *grace ;* and our claims would no more depend on *mercy*, but on justice; a sentiment the very opposite of gospel-doctrine. If a friend gives me, who am a debtor, a sum of money sufficient to pay off my debt, my creditor is bound as much on the score of *justice* to give up my bond of payment when I deliver to him this money, as if it had been all earned by my own industry. It is no concern of his, how I obtain the money.

(b) Δικαιοσύνη Θεοῦ means *God's fidelity* or *veracity* in the bestowment of grace according to the promises of the gospel. So Beza, Piscator, Turretin, Locke, Bohme, and others.

But how can God's *fidelity* or *veracity*, or any other of his attributes, be ἐκ πίστεως, or διὰ πίστεως, or ἐπὶ τῇ πίστει?

(c) God's vindictive justice. So Origen, Theodoret, Grotius, Wetstein, Marckius, Bretschn. (Lex.), Fritsche, and some others.

But vindictive justice is manifested in the *punishment* of sinners, not in their pardon. The δικαιοσύνη here is that which *pardons*.

(d) Rewarding justice, i. e., that which bestows favors on the virtuous. So Calov, Storr, and others.

But how can this attribute of God be *by faith*, and *by faith in Christ?*

(e) Goodness of God. So Schoettgen, Morus, Voorst and others.

But here again, goodness, considered simply in the light of a divine attribute, cannot be regarded as what the apostle means to designate; for how can this be ἐκ πίστεως?

II. Δικαιοσύνη Θεοῦ is regarded as something which belongs to men ; either as an attribute, quality, etc., or else as a state, condition, etc., of which God is the author or giver; so that Θεοῦ is construed as *Gen. auctoris.* But here again, there is some variety of opinion ; for,

(a) Some hold that δικαιοσύνη means *internal righteousness, virtue,* or *holiness* such as the gospel requires. So Ammon, Schleusner, Tholuck, Paulus, Schultz, Winer, Wahl, Glockler, and others. But some of them explain this, as meaning *the way and manner of obtaining this holiness.*

So far as Rom. i. 17 is concerned, this is a possible sense. But the phrase δικαιοσύνη is so often employed by Paul to designate *pardon, forgiveness,* or at least a state of *pardon* or of *being forgiven*, that it cannot well be supposed it is here employed in a different sense, in proposing the theme which the apostle afterward discusses.

That δικαιοσύνη θεοῦ .... ἐκ πίστεως had a direct reference, in the writer's mind, to liberation from punishment and the obtaining of salvation, seems to be clear from the quotation which he immediately makes from the Old Testament, in order to sanction the sentiment which he had uttered, viz. δίκαιος ἐκ πίστεως ζήσεται, *he who is just*, *i. e.*, he who is accepted or regarded as δίκαιος, *shall obtain life by faith*, *i. e.*, shall be happy by faith (not by merit). Such then is the δικαιοσύνη Θεοῦ. It bestows unmerited favor on perishing sinners; not on him who has fulfilled the law, (for who has done this?) but on him who believes on Jesus; comp. Romans iv. 3—5.

Such a δικαιοσύνη, which is from God, or is of divine appointment, is revealed *in* or *by* the gospel, ἐν αὐτῷ ἀποκαλύπτεται; for αὐτῷ refers to τὸ εὐαγγέλιον in ver. 16. The apostle does not mean to say, that nothing respecting such a faith was before revealed; for he appeals immediately to the Old Test. Scriptures, in order to confirm the sentiment which he had just uttered. But the gospel, in the first place, makes such a revelation one of its *most prominent* features; and therefore, secondly, justification by faith is revealed in it *more fully* and *explicitly* than it ever had been before. In the like way, life and immortality are said to be brought to light by the gospel, 2 Tim. i. 10.

The phrase, ἐκ πίστεως εἰς πίστιν, a controverted, and (by reason of its connection) very difficult phrase. The main question is, whether ἐκ πίστεως is to be joined with δικαιοσύνη, or whether it belongs in sense to εἰς πίστιν, so that ἐκ πίστεως εἰς πίστιν would make a kind of *climactic* expression, which would be equivalent to the following phrase, viz., 'from a lower to a higher degree of faith.' In this latter way Theophylact understood it; for he says, οὐ γὰρ ἀρκεῖ τὸ πρώτως πιστεῦσαι, ἀλλ' ἐκ τῆς εἰσαγωγικῆς πίστεως δεῖ ἡμᾶς ἀναβαίνειν εἰς τὴν τελειότεραν πίστιν; *i. e.*, 'our first belief is not sufficient, but we must ascend from our inceptive faith to a more perfect degree of it.' So Clemens Alex. (Strom. V. 1): Κοινὴ πίστις καθάπερ θεμέλιος, καθὼς ὁ Κύριος λέγει, ἡ πίστις σου σέσωκέ σε; *i. e.*, 'a common faith is as it were a foundation, as Christ said: Thy faith hath saved thee.' He then goes on to say, that 'a τελεία πίστις is one which can remove mountains; on which account the apostles themselves made this request: Lord, we believe, help thou our unbelief!'

Tholuck approves of this exegesis; and it is substantially the same as that which has been defended by Melancthon, Beza, Calov, Le Clerc, and many others. But three difficulties seem to

ROMANS I. 17   35

lie in the way of admitting it; the first, that it does not appear at all to answer the exigency of the passage; the second, that the *usus loquendi* of Paul's epistles is against it; the third, that the context is evidently repugnant to it.

(a) The exigency of the passage. The exegesis in question would make Paul's main *thesis* to be this: 'The justification which God bestows, (or, according to Tholuck, the fulfilling of the law which he requires,) is revealed in the gospel, from a lower degree of faith to a higher, *i. e.*, (as I suppose is meant,) it is so revealed, as that men are required to advance from a lower to a higher degree of faith. But this would indeed be a most singular mode of expressing such a sentiment; one of the last which the usual method of thought and expression can well be supposed to devise. One might expect, if this idea is intended to be contained in the passage, that the writer would have said: Δικαιοσύνη Θεοῦ ἐν αὐτῷ ἀποκαλύπτεται ἵνα προβαίνωμεν (or προβῶμεν) ἐκ πίστεως εἰς πίστιν; or at least that some mode of expression like this would have been employed. But if the sense be not, that justification is so revealed by the gospel as that men are required to advance from a lower to a higher degree of faith, then, after all, ἐκ πίστεως must be joined in effect with δικαιοσύνη, and we must say,'The justification which is ἐκ πίστεως εἰς πίστιν, is revealed,' etc.

This sentiment then does not fit the *exigency of the passage;* since it represents the apostle, not as proposing the grand theme of gratuitous justification (which is evidently the main subject of his epistle), but as proposing the *climactic* nature of the faith connected with justification, as his great topic. How can this well be imagined by a considerate reader of his epistle?

(b) It is against the usus loquendi of homogeneous passages; e. g., Rom. iii. 22, δικαιοσύνη Θεοῦ διὰ πίστεως (altogether of the same tenor as δικαιοσύνη Θεοῦ . . . . ἐκ πίστεως in our verse); Rom. iii. 30, ὃς δικαιώσει . . . . ἐκ πίστεως, καὶ . . . . διὰ πίστεως· Rom. iv. 11, σφραγῖδα τῆς δικαιοσύνης, τῆς πίστεως· Rom. iv. 13, διὰ δικαιοσύνης πίστεως· Rom. v. 1, δικαιωθέντες ἐκ πίστεως· Rom. ix. 30, τὰ ἔθνη . . . . κατέλαβε . . . δικαιοσύνην τὴν ἐκ πίστεως· Rom. ix. 32, ὅτι οὐκ [Ἰσραὴλ ἦν διώκων δικαιοσύνην] ἐκ πίστεως· Rom. x. 6, ἡ δὲ ἐκ πίστεως δικαιοσύνη· and so in the other epistles of Paul, *e. g.*, Gal. ii. 16, [δικαιοῦται ἄνθρωπος] διὰ πίστεως· Gal. iii. 8, ἐκ πίστεως δικαιοῖ τὰ ἔθνη ὁ Θεός· Gal. iii. 11, ὁ δίκαιος ἐκ πίστεως ζήσεται (a quotation); Gal. iii. 24, ἵνα ἐκ πίστεως δικαιωθῶμεν· Gal. v. 5, ἐκ πίστεως ἐλπίδα δικαιοσύνης ἀπεκδεχόμεθα· Phil. iii. 9, δικαιοσύνην . . . . τὴν διὰ πίστεως· Heb. xi. 7, τῆς κατὰ πίστιν δικαιοσύνης; et alibi sæpe. These are enough to show what Paul (I had almost said everywhere, and always) presents to our view, in respect to the subject of justification. Can there

be any good reason to apprehend, that in proposing the *theme* of his whole epistle, he should not propose the same *justification by faith* of which he afterwards so amply treats?

'But how could Paul separate ἐκ πίστεως so far from δικαιοσύνη, if he means that the former should qualify the latter?' I answer, δικαιοσύνη, as here employed, has already a noun in the Genitive (Θεοῦ) connected with it. The writer could not say ἡ ἐκ πίστεως δικαιοσύνη Θεοῦ (which would, I believe, be without a parallel); nor was it apposite to say, δικαιοσύνη Θεοῦ ἐκ πίστεως, because the writer was hastening to say, that God's appointed method of justification *was revealed* in the gospel. When this idea, which was uppermost in his mind (because he had just said that *he was not ashamed of the gospel*), was fully announced, the writer proceeds immediately to specify more particularly the δικαιοσύνη in question. It is a δικαιοσύνη ἐκ πίστεως, in accordance with which he has, in almost numberless examples, elsewhere made declarations.

The easiest and most direct solution is, to suppose δικαιοσύνη to be repeated here before ἐκ πίστεως. The sentence would then run thus: Δικαιοσύνη γὰρ Θεοῦ ἐν αὐτῷ ἀποκαλύπτεται [δικαιοσύνη] ἐκ πίστεως, κ. τ. λ. or γενομένη may be supplied by the mind, before ἐκ πίστεως. In this way, ἐκ πίστεως is *epexegetical* merely of what precedes. The idea conveyed by δικαιοσύνη is resumed by the mind, and it is made still more definite by this adjunct.

(c) That this is the real sentiment and design of the apostle, seems quite clear from the quotation which he forthwith makes in order to confirm what he had said, viz. ὁ δὲ δίκαιος ἐκ πίστεως ζήσεται. Does not δίκαιος ἐκ πίστεως clearly and unavoidably correspond with the δικαιοσύνη .... ἐκ πίστεως which immediately precedes?

I merely add, that Flatt, Bengel, Hammond, and others, interpret the passage in the same way as I have done. The more I study the passage, the more difficulty I feel in construing it as meaning *revealed from faith to faith.* What can be the meaning of *revealed* FROM *faith?* And if ἐκ πίστεως does not qualify ἀποκαλύπτεται, then it must qualify δικαιοσύνη, in which case the meaning that I have given seems nearly certain. And so Reiche construes ἐκ πίστεως, connecting it with δικαιοσύνη, and supposing γενομένη to be implied before it, which is admissible.

In respect to the thing itself, viz. *justification by faith,* faith designates the *modus in quo,* or the *means by which;* not the *causa causans seu efficiens, i. e.,* not either the meritorious or efficient cause or ground of forgiveness. Everywhere the apostle represents *Christ* as this cause. But faith (so to speak) is a *conditio sine qua non;* it is a taking hold of the blessings proffered by the gospel, although it is by no means the cause or ground of their being offered. If the readers of this epistle will keep in mind these simple and obvious truths, it will save them much perplexity. *Justification by faith*, is an expression designed to point out *gratuitous justification* (Rom. iv. 16), in distinction from that which is by merit, *i. e.*, by *deeds of law*, or entire obedience to the precepts of the law. The word *faith*, as used in this phrase, is designed to show, that the justification which we are now considering can be conferred only on *believers*, and that it is to be distinguished from δικαιοσύνη ἐξ ἔργων, *i. e.*, meritorious justification. It is not designed to show that faith is, in any sense, the *meritorious* or *procuring* cause or ground of justification.

In order to be believed, for belief, εἰς πίστιν. Such a use of the Acc. with εἰς is exceedingly frequent in Paul's epistles. It is equivalent to the Infinitive mood with the article before it; *e. g.*, in ver. 5, above εἰς ὑπακοὴν = εἰς τὸ ὑπακουϑῆναι; so in ver. 16, εἰς σωτηρίαν = εἰς τὸ σωϑῆναι, et sic al. sæpe. The reason why the apostle adds εἰς πίστιν seems to be because he had said εἰς σωτηρίαν παντὶ τῷ πιστεύοντι. In accordance with this he here says, that *gratuitous justification* (δικαιοσύνη ἐκ πίστεως) is revealed, so that all, both Jews and Greeks (Ἰουδαίῳ τε πρῶτον καὶ Ἕλληνι) may *believe* and be saved; *i. e.*, they can be saved through *belief*, and in this way only. Or we may construe εἰς πίστιν as Reiche does, viz. δικαιοσύνη is revealed *to belief*, *i. e.*, to believers; comp. iii. 21.*

If ἐκ πίστεως is to be attached to ἀποκαλύπτεται, I should think the sentiment must be, that 'the gospel is revealed by means of faith, *i. e.*, by means of those who have faith in Christ, and in order to promote faith,' thus making a kind of *paronomasia*, to which the writings of Paul are by no means a stranger. But I cannot apprehend this to be the true sentiment.

It should be remarked here, that faith is represented as the necessary condition of δικαιοσύνη Θεοῦ, and also that this is revealed to those who have faith, or at least for the sake of promoting faith. Thus the gospel scheme seems to begin and end (as it were) with faith, 'He that *believeth* shall be saved.'

In accordance with what is written, καϑὼς γέγραπται, *agreeably to what is written*, viz. in the Scriptures. The Talmudists very

---

* If ἐκ πίστεως be joined with the verb ἀποκαλύπτεται to express "the condition or subjective ground of the action, i. e the humble and trustful surrender of the soul, and εἰς πίστιν be referred to the individuals to whom the δικαιοσύνη is made known (or rather definitely and particularly to the faith in the individuals), the believers, τοὺς πιστεύοντας, both the grammatical construction and the connected train of thought should seem to be best preserved.

often appealed to the Scriptures in the like way, by the formulas חִינוּ דְכְתִיב, *as it is written;* הֵינוּ הָךְ דִּכְתִיב, *according to that which is written;* or הִיכָּה דְּאָמַר הַפָּסוּק, *as the Scripture says.* It is not necessary to suppose, in all cases of this nature, that the writer who makes such an appeal, regards the passage which he quotes as specific *prediction.* Plainly this is not always the case with the writers of the New Testament; as nearly all commentators now concede. Compare, for example, Acts xxviii. 25, seq. Rom. viii. 36. ix. 33. x. 5. xi. 26. xiv. 11, etc. Such being the case, it is not necessary that we should interpret the passage which follows (Hab. ii. 4.), as having been originally designed to describe *gospel justification by faith;* for plainly the connection in which it stands does not admit of this *specific* meaning. But it then involves the same *principle* as that for which the apostle is contending, viz., that 'the means of safety is confidence or trust in the divine declarations.' The prophet Habakkuk sees, in prophetic vision, "troublous times" coming upon Judæa; and he exclaims צַדִּיק בֶּאֱמוּנָתוֹ יִחְיֶה, ὁ δίκαιος ἐκ πίστεως ζήσεται, *the pious man shall be saved by his confidence or faith,* viz., in God. It was not, then, by relying on his own merit or desert that safety could be had; it was to be obtained only in the way of believing and trusting the divine declarations. Now the very same *principle* of action was concerned in so doing at that time, which is concerned with the faith and salvation of the gospel. Of course the apostle might appeal to this declaration of Habakkuk, as serving to confirm the *principle* for which he contended.

Dr. Knapp and many others join ἐκ πίστεως with δίκαιος, and then translate the passage thus: *The just by faith shall live; i. e.,* he who possesses faith shall be happy. The sentiment is true; but it does not comport, I apprehend, with the design of Habakkuk, who must have written בֶּאֱמוּנָתוֹ if he intended this, and not (as he has done) בֶּאֱמוּנָתוֹ.

If it be viewed as a simple *illustration of a general principle,* all difficulty about the quotation vanishes. As the Israelite, in the time of Habakkuk, was to be saved from evil by means of *faith,* so Jews and Gentiles are now to be saved by means of *faith.*

To the whole I subjoin the brief comment which J. A. Turretin has so strikingly given, in his *Prælectiones* on the epistle to the Romans: "Apostolus noster, ubi agit de justificatione et salute hominum, sæpe vocat *justitiam Dei* eam justificationis rationem quam Deus hominibus commonstrat, et cujus ope eos ad salutem ducit." Again: "*Justitia Dei* . . . . est ipsamet hominis justificatio, seu modus quo potest justus haberi apud Deum, et salutis particeps fieri;" a definition of which one may almost say: *Omne tulit punctum.*

Turretin has, indeed, construed ἐκ πίστεως εἰς πίστιν nearly as Tholuck has done. But the *usus loquendi* of Paul in such constructions is decidedly against him: *c. g.*, Rom. vi. 19, 'Since ye have yielded your members as servants of impurity, καὶ τῇ ἀνομίᾳ εἰς ἀνομίαν, *and to iniquity for the commission of wickedness*, so should ye yield your members as servants τῇ δικαιοσύνῃ εἰς ἁγιασμόν *unto righteousness, in order that ye may practise holiness;*' 2 Cor. ii. 16, '[The gospel is] to some ὀσμὴ θανάτου εἰς θάνατον, and to others, ὀσμὴ ζωῆς εἰς ζωήν, *a savor of death to the causing of death, and a savor of life to the causing of life.*' In these and all such cases, the Accusative with εἰς before it, denotes the *end*, or *object*, to which the thing that had just been named tends. So must it be, then, in the text; the [δικαιοσύνη] ἐκ πίστεως is revealed or declared to the world εἰς πίστιν, *i. e.*, in order that it may be received or believed.

(18) *For the wrath of God from heaven, is revealed against all ungodliness and unrighteousness,* ἀποκαλύπτεται γὰρ .... ἀνθρώπων. The γάρ with which this verse is introduced, refers doubtless to an *implied* thought in the mind of the writer, intervened between verses 17 and 18, viz. 'This δικαιοσύνη Θεοῦ is now the only δικαιοσύνη possible for men.' The sequel shows this; since it is designed to prove that all men are in a state of sin and condemnation, and can be saved only by *gratuitous* pardon. Ὀργὴ Θεοῦ, literally, *the wrath of God, divine indignation,* or (to use a softer phraseology) *God's displeasure.* That the phrase is *anthropopathic* (*i. e.*, used as speaking of God after the manner of men), will be doubted by no one who has just views of the divine Being. It is impossible to unite with the idea of complete perfection that of anger in the sense in which we usually cherish it; for with us it is a source of misery and sin. To neither of these effects of anger can we properly suppose the divine Being to be exposed. His *anger*, then, can only be that feeling or affection in him, which moves him to look on sin with disapprobation, and to punish it when connected with impenitence. We must not, even in imagination, connect this in the remotest manner with *revenge;* which is only and always a *malignant* passion. But vengeance, even among men, is seldom sought for against those whom we know to be perfectly impotent, in respect to thwarting any of our designs and purposes. Now as all men, and all creation, can never endanger any one interest (if I may so speak) of the divine Being, or defeat a single purpose; so we cannot even imagine a motive for *revenge*, on ordinary grounds. Still less can we suppose the case to be of this nature, when we reflect that God is infinite in wisdom, power, and *goodness.* It would be quite as well (nay, much better) to say, that when the Bible

attributes *hands, eyes, arms,* etc., to God, the words which it employs should be literally understood, as to say that when it attributes *anger* and *vengeance* to him, it is to be literally understood. If we so construe the Scriptures, we represent God as a malignant being, and class him among the demons; whereas by attributing to him *hands, eyes,* etc., we only commit the sin of *anthropomorphism.*

The lexicons make ὀργὴ to signify *punishment.* By way of consequence, indeed, punishment is *implied.* But ὀργὴ Θεοῦ is a more fearful phrase, understood in the sense of divine displeasure or indignation, and more pregnant with awful meaning if so rendered, than it is if we give to it simply the sense of κόλασις, as so many critics and lexicographers have done.

'Απ' οὐρανοῦ, another *locus vexatus.* Is it to be joined with Θεοῦ; or should we refer back to ἀποκαλύπτεται, and construe it as implying the method in which the divine displeasure is made known? The latter way is the one which almost all commentators have chosen, although there is almost an endless diversity among them as to the meaning of ἀπ' οὐρανοῦ. E. g. (1) The *heavens* declare the glory of God, and so point men naturally to his worship, and by consequence warn them to forsake sin. (2) Storm, tempest, hail, thunder, lightning, etc., *from heaven,* declare the wrath of God against sin. (3) Christ will be revealed *from heaven,* at the last judgment, to punish sin; so Chrysostom, Theodoret, Theophylact, Limborch, etc. (4) Judgments which come from God, who is in heaven, testify against sin; so Origen, Cyril, Beza, Calvin, Bengel, etc. (5) In consequence of an appointment of heaven, the divine displeasure against sin is testified by conscience in every breast. (6) The displeasure of God against sin is revealed, through divine appointment, or by the arrangement of the supreme Being.

This last interpretation I think to be nearly right. But the *usus loquendi* (which seems unaccountably to have been overlooked here) enables us to be more explicit. In Heb. xii. 25, the apostle says: "If they escaped not who rejected τὸν ἐπὶ γῆς . . . . χρηματίζοντα, *him who on earth* [at Mount Sinai] *warned them,* much more shall we not escape, if we reject τὸν ἀπ' οὐρανῶν [χρηματίζοντα] *him* [who warneth us] *from heaven;*" comp. Mark i. 11, where a voice ἐκ τῶν οὐρανῶν says: "This is my beloved Son," etc. Now if such phraseology be compared with Matt. v. 45, τοῦ πατρός ὑμῶν τοῦ ἐν οὐρανοῖς· vi. 1, πατρὶ . . . . ἐν τοῖς οὐρανοῖς· vi. 9, πάτερ ἡμῶν ὁ ἐν τοῖς οὐρανοῖς, et al. sæpe, it would seem sufficiently plain, that *God coming from heaven* where he dwells, or *God belonging to heaven,* is intended to be designated by the phrase Θεοῦ ἀπ' οὐρανοῦ. So Reiche. That ἀπό, in multitude of cases, is put before a noun of *place*, in order to designate that one belongs to it, scarcely needs to be suggested; *e. g.*, Matt. ii. 1. iv. 25. 2 Thess. i. 7. John i. 45. xxviii. 21, et al. sæpe. The sentiment I take to be this: 'The God of heaven, or the God who dwells in heaven, *i. e.*, God supreme, omnipotent, has revealed his displeasure against sin;' and, therefore, escape from punishment can be only by the δικαιοσύνη Θεοῦ.

How the revelation of God's displeasure is made, is disclosed by the sequel. To the heathen it is made by God's works and their own consciences, Rom. i. 20, 32. ii. 14, 15.

'Ασέβειαν, *impiety* towards God (from a privative and σέβομαι *to worship*); ἀδικίαν, *injustice, unrighteousness*, toward men.

Who keep back or *hinder the truth by iniquity,* τῶν τὴν . . . . κατεχόντων. So the verb κατέχω most naturally means; comp. Luke iv. 42. Philem. ver. 13. 2 Thess. ii. 6, 7. It also means *to hold firmly, to grasp hold of, to take possession of and retain*, etc., as may be seen in the lexicons; but these meanings do not fit well here. Theophylact explains κατεχόντων by καλύπτειν, σκοτίζειν. The meaning seems to be: 'Who hinder the progress or obstruct the power of truth, in themselves or others.'

But of what truth? 'Αλήθεια cannot here mean the *gospel*; because the writer goes on immediately to say, that the *light of nature* sufficed to teach the *heathen* better, than to restrain the ἀλήθεια in question. 'Αλήθεια is here, then, that truth which the light of nature taught respecting *the eternal power and Godhead* of the Creator. When the apostle says in ver. 18, τῶν τὴν ἀλήθειαν ἐν ἀδικίᾳ κατεχόντων, in his own mind he singles out of the ἀνθρώπων *(all men)* whom he has just mentioned, the heathen or Gentiles, whose vicious state he immediately proceeds to declare. This is the theme for the remainder of the first chapter.

Ἐν ἀδικίᾳ may mean *by iniquity,* ἐν standing before the *means* or *instrument*, as usual; or else it is used adverbially = ἀδίκως. Reiche prefers the latter sense; which is agreeable to idiom.*

CHAP. I. 19—32.

THE apostle, having alluded to the heathen or Gentiles, as those 'who hinder the truth through unrighteousness,' now proceeds to illustrate and confirm his charge against them. God has disclosed in the works of creation his eternal power and Godhead, and thus so clearly, that they are without excuse for failing to recognize it, verses 19, 20. And since they might have known him, but were ungrateful, and

---

* The former, however, seems to us to be the meaning here. There is a sort of contrast between ἀλήθειαν and ἀδικία. The truth, the right, which is communicated to all is checked in its development by the love and practice of the wrong.

refused to glorify him, and darkened their minds by vain and foolish disputations; and represented the eternal God to be like mortal man, and even like the brutes which perish; God gave them up to their own base and degrading lusts, as thus rendering the creature the honor that was due to the Creator, verses 21—25. Yea, he gave them up to the vile and unnatural passions which they cherished, verses 29, 30, and these they not only commit themselves, although they know them to be worthy of death, *i. e.*, of condemnation on the part of the Divine lawgiver, but by their approbation they encourage others to commit the like offences.

Such being the state of facts in regard to the heathen world, it follows of course that they *justly* lie under the condemning sentence of the divine law. It is not the object of the apostle to prove that every individual heathen is guilty of each and all the sins which he enumerates; much less does he intend even to intimate that there are not other sins, besides those which he enumerates, of which the Gentiles are guilty. It is quite plain, that those which he does mention, are to be regarded merely in the light of a *specimen*. Nor will the charges which he here makes, prove that every individual of the Gentile world was, at the moment when he was writing, guilty of all the things preferred against the heathen. If we suppose that there might then have been some virtuous heathen, (a supposition apparently favored by Rom. ii. 14), such persons must have abstained from the habitual practices of the vices named, and from others like them. But it suffices for the apostle's purpose, to show that they once had been guilty of them; which of course was to show their absolute need of salvation by a Redeemer, *i. e.*, of gratuitous pardon procured through him. The case may be the same here, as that which is presented in chap. ii. iii., where a charge of universal guilt is brought against the Jews. Certainly this was not designed to prove that there then existed no pious Jews, who were *not* liable to such charge in its full extent, at the moment when the apostle was writing. Nay, it was of course true to *some* extent, even of the pious, at the time when Paul was writing, that they daily committed sin in some form or other, and the same was true of pious Gentiles, if indeed there were any such. *All men*, then, were guilty before God, although all men might not practise the particular vices which the apostle named, when he was writing. It matters not for his purpose to prove this. All who could sin, had sinned, and did then sin, in some way or other, all this is now, and always has been true. Of course, all have fallen under the condemnation of the divine law, and salvation by the grace proffered in the Gospel, is the only salvation which is possible for them.

The question *when* men *begin* to sin, it is not the object of the apostle here to discuss. Nor is it even the *degree* of their depravity, which is his main design to illustrate and prove. The *universality* of it is the main point, and it is all which is essential to his argument. To this universality Paul admits of no exception, but then we are of course to understand this, of those who are capable of sinning. It is thus that we interpret in other cases. For example, when it is said "He that believeth not, shall be damned," we interpret this of those who are capable of believing, and do not extend it beyond them. With the question, *when* individuals are capable of believing or of sinning, I repeat it, Paul does not here concern himself. Neither mere infancy, nor entire idiocy, is the object of his present consideration. He is plainly speaking of such, and only of such, as are capable of sinning; and these, one and all, he avers to be sinners, in a greater or less degree. Such being the fact, it follows, that as "the soul which sinneth must die," so, if there be any reprieve from this sentence, it must be obtained only by pardoning mercy through a Redeemer.

I add merely, that the clause τῶν τὴν ἀλήθειαν ἐν ἀδικίᾳ κατεχόντων, properly belongs to that division of the discourse which we are now to examine; but the connection of it with the general proposition in the preceding part of ver. 18, is made so intimate by the present grammatical structure, that I deemed it best not to disjoin them in the commentary.

(19) The idea of the preceding verse is here expanded and enforced by showing that to all men is made, in the works of na-

ture, a revelation so plain of the eternal power and Godhead of Jehovah, that nothing but a wilful and sinful perversion of the light which they enjoy, can lead them to deny this great truth. *Because that which might be known concerning God was manifest to them,* διότι . . . . αὐτοῖς. Διότι = διὰ τοῦτο ὅτι and equivalent in logical force here to γάρ, stands before a clause which assigns a reason why the apostle asserts that the heathen *hinder the truth by iniquity.* The amount of the proof which follows is, (1) That the truth was knowable. (2) That nothing but base and evil passions keep men from acknowledging and obeying it.

The knowledge of God, τὸ γνωστόν τοῦ Θεοῦ, or *that concerning God which is knowable* or *known.* The meaning *that which is knowable,* seems on the whole to be best; and that τὸ γνωστόν may be thus rendered we can have no doubt, when we compare τό νοητόν, *intelligible,* τὸ αἰσθητόν *quod perceptum sit,* τὸ ἀόρατον *quod non visum sit, i. e.,* invisible, etc. Buttmann (Gram. § 92. Anm. 3, comp. my N. Test. Gramm. § 82, Note 1,) seems to have decided this point, however, beyond any reasonable doubt. He says, indeed, that *verbals* in -τός frequently correspond to the Latin participles in *-tus ;* so πλεκτός *stricken,* στρεπτός *perverted,* ποιητός *made, factus,* etc. But "more commonly," he adds, "they have the sense of *possibility,* like the Latin adjectives in *-ilis,* or the German ones in *-bar ;* as στρεπτός *versatilis,* ὁρατός *visibilis,* ἀκουστός *audibilis.*" This appears more fully when ἐστί is joined with these adjectives or verbals; *e. g.,* βιωτόν ἐστι, one can live, (*quasi,* 'it is live-able'); τοῖς οὐκ ἐξιτόν ἐστι, they cannot go out, (*quasi* 'to them it is not go-able'). Plato also frequently uses the very word under examination, in connection with δοξαστόν, *e. g.,* τὸ γνωστὸν καὶ τὸ δοξαστόν, *that which is knowable and that which is supposable,* de Repub. Lib. v.*

Concerning God, τοῦ Θεοῦ, Θεοῦ being *Genitivus objecti,* as grammarians say. For an extended statement of the latitude of the Genitive, in regard to the many various relations which it expresses, see N. Test. Gramm. § 99. Examples in point are Matt. xiii. 18, παραβολὴ τοῦ σπείροντος, *the paralle* CONCERNING *the*

---

* Both the verbal form of the word and classical usage undeniably sanction the meaning: "that which may be known," if the context favors that interpretation. But, if we take this in its most extended signification: "all that could be known," it cannot of course be true; since the Gentiles have not all possible knowledge of God from the light of nature. — On this account Luther, De Wette, Meyer and others not without reason translate: "that which is known." So Alford: "The objective knowledge patent and recognized in creation;" "that universal objective knowledge of God as the Creator which we find more or less in every nation under heaven, and which as matter of historical fact, was proved to be in possession of the great Gentile nations of antiquity."

sower; 1 Cor. i. 18, ὁ λόγος ὁ τοῦ σταυροῦ, *the declaration* CON-
CERNING *the cross.* So λόγος τινός a *report* CONCERNING *any
one*, Xen. Cyrop. vi. 3. 10. viii. 5. 28. Comp. Luke vi. 12.
Rom. xiii. 3. John xvii. 2. Heb. ix. 8, et alibi.

Among them, ἐν αὐτοῖς. So ἐν often means; *e. g.*, Matt. ii. 6,
ἐν οἷς *among whom;* Rom. xi. 17. 1 Cor. iii. 18, etc. The sense
would then be: 'What may be known [by the light of nature]
concerning God, was manifest among them,' *i. e.*, in the midst of
them, or before their eyes. The more probable sense, however,
seems to be *in them, i. e.*, in their minds or consciences; comp.
Rom. ii. 15. Acts xiii. 15. Some prefer to render ἐν αὐτοῖς as
they would the simple Dative αὐτοῖς, viz., *to them,* and appeal to
such examples as 1 Cor. xiv. 11. Matt. xvii. 22. Luke xxiii. 31.
xii. 8, and even to Acts iv. 12. 1 Cor. ii. 6. 2 Cor. iv. 3. But
the preceding method of construction is plainly the more certain
and simple one. Tholuck and Reiche accordingly prefer to render ἐν αὐτοῖς *in them;* and they interpret it as referring to their
moral sense, by which they may come to discern and judge of the
evidences of divine power and Godhead. That ἐν before the
Dative, can never be properly considered the same thing as the
simple Dative, seems to be conclusively shown by Winer, N.
Test. Gramm. p. 177, ed. 3.

The γάρ in ὁ Θεὸς γὰρ αὐτοῖς ἐφανέρωσε is γάρ *confirmantis.*

(20) *For the invisible things,* etc., τὰ γὸρ . . . . καὶ θειότης,
may be regarded as a *parenthetic* explanation. The γάρ here
is also γάρ *confirmantis vel illustrantis;* it stands before an
assertion designed to illustrate and confirm the preceding
declaration. Ἀόρατα, means the attributes or qualities of the divine Being; which are ἀόρατα, invisible, because they are not
objects of physical notice, *i. e.*, are not disclosed to any of our
corporeal senses. Of course the expression refers to the attributes belonging to God considered as a *spirit;* 1 Tim. i. 17.

Since the creation of the world, ἀπὸ κτίσεως κόσμου. That ἀπό
may be rendered *since,* scarcely needs proof; *e. g.*, ἀπὸ καταβολῆς
κόσμου, ἀπ' ἀρχῆς, ἀπὸ τῆς ὥρας ἐκείνης, etc.; see Lex. in
verbum. So far as the *usus loquendi* is concerned, it might be
rendered *by, by means of,* a sense which ἀπό very frequently has,
but τοῖ ποιήμασι would then be tautological. By τὰ ἀόρατα αὐτοῦ
. . . . καθορᾶται, the writer means to say, that *ever since* the
world was created, the evidences of eternal power and Godhead
have been visible to the mind; which indeed, must be as true as
that they are now visible.

By the things which are made, τοῖς ποιήμασι, *i. e.*, by the natural
creation. Ποιήμασι, might be rendered *by his operations,* inasmuch as nouns ending in the neuter -μα not unfrequently in the

Hebrew-Greek have the same meaning as those which end in -σις; *e. g.*, δικαίωμα, δικαίωσις, *justification*. If it were thus rendered, the sense would be, that the operations of God in the world of nature continually bear testimony respecting him. This is not only true, but a truth scarcely less striking, as it now appears to us through the medium of astronomy, natural philosophy, and physiology, than that which is developed by *creative* power. Nevertheless, as the discoveries of modern science were unknown to the heathen, so it seems most congruous here to explain ποιή-μασι* by *things made, the natural creation*, which the heathen, in common with all others, were continually reminded of by their external senses.

The due result of serious notice is, that τὰ ἀόρατα τοῦ Θεοῦ may be *νοούμενα, apprehended by the mind, understood*. Νοούμενα καθορᾶται means, *are distinctly seen, are intelligibly perceived*, *i. e.*, they are so, or may be so, by the aid of the things which have been made. In other words: God's *invisible* attributes, at least some of them, are made as it were *visible, i. e.*, are made the object of clear and distinct apprehension, by reason of the natural creation. So the Psalmist: "The heavens declare the glory of God," etc., Ps. xix. 1, 2.

But what are the *attributes of God* which are thus plainly discernible by his works? The answer is, ἥ τε ἀΐδιος αὐτοῦ δύναμις καὶ θειότης, *both or even his eternal power and Godhead*. This clause is epexegetical of τὰ ἀόρατα αὐτοῦ. Δύναμις must here have special reference to the *creative power* of God; and this seems to be called ἀΐδιος, because it must have been possessed antecedently to the creation of the world, or before time began. Still, although δημιουργία (creative power), as Theodoret says, is here specially meant, I apprehend that the sense of δύναμις is not restricted to this. He who had power to *create*, must of course be supposed to have power to wield and govern.

Θειότης is distinguished by Tholuck and others, from Θεότης, for they represent the latter as signifying *the Divinity* or *the Divine nature*, while the former is represented as meaning the *complexity of the divine attributes, the sum* or *substance of divine qualities*.† I cannot find any good ground, however, for such a distinction.

---

* The two ideas may be included in the word, that of creation and preservation.

† There seems to be some ground for the distinction made by De Wette, Alford and others between θειότης as used here and θεότης in Col. 2: 9. The former word here refers to "those vestiges of God which men may everywhere trace in the world around them," as "his majesty and glory," but the latter word in Colossians designates "the essential and personal Godhead of the Son." See Trench's Syn. of the N. Test., De Wette's Comm., et al.

Θεότης is the *abstract* derived from Θεός; and from this latter word is formed the *concrete* or *adjective* derivate Θεῖος, *divine*. Τὸ Θεῖον of course means *divinity*; and from this comes another regular abstract noun Θειότης, with the same signification. So Passow: Θειότης, *Gottlichkeit, göttliche Natur,* i. e. *divinity, divine nature.* He then adds: "In particular, divine greatness, power, excellence, eminence," etc.; *i. e.,* Θειότης designates the *divinity* with special reference to these qualities—the identical manner in which the word is employed in our text. The same lexicographer defines Θεότης *the Godhead, the divine Being, divine excellence.* In the same sense, viz., that of Godhead, Divinity, is τὸ Θεῖον plainly used in Acts xvii. 29. So Θειότης Wisd. xviii. 9. So Clemens Alex. (Strom. V. 10), τὸ μὴ φθείρεσθαι, Θειότητος μετέχειν ἐστί, *not to perish, is to be a partaker of Godhead or Divinity.*

If Θειότης be interpreted here as a word designating "the sum of *all* the divine attributes," we must regard *natural theology* as equally extensive with that which is revealed, so far as the great doctrines respecting the Godhead are concerned. Did the apostle mean to assert this? I trust not. I must understand Θειότης, then, as designating *Divinity, divine nature, divine excellence* or *supremacy, i. e.,* such a station, and condition, and nature as make the Being who holds and possesses them to be truly divine, or God. *Eternal power* and *supremacy* or *exaltation* appear, then, to be those qualities or attributes of the divine Being, which the works of creation are said by the apostle to disclose. And when examined by the eye of philosophy and reason, the evidence appears to be of the very same nature which he has here designed. At all events, the heathen never have made out any very definite and explicit views of God as *holy* and *hating sin;* not to speak of other attributes, of which they had quite imperfect and unsatisfactory views.

On this deeply interesting subject, viz., the disclosure of the natural world in respect to the Creator, Aristotle has said an exceedingly striking thing (De Mundo, c. 6), πάσῃ θνητῇ φύσει γενόμενος ἀθεώρητος, ἀπ᾽ αὐτῶν τῶν ἔργων θεωρεῖται ὁ Θεός, *God, who is invisible to every mortal being, is seen by his works.* Comp. also Wisd. xiii. 1—5.

So that they are without excuse, εἰς τὸ εἶναι αὐτοὺς ἀναπολογήτους. Εἰς τό, followed by an Inf., is often used in the same manner as ὥστε; *e. g.,* Luke v. 17. Rom. iv. 18, vii. 4, 5. xii. 3. Εἰς τὸ κ. τ. λ., is joined in sense with ὁ Θεός γὰρ αὐτοῖς ἐφανέρωσε (the first clause in ver. 20 being a parenthesis); *i. e.,* 'God has exhibited, in his works, such evidences of his eternal power and Godhead, that those are without any excuse *who hinder the truth by reason of their iniquity.*' That the apostle means to characterize the heathen by all this, is clear from the sequel.

(21) *Because that having known God,* διότι γνόντες τὸν Θεόν. The διότι here is considered by Glockler as co-ordinate with that in ver. 19 ; and both the clauses in vers. 19, 20, and in vers. 21—23 he considers as *protases* to διὸ κ. τ. λ. in ver. 24 seq. The sense then is: '*Because* the knowledge of God was disclosed to them, etc.,—*because,* when they knew God, they did not glorify him, etc.,—διό, *therefore* God gave them over,' etc. But διότι cannot stand in the real protasis of a sentence that is independent of a preceding one; see examples of its use in the Concordance. We must consider the διότι in ver. 19, then, as prefatory to a reason why the heathen suppress the truth iniquitously; and the διότι in ver. 21 as prefatory to a reason why *they are without excuse.* In the same way γάρ often follows in two and even three successive clauses, prefatory to successive reasons for successive assertions.

Γνόντες here is employed in a sense that comports with the meaning of τὸ γνωστὸν in ver. 19, and may mean either *actual knowledge,* or *opportunity to know, being furnished with the means of knowing, having the knowledge of God plainly set before them.*

They glorified him not as God, neither were thankful, οὐχ ὡς . . . . εὐχαρίστησαν; *i. e.,* they paid him not the honor due to him as the Creator and Governor of all things, nor were they thankful for the blessings which he bestowed upon them. The particle ἤ, after a *negative* clause, means *nor, neither.*

But indulged foolish imaginations or *vain thoughts,* ἀλλ' ἐματαιώθησαν . . . . αὐτῶν. So we may render the passage, if we follow the more common meaning of ματαιόω, which not unfrequently corresponds to the Hebrew סָכַל, הִסְכִּיל, *insipide, stulte agere.* The Vulgate renders ἐματαιώθησαν by *evanuerant,* and Erasmus by *frustrati sunt;* and to the like purpose many critics have interpreted it. But the evident intention of the writer seems here to be, to describe a state of mind or feeling, not to express the result of it. Διαλογισμοῖς may be translated *thoughts, reasonings,* or *disputations;* for the word has each of these senses. The first seems the most appropriate here, on account of the clause which immediately follows, and which shows that *the state of the interior man* is designed to be described. It should be noted, moreover, that διαλογισμός, as meaning *thought* or *imagination,* is commonly taken in *malam partem, i. e.,* as designating *bad thoughts, evil imaginations, e. g.,* Matt. xv. 19. Mark vii. 21. Is. lix. 7 (Sept.) 1 Cor. iii. 20.

If we construe the words before us in this way, the sense will be: 'They foolishly or inconsiderately indulged evil imaginations,' *i. e.*, base and degrading views respecting the nature and attributes of God, and the honor due to him, as the sequel (vers. 22—25) shows, particularly ver. 23.

But there is another sense of the expression before us, which I am strongly tempted to adopt. The Hebrew הֶבֶל, *vanitas*, ματιότης, μάταια, as is well known, is often employed to designate idols and idolatry. Hence μάταια is frequently employed by the Septuagint to designate idols; *e. g.*, 2 Kings xvii. 15. Jer. ii. 5. viii. 19. Amos ii. 4. 1 Kings xvi. 13, etc. So also in the New Testament, Acts xiv. 15. From this usage, as one might naturally conclude, the verb ματαιόω (which means literally μάταιον *facere vel fieri*) sometimes means, *to be devoted to* μάταια, *i. e.*, to idols; *e. g.*, 2 Kings xvii. 15. Jer. ii. 5. ἐματαιώθησαν, *they became devoted to idolatry*, or *to vanities* (which is the same thing). The phrase in our verse is plainly susceptible of the like rendering, viz., *In their evil imaginations* or *by reason of their wicked devices, they became devoted to idolatry*, or *devoted to vanities* (which has the same meaning).*

But on the whole, it is safer perhaps to regard the clause before us a kind of parallel with the one which follows; in which case, the first asserts that the heathen foolishly indulged in wicked devices, and the second, that in consequence of this, their inconsiderate minds became darkened. The clause under examination will then be of the like tenor with ver. 22.

And their inconsiderate mind was darkened, καὶ ἐσκοτίσθη .... καρδία. Καρδία, like the Hebrew לֵב very often means, *animus, intellectus, the mind;* and this is plainly its meaning here. — Ἀσύνετος means *stolidus, insipiens*, or *imprudens*, which latter word means, *wanting in consideration and foresight*. I hesitate between this meaning, and that of *stolidus* in the sense of the Hebrew נָבָל, *i. e., impious, wicked*. The καρδία which had foolishly indulged evil imaginations respecting God, may be truly characterized either as *inconsiderate* or as *impious*. On the whole, the latter seems to convey rather the most energetic meaning; but the former accords better with the idea, that the second clause (now under examination) is parallel with the clause which precedes it.

It will be observed by the attentive reader, that the apostle here represents *the darkening of the mind* to be *a consequence* of the wicked imaginations which the heathen had indulged. Men

* Although this word may be used here in a general sense, yet there can be little doubt that it was chosen with reference to the allusion in it to idol-worship, one of the ways in which the heathen showed their evil imaginations.

had once a right knowledge of the true God; they all have opportunity to be acquainted with his true attributes. But in this condition, they choose foolishly to indulge in wicked devices and imaginations; and in consequence of this, they lose even what light they possessed ἐσκοτίσθη ἡ ἀσύνετος αὐτῶν καρδία.

(22) *Professing themselves to be wise, they became fools,* φάσκοντες .... ἐμωράνθησαν. The antithesis of the sentiment here is strong.

The pretensions of many heathen philosophers to *wisdom*, are well known. From these sprung the names φιλόσοφοι, φιλοσοφία, σόφοι, σοφισταί, etc. Φάσκω means *to declare, to affirm;* which, in the present case, means the same as *to profess*. So the Greeks used φάσκω; *e. g.*, οἱ φιλοσοφεῖν φάσκοντες, *those who profess to philosophize*. To the same purpose Cicero says: " Qui se sapientes esse profitentur," Quæst. Tusc. I. 9.

(23) *And exchanged the glory of the immortal God, for an image like to mortal man, and fowls, and quadrupeds, and reptiles,* καὶ ἤλλαξαν .... ἑρπετῶν. The phrase τὴν δόξαν τοῦ ἀφθάρτου Θεοῦ means *the majesty and excellence of the eternal God,* or *the glorious and eternal God.* In ἤλλαξαν .... ἐν ὁμοιώματι, the Dative with ἐν before it follows the verb. In such cases the usual construction is to put the simple Dative after the verb, *i. e.*, the dative of the noun designating the thing *for* which another is exchanged; *i. e.*, Lev. xxvii. 10, οὐκ ἀλλάξει .... καλὸν πονηρῷ. Ibid. ἀλλάξῃ .... κτῆνος κτήνει. Lev. xxvii. 33. Ex. xiii. 13. The classic writers usually say, ἀλλάσσειν τί τινος, or τὶ ἀντί τινος; but sometimes ἀλλάσσειν τί τινι. I find no construction like this in ver. 23, except in Ps. cv. 20, where in the Sept. ἠλλάξαντο τὴν δόξαν αὐτοῦ ἐν ὁμοιώματι μόσχου occurs. Tholuck says, that ἐν ὁμοιώματι stands for εἰς ὁμοίωμα, and he construes it here as meaning *the transmuting of one thing into another, i. e.,* making out of one thing something different from it. But this is not the common use of ἀλλάσσω, in cases like ours, although the verb occasionally admits of this sense (see ver. 26 below, where, however, the Accusative with εἰς is employed). But usually it means *to commute one thing* FOR *another* (not to transmute one thing *into* another). Nor can it be the design of Paul to say, that the heathen changed the glorious and immortal God into an image of perishable man and animals, (for how could they do this?) but to say that they exchanged the former (as an object of worship) for the latter; which is the exact state of the case.

Such being the fact, both as to the sense of the passage and the more usual construction of the verb ἀλλάσσω, I must regard ἐν ὁμοιώματι here as being of the same import and design as the simple Dative unattended with the preposition; of which examples are not wanting in the New Testament, and which Ps. cv. 20, confirms.

The phrase ἐν ὁμοιώματι εἰκόνος is like the Hebrew דְּמוּת צֶלֶם, *the resemblance of the image*, i. e., an image *resembling* or *like unto*. Φθαρτοῦ is designed as the antithesis of ἀφθάρτου, and means *frail, perishable, mortal*.

Πετεινῶν κ. τ. λ. How extensively such idolatry as is here described, has been and still is practised among the heathen, is too well known to need any formal proof in the present case. Juvenal (Sat. xv.) has drawn an admirable picture of Egyptian superstitions. The following lines are sufficiently graphic:

> "Quis nescit . . . . qualia demens
> Ægyptus portenta colat? Crocodilon adorat
> Pars hæc; illa pavit saturam serpentibus Ibim.
> . . . .
> Oppida tota canem venerantur, nemo Dianam."

And after saying that they worshipped various productions of the earth, and even culinary vegetables, he exclaims:

> "O sanctas gentes, quibus hæc nascuntur in hortis
> Numina!"

Comp. Ps. cxv. cxxxv. 15, seq. Is. xliv. 9—17, where is a most vivid description, in some of its traits not unlike to the hints in Horace, Lib. I. Sat. 8.

(24) Such was the impiety and folly of the heathen. Even their philosophers and learned men could not be exempted from part of the charges here brought against the Gentiles. On account of such sins, God even gave them up to their own lusts; διὸ καὶ παρέδωκεν . . . . ἀκαθαρσίαν, *wherefore God even gave them up, in the lusts of their hearts, to impurity* ;* i. e., God gave them over to the pursuit of their lusts, and to the dreadful consequences which follow such a course, because they were so desperately bent upon the pursuit of these objects, and would hearken to none of the instructions which the book of nature communicated. The imputation is, that in apostatizing from the true God, and betaking themselves to the worship of idols, they had at the same time been the devoted slaves of lust; which indeed seems here also, by implication, to be assigned as the reason or ground of their apostasy. Every one knows, moreover, that among almost all the various forms of heathenism, impurity has been

---

* The καί after διό may import· "as they advanced in departure from God, so God also on his part gave them up. *His* dealings with *them* had a progression likewise."—Alford.

either a direct or indirect service in its pretended religious duties. Witness the shocking law among the Babylonians, that every woman should prostitute herself, at least once, before the shrine of their Venus. It is needless to say, that the worshippers of Venus in Greece and Rome practised such rites; or that the *mysteries* of heathenism, of which Paul says "it is a shame even to speak," allowed a still greater latitude of indulgence. Nor is it necessary to describe the obscene and bloody rites practised in Hindostan, in the South Sea and the Sandwich Islands, and generally among the heathen. Polytheism and idolatry have nearly always been a religion of *obscenity* and *blood*. This the apostle plainly intimates.

The διό here = διὰ ὅ, *on account of which, for which reason*. For *substance* it has the same sense with διότι; yet it is employed more frequently in the way of *illation*, while it has a more specifically *relative* meaning than διότι. Thus διότι in ver. 19, stands at the head of a declaration intended to illustrate and establish the truth of the preceding assertion; so again of διότι in ver. 21; but διό in ver. 24, stands at the head of an *illation* from all the preceding premises in verses 19—23.

Gave up, gave over, παρέδωκε, *i. e.*, left them to pursue their own desires, without checking them by such restraints as he usually imposes on those who are not hardened and obstinate offenders. It seems here neither to denote an active 'plunging into sin,' on the one hand; nor a 'mere inactive letting alone,' on the other; but a withholding, by way of just retribution for their offences, such restraints as I have just described. The verb παραδίδωμι is commonly employed to designate *delivering over* to prison (Acts viii. 3), to bonds (2 Pet. ii. 4), to the executioner or condemning judge (Matt. xviii. 34, xxvii 2, 26). So here it is *a giving* or *delivering over* to the consequences of their own lusts, *i. e.*, a judicial abandonment of wicked heathen.*

In their lusts, ἐν ταῖς ἐπιθυμίαις, *i. e.*, God gave them up [being] in their lusts, εἰς ἀκαθαρσίαν κ. τ. λ. But most critics construe ἐν here as meaning *by* in the sense of *on account of, by reason of*. The sense is good, indeed, when rendered in this way, and the *usus loquendi* above exception; see Bretschn. Lex. ἐν No. 6. ed. 2nd. But I prefer to render it in the following way, viz. *God gave up them* [ὄντες being] *in their lusts* etc.; *i. e.*, he gave them up who were filled with lust, he gave them up to the pursuit of it, he abandoned them to the perverse desires of their own hearts, and to the consequences which would follow. In this way, ἐν

---

* Alford says: "As sin begets sin, and darkness of mind deeper darkness, grace gives place to judgment, and the divine wrath hardens men and hurries them on to more fearful degrees of depravity."

ταῖς ἐπιθυμίαις τῶν καρδιῶν becomes equivalent to an adjective qualifying αὐτούς. Of a usage like this in respect to the dative, with ἐν before it, the New Testament affords most ample proofs; *e. g.*, Luke iv. 32, ἐν ἐξουσίᾳ ἦν ὁ λόγος αὐτοῦ, *his word was powerful;* Rev. i. 10, ἐγενόμην ἐν πνεύματι, *I was inspired;* John xvi. 25, ἐν παροιμίαις λαλεῖν, *to speak parabolically;* John v. 5, ἐν ἀσθενείᾳ ἔχων, *being weak;* Rom. xvi. 7, οἱ γεγόνασιν ἐν Χριστῷ, *who became Christians;* and thus very often, as may be seen in Bretschn. Lex. ἐν, No. 5. Comp. Ps. lxxxi. 13. Ἐν employed in this way, may be called *ἐν conditionis;* inasmuch as the noun before which it stands, serves to designate *condition, habitude,* or *relation.* Ἐν thus employed agrees with the so-called ב *predicate* of the Hebrews, *i. e.,* ב prefixed to a noun which is employed in the sense of an adjective.

To the practice of impurity, εἰς ἀκαθαρσίαν, where εἰς before the Accusative denotes, as usual, *the object for which* anything is, or is done. The sense is the same as εἰς τὸ ποιεῖν τὴν ἀκαθαρσίαν.

To dishonor their own bodies among themselves, or *that their own bodies should be mutually dishonored,* τοῦ ἀτιμάζεσθαι . . . . ἐν ἑαυτοῖς, (ἀτιμάζεσθαι in the Passive). Τοῦ ἀτιμάζεσθαι is constructed after παρέδωκε implied. This Infinitive with τοῦ has, until recently, been generally reckoned as an imitation of the Hebrew Inf. with ל; but Winer (N. Test. Gramm. § 45. 4, ed. 3rd) has shown abundantly that it is very common in the Greek classics; see my N. Test. Gramm. § 138. The older critics used to solve this form of the Infinitive (where τοῦ intimates *design, object, end*), by supplying ἕνεκα or χάριν before it. Winer constructs τοῦ ἀτιμάζεσθαι, in the present case, by making it the Genitive after ἀκαθαρσίαν. I prefer the other method, which makes the clause *epexegetical. Among themselves,* ἐν ἑαυτοῖς. For this frequent sense of ἐν, see Bretschn. Lex. ἐν I. 6.

(25) A repetition of the idea contained in ver. 23 — καὶ ἤλλαξαν κ. τ. λ., but with some additions. Οἵτινες μετήλλαξαν . . . . ψεύδει *who exchanged the true God for a false one.* Ἀλήθειαν τοῦ Θεοῦ = τὸν ἀληθῆ Θεόν. More usually it is the *latter* of two nouns which is employed as an adjective in order to qualify the former; but sometimes the first noun performs the office of an adjective; compare Heb. Gramm. § 440. *b.* Both ἀλήθειαν and ψεύδει are examples of the *abstract* for the *concrete;* ψεύδει corresponding to the Hebrew הֶבֶל, שָׁוְא, שֶׁקֶר, which are so often employed to designate idols. In regard to μετήλλαξαν . . . . ἐν τῷ ψεύδει, see on ἤλλαξαν . . . . ἐν ὁμοιώματι in verse 23. But ἀλήθεια may be rendered *true worship,* and ψεύδει *false worship.*

And worshipped and served the creature more than the Creator, καὶ ἐσεβάσθησαν . . . . κτίσαντα. — Σεβάζομαι signifies *to venerate, to worship*, and designates the state of mind in the worshipper. The Aorists passive often have the sense of the Middle voice, and so, therefore, not unfrequently have an active sense, as here: N. Test. Gramm. § 61, 1. Λατρεύω designates either internal worship (see ver. 9 above), or external. Here, as it is joined with σεβάζομαι, it more naturally designates the *external* rites of the heathen religion. — *the creature, created things*, τῇ κτίσει; see the close of verse 23. — Παρά, *more than, above;* compare Luke iii. 13. Heb. i. 4. iii. 3. ix. 23. xi. 4. etc.; and see Bretschn. Lex. παρά III. 2. e. But here παρά may be rendered, *rather than*.

Who is blessed forever, Amen, ὅς ἐστιν . . . . ἀμήν. Doxologies of this nature are not unusual in the writings of Paul; see Gal. i. 5. Rom. ix. 5. 2 Cor. xi. 31. The Jewish Rabbies from time immemorial have been accustomed to add a doxology of the like nature, whenever they have had occasion to utter any thing which might seem reproachful to God. The Mohammedans have borrowed this custom from them, and practise it to a great extent. Tholuck mentions an Arabic manuscript in the library at Berlin, which contains an account of heresies in respect to Islamism; and so often as the writer has occasion to name a new heretical sect, he immediately adds: 'God be exalted above all which they say!' — Εὐλογητός means *worthy of praise, deserving to be extolled*.

Amen, ἀμήν, the usual response of the Hebrew solemn assemblies to the words or precepts of the law, when read; see Deut. xxvii. 15 — 26. The Hebrew אָמֵן means *verum, certum, ratum sit, i. e., ita sit;* which is the usual sense of ἀμήν in the New Testament, as in Rom. ix. 5. xi. 36. Gal. i. 5. Eph. iii. 21, et al. sæpe. As to the custom of public religious assemblies in respect to using this word, see 1 Cor. xiv. 16. It is to be understood as a solemn expression of assent to what has been said, and an approbation of it on the part of those who use it.

(26) As ver. 25 is a repetition and amplification of the sentiment in ver. 23.; so vers. 26, 27, are a repetition and amplification of the sentiment in ver. 24. There is the same connection in both cases; *e. g.*, after asserting the idolatry of the heathen in ver. 25, the apostle proceeds (as in ver. 24) to say: *on account of this* [their idolatry] *God gave them up to base passions*, διὰ τοῦτο . . . . ἀτιμίας. For the sense of παρέδωκεν ὁ Θεός, see verse 24. — Πάθη ἀτιμίας, *base passions* where ἀτιμίας (the latter of two nouns in regimen) holds the place of an adjective, agreeable to common usage; see the remarks on verse 25.

For their women exchanged their natural usage, into that which is unnatural or against nature, αἵ τε γὰρ . . . . φύσιν. Παρά not unfrequently has the sense here assigned, as may be seen in the lexicons; comp. Acts xviii. 13. So Plato παρὰ φύσιν ἡδόνη, *unnatural pleasure*. Τὴν φυσικὴν χρῆσιν means *usus venereus*. But whether the apostle refers here to the Greek τριβάδες or ἑταιρίστρια, or to those who were guilty of prostituting themselves in the vile and unnatural manner mentioned in verse 27, it would be difficult to determine; nor is it necessary. Those who wish to trace evidences of the facts alluded to, may consult Seneca, Ep. 95. Martial Epigr. I. 90. Athenæus, Deipnos. 13. p. 605. Tholuck on the State of the heathen World, in Neander's *Denkwürdigkeiten*, I. p. 143 seq., translated in the *Biblical Repository*, vol. II. Sucton. Nero, 28.

(27) *In like manner, also, the males, leaving the natural use of the female, burned in their lust toward each other,* ὁμοίως τε καὶ .... ἀλλήλοις. Literally ὁμοίως τε καὶ may be rendered *moreover, in like manner too*. Τὲ καὶ is often employed in enumerating particulars, in order to designate an intimate connection between them. This it signifies in a more emphatic manner than καὶ simply; and in this respect the Greek τέ answers well to the Lat. *que*. Τέ is employed rather to annex *clauses* than *words*, and in this respect differs from καί; at the same time τέ is more commonly connected only with clauses which are not necessary to complete the sentence in itself, but are epexegetical, *i. e.*, serve for confirmation, illustration, amplification, etc. But in this instance, some good Codd., and many versions and fathers, read δέ instead of τέ; and δέ is preferred by many critics.

The evidences of the fact here stated by the apostle are too numerous and prominent among the heathen writers to need even a reference to them. Virgil himself, ' the *chaste* Virgil,' as he has been often called, has a *Corydon amabat Alexin*, without seeming to feel the necessity of a blush for it. Such a fact sets the whole matter in the open day. That at Athens and Rome παιδεραστία was a very common and habitual thing, needs no proof to one who has read the Greek and Latin classics, especially the amatory poets, to any considerable extent. Plutarch tells us that Solon practised it; and Diogenes Laertius says the same of the Stoic Zeno. Need we be surprised, then, if the same horrible vice was frequent in the more barbarous parts of Greece and the Roman empire? Would God that nations called Christian were not reproachable with it; and that the great cities of the old world (possibly of the new also), did not exhibit examples of it almost as flagrant as those of Greece and Rome!

Males with males doing that which is shameful, ἄρσενες .... κατεργαζόμενοι. A further description of what the writer means, so as to leave no doubt about the design of the preceding affirmation.

And receiving in themselves the reward which is due to their error, καὶ τὴν . . . . ἀπολαμβάνοντες. The apostle doubtless means, here, the evil consequences, both physical and moral, which followed the practices on which he is animadverting. In respect to the first, their bodies were weakened, their health impaired, and premature old age came on both in a mental and physical respect. With regard to the second, what else could be expected from those who sunk themselves far below the brute creation, but that their moral sense would be degraded, their conscience "seared with a hot iron," and all the finer feelings and delicate sensibilities of life utterly extinguished? No example in the whole brute creation can be produced, which resembles the degradation of the παιδερασταί; and it follows, by an immutable law of a sin-hating God which is impressed on the very nature of all moral beings, that degradation and shame should result from the gratification of viler than beastly appetites. The despots, princes, and rich men of the East, who practise polygamy and keep extensive harems, are usually *superannuated* by the time they are *forty* years of age; how much more might this be naturally expected, as to the offenders mentioned in the verses under examination?

(28) *And inasmuch as they did not like to retain God in their knowledge,* καὶ καθὼς . . . . ἐν ἐπιγνώσει. Δοκιμάζω usually means *to try, prove, examine,* etc. But a secondary sense of the word is, *to approve, to choose;* like to δόκιμος *approved, accepted, agreeable,* etc. The apostle means here to say, that the heathen voluntarily rejected the knowledge of the true God, which, to a certain and important extent, they might have gathered from the book of nature so widely spread open before them—Ἔχειν ἐν ἐπιγνώσει may be considered as equivalent to ἐπιγνώσκειν; or, which is still better, to designate that failure *to retain in their knowledge* what God had revealed to them in the book of nature, which book the apostle accuses them of neglecting.

God gave them up to a reprobate mind, παρέδωκεν . . . . νοῦν.— See on ver. 24 for παρέδωκεν.—Ἀδόκιμος is the negative or antithesis of δόκιμος; and therefore means *reprobate, that which is to be rejected, unapproved.* Beza has rendered this adjective as though it had a neuter *active* sense, *a mind incapable of judging.* But the *usus loquendi* will not bear this; although adjectives in -ιμος sometimes have an active sense; see Buttm. ausfuhrl. Sprachl. 2 Abth. p. 341. The meaning here of ἀδόκιμον νοῦν is *wicked* or *vile mind,* which is deserving of condemnation or execration. There is here an evident paronomasia of ἀδόκιμον with ἐδοκίμασαν.

To do those things which are disgraceful, ποιεῖν τὰ μὴ καθήκοντα, *i. e.*, which are indecorous, shameful. God, in his righteous judgment, abandoned those who practised such vices to the legitimate consequences of their own passions and conduct.

(29) *Filled, full of, abounding in,* πεπληρωμένους, The construction, if completed, would be [παρέδωκεν αὐτοὺς ὁ Θεὸς] πεπληρωμένους κ. τ. λ.; so that πεπληρωμένους agrees with αὐτοὺς in the preceding verse. It is here followed by the *Dative* of the succeeding nouns; and so in some other cases, Wahl's Lex. under πληρόω. The Genitive is more common after verbs of *abounding*.

Ἀδικίᾳ is a *generic* word here, *iniquity, sin,* which comprehends all the particular vices that are afterwards named.—Πορνείᾳ is omitted in some manuscripts, viz. A. B. C., several younger MSS., and some of the versions and fathers. In some, it is placed after πονηρίᾳ. The enumeration seems quite incomplete without it; as it is a sin which most of all was universal among the heathen. In the New Testament, the πορνείᾳ has an extended sense, comprehending *all illicit intercourse,* whether fornication, adultery, incest, or any other *venus illicita.*

Malice, πονηρίᾳ, *i. e., versuta et fallax nocendi ratio,* as Grotius defines it. *Malice* is a wicked desire or intention of doing harm to others, in a fraudulent and deceitful manner. This word is omitted in D. E. G. in codd. Clar. Boern.; which generally read, ἀδικίᾳ, κακίᾳ, πορνείᾳ, πλεονεξίᾳ, κ. τ. λ.—Πλεονεξίᾳ, *covetousness.* Where luxury abounds, and devotedness to sinful pleasures, there a thirst for gold will also reign, because it is necessary to supply the means of pleasure. Petronius strikingly represents Rome as covetous of the wealth of other nations, in the following manner:—

. . . . Si quis sinus abditus ultra,
Si qua foret tellus quæ fulvum mitteret aurum,
Hostis erat, fatisque in tristia bella paratis
Quærebantur opes.

Mischief, κακία, among the Greeks, was the antithesis of ἀρετή, when taken in a *generic* sense. But when taken (as here) in a *limited* one, it means *the habit of doing mischief,* or *harm to others* in any way. It differs from πονηρία, *malice,* inasmuch as that more particularly designates a state of mind, and the craftiness by which the purposes it forms are to be executed. Κακία means any kind of *injurious treatment.*

Full, μεστούς is of the same meaning as πεπληρωμένους; but it seems to be introduced here with the genitive merely for the sake of varying the construction. The ellipsis is as before, [παρέδωκεν αὐτούς ὁ Θεὸς] μεστούς κ. τ. λ.—*Envy,* φθόνος, seems to be a widely spread passion of the human breast. It exists at almost all times and in all places, where one part of the community is, or is thought to be, more happy or distinguished than another. This passion was in the highest degree predominant at Rome. — *Murder or manslaughter*, φόνος, both public and private, legalized and forbidden, was extremely frequent at Rome; *e. g.*, the gladiatorial fights, the destruction of slaves, the executions by the Roman emperors' orders, and deaths by poison, assassination, etc. — *Strife*, ἔρις of course followed on in such a train. — *Deceit*. δόλος is strikingly exemplified by a verse of Juvenal: "Quid Romæ faciem? Mentiri nescio," Sat. III. 41. — *Malevolence*, κακοήθεια, particularly that species of it which perverts the words and actions of another, and puts a wrong construction on them in order to gratify a love of mischief, when it was easy and proper to put a good construction upon them. It differs *specifically*, therefore, from πονηρία.

(30) *Backbiters*, Ψιθυριστής, *i. e., a slanderer in secret.* — Κατάλαλος, *a slanderer in public.* — *Haters of God*, θεοστυγεῖς. Grotius says, it should be written θεοστύγεις, *i. e.*, with the tone or accent on the penult, in order to have an *active* sense. But this is not necessary; for Suidas defines θεοστυγεῖς (oxytone) by οἱ ὑπὸ θεοῦ μισούμενοι, καὶ οἱ θεὸν μισοῦντες. In the same manner Passow gives the meaning of the word. That the *active* sense is here required, the context clearly shows; inasmuch as the vices of men are here designated, not the punishment of them.* — *Reproachful*, ὑβριστάς, *i. e.*, lacerating others by slanderous, abusive, passionate declarations. — *Proud*, ὑπερηφάνους, *i. e.*, looking with disdain upon others, and thinking highly of themselves. — *Boasters*, ἀλαζόνας, *i. e.*, glorying in that which does not belong to them, whether wealth, learning, talents, or anything else. — *Inventors of evil things*, ἐφευρετὰς κακῶν. This doubtless refers to the inventions in luxuries, vices, etc., which were constantly taking place in the great cities of ancient times, where there was a competition in pleasures among the wealthy. *Disobedient to parents*, γονεῦσιν ἀπειθεῖς; a vice exceedingly common among the heathen, multitudes of whom cast out their parents, when they are old, to perish from hunger, or cold, or by the wild beasts. The accusative cases, throughout this and the following verses, are all governed by παρέδωκεν brought forward from verse 28.

. (31) *Inconsiderate*, ἀσυνέτους, or *foolish*; compare verses 21, 22. — *Covenant breakers*, ἀσυνθέτους, *perfidious*. — *Destitute of natural affection*, ἀστόργους. The writer probably refers here,

---

* It is doubtful whether this word can mean "haters of God;" all classical usage favors the meaning "hated of God." See Meyer, Ruckert, De Wette, etc. The tone too should be on the final syllable.

to the usual practices among the heathen of exposing young children to perish, when the parents had more of them than they thought themselves able to maintain, or had such as they did not wish to take the trouble of bringing up. Tertullian (in Apologetico) repeats this accusation against them in a tremendous manner : " .... qui natos sibi liberos enecant ... crudelius in aqua spiritum extorquetis, aut frigori et fami et canibus exponitis." — *Implacable*, ἀσπόνδους, *qui pactum non admittit*. Some manuscripts (A. B. D. E. G. et al.) omit the word; but still its authority does not seem fairly to be doubtful. This is a well-known trait of the heathen character, exemplified in a most striking manner by the *Aborigines* of this country. — *Unmerciful*, ἀνελεήμονας, or *destitute of compassion*. What, for example, are or were the provisions made for the poor and suffering, among the heathen?

(32) *Who knowing the ordinance of God,* οἵτινες .... ἐπιγνόντες. Ἐπιγνόντες used like γνόντες in ver. 21; where see remarks. In Rom. ii. 14, 15, Paul asserts that 'the heathen who have no written law (revelation), are a law to themselves, for they give evidence that the requisitions of the divine law are written upon their hearts.' He refers of course, in these and the like expressions, to leading and principal traits of moral duty. So in our text, when he speaks of the Gentiles as *knowing God*, he means, that the disclosures made respecting God in the works of nature, and respecting the duties which he demanded of them in their own consciences or moral sense, were of such a kind as fairly to give them an opportunity of knowing something respecting the great outlines of duty, and of rendering them inexcusable for neglecting it.

Ordinance, τὸ δικαίωμα, or *statute, precept*. The Seventy employ it often, in order to translate the Hebrew חק, משפט, מצוה. The use of δικαίωμα in such a way, seems to be quite *Hellenistic*. Suidas, however, defines it thus: δικαιώματα ; νόμος, ἐντολαί. Clear cases of usage in such a sense, are 1 Macc. i. 13. ποιεῖν τὰ δικαιώματα τῶν ἐθνῶν, and Test. xii. Patriarch., ποιεῖν τὰ δικαιώματα Χυρίου, καὶ ὑπακούειν ἐντολὰς Θεοῦ; Fabric. Cod. Pseudep. I. 603.

What the δικαίωμα or חק is which the heathen knew or might have known, is now declared, viz.. ὅτι οἱ .... εἰσίν, *that they who do such things* [such as he had just been mentioning], *are worthy of death*. As the affirmation here has respect to those who did not enjoy the knowledge of a written revelation, so *death* can hardly be taken in the *full* and exact *scriptural* sense of the word; (on this sense, see the remarks on Rom. v. 12). It must, however, be taken in a sense strictly analogous with this, viz., as meaning *punishment, misery, suffering*. The very nature of the term implies this. That the word θανάτου is *figuratively*, not literally employed here, is sufficiently plain from an inspection of the catalogue of vices which the apostle had just named. Surely he does not mean to say, that *all* of these deserved capital punishment from the civil magistrate in the *literal* sense; and that this was a case so plain, that the heathen themselves clearly recognized it.

Since crimes in many cases are the result of a sudden *impetus* of passion and temptation, in the midst of which men abandon reflection, it requires, in the main, a higher degree of depravity coolly to applaud and deliberately to justify and encourage wickedness already committed or to be committed, than it does to commit it in the moment of excitement. Hence the apostle considers this as the very climax of all the charges which he had to bring against the heathen, that they not only plunged into acts of wickedness, but had given their more deliberate approbation to such doings. *Not only do the same things, but even commend those who do them,* οὐ μόνον . . . . πράσσουσι. It is often the case, that wicked men, whose consciences have been enlightened, speak reproachfully of others who practice such vices as they themselves indulge in. Few profligate parents, for example, are willing that their children should sustain the same character with themselves. But when we find, as in some cases we may do, such parents encouraging and applauding their children in acts of wickedness, we justly consider it as evidence of the very highest kind of depravity.

There is some variety in the readings of the MSS. and Version, as to ἐπιγνόντες, but not enough to render its authority doubtful.

It is of such depravity as this, that the apostle accuses the heathen. And justly; for even their philosophers and the best educated among them, stood chargeable with such an accusation. For example; both the Epicureans and the Stoics allowed and defended παιδεραστία and incest, numbering these horrid crimes among the ἀδιάφορα, *things indifferent*. Aristotle and Cicero justify revenge. Aristotle (Polit. I. 8) represents war upon barbarous nations to be nothing more than a species of *hunting*, and as altogether justifiable. The same writer justifies forcible abortion, Polit. VII. 16. Other philosophers represent virtue and vice as the mere creatures of statute and arbitrary custom; or (to use the words of Justin) they maintain, μηδὲν εἶναι ἀρετὴν μηδὲ κακίαν, δόξῃ δὲ μόνον τοὺς ἀνθρώπους ἢ ἀγαθὰ ἢ κακὰ ταῦτα ἡγεῖσθαι, *that there is nothing either virtuous or vicious, but that things are made good or evil merely by the force of opinion.*

This is sufficient to justify the declaration of the apostle; for if philosophers thought and reasoned thus, what must the common people have done, who were more exclusively led by their appetites and passions? The picture is, indeed, a dreadful one; it is truly revolting in every sense of the word. But that it is just, nay, that it actually comes short of the real state of things, particularly on the score of impurity and cruelty, there cannot be the least doubt on the part of any man who is acquainted with the ancient state of the heathen world, and of Rome in particular. Poets, philosophers, and historians, have confirmed the words of Paul; and the relics of ancient cities in Italy, (in pictures, carvings, statues, etc.)—cities destroyed near the time when the apostle lived—bear most ample testimony to what he has said of their lasciviousness and shameless profligacy. One has only to add, with the deepest distress, that in many of the great cities or countries called Christian, there is fearful reason to believe that there are abominations practised in various respects, which even exceed any inventions of heathen depravity. How often is one obliged to exclaim with the apostle, παρέδωκεν αὐτοὺς ὁ Θεός! The evidence of this lies in more than beastly degradation.

It is hardly necessary to repeat here that Paul does not mean to assert of every individual among the heathen, that he stood chargeable with each and every crime here specified. This is impossible. He means only to say, that these and the like vices (for surely they were guilty of many others), were notorious and common among the heathen; and that every individual capable of sinning, philosophers and common people, stood chargeable, in a greater or less degree, with some of them. In this way he makes out a part of his main proposition, viz. that *all men are under sin;* consequently that *all are in a lost condition,* or *in a state of condemnation.* These declarations being established, it follows of course that *all men need a Saviour, and can be delivered from the curse of the divine law, only by means of atoning blood, which procures gratuitous pardon for them.*

That the apostle has been here describing the *heathen*, is clear from verses 20—23, where all that is said applies in its proper force only to them.

That the heathen had a *moral sense*, is clear from Rom. ii. 14, 15. One may even suppose it to be probable that some of them did to a certain extent, obey this internal law; at least, we may well suppose that they *could* obey it. This seems to be implied in Rom. ii. 26, and perhaps in Acts x. 36. It is on this basis that the apostle grounds his charges of guilt against them. They *knew*, at least they might have known, that what they did was against the law of nature, against their *consciences*, against their internal persuasion with respect to right and wrong. Consequently they were verily guilty in the sight of God; not for transgressing the precepts of a revelation never made known to them, but for violating a law that was within them, and shutting their eyes against the testimony of the natural world. Most clearly and fully does the apostle recognize and teach all this, Rom. ii. 12—16, 26, 27. Consequently no one can accuse God of injustice, because he blames and condemns the heathen; for he makes the law which was known to them the measure of their blame and condemnation (Rom. ii. 12, seq.), and not a revelation with which they were not acquainted.

It is clear then that the Gentiles need a Saviour; it is equally clear that they need gratuitous justification, and that they must perish without such a provision for them. It remains then to be seen, whether the same things can be established with respect to the Jews.

On the method of establishing the declaration which the apostle makes concerning the depravity of the Gentiles, it may be proper here to add a single remark. He goes into no formal *argument*. In the passage which we have been considering, he does not even appeal (as he sometimes does, Tit. i. 12), to the testimony of their own writers. The ground of this must be, that facts were plain, palpable, well known, and acknowledged by all. In particular, he was well assured that the Jewish part of his readers would call in question none of the allegations which he made in relation to the vices of the Gentiles. There was no need, therefore, of any more formal proof on the present occasion. We shall see that the writer occupies more time, and makes greater effort, to confirm his declarations respecting the Jews.

Reiche, in his recent Commentary (p. 173 seq.), labors to show, that the *giving over* of the heathen to their lusts, etc., must mean an *active* hardening of them, or demoralization of them on the part of God. This, however, he does not consider as the apostle's real opinion, but only his argument κατ' ἄνθρωπον, *i. e.*, in conformity with the Jewish prejudices and modes of argument in respect to the heathen. In like manner he considers the criminality which the apostle attaches to idol-worship, in verses 21—25, to be an allegation κατ' ἄνθρωπον. One is pained to meet with not a few remarks of this nature, in a work as valuable in many respects as the Commentary of this writer is. What means the *second* commandment? And what, all the zeal testified through the Old Test. against the sin of idol-worship? And how was the apostle to convict the *Gentiles* at Rome, by employing a mere κατ' ἄνθρωπον, Jewish opinion or prejudice, as an argument against them? Neither the frankness, the sincerity, nor the good sense of the apostle, will permit me to accede to such sentiments.

CHAP. II. 1—29.

THE apostle, having thus concluded his short but very significant view of the *heathen* world, now turns to address his own nation, the Jews, in order to show them that they stood in need of the mercy proffered by the Gospel, as really and as much as the Gentiles. But this he does not proceed to do at once, and by direct address. He first prepares the way by illustrating and enforcing the general proposition, that all who have a knowledge of what is right, and approve of it, but yet sin against it, are as really guilty as those who are so blinded as not to see the loveliness and excellence of virtue, and who at the same time transgress its precepts. This he does in verses 1—8; in which, although he had the Jews constantly in mind, he still advances only general propositions, applicable in common to them and to others; thus preparing the way, with great skill and judgment, for a more effectual charge to be made specifically against the Jews, in the sequel of his discourse.

The words of Turretin (Expos. Epist. Pauli ad Rom. in cap II.) are in point here: "Postquam ostendisset apostolus epistolæ suæ capite primo, Gentes ex propriis operibus justificari non potuisse, eo quod deploratissimus eorum status esset, idem jam Judæis capite II. demonstrare aggreditur. Verum id facit dextre nec mediocri solertia, statim ne nominatis quidem Judæis, positisque generalibus principiis, quorum veritatem et equitatem negare non poterant; quo facto, sensim eorum mentionem injicit, tandemque directe eos compellat, vividaque et pathetica oratione eorum conscientiam pungit, facitque ut de propriis peccatis volentes nolentes convincantur. Et in his quidem omnibus, deprimit supercilium Judæorum, qui cæteras gentes summo contemptu habebant, iisque se longe meliores et Deo acceptiores gloriabantur. At vero, non negatis Judæorum ad cognitionem quod attinet præerogativis, ostendit eos, ad mores quod spectat, quæ pars est religionis longe præcipua, Gentibus haudquaquam meliores fuisse, proindeque Dei judicio et damnationi haud minus obnoxios fore."

In verses 9—16, the apostle shows that the Jews must be accountable to God as really and truly, for the manner in which they treat the precepts contained in the Scriptures, as the heathen for the manner in which they demean themselves with respect to the law of nature, and that each must be judged, at last, according to the means of grace and improvement which he has enjoyed.

In verses 17—29 he advances still farther, and makes a direct reference to the Jews. He shows here, that those who sin against higher degrees of knowledge imparted by revelation, must be more guilty than those who have offended merely against the laws of nature, i. e , he plainly teaches the doctrine, that guilt is proportioned to the light and love that have been manifested, and yet been abused. The very *precedence* in knowledge, of which the Jews were so proud and so prone to boast, the apostle declares to be a ground of *greater* condemnation, in case those who possessed it sinned against it, a doctrine consonant as truly with reason and conscience, as it is with the declarations of the Scriptures; compare John iii. 19. xv. 22—24. ix 41

(1) *Therefore thou art without excuse, O man, every one that condemneth,* or *whosoever thou art that condemneth,* διό . . . . κρίνων.—Διό *is made up of* διά *and* ὅ, *and we cannot avoid the conclusion that the word is, in its own proper nature,* illative. To my own mind, the connection appears to be thus: 'Since it will be conceded, that those who know the ordinances of God against such vices as have been named, and still practise them and applaud others for doing so, are worthy of punishment; it follows (διό, *therefore*) that all who are so enlightened as to disapprove of such crimes, and who still commit them, are even yet

more worthy of punishment.' The apostle here takes the ground, that those who were so enlightened and instructed by revelation as to condemn the vices in question, would of course sin against motives of a higher kind than those which influenced the heathen who were possessed of less light. It must be conceded, indeed, that συνευδοκοῦσι in i. 32 is designed to aggravate the description of the guilt which the heathen incurred, (and in fact it does so); yet it will not follow, that the sin of these heathen would not have been still greater, had they enjoyed such light from revelation, as would have led them fully to condemn those very sins in their own consciences, while they yet practised them. The main point, in the present chapter, seems to stand connected principally with the greater or less light as to duty. The heathen with less light went so far in vice as even to approve and applaud it, as well as to practise it; the Jew with more light was led irresistibly, as it were, to condemn such sins, but with all this light, and against all the remonstrances of his conscience, he violated the same precepts which the heathen violated. Now what the apostle would say, is, that he who sins while he possesses light enough to condemn the vice which he practises, is really and truly guilty, as well as he who sins while approving it. He takes it for granted that his readers will concede the point which he has asserted respecting the guilt of the heathen; hence he draws the inference (διό), that on the like grounds they must condemn every one, who, like the Jew, sins against the voice of his conscience and against his better knowledge.

In like manner Flatt makes out the connection of διό here: " Διό, *because* thou knowest τὸ δικαίωμα τοῦ Θεοῦ; because thou knowest, that according to the divine decision they are worthy of punishment who practise such vices; because thou thyself dost acknowledge this δικαίωμα Θεοῦ, so thou canst not excuse thyself for committing the like sins." Πᾶς ὁ κρίνων is indeed a *general* proposition: but this is plainly a matter of intention on the part of the writer. He means to include the Jews in it; but at the same time he commences his remarks on them in this general way for the very purpose of approaching gradually and in an inoffensive manner the ultimate point which he has in view.

For wherein (i. e., in respect to what) thou condemnest another, thou passest sentence of condemnation upon thyself, ἐν ᾧ γὰρ . . . . κατακρίνεις; or, *in condemning another, thou passest sentence on thyself.*—Ἐν ᾧ, *in respect to, with reference to;* it might be translated, *because that, inasmuch as,* like the Hebrew באשר. The idea then would be: 'For the very act of condemning another, is passing sentence upon thyself.' The former explanation is preferable: 'Thou who condemnest, dost pass sentence on thyself in respect to the very point which is the subject of condemnation;' *i. e.*, thou, who condemnest the practice of the vices just named, inasmuch as thou practisest the very same vices, dost come under thine own condemnation. Χρίνω may here, as oftentimes, have the same sense substantially as κατακρίνω; compare Matt. vii. 1. Luke vi. 37. Rom. xiv. 3, 4, 10, 13, 22. 1 Cor. iv. 5. Col. ii. 16; or we may render the passage thus: 'With that [sentence] which thou dost pass,' or *'while* thou passest sentence' (ἐν ᾧ *while*, Mark ii. 19. Luke v. 3. John v. 7), viz. on the heathen, 'thou dost condemn thyself.'

The γάρ in this clause is γάρ *illustrantis vel confirmantis;* for the sentiments which follow are designed to show, that πᾶς ὁ κρίνων is *inexcusable*, inasmuch as he stands chargeable himself with the very crimes which he censures in others.

Since thou who condemnest, doest the same things, τὰ γὰρ .... ὁ κρίνων. The apostle asserts this, and leaves it to the conscience of his readers to bear witness to the truth of it, and to make the application. As in the case where the woman taken in adultery was brought before the Saviour, and he said to her accusers: "He that is without sin, let him cast the first stone," and all withdrew because of conscious guilt; so here, the apostle says: 'Every one who condemns the heathen for the crimes specified, [he was well aware that the Jews did this with a loud voice], condemns himself, because he is guilty of the like vices.' No arguments or testimony was necessary here, for Paul knew that the consciences of his readers would at once bear witness to the truth of his allegations. He therefore leaves it to their consciences. But still, external testimony to the facts alleged is not wanting. That the Jews of this period were grossly corrupt, is certain from the accusations which Jesus so often brought against them, as recorded in the Gospels. We may make the appeal to Josephus also, and in particular to the description which he gives of Herod and his courtiers.

(2) *For we know that the judgment of God is according to truth, against those who do such things,* οἴδαμεν δὲ .... πράσσοντας. Δέ may be occasionally a proper and simple *continuative* of discourse; but such a sense without some indication of diversity or antithesis, is not usually to be attached to it. Not unfrequently it assumes the place of a *casual* particle, and is equivalent to γάρ; not because δέ of itself has the same signification as γάρ, but because it connects sentences, or parts of sentences, which have a *causal* relation. 'In such cases it may be translated *for, since,*' etc. Here I take the connection of thought to be simply this: 'Thou art without excuse, who,' etc. .... *i. e.*, thou shalt not escape condemnation, '*for* we know that the judgment of God,'

etc. Reiche gives δέ an *adversative* sense; and to do so, he makes the sentiment opposed to be the supposition that 'God would not judge men.' But the preceding context does not supply this; and the above method of interpretation, which is grounded on the context, is more simple and obvious, and is equally conformed to idiom. — Κρίμα Θεοῦ means *sentence of condemnation on the part of God*, Θεοῦ being *Genitivus auctoris*. — Κατὰ ἀλήθειαν may (1) be taken (as usual in the classics) for *truly, verily; i. e.*, just in the same sense as ὄντως, ἀληθῶς. This would make a good meaning in our verse; but not the best. (2) It may mean the same as κατὰ δικαιοσύνην, *agreeably to justice*, inasmuch as ἀλήθεια often means *vera religionis doctrina, vera atque salutaris doctrina*, etc. So Beza, Tholuck, and others. (3) A better sense still seems to be, *agreeably to the real state of things, in accordance with truth* as it respects the real character sustained by each individual. The sentiment then is: 'Think not to escape the judgment of God, thou who condemnest the vices of the heathen, and yet dost thyself practise them; whatever thy claims to the divine favor on account of thy birth or thy spiritual advantages may be, remember that the judgment of God will be according to the true state of the case, according to the real character which thou dost sustain.'

Such things, τὰ τοιαῦτα, viz. such as he had just been mentioning.* Observe that the apostle does not accuse the πᾶς ὁ κρίνων here of the very same thing in all respects; nor is it to be understood, that every individual among the Jews, or even that any one, was chargeable with each and every vice which he had named. Enough that any one or more of these vices might be justly charged on all. And even if it could be said, that there might be individuals who gave no *external* proofs to men that they were guilty of any of these vices; there certainly were none who were not more or less guilty, in the sense in which our Saviour declares in his Sermon on the Mount that men may be guilty of murder and adultery, *i. e., spiritually, internally, mentally*.

(3) *Dost thou think this, then, O man, who condemnest those that do such things, and doest the very same things, that thou shalt escape the judgment of God?* Λογίζῃ δὲ .... Θεοῦ. Δέ being in its proper nature *adversative*, it is very naturally employed in replies, answers, or questions which are designed to be in opposition to something which another may have said, or may be supposed to cherish in his thoughts. It gives *energy* to the reply in

---

* See a similar use of τὰ τοιαῦτα in Class. Greek, e. g. Xen. Memorab. I. 5 2.

Greek; but it cannot always be translated into our own idiom, whose particles are often so insignificant compared with the Greek ones. In the present case, it must be rendered *then*, which makes the sentence in English approach very near to the energetic form of the Greek.

The sense of the verse appears to be as follows: 'Thou who condemnest others for vicious indulgences and still dost thyself practise the same, dost thou suppose, that while they cannot escape thy condemning sentence, thou canst escape the sentence of him who is of purer eyes than to behold iniquity?' Well has Chrysostom paraphrased it: τὸ σὸν οὐκ ἐξέφυγες κρίμα, καὶ τὸ τοῦ Θεοῦ διαφεύξῃ; *thou hast not escaped thine own condemnation; and shalt thou escape that of God?* *

(4) *Or dost thou despise* (treat with contempt) *his abounding goodness, and forbearance, and long suffering,* ἢ τοῦ .... καταφρονεῖς; The word πλοῦτος is often employed by Paul in order to designate *abundance, copiousness;* e. g., Eph. i. 7. ii. 7. i. 18. iii. 16. Rom. ix. 23. xi. 33, et alibi. The Seventy frequently employ it to translate הָמוֹן and חַיִל. Here πλούτον supplies the place of an adjective, and means *abundant* or *abounding;* comp. Heb. Gramm. § 440. b. *Kindness, benignity,* χρηστότητος. *Holding in,* ἀνοχῆς, *i. e.,* checking or restraining indignation, forbearing to manifest displeasure against sin. Μακροθυμίας, *longanimitas,* אֶרֶךְ אַפַּיִם, *slowness to anger, forbearance to punish.* Both words (ἀνοχῆς, and μακροθυμίας) are of nearly the same import, and serve, as synonymes thus placed usually do, to give *intensity* to the expression. The meaning is as if the apostle had said: 'Despisest thou his abounding kindness and distinguished forbearance to punish?' The apostle means to say here, that all the distinguished goodness which the ὁ κρίνων enjoyed, in consequence of his superior light, was practically neglected and contemned by him, inasmuch as he plunged into the same vices which the ignorant heathen practised.

Not acknowledging that the goodness of God leadeth thee to repentance, ἀγνοῶν .... ἄγει. Ἀγνοῶν in the sense of *not recognizing* or *acknowledging*. Γινώσκω and the Hebrew יָדַע often mean *to recognize, to acknowledge;* as may be seen in the lexicons.—Τὸ χρηστόν, i. q., χρηστότης, by a common usage of the Greek tongue; compare τὸ γνωστόν in i. 19.—Ἄγει, *leads;* but as verbs often designate a tendency towards the action which they usually designate, as well as the specific action itself, so here the *tendency* or *fitness* to accomplish the end is designated; com-

---

* The apostle seems to have in mind here the feeling of the Jews that only the Gentiles were to be judged under the Messianic reign, whilst all Israel should be treated as children. See Meyer's Comm.

pare John v. 21, ἐγείρει, *has the power* or *faculty to raise up;* ζωοποιεῖ, *has the power of giving life;* Rom. i. 21, γνόντες, *having opportunity to know.* The sentiment is, that the goodness of God which the ὁ κρίνων enjoys in a peculiar manner, and which is manifested so highly in his forbearance to punish, is intended to teach him gratitude for God's blessings, and of course sorrow (μετάνοιαν) for his offences in respect to that course of conduct which such a principle would dictate. Let the reader compare, for the sake of deeply impressing on his mind so important and striking a sentiment, the passages in 2 Pet. iii. 9. Ezek. xviii. 23, 32. xxxiii. 11.

(5) *According to thine obstinacy, however, and impenitent heart,* or *according to thy hard and impenitent heart,* κατὰ δὲ .... καρδίαν. With δέ the antithesis is sometimes implied merely, by what is said in the context, and not expressed. Here I take the antithetic sentiment to be: "Thou art indeed hoping to escape the judgment of God, but instead of this thou art heaping up treasures of wrath," etc. * Δέ, here rendered *however*, naturally refers back to ver. 3, and is properly *adversative* to the thought which the impenitent man cherishes. Σκληρότης means *insensibility* of heart or mind, a state in which one is not duly affected by considerations presented to his mind. — Ἀμετανόητον καρδίαν means a heart not so affected as to sorrow for sin, through the goodness of God which is designed to produce such an effect. It is by such spiritual insensibility or stupidity, that a sinner is aggravating his condemnation; so the next clause.

Thou art treasuring up for thyself wrath in the day of wrath, when the righteous judgment of God shall be revealed, θησαυρίζεις .... τοῦ Θεοῦ. Θησαυρίζεις, *to treasure up, i. e.*, to lay up in store, to accumulate, to increase. In the choice of this term, there is a tacit reference of the mind to the preceding τοῦ πλούτου τῆς χρηστότητος; — Σεαυτῷ, *for thyself*, Dativus *incommodi* (as grammarians say); compare Rom. xiii. 2. Matt. xxiii. 31. James v. 3. See N. Test. Gramm. § 104. 2, Note 1.—Ὀργήν, *wrath*, includes also the *punishment* which is the natural consequence of wrath. A *day of punishment* is called, in the Old Testament, יוֹם אַף יְהוָֹה, יוֹם זַעַם, יוֹם נוֹרָא, *i. e.*, a day when the displeasure of Jehovah is manifested.

In the day of indignation, or *punishment,* ἐν ἡμέρᾳ ὀργῆς, *i. e.*, ὀργὴν [τὴν ἐσομένην] ἐν ἡμέρᾳ ὀργῆς, indignation that will be shown

* Is it not better here with De Wette and Meyer to consider δέ as strictly adversative, and introducing the contrast of the preceding clause · ὅτι—ἄγει ? The goodness of God leads (i e. this is its object and natural effect unresisted) thee to repentance, but in accordance with thine obstinacy and impenitent heart, thou art, etc.

or executed, etc.— Καὶ ἀποκαλύψεως καὶ δικαιοκρισίας may be taken as a Hendiadys, and rendered *of revealed righteous judgment.* The meaning is: 'When God's righteous judgment shall be revealed, *i. e.*, in the great day of judgment.' Griesbach, with a majority of MSS., omits the second καί; which makes the reading more facile.

(6) *Who will render to every man according to his works,* ὃς ἀποδώσει . . . . αὐτοῦ, *i. e.*, who will make retribution to every man, according to the tenor of his conduct. Ἔργα means here, as often elsewhere, all the developments which a man makes of himself, whether by *outward* or *inward* actions; compare John vi. 27. Rev. xiv. 13. xxii. 12. The word is indeed more commonly used to designate *something done externally;* but it is by no means confined to this sense. Thus ἔργα νόμου means *any work which the law demands;* ἔργα Θεοῦ means *such works as God requires;* and in cases of this nature it will not be said, I trust, that God and his law do not require anything but *external* works. Many theories respecting future reward, have been made from this verse. The apprehension that Paul here contradicts *salvation by* GRACE, and makes it to depend on the merit of works, has no good foundation. The *good works* of the regenerate are imperfect. No man loves God with *all his heart* and his neighbor *as himself.* But there is some real goodness in the works of the truly sanctified; and this will be rewarded, imperfect as it is, not on the ground of law (which would demand entire perfection), but on the ground of *grace*, which can consistently reward imperfect good works. Thus the *grace* of the gospel and the *reward* here promised to good works, are altogether consistent. But those who remain impenitent and unbelieving, stand simply on *law-ground* as to acceptance, and must therefore be punished according to the measure of their sins.

(7) *To those who by patient continuance* or *perseverance in well-doing, seek for glory, and honor, and immortality,* or *immortal glory and honor,* [he will render] *eternal life* or *happiness,* τοῖς μὲν . . . . αἰώνιον.—Μέν has its corresponding δέ in v. 8., introducing a contrast.—Ὑπομενήν means *perseverance* or *patient continuance.*—Κατά, before the Accusative, frequently designates the *modus* in which anything is done, or the state and condition in which it is; *e. g.*, κατὰ τάξιν, κατὰ ζῆλον, κατὰ γνῶσιν, etc.— Ἔργον here has the epithet ἀγαθοῦ, in order to distinguish it from the generic ἔργα used in the preceding verse.—Δόξαν καὶ τιμὴν καὶ ἀφθαρσίαν is cumulative or intensive; *i. e.*, it expresses happiness or glory of the highest kind. We may translate the phrase thus: *immortal glory and honor,* making ἀφθαρσίαν an adjective; or we may render it, *glorious and honorable immor-*

tality, or *honorable and immortal glory*. The idea is substantially the same in all; but the first seems most congruous as to the method of expression. The joining of τιμή and δόξα in order to express *intensity*, is agreeable to a usage which is frequent in the New Testament; *e. g.*, 1 Tim. i. 17. Heb. ii. 7, 9. 2 Pet. i. 17. Apoc. iv. 9, 11. So the Hebrew, הוֹד וְהָדָר.

The interpretation given above is the usual one, for substance, adopted by the great body of the commentators. But some prefer the following arrangement: τοῖς μὲν [ἀποδώσει], καθ' ὑπομενὴν ἔργον ἀγαθοῦ, δόξαν καὶ τιμὴν καὶ ἀφθαρσίαν, ζητοῦσι ζωὴν αἰώνιον, *i. e.*, 'to those [will he render], according to their perseverance in well-doing, glory and honor and immortality, [even to those who] seek eternal life.' But when it is said in defence of this, that it is incongruous to speak of SEEKING *glory, and honor, and immortality*, and therefore ζητοῦσι must be joined with ζωὴν αἰώνιον, I acknowledge myself incapable of perceiving the weight of the argument. What is *glory*, but future happiness? What is *honor*, but the divine approbation? And what is *immortality*, but the perpetuity of these? And what is there more incongruous in seeking these, than in seeking ζωὴν αἰώνιον? ζητεῖν, means *to labor for, earnestly to desire, to strive for with effort;* and all this the Christian certainly may and must do, in respect to glory, and honor, and immortality. The suggestion, that 'to seek after immortality would have no sense, because we are and must be immortal,' does not apply in this case; for it is not after immortality simply considered that we are to seek, but after an *immortality of glory and honor*. Besides, there is such an unnatural chasm between τοῖς and ζητοῦσι, in case we adopt this interpretation, as should be admitted only from a *necessity*, which does not here exist.

(8) *But to those who are contentious*, τοῖς δὲ ἐξ ἐριθείας. The Genitive of a noun with ἐκ (ἐξ) is often employed as an adjective in designating some particular description of persons or things. Thus ὁ ἐξ οὐρανοῦ = οὐράνιος; ἡ ἐκ φύσεως, *natural;* τὸν ἐκ πίστεως, *credens;* ὁ ἐξ ὑμῶν, *yours;* οἱ ἐκ περιτομῆς, *the circumcised;* so the classical οἱ ἐκ στοᾶς, etc. The objections against such a sense of ἐξ, have no good foundation. The apostle means here to designate those who contend against God, or rebel against him. The Seventy use ἐρεθίζω in order to translate מָרָה, Deut. xxi. 20. xxxi. 27. What it means, moreover, is explained in the next clause by ἀπειθοῦσι. The derivation of ἐριθείας from ἐριθεύω, to *work in wool, to make parties*, etc., is quite unnatural. It doubtless comes from ἔρις, ἐρεθίζω, as the sense of the word in the N. Test. clearly shows.*

* The derivation of this word from ἔριθος or ἐριθεύω seems now to be

And are disobedient to the truth but obedient to unrighteousness, καὶ ἀπειθοῦσι . . . . ἀδικίᾳ. Here (in a subordinate member of the *apodosis* of the sentence begun in verse 7) is a second μέν which is *protatic*, and another δέ *apodotic*. The contrast of the two respective clauses in which they stand, is made very plain by ἀπειθοῦσι and πειθομένοις. We have no words capable of designating such nice shades of relation as μέν and δέ signify here, and in like cases; although they are very plain and significant to the practised critic. I have not in this case attempted an exact translation, the nearest to the original that I am able to come, is as follows: *even those who disobey indeed the truth, but obey unrighteousness*. How imperfect an exhibition this is of the nicer coloring of the Greek expression, every one must feel who has "διὰ τὴν ἕξιν τὰ αἰσθητήρια γεγυμνασμένα πρός διάκρισιν."

* Ἀληθείᾳ here means *true doctrine*. As the proposition of the apostle is *general* here, *i. e.*, as it respects all, whether Jews or Gentiles, who disobey the precepts of religion and morality, so ἀληθείᾳ must be taken in a latitude that embraces the truth of both natural and revealed religion. Ἀδικίᾳ, as in i. 18, the antithesis of ἀληθείᾳ, means *that which is unrighteous, that which the truth forbids*.

Indignation and wrath, ὀργὴ καὶ θυμός. Ammonius says: θυμός *is of short duration, but* ὀργή *is a long-continued remembrance of evil.* These words do not seem, however, to be used here with any specific difference, both meaning *excitement, the feeling of strong excitement, indignation*, etc., but the accumulation of synonymous terms, as often, is intensive. The construction of these nouns in the Nominative case, is an evident departure from the structure in the preceding verse, (called by Grammarians ἀνακόλυθον) where ζωὴν αἰώνιον is in the Accusative governed by ἀποδώσει understood. Here ὀργὴ καὶ θυμός are the Nominative to ἔσονται implied.

(9) Θλίψις καὶ στενοχωρία are in the same construction as ὀργὴ καὶ θυμός, *i. e.*, with ἔσται understood, and designate the effect of the latter. The meaning is, *intense anguish, great suffering.* These two words, used in the way of expressing *intense suffering*, are often joined by classic writers; and so in Hebrew we have צָרָה וְצוּקָה Is. xxx. 6. The literal sense of the words, according

---

generally acknowledged, although formerly Prof. S. and others derived it from ἔρις, *strife*. But such passages as 2 Cor. 12: 20, Gal 5: 20, where ἐριθεία is distinguished from ἔρις, oppose this derivation Alford and some others understand it here in accordance with the first meaning of the word ἐριθεύω, as signifying "*self-seeking*," but perhaps the apostle rather intends to designate that opposition to God which is the result of self-seeking.

to their etymology, would be *pressure* and *narrowness* or *want of room* (the former objective and the latter subjective); but the literal sense is abandoned, and the tropical one here employed. The ninth verse is a repetition of the general sentiment contained in ver 8; while the 10th verse repeats the sentiment of verse 7. This repetition, however, is evidently not merely for the sake of emphasis, but with the design of making a *specific* application of the threatening to all classes, both Jews and Gentiles.

Upon every soul of man, ἐπὶ πᾶσαν ψυχὴν ἀνθρώπου, *i. e.,* upon every man. In Hebrew, the *soul* of the righteous, of the wicked, etc., means the righteous, the wicked, etc. So here, *the soul of man* means *man; i. e.,* by metonymy, a leading or conspicuous part of man, is put for the whole person.— *First of the Jew, and then of the Greek,* Ἰουδαίου . . . . Ἕλληνος, *i. e.,* the Jew, to whom a revelation has been imparted, shall be judged and punished first in order, because he sustains a peculiar relation to revealed truth which calls for this; compare i. 16. Here the apostle openly shows, that what he had been thus far saying only in *general* terms, is applicable to *Jews* as well as to Greeks.

(10) *But glory, and honor, and peace, to every one who doeth good, first to the Jew, and then to the Greek,* δόξα δὲ . . . . Ἕλληνι. That is, both threatenings and rewards are held out to the Jews and Greeks, in the same manner, and on the same condition. This verse is a repetition of verse 7, with the addition of Ἰουδαίου τε πρῶτον καὶ Ἕλληνος. But here εἰρήνη is substituted for ἀφθαρσίαν there. Εἰρήνη may be considered as the opposite of that *enmity* and *disquietude* in which unsanctified men are involved, as it respects God. *Intensity* of affirmation is intended here, as in the preceding verse.

(11) *For with God there is no partiality,* or *no respect of persons,* οὐ γὰρ . . . . Θεῷ. The Hebrew נָשָׂא פָנִים means *to deal partially,* to look not at things, but at *persons,* and pass sentence accordingly. The phrases πρόσωπον λαμβάνειν or βλέπειν, and also προσωποληψία, are entirely Hebraistic in their origin; the classic writers never employ them. The apostle here explicitly declares, that there is no difference in regard to the application of the general principle which he had laid down, the Jew as well as the Greek being the proper subject of it. The γάρ at the beginning of the verse is γάρ *confirmantis.*

(12) A confirmation or explanation of what he had just said in the preceding verse; for if God judges every man according to the advantages which he has enjoyed, then there is no *partiality* in his proceedings; and that he does, the present verse explicitly declares.

Since as many as have sinned without a revelation, shall perish without a revelation, ὅσοι γὰρ . . . . ἀπολοῦνται. Νόμος, like the Hebrew תורה, often means *the Scriptures, the revealed law ;* e. g., Matt. xii. 5. xxii. 36. Luke x. 26. John viii. 5, 17. 1 Cor. xiv. 21. Gal. iii. 10. Matt. v. 18. Luke xvi. 17. John vii. 49, et alibi. Here most plainly it means *the revealed law, revelation,* or *the Scriptures;* for verse 15 asserts directly that the heathen were not destitute of *all* law, but only of an *express* revelation. The classical sense of ἀνόμως would be *unlawfully,* = παρανόμως. But plainly this meaning is here out of question. Ἀνόμως ἀπολοῦνται means, that, when adjudged to be punished, they shall not be tried by the precepts of a *revealed law* with which they have never been acquainted, but by the precepts of the *law of nature* which were written on their own hearts; see verse 15.

And so many as have sinned under revelation, will be condemned by revelation, καὶ ὅσοι . . . . κριθήσονται. Here νόμος is employed in the sense pointed out in the preceding paragraphs. Ἐν νόμῳ, *in a state of law, i. e.,* of revealed law or revelation, with ἐν *conditionis,* as we may call it; for ἐν is often put before nouns designating the state, condition, or relation of persons or things; see Bretschn. Lex. ἐν, No. 5. It is equivalent to ἔννομοι, 1 Cor. ix. 21, νόμον ἔχοντα, Rom. ii. 14. The sentiment is, that those who enjoyed the light of revelation (as the Jews had done) would be condemned by the same revelation, in case they had been transgressors. The ὅσοι employed in this verse is of the most general signification = *quicunque;* οἵτινες would have a relative and *limited* sense.

(13) This declaration is followed by another which is designed to illustrate and confirm it, and which is therefore introduced with another γάρ. *For not those who hear the law are just with God, but those who obey the law shall be justified,* οὐ γὰρ . . . . δικαιωθήσονται, *i. e.,* not those to whom a revelation has been imparted, and who hear it read, are counted as righteous by their Maker and Judge, but those who obey the law shall be counted righteous. The apostle here speaks of οἱ ἀκροαταί τοῦ νόμου, with reference to the public reading of the Scriptures every Sabbath day. The sentiment is: 'Not those who merely enjoy the external privilege of a revelation, but those who *obey* the precepts of such a revelation, have any just claim to divine approbation.

(14) To this sentiment the apostle seems to have anticipated that objections would be made. He goes on to solve them, or rather to prevent them by anticipation. He had said that Jew and Gentile, without distinction, would come under condemnation for disobedience to the divine law, and also be rewarded for obedience (verses 9, 10); he had declared that there is no partiality with God, and that all would be judged by the precepts of law

(verses 11, 12); he had intimated that those who were the hearers of the law (the Jews) would not on that account be accepted, but only those who obey it. It was natural now for some objector to say: 'The Gentiles have no revelation or law; and therefore this statement cannot be applied to them, or this supposition cannot be made in relation to them.' The answer to this is, that the Gentiles have a law as really and truly as the Jews, although it is not written on parchment, but on the tablets of their hearts. That verse 14 is designed to illustrate the fact, that the Gentiles are under a law, in the same manner as verse 13 (οἱ ἀκροαταὶ τοῦ νόμου) is designed to show that the Jews are under a law, there seems to be no good reason to doubt. The γάρ then in verse 14, is γάρ *illustrantis et confirmantis*.

An objection to this has often been made, viz., that in this way we may represent the apostle as affirming, that there were some of the heathen who did so obey the law as to be just before God. But the apostle no more here represents the heathen as actually attaining to this justification, than he represents the Jew as actually attaining to it in verse 13. Surely he does not mean to say in verse 13, that there are any Jews who are actually ποιηταὶ τοῦ νόμου in the sense which he attaches to this phrase; compare chap. iii. 19, 20, 23, 27, 30, 31. He is merely illustrating a *principle*, in both cases. The Jew expected justification on account of his *external* advantages. 'No,' says the apostle, 'this is impossible; nothing but *entire* obedience to the divine law will procure justification for you, so long as you stand merely on your own ground. And here the heathen may make the like claims. If you say that a heathen man has no law, because he has no revelation; still I must insist that he is in as good a condition with respect to actual justification, as you Jews are; for although he has no Scripture (and in this respect, no law), yet he has an *internal* revelation inscribed on his heart, which is a rule of life to him, and which, if perfectly obeyed, would confer justification on him, as well and as truly as entire obedience to the *written* law could confer it upon you. The principle is the same in both cases. You can claim no pre-eminence in this respect.'

If it is understood that the apostle is only *laying down*, or *illustrating a principle here*, NOT *relating a historical fact;* all difficulty about the sentiment of the passage is removed. Certainly there is no more difficulty in ver. 14, than must arise in regard to the ποιηταὶ τοῦ νόμου of ver. 13. The writer means to say neither more nor less, than that *the Gentiles may have the same kind of claims to be actually justified before God as the Jews* (which of course has an important bearing on ver. 11); but, as the sequel shows most fully, *neither Jew nor Gentile has any claim at all to justification, since both have violated the law under which they have lived.*

Do in their natural state such things as revelation requires, φύσει .... ποιῇ. Φύσις, in a classical sense, means *the nature* or *natural state* of a thing, *the natural condition* of any thing; just in the same way as we use the word *nature* in our own language; *e. g.*, the Greeks said ὁ κατὰ φύσιν θάνατος, *natural death ;* ὁ κατὰ φύσιν πατήρ, *natural father ;* φύσιν ἔχει γένεσθαι, *it naturally happens,* etc. In the verse before us, Φύσει is equivalent to μὴ νόμον ἔχοντα; *i. e.*, it designates those who were acquainted with the precepts of natural religion only, and were destitute of special revelation. The dative case (φύσει), here, as often, expresses the state or condition of anything; *i. e., Dativus conditionis*. As to τὰ τοῦ νόμου, it means either ἔργα νόμου (see ver. 15), or else δικαιώματα νόμου, etc. *Those things belonging to the law* designates, of course, such things as the law requires.

These having no law, are a law unto themselves, οὗτοι .... εἰσι νόμος. The construction is changed when οὗτοι (masc. gender) is employed; which is *constructio ad sensum,* ἄνθρωποι being understood. What is meant by ἑαυτοῖς εἰσι νόμος, is explained in the following verse.

(15) *Who show that the work which the law requires is written upon their hearts,* οἵτινες .... αὐτῶν. Οἵτινες refers to the Gentiles. — *The work* or *duty of the law,* τὸ ἔργον τοῦ νόμου, *i. e.*, that which the law demands. So, plainly, this much controverted passage should be rendered, if we compare it with other phrases of the like tenor ; *e. g.*, 2 Thess. i. 3, ἔργον τῆς πίστεως, *work such as faith demands ;* 1 Thess. i. 11, ἔργον πίστεως, *such works as faith requires ;* John vi. 28, 'What shall we do that we may perform τὰ ἔργα τοῦ Θεοῦ, *such works as God requires ;* to which the answer is (ver. 29.) 'τὸ ἔργον τοῦ Θεοῦ, *the work which God requires,* is, that ye should believe, etc.; John ix. 4, τὰ ἔργα τοῦ πέμψαντός με, *works enjoined by him who sent me ;* 2 Tim. iv. 5, ἔργον εὐαγγελιστοῦ, *duty which the evangelical office demands ;* et sic alibi. With these plain cases of usage before us, there is no need of endeavoring to prove, as some have done, that ἔργον is here merely *periphrastic, i. e.*, that ἔργον τοῦ νόμου means the same as νόμος. That such a *usus loquendi* is not unknown to the Greeks, may indeed be shown ; *e. g.*, τὸ τῆς φιλοσοφίας ἔργον, ἔνιοί φασιν, ἀπὸ βαρβάρων ἄρξαι, *philosophy (some say) took its rise from barbarians.* Aristotle (Rhet. i. 15. 6) says: ποιεῖν τὸ ἔργον τοῦ νόμου, *to do what the law requires.* The *periphrastic* use of χρῆμα and πρᾶγμα in this way, is well known. But it is wholly unnecessary to have resort to this, when the expression ἔργον νόμου can be so easily explained without it. It means plainly, *such work,* or *duty as the law requires.*

This, *i. e.*, precept enjoining this, *is written on the hearts or minds* of the Gentiles. Γραπτόν is of course to be understood figuratively; and the idea conveyed by the whole expression is, that the great precepts of moral duty are deeply impressed on our moral nature, and co-exist with it, even when it is unenlightened by special revelation. There is also an allusion in γραπτόν to the written law of the Jews; this was written on *tablets*, that on *the heart*. Καρδία, like the Hebrew לֵב, very often stands for *mind* as well as *heart*. Γραπτόν ἐν ταῖς καρδίαις is used as the antithesis of γραπτὸν ἐν πλαξὶ λιθίναις, which characterized the revealed law of Moses; 2 Cor. iii. 3.

What was meant by the expression just considered, the apostle goes on to show by adding two epexegetical clauses. *Their conscience bearing witness* Συμμαρτυρούσης αὐτῶν τῆς συνειδήσεως, viz., τῷ αὐτῷ, *to it*, to the same ἔργον νόμου. That is, the evidence that what the law of God requires is inscribed on the minds of the heathen, is the testimony of their consciences to such moral precepts. Some understand συμμαρτυρούσης as meaning, that the conscience bears testimony *in conjunction* with the heart or mind; but compound verbs, like συμμαρτυρέω, not unfrequently have substantially the same sense as the simple forms, or the same with a little intensity. So συμμαρτυρέω is employed in Rom. ix. 1. And in our text, *written in their hearts* or *minds* is explained by adding, *the conscience bearing testimony*, viz., to the precepts in question. This is the evidence that these precepts are engraved upon the minds of natural men. The apostle does not mean to say, that there are two testimonies, one of the mind and another of the conscience; but that the conscience testifies to the fact which he had alleged in regard to the mind.

The apostle now adds a second confirmation of the fact, that the demands of the moral law are inscribed on the heart of men in a state of nature; viz., *their thoughts alternately accusing or excusing them*, καὶ μεταξὺ .... ἀπολογουμένων. Μεταξὺ ἀλλήλων, *between each other, at mutual intervals, alternately, i. e.*, in succession, first one kind of thoughts, *i. e.*, approbation; then another kind, *i. e.*, disapprobation.— Λογισμός means *ratiocination, judgment, reflection*. It designates a more deliberate act of the mind than a mere ἐνθύμημα or ἐνθύμησις. — Κατηγορούντων, *accusing*, in case the actions were bad; ἀπολογουμένων, *defending*, in case they were good. After each of these participles, ἑαυτούς or ἄνθρωπον is implied.

The meaning of this clause is not, as has frequently been supposed, that one man blames or applauds another, or that men mutually blame and applaud one another, (although the fact itself is true); but that in the thoughts or judgment of the same individual, approbation or condemnation exists, according to the tenor of the actions which pass in review before him. Thus the voice of conscience, which proceeds from a moral feeling of dislike or approbation, and the judgment of the mind when it examines the nature of actions, unite in testifying, that what the moral law of God requires is impressed in some good measure on the hearts even of the heathen.

To deny that men can have any sense of moral duty or obligation, without a knowledge of the Scriptures, is erroneous; for the apostle's argument, in order to convince the Gentiles of sin, rests on this as a basis. And if it be alleged, that in this way the necessity of a revelation is superseded; I answer, not at all. The knowledge of some points of moral duty, or the power to acquire such knowledge, is one thing; a disposition to obey the precepts of natural religion is another. The latter can be affirmed of few indeed among the heathen of any age or nation. Again; faculties adapted to discover the path of duty are one thing, the use of them so as effectually to do this is another. The former the apostle asserts; the latter he denies. And justly; for after all, what have the heathen done and said which renders the gospel in any measure unnecessary? Little indeed; in some respects we may say, nothing. What *authority* had their precepts over them? And how was it with them as to doubts and difficulties about some of the plainest principles of morality? Their minds were blinded by their passions. Hence the voice within them was not listened to; but this does not prove that God left himself without sufficient witness among them. The apostle most plainly and fully asserts that he did not.

(16) *In the day when God shall judge the secret things of men,* ἐν ἡμέρᾳ . . . . ἀνθρώπων. But with what must we connect ἐν ἡμέρᾳ, Most commentators have said: 'With κριθήσονται verse 12, making verses 13, 14, 15, a parenthesis.' So Knapp, Griesbach, and others. This would then compare, as to construction, with Rom. i. 2 — 6. v. 13 — 18, and many other passages in Paul's epistles.

Others, as Beza, Heumann, Winer, join ἐν ἡμέρᾳ with δικαιωθήσονται at the end of verse 13, and make verses 14, 15, a parenthesis.

Bengel and Chr. Schmidt join ἐν ἡμέρᾳ with ἐνδείκνυνται in verse 15, making the sentiment to be, that in the day of judgment it will appear manifest to all, that men's consciences have testified in favor of the law of God, etc.

Somewhat different in sense from this, is the exegesis of Jerome, Theodoret, Chrysostom, Theophylact, Œcumenius, Calvin, Erasmus, and others; viz., that ἐν ἡμέρᾳ stands connected immediately with the participles κατηγορούντων and ἀπολογουμένων, which makes the passage to mean, that in the judgment-day the consciences of the heathen will accuse them of all that Paul has charged upon them. Several of these commentators, however, think that Paul means only to say, that *a fortiori* their consciences will then accuse them; without meaning to say, that they do not accuse them in the present life.

To this last interpretation Tholuck seems to accede. But I cannot accord with this exegesis, because the object of the writer, in verses 13—15, seems plainly to be merely a justification or confirmation of what he said in verse 12, viz., that the heathen who had *no revelation*, still had a *law* which they were bound to obey, and by which they must be judged. How does Paul establish this? By an appeal to the fact that they have a conscience or a moral sense, and that they pass judgment of a moral nature upon their own actions. To say that this conscience and moral sense will be developed at the judgment-day, is saying what is not sufficiently apposite to his purpose. At the judgment-day, the heathen will be tried by what? By the law under which they were placed, and under which they acted, in the present life. What was this law? That of conscience or moral sense. Then the *accusing* and *excusing*, which are appealed to as evidence of this moral sense, are exercised in the present world; *i. e.*, its exercise *here* must of course be appealed to in order to sustain the apostle's argument, by which he designs to establish their present guilt.

For these reasons I must accede to the prevailing opinion among critics, viz. that ἐν ἡμέρᾳ is either to be joined with κριθήσονται in ver. 12, and that vers. 13—15 are a *parenthetic* explanation or confirmation of ver. 12; or (which I think preferable) make verses 11—15 parenthetic, and unite ver. 16, ἐν ἡμέρᾳ κ. τ. λ. with ver. 10.*

Τὰ κρυπτὰ augments the force of the affirmation; 'God will not only bring into judgment the *external* actions of men, but all their *secret* thoughts, desires, and affections.' Tholuck understands it as referring to the secret judgment of the mind or conscience, mentioned in the preceding verse, and makes the sense to be, that God will bring into *open* judgment all the *secret* judgments of the mind. But does this accord with the nature of the case? It is not the moral judgment of the mind, when it accords with the

---

* This last view is defended by Alford and seems open to no objection but the great length of the parenthetic clauses that intervene, which in such a writer as Paul is not serious. See Introd. Meyer however connects this with verse 13. De Wette, with the preceding participles, and Olshausen with ἐνδείκνυνται in verse 15

decision of the divine law (as is here supposed), which the apostle means to represent as judged by God; for these are not matters of punishment, when they are correct; but it is the secret wickedness of men, as well as their open vices, that will make the final judgment a time of awful terror. That such a view of the subject is here intended, seems to me quite plain; and so Turretin, Flatt, and most others. To the very same purpose Paul speaks in 1 Cor. iv. 5, where he represents the day of judgment as the time, when God will bring to light τὰ κρυπτὰ τοῦ σκότους . . . . καὶ τὰς βουλὰς τῶν καρδίων.

According to the Gospel which I preach, κατὰ τὸ εὐαγγέλιόν μου; compare 2 Tim. ii. 8. 1 Cor. xv. 1. Some have understood this of a *written* gospel of the apostle; but without any good critical or historical evidence.

By Jesus Christ, διὰ Ἰησοῦ Χριστοῦ. Compare Acts xvii. 31. John v. 27, 22. xvii. 2. Acts x. 42.

By affirming that *God will judge* τὰ κρυπτὰ *according to his gospel*, Paul seems to intimate, that a judgment-day is not plainly revealed by the light of nature; or, at least, that the *extent* of the sentence which will be passed at that time, is not understood by the heathen. Notions of reward and punishment, in some form or other, belong to almost all the systems of heathenism; but such explicit views of a judgment-day as the gospel gives, are nowhere else to be found.

As the *secrets* of all hearts are to be revealed and judged, in the great day of trial, what but *Omniscience* is capable of passing sentence? To God alone is ascribed the power and prerogative of searching the heart; see 1 Sam. xvi. 7. 1 Chron. xxviii. 9. xxix. 17. Ps. vii. 9. Jer. xi. 20. xvii. 10. Rom. viii. 27. To Christ the same power is ascribed in Acts i. 24. Rev. ii. 23, besides the present passage. How can the Supreme Judge of all the human race be less than *omniscient;* How can he do *full* and *impartial* justice, with any knowledge short of *omniscience?*

(17) The attentive reader cannot help observing the skill and address which Paul exhibits in this chapter, in showing that his kinsmen the Jews are even more guilty than the Gentiles, and consequently that salvation by grace is the only salvation which is possible for them. In verses 1 — 8, he discusses the subject on general grounds, bringing forward considerations applicable either to Jew or Gentile, but not once naming either. In verses 9 — 16, he makes the application of these considerations to both, and shows why both are to be considered as transgressors of the divine law, the one having sinned against the revelation contained in the Scriptures, the other against that which the

book of nature discloses. But he has not yet done with the subject. Guilt is proportioned to light and love abused. He ventures therefore, in the next place, to prefer a heavier charge against the Jews than he had done against the Gentiles. He takes them on their own ground; admitting, for the sake of argument, all the claims to pre-eminence which they were accustomed to advance, he then shows that these only increase their guilt so much the more, in case of disobedience.

If now thou art surnamed Jew, εἰ δέ .... ἐπονομάζῃ. The reading ἰδέ (from which comes our English version *behold*), is found in very few manuscripts, and is of no good authority. The only difficulty with εἰ δέ is, that it makes a *protasis*, to which there seems at first view, to be no corresponding *apodosis*. However, this is not in reality the case; for vers. 21 seq. make in substance an *apodosis*. The relation between the two parts stands thus: 'If now thou art called a Jew, etc., *i. e.*, if thou dost in fact enjoy a high pre-eminence as to privileges, ... then how dost thou transgress the very law which thou teachest, and of which thou dost make thy boast?'

Ἰουδαῖος, a name of honor, much coveted by the Jews; comp. Gal. ii. 15. Phil. iii. 5. Rev. ii. 9. — Ἐπονομάζῃ, more formal and solemn than ὀνομάζῃ. It is appropriate also; inasmuch as Ἰουδαῖος is a surname, which may be added to the individual name of every Hebrew.

Thou restest upon the law, ἐπαναπαύῃ τῷ νόμῳ, or *thou leanest upon the law.* Ἐπαναπαύω corresponds to the Hebrew, נִשְׁעַן, *to lean upon, to restore, to prop up one's self by;* see 2 Kings vii. 2, 17. ἐπανεπαύετο τῇ χειρὶ αὐτοῦ. This verb is also used in the sense of *adhering to;* see 1 Macc. viii. 12. Either meaning gives a good sense in the verse before us. The first, is the more usual sense of the word, and altogether apposite. The Jew *leaned upon* the law, as defending his claims to precedence and to acceptance with God. — Νόμῳ of course means here the *Mosaic law,* or the *Jewish Scriptures.*

And gloriest in God, καὶ .... Θεῷ; *i. e.*, dost claim to thyself honor or glory, because Jehovah, the only living and true God, is thy God; compare Deut. iv. 7. Ps. cxlvii. 19, 20. 2 Sam. vii. 23. It was on this account that the Jew felt himself so far elevated above the Gentile, and so disdained all comparison with him. For the construction of καυχᾶσαι with ἐν and the Dative case, see Wahl on the word. For the form, καυχᾶσαι, 2nd person singular, see New Testament Gramm. § 71. 5; also verse 23.

(18) *And art acquainted with* [*his*] *will, and canst distinguish things that differ,* καὶ .... διαφέροντα. Γινώσκεις, *knowest, art acquainted with,* designates what the Jews were accustomed to

say of themselves; or if viewed simply as a declaration of the apostle, the meaning is: 'Thou hast the means of knowing, thou art instructed in.' Τὸ θέλημα, *his will;* where almost all the commentators say that αὐτοῦ or τοῦ Θεοῦ is to be supplied after θέλημα. But this is unnecessary; for, as is well known, the article frequently has the sense of a pronoun; see Middleton on the Greek article, chap I. § 3. *e. g.,* Acts xvii. 28, τοῦ γὰρ γένος ἐσμέν, *for we are of* HIS γένος. See New Testament Gramm. § 94.

Δοκιμάζεις may mean either to *distinguish* or *to approve;* the word having both these meanings in the New Testament and in the classics. So διαφέροντα may mean *things that differ,* or *things that excel;* the *usus loquendi* in both senses being equally certain. So some explain the phrase as meaning: 'Thou approvest the things which are excellent.' I prefer the other sense, because the idea of *knowledge* or *instruction* is the one here intended to be urged; as is plain from the sequel. Such being the case, *to distinguish things that differ* is more characteristic of this, than the other rendering is, and therefore more appropriate. *Things that differ,* are virtue and vice, *i. e.,* lawful and unlawful, praiseworthy and base things, etc.

Being instructed by the law, κατεχούμενος ἐκ τοῦ νόμου; *i. e.,* being taught or enlightened by the Scriptures.

(19) *Thou art confident moreover that thou thyself art a guide of the blind,* πέποιθάς τε . . . . σκότει. This is figurative language, designed to show in a strong light the claims to superiority over the Gentiles, which were made by the Jews. *A guide to the blind* signifies one who is an instructor by means of superior knowledge, *i. e.,* an instructor of those who are in a state of gross ignorance, viz., the Gentiles; see Matt. xv. 14.— *A light to those who are in darkness,* φῶς τῶν ἐν σκότει, the same idea by the use of another figure. Compare Is. xlix. 6. Luke ii. 32. John i. 8, 9, 4, 5, respecting the signification of the word *light.*— Σκότος here, as often elsewhere, designates a state of ignorance.

(20) *An instructor of the ignorant, a teacher of little children,* παιδευτὴν . . . . νηπίων. Ἄφρων means *one who has not mental skill* or *consideration;* secondarily, *an ignorant person.*— Νηπίων of course here means, *children* of such an age as that they may receive instruction. I have therefore rendered it *little children,* in preference to *babes,* which naturally designates those not sufficiently mature for instruction.

Having the delineation (or *form*) *of true knowledge in the Scriptures,* ἔχοντα . . . . ἐν τῷ νόμῳ. Μόρφωσιν may be used in a bad or good sense. In a bad sense it occurs in 2 Tim. iii. 5, where *the form* (μόρφωσιν) *of godliness* is opposed to the *power of* it, *i. e.*, hypocritical pretences to piety are opposed to the real exercise of it. But the verb μορφόω is used in a good sense in Gal. iv. 19, 'until Christ μοφωθῇ be *formed* in you.' The synonyme of μόφωσις, viz., ὑποτύπωσις, is used in a good sense, 2 Tim. i. 13, 'hold fast ὑποτύπωσιν of sound doctrine,' etc. Μόρφωσις means *form, external appearance;* also, *delineation, sketch, i. e.*, imitated form. I understand it in the good sense, *i. e.*, as meaning *delineation* in our verse, because the apostle is enumerating the supposed, or rather the acknowledged, advantages of the Jews. One of these was, that *true knowledge* (in distinction from the philosophy falsely so called of the Greeks) was in their possession, or at least in their power.

Of true knowledge, τῆς γνώσεως καὶ τῆς ἀληθείας; a Hendiadys in which the latter noun qualifies the former. The meaning of the whole is 'Est tibi vera sapientia in lege adumbrata.'

(21) *Dost thou, then, who teachest others, not instruct thyself?* ὁ οὖν .... διδάσκεις; This constitutes in reality, although not formally, the apodosis to the protasis which commences with εἰ δέ in verse 17. *Argumentum ad hominem;* for it is as much as to say: 'Thou pridest thyself in thy superior knowledge, and requirest all others to sit at thy feet in the humble capacity of learners; making these lofty professions, now, art thou thyself at the same time ignorant of what thou professest to know?' The apostle implies by this, that many of the Jews were criminally ignorant. Reiche finds the apodosis in verse 25; Glockler, in verse 23; alii aliter. The οὖν in verse 21, as well as the nature of its contents, seems to me to point plainly to the apodosis. Dr. Knapp has omitted the sign of interrogation after διδάσκεις, κλέπτεις, etc.; plainly to the disadvantage of the sense. The interrogation is, indeed, not one of doubt or simple inquiry, but is designed for reproof and conviction. It is, moreover, better accordant with the apostle's mode of reproof in this epistle, to suppose him here to be making interrogations (in the manner above stated), than to suppose him *directly* to make the charges, at first; as Dr. Knapp's pointing would indicate.

Thou who proclaimest that [men] *must not steal, dost thou steal?* ὁ κηρύσσων .... κλέπτεις; Dost thou practise the very vice, against which thou dost so loudly protest? Κηρύσσειν, *publicly to proclaim;* in respect to a teacher of religion or morality it means *to preach.*

(22) *Thou who forbiddest to commit adultery, dost thou commit adultery?* ὁ λέγων .... μοιχεύεις; A crime very common among the Jews; for even the Talmud accuses some of the most celebrated Rabbies of this vice. Ὁ λέγων μή, *forbiddest,* lit. *who sayest: Not.*

Dost thou who abhorrest idols, commit robbery in sacred things?
ὁ βδελυσσόμενος . . . . ἱεροσυλεῖς; Since the Babylonish captivity, the Jews have always expressed the greatest abhorrence of idolatry. But still, the real criminality of idolatry consists in taking from the only living and true God that which belongs to him, and bestowing it upon something which is worthless and vain. Now the Jews, who were prone to keep back tithes and offerings (Mal. i. 8, 12, 13, 14. iii. 10. Mark vii. 11), by so doing robbed God of that which was due to him, notwithstanding they professed a great abhorrence of idolatry which committed the like sin. I apprehend, however, that the word ἱεροσυλεῖς is here used in a somewhat wider extent than this interpretation simply considered would imply, *i. e.*, that it designates every kind of act which denies to God his sovereign honors and claims.

The exegesis of this word which assigns to it a *literal* sense, viz., that of *committing sacrilege, i. e.*, of robbing the temples of idols and converting their riches to individual use (contrary to the precept in Deut. vii. 25, 26), wants an *historical* basis for its support. When and where were the Jews accustomed to act in this manner? Yet Chrysostom, Theophylact, Le Clerc, Koppe, Rosenmuller, Fritsche, and others, have defended this interpretation.*

(23) *Thou who gloriest in the law, by the transgression of the law dost thou dishonor God?* ὃς ἐν . . . . ἀτιμάζεις; As God was the author of the law, or supreme legislator, so the transgression of it was a dishonoring of him, a contemning or setting light by his authority. For the construction and form of καυχᾶσαι, see note on verse 17 above; also comp. in Matt. v. 36. viii. 2. Mark. i. 40. ix. 22. Luke xvi. 25. 1 Cor. iv. 7. Rom. xi. 18, the like forms.

(24) *For the name of God is blasphemed on your account, among the Gentiles; as it is written,* τὸ γὰρ . . . . γέγραπται. Γάρ *confirmantis.*— Δι' ὑμᾶς may possibly mean *by you, i. e.*, by you as authors or agents; like ζῶ διὰ τὸν Πατέρα, *vivo Patre vitæ meæ auctore,* John vi. 57 ; or like ζήσεται δι' ἐμέ, ibid., et sic alibi. But the most natural meaning of δι' ὑμᾶς here is *on your account, i. e.*, you being the cause or ground of the blasphemy in question. The passage quoted seems to be Isaiah lii. 5 ; where, however, the Sept. has δι' ὑμᾶς διαπαντὸς τὸ ὄνομά μου βλασφημεῖται ἐν τοῖς ἔθνεσι, varying in manner at least from the text quoted by the

---

* Both Acts 19. 37 and Josephus Antt. 4 8. 10 would imply the propriety of such an implication against the Jews, but it is perhaps more probable that a robbing of the temple of God, i. e withholding and appropriating to private use. the legitimate temple-offerings is meant here. See Josephus, Antt. 8 2. 5 and 22. 6 2.

apostle. However, such variations are common in the New Testament text. The Hebrew runs thus: וְתָמִיד כָּל־הַיּוֹם שְׁמִי מִנֹּאָץ, the sense of which is that the heathen blasphemed the name of Jehovah, because his people (by reason of their sins) were subjected to captivity. In the like manner Paul accuses the Jews of causing the name of Jehovah to be reproached among the Gentiles, because of the transgression against his laws which they committed. The original passage is not a proper *prediction*, but a simple declaration of a fact then existing. Paul quotes it here, for the sake of declaring that the same thing was true in his day; *i. e.*, he expresses his own views and asserts facts, in the language of an ancient prophet. The γάρ at the beginning of the verse shows that the design of the verse is, to illustrate and enforce the declarations contained in ἀτιμάζεις. Ἐν τοῖς ἔθνεσι, is a *circumstance* added in the Sept. and by the apostle. It is not expressed in the Hebrew, but it is evidently *implied*. The meaning of the whole is, that the heathen themselves are led to blaspheme the name of God by the flagrant vices of the Jews; which was a heavy charge, and allowing its truth, it served abundantly to illustrate and confirm the declaration, that the Jews brought dishonor upon God by their offences — dishonor even from others. Of course their sins must have been great and conspicuous.

(25) *Circumcision indeed is profitable, if thou dost obey the law*, Περιτομὴ . . . . πράσσῃς. — Μέν here belongs to the protasis, the apodosis to which commences with ἐὰν δέ. The γάρ in this verse is omitted in many MSS. and Versions. Still, it has sufficient support to claim a place in the text. Although γάρ always implies some *preceding* sentiment to which it refers, yet this is not always *expressed*, but not unfrequently left to the mind of the reader to supply. In such a case we may sometimes render γάρ by *indeed, to be sure, truly*, although not strictly an adverb, (see Passow Lex. γάρ). Here, as it seems to me, the sentiment in the writer's mind before writing γάρ was: 'Thou hast no reason for glorying in the law; for (γάρ) circumcision [the symbol or token of admission to the privileges of a Jew] will not avail thee in case thou transgressest the law, as in reality thou dost.' In such a connection of thought, which is naturally deduced from verses 23, 24, the appropriateness of γάρ is sufficiently plain. In the case before us, verse 25, seq. are not a direct deduction from the preceding paragraph, but an illustration of a similar nature, designed to show that the Jew can claim no moral preference over the Gentile, on the mere ground of *external* privileges. As this is the main position of the apostle in this stage of his discussion, we might supply before γάρ in verse 25, the general thought, viz., 'The Jew has no precedence in the matter of justification over

the Gentile; for (γάρ) circumcision profits only when he does not transgress the law ; and this never can be affirmed of the Jew.' But the manner in which the connection is made out above, connects γάρ with the more immediate context, and the παραβάσεως of verse 23, and παραβάτης of verse 25 show that the writer had such a connection in his mind.

But if thou becomest a transgressor of the law, thy circumcision becomes uncircumcision, ἐὰν δὲ . . . . γέγονεν; *i. e.*, if thou dost not obey the law, then the privileges to which thou art entitled as a Jew, will not save thee; thou wilt not be considered or treated as any better than an uncircumcised person, *i. e.*, a Gentile or heathen man. In a word, not *external* privileges or pre-eminence, in themselves considered, but the use which is made of them, entitles any one to divine approbation or favor.

How much the Jews attributed to circumcision, is strikingly illustrated in a passage of the Talmud (Shemoth Rabba, sect. 19. fol. 118): "Said Rabbi Berachias, When heretical, apostate, and impious Jews say: 'We cannot go down to hell because we are circumcised;' what does the blessed God do? He sends his angel, et præputia eorum attrahit, ut, ipsi præputiati [uncircumcised] in infernum descendant."

(26) *If, moreover, the uncircumcised keep the precepts of the law,* ἐὰν οὖν . . . . φυλάσσῃ. Οὖν here, as often, serves merely for the *external* connection of vers. 25, 26, and not to point out a logical inference, deduction, etc. It might be rendered *then* or *so*. But verses 25, 26 seem to be simply *parallel* cases; and if so, *moreover*, is a more appropriate rendering. Ἀκροβυστία, abstract for concrete, as exhibited in the translation.—Δικαιώματα, *precepts*, משפטים.

Shall not his uncircumcision be counted for circumcision? οὐχὶ ἡ . . . . λογισθήσεται. That is, shall not he, in a heathen state, be accepted as readily as a Jew who obeys in a state of circumcision? In other words: Neither circumcision, nor the want of it determines our deserts in view of our Maker and Judge; but a spirit of filial obedience. "If ye love me, ye will keep my commandments."—Εἰς περιτομήν is after the Hebrew analogy, which puts ל before a noun designating that into which another thing has been changed, or which it has become, *e. g.*, היִיתֶם לַאֲנָשִׁים, *be men*, 1 Sam. iv. 9; 'Jehovah made the rib לְאִשָּׁה, *a woman*, Gen. ii. 22. The parallel between ἀκροβυστία γέγονεν in ver. 25, and εἰς περιτομὴν λογισθήσεται ver. 26, is very obvious.

The *possibility* that a heathen might keep the law, is here most plainly admitted; but this gives no ground for saying that such a case has ever *actually* existed. Still, the principle enforced is the same; and the assumption of such a case gives great force to the apostle's reasoning.

(27) *Yea, he who keeps the law in his natural uncircumcised state, shall condemn,** καὶ κρινεῖ . . . . τελοῦσα. Καί *affirmantis,* qualifying κρινεῖ. Ἐκ φύσεως between the article and its following noun, takes of course the place of an adjective. Φύσις plainly means here what we call *a state of nature,* in distinction from a state in which a revelation is enjoyed. The apostle states here and in the preceding verse, as before remarked, *a principle* for illustration merely; he does not aver, that what he describes, is matter of *historical fact*; for this would contradict the whole tenor and object of his reasoning in general, which is to show that *all men without exception have sinned,* and therefore that all without exception must be saved by grace through faith in Christ, and can be saved only in this way. The efforts to prove from such passages as the present that there have been heathen who kept the whole law of God, are surely fruitless. The main argument of the apostle himself falls to the ground, if this be once admitted. It seems quite plain, that the whole is merely a *supposed* case — supposed for the sake of illustrating a principle; and in the process of argumentation, nothing is more common than this.

Thee who art a transgressor of the law, although enlightened by the Scriptures and a partaker of circumcision, Σὲ τὸν . . . . νόμου. Διὰ γράμματος καὶ περιτομῆς here coming between the article τόν and its corresponding noun παραβάτην, evidently perform the office of *adjectives* qualifying παραβάτην. The διά here is διά *conditionis vel status,* if I may so speak. Διά is not unfrequently placed before nouns which designate *state or condition*; *e. g.,* Rom. iv. 11, those who believe δι' ἀκροβυστίας, *in an uncircumcised state*; 2 Cor. ii. 4, I have written this διὰ πολλῶν δακρύων, *in a state of much weeping*; 2 Cor. v. 10, that every one may receive τὰ διὰ τοῦ σώματος, [according to] *the things done in a bodily state*; Heb. ix. 12. 2 Pet. i. 3. 1 John v. 6; see Bretschn. Lex. διά I. 2. *c.* The idea intended to be conveyed by the apostle, is quite plain; viz. 'If a Gentile should do what the law requires, would not this show that you are worthy of condemnation who transgress the law, although you enjoy the light of revelation and the privileges which a state of circumcision confers?'

(28) *For he is not a Jew who is one externally;* οὐ γὰρ . . . . ἐστιν; *i. e.,* who is descended from Abraham, is circumcised, and

---

* Κρινεῖ, literally *shall judge,* here means, *shall condemn.* i. e by their example put to shame, or as κατακρίνω is used in Matt. 12: 41, 42, "rise in judgment against."

enjoys the privileges of a written revelation, is not a Jew in the important and spiritual sense of the word; he is merely an *external* (not an internal) Jew. The grammatical construction completed without any ellipsis, would be, ὁ ἐν τῷ φανερῷ ['Ιουδαῖος], οὐκ 'Ιουδαῖος ἐστιν.

Nor is that which is external, [merely] *in the flesh, circumcision,* οὐδὲ ἡ ἐν . . . . περιτομή; *i. e.*, that is not circumcision in its high and true sense, which is merely external, which pertains merely to the flesh. The sentence filled out would read thus: οὐδὲ ἡ ἐν τῷ φανερῷ [περιτομή], ἐν σαρκὶ [περιτομή], περιτομή [ἐστι], *i. e.*, true περιτομή.

(29) *But he who is a Jew in the hidden part,* ἀλλ' ὁ ἐν . . . . 'Ιουδαῖος; *i. e.*, who is spiritually or internally a Jew, such a one only deserves the appellation 'Ιουδαῖος. The clause filled out would stand thus: ἀλλ' ὁ ἐν τῷ κρυπτῷ 'Ιουδαῖος ['Ιουδαῖός ἐστιν]; which latter clause the mind of the writer supplied from the first part of ver. 28.

And the circumcision of the heart, a spiritual not a literal one, καὶ περιτομὴ . . . . γράμματι, [is the true circumcision.] There is the same ellipsis here, as in the preceding clause, περιτομή ἐστιν being understood after οὐ γράμματι. The words πνεύματι οὐ γράμματι, most interpreters construe as referring to the Holy Spirit and to the precepts of the law; *i. e.*, circumcision of the heart wrought by the operation of the Holy Spirit, not by following merely the literal precepts of the law. The sense is good, and the doctrine true; but I apprehend that the writer here uses πνεύματι and γράμματι merely as adjectives or adverbs to characterize more graphically the περιτομὴ καρδίας which he had just mentioned.

Whose praise is not of men, but of God, οὗ ὁ ἔπαινος . . . . Θεοῦ; that is, the praise of the Jew, who is truly a Jew after the hidden or internal man, is not of men but of God. "Man looketh on the outward appearance, but God looketh on the heart." The Jews considered it as a great privilege and a ground of high pre-eminence over others, that they were descended from Abraham, were circumcised and were entrusted with the Scriptures. 'All this,' says the apostle, 'does not entitle them in the least degree to the praise of God. The state of the heart in the internal man, is what he considers; and this alone is of any real moral value in his sight.' 'You,' says he, 'who are nothing more than *external* Jews, are not Jews in the high and noble sense which will make you to be heirs of the grace of life or of the promises of God. You have, because of your external privileges, no pre-eminence over the heathen on the score of *moral accountability*. All men, in regard to such an accountability, stand on a level, for each will be judged according to the law under which he acted; the Gentiles by the law of nature, the Jews by revelation.'

CHAP. III. 1—20.

NOTHING was more natural than for the Jew, who had entertained the most elevated notions of the advantages to which he was entitled from his *external* privileges, to feel strong objections to such a representation of the apostle as reduced Jews and Gentiles to a level in a *moral* respect. The Jew is represented accordingly as indignantly asking 'Of what advantage then can Judaism be?' The apostle replies in verse 2, that it is advantageous in many ways, and especially in that more light was conferred by it. But the Jew further inquires, how the apostle's views could be reconciled with God's fidelity to the promises which he had made to the Jews, ver. 3 The apostle replies, that this fidelity must not for a moment be called in question, but that we must adopt the sentiment of David (Ps. li 4) in regard to this, ver 4 The Jew still dissatisfied, urges further 'If the sins of the Jewish nation serve to render more conspicuous the justice of God, is it not unjust that he should punish us?' ver 5 Not at all, replies the apostle, for on the same ground you might object to the truth, that God will judge the world, and of course punish the wicked, for his justice will be displayed in such a way as to redound to his glory, ver 6. The Jew again asks 'If God's faithfulness becomes more conspicuous by my unfaithfulness, why should I be condemned?' ver 7. To which the apostle replies that he might just as well say. 'Let us do evil that good may come,' which in fact some did charge him with saying, although they deserved condemnation for so doing, inasmuch as the charge was false

The Jew again asks, with evident disappointment, 'How then have we Jews any pre-eminence over the Gentiles?' To which the apostle replies You have none, in respect to the matter that I am discussing. *All are sinners* Your own Scriptures do abundantly bear testimony that your nation are transgressors, as well as the heathen. Prophets of different ages have borne testimony which conveys charges of the most aggravated nature, vers 10—18 Now as what is thus said in the Scriptures was plainly said concerning the Jews, it follows, that your own sacred books bear testimony to the same doctrine which I affirm to be true Consequently the whole world, Jews and Gentiles, are guilty before God, ver 19, for by *works of law* none can be justified, inasmuch as the law condemns all transgressors, and sets forth their criminality instead of declaring their justification, ver 20

(1) *What advantage then hath the Jew?* or, *what pre-eminence hath the Jew?* Τί οὖν . . . . Ἰουδαίου;— Οὖν, *then,* is very often joined with τί in interrogatives. Both words united signify as much as to say: 'Allowing what you affirm, then how can this or that take place, or how can it be so or so?'— Περισσόν signifies *that which exceeds* or *abounds, precedence, præstantia.* Sentiment: "If what you say is true, then how is the Jew in any better condition than the Gentile, or what pre-eminence has he over him?'

Or what is the advantage or *profit of circumcision?* Ἢ τίς . . . . περιτομῆς. That is, if the Jew is subject to the same condemning sentence as the Gentile, of what use is the rite of circumcision, and the relation in which it places him to the people of God?

(2) *Much* [advantage] *in many respects*, or *in every respect*, Πολύ . . . . τρόπον. Rendered in this latter way, πάντα would refer of course to something in the preceding context, and *every respect* would mean, every one already touched upon, e. g., in ii. 17—23. Literally interpreted, πάντα must mean *in all respects*. But the real sense of the phrase here is better given by the translation, *in various* or *many respects, in a variety of ways*.

The principal one however is, that they were entrusted with the oracles of God, πρῶτον μὲν γὰρ . . . . Θεοῦ. Beza renders πρῶτον, *primarium illud est quod.* Πρῶτον clearly means, in some cases, *imprimis, maxime omnium, particularly, specially, most of all;* e. g., Matt. vi. 33. Luke xii. 1. 2 Pet. i. 20. iii. 3. 1 Tim. ii. 1. In these cases, it does not signify *first* in such a sense as implies a *second* in order, but *first* as the most eminent or most important thing in the writer's mind or intention; like the Hebrew רֵאשִׁית, e. g., רֵאשִׁית גּוֹיִם, the most distinguished of nations, Num. xxiv. 20. Amos. vi. 6.— Tholuck suggests, that μέν renders it probable that a *protasis* is here intended, although he does not think this decisive. And truly it is not decisive; for μέν is not unfrequently used without any δέ following, both in the classical writers and in the books of the New Testament; e. g., 2 Cor. xii. 12. 1 Thess. ii. 18. Rom. vii. 12. xi. 13. x. 1, where " explicationi inservit: " and so μὲν γάρ in Acts xxviii. 22. 2 Cor. ix. 1. xi. 4. Heb. vi. 16. vii. 18; μὲν οὖν, Acts xxvi. 9. 1 Cor. vi. 4, 7, et alibi. Μὲν γάρ, in cases such as those just cited, seems evidently designed to answer the place of the Latin *equidem, quidem,* i. e., to give *intensity* to a declaration; and μέν may in such cases be called μέν *intensivum*, or μέν *concessivum*, viz., implying that what is asserted, is supposed to be conceded; or at least that the speaker thinks it plainly ought to be conceded. It is indeed true, that μέν may be said *always* to imply that another and different or opposite sentence or declaration must follow, but the omission of this declaration in cases where it can be easily and naturally supplied by the reader is frequent. In the case before us the implication is, that to Jews were committed the divine oracles, and not to other nations; *i. e.,* [οἱ Ἰουδαῖοι] μὲν γὰρ ἐπιστεύθησαν τὰ λόγια τοῦ Θεοῦ, [τὰ ἄλλα ἔθνη δὲ οὐκ ἐπιστεύθησαν, κ. τ. λ.]

Γάρ here has indeed of itself no necessary connection with or influence upon the μέν; and may be considered as γάρ *illustrantis*, *i. e.,* γάρ standing before a clause designed to illustrate or confirm what precedes.

The two particles μὲν γάρ imply, that the advantage [πρῶτον] of the Jew, it must be conceded, lay specially in his having the gift of a revelation filled with precious promises to him. We may translate (ad sensum) thus: 'A peculiar advantage, as you must concede, is, that,' etc.; or, 'The most important advantage is,' etc.'; both having substantially the same sense.

The words ὅτι .... Θεοῦ are not to be construed by taking λόγια as a Nominative, for this word is the Accusative after ἐπιστεύθησαν. It is a principle of the Greek language, that where a verb in its *active* voice governs the Accusative of a *thing* and the Dative of a *person*, the Accusative is retained after a verb of the *passive* voice. Such is the case with πιστεύω; see Luke xvi. 11. John ii. 24; compare for the passive voice, 1 Cor. ix. 17. Gal. ii. 7. 1 Thess. ii. 4. 1 Tim. i. 11. Tit. i. 3. So frequently in the classics; Lex. in verb., also N. Test. Gramm. § 108. 6.

Oracles, λόγια, like the דָּבָר of the Hebrews, means any kind of divine response or communication, *effatum divinum*. Here, as verse 3 shows, the λόγια has special reference to those oracles which contain *promises* respecting the Messiah, the Jewish nation, etc.

In regard to the general sentiment of the verse, it is as much as to say, that more light, and better spiritual advantages were bestowed upon the Jews than upon the Gentiles. Access to the Scriptures would give more light; the promises offered encouragement to a life of piety; and in consequence of the state in which revelation placed the Jews, to them were made the first offers of the gospel. It should be remarked here, that the apostle contents himself for the present with naming merely one ground of advantage which the Jew had. The pressure of objections seems to have occasioned his omission of other grounds of precedence. The reader will find others in chap. ix. 1. seq.

(3) *What then?* τί γάρ; The usual mode of asking questions, γάρ being very often joined with an interrogative; see Passow on γάρ. It seems to be γάρ *intensivum*, in most of such cases; as Acts xvi. 37, οὐ γάρ, *not at all*, 2 Tim. ii. 7. Job vi. 8. Phil. i. 18. In the present case, γάρ has reference to what had been said in the preceding verse. The course of thought appears to be thus: 'What then shall we say to this, viz., to that which I am now about to suggest?' That is; 'Allowing what you have said to be true, then if some of the Jews were unfaithful, as you intimate, would not this detract from the veracity of the divine promises?'

If some were unfaithful, will their unfaithfulness render void the faithfulness of God? εἰ ἠπίστησαν .... καταργήσει; That is, if some of the Jews have been unfaithful to the covenant, and are in no better condition than the heathen, how will this consist with the fidelity of God in respect to his promise made to the Jewish nation ? — 'Ηπίστησαν is from ἀπιστέω, which comes from ἄπιστος, *unfaithful*, (πιστός often means *faithful*). 'Απιστέω therefore means, *not to be* π ι σ τ ό ς, i. q., *to be unfaithful, treacherous,* etc., viz., in respect to their covenant with God. The meaning is: 'If the Jews practically disregard, *i. e.*, would not dutifully receive and obey, divine revelation, etc.' — Πίστιν, *fidelity, faithfulness in keeping promises;* compare Matt. xxiii. 23. 2 Tim. ii. 13, and perhaps Gal. v. 22. 1 Tim. i. 4, 19. Rev. ii. 19. xiii. 10. The μή before ἀπιστία αὐτῶν is *interrogative* and employed here (as usual) in a question to which a *negative* answer is of course expected; see New Testament Gramm. § 153, 4.

Μὴ γένοιτο, *hoc minime eveniat! Let not this be supposed;* or *not at all, by no means!* Optative of γίνομαι joined with a negative. This should be included in verse 4. The Hebrew חָלִילָה corresponds to this.

(4) *But let God be* [*accounted*] *true, and every man false,* γινέσθω δὲ . . . . ψεύστης. 'Αληθής means *veracious, faithful to his word* or *promise*. Ψεύστης is the opposite of ἀληθής. The meaning is: Let God be regarded as faithful although all men should thereby be deemed guilty of unfaithfulness; *i. e.*, much more becoming and proper is it, that men should impute unfaithfulness to themselves than to God. The second δέ I have rendered *and* here, although it appears *adversative*. The sentiment is not injured by this version, and the repetition of *but* is avoided.

To confirm the pious sentiment which he had just uttered, the apostle appeals to an expression of David (Ps. li. 7), where, in signifying his penitence in view of his past transgressions, he says (Sept. Ps. l. 4): "Against thee only have I sinned, and done this evil in thy sight, ὅπως ἄν . . . . κρίνεσθαί σε, *so that thou mayest be justified when thou speakest* (or *in thy words* בְּדָבְרֶךָ), *and be clear when thou art judged*." The Psalmist means to say that as he had sinned in a grievous manner against God, so God is to be justified and acquitted altogether, when he reproves him for his sin and pronounces against it the sentence of condemnation. So Paul: 'Let us not,' says he, 'attempt to justify ourselves when we are accused of being unfaithful; but let us justify God in all respects, when he condemns our conduct and vindicates his own.'

The words ἐν τοῖς λόγοις σου mean, *when thou utterest reproof* or *condemnation, i. e.*, the connection in which it stands gives it of necessity such a turn. — Νικήσῃς, *mightest overcome,* Hebrew תִּזְכֶּה, *mightest be pure, i. e.*, mightest be adjudged to be pure, held to be guiltless or faultless. So in Rabb. Hebrew, and in the

Gemara זכה means *vincere in causa*. He who in a judicial contest was adjudged to be *pure* or *guiltless*, of course was the victor; and on this account the Septuagint νικήσῃς (adopted by the apostle) is a translation of the Hebrew *ad sensum*, although not *ad verbum*.

Flatt, Reiche, and others construe ἐν τῷ κρίνεσθαί σε as in the *passive* voice. The Hebrew runs thus: בְּשָׁפְטֶךָ . . . . בְּדָבְרֶךָ, *when thou speakest . . . . when thou judgest*, or *in the judgment of thee, i. e.*, when thou art judged. The sense here seems plainly to require us to understand the meaning as *passive;* for the apostle designs to say, that when the doings of God are judged of by his creatures, he must be acquitted. So in the present case, he must be acquitted of all *unfaithfulness*. The Psalmist (Psalm li. 7) employs the verb תִּזְכֶּה in its *active* sense, meaning, that when God condemns *he will act justly*. The use which the apostle makes of the sentiment, is of the same nature; for he would say: 'In pronouncing sentence or condemnation upon men, thou art to be justified, and if thou art called in question for this, thou wilt prove to be victor, or come off clear in the contest.'

(5) *But if our unrighteousness commend the righteousness of God*, εἰ δὲ . . . . συνίστησι. Δέ " addit vim interrogationi, et usurpatur præsertim interrogatione repetitâ," Bretschn. Lex. δέ 3. *b*. The sense of δέ is plainly *adversative* here.—Ἀδικία is here the *generic* appellation of sin, for which a *specific* name (ἀπιστία) was employed in ver. 3, and ψεῦσμα is used in ver. 7. In like manner, the δικαιοσύνη in ver. 5, which is a *generic* appellation, is expressed by a specific one (πίστιν) in ver. 3, and by ἀλήθεια in ver. 7. The idea is *substantially* the same, which is designated by these respectively corresponding appellations. *Fidelity, uprightness, integrity*, are designated by πίστιν, δικαιοσύνην, and ἀλήθεια; while ἀπιστία, ἀδικία, and ψεύσματι, designate *unfaithfulness, want of uprightness*, and *false dealing*. All of these terms have more or less reference to the בְּרִית, *covenant*, or *compact* (so to speak), which existed between God and his ancient people. But in the present verse, they are to be taken in a sense somewhat more enlarged.

Δικαιοσύνην Θεοῦ does not here mean (as it does in most cases where it is used in this epistle), the *justification which is of God;* it designates the *divine justice*, as the context clearly shows. For here the apostle (or the objector) is speaking of that attribute of God, *which is concerned with the judging and punishing of offenders*. Of course, the *retributive* justice of God must be understood by δικαιοσύνην Θεοῦ.

Sets off to advantage, συνίστησι, *renders conspicuous*.— Τί ἐροῦμεν; *what shall we say?* That is, how can we persevere in maintaining that the unbelieving part of the Jewish nation will be cast off, so long as even their very unbelief will be instrumental in setting off to more advantage, or in rendering more conspicuous, the retributive justice of God, and so of causing the more glory to his name? The equivalent of τί ἐροῦμεν, is common in the Rabbinic writings, where it runs thus: מַאי אִיכָּא לְמֵימַר, *quid est dicendum?* This is usually expressed by the abbreviation מאל.

Is God unjust, who inflicts punishment? μὴ ἄδικος .... ὀργήν; If the interrogation were made by μὴ οὐ, *is not*, etc., the solution of the sentence would be easy. But μή corresponds to the Latin *numne*, and asks a question to which *a negative* answer is usually expected. The Attics employed it, however, with somewhat greater liberty, and in cases where a negative answer did not of course follow. On the contrary, οὐ is used as an interrogation, where an *affirmative* answer is of course expected. For an example of both cases; Μὴ δοκεῖ σοι τοῦτο εἶναι εὔηθες; *Does this seem to you foolish?* Ans. No. Οὐ καὶ καλόν ἐστι τὸ ἀγαθόν; *Is not a good thing something excellent?* Ans. Yes. We cannot translate, therefore, as Turretin and many others have done: *Nonne injustus Deus, dum infert iram? i. e.,* is *not* God unjust, etc.? This would indeed make the sentiment more easy and intelligible, when viewed as coming from the objector; for that it is to be attributed to him appears from the sequel, κατὰ ἄνθρωπον λέγω. After all, however, nearly the same sentiment comes out of the passage in another way. The objector asks: Τί ἐροῦμεν; μὴ ἄδικος κ. τ. λ.; That is; Can it be now that God deals unjustly in the infliction of punishment [as your positions would seem to indicate]?' The answer is in the *negative* of course: μὴ γένοιτο. The objector means by the question which he puts, the same thing as to say; 'I cannot believe your representation, for it would make God unjust.'

The immediate *occasion* for such a question on the part of the objector, is furnished by the sentiment of the preceding verse. God, says the apostle, is to be justified in his condemning; yea, he is altogether to be vindicated in it, even if all men are by him found guilty of unfaithful and treacherous dealing. 'But,' replies the objector, 'on your ground we may go on and say, that glory redounds to God because of such dealing on the part of men; for this gives opportunity for God to display his justice to greater advantage than it could otherwise have been displayed. Why not, now, carry these considerations forward, and come to the result to which they would naturally lead? Why not conclude, that God is unjust when he inflicts punishment? For this would seem to be a necessary consequence, if it be true that his justice is displayed to the greatest advantage by reason of the wickedness of men, and he thus gets to himself the more honor and glory.

Tholuck attributes μὴ ὁ Θεὸς, κ. τ. λ. to the apostle himself, as an answer to the preceding question. But the κατὰ ἄνθρωπον λέγω and the μὴ γένοιτο which follow, seem to me clearly to decide against this.

I speak after the manner of men, κατὰ ἄνθρωπον λέγω; *i. e.*, I speak as men are often accustomed to do. The expression itself is *general*; but the class of men whom the writer has in mind here, are plainly the objectors to his doctrine. The expression κατὰ ἄνθρωπον λέγω may mean: *I speak more humano, i. e.*, in such a manner as is intelligible to men; so ἀνθρώπινον λέγω, in Rom. vi. 19; and κατὰ ἄνθρωπον λέγω, in Gal. iii. 15. In the sense *first* attributed to the phrase, the Greek and Latin writers often use the like expression; *e. g.*, Aristoph. Ranæ, ver. 1090, ὃν χρὴ φράζειν ἀνθρωπεῶς, *which one must describe in a way that is usual among men;* Athen. Deipnos. Tom. III. Lib. IX. 29, ἀνθρωπίνως λαλεῖν, *to speak like other folks.* So Cicero: *hominum more dicere,* de Div. II. 64. In like manner the Rabbins, when they wish to express what is commonly understood or affirmed by men in general, say : כְּמוֹ דְּאָמְרִי אֱנָשִׁי, *as men usually affirm,* or *say*.

(6) *By no means*, μὴ γένοιτο. This is the *negative* answer, given by the apostle to the question: Μὴ ἄδικος κ. τ. λ.

Otherwise, how shall God judge the world? ἐπεὶ πῶς . . . . κόσμον; *i. e.*, if it is not to be denied that God is unjust, or if we must concede that he is unjust, then how shall we admit the doctrine of a future or general judgment? — 'Επεί, *otherwise;* comp. Rom. xi. 6, 22. 1 Cor. v. 10. vii. 14. xiv. 16. xv. 29. Heb. x. 2, et alibi. The question, 'How shall God judge the world?' is founded on the concessions or established opinion of the Jews respecting a judgment-day, which were well known to the apostle. The expression implies as much as to say: 'You Jews concede that there will be a time of judgment, when God will punish the wicked and reward the righteous. But how can this be, if your objections have any force? The retributive justice of God will be rendered conspicuous, when the wicked shall be condemned and punished, and God will be glorified thereby, just as in the present case; if this then be a reason why God should not punish, it is a reason why there should be no judgment; and in order to be consistent, you must deny this also.'

Some contend that κόσμος here means only the *heathen;* and Reiche has endeavored, at great length, to establish this interpretation. But I do not see anything to be gained from it. The Jews admitted a *general* judgment as well as a judgment of the heathen. Why then could not Paul argue from this as well as from the other? The *nerve* of the argument is the same in both cases; and this is, that 'because God brings good out of evil, he is not therefore bound to remit the punishment of the evil, which must be inflicted at the day of judgment.'

(7) *Still, if the truth of God has abounded the more unto his glory, on account of my false dealing,* εἰ γὰρ .... αὐτοῦ. Tholuck understands these to be the words of the apostle. To me they appear very plainly to be the words attributed to the objector.* The γάρ at the beginning of the verse refers to an implied thought in the mind of the objector, viz., 'My objection is still valid; for (γάρ) if the truth,' etc. As to ἀλήθεια and ψεύσματι, see on verse 5. Ἀλήθεια here means, God's *faithful dealings* with his people, both in his threats and promises; Ψεύσματι means their *unfaithfulness* as to his covenant, their false and treacherous dealings in respect to their vows and obligations. Sentiment: 'If the veracity and faithfulness of God are rendered more conspicuous, and this unto his own glory, by the false and deceitful conduct of his covenant people, why,' etc. Reiche insists here, that ἀλήθεια must refer to *true religion* in opposition to *idolatry* (ψεῦσμα); and so he makes out the verse to apply to the *heathen*. Why then does he not refer ἀληθής and ψεύστης, in verse 4, to the heathen? Is it not evident that the *nouns* here merely correspond to the *adjectives* there?

Then why am I still condemned as a sinner? τί ἔστι .... κρίνομαι; That is, why should I suffer punishment on account of that very thing which has contributed to the glory of God, inasmuch as it has occasioned the greater display of his perfections?

(8) *Shall we then* [say], *(as it is slanderously reported, and as some affirm that we do say): Let us do evil that good may come?* καὶ μὴ .... ἀγαθά; As μή is simply *interrogative* here, it cannot be rendered (as in our English version), *not*. Μή is connected with ἐροῦμεν or λέγωμεν understood, as appears from the following clause with ὅτι; or it may be connected simply with ποιήσωμεν. The answer of the apostle is by a question which strongly implies disapprobation of the sentiment in the preceding clause;

---

* It is a matter of some question, whether it is not better to take this verse as an extension of the reasoning of the preceding verse, and not as the language of the objector. The course of thought then is: How shall God judge the world; for if the truth of God is established by my wickedness (unfaithfulness) why am I to be judged as a sinner, i. e. suffer for that which contributes to God's glory. And [why] should we not ... do evil that good may result from it? the punishment of which (evil doing) is just.

'Shall we then speak out and say: Let us do evil that good may come? as some do actually, although slanderously, accuse us of saying.' Ὅτι, as often in the N. Test. and classic Greek, simply marks *cited words*, viz., the words ποιήσωμεν κ. τ. λ. Or the whole may be construed thus: *Shall we say, then, that we may do evil,* etc. Καί is here a *continuative* of the apostle's reply to the objector. Βλασφημούμεθα, literally, *we are slanderously reported,* viz., it is slanderously reported that we say, etc.

The occasion given for the enemies of the gospel thus to slander Paul and others, was, that he preached the doctrine, that God would be glorified by the display of his justice in the condemnation of sinners, and that where sin abounded grace did much more abound; doctrines easily abused by a carnal mind, but which contain truths awful and delightful. Would God that abuse of them might have never extended beyond the apostolic age!

Whose condemnation is just, ὧν τὸ κρῖμα ἔνδικόν ἐστι. He means, that the condemnation of those who falsely attributed such doctrines to the apostles and other preachers, was just; in other words, that their offence was of such a nature as to deserve punishment.*

(9) *What then?* τί οὖν; The question is by the objector; and οὖν, in such a connection, implies as much as to say: 'What now can be gathered from all this?'

Have we [Jews] *any preference?* προεχόμεθα; That is, allowing all that you have said to be true, what preference now can we assign to the Jews? Προεχόμεθα may be construed as in the Passive, *i. e.*, are we preferred?—Have we any precedence? So in Plut. de Stoic. τοῖς ἀγαθοῖς πᾶσι προσήκει, κατ' οὐδὲν προεχομένοις ὑπὸ τοῦ Διός, *i. e.*, this is necessary for the good, *who are not indulged at all with a preference* by Jupiter.

None at all; οὐ πάντως; *i. e.*, none as it respects the great point in debate, viz., whether all men are sinners before God, and under the condemning sentence of his law. So the latter part of the verse leads us to explain the sentiment; and a comparison with vers. 1, 2, above, and ix. 1—5, will oblige us thus to interpret it; for superiority of another kind, *i. e.*, in external advantages, is there directly asserted of the Jews by the apostle himself.

For we have already made the charge (ch. i. and ii.) *against both Jews and Gentiles, that they are all under sin,* προῃτιασάμεθα

---

* Is it not more natural to refer the ὧν to those who would maintain the sentiment contained in the words: "Let us do evil," etc, than to suppose that the apostle turns aside to characterize the conduct of those who defame him. So Meyer, De Wette, Alford, and others.

. . . . εἶναι. Προαιτάομαι does not mean directly *to prove*. Αἰτία is *accusation, cause, ground, reason;* hence the verb αἰτιάομαι means *to accuse, to show cause*, etc.: generally in a *bad* sense, implying the preferring or supporting of a charge against any one. So the apostle means to say, that having already advanced or supported the charge against Jews and Gentiles of being sinners without exception, and of standing in need of the mercy proffered by the gospel, of course he cannot now concede, that the Jews have any exemption from this charge, or any ground of preference to the Gentiles, so far as the matter of justification is concerned. Ὑφ' ἁμαρτίαν means, *under the power*, or *control of sin*, subject to its dominion.

(10) Καθὼς γέγραπται κ. τ. λ. What is the object of this appeal? Evidently it is to illustrate and confirm the point now in debate. And what then is this point? Why plainly, that the Jews have no preference over the Gentiles, so far as their guilt and inability to justify themselves are concerned. The apostle had just said (in answer to the question put by a Jew, Have we any pre-eminence?) Οὐ πάντως. Why not? Because he had already shown reason why the Jews, as well as the Gentiles, are involved in the charge of universal guilt; therefore, both were in the same condition, with respect to their need of a Saviour. The quotations then, have special reference to the Jews. So Chrysostom, Calvin, Grotius, Tholuck, Flatt, and others; and so verse 19 obliges us to construe the quotations in question.

The quotations are taken from various parts of the Hebrew Scriptures, and mostly in the words of the Septuagint. The general strain and object of them is to show, that in ancient times charges of guilt were made against the Jews, not less aggravated than those now made by the apostle. The Jew could make no satisfactory reply to this, so long as he allowed the full weight and authority of the Old Testament. The apostle then, by adducing such charges from the Jewish Scripture, says in effect: 'You cannot accuse me of making strange and novel charges against you. Your own Scriptures are filled with charges of the like nature.' See further v. 19.

Let us proceed to consider each of the quotations separately. Ὅτι οὐκ . . . . εἰς, is a quotation *ad sensum* of Ps. xiv. 1; where the Hebrew has אֵין עֹשֵׂה טוֹב; and the Septuagint, οὐκ ἔστι ποιῶν χρηστότητα, οὐκ ἔστιν ἕως ἑνός. In Ps. liii. (a repetition of Ps. xiv.), the Septuagint has simply οὐκ ἔστι ποιῶν ἀγαθόν; while the Hebrew is the same as above. It would seem, therefore, that the apostle had his eye or his mind upon Ps. xiv., when he made the quotation before us; and that he has varied from the *diction*, but followed the *sense* of the original. Instead of saying *there is none that doeth good*, he says, *there is none righteous* (idem per alia verba). The οὐδὲ εἷς of our text, evidently corresponds to the Septuagint οὐκ ἔστιν ἕως ἑνός.

(11) Οὐκ ἔστιν συνιῶν .... Θεόν, corresponds to the Hebrew הֲרֵשׁ מַשְׂכִּיל דֹּרֵשׁ אֶת־אֱלֹהִים, *whether there is any one who understandeth, who seeketh after God,* Ps. xiv. 2. The question in the Hebrew implies a *negative*; and a simple negative is made by Paul, who says, οὐκ ἔστιν κ. τ. λ. The Septuagint runs literally: Εἰ ἔστι συνιῶν ἢ ἐκζητῶν τὸν Θεόν. Paul has cited *ad sensum*, and nearly *ad verbum*. Συνιῶν instead of συνιείς, as from συνιέω the old root. See § 81 of New Test. Gramm. Comp. § 80.

(12) Πάντες .... ἑνός, cited exactly from the Septuagint version of Ps. xiv. 3. The Hebrew runs thus:

הַכֹּל סָר יַחְדָּו נֶאֱלָחוּ אֵין עֹשֵׂה טוֹב אֵין גַּם אֶחָד

Whether all have gone out of the way and together become corrupt? None doeth good, not even one. Paul omits, as the Septuagint also does, the interrogatory sense of the first clause, made by הַכֹּל (which is co-ordinate with הֲיֵשׁ in the preceding verse), and renders simply: Πάντες ἐξέκλιναν; altogether *ad sensum*.

The word συνιῶν in verse 11 means *to have an enlightened knowledge*, viz. of God and duty. — Ὁ ἐκζητῶν (Heb. הַדֹּרֵשׁ) means, *to worship God, to seek* him in acts of devotion, meditation, etc., *to be a devoted worshipper.* — Ἐξέκλιναν in verse 11 means, *have departed from* the right way, from the paths of piety and happiness. — Ἠχρειώθησαν, *have become corrupt,* literally *have become unprofitable* or *useless.* But as the meaning is here a *moral* one, the first rendering is the most appropriate.

In regard to the *original* meaning of these quotations, there seems not to be much room for dispute. Who is it of whom the Psalmist is speaking? It is נָבָל, ὁ ἄφρων, as ver. 1 determines. But are *all* men without exception ἄφρονες? Whatever may be the fact, yet it is not *here* asserted; for in ver. 4 the *workers of iniquity* are expressly distinguished from *my people.* In verse 5, *the generation of the righteous* is distinguished from *the workers of iniquity.* It is plain, then, that the Psalmist is here describing two parties among the Hebrews; the one wicked, yea altogether corrupt; the other righteous, *i. e.*, belonging to the true people of God.

The application of this passage by the apostle is plain. All unbelievers, all who put not their trust in Christ, are of the same character with those wicked persons whom the Psalmist describes;

and what is now true of them, was once true of present believers, *i. e.*, before they became penitent.

(13) Τάφος . . . . ἐδολιοῦσαν, verbatim with the Septuagint version of Ps. v. 10 (v. 9); which runs thus in the Hebrew:

קֶבֶר פָּתוּחַ גְּרֹנָם לְשׁוֹנָם יַחֲלִיקוּן

An open sepulchre is their throats; with their tongues do they flatter, speak deceitful things. Sentiment: 'As from the sepulchre issues forth an offensive and pestilential vapor; so from the mouths of slanderous persons issue noisome and pestilential words.' Or if it may mean, as some suppose, that 'their throat is like an open sepulchre, swallowing up and destroying all' (Reiche, Barnes), then what is the sense of *their tongues*? This shows that *noisome and pestilential falsehood and flattery or deceit*, is the idea which is intended to be expressed.— Ἐδολιοῦσαν, *speak deceit, deceive*, stands for ἐδολίουν, Imperfect active; see N. Test. Gramm. § 65. 8.

Ἰὸς ἀσπίδων ὑπὸ τὰ χείλη αὐτῶν, accords verbatim with the Septuagint version of a part of Psalm cxl. 4. (cxl. 3). The Hebrew runs thus: חֲמַת עַכְשׁוּב תַּחַת שְׂפָתֵימוֹ, *the poison of asps, or of the adder, is under their lips*; *i. e.*, their words are like poison, they utter the poisonous breath of slander. The phrase before us gives intensity to the preceding description; all of which, however, is not intended to designate merely some specific kind of slander, but the sinful exercise of *the tongue*, which (as James expresses it) is πῦρ, ὁ κόσμος τῆς ἀδικίας, iii. 6.

In the passages quoted in this and the following verse, the persons characterized are the enemies of David. What was said of them may be applied, as the apostle here intimates by the quotation, to all those who refused submission to 'David's Lord that sat upon his throne.'

(14) Ὧν τὸ . . . . γέμει, runs thus in the Septuagint: Οὗ ἀρᾶς τὸ στόμα αὐτοῦ γέμει καὶ πικρίας καὶ δόλου (Ps. ix. 7), which corresponds to the Hebrew in Psalm x. 7, אָלָה פִּיהוּ מָלֵא וּמִרְמוֹת, excepting that οὗ is added by the Seventy, and also δόλου. The apostle has quoted the Hebrew as it would seem, and exactly *ad sensum*, the suffix pronoun in פִּיהוּ being *generic*, and indicating a real *plurality*, which Paul expresses by ὧν.

Πικρίας is used to translate the Hebrew מִרְמוֹת, which literally signifies *fraud, deceit*. But as *false accusations* are here meant, which tend to destroy reputation and confidence, and proceed from *bitterness* of spirit, so πικρία (*bitterness*) is employed to characterize them, it being used *ad sensum* in a general way. Or did the Seventy read מְרֹרוֹת, *bitterness*?

(15 —17) Ὀξεῖς .... ἔγνωσαν, abridged from Is. lix. 7, 8. The Septuagint and Hebrew run thus:

Οἱ πόδες αὐτῶν ἐπὶ πονηρίαν τρέχουσι, ταχινοὶ ἐκχέαι αἷμα, καὶ οἱ διαλογισμοὶ αὐτῶν διαλογισμοὶ ἀπὸ φόνων· σύντριμμα καὶ ταλαιπωρία ταῖς ὁδοῖς αὐτῶν, καὶ ὁδὸν εἰρήνης οὐκ οἴδασι.	רַגְלֵיהֶם לָרַע יָרֻצוּ וִימַהֲרוּ לִשְׁפֹּךְ דָּם נָקִי מַחְשְׁבוֹתֵיהֶם מַחְשְׁבוֹת אָוֶן שֹׁד וָשֶׁבֶר בִּמְסִלּוֹתָם׃ דֶּרֶךְ שָׁלוֹם לֹא יָדָעוּ׃

Here the expressions are altogether of a *general* nature, as they stand in the prophet, and plainly characterize a great part of the Jewish nation in the time of the writer; compare Is. lix. 2, 4, 9 — 15. Of course this is still more directly to the apostle's purpose, than the preceding quotations. Those correspond with his intention in the way of *implication* ; but the present quotation corresponds in the way of direct *analogy*.

An inspection of the *original* will disclose how much the apostle has abridged it in his quotation. Ὀξεῖς is substituted for ταχινοί in the Septuagint; and the clause: "their thoughts are thoughts of evil," is omitted. Both the Seventy and Paul omit the Hebrew נָקִי in the phrase דָּם נָקִי, *innocent blood.*—Ἐκχέαι, 1 Aorist Inf., comes from ἐκχέω, Fut. ἐκχεύσω (in the New Testament ἐκχεῶ, the Attic Fut., N. Test. Gramm. § 65. 3), 1 Aor. ἐξέχεα after the manner of verbs in λ, μ, ν, ρ. A few verbs thus form the first Aorist. See Gramm. § 65. 10.

Sentiment: 'They are ready and swift to engage in crimes of the highest degree ; *destruction and misery attend their steps, i. e.*, wherever they go, they spread destruction and misery around them. The way of happiness they take no knowledge of, or they give no heed to what concerns their own true welfare or that of others.'

(18) Οὐκ ἔστι .... αὐτῶν, is exactly quoted from the Septuagint, and corresponds for substance to the Hebrew. The Hebrew original is in Psalm xxxvi. 1, and it runs thus: אֵין פַּחַד אֱלֹהִים לְנֶגֶד עֵינָיו, *there is no fear of God before his eyes;* i. e., he has no reverence for God, no fear of offending him which puts any effectual restraint upon his wickedness.

(19) *Now we know that whatsoever things the law saith, it addresses to those who are under the law,* οἴδαμεν δὲ ..... λαλεῖ; i. e., we know that whatever the Old Test. Scriptures say, when they speak in the manner now exhibited, they address it to those who are in possession of these Scriptures, viz., to the Jews.—Δέ continuativum, *nunc*, German *nun*, English *now*, in the sense of a *continuative.*— Τοῖς ἐν τῷ νόμῳ, *those who have a revelation* or

are under the law; ἐν conditionis, compare what is said on ἐν under chap. i. 24.

The object of the apostles is to show, that the Jews can in no way avoid the force of what is here said. It was originally addressed to the Jews, in a direct manner. What he has quoted was indeed spoken at different times, to different classes of persons, and uttered by various individuals. But still the *principle* is the same. *Jews* are addressed; and the Jews are accused in the very same manner, *i. e.*, with equal force, by their own prophets whose authority is acknowledged, as they were accused by Paul. The *principle* then by which such an accusation is to be supported, is thus established. As to the actual application of this, and the *facts* respecting the conduct and character of the Jews in the apostle's time; all the writings of the New Testament, of Josephus, and others, and the direct assertions of Paul in this epistle, go to show that no injustice at all was done to them in the present case.

It is this principle, which the apostle has in view to establish by all his quotations, viz., that in consistence with the fidelity of God to his promises, and consistently with the ancient Scriptures, the Jews might be charged with wickedness even of a gross character, and such as brought them as truly as the polluted heathen under the curse of the divine law; and this he does entirely establish. When thus understood, there remains no important difficulty respecting the quotations. These proofs from Scripture were not needed to settle the question about the depravity of the *Gentiles*. The character of the heathen was too palpable to be denied. That of the Jews, indeed, was scarcely less so in the eyes of others; but still, they themselves expected to escape divine justice, on the ground of being God's *chosen people*. All expectation of this nature is overturned by the declarations and arguments of the apostle, in chapters ii. iii. of this epistle.

Such as undertake to prove *universal* depravity directly from the texts here quoted, appear to mistake the nature of the apostle's argument, and to overlook the design of his quotations. It is impossible to make the passages in the Old Testament, as they there stand, to be *universal* in their meaning, without doing violence to the fundamental laws of interpretation. And surely there is no need of doing thus. The whole strain of the apostle's argument at large, goes to establish universal depravity; I mean the universal depravity of all who are *out of Christ*, and are capable of sinning. The doctrine is safe, without doing violence to any obvious principle of exegesis; which we never can do with safety. I need scarcely add, that Flatt, Tholuck, and

ROMANS III. 19.

nearly all distinguished commentators of the present day, so far as I know, agree in substance with the interpretation which I have now given.

So that every mouth must be stopped, and the whole world become guilty before God, Ἵνα πᾶν . . . . Θεῷ. Ἵνα has here the *ecbatic* sense, not the *telic;* for to assert that the Old Test. was written principally to stop the mouths of the guilty, would be a singular position indeed. See Tittmann on ἵνα, in the Bibl. Repository, No. I. of 1835.— Πᾶν στόμα φραγῇ, *i. e.*, every man, all men, whether Jews or Gentiles, must be convicted of sin, and be unable to produce anything to justify their conduct; compare Job v. 16. Ps. cvii. 42. The phraseology is borrowed from the custom of gagging criminals, *i. e.*, stopping their mouths in order to prevent apology or outcry from them, when they were led out to execution.— Ὑπόδικος, *reus, i. e.*, guilty, deserving of condemnation.

But how extensive is the conclusion here? (1) It extends to *all* who are out of Christ. I draw this conclusion, not so much from the mere forms of expression, such as πᾶν στόμα and πᾶς ὁ κόσμος, as I do from the nature and object of the apostle's argument. What is this? Plainly his design is, to show that there is but *one* method of acceptance with God now possible; and this is in the way of gratuitous pardon or justification. But why is this necessary in *all* cases? The answer is: Because all have sinned. Certainly, if those who do not believe in Christ cannot obtain pardon without him, this is because they are sinners, and have no claim on the score of justice or law.

But (2) All who are in Christ, *i. e.*, are justified, have once been sinners, and do still commit more or less sin, for which pardoning mercy becomes necessary. Once they were among the impenitent and unregenerate. What the apostle asserts then, in our text, of *all* men, need not be limited, and should not indeed be limited, merely to those who are out of Christ at any particular time, but may be extended to all who were ever out of him.

According to the apostle's own commentary on this doctrine in chap. iv., it appears that even Abraham and David, as well as the grossest sinners, were justified only in a *gratuitous* way, being utterly unable to obtain the divine approbation, on the ground of perfect obedience. The plain inference then is that all men are sinners, and that none therefore can be saved by their own merits. So verse 20 virtually declares; and verse 23 says explicitly.

In form, the argument of Paul extends only to those who are *out of Christ;* but as this has once been the condition of all men without exception, so in *substance* it embraces all men without exception, who "by nature are children of wrath, being children of disobedience;" for "that which is born of the flesh, is flesh."

I cannot forbear to repeat that it seems to me a wrong view of the apostle's meaning in verses 10 — 19, which regards him as laboring to prove directly the universality of men's depravity, merely by the *argument* which these texts afford. Paul has other sources of proof, besides that of argument; for if he himself was an *inspired* apostle, then surely his own declarations respecting the state of the heathen or Jews, were to be credited on just the same grounds as those of the ancient Psalmist and of the Prophets. Why not? And then, why should we be solicitous to show that everything in Paul's epistle is established by *argumentation*? Had the apostle no other way of establishing truth, except by argumentation? Are not his own declarations, I repeat it, as weighty and credible as those of the ancient prophets? If so, then we need not be anxious to retain the argument as a *direct* one, in verses 10 — 19. Enough that it *illustrates* and *confirms* the PRINCIPLE which the apostle asserts, and for which he contends. The argument from this principle is irresistible, when we once concede that Christ is the only Saviour of all men without exception; for this cannot be true, unless all men without exception are sinners. Of course I mean, all who are capable of sinning.

(20) *Because that by works of law shall no flesh be justified before him*, διότι .... αὐτοῦ. Διότι, *on account of, because that, for.* In this sense it differs little or nothing from γάρ. It is not employed, as some contend, to designate a *logical* conclusion from premises, *therefore;* but stands before a clause which assigns a reason or ground of something already affirmed. The appeal of Bretsch. (lex.) to Acts xvii. 31. Rom. i. 21. viii. 7. 1 Pet. ii. 6, does not at all support his conclusion, διότι being employed in all these cases as above stated.

Works of law, ἔργων νόμου, *i. e.*, such works as law requires; just as ἔργα Θεοῦ means, 'such works as God requires or approves; and so ἔργα τοῦ Ἀβραάμ, John viii. 39, τὰ ἔργα τοῦ πατρός ὑμῶν [τοῦ διαβόλου], John viii. 14; τὰ ἔργα τῶν Νικολαϊτῶν, Rev. ii. 6; and so ἔργα τῆς πόρνης — τῆς σαρκός — τοῦ διαβόλου — τῆς πίστεως, etc. From these and a multitude of other examples, it appears entirely plain that ἔργα and ἔργον, followed by a Genitive which qualifies them, mean something to be effected or done, which is agreeable to the command, desire, nature, etc., of the thing which is designated by the Genitive noun.

Concerning this usage, there is no just room to doubt. But the sense of νόμου has been thought to be less obvious. Does νόμος then mean *ceremonial law*, or *revelation* in general, or *the moral law* whether revealed or natural? The *object* or *design* of the writer must determine this. What then is the object of Paul in the present case? Surely it is, to show that both Gentiles and Jews need that gratuitous justification which the gospel proclaims, and which Christ has procured; compare iii. 9, πᾶν στόμα and πᾶς ὁ κόσμος in iii. 19, πάντες in ver. 23, together with ver. 29. Cf. also chap. i. 19 — 32 with ii. 17 — 29. Nothing can be more certain than that the conclusion of the apostle is a *general* one, having respect to Jew and Gentile both. But how can it be apposite to say, in respect to the Gentiles, that they cannot be justified by the *ceremonial* law? Were the Gentiles sinners, because they had not kept the *ritual* laws of Moses? So the apostle does not judge; see ii. 14, 15, 26. How, then, can he be supposed to say in reference to the Gentiles (for the present verse refers to them as well as to the Jews), that *by the law is the knowledge of sin?* What knowledge of the *ceremonial* law of Moses did the heathen possess?

The transgressions of the *ritual* law are also no part of the accusation which the apostle here brings against the Jews. In chap ii. 17 — 29, he accuses them of breaking *moral* laws; and after having enumerated a long catalogue of crimes common among the Gentiles in chap. i. 19 — 32, he goes on immediately to intimate in chap. ii. 1, seq., that the Jews were chargeable with the same or with the like crimes. In ii. 14, seq., and ii. 26, seq., he intimates that the law, inscribed upon the consciences and minds of the heathen, inculcated those very things with regard to which the Jews were sinners. In iii. 9, seq., he brings Jews and Gentiles under the same accusation, explicitly charging all with being sinners, and sinners against a law which was common to both.

Again; when it is asked in Rom. vi. 15, *Shall we sin because we are not ὑπὸ νόμον but under grace?* what sense would there be in this question (which is supposed to be urged by an objector), provided the *ceremonial* law be meant? Would he in reason ask the question: 'Have we liberty to break the *moral* law, *i. e.*, to sin, because we are not under the ceremonial?' Or, 'because the *ceremonial* law will not justify us, may we not break the *moral* law?' Yet νόμον in Rom. vi. 15, is plainly of the same nature as νόμος in iii. 20.

Finally; the apostle everywhere opposes the δικαίωσις or δικαιοσύνη of the gospel, to that justification which results from works in general, works of any kind whatever; *e. g.*, 2 Tim. i. 9. Eph. ii. 8, 9. Tit. iii. 5. Rom. iv. 2 — 5, 13 — 16. iii. 27. xi. 6.

and in many other places. In all such cases, *justification by works* means a *meritorious* justification, while that which is by faith means a *gratuitous* justification.

From all this it results, that νόμου must here mean the *moral law*, whether written or unwritten, *i. e.*, law in general, any law whether applicable to Gentile or Jew, any rule which prescribes a duty by obedience to which men might claim a promise of reward. Neither is this duty limited to what is *external* merely. It also has reference to *the state of their heart and feelings*. So Paul teaches most explicitly, in Rom. ii. 28, 29, in Rom. ii. 16, and often elsewhere.

Understood in this way, the phrase ἔργα νόμου is plain. Neither Jew nor Gentile can be justified before God on the ground of obedience; "all have sinned and come short of the glory of God;" each one has broken the law under which he has acted; the Gentiles, that which was written on their minds and consciences, ii. 14, 15; the Jews, that which was contained in the Scriptures, ii. 27. Now as the law of God, revealed or natural, requires *entire* and *perfect* obedience, just so far as it is known and understood, or may be so without criminal neglect on the part of men; and since "the soul which sinneth must die," and "he who offendeth in one point is guilty of all;" it follows of necessity that all men, whether Jews or Gentiles, while in an unconverted state, are under the condemning sentence of the law; and therefore that they cannot possibly claim acceptance with God on the ground of perfect obedience. They can indeed expect nothing but condemnation and misery from the exercise of simple *retributive* justice toward them under a pure system of law; for "all have sinned," and therefore "all have come short of the glory of God."

In no other way, as it seems to me, can the general course of argument by the apostle be understood and interpreted so as to preserve consistency with the other parts of this epistle, and with his other writings, or so as to harmonize with the particular design and object of the writer. Accordingly Storr, Flatt, Tholuck and many others have explained ἔργων νόμου substantially in the same manner as I have done. I add merely, that the question here is, whether men in their present state and character, as *actual* transgressors, can be justified by the law. The generic and *abstract* question, whether human nature is *capable* of fulfilling the law, is not the subject of discussion, and is a question of no moment, so far as the simple doctrine of justification is concerned; inasmuch as all men born in the natural way, who are capable of sinning, do sin.

Δικαιωθήσεται, see on δικαιοσύνη in i. 17, where the verb

δικαιόω is also explained. It means here *to be accepted and treated as having fully kept the precepts of the law.* — Οὐ πᾶσα .... σάρξ = לֹא כָל־בָּשָׂר, *no one;* a true Hebraism in all respects, which would hardly have been intelligible to a mere Attic Grecian.

If *all the world* are ὑπόδικος τῷ Θεῷ, then must it be true that none can be δίκαιος before him in a legal sense, *i. e.*, on the ground of perfect and meritorious obedience. Ἐνώπιον αὐτοῦ = לְפָנָיו, *in his view, in his sight, in his presence.* The mind of the writer here contemplates mankind as standing before the divine tribunal, in order to be judged of the things done in the body.

For by law is the knowledge of sin, διὰ γὰρ .... ἁμαρτίας. The γάρ here introduces a reason or ground why *works of law* will not justify. The law condemns but does not justify; and this, because men have broken it. Νόμου here must evidently mean the same as it does in the clause ἐξ ἔργων νόμου, which clearly signifies any law of a moral kind, either natural or revealed. Turretin understands νόμου, in the phrase before us, as meaning the Jewish Scriptures. But, as the preceding phrase is general, it must be understood so here. All law is a rule of action, in the most extensive sense of this word, embracing the internal as well as the external developments of the human soul. By this rule all actions are to be scanned; the Gentiles are to scan theirs by the law written upon their own minds, ii. 14, 15; the Jews by their own Scriptures. The precepts of law, whether natural or revealed, by commanding this and prohibiting that serve to make known the nature of sin: for all sin is ἀνομία, *want of conformity to the law.* The simple design of the apostle, in saying διὰ γὰρ νόμου ἐπίγνωσις ἁμαρτίας, is to remind those whom he addressed, that the law (any law either natural or revealed), so far from holding out to men who are *sinners* the prospect of justification before God and promising them acceptance with him, is the very means of bringing them, by its disclosures respecting the nature and guilt of sin, to a knowledge of their unhappy and desperate condition, inasmuch as it shows them that they are exposed to its full penalty for every transgression which they have committed. The word ἐπίγνωσις is stronger than the simple word γνῶσις; and in this way the apostle means to intimate the clear knowledge of sin which the law communicates.

CHAP. III. 21—31.

The apostle having shown that both Jews and Gentiles are all under sin, and therefore are obnoxious to the penalty of the divine law, he now proceeds to show more definitely that *gratuitous* pardon or justification is the only way of salvation now open for men. This way of salvation is disclosed in the Old Testament Scriptures, verse 21; even that justification which is proposed to all men without distinction, and conferred on all who believe in Christ, verse 22. No difference can be made, as to the need of such a justification, between the Jew and Gentile, inasmuch as all without exception are sinners, and therefore stand in the same need of gratuitous pardon, verse 24. Christ is set forth to all men as a propitiatory offering or sacrifice, the efficacy of which may be experienced by faith in his blood, and thus God manifests to the world the provision which he has made for the forgiveness of all sin, and discloses a way in which his holy regard to justice may be preserved, and yet his pardoning mercy bestowed on the penitent believer in Jesus, verses 25, 26. All boasting then on the ground of our own merits, is entirely excluded, because justification by faith, from its own nature, must be wholly gratuitous, verse 27. The conclusion is forced upon us from all this, that we are *gratuitously* justified, and not on the ground of merit, verse 28. All are justified on the same ground, because God stands in the same relation to both Jews and Gentiles, verse 29, both the circumcised and the uncircumcised are justified by faith, verse 30. The Old Testament Scriptures also (as was before said, verse 21) teach the very same doctrine, verse 31.

(21) *But now, the justification without law which is of God, is revealed*, νυνὶ δὲ .... πεφανέρωται. Νυνί, *now, i. e.*, under the gospel dispensation, in distinction from ancient times, or former days.* Δέ " particula *discretiva*, opposita conjungens." — Χωρὶς νόμου, *without law, i. e.*, without the aid or concurrence of law, or in such a way as not to be by means of law, or in a way different from or contrary to that of *legal* justification which rests solely on the ground of *perfect* and *meritorious* obedience. Χωρὶς νόμου, may be interpreted as qualifying δικαιοσύνη Θεοῦ, or it may possibly be joined in sense with πεφανέρωται. The meaning in either case may perhaps be substantially the same. But both its position in the sentence, and its more appropriate meaning when thus construed, favor its connection with δικαιοσύνη Θεοῦ. Δικαιοσύνη Θεοῦ see on i. 17. — Πεφανέρωται, *is disclosed, manifested, revealed*, viz., in or by the gospel.

Which is testified, i. e., plainly and openly declared, *by the law and the prophets*, μαρτυρουμένη .... προφητῶν, *i. e.*, by the Old Testament Scriptures; compare Matt. v. 17. vii. 12. xi. 13. xxii. 40. Luke xvi. 16. John i. 45. 4 Macc. xviii. 10. The apostle would affirm that he teaches no new thing; he only repeats what in substance has been declared in the Old Test. respecting *gratuitous* justification. And when he says νυνὶ ..

---
* It cannot be doubted that this gives a true idea, but it may be questioned whether νυνί strictly refers to time, whether it is not simply *deductive, as things are, now*.

πεφανέρωται, *is* NOW *revealed,* in the preceding part of the verse, he means that this shall be *emphatically* (not absolutely) understood; otherwise the same verse would contain a contradiction of itself. He designs to say, that gratuitous justification is more fully and amply revealed by the gospel. What is merely hinted in the declaration before us, Paul goes on fully to develop in chapter iv.

(22) What that *righteousness of God,* δικαιοσύνη Θεοῦ, is, which is *without the law,* χωρὶς νόμου, the apostle next proceeds explicitly to develop. *The justification then which is of God by faith in Jesus Christ,* δικαιοσύνη δέ . . . . 'Ἰησοῦ Χριστοῦ. This explanation makes it clear as the noon-day sun, that δικαιοσύνη Θεοῦ, in this connection, does not mean, righteousness or the love of justice, as an *attribute* of God. For in what possible sense can it be said that God's righteousness or justice (as an essential *attribute*) is by faith in Christ? Does he possess or exercise this attribute, or reveal it, by faith in Christ? The δέ does not stand here as *adversative* to χωρὶς νόμου, but seems plainly to introduce a clause which is a *resumption* of the preceding δικαιοσύνη Θεοῦ for the sake of further explanation. The Attics often employed δέ as a sign of *resumption.* In such a case, it is equivalent to our, *and so, therefore, then.* The shade of thought appears to be this: 'As it is a justification χωρὶς νόμου, *then* or *therefore* (δέ) it is a justification by faith;' or the sense will be good if we construe thus: 'a justification χωρὶς νόμου, *namely* (δέ) a justification by faith.' But this latter usage of δέ without any *adversative* sense in any respect, seems hardly admissible.

By Christian faith, διὰ πίστεως Ἰησοῦ Χριστοῦ, *i. e.,* by that faith of which Jesus Christ is the object, Ἰησοῦ Χριστοῦ being *Genitivus objecti;* for most clearly it is not faith which belongs to Christ himself, but the faith of sinners towards him. The meaning of the apostle is, that the gratuitous justification which the gospel reveals, is that which is to be had by believing and trusting in Christ as our Redeemer and Deliverer; compare vers. 23 — 26. Faith, indeed, is not to be regarded as the meritorious cause or ground of justification (which is wholly *gratuitous,* ver. 24), but only as the means or instrument by which we come into such a state or relation, that justification can, consistently with the nature and character of God, be gratuitously bestowed upon us.

To all and upon all, εἰς πάντας καὶ ἐπὶ πάντας. Luther understands ἐρχομένη before εἰς πάντας, i. e., [δικαιοσύνη Θεοῦ ἐρχομένη] εἰς πάντας. The sense is good; but can we not better construe εἰς πάντας as connected with πεφανέρωται? Φανερόω usually takes the simple Dative after it in such cases; but the New Testament writers often use the Accusative with εἰς instead of the simple Dative, or the Dative with ἐν; see Bretschn. Lex. εἰς 5. b.

Ἐπὶ πάντας appears to mark the subjects, who receive the δικαιοσύνη in question; which is clear from the τοὺς πιστεύοντας that follows and qualifies it. I am aware, indeed, that many commentators suppose that πιστεύοντας belongs equally to both cases of πάντας. But may we not suppose, that εἰς πάντας denotes to whom the proclamation of δικαιοσύνη, *gratuitous pardon*, is made, *i. e.*, that it is made to all men? Καὶ ἐπὶ πάντας τοὺς πιστεύοντας I should then consider as a kind of parenthesis thrown in to guard against the idea that the actual bestowment of justification is as universal as the offers of it. The offer is made to all men without exception; *believers* only, however, are entitled to the actual reception of it. My reason for supposing such a parenthesis here, is that the writer immediately resumes the generic or universal idea, οὐ γάρ ἐστι κ. τ. λ., which shows that his mind is intent on the illustration of εἰς πάντας, as his principal proposition. Besides this, the clause ἐπὶ πάντας τοὺς πιστεύοντας is omitted in A., B., C., Copt., Æth., Arm., Clem., Origen; which shows at least that it was not deemed essential to the *principal* sentiment. As the main object is to show, that there is no exception at all as to the need of that justification which the gospel proposes, Paul only suggests, here and there by the way, the extent in which the justification proposed is actually bestowed — ἐπὶ πάντας τοὺς πιστεύοντας . . . . καὶ δικαιοῦντα τὸν ἐκ πίστεως Ἰησοῦ (ver. 26).

It is by overlooking these nicer shades and connections of thought in this paragraph, that many critics have come to the conclusion, that no difference exists here between εἰς πάντας and ἐπὶ πάντας.* Before ἐπὶ πάντας either ἐστί or rather ἡ δικαιοσύνη ἐστί seem to be implied; and then ἐπί is used in the sense of *ad commodum, for;* comp. Heb. viii. 8. xii. 10; see also Bretschn. Lex. ἐπὶ, III. 5.

For there is no distinction or *difference*, οὐ γάρ ἐστι διαστολή, *i. e.*, in regard to the matter of justification by faith or gratuitous justification; there is no distinction whatever between Greek and Jew; for as all have sinned, so justification by *deeds of law*, *i. e.*, by perfect obedience to the law, is an impossible thing, inasmuch as it is impossible that a sinner should lay in any proper claim to such a justification. The γάρ here is γάρ *illustrantis* vel

---

* The repetition of prepositions before a word with a shade of difference in meaning for the sake of intensity or distinctness, as here *for* all, i e "for the benefit of all," and *upon* all, i e. "so as to be shed down on all," is common in Paul's writings; see Winer, N. Test. Idioms, § 54, 6, and Alford and Meyer's Commentaries.

confirmantis, the sequel being designed to illustrate and confirm the affirmation made above, viz., that the justification which is of God without law, *i. e.*, *gratuitous* justification, is revealed εἰς πάντας.

(23) *For all have sinned, and come short of divine approbation,* or *of the glory which God bestows,* πάντες γάρ . . . . Θεοῦ. The γάρ here is again γάρ *illustrantis* vel *confirmantis*, *i. e.*, it introduces the reason why there is no *difference*, διαστολή. Ὑστερέω comes from ὕστερος, *last*, and sometimes means (as its etymology would indicate) *to be last* or *inferior*, 1 Cor. xii. 24. viii. 8. 2 Cor. xi. 5. xii. 11. The passive voice is used in the same sense (for substance) as the active; ὑστερέω meaning *deficio*, *destituo*, and ὑστερέομαι, *destituor*, *I am wanting in*, *I am deficient in*. The idea in our text is that of *failing*, *being deprived* or *destitute of*, and the verb governs the Gen. by the usual principles of syntax.

The divine approbation, δόξης τοῦ Θεοῦ. So indeed most commentators translate it; and with good philological support, inasmuch as δόξα often and even commonly means *praise, approbation*, in the classics, and has a like sense in the N. Test., *e. g.*, John v. 41, 44. vii. 18. viii. 50, 54. xii. 43. Nevertheless, as δόξα very often means, by N. Test. usage, *a glorified state, a glorious condition, supreme happiness*, it may be so taken here, and Θεοῦ may be construed as *Genitivus auctoris*, so that δόξης τοῦ Θεοῦ would mean, *the glory which God bestows*, or of which God is the author. So Semler, Morus, Bohme, Chrysostom, Beza, Hammond, Bengel, Glockler, and others. But still as the subject is here that of *justification*, viz., acquittal, δόξης may appositely be employed in the *classical* sense of *opinion* (here *good opinion, approbation*), *i. e.*, the approbation of the final judge of men, when they stand before his tribunal. The idea would then be, that inasmuch as all men have broken the law of God, they cannot expect his approbation in the day of trial, upon the ground of their own merits. Hence the necessity of some other method of justification different from that which is *by works of law*.

(24) *Being justified freely by his grace through the redemption which is by Christ Jesus,* δικαιούμενοι . . . . Ἰησοῦ. The apostle has previously declared that all have sinned, and thus rendered a sentence of acquittal and reward impossible on the ground of *law*. He now asserts the counterpart of this, viz., that all who obtain justification must obtain it *gratuitously* and only by virtue of the redemption that Christ has accomplished; a proposition which contains the very essence of all that is peculiar to the gospel of Christ, or that can make a solid foundation on which the hopes of perishing sinners may rest.

The ellipsis before and after δικαιούμενοι may be filled out thus: [πάντες] δικαιούμενοί [εἰσι]; for δικαιούμενοι here evidently stands in the room of a verb. In fact, verses 23, 24, are really two different sentences; while the present grammatical construction of them makes but one. — Δωρεάν, *gratuitously, in the way of mere favor*. Δωρεάν (Heb. חִנָּם) comes from δωρεά, *donum gratuitum, beneficium;* and this, with δῶρον, *munus*, δώρημα, *beneficium*, and δωρέομαι, *dono*, all originate from δίδωμαι or διδόω, *to give*. By his grace, τῇ αὐτοῦ χάριτι, epexegetical of δωρεάν, and added to give intensity to the whole sentence or affirmation; comp. Eph. ii. 8, 9. 2 Tim. i. 9. Tit. iii. 4, 5. *Redemption*, ἀπολυτρώσεως. The force of this word may be best seen by recurring to its root λύτρον, which means, 'the price of ransom paid for a slave or a captive, in consequence of which he is set free.' Λυτρόω and ἀπολυτρόω both mean, *to pay the price of ransom;* ἀπολυτρόω is somewhat *intensive*, and = *pay off*. Accordingly λύτρωσις and ἀπολύτρωσις mean, (1) *The act of paying this price;* and (2) The consequences of this act, viz. *the redemption* which follows it. In this way the idea of ἀπολύτρωσις comes at times to be merely generic, *i. e., liberation, deliverance.*. — Τῆς ἐν Χριστῷ Ἰησοῦ designates the author of our redemption, viz., him who paid the ransom and procured our freedom, when we were the slaves and captives of sin and Satan, and exposed to the wrath of God, i. 18. The sequel defines more exactly what the writer understands by ἀπολυτρώσεως in this place.

(25) The most important word in the translation of the first clause of this verse, is ἱλαστήριον. In classic Greek it is equivalent to the adjective ἱλάσιμος, *propitiatory, atoning;* which comes directly from ἱλασμός, *atonement, propitiation;* which with ἱλαστικός, ἱλαστήριος, and ἵλασμα comes from ἱλάσκομαι or ἱλάομαι (ἱλέομαι Att.), always employed by Homer to designate *the making of propitiation* or *atonement* to the gods. The later Greeks sometimes used ἱλάσκομαι in the sense of *being propitious*.

In our text ἱλαστήριον is best considered as a noun, although it may be an adjective used in an elliptical way, like other adjectives of a similar nature; *e. g.*, χαριστήριον, σωτήριον, τὰ ἐτήσια τὰ γενέθλια, etc., with θῦμα, *offering or sacrifice* to be supplied.

The Seventy employ ἱλαστήριον, sometimes joining it with ἐπίθεμα, Ex. xxv. 17; but usually omitting ἐπίθεμα and using ἱλαστήριον alone, in the same sense which both words would give; *e. g.*, Ex. xxv. 18, 19, 20 bis, 22. xxxvii. (Sept. xxxviii.) 6, 7, 8, 8 bis. Lev. xvi. 2, 13, 14, 15, etc. In all these cases whether ἱλαστήριον has ἐπίθεμα expressed or not, the Hebrew word is כַּפֹּרֶת, *covering*, viz. the covering of the ark of the covenant in the most holy place, which was overlaid with pure gold (Ex. xxv. 17), over which the cherubim stretched out their wings (Ex.

xxv. 20), and which was the throne of Jehovah in his earthly temple, the place from which he uttered his oracles, and communed with the representatives of his people, Ex. xxv. 22; comp. Ex. xxxvii. 6 — 9. Into the inner sanctuary where the ark was, the high-priest entered but once in a year (Heb. ix. 7), when he sprinkled the כַּפֹּרֶת ἱλαστήριον [ἐπίθεμα] with blood, in order to make propitiation for the sins of the people, Lev. xvi. 2, 15, 16. In like manner with the Seventy, Philo calls the כַּפֹּרֶת, πῶμα ἱλαστήριον and ἐπίθεμα ἱλαστήριον, i. e., a *propitiatory covering;* Vita Mosis, III. 668. (Frankf. ed.) Also in de Prof. p. 465. But Paul was not necessarily limited to that, inasmuch as the common Greek idiom afforded him another combination of ἱλαστήριον, viz. ἱλαστήριον θῦμα, *propitiatory sacrifice* or *offering.* So Dio Chrysostom, Orat. II. 184, ἱλαστήριον Ἀχαιοὶ τῇ Ἀθηνᾷ. So Josephus, ἱλαστήριον μνῆμα, *a propitiatory monument,* Antiq. XVI. 7. 1. So in 4 Macc. xvii. 22, ἱλαστηρίου θανάτου αὐτοῦ. Symmachus in Gen. vi. 14, ἱλάσεις ἱλαστήριον. Some, as Origen, Erasmus, and Luther, have interpreted the word here in accordance with the usage in the LXX., but Hesychius, Grotius, Turretin, Tholuck, Alford, Meyer, and others, in accordance with Greek idiom as above stated. I most fully agree with the latter interpretation, since the phrase ἐν τῷ αἵματι αὐτοῦ, which follows, seems to refer to the αἷμα of the ἱλαστήριον. It may be said, that if Christ be represented as the *mercy-seat* which was sprinkled with propitiatory blood, αἵματι αὐτοῦ may refer to this. But such an image is unnatural, if the analogy of the Jewish mercy-seat be consulted; for then Christ would be represented as a mercy-seat, sprinkled with his *own* blood. But if ἱλαστήριον means a *propitiatory sacrifice,* the usage is altogether congruous; inasmuch as the blood was sprinkled round about upon the altar, where the sacrifice was laid, Lev. i. 5, 11. iii. 8.

The use of προέθετο favors this latter meaning. In the classics, προτίθημι means: (1) *To lay before, to set before, e. g.,* to set anything before one to eat; also to set a mark before one, or a punishment, or a reward; *i. e., to propose.* (2) *Publicly to expose* or *to hold up to view, e. g.,* to expose goods, wares, etc., for inspection and sale; also to *declare* enmity, war, hatred, etc. (3) To *prefer;* which is the least common signification. In the New Testament προτίθημι is sometimes used in the sense of *purposing, decreeing, constituting; e. g.,* Rom. i. 13. Eph. i. 9. So also in Joseph. Antiq. IV. 6, 5. But with this meaning the verb is *intransitive,* and of course is not followed by the Acc. case.

Of these various meanings, the second classical one seems plainly to be that which is best adapted to our text; as it best agrees with the εἰς ἔνδειξιν and πρὸς ἔνδειξιν which follow. Ὅν προέθετο ὁ Θεὸς ἱλαστήριον may then be rendered, *whom God hath openly exhibited to the world as a propitiatory sacrifice.* But suppose now that we construe ἱλαστήριον as meaning *mercy-seat,* there is *incongruity* in the image, as the *mercy-seat* was not exhibited to the view of those for whom atonement was made; the high-priest only saw it once in each year, on the great day of atonement. To avoid this evident incongruity, one must render προέθετο, *constituit;* and then the evident reference made by it to εἰς ἔνδειξιν and πρὸς ἔνδειξιν, is lost or obscured.

By faith, διὰ τῆς πίστεως, *i. e.,* this sacrifice then produces its propitiatory effect, when faith is exercised in the blood, *i. e.,* death of the victim which is offered. In other words; Christ makes expiation which is effectual for such only, as trust in his atoning blood, *i. e.,* who believe in him as the "Lamb of God which taketh away the sin of the world." So Glockler and others. Διὰ τῆς πίστεως may also be connected with δικαιούμενοι or with προέθετο; so Reiche and others; but not to so good purpose, nor so naturally, as with ἱλαστήριον.*

By his blood, ἐν τῷ αἵματι αὐτοῦ, *i. e., by his bloody death;* the expression and image being borrowed from the expiatory blood of the ancient sacrifices. Faith in his blood or in the death of Jesus, as the means of expiation, seems to be the distinguishing trait above all others of true Christianity. The phrase ἐν τῷ αἵματι αὐτοῦ may also be connected with δικαιούμενοι; (so Reiche, Winzer, Fritsche, and others); or it may be connected with ἱλαστήριον, and still the same sentiment for substance be retained. (So Chrysostom, Theodoret, Vitringa, Calov, and others.)

In order to declare, etc., εἰς ἔνδειξιν . . . . πρὸς ἔνδειξιν. Εἰς before ἔνδειξιν is equivalent to πρός in verse 26, and πρὸς ἔνδειξιν is co-ordinate with εἰς ἔνδειξιν and sustains the same relation to the *first* part of the whole sentence. The prepositions εἰς and πρός stand before the Accusative case, and before the Infinitive mode used as a noun in the Accusative, in order to designate the *intention, object, purpose, design, end,* etc., of any thing; *e. g.,* εἰς ζωήν, *in order to obtain life,* εἰς τὴν ἀνομίαν, *in order to commit iniquity,* εἰς ὅ, *for which purpose,* εἰς τοῦτο, *for this purpose,* εἰς τὸ ἐμπαῖξαι, *in order to mock.* So in Matt. xx. 19, εἰς τὸ σταυρωθῆναι, *in order to be crucified,* and so in numberless instances; see Bretsch. Lex. εἰς 3. The same thing is true of πρός; *e. g.,* πρὸς τὸ θεαθῆναι, *in order to be seen,* Matt. vi. 1;

---

* It seems best here to consider the clauses διὰ τῆς πίστεως and ἐν τῷ αἵματι, as distinct and disconnected clauses, the former indicating "the subjective means of the appropriation of the propitiatory sacrifice; and the latter, the objective means of the propitiation made by Christ." See De Wette, Meyer, and Alford.

πρὸς παραχειμάσαι, *for the sake of passing the winter*, Acts xxvii. 12; πρὸς τὸ ἐπιθυμῆσαι, *in order to lust*, Matt., v. 28; πρὸς οἰκοδομήν, *for the sake of edification*, Rom. xv. 2; πρὸς ἐντροπήν, *for the sake of shaming you*, 1 Cor. vi. 5, et al. sæpe; see Bretschn. Lex. πρός, III. *c*. The arrangement of the thought stands thus: ὃν προέθετο ὁ Θεὸς ἱλαστήριον .... εἰς ἔνδειξιν, ὃν προέθετο ὁ Θεὸς ἱλαστήριον .... πρὸς ἔνδειξιν; which arrangement fully exhibits what I mean, by saying that the expressions are *co-ordinate*. And this arrangement seems to be plainly and fully confirmed, by the antithetic comparison of προγεγονότων (*past*) in one clause, and ἐν τῷ νῦν καιρῷ (*present*) in the other.

Of his justification, τῆς δικαιοσύνης αὐτοῦ, *i. e.*, of the justification which he proffers, or of which he is author. Ambrose, Locke, and others, understand δικαιοσύνης as meaning *veracity;* Theodoret, Socinus, Grotius, Bolten, Koppe, and Reiche, explain it as meaning *goodness;* like the Hebrew צְדָקָה. Flatt renders it *sanctitas;* Tholuck says that δικαιοσύνη, in Paul's writings, always means *righteousness* or *holiness;* in which he is most surely mistaken. To my own mind nothing can be plainer, than that δικαιοσύνης has the same sense here as in chap. i. 17, and as in verse 22 above: where it seems too plain to be mistaken. What can be more congruous, than that it should be taken here in a sense which is homogeneous with δικαιωθήσεται in verse 20, and δικαιούμενοι in verse 23?*

What now is the sentiment which is in accordance with this? It is as follows: 'God has openly exhibited Christ to the world as a propitiatory offering for sin, unto all who believe in him, in order that he might fully exhibit his pardoning mercy (his δικαιοσύνη) in respect to the forgiveness of sins under the past and present dispensation.'

Is not this plain and consistent sentiment, congruous with the design of the writer and with the nature of facts? How or why so much difficulty should have been made about the word δικαιοσύνης here, I am not able to explain. One good rule in the explanation of Scripture is, that the same writer, on the same topic, and in the same connection of reasoning and thought, must be construed as using the same phraseology in the same sense. All I ask here is, that a maxim so plain and reasonable should be observed. And where is the "repetitio" alleged by Turretin, in this case? Where has the apostle before said, that God had openly proposed to the world the propitiatory sacrifice of Christ,

---

* If we consider δικαιοσύνη to indicate the *justice* of God, as most modern commentators do, the idea is equally forcible. For God's justice as a judge in overlooking the sins of those in past ages is exhibited in the sacrifice of his Son, to which he had regard in all his dealings with them.

in order to exhibit his pardoning mercy for sins committed under the old and under the new dispensation? And as to the "frigida;" if there be any one sentiment in the whole New Testament, respecting the efficacy of the atoning blood of Jesus with regard to power and extent, which stands at the head of all others, the sentiment here developed holds this very place. It has its express parallel only in Heb. ix. 15.

Through remission by the forbearance of God of sins formerly committed, διὰ τὴν . . . . Θεοῦ. That διά not unfrequently has the meaning *in respect to, in regard to*, may be seen by consulting Matt. xviii. 23, διὰ τοῦτο, *in respect to this*, viz., the sentiment which Jesus had just uttered. So also, with another shade of sense, Matt. xxi. 43. xxiii. 34, διὰ τοῦτο, *for the sake of this, on account of this*; Mark xi. 24. Luke xi. 49. 1 Thess. iii. 7, διά, *on account of.* So Flatt on our verse: διά, *in Rucksicht auf*, i. e., *in respect to.* But still, I do not take διά here as meaning merely *in respect to, in regard to.* A common meaning of it is, *per, propter.* Here I understand it is designating the manner in which δικαιοσύνη has exhibited itself, viz., *by* or *through remission*, etc. So Reiche. But there is another sense still in which it may be here interpreted; viz., *on account of, for the sake of*, remission, etc. This would make it co-ordinate with εἰς ἔνδειξιν κ. τ. λ., and with πρὸς ἔνδειξιν κ. τ. λ.; and it would be rather more consonant with usual Greek idiom as to the meaning of διά. We should then have *three* co-ordinate clauses explanatory of προέθετο κ. τ. λ., instead of two. I should embrace this last interpretation, were it not that εἰς ἔνδειξιν and πρὸς ἔνδειξιν seem rather to favor the reception of only *two* co-ordinate clauses. The variation of the *prepositions*, in this case, would make nothing decisive against such an exegesis. Paul often varies them, where the sense is designed to be substantially the same. On the whole, the clause διὰ τὴν πάρεσιν . . . . Θεοῦ may be best regarded as epexegetical of the preceding δικαιοσύνης αὐτοῦ, viz., his δικαιοσύνη was manifested *on account of, in respect to*, the remission of sins committed in former times, etc.

Πάρεσιν (from παρίημι) means *remission, passing by, dismissing*, etc.; and therefore it has the same sense with ἄφεσιν, as we should expect from the etymology of the word. — Προγεγονότων, *formerly done, committed in times before*. In the sense of *done, taken place*, or *committed*, γίνομαι is often used with respect to *actions*; *e. g.*, Matt. vi. 10. Luke x. 13. xxiii. 24. ix. 7. xiii. 17, et alibi.

(26) *During the forbearance of God*, ἐν τῇ ἀνοχῇ. The uniting of this clause with verse 26, seems to be a mistake in Robert Stephens; for it is better connected with the preceding verse,

and has reference either to πάρεσιν or προγεγονότων ἁμαρτημάτων. But to which of these? Does the writer mean to say, *remission . . . . through the forbearance of God*, to punish sin; or *sins formerly committed, while God forbore to punish*? The latter sense might be made out; for ἐν often has the sense of *during, dum est; e. g.*, Matt. xii. 2, ἐν σαββάτῳ, during the Sabbath, Matt. xiii. 4, ἐν τῷ σπείρειν, *during the action of sowing;* John ii. 23, ἐν τῇ ἑορτῇ, *during the feast;* John vii. 11. Acts viii. 33. xvii. 31. Rev. i. 10. But the former sense is preferable, and gives the idea of *remission* as introduced by, or connected with *forbearance to punish*. Both together make the idea of *justification* an intensive one. As to the general sentiment of the clause, it has in some respects a parallel, in Acts xvii. 30. "As to the times of this ignorance, ὑπεριδὼν ὁ Θεός," *i. e.*, God forbore punishment. But in our text the apostle speaks of the actual *remission* of sin which is connected with justification, *i. e.*, the pardon of sin.

For the meaning of πρὸς ἔνδειξιν τῆς δικαιοσύνης αὐτοῦ, see explanation of εἰς ἔνδειξιν τῆς δικαιοσύνης αὐτοῦ in verse 25. *At the present time*, ἐν τῷ νῦν καιρῷ, *i. e.*, under the new dispensation. Thus has the apostle shown, that the propitiatory sacrifice of Christ extends, with respect to its efficacy, to all ages of the world, to all generations and nations, where such a faith as God requires is exhibited. See the parallel sentiment in Heb. ix. 15. It is implied also in other passages of the New Testament, not unfrequently; but it is no where else so explicitly asserted. The sentiment shows, moreover, in what light the apostle viewed the death of Christ. If this were to be regarded only as the death of a martyr to the truth, or as an example of constancy, etc., then how could its efficacy take hold on προγεγονότων ἁμαρτημάτων, whatever it might do as to those who lived *after* his death took place? This question seems to suggest the necessity of ascribing a *vicarious* influence to the death of Jesus; for how else can it avail for the forgiveness of sins committed in early ages?

Reiche, Barnes, and some others, reject the idea that προγεγονότων refers to *past ages*, and think that the text requires no more than to understand it as designating the *past sins* of each individual living under the gospel. But what inducement the apostle could have to put in προγεγονότων on such a ground, or how προγεγονότων ἁμαρτιῶν could differ from the simple ἁμαρτιῶν, as individually applied, I do not see. Less still do I feel the force of his remark, that it would be difficult, on the ground of the exegesis which I adopt, to avoid the conclusion that all men will be saved; for the apostle has fully avoided any conclusion of this nature, as to the time *before* or *since* the gospel was published, by stating that salvation is ἐπὶ πάντας τοὺς πιστεύοντας. Besides, ἐν τῷ νῦν καιρῷ is evidently emphatic and antithetic; and the antithesis can be found only in προγεγονότων ἁμαρτιῶν. The question is, 'whether Christ is the only Saviour of the race of man;' and this naturally extends to *past* ages, as well as present. Such a view exceedingly ennobles the whole subject, and is altogether consonant with the epistle to the Hebrews. Comp. Rom. v.

That he might be [shown to be] *just, and yet the justifier of him that believeth in Jesus,* εἰς τὸ εἶναι .... Ἰησοῦ, *i. e.*, has the faith of a Christian. Here again is a great diversity of sentiment concerning δίκαιον. Some make δίκαιον to signify *kind, benignant,* for which they appeal to Matt. i. 19. John xvii. 25. 1 John i. 9, and the frequent signification of the Hebrew צָדִיק and צְדָקָה. But although the word is capable of this sense, the connection does not seem to admit it here, as it would make tautology. The difficulty seems to be, that commentators have overlooked the logical connection of the whole clause. The εἰς τό at the beginning of it, shows that it has a like object with εἰς ἔνδειξιν, and πρὸς ἔνδειξιν, with, however, this difference, that in εἰς τὸ εἶναι δίκαιον κ. τ. λ, the writer looks back to the whole sentiment proposed in verses 21—24; which is, that all men are sinners, that a regard merely to law, *i. e.*, justice merely on the part of God (he being δίκαιος merely) does not in itself permit justification by overlooking or setting aside the penalty against sin, and that the death of Christ is an expedient of infinite wisdom, by which the full claims of the law may be admitted, and yet the penalty avoided, because a moral compensation or equivalent has been provided by the sufferings of him who died in the sinner's stead. Here then are two things conspicuous, in this wonderful arrangement of wisdom and benevolence; *the first*, that God will not give up the penalty of his law without an adequate substitute for it, for he is δίκαιος, *i. e.*, he retains a high and immutable regard to justice or rectitude, he is unwilling to sacrifice any part of the purity and strictness of his law, which is 'holy, and just, and good;' *the second*, that God has still provided a way by which he may retain all his regard to justice, and his law remain without being in any measure dishonored or sacrificed, and yet the penitent sinner may be pardoned and treated as though he had yielded perfect obedience to it. These I take to be the sentiments conveyed by δίκαιον and δικαιόντα in this passage. Bengel has happily expressed it; "Summum hic paradoxon evangelicum; nam in lege conspicitur Deus et condemnans, in evangelio justus ipse et justificans, peccatores." As I can find no case in which δίκαιος appears to mean either *justified* or *justifying*, I must retain the sense of *just* in this place.

The believer in Jesus, τὸν ἐκ πίστεως Ἰησοῦ is like οἱ ἐκ περιτομῆς, οἱ ἐξ ἐρεθείας, literally, *him who is of the faith, who believes in Jesus*, i. e., the true Christian believer. Ἰησοῦ is the Gen. of the *object*.

(27) *Where then is boasting or glorying?* ποῦ οὖν ἡ καύχησις; That is, if what I have said be true, viz., that all men, both Jews and Gentiles, are sinners, and can be justified only by grace through the redemption that is in Christ Jesus; then it follows, that all boasting of their own merits, all occasion of glorying in their special privileges is entirely excluded. This has a special reference to the Jews, who were so prone to boast of these things.

By what law or economy? διά ποιοῦ νόμου; Νόμου appears to be used here in the sense of *religious economy* or *dispensation*, i. e., that which ordered or regulated the lives of men, and prescribed the reward of actions either good or bad. Τῶν ἔργων; i. e., is it excluded, διά νόμου τῶν ἔργων; Is it excluded by that economy or rule of life, which places justification on the ground of perfect obedience to the law, i. e., of entirely performing all those *works* which the law demands?

Nay, but by the economy or *rule of faith*, οὐχὶ . . . . πίστεως. That is, faith being the condition of justification under the gospel arrangement or νόμος, this excludes all claims of desert on the part of the sinner. The very statement of itself shows, that although faith is a *conditio sine quâ non* of justification, yet it is *not* the *meritorious* or *procuring* cause of it. Νόμου πίστεως means *that arrangement which makes faith necessary to salvation*, but which, at the same time, bestows salvation merely as a gratuity.

(28) *We conclude, therefore, that a man is justified by faith, without the deeds of the law*, Λογιζόμεθα . . . . νόμου, i. e., we reckon or count it as certain, that men are justified in a *gratuitous* manner through faith in Christ, and not by perfect obedience to the law or by perfectly doing those things which the law requires. See remarks on chapter iv. 5. For γάρ here, some Codices, etc., have οὖν; which gives a better sense, inasmuch as the conclusion here is a *logical* inference and not a mere *casual* suggestion But as the weight of authority is on the side of γάρ, I have followed this in the regular version.

Luther translates πίστει, ALLEIN durch den Glauben, i. e., by faith *only*, thus adding *only* to the text. And such were his views on this subject, that he rejected the epistle of James from the canon of the New Testament, because he thought that the second chapter of this epistle taught a doctrine different from that which Paul here inculcates. See Excursus II. for a brief view of this subject.

(29) *Is he the God of the Jews only? Is he not also of the Gentiles?* ἢ Ἰουδαίων .... ἐθνῶν; That is, why should it not be acknowledged, that "the God of the spirits of all flesh," who "has made of one blood all the nations that dwell upon the face of the earth," and who of old was named עֶלְיוֹן קֹנֵה שָׁמַיִם וָאָרֶץ — sustains the same relation to the *Gentiles* as to the Jews, and will admit them to the like privileges? The ἤ here is interrogative, and implies that the person who is addressed will agree in the answer with the person who puts the question; so nicely are the Greek interrogative signs adjusted.

(30) *He should, he must be so regarded.* Ναὶ, καὶ [Θεὸς] ἐθνῶν. To confirm this he adds: *Since it is one and the same God, who will justify the circumcised by faith, and the uncircumcised by faith,* ἐπείπερ .... πίστεως. Εἷς, *one and the same;* so Luke, xii. 52. 1 Cor. x. 17. xi. 5, et al. — Ἐκ πίστεως and διὰ τῆς πίστεως are of the same import; for both ἐκ and διά are placed before the Genitive denoting the *instrumental* cause, in almost numberless examples. — Περιτομήν and ἀκροβυστίαν are examples of the *abstract* put for the *concrete* = Jews and Gentiles.

(31) *Do we then make void the law through faith?* νόμον οὖν .... πίστεως; That is, do we counteract or annul the Old Test. Scriptures, by inculcating *gratuitous* justification? So I feel obliged to construe νόμον here, when I compare this verse with verses 20, 21, and with chap. iv. where the object of the writer throughout is, to show that the Old Testament inculcates the same doctrine as that which he here urges. So Flatt, Koppe, Chrysostom, and others. This exegesis is quite plain from the fact that the apostle immediately proceeds to answer the objection here made, by showing that the Old Testament actually teaches the doctrine in question.

We confirm the law, νόμον ἱστῶμεν; *i. e.,* we inculcate that which entirely accords with the Old Testament, and serves to confirm it. Ἱστῶμεν is the unusual *contract-form*, from ἱστάω instead of ἵστημι.

How *gratuitous justification* can be said to confirm or establish the *moral* law (as this text has been often explained), it seems difficult to make out. It would seem to be the *atonement* which goes to establish the claims of the moral law; how can *remission of the penalty* of itself establish such a law? That the doctrine of justification by faith does not, indeed, overthrow moral obligation; yea, that such a justification even serves in a most important way to promote holiness of life; the apostle shows in chap. vi. But his present concern is with the objection made to his sentiments, viz., the objection that he is weakening the force of the ancient Jewish Scriptures. Accordingly, he discusses the question at large in the following chapter.

CHAP. IV. 1—12.

The writer now proceeds to show, that the Scriptures of the Old Testament do in fact confirm the view which he had given of *gratuitous* justification. Even Abraham, notwithstanding his peculiar covenant relation to God, had no cause of glorying before him, verses 1, 2 ; for the Scripture asserts, that *Abraham's faith was imputed to him for righteousness*, and consequently that he was gratuitously justified, verses 3, 4. So also David speaks of the subject of justification, representing it as *gratuitous* forgiveness, not as acceptance *pro meritis*, verses 6—8. Neither can such forgiveness belong only to those who are circumcised, *i. e.*, to Abraham and his natural posterity, for Abraham himself was justified *antecedently* to his circumcision ; and he received this rite merely as a token of confirmation in respect to the blessing already bestowed, and in order that he might be a spiritual father *i. e*, an eminent pattern or exemplar of spiritual blessings, both to Gentiles and Jews, verses 9—12

Verses 1—12 might be divided into three distinct parts, viz , (1) Verses 1—5, the justification of Abraham was *gratuitous* (2) Verses 6—8, David discloses the same views as to the method of acceptance with God. (3) Verses 9—12, circumcision was not, and could not be any ground at all of the justification of Abraham. I have, however, chosen to connect these under one general head because I view the third particular as the answer to the question in verse 1, and the first and second particulars as being preparatory to this, and also as having respect to the main design of the writer, which is, to show that the Old Testament Scriptures do in fact exhibit the same views of justification which he has given in the preceding context.

(1) *What then shall we say that Abraham our father obtained in respect to the flesh?* τί οὖν .... κατὰ σάρκα; This question is parallel with those in chap. iii. 1. The apostle evidently suggests it as one which an opponent to his views would naturally ask. The import of it is: 'How then will your doctrine concerning justification as entirely gratuitous, agree with the views which the Scripture leads us to take of Abraham? Had he no advantage from his precedence and privileges? Was the covenant and rite of circumcision, by which he was distinguished from all the rest of the world, of no avail in his case?' Such is evidently the tenor of the discourse, whether we suppose the apostle to put such interrogations in his own person, or in that of his opponent.

Then, οὖν, *i. e.*, on the ground which you take, what can we say, etc.? The use of οὖν in questions where objections are raised, is very common among the Greeks. *Our father*, τὸν πατέρα ἡμῶν, shows that the objector here is supposed to be a Jew.

— Εὑρηκέναι, *obtained;* comp. Luke i. 30. Heb. ix. 12, — Κατὰ σάρκα is a controverted phrase here. Should it be united in sense with τὸν πατέρα ἡμῶν? Or must we join it with εὑρηκέναι? If the question here concerned the relation of Abraham respectively as a *spiritual* father and as a *natural* one, we should feel in a measure necessitated to join κατὰ σάρκα with τὸν πατέρα ἡμῶν. Chrysostom, Erasmus, Limborch, and others, do thus join it; and some manuscripts, in accordance with such views, placed εὑρηκέναι *before* τὸν πατέρα ἡμῶν. But as the weight of authority is against these; as the *hyperbaton* or transposition, taking the text as it now stands, would be abrupt and improbable if we should join κατὰ σάρκα with τὸν πατέρα ἡμῶν; and especially as κατὰ σάρκα would not then add anything to the idea designated by τὸν πατέρα ἡμῶν; so it would seem to be more eligible, to regard κατὰ σάρκα as qualifying εὑρηκέναι. One meaning which has been given here to σάρξ, is *external privileges* or *advantages;* and the appeal is made to 1 Cor. x. 18. Phil. iii. 3. Gal. vi. 12, in order to confirm this; but these texts all plainly relate to circumcision. Σάρξ sometimes means *that which is external* or *physical,* in distinction from that which is internal or spiritual; *e. g.,* Gal. iv. 23. Rom. ix. 8. In accordance with this general idea, and with probability on their side, Wetstein, Venema, Michaelis, Koppe, Bretschneider (Lex.), and others, understand by κατὰ σάρκα in our text, *circumcision;* σάρξ being frequently used to designate the physical member which was circumcised, or fleshly circumcision, *e. g.,* Phil. iii. 3. Gal. vi. 12. 1 Cor. x. 18. Eph. ii. 11. Col. ii. 13; comp. Gen. xvii. 11, 14, 24, 25. Tholuck makes the objection to this exegesis, that the apostle does not undertake, in the sequel, to show that *circumcision* was not the ground of Abraham's justification, but that *works* were not. He also suggests, that the second verse seems to construe κατὰ σάρκα as being equivalent in sense to ἐξ ἔργων, Calvin renders κατὰ σάρκα, *naturaliter;* and Grotius, *propriis viribus;* to support which appeal has been made to Matt. xvi. 17. Gal. i. 16; but there the phrase is, *flesh and blood.* But if we consider κατὰ σάρκα as the opposite of κατὰ πνεῦμα, and regard πνεῦμα as designing the *gracious spiritual influences* vouchsafed to believers under the gospel, the meaning of κατὰ σάρκα would then be: 'In respect to efforts by one's own natural powers, or efforts made in one's own strength.' This is the interpretation which for substance Tholuck defends.* If

---

* The use of ἔργων in the plural in verse 2, favors this more general meaning of σάρξ. Hence Olshausen says · "We may best understand σάρξ of the outward in general (Gal. 3: 3) as contrasted with πνεῦμα, the inward and life giving." Alford: it ' refers to that department of our being from which spring works, in contrast with that in which is the exercise of faith;" see chap. 8. 4, 5 — See also Meyer and De Wette.

however κατὰ σάρκα is to be taken as qualifying εὑρηκέναι (and so the present text compels us to take it), I must prefer the predominant sense of it in the epistles of Paul, viz., *in respect to circumcision;* comp. iii. 1. where the very same question is put in a more literal way. The meaning of the question would then be: What good or advantage has Abraham our father obtained, in respect to the distinguishing rite which separated him from all the world and consecrated him to God? The apostle in answer to the like question in chap. iii. 1. shows that the Jewish nation were all under sin and under condemnation, and that they can therefore lay no claim to justification on the ground of external privileges. The objector, however, not satisfied with this general answer, wishes now to know in particular whether we can justly hold that no pre-eminence was given to Abraham on account of the covenant and the rite of circumcision. The apostle in his answer *tacitly* admits, that Abraham enjoyed some advantage on account of his external privileges. He admits the same thing *expressly* of the whole Jewish nation, iii. 2. But as to the great subject in question, viz., *gratuitous justification,* Paul avers at once that Abraham was not justified at all on the ground of his external advantages, or of any merit; for then he would have had matter of boasting. But this he has not before God; whatever may be the praise which his privileges or his conduct in general may deserve from men.

The apostle as we shall see makes good use of the case of Abraham, in the sequel, v. 10, seq., in refuting the assumption of the objector.

(2) *For if Abraham was justified by works, he has ground of boasting,* εἰ γὰρ . . . . καύχημα. This is the real response of the apostle, which is marked by the nature of the sentiment. Γάρ, as is often the case, refers to something *implied:* οὐ καύχησις. The apostle means to say that Abraham had no καύχησις (comp. iii. 17), *i. e.*, no ground for attributing justification to his own merits; and γάρ introduces the reason why he has no ground of glorying in his own works.

When the apostle says, εἰ, *if,* etc., he makes a supposition which he regards as untenable; for this is indicated by the Ind. Præter (ἐδικαιώθη) joined with εἰ; see New Testament Grammar, § 129. 3. d. We should naturally have expected after this, that the Imperf. εἶχε ἄν (instead of ἔχει) would have been used in the *apodosis* of this conditional sentence. The use of the present instead of this shows a design on the part of the writer to say, not only that Abraham *would have had* ground of glorying, in case of perfect obedience, but that the same would have continued down to the then present time.

But not [*i. e.*, he had no ground of boasting] *before God*, ἀλλ' . . . . Θεόν. Whatever advantage then the Jew might attribute to Abraham, he could not justly attribute that of obtaining justification by his own privileges or merits. So the writer goes on to prove from the Jewish Scriptures. Οὐ πρὸς τὸν Θεόν may be considered either as referring to ἔχει καύχημα or to ἐξ ἔργων ἐδικαιώθη. The sense will be substantially the same. The immediate antecedent, in such a case, has the preference; and therefore I consider it as referring to ἔχει καύχημα.

Many critics, as Beza, Grotius, Semler, Koppe, Tholuck, and Rückert, understand the reasoning of the apostle in this verse thus: 'If Abraham were justified by works, then he would have cause of glorying; he had glory indeed among *men* on this account, but *not* before *God*.' 'Ἀλλά in this case, is understood as *concessive* (in part) and at the same time *adversative*. But the sequel in verses 4, 5, introduced by γάρ *confirmantis*, shows, that the apostle's object is to prove simply, that Abraham had no ground of acceptance *before God* on account of his works or merit, but that he was justified altogether in a *gratuitous* manner. The apostle is not then discussing the question, whether Abraham had any ground of praise or justification from *men*, and the mode of reasoning stated above would be altogether inapposite to the writer's design. Besides, if Abraham were justified by works, according to the supposition made, then he would have the praise of God as well as of men; so that the denial here of such a praise would contradict the nature of the case and other Scriptures; comp. ii. 6, 29. See Reiche's refutation of the above exegesis.

The reasoning of the apostle may be simply stated thus: 'If Abraham had been justified by his own merit, then he would have ground of glorying: but he has no ground of glorying before God; [therefore he was not justified by his merit.'] The conclusion is omitted by the apostle, apparently on the ground that every intelligent reader's mind will supply it. That he supposes such a conclusion is clear from verses 3, 4.

(3) *For what saith the Scripture? And Abraham believed God, and it was counted to him for righteousness;* see Gen. xv. 6, which runs thus: "And he [God] counted it to him [Abraham] as righteousness." Instead of the *active*, the apostle (with the Seventy) employs the *passive* form, but the idea is for substance the same. But what is λογίζεσθαι εἰς δικαιοσύνην?

The word λογίζεσθαι usually means, *to reckon to one what he actually possesses*, or *to impute that to him which actually belongs to him*, *i. e.*, to treat him as actually possessing the thing or quality reckoned to him; *e. g.*, Ps. cvi. 31. (cv. 31) where the good deed of Phinehas in slaying the polluted Israelite and Midianitish woman, 'was counted to him for righteousness' (Num. xxv. 6, seq.); 2 Sam. xix. 19, where Shimei prays David: μὴ λογισάσθω ὁ Κύριός μου ἀνομίαν, *i. e.*, the iniquity which Shimei himself had done. The same in Ps. xxxii. 2 (xxxi. 2), where David pronounces the man blessed, to whom the Lord does not *impute* iniquity (οὐ μή λογίζεται ἀνομίαν). In Lev. vii. 8 (vii. 18) the Sept. has οὐ λογισθήσεται αὐτῷ, viz., the informal and untimely offering which any one makes, *shall not be reckoned to him* as an offering. So in Lev. xvii. 4, if a man kill a victim for sacrifice without bringing it to the door of the tabernacle, " blood," *i. e.*, bloodguiltiness, " *shall be imputed to him*, ἐκεινῷ λογισθήσεται . . . . αἷμα." So also Num. xviii. 27, and Prov. 27: 4. These are all the instances in the Old Test. where the word חשׁב, = λογίζομαι, is employed in designating any action, word, or thing, as imputed or reckoned to a *person;* and in all these, it is uniformly one's *own* doings, words, or actions, and not those of *another*, which are imputed. The verb חשׁב is indeed often employed in other cases; but only in the sense of *thinking, supposing, imagining, devising;* or else as signifying *making account of, regarding*, or *esteeming;* all of which cases have no direct bearing on the present investigation.

In the New Test. the word λογίζομαι is often employed, like the Hebrew חשׁב, in the sense of *thinking, computing, reckoning, esteeming, considering, devising, meditating*, etc.; in which senses it has no direct bearing on our present enquiry. The only cases that are apposite to our purpose, are those in which something is *imputed* or *counted to persons*. These, independently of the instances which relate directly to Abraham's case, are 2 Cor. v. 19, where it is said: " God was in Christ, reconciling the world to himself, not *imputing* (μὴ λογιζόμενος) to them their trespasses, *i. e.*, their *own* sins. In 2 Tim. iv. 16, Paul says of those who forsook him: " μὴ αὐτοῖς λογισθείη, *let it not be imputed to them,*" *i. e.*, let not their offence be reckoned to them. All the other cases in which λογίζομαι is employed in the sense of *reckoning something to an individual*, are of one tenor, and have respect either to Abraham himself, or else to those whose case is compared with his. These may be found in Rom. iv. 3, 4, 5, 6, 8, 9, 10, 11, 22, 23, Gal. iii. 6. James ii. 23. In Rom. v. 13, ἐλλογεῖται is construed by many as meaning *imputed* or *counted*, but I apprehend the true meaning to be *regarded, made account of*. In Philem. ver. 18, the same word again occurs, and there in the sense of *reckon*, or *put to the account of*. But this is a different word from λογίζομαι, which is now before us, and is never employed in respect to the matter of justification. In all the cases of λογίζομαι as applied to Abraham's faith, or to that of others who follow his example, it is only *his* or their *own faith*, which is counted for righteousness; not the faith of others put to their account.

The form of the expression λογίζομαι εἰς, is purely Hebraistic; and nothing except resort to the Hebrew idiom can avail in solving the difficulty of its explanation. The Hebrews had two modes of expression when they said that *one thing was counted or reckoned as another*. (1) The thing counted or reckoned was put in the Accus. after חָשַׁב; and the thing for which or as which it was counted, was put in the Dat. with לְ (= εἰς) before it; *e. g.*, Job xiii. 24, וַתַּחְשְׁבֵנִי לְאוֹיֵב, *and thou dost count me for an enemy*. In like manner, Job xli. 19, 24. xix. 15. xxxiii. 10. 1 Kings x. 21. Lam. iv. 2, where the Pass. retains the Dat. after it. (2) The thing counted was put in the Acc. as in No. 1, while the thing for which it was counted took the particle כְּ before it; *e. g.*, Job xix. 11. וַיַּחְשְׁבֵנִי כְצָרָיו, *and he counts me as his enemy*. So Isa. xl. 15. Num. xviii. 27. Once (Ps. lxxxviii. 5) we have עִם (*with*) instead of כְּ (*as*.)

In accordance with the first mode (the Acc. of the thing and the Dative of the person with לְ) are most of the cases where anything is said to be *reckoned* or imputed to individuals; *e. g.*, Ps. xxxii. 2. (xxxi. 2.) Gen. xv. 6. 2 Sam. xix. 26; and with the Pass. voice retaining the Dat. after it, Lev. vii. 18 (vii. 8.) xvii. 4. Num. xviii. 27. Prov. xxvii. 14. In Ps. cvi. 31, we find לְ both before the *thing* reckoned and the *person* to whom it is reckoned.

The form λογίζομαι εἰς, or λογίζομαι ὡς or ὥσπερ, is employed by the Sept. for חָשַׁב לְ, *e. g.*, εἰς for לְ in Job xli. 24 (23). Lam. iv. 2; ὥσπερ for לְ in Job xli. 19 (18.) xxxiii. 10. In like manner, ὡς is put for כְּ, in Num. xviii. 27. Is. xl. 15. Job xix. 11. (ὥσπερ.) There can be no important difference between the Hebrew, or the corresponding Greek expressions: λογίζομαι εἰς and λογίζομαι ὡς or ὥσπερ. And in our text, whether we say with the apostle: καὶ ἐλογίσθη αὐτῷ εἰς δικαιοσύνην, *and it* [*i. e.*, Abraham's act of believing] *was counted to him for righteousness;* or, in more exact conformity with the shape of the Hebrew; καὶ αὐτὸ ἐλογίσατο αὐτῷ ὡς δικαιοσύνην, i. e., *he* [God] *imputed it* [the act of believing] *to him as righteousness;* the sense is one and the same.

The *gratuity* then of Abraham's justification cannot be made out, as it would seem, merely from the *mode* of expression here employed. This decides no more than that God reckoned Abraham's faith as a *righteousness* or *righteous act*. And so the same thing is said of the act of Phinehas, Ps. cvi. 31. And in general, where one's own act is said to be imputed to him, whether it be a good or bad one, the meaning is not of course that it is *gratuitously* imputed to him, but that it is imputed to him because it belongs to him, and therefore the imputation or reckoning to him accords with the reality.

On this account some commentators have considered Paul here as putting a forced sense upon the words of Gen. xv. 6, which they say, decides nothing more than that God counted to Abraham an act of faith as righteousness, which was indeed such an act, and therefore deserved to be so counted. *Faith* thus seems a DUTY, and therefore to be placed on the same ground with all other duties; and Christ himself calls it the *work of God*, viz., the work which God requires, John vi. 29. How then, they ask, can this prove the gratuitous justification of Abraham? Due consideration of the nature of the case will help, I trust, to remove this difficulty.

There are but two possible methods of acceptance with God, or of justification before him; the one by complete obedience to the law of God, and therefore on the ground of *merit;* the other, by gratuitous pardon vouchsafed to him who has broken the law. The first method of justification Paul mentions, is impossible, under the present circumstances of men and with their present character; and consequently that *gratuitous* justification is the only way of acceptance. Now Abraham either kept all the law, or he did not. It is taken for granted, (as well it might be, after what the apostle had said,) that *he did not*. Justification on the ground of *merit* then, is out of all question. There remains therefore only *gratuitous* justification.

But because justification is *gratuitous*, it does not follow that there is no *condition* on which the gratuity is to be bestowed, no regard to character, state of mind, penitence, confidence in proffered mercy, or anything else. The gospel with all its freeness and largeness of beneficence, promises salvation only to those *who believe*. "He that believeth, shall be saved."

Here then is the general principle, the *conditio sine qua non*, of free and unmerited pardon and acceptance. And the example of Abraham confirms this principle. He *believed*, and righteousness was counted to him. But this could have been done in no other way, than that by belief he was brought within the pale of offered mercy. If a man commits one sin, and thus comes under the curse of the law, all hopes of acceptance or salvation on *law-ground* are utterly at an end. But here Abraham, a sinner, once probably an idolater (Josh. xxiv. 14,) was accepted and treated as righteous, when he exercised an act of faith, which is the necessary condition of gratuitous pardon. Now this could not have taken place, if Abraham had not been *gratuitously* accepted. The gospel condition of gratuitous justification was complied with by him, *i. e.*, he exhibited faith; and so acceptance, such as the gospel promises, was the consequence of this faith, or was connected with it.

We are not to understand the apostle to assert that Abraham's faith, as such, was in the particular instance related in Gen. xv. 1—5, the principal ground or *meritorious* cause of his final and complete justification. This would defeat the express declarations of verses 4, 5. In these he takes it for granted, that Abraham could plead no merit, and make no claim on the score of simple justice; and that *justification by faith* does of necessity imply, (as truly it does and must imply,) that the acceptance in such cases is a matter of mere *gratuity*, and not of merit or desert.

Faith then may be a *duty* and a *work*, and may be necessary to gratuitous justification, and may be required because it is reasonable in itself and necessary in order to prepare the sinner for justification; and yet the man who is already a sinner can put in no claim for acceptance on the ground of *merit*, because he exercises faith. Acceptance in this way must of course be *gratuitous*.

Why then does not the apostle establish his point, when he shows that Abraham was accepted in consequence of *believing*, and not because he had obeyed the whole law? No act of Abraham, after he had once fallen under the curse of the law, could of itself redeem him from that curse. Nothing that he did, or could do, would atone for past sins. And no act that he did would be *perfect*. Acceptance therefore on the ground of merit, was impossible in these circumstances; and any act of his, either faith or any other, if counted at all for righteousness, must be so counted *gratuitously*. But if so, then the very point which Paul is laboring to establish, is confirmed.

It is the *nature of the case* then, and not the diction merely which is employed, that shows what it is which is here proved by the apostle. We might indeed make some appeal to the nature of the language. We might say, that *faith* is not properly *obedience to the law*, as such; certainly, it is not *entire* obedience. Nor was the faith that was exercised by Abraham full and perfect. At least we may argue this from the imperfect condition of any and every sinful man. That it should be *counted for righteousness*, then, would seem to imply, that it was counted for something which in and of itself it was not, *i. e.*, it was not a *perfect* righteousness such as the law demands. To count it then for a righteousness would imply an act of *grace* on the part of

God. Not that the apostle means to say, that God actually, in his own real estimation, judged Abraham's faith to be a different thing from what it was, and a perfect virtue which of itself could claim acceptance with him. It is impossible for a moment to suppose this; because it would be supposing that God puts a wrong estimate upon things. We come therefore of necessity to the conclusion, that *counting for righteousness* means, *to accept and treat as righteous*. More than this we cannot suppose, without at the same time supposing, that God makes in his own mind an estimate of things different from what they really are.

It is highly important that the reader should here call to mind, also, that Paul is not now laboring to show in what relation Christ stands to all that find acceptance, as the meritorious cause or ground of their pardon. He had already shown this, in the preceding chapter. The simple point now before him is, whether justification through this Saviour is *meritorious* or *gratuitous*. Hence he does not say here, that the righteousness of Christ became the righteousness of Abraham by imputation or transfer. It was inapposite to his present purpose to discuss this point. He simply avers, that the *conditio sine qua non* of gratuitous justification was complied with by Abraham, who therefore was justified in a *gratuitous* manner. Whatever other parts of Scripture may teach in relation to the imputed righteousness of Christ, no declaration on that point is to be found here. Abraham's *own faith*, and an individual act of it, viz., his giving credit to the divine promises, is the subject of the apostle's assertions.

In a word; the shape of Paul's argument appears to me as being substantially this, viz., 'justification is *gratuitous;* for righteousness was not counted to Abraham on the ground of perfect obedience, but in consequence of his compliance with the necessary condition of gratuitous justification, *i. e.*, in consequence of his exercising faith. Now if he was accepted and treated as just on such ground, it follows of necessity that he could not have been accepted on the ground of merit, and consequently that his justification was *gratuitous*.' And if the justification of Abraham, the most eminent of all the Hebrew saints, was a mere matter of gratuity, it must certainly be so in case of all others. And thus the object of the apostle is gained by an illustration and confirmation of the principle which he is endeavoring to inculcate.

(4) *To him who worketh,* τῷ ἐργαζομένῳ (Midd. voice), *i. e.*, to him who performs all the ἔργα νόμου, to him who yields entire obedience* to the precepts of law; compare the remarks on ἔργα

---

* This idea should seem rather to be implied than directly expressed *To him who worketh,* i. e. to him who is a laborer *works for hire,* viz. here, to him who doeth the works of the law, depends upon obedience to the law,

νόμου under iii. 20 above. Ἐργαζομένῳ here is equivalent to ὁ ποιῶν τὰ ἔργα; comp. iii. 20, 27, 28. ii. 15; also verse 6. below. Luther translates: *Der mit Werken umgehet;* Beza: *Is qui ex opere est aliquid promeritus.* Tholuck defends Luther's version. To me it seems to convey truth, but not the *whole* truth. Better has Turretin said: *Per eum qui operatur* non intelligimus . . . . eos qui bona opera faciunt, sed eos qui perfectè implērunt legem Dei absque ullo defectu. It has been objected to this interpretation that in this way all rewards would be excluded, inasmuch as no man is perfect. But is it not true that all rewards of *merit* on law-ground, *i. e.*, that of entire perfection, are excluded? It seems to be a very clear doctrine of the New Testament, that the good works which are rewarded, are *gratuitously* rewarded in proportion to their desert of reward. *Imperfect* good works can now be accepted and rewarded, through grace by Christ, which under a law-system could put in no claim for reward or acceptance; a principle that does not seem to be generally understood.

Reward is not rewarded or *counted as a matter of grace,* ὁ μισθὸς . . . . χάριν; *i. e.*, it is his just *due*, as the sequel (ἀλλὰ κατὰ ὀφείλημα) shows: a due in consequence of the promise or engagement of reward which the law contains, and not because the obedience of men can really profit the Divine Being, so as to lay him under obligations on this account.

(5) *But to him who does not yield perfect obedience,* τῷ δὲ μὴ ἐργαζομένῳ; plainly the opposite of the first part of the fourth verse. The meaning is: 'To the sinner who has not exhibited perfect obedience, but πιστεύοντι κ. τ. λ., who believeth on him who justifieth the ungodly,' *i. e.*, on Christ who died for sinners, and on account of whose death they are justified; comp. v. 8 — 10. iv. 25. 1 Pet. iii. 18. Heb. ix. 28, et al.

Some commentators suppose that Paul means to characterize Abraham specifically, by the μὴ ἐργαζομένῳ and τὸν ἀσεβῆ in verse 5. But the propositions in verses 4, 5, are of wider extent than an individual case, and they declare a general truth of which Abraham's case is only a particular example or illustration.

His faith is counted as righteousness, λογίζεται . . . . δικαιοσύνης; *i. e.*, through belief in Christ who died for sinners, he comes to be treated or accepted as if he were himself righteous; in other words, through the favor of God he is freed from the penalty of the law, and accepted and treated as he would be, had he been perfectly obedient. The meaning of the phrase, *counted for righteousness,* is of course the same here as in ver. 3; and in

reward is not counted or reckoned as a matter of grace [as it was to Abraham], but as a matter of debt.

both cases it is very plain, that it signifies *gratuitous* or *unmerited* justification on the grounds already explained. We may add here, that by the apostle's own explanation in the context, this justification is one which is *of grace*, κατὰ χάριν (24), and *without works*, χωρὶς ἔργων (verse 6.)

The whole matter lies in a short compass: 'On the ground of works, *i. e.*, of perfect obedience and therefore of merit, none can be justified, because all are sinners. If any then are justified at all, it must be of *grace;* but this grace, although *freely* bestowed and without any just claims on the part of the sinner, is still *not unconditionally* bestowed. *Faith* in him who died to save sinners, is requisite to prepare one for the reception of pardon, yet faith is not in any *legal* sense the meritorious ground of justification; and he who is justified in this way, as a consequence of his faith, is still justified in a manner altogether gratuitous.'

(6) *In the like manner, also David congratulates the man*, καθάπερ καὶ .... ἀνθρώπου. The example of David is now added to that of Abraham, in order to show (what he had before asserted in iii. 31) that he does not disannul the Old Testament Scriptures by avowing the doctrine of *gratuitous* justification. *Utters congratulation*, λέγει μακαρισμόν. Μάκαρ means *happy;* μακαρίζω, to *call* or *pronounce one happy, i. e.*, congratulate; and of course μακαρισμός means *congratulation*, not happiness. I have accordingly used the word *congratulate* in the translation here, not the words, *utters praise, eulogizes, praises*, etc. *Felicem dicere* the Latins could say; and we might translate *pronounceth happy*, etc., as I have done in the version. ῟Ωι ὁ Θεός .... ἔργων, *i. e.*, whom God accepts and treats as righteous χωρὶς ἔργων, without entire obedience to the law, without having done all the works which the law enjoins; comp. verse 5 above. *To impute righteousness without works*, is equivalent to: *to count faith for righteousness;* and both are designed to designate *gratuitous* justification.

Δικαιοσύνη here and elsewhere in this chapter where the same phraseology occurs, is plainly not to be understood in the sense of *justification* (which is the more common meaning of it in our epistle,) but in the usual sense of הְקָצָּ. To say that *faith was counted for* JUSTIFICATION, would make no tolerable sense; but to say — *it was counted as complete obedience*, would be saying just what the apostle means to say, viz., that the believer is gratuitously justified, in the manner that has been explained above.

(7) *Happy, greatly privileged*, μακάριοι. — *Are remitted*, ἀφέθησαν, from ἀφίημι, to *remit, forgive* — 'Whose sins ἐπεκαλύφθησαν, *are covered;*' a figurative expression, not unfrequently

applied to the remission of sins. *To cover* or *conceal*, is to remove from sight or notice; and sins which are left out of sight and out of notice, of course are sins which are not punished. Comp. in Is. xxxviii. 17. Mic. vii. 19. Job xiv. 17.

(8) *Happy the man, to whom the Lord imputeth not iniquity!* *i. e.*, the sin which he has committed. The meaning is: 'Happy the man who obtains forgiveness of his sins, and is accepted and treated as if he were righteous.' *To impute one's own iniquity to him*, is to hold him accountable for it in respect to the demands of punitive justice.

To cover sins and impute not iniquity, means to pardon sin and to treat with favor; and this is substantially the same thing which is designated by *counting faith for righteousness; i. e.*, both forms of expressions denote *gratuitous acceptance with God*.

The apostle has now prepared the way to refute the special allegation designed to be made by the question in verse 1, τί οὖν ἐροῦμεν Ἀβραὰμ τὸν πατέρα ἡμῶν εὑρηκέναι κατὰ σάρκα; He has shown that acceptance on the ground of merit or perfect obedience is out of the question; for even Abraham and David were justified through faith gratuitously, and not ἐξ ἔργων. No ground of boasting, then, could be claimed by either of these conspicuous individuals. It was *grace only* that saved them. But if it is true in the general sense here stated, that salvation is in all cases entirely a matter of *gratuity*, a question still remains, viz. Is this gratuity bestowed as the Jews would claim, only on those who are circumcised, *i. e.*, on the Jews only, or is it also granted to the Gentiles. The apostle now proceeds to the special consideration of the question about circumcision, which was first asked in chap. iii. 1, and again virtually repeated by the εὑρηκέναι κατὰ σάρκα in chap. iv. 1.

(9) [Is] *this congratulation then respecting the circumcised* [only], *or also the uncircumcised;* ὁ μακαρισμὸς . . . . ἀκροβυστίαν; That is, granting there is cause for pronouncing blessed the man whose sins are forgiven and whose iniquities are covered, still it may be asked: 'Does gratuitous pardon belong only to the circumcised Jew, or are God's promised mercies bestowed also on the idolatrous heathen?'

Λέγομεν γάρ supposes an *implied* answer in the *affirmative* to the preceding questions, viz., 'The privilege belongs also to the uncircumcised.' That such must be the case, the apostle now proceeds to show, by the allegation that Abraham was justified in an *uncircumcised* state. The inference is, that David could not mean to exclude such cases as that of Abraham himself. In this way the γάρ is easily accounted for here, as referring to some *implied* sentiment. For a like *aposiopesis* of the answer to a question, see iv. 2. et al.

(10) *How then was it counted? While he was in a state of circumcision or of uncircumcision? Not in a state of circumcision, but of uncircumcision?* πῶς οὖν . . . . ἀκροβυστία; In ἐν περιτομῇ κ. τ. λ., the ἐν stands (as often) before the Dative of a noun designating state or condition. The design of the writer is plain. Abraham's *faith was imputed to him for righteousness, i. e.*, he was gratuitously justified *before* the covenant of circumcision was made with him, and of course before he was a partaker in this rite. Consequently the privilege in question is not limited to those who are circumcised, and therefore does not depend on circumcision.

(11) *And he received the sign of circumcision as a seal of the righteousness by faith, which* [he obtained] *while in a state of uncircumcision,* καὶ σημεῖον . . . . ἐν ἀκροβυστίᾳ. That is, circumcision was not the cause or ground of his faith being counted for righteousness, or of his being gratuitously justified; it was merely a *seal, i. e.*, a token of confirmation (for such is σφραγίς, 1 Cor. ix. 2. 2 Tim. ii. 19) in respect to the blessing which he had before obtained. The allusion in the language is to the practice of confirming written instruments, by seals placed on them in token of ratification. Τῆς δικαιοσύνης τῆς πίστεως, might here be rendered *of the justification which is by faith;* but the idiom of this chapter rather points us to a different version. There is, however, no ground for mistake here, inasmuch as the qualifying words τῆς πίστεως in connection with what had before been said, sufficiently guard against it. We might naturally expect the *article* here, viz., τὸ σημεῖον τῆς περιτομῆς, inasmuch as the thing is specific and monadic; but for this very reason also, the article may be omitted, because there is no danger of mistake; see New Test. Gramm. § 89, 2 *a. b.*

Σημεῖον means *a symbol, a token, an external visible mark.* In τῆς ἐν ἀκροβυστίᾳ the τῆς is referred by many to πίστεως; but the nature of the case seems plainly to demand, that it should be referred to the compound idea designated by τῆς δικαιοσύνης τῆς πίστεως.

The circumstance here related is fatal to the claims of the bigoted Jew, with respect to circumcision. But the apostle is not satisfied with this simply; he advances farther, and claims that 'Abraham was not only justified before he was circumcised, but this was done for the very purpose of confirming the truth which he is proclaiming. He was justified before the covenant of circumcision, *in order that he might be the father of all those who believe in a state of uncircumcision, so that righteousness might also be imputed to them,* εἰς τὸ εἶναι . . . . δικαιοσύνην.' That is; God, in justifying Abraham before he was circumcised, did intend to make him a father, *i. e.*, an eminent leader, pattern, or example, to Gentile as well as Jewish believers, and to show that righteousness might be imputed to the uncircumcised as well as to the circumcised. Δι' ἀκροβυστίας is an example of διά *conditionis*, *i. e.*, of διά before a noun in the Genitive which designates state or condition, and is equivalent to the Dative with ἐν as used above. Εἰς τὸ λογισθῆναι κ. τ. λ., designates the consequence, or the object in respect to which *paternity* and *sonship* existed, viz., that of being gratuitously justified, *i. e.*, of having righteousness imputed to them, which means the same thing. The καί in this clause is omitted in A., B., several MSS. minusc., and some versions. It is unnecessary; but still it does not mar the sense, as may be seen in the version.

(12) In all this, moreover, the apostle admits that there was another object in view, viz., that Abraham should be the spiritual father of the *circumcised*, as well as of the uncircumcised, *i. e.*, that he should be an eminent example to all, both Jews and Gentiles, of that gratuitous justification which God bestows on men, and which is universally proffered under the gospel dispensation. So the sequel: *And* [in order that he might be] *the father of those who are circumcised, of those who are not only of the circumcision, but walk in the steps of that faith which our father Abraham had while in a state of uncircumcision,* καὶ [εἰς τὸ εἶναι αὐτὸν] πατέρα, ... 'Ἀβραάμ. The connection requires us to understand the apostle as asserting, that the sign of circumcision which Abraham received, as a seal of the righteousness of faith or a token of confirmation in respect to his gratuitous justification, was received by him in order that he might be the spiritual father of such Jews as imitated his example, as well as of Gentiles. The writer clearly makes the same distinction here, that he does in chapter ii. 28, 29. Not the literal posterity only of Abraham, or only his descendants by natural generation who received the external sign of circumcision in their flesh, were the children of this patriarch in the sense here intended. *To walk in the steps of Abraham's faith,* means to follow the example of Abraham, to possess and exercise a faith like his. It is to such and only to such, that Abraham is a *spiritual* father.

This last clause of the verse renders very plain what is meant, when Abraham is called the *father* of both Gentile and Jewish believers. The word אָב, πατήρ employed in this way, designates (as before remarked) an *examplar, a pattern, a leading and eminent example* after which others copy; compare for such a sense, Gen. iv. 20, 21. John viii. 38, 41, 44, where the devil is called the *father* of the wicked Jews; comp. also 1 Macc. ii. 54. So in the verse before us, the *children* of Abraham are those *who walk in the steps of his faith, i. e.*, imitate his example.*

One difficulty remains in respect to τοῖς στοιχοῦσι. The repetition of the article before it here seems as if the writer intended to distinguish those whom it designates, from the τοῖς οὐκ ἐκ περιτομῆς μόνον which (by placing the οὐκ before τοῖς) would mean, *not only to those of the circumcision;* and then ἀλλὰ καὶ τοῖς κ. τ. λ. would mean, *but also to those who walk*, etc., *i. e.*, but also to Gentiles who imitate Abraham's faith. To this purpose the Syriac version, the Vulgate, Theodoret, Anselm, Castalio, Grotius, Koppe, and others. But the objection to this is, that heathen believers have already been mentioned in the preceding verse; and that the writer seems plainly here intending to characterize such Jews, and only such, as were the spiritual children of Abraham, *i. e.*, to whom he was a spiritual father. The repetition of the article before στοιχοῦσι in this case is indeed peculiar; Tholuck calls it a *solecism,* and Ruckert says it is not to be tolerated. I regard it, however, as a *resumption* of the sentence begun with the preceding τοῖς, and interrupted by the οὐκ ἐκ περιτομῆς μόνον ἀλλὰ καὶ, the former part of which has the sense of an adjective qualifying the τοῖς; but inasmuch as the resumption gives a new characteristic, it was necessary that the Part. στοιχοῦσι should have the article; as in other like cases. In this view Reiche fully concurs.

CHAP. IV. 13—17.

THE apostle now proceeds to another illustration and confirmation of his assertions respecting gratuitous justification. The Jew gloried in belonging to a nation to whom God had given a revealed law, and looked upon the pre-eminence which this gave him, as a proof that God would treat him with special favor in a spiritual respect. In order to take away all ground of glorying in this manner, the apostle here proceeds distinctly to remind them, that Abraham was not justified by any such privilege, the law having been given more than four hundred years after the time in which he lived. Such, then, as are his spiritual children, *i. e*, such as are justified on grounds like those on which he was justified, cannot regard the *law* as the ground of their justification.

The proof of the writer's position could not fail to make a deep impression on the mind of a serious Jew. 'Abraham did not receive promises for himself and his

---

* The idea of priority in a particular course is doubtless prominent in the designation of *father*, as used here. "Abraham is called the 'father of the faithful,' as their leader, from being the first conspicuous example of faith recorded in the Scriptures," and as being the head of the whole family of believers So he is called the father of the circumcision in this verse, as being the first who was circumcised. Cf. also the use of the word in Gen 4: 20.

seed, on account of the law or by means of the law, but gratuitously, *i e*, by the righteousness of faith, verse 13. Now if the possession of the law, or obedience to it, were necessary to constitute Abraham and his seed heirs of the promises, then heirship by faith, and the promises connected with this, would be annulled, because these were granted to Abraham before the giving of the law, verse 14. The law, moreover, is so far from being the ground of such promises, that it is a means of indignation on the part of God towards sinners, *i e.*, a means of their punishment; for it is the prohibitions of the law which constitute and define transgressions, and if there were no law, there could be no transgression, verse 15. Such being the case, the promises are not made on the ground of law, but through the instrumentality of faith, *v. e.*, gratuitously, in order that all the seed might be assured respecting them, both Gentiles who have not the law, and Jews who have it, provided they have like faith with Abraham, the spiritual father of all, verse 16. The Scripture points out such a relation of Abraham to all true believers, and he is regarded as sustaining such a one, by him who raises the dead to life, and calls things out of nothing into existence, verse 17.

(13) *For not by the law was the promise made to Abraham, or to his seed,* οὐ γὰρ .... σπέρματι αὐτοῦ. Γάρ introduces a confirmation of the preceding declaration, that Abraham was the *spiritual* father of both Jews and Gentiles, πατέρα πάντων τῶν πιστευόντων, etc., not by any external right or privilege, but through faith.—*Through law, by means of the law,* διὰ νόμου. The writer designs by it either to designate the *possession* of the law, the privilege of living under it, and being the depositary of it, or else he means *obedience* to it. I am inclined to give it the former sense here, on account of the οἱ ἐκ νόμου in verse 14, which rather designates such as live under the law than those who fulfil it.

What the *promise* made to Abraham and his seed was, the writer proceeds to tell us, viz, *that he should be heir* or *possessor of the world,* τό κληρονόμον .... κόσμον. This expression is found literally in none of the passages which contain the promises made to Abraham, Gen. xii. 1—3. xv. 1—6. xvii. 1—8. But in Gen. xv. 5, is a promise, that the seed of Abraham should be like the stars of heaven for multitude; and in Gen. xvii. 5, it is said: "A father of many nations have I made thee." That the apostle had his mind intent upon this text, is plain from verse 17 in the sequel. When he says, then, that *the promise was that Abraham should be heir of the world,* his meaning evidently is, that the seed of Abraham (in the sense here meant, viz, his spiritual seed), should be co-extensive with the world, or (to use the phraseology employed in another of the promises made to Abraham), "in him should all the families of the earth be blessed." Taken in the sense now adverted to, the phrase before us would imply, that the spiritual seed of Abraham should be co-extensive with the world, *i. e.*, should be of all nations. But there is a somewhat more figurative way of understanding the phrase *to be heir of the world,* viz., to take it as an expression that designates the receiving of great and important blessings. In such a way most clearly are יָרַשׁ הָאָרֶץ, κληρονομεῖν τὴν γῆν to be taken, Psalms xxv. 13. xxxvii. 9, 11, 22, 29. Prov. ii. 21. Matt. v. 5. The former method of exegesis, however, is here to be preferred, on the ground, that ver. 17 develops the fact, that Paul here had a *special* meaning in reference to the *extent* of Abraham's spiritual seed.

In regard to that *seed* of Abraham to whom the promise was specially made; who can this be but the Messiah? Who else of Abraham's seed was to be possessor of all the earth, particularly in a *spiritual* sense? That Paul himself had such a view of this subject, is made quite certain by Gal. iii. 16. It is true, indeed, that in respect to the promises of a *temporal* nature made to Abraham, his *literal* descendants were the partakers and heirs of them; see Gen. xvii. 8. xv. 18. So also were they, that is, some of them, heirs of spiritual promises. But the specific promise to which the apostle alludes in our text, seems to have been made with reference to Christ, at least it seems to have been entirely fulfilled only in him, Gal. iii. 16.* Reiche construes the promise here as having respect to a *new world*, like that which the Millenarians expect, after the end of the present order of things; which implies a method of interpreting the *Messianic* prophecies that cannot be defended on the ground of rational exegesis.

The promise in question was not διὰ νόμου, *i. e.*, on account of any privileges connected with the giving of the law, for the law was not yet given; but it was διὰ δικαιοσύνης πίστεως, *through the righteousness of faith;* see on iii. 22.

(14) *If now they who are of the law, are heirs,* εἰ γὰρ . . . . κληρονόμοι; *i. e.*, if they who live under the law and enjoy its privileges, are heirs of the promise made to Abraham and his seed. Γάρ here is prefixed to an additional clause designed to confirm what precedes. Οἱ ἐκ νόμου may mean, either those who rest upon the law, *i. e.*, make their boast of having fulfilled it and so expect justification from it (in which way Tholuck and many others have understood it); or it may mean, those who enjoy the privileges and the distinction which a revelation confers. I prefer the latter sense as being more consonant with the special object of the apostle; which here is to prove that no external rites or privileges can be the ground of justification before God.

* Although the promises here referred to were only fulfilled through the agency and in the person of Christ, yet it may be questioned whether the *seed* of Abraham here refers definitely to him. It should seem rather to refer to the whole posterity of Abraham, to whom in connection with him, as their head, the promise was made.

Faith is rendered of no effect, and the promise is made void, κεκένωται . . . . ἐπαγγελία. The reason of this is, that the promise was made to Abraham and his seed in consequence of faith, and therefore gratuitously; but if those only who enjoy the privilege of living under the law are heirs of the promise, and are so without walking in the steps of Abraham as to faith, then the promises to Abraham are of no effect. In a word, the ground of justification taken by those who plead for it ἐκ νόμου, is entirely diverse from and opposed to that by which Abraham was justified, and on which the promises were made to him; and if they are in the right, the promises made to Abraham are of course null, because a new condition unknown to him and different from that under which he obtained blessings, would thus be introduced.

(15) *For the law is the occasion of wrath; for where there is no law, there is no transgression,* ὁ γὰρ νόμος . . . . παράβασις. A reason is here assigned why the promise would be made void, on the ground suggested; and this is, that the law was actually the occasion of bringing upon the Jews divine displeasure, by reason of their offences against its precepts. It is on this account that the verse is introduced by γάρ *causal* If there were no law, then there would be no transgression or sin. All sin is ἀνομία, *i. e.*, want of conformity to the law of God, either as to omission or commission. Now as all men do sin, the law against which they offend (inasmuch as it prohibits and condemns sin) is the instrument of their *condemnation*, not of their justification. This is indeed no fault of the law, which is of itself "holy and just and good" (Rom. vii. 12); the fault lies with the transgressor. But when such transgressor appeals to the law as the ground of his justification, he must be told (as he is here told) that the law, instead of delivering him from death or justifying him, condemns him to death; nay, that its precepts, although holy and just and good in themselves and worthy of all respect and obedience, are nevertheless the occasion (the innocent occasion indeed) of the sinner's guilt and ruin. The fault lies in him; but still, if there had been no precepts to transgress and no penalty connected with transgression, then he would not have been a transgressor. It is on such ground that the apostle (chap. vii. 7—13) declares most explicitly, that "he had not known sin, except by the law;" that "sin, taking occasion by the law, wrought in him all manner of concupiscence;" that "without the law sin was dead," *i. e.*, the power of sin was inefficacious; but still, that "the law is holy and just and good," and all the fault lies in the transgressor. Chap. vii 7, seq., is indeed an ample commentary on the sentiment expressed in the verse before us.

Admitting the truth of the apostle's representation, it follows, that those who have no knowledge of law, *i. e.*, *no moral sense of any moral precept*, cannot be transgressors. This is plainly and palpably the doctrine which he teaches; a doctrine which is sanctioned by the fundamental principles of our moral nature, and essential to the idea of right and wrong. In common cases, we never pronounce any man to be an offender against a moral law, unless he is *an intelligent, rational, moral, free agent.* Any one of these qualifications being found wanting, we absolve him from guilt. And does not Paul the same? But this does not settle the question *when* men begin to be such agents; for plainly they may be moral and free agents before they can read the Scriptures. The question as to the *time when* sinning begins, in each individual case, can be settled only by Omniscience. Why should we not be content to leave it with 'the Judge of all the earth, WHO WILL DO RIGHT?'

The second γάρ in this verse introduces a reason or ground of the assertion immediately preceding; that the law is the occasion or instrument of condemnation. How does this appear? In this way, viz., because that where there is no law, there is no transgression.

(16) Because then the law does in fact never justify, but only condemn, it follows that if justification be at all bestowed on sinners, it must come in some other way than by law. *On this account it was of faith, so that it must be of grace,* διὰ τοῦτο . . . χάριν; *i. e.*, the promise is through faith, so that it must be gratuitous, since there is no way left in which it could be bestowed on the ground of merit. See the notes on verses 4, 5, above. We must of course suppose ἡ ἐπαγγελία γίνεται to be implied before ἐκ πίστεως; in which case the mind reverts to the idea at the close of verse 14. The ἵνα before κατὰ χάριν is doubtless to be taken in the *ecbatic* sense, *ita ut, so that,* indicating *event,* not purpose. The reasoning then stands thus: 'The promise was of *faith* as the condition, so that it must of course be gratuitous.' *In order that the promise might be sure to all the seed,* εἰς τὸ εἶναι . . . . σπέρματι. On any other ground than that of *grace* or *gratuity,* the promise could not be sure either to Abraham or to his seed; for if it were to be fulfilled only on condition of entire obedience to the law, then would it never have a fulfilment, inasmuch as no mere man ever did or will exhibit perfect obedience. Διὰ τοῦτο in this verse extends to the whole of the reasoning which precedes, and which goes to show that justification or the promises of pardon and acceptance must be on *gratuitous,* and not on meritorious grounds.

Not only to him who is under the law, but to him who is of the faith, of Abraham, οὐ τῷ .... . . 'Αβραάμ ; *i. e.*, the promise is sure of fulfilment to both Jew and Greek, that is, to all men without distinction, to all τοῖς στοιχοῦσι τοῖς ἴχνεσι τῆς ἐν τῇ ἀκροβυστίᾳ πίστεως τοῦ πατρός ἡμῶν 'Αβραάμ. The reader should note, that μόνον belongs to οὐ τῷ, not to ἐκ τοῦ νόμου.

(17) This last idea, viz., that Abraham is the spiritual father of both Jews and Gentiles, the apostle now takes occasion farther to illustrate and confirm, by a reference to the Jewish Scriptures. *Who is the father of us all; (as it is written : A father of many nations have I made thee,)* ὅς ἐστι .... τέθεικά σε. Τέθεικά σε is the Septuagint rendering of נְתַתִּיךָ, the Hebrew נָתַן frequently meaning *to put, place,* or *constitute;* in which meaning it is often followed by the Septuagint and New Testament, by the use of τίθημι. There is a question whether the original in Gen. xvii. 5, means anything more than that the *literal* posterity of Abraham should be very numerous. Tholuck and many commentators so construe it; but it seems clear to me, that the apostle viewed it as having reference to a *spiritual* seed. This is made quite certain by comparing Gal. iii. 7. Rom. ii. 28, 29. iv. 11, 12, 16, 18. The embarrassment as to the interpretation of Gen. xvii. 1—8, seems to arise principally from the fact, that promises of both a temporal and spiritual nature are there made. A *double paternity* (so to speak) is assigned to Abraham; many nations are to descend from him *literally;* his literal seed are to possess the land of Canaan. But he is also to become the *spiritual* father of 'many nations,' (*i. e.*, an eminent pattern or exemplar in regard to faith, and justification by it, see verse 12 above), and in him are '*all the families* of the earth to be blessed,' Gen. xii. 3.

Such a father he was *in the sight of God, whom he confided in or believed*, κατέναντι οὗ .... Θεοῦ. Κατέναντι is equivalent to the Hebrew נֶגֶד, לִפְנֵי, לְנֶגֶד, בְּעֵינֵי, *in the sight of, in the view of, before*. The sentiment is this: ' Abraham is the father of many nations, in the sight of that God in whom he trusted, or whose word he believed ;' *i. e.*, God views him and has constituted him the spiritual father of many nations. The construction of the verse is difficult, but I regard the real sense of it to be the same, as if the arrangement in Greek were thus: Κατέναττι Θεοῦ οὗ [= ᾧ] ἐπίστευσε. The οὗ is to be considered as a case of *attraction*, as grammarians say. Cf. John ii. 22. Mark vii. 13. Luke ii. 20. Acts vii. 17, 45. 1 Pet. iv. 11. John xv. 20, etc.; but in all these cases, the noun *precedes* the pronoun which conforms to it. Examples, however, of the like nature with the present, are the following, viz., Mark vi. 16, ὃν ἐγὼ ἀνεκεφάλισα Ἰωάννην, οὗτός ἐστι; Acts xxi. 16. ἄγοντες παρ' ᾧ ξενισθῶμεν Μνάσωνι; Rom. vi. 17, εἰς ὃν παραδόθητε τύπον διδαχῆς ; in which examples, indeed, the *noun* conforms to the pronoun as to its case; but this makes no important difference, inasmuch as the conformity may be of either kind, *i. e.*, of the noun to the pronoun, or the pronoun to the noun; see New Test. Gramm. § 113. 2, 3.* If we regard οὗ ἐπίστευσε as a circumstance thrown in, and to be mentally included in a parenthesis, the difficulty of the sentence will be removed. The present construction is somewhat anomalous as to the order of words; for the usual order would be thus: Κατέναντι Θεοῦ οὗ ἐπίστευσε, κ. τ. λ.

Who giveth life to the dead, and calleth the things which are not, as if they were, τοῦ ζωοποιοῦντος .... ὄντα. To express the idea of divine, almighty power, is plainly the object of this passage. This is does by asserting that God raises the dead, and exercises creative and controlling power. In regard to τοῦ ζωοποιοῦντος τοὺς νεκρούς, it may mean generally, that God has the power to raise the dead, and that he exercises it; or it may have a special reference to God's promises to raise up a numerous progeny from Abraham, who was dead as to the power of procreation; comp. Heb. xi. 17—19, and verse 19 below. In either case the meaning is good. In the first it is more energetic; in the second, more appropriate to the special object of the writer. Καλοῦντος τὰ μὴ ὄντα ὡς ὄντα is Hebraistic in its manner. Καλέω is sometimes employed like the Hebrew קָרָא, *i. e.*, to designate the idea of *commanding a thing to be* or *exist*, which did not before exist; *e. g.*, Is. xli. 4. xlviii. 13; comp. 2 Kings viii. 1. Isaiah xxii. 12. Comp. also 2 Macc. vii. 28, ἐξ οὐκ ὄντων ἐποίησεν αὐτὰ ὁ Θεός, which resembles in sense the phrase before us; also Philo de Creat. p. 728, τὰ μὴ ὄντα ἐκάλεσεν εἰς τὸ εἶναι. The reference in the mind of the writer, when he used the phrase before us, no doubt was to Gen. i. 3, seq. *The calling of things that are not*, is to command that they shall exist, in order to fulfil the purposes which the Creator has in view by bringing them into existence. This latter circumstance seems to have been overlooked; and thus has arisen great perplexity among interpreters. 'How,' it has been asked, 'could God call into existence things that are not, as if they were?' A seeming paradox, indeed, if literally interpreted; for things that already are, cannot be called into existence. After all, the meaning of the apostle is not simply *bidding to exist* (καλοῦντος), but also *directing, disposing of, commanding* in any way and for any purpose, the things called. 'God,' says he, 'can call into existence things that now have no existence, and employ them for his purposes, just as he directs and disposes of

* This attraction from the Dative is so unusual, that most modern commentators prefer to make out the construction thus: κατέναντι τοῦ Θεοῦ, κατέναντι οὗ ἐπίστευσε, *before God in whose sight he believed;* cf. Luke 1. 4.

140 ROMANS IV. 18.

things that already ⁓exist; God calls τὰ μὴ ὄντα just as he does τὰ ὄντα; things that do not now exist, are at his disposal as really and truly as things that do exist, *i. e.*, they can be made to exist and to subserve his purpose, in the same manner as things do which now already exist.' If any one still feels a difficulty, he may solve the sentence in this simple way, viz., καλοῦντος τὰ μὴ ὄντα ὡς [ἐκάλεσεν] ὄντα, *i. e.*, calling into existence (Gen. i. 2. Ps. xxxiii. 6) things that are not, as [he called into existence] things that are. The sense would be for substance the same.

CHAP. IV. 18—25.

THE apostle now proceeds to a more detailed and animated description of Abraham's faith. First he hoped, when to all human appearance there was no ground of hope, that he might become the father of many nations through the birth of a son, verse 18. His strong faith led him to overlook his own extreme old age and that of Sarah, verse 19; to trust with full confidence in the simple promise of God respecting a son, thus giving glory to God by reposing in him such an unlimited trust, and by being so fully persuaded that he would perform what he had promised, vers 20, 21. On this account he was justified through his faith, verse 22, nor was this fact recorded merely for his sake, but also for our sake, that we may be inspired with the hope of attaining to the like justification, provided we believe in the declarations of him who raised up Jesus from the dead, and proposed him to the world as the object of saving belief, inasmuch as he died for our offences, and rose again in order that we might be justified. v. 23—25.

(18) *Who against* [all apparent] *ground of hope, believed in hope that he should become the father*, etc.,* ὃς παρ᾽ ἐλπίδα ἐπ᾽ ἐλπίδι ἐπίστευσεν. The ὅς, κ. τ. λ. here is co-ordinate with the ὅς, κ. τ. λ. in ver. 16. But though co-ordinate as to construction, it is not merely epexegetical, but adds some new declarations respecting the strength of Abraham's faith. The expression παρ᾽ ἐλπίδα ἐπ᾽ ἐλπίδι, is what the Greeks call ὀξύμωρον [*oxymoron*], *i. e., a sharp, pointed,* and apparently contradictory *saying;* like the Latin *spes insperata, ignavia strenua*, etc. The παρ᾽ ἐλπίδα, *beyond* or *against hope*, in this case, refers to the circumstances recounted in ver. 19. For the like sense of παρά, see Acts xviii. 13.

According to what has been said, κατὰ τὸ εἰρημένον, viz., in Gen. xv. 5.— Οὕτως, *so*, viz., like the stars in respect to number, to which Abraham had just been pointed, *i. e.*, innumerable; comp. Ps. cxlvii. 4.

---

* *That he should become*, literally "*in order to his becoming*, etc. (i. e. as a step in the process of his becoming, and one necessary to that process going forward)."— *Alford.*

(19) *Not being weak*, μὴ ἀσθενήσας, *i. e.*; being strong. The Greeks call this mode of expression λιτότης, *smallness, slenderness*, or μείωσις, *diminution;* because it seemingly, though not really, diminishes from the full strength of the *positive* form. The word ἀσθενήσας here seems to be chosen in reference to the state of the patriarchal pair, who were weak in body. Their faith was in an *opposite* condition, μὴ ἀσθενήσας. These words begin a third co-ordinate clause, both the others beginning with ὅς, as already noted.

In faith, τῇ πίστει, Dative of condition, *in respect to faith, i. e.,* having strong confidence.

He did not regard, οὐ κατενόησε.* — *Already dead*, ἤδη νενεκρωμένον, *i. e.*, inefficient with regard to procreation; comp. Heb. xi. 12. Gen. xvii. 17. *About*, που, (adv.) which sense it has when it is *enclitic*, as here; *about* 100 *years of age*, ἑκατονταέτης που. — Καί, *nor*, inasmuch as it follows οὐ in the preceding clause. So in Hebrew, ו following לֹא means *nor*, Hebrew Gramm. § 358. Note. — Τὴν νέκρωσιν τῆς μήτρας = τὴν μήτραν τὴν νενεκρωμένην. Comp. the age of Sarah (90) at this time, Gen. xvii. 17.

(20) *He did not doubt*, οὐ διεκρίθη, *did not hesitate;* comp. Rom. xiv. 23. James i. 6. ii. 4. Matt. xxi. 21. Mark xi. 23. — *Respecting the promise of God, through*, or *by reason of an unbelieving spirit*, εἰς δὲ τὴν ἐπαγγελίαν . . . . ἀπιστίᾳ. The δέ here is *adversative* in respect to the preceding circumstances, and may be translated, *still, but*, or *however*. The Dat. of ἀπιστίᾳ is construed agreeably to idiom; see New Test. Gramm. § 106. 5.

But he was confident through faith, he firmly and confidently believed, ἀλλ᾽ ἐνεδυναμώθη τῇ πίστει, the opposite of the preceding expression; τῇ πίστει, the Dative of manner or means; see New Test. Gram. ut supra.

Giving glory to God, Δοὺς δόξαν τῷ Θεῷ. The Hebrew שִׂים כָבוֹד לַיהוָה means, to show by our actions that we acknowledge any attribute of God; which is ascribing to him what belongs or is due to him. So here, Abraham, by the strength of his confidence, did in the highest manner ascribe to God omnipotence and veracity. Comp. John ix. 24. Josh. vii. 19. The meaning of the phrase as here employed by the writer, is given in the next verse.

(21) *Being fully persuaded*, καὶ πληροφορηθεὶς ὅτι κ. τ. λ., a repetition or epexegesis of what the preceding clause asserts. "Being strong in faith" there, is equivalent to πληροφορηθεὶς

* Lachmann, following MSS. A C, Alford and others, omit the οὐ before κατενόησεν; and then the meaning is: not being weak in the faith, he knew well, was well aware that his body, etc., but (v. 20, εἰς δὲ) did not, etc. The majority of critics retain the οὐ.

here; comp. Heb. x. 22.— *What he had promised*, ὃ ἐπήγγελται. The Perf. pass. not unfrequently has an *active* sense, inasmuch as it serves for the Perf. Middle as well as the Passive, (New Test. Gramm. § 61. 2.) So in Acts xiii. 2, προσκέκλημαι, *I have invited*. Acts xvi. 10. 1 Pet. iv. 1. John ix. 22.— Καὶ ποιῆσαι, *also to perform*, καί in the sense of *etiam*, *quoque*, as it often is, *i. e.*, καί *intensive*.

(22) *Wherefore* [his belief] *was counted to him as righteousness*, διὸ . . . . εἰς δικαιοσύνην ; in other words, through his faith he was counted or treated as righteous, he was admitted to the divine favor. See on verse 5 above. The καί before ἐλογίσθη I have interpreted as *intensive*. If otherwise taken, it may be solved thus : *Wherefore, also, it was imputed*, etc.

(23, 24) Nor was this method of justification and acceptance limited to Abraham. The history of it is recorded as an example, for the encouragement and imitation of all others down to the latest period of time. Those who believe in him who raised up Jesus from the dead (comp. ver. 17 above), *i. e.*, those who believe in what God has done and said with respect to the Messiah, the only foundation of the sinner's hope, will be justified through their faith, in like manner as Abraham was by his.

(25) *Was given up*, παρεδόθη, viz., to death, Matt. xxvi. 2.— Διὰ τὰ παραπτώματα ἡμῶν, comp. Is. liii. 12, 5. 6. 8. Gal. i. 4. ii. 20. Tit. ii. 14. 1 Pet. ii. 24.

On account of our justification, διὰ τὴν δικαίωσιν ἡμῶν, *i. e.*, our acceptance with God. Christ rose from the dead, in order that this great and glorious work might be completed. The *primary* object of his death is here stated as being *expiatory*, *i. e.*, as having a special influence on that part of *justification* which has respect to remitting the penalty of the divine law. But as justification, in its *full* sense, comprehends not only forgiveness, but the accepting and treating of any one as righteous, it implies of course the advancement of the pardoned sinner to a state of glory. The resurrection of Christ was connected with this; for if "Christ be not risen, then our faith is vain." His resurrection was preparatory to his receiving the kingdom given him of the Father, and thus was necessary in order to complete the redemption of those who believe in him.

Reiche maintains, that the whole work of Christ, is to be considered as *one ;* and that we are not at liberty to ascribe more efficacy to his death than to any of the actions of his life. Of course he disallows the idea of a *vicarious sacrifice*, in any proper sense of these words ; and he maintains that God, for Christ's sake and for some reasons not stated by the sacred writers, forgives and accepts the sinner. But, although the incarnation and obedience of Christ constitute an important part of his mediatorial work, still it seems perfectly clear that the New Testament ascribes *peculiar* efficacy to the sufferings and death of Christ; and to my mind, the doctrine of the *atonement* or the *vicarious sufferings and death of Christ*, is fundamental to the very essence of Christianity as distinguished from other systems of religion.

CHAP. V. 1—21.

THE apostle having thus shown, (*a*) That all men, Jews and Gentiles, are sinners; (*b*) That they are therefore under the condemning sentence of the divine law; (*c*) That the only method of escape from the execution of this sentence, is by gratuitous pardon, *i. e.* by justification obtained through the death of Christ, and (*d*) That all this is no new doctrine, but one inculcated in the Old Testament both by declaration and example; he next proceeds, in chapter v, to exhibit the blessed fruits of this pardon or justification (1) We have peace with God (with whom we were before in a state of enmity, being alienated from him, compare verses 6—10), and we enjoy, through Christ, free access to a state of favor with God, and thus are led to rejoice in the hope of future glory, verses 1, 2. (2) We are supported and comforted in all our afflictions during the present life; nay, we may even rejoice in them as the instruments of spiritual good to us, verses 3—5. (3) All this good is rendered certain, and the hope of it sure, by the fact that Christ, having died for us while in a state of enmity and alienation, and having thus reconciled us to God, will not fail to carry on and complete the work which he has thus begun, verses 6—10. (4) We may now therefore rejoice in God (who is as truly *our* covenant God as he has been that of the Jews), on account of the reconciliation which Christ has effected, verse 11.

(5) This state of reconciliation or filial relation to God, is *extended to all* men, *i. e.*, in some respects actually bestowed on all, and in others proffered to all, laid open for all, rendered accessible to all, in like manner as the evils occasioned by the sin of our first ancestor have in some respects extended to all, and in others are liable to be incurred or suffered by all; yea, such is the *greatness* of Christ's redemption, that the blessings procured by his death far exceed the evils occasioned by the sin of Adam (verses 12—19), they even exceed all the evils consequent upon the sins of men, who live under the light of revelation, verses 20, 21. The *certainty* of salvation, then, under such a dispensation as this, would seem to be made quite evident.

Such appears to me the sum of what is taught in chap v. The difficulties attending the interpretation of this passage, I readily acknowledge, and have long and deeply felt. To the study of them I have devoted much more time, than to any other equal portion of the Holy Scriptures I do not persuade myself, however, that I have succeeded in all respects with regard to the solution of them; much less do I expect that what I shall propose will be satisfactory to the minds of all others. What I could do, I have done; if others succeed better, it will be a matter of sincere joy to me. One thing I cannot help remarking here, which is, that any exegesis of verses 12—21, which represents the contents as irrelevant to the tenor of the context both before and after these verses, must wear the air, of course, of being an improbable one. Never have I found more difficulty, however, than in satisfying myself of the relation which verses 12—21 do in fact hold toward the context, and in particular how they bear upon the theme discussed in verses 1—11. The result of all my investigations is given, as to substance, under No. 5 above

Tholuck states his result a little differently. "To render more conspicuous the fruits obtained by redemption, the apostle contrasts the state of mankind *as a whole*, and as being in the misery of their unredeemed condition, with the state of mankind *as a whole*, in their happiness as partakers of the benefits of redemption. By a striking parallel, he exhibits mankind in Adam the head and source of our race as sinful; and in Christ the head and source of it, as redeemed; and he so represents this, that redemption appears to be the greatest and most important occurrence which has taken place with regard to mankind — the central point of all spiritual life and all happiness" (Comm über Rom p. 168 edit. 2) Whether this summary comes nearer than my own to the true exhibition of the contents of verses 12 — 21; in particular, whether it harmonizes better with the context; I submit to the reader to decide, when he shall have carefully studied the whole. In the mean time, I acknowledge with gratitude the important aid that I have received from the Commentary of the above named excellent writer

The reader will find a more detailed statement of the contents of different passages at the commencement of the commentary on them.

(1) *Then*, οὖν, concessive and continuative. It does not here express the force simply of *syllogistic* conclusion, but resumes and alludes to the preceding arguments and illustrations, and takes for granted the fact stated by δικαιωθέντες. This last word has here peculiar reference to *pardon of sin*, *i. e.*, having been pardoned or justified.

By faith, ἐκ πίστεως, i. e., *gratuitously*, through *belief* instead of perfect obedience; see on chap. iv. 5 above.

We have peace, εἰρήνην ἔχομεν; here in opposition to a state of enmity to God, or a state of alienation from him; see verse 10. Several important MSS., A., C, D., 71., al., and some versions and fathers, read ἔχωμεν (Subj.); but Paul does not mean to say merely that *we may have* peace, but that we are in actual possession of it.*

Διὰ τοῦ K. I. Χριστοῦ, viz., by the reconciliation which he has effected, see verse 11.

(2) *By whom also*, δι' οὗ καί. — *Access*, τὴν προσαγωγήν, as well as reconciliation; comp. Eph. ii. 18. iii. 12. We have obtained access εἰς τὴν χαρὶν ταύτην, *i. e.*, either *to this state of favor* or *grace*, in which we now stand or are; or, as Tholuck, Reiche, and some others : ' We have obtained access [to God] by belief (τῇ πίστει) in that grace in which we continue.' The former seems to be the most facile sense; the latter, most conformed to idiom. Προσαγωγή seems to imply that God is the object of access; so it is expressed in Eph. ii. 18. 1 Pet. iii. 18, and *implied* (as here) in Eph. iii. 12. Besides, the *object* of belief is generally indicated by εἰς; which would favor the view of Tholuck. — *We have become possessed of, we have obtained*, ἐσχήκαμεν. As the *Perf*. is here employed (and not *Pres*. as above), it would seem that the *access*

* Lachmann adopts the reading ἔχωμεν, and it must be confessed that there is strong MS authority for it. If it be adopted, the Subjunctive must be considered as hortatory: *Let us have peace*, etc.

here spoken of must refer to the pardoned sinner's *first* access to God, after his forgiveness.

We stand, ἐστήκαμεν, the Perf. being used in this verb, because the Present has not a *neuter* sense. See New Test. Gramm. § 50. 3, Note 2.

And we rejoice, καὶ καυχώμεθα ; *i. e.*, in addition to a state of peace with God and access to him, we are filled with joy, *in the hope of that glory which God will bestow*. Θεοῦ is here *Genitivus auctoris*.

(3) *And not only so, but we also rejoice*, οὐ μόνον δέ, ἀλλὰ καὶ καυχώμεθα κ. τ. λ., etc. Δέ continuative and discretive. The ellipsis after οὐ μόνον δέ is plain ; *i. e.*, 'not only [do we rejoice in hope of future glory], but,' etc. Ἐν after καυχάομαι, as not unfrequently, stands before the object of the verb ; *e. g.*, in Rom. ii. 17. Gal. vi. 13, etc. The apostle does not mean to say, that the Christian exults in pain and sorrow as such ; but that as a means of spiritual good he exults in them, and is enabled by divine grace to triumph over them.

Knowing, having assurance, εἰδότες ; viz., from our relation to God, and from his gracious purposes toward us. Confidence in him gives assurance.

Produces patience or *perseverance*, ὅτι . . . . κατεργάζεται. Neither of these virtues can be exercised without sufferings and trials. *Patience* is steadfast and submissive endurance of evils. Afflictions are essential to the cultivation of this virtue. They are not, indeed, the direct and efficient cause of patience ; but they are at least an occasion or instrumental cause.

(4) *Trial* or *approbation*, δοκιμήν. Either rendering is correct; for perseverance or patience in the enduring of afflictions makes thorough *trial;* and the same virtue secures *approbation*. I prefer the second meaning, viz., *approbation ;* because it more naturally connects itself with the ἐλπίς that follows. Comp. δοκιμάζω, which means *to try*, and also *to approve*.

Hope, ἐλπίδα, which springs of course from the approbation bestowed on patient endurance of suffering for virtue's sake.

(5) *Will not disappoint*, οὐ καταισχύνει ; as the sequel shows. So the Hebrew, לֹא יֵבוֹשׁ. The δέ before this clause and two others in verse 4, is continuative and discretive.

Ὅτι ἡ ἀγάπη τοῦ Θεοῦ κ. τ. λ. The *first* reason given why the Christian's hope will not disappoint him, is that *the love of God is diffused* (ἐκκέχυται) *in his heart* or *mind;* and this, by that Holy Spirit which is imparted to him, *i. e.*, by the gracious influence of that Spirit who dwells in the hearts of believers ; 1 Cor. vi. 19. iii. 16. 2 Cor. vi. 16. 2 Cor. i. 22, where the spirit which is in the hearts of believers is called their ἀῤῥαβών, *the pledge* of their future happiness, the pledge that their salvation is secure. Comp. also Eph. i. 13, 14, where the same sentiment is fully expressed. The *love of God* here evidently means *his love toward us;* as verse 8 plainly shows. His love *shed abroad* in the hearts of Christians means, that a full and satisfactory conviction respecting his love is bestowed; and the manner of bestowing or giving such a sense of his love is here designated, viz., by the influence of the Holy Spirit.

CHAP. V. 6—10.

VERSES 6—10 constitute a kind of episode (if I may so speak), and contain an illustration and confirmation of the sentiment expressed in verse 5. viz, that *the Christian's hope will not disappoint him.* To show that this is truly the case, the writer goes on to produce an illustration, which exhibits an argument of the kind called *a majori ad minus*, i. e, 'if Christ has already done the greater thing for you, viz, reconciled you to God, when you were in your sinful state, how much more will he *complete* the work, the greatest and most difficult part of which has already been accomplished?'

In this view the passage before us seems to be more direct, in respect to *the perseverance of the saints*, than almost any other passage in the Scriptures which I can find The sentiment here is not dependent on the *form* of a particular expression (as it appears to be in some other passages); but it is fundamentally connected with the very nature of the argument.

(6) Ἔτι γὰρ Χριστὸς ὄντων ἡμῶν. The variety of readings is here considerable; *e. g.*, εἴγε, B., Syr., Erp., Copt.; εἰ γὰρ, Isid., Pelus., August.; εἴ τι, F., G.; εἰς τί, (ut quid), Ital., Vulg., Iren., Ambros., Pelag.; which all probably originated either from the supposed unusual location of ἔτι, or else from an apprehension that ἔτι in verse 8 rendered it unnecessary or improbable here. In like manner many MSS. and Versions have an ἔτι after ἀσθενῶν here; which Griesbach and Koppe admit into the text, but Knapp and Vater reject. It probably arose from some of the *lections*, which began with this verse, and transposed the ἔτι, for convenience' sake in reading, as it would not appear seemly at the beginning of a lection. The position of ἔτι seems designed for the sake of emphasis; comp. Matt. xii. 46. xvii. 5. Mark v. 35. xii. 6, and specially Heb. ix. 6, ἔτι τῆς πρώτης σκηνῆς ἐχούσης στάσιν, where ἔτι belongs to ἐχούσης. — Γάρ here introduces proof that the hope of the Christian will not disappoint him.

While we were yet, or *we yet being*, ἔτι ὄντων ἡμῶν. — Ἀσθενῶν, literally *destitute of strength;* here, as generally expounded, in a *moral* sense, *i. e.*, destitute of moral vigor, without holy energy, in a state of moral indisposition or infirmity. So Prov. xxiv. 16, οἱ ἀσεβεῖς ἀσθενήσουσιν ἐν κακοῖς, the ungodly *are weak* in their evil ways, *morally weak*. Various modifications of the word ἀσθένεια may be found in Gal. iv. 9. Heb. iv. 15. v. 2. vii. 18. In Heb. iv. 15, the nature of the appeal seems to show, that the writer supposes Jesus himself to have possessed ἀσθένεια like our own; but he takes care to add, χωρὶς ἁμαρτίας; so that while he had the susceptibility of being tempted and tried (πεπειρασμένον κατὰ πάντα καθ' ὁμοιότητα) in all respects as we are, which seems to be the ἀσθένεια here characterized, he still remained " holy, harmless, undefiled, and separate from sinners." It is not susceptibility of being tempted, then, which makes any one a sinner. However, in our text, ἀσθενῶν seems to be used in a more emphatic sense than in Heb. iv. 15. v. 2 ; for it is immediately exchanged for ἀσεβῶν, and in verse 8 for ἁμαρτωλῶν. This shows that actual development of character by some kind of voluntary action is meant, and not merely *vitiositas* or *peccabilitas;* for ἀσεβής and ἁμαρτωλός are not applied to mark these qualities, but to mark character that is developed.

After all, however, the doubt forces itself on my mind, whether ἀσθενῶν does not here characterize *weakness* or *inability* of the sinner as to saving himself, having once come under the condemning sentence of the law. In Heb. vii. 18, the law is asserted to be ἀσθενής, because it can afford no help to the sinner who is condemned by it. What now if we suppose the apostle to mean here, that ' when we were under the curse, and *unable* to save ourselves, Christ then interposed?' The sense is surely good, and the apparent *tautology* made by ἀσεβῶν, when it is construed in the usual way, is avoided.

In due time, κατὰ καιρόν, *at an appointed* or *set time*, viz., that fixed upon in the counsels of God. Comp. Sept. in Job v. 26. Isa. lx. 22 ; comp. also Luke xxi. 24, 8. Heb. xi. 11. Comp. τὸ πλήρωμα τοῦ χρόνου in Gal. iv. 4.

For [us] *who were ungodly*, ὑπὲρ ἀσεβῶν, i. e., ὑπὲρ ἀσεβῶν [ἡμῶν]. It is plain that ἀσεβῶν here characterizes the same class of persons who were called ἀσθενῶν in the preceding clause. It means *impious, those who do not reverence* or *fear God*.— Ὑπέρ, *for, on account of, instead of, i. e.,* in our room or stead.— So the comparison in the next verse, where dying ὑπὲρ ἀγαθοῦ and ὑπὲρ δικαίου is mentioned, obliges us to interpret this. Even Ruckert concedes that the meaning here must be *loco nostro, vice nostrâ*. Reiche admits that this is the *symbolical costume* of the language; but that the idea of *vicarious sacrifice* is to be *objectively* admitted, he arbitrarily deems to be entirely out of question.

(7) Γάρ *illustrantis ;* for the sequel is designed to illustrate the great benevolence which the death of Christ displayed, and which

is proposed to our view in verses 5, 6. Δικαίου is here used in distinction from ἀγαθοῦ. Often these words are *synonymous;* yet they are capable of distinct use, and in classic usage they are not unfrequently distinguished from each other. *E. g.,* Cicero: "Recte *justum* virum, *bonum* non facilè reperiemus;" de Offic. III. 15. Again: "Jupiter *Optimus* dictus est, id est, *beneficentissimus.*' So in the Talmud (Pirque Abhoth, 5, 10) it is said: "There are four kinds of men; (1) Those who say: What is mine is mine, and what is thine is thine; these are the *middling* men. (2) Those who say: What is mine is thine, and what is thine is mine; these are the common people. (3) Those who say: What is mine is thine, and what is thine is thine; these are the חסידים, *i. e.,* ἀγαθοί. (4) Those who say: What is mine is mine, and what is thine is mine; these are the רְשָׁעִים." So (by the Seventy) חסיד, usually = ὅσιος, צַדִּיק, δίκαιος. Δίκαιος may be used to designate a person who is *innocent* merely; so in the Septuagint, Ex. xxiii. 7. Gen. xviii. 23, seq. So in the New Testament, Matt. xxvii. 19, 24. It corresponds also to the Hebrew נָקִי, Prov. i. 11. vi. 17. Joel iii. 19. In using δίκαιος, therefore, as designating a character somewhat different from ἀγαθός and inferior to it, the apostle has not varied from sacred and classic usage. Δίκαιος clearly means here, *one who is just* in the common sense of the word, *one who is free from crimes* cognizable by law, *one who does not defraud,* etc. For such a one, the apostle says, it would be rare to find any person willing to volunteer the sacrifice of his life.

Although for the ἀγαθός, i. e., the benevolent or rather *the beneficent man,* (the חסיד), *some one perhaps might venture even to lay down his life.* This has in fact not unfrequently been done. The difference between the readiness of men to hazard their lives for a man of peculiar and overflowing benevolence of heart, and for a man who merely pays a nice regard to *meum* and *tuum,* is very plain to every observer who has a feeling heart. Reiche and Tholuck suppose ἀγαθός here to designate a *kind benefactor,* in distinction from a simple δίκαιος. To this I see no objection; for it makes the contrast between δίκαιος and ἀγαθός the more striking; and is well founded in the nature of the idiom. I may add, that the sequel is rendered the more striking by it. Besides, the use of the *article* here before ἀγαθοῦ shows that a *specific* benefactor is thought of by the writer. The article is here = to the pronominal adjective *his.*

The γάρ in this second clause may (as usual in such cases) be taken as *affirmative* (ja, allerdings, Passow), and we might translate thus: *Perhaps, indeed, for the benefactor,* etc. I have rendered it *although* in the version; not because γάρ of itself means *although*, but because the relation of the sentiment demands such a rendering, in order to make the sense explicit to us. The καί before τολμᾷ is undoubtedly *καί intensivum;* but standing before such a connection as τολμᾷ ἀποθανεῖν, it may be joined with either verb, as the sense requires. Here it is better to join it with ἀποθανεῖν — *would venture even to die.* What he had just said was: 'Scarcely will any one die for a just man ;" now he says: ' Still it may be, that some one will venture *even to die* for a benefactor.' *Will even venture* does not put the emphasis in the right place.

(8) Yet the grace of the gospel has far surpassed any exhibition of human benevolence. He [God] *commends,* συνίστημι, *displays,* — Ἀγάπην, *benevolence,* רַחֲמִים *compassionate kindness.* — Ὑπὲρ ἡμῶν, *in our stead,* or *on our account.* In either way of rendering the sense here must be, that the death of Christ saved us from that which we as ἁμαρτωλοί deserved. Ἁμαρτωλοί means *those who err* in heart and life.

(9) *Much more, then, being justified, i. e.,* acquitted as to our past offences, *by his blood, i. e., shall we be saved by him from* [future] *indignation,* πολλῷ οὖν . . . . ἀπὸ τῆς ὀργῆς. In other words : ' If Christ by his death has accomplished our reconciliation, while we were in a state of enmity; *a fortiori* we may expect that the great work, thus begun and accomplished as to the most difficult part, will be completed.' That αἵματι αὐτοῦ means the same thing as the death of Christ, *i. e.,* that it here directly refers to the preceding ἀπέθανε, does not admit of any reasonable doubt.

(10) A repetition of the same general ideas, in which the sentiment of the whole is compressed and rendered prominent. Γάρ *confirmantis.* Θανάτου κ. τ. λ. here corresponds to τῷ αἵματι αὐτοῦ in the preceding verse. — Ἐν τῇ ζωῇ αὐτοῦ, the antithesis of θανάτου αὐτοῦ. Meaning: 'If we were reconciled to God, when enemies, by a *dying* Saviour ; *a fortiori* shall we, when thus reconciled, attain salvation through a *living* one ;' *i. e.,* if Christ in his humble and suffering state reconciled us to God, much more in his exalted and glorified state (ἐν τῇ ζωῇ αὐτοῦ) will he complete the work thus begun ; comp. Rom. iv. 21, where is the same sentiment. Ἐν before ζωῇ is evidently used in a different sense from διά before θανάτου.

The scriptural view of *reconciliation* is, that the *offending* party becomes reconciled to the other. The verb καταλλάσσω properly means *to change, exchange;* and it is here employed to designate the change of the sinner's mind, who was "at enmity with God," to that state in which he comes to love and reverence him.

(11) *And not only*, οὐ μόνον δὲ, [do we rejoice in afflictions, verse 3, as tending to produce a hope of glory which the death of Christ has rendered *sure* and *certain*], *but we rejoice*, ἀλλὰ καὶ καυχώμενοί [ἐσμεν] *in God*, viz., as our God, our covenant God, our supreme and eternal joy; comp. Rev. xxi. 3. Heb. viii. 10. Zech. viii. 8. Jer. iv. 2; also John viii. 41, 54. Rom. ii. 17, which last passage shows the claims of the Jews in respect to their covenant relation with God. The apostle means to intimate, that all which the Jews boasted of, is in reality secured to Christians. The use of καυχώμενοι here, instead of a proper verb as in verse 3, is substantially *Hebraistic;* for in Hebrew the change of construction from a verb to a participle, and *vice versa*, is very common.

The verse before us is a *summary* or *consummation* of all the grounds of rejoicing; for to rejoice in God as our God, expresses the consummation of all the Christian's happiness. In respect to form or mode of expression, it constitutes a diverse head; and it is one which in fact is really diverse in this respect, viz., that it is more *generic* than the preceding declarations. The phrases in verses 1, 3, and 11, καυχώμεθα — οὐ μόνον δὲ ἀλλὰ καὶ — οὐ μόνον δὲ ἀλλὰ καί — present the natural division of the apostle's discourse, and correspond to our 1st, 2nd, 3rd, in English. Some critics, however, think that verse 11 refers merely to the καταλλαγέντες σωθησόμεθα of the preceding verse, and construe thus: 'But we are not only reconciled and saved, but also rejoice,' etc. The sense is good; but the method above stated seems to me, on the whole, to be preferable. The phrase τὴν καταλλαγὴν ἐλάβομεν receives its *form* from the expression in verse 10, κατηλλάγημεν κ. τ. λ. The word means *reconciliation;* and such is the sense in which our English translators here used the word *atonement* (quasi *at-one-ment*).

CHAP. V. 12—19.

The *main* design of this passage seems, indeed, to be plain, although the detail is attended with difficulty. It is this, viz., to impress on our minds the *certainty* of salvation through redeeming blood, and to exalt our views respecting the *greatness* of the blessings which Christ has procured for us, by a comparison of them with the evil consequences which ensued upon the fall of our first ancestor, and by showing that the blessings in question not only extend to the removal of these evils, but even far beyond this, so that the grace of the gospel has not only abounded but *superabounded*. These objects appear also to be united with the intention, to exhibit the *extent* to which the blessings in question are actually diffused or proffered

A *synopsis* of what is particularly taught in verses 12—19, may be comprised in the following particulars; viz., (a) Sin entered into the world [commenced] by the offence of Adam, and death, i.e., misery or loss of happiness, came in as the necessary result of it In like manner death came upon all men, because that all have sinned, verse 12.

(b) It is indeed true, that all men have been subjected to death: for that even those who did not live under the light of revelation, nor were made acquainted with any *express* commands of God, have been so, is proved from the fact, that all those who lived between Adam and Moses were sinners, and therefore lay under sentence of death, verses 13, 14

(c) Adam, who was the occasion of introducing sin into the world, and of bringing sin and death upon all men, may be considered as a τύπος of Christ, in respect to the influence which he has had on others, (but not as to the *kind* of influence, or as to the *degree* of it, for here is a wide diversity;) verse 14. last clause.

(d) That the *kind* and *degree* of influence which Adam had on all men is not like that which Christ has on them, is plain, (1) *As to the* KIND *of influence*, from the fact that Adam occasioned the *condemnation* of all men, but Christ delivers mankind from condemnation, and bestows eternal happiness on them, verse 15 (2) *As to the* DEGREE *of influence*, because the condemnation of which Adam was the occasion has respect only to *one* offence, while the pardon which Christ procured extends to *many* offences, verse 16 Hence (3) If death reigned over men because of one offence, much more shall they reign in life who through Christ receive pardon for *many* offences and a title to future blessedness, verse 17 In other words, if *evils* through *one* offence spread so wide, then *blessings* through the pardon of *many* offences more than counterbalance them.

Having thus guarded his readers against extending the idea of τύπος to points of which it cannot properly be predicated, and having shown that the influence of Christ on the human race is exactly the *reverse* of that of Adam, in respect to its *kind* or *nature*, and also that it far surpasses it in *degree*, the apostle now comes to the consideration of the real points of similitude between Adam and Christ, viz, the *universality* or *extent* of influence as excited through the act of one, *i e*, by what one individual has done This he states as follows

(e) As the consequences of Adam's sin were extended to all men, so the consequences of Christ's obedience [viz. unto death] are extended to all; *i. e*, Jews and Gentiles may all come on an equal footing into the kingdom of Christ, or the blessings which the gospel proffers are in some respects actually bestowed on all men without exception, and in others made equally accessible to all men, and to all on the same terms or conditions, verse 18, 19. All this was accomplished, in each case, by the act of one individual.

It seems to be plain, that the particular object of the writer is developed in verses 15—17, and 20, 21, and from these his object would appear mainly to be (as before stated,) ' to impress our minds with the *certainty* of salvation which is by grace, and to *magnify the riches* of that grace which is bestowed through Jesus Christ ' This the writer undertakes to accomplish by a comparison of the evils removed by Christ and the blessings bestowed, with the mischiefs occasioned by the fall of our first parents. Moreover, it is certain that inasmuch as all men have been injured by the fall, so it is a merciful and proper and benevolent arrangement on the part of God, that the blessings procured by Christ should be bestowed on all, or at least proffered to all, and in this way, the fact that he is the God of the Gentiles as well as the Jews, and that salvation is and ought to be accessible to the former as well as to the latter — a truth for which Paul so often and earnestly contends—see ni 29—31 iv. 1—25—is more fully illustrated and more satisfactorily and triumphantly evinced. We have then, according to this view of the matter, three objects to be accomplished by verses 12—21; viz , *to display and more fully evince the* CERTAINTY, *the* GREATNESS, *and the* EXTENSIVE NATURE *of that salvation which Christ* wrought In this general statement Ruckert agrees, in his recent Commentary.

(12) *Therefore*, διὰ τοῦτο. So it is usually translated, viz., as *illative*, and as showing that what follows is a *consequence* or *deduction* from what has gone before.

Some have however converted the words διὰ τοῦτο, into a mere *formula of transition;* e. g., Schleusner makes them so here; and Wahl represents διὰ τοῦτο as having such a sense in Matt. xiii. 52. These words might then be rendered, *moreover, further.* But such a meaning cannot be supported by reasoning which is strictly philological.

Schott understands διὰ τοῦτο, in his able Essay on Rom. v. 12 —14 (*Opusc.* vol. i. p. 318. seq.) as indicating an *occasion,* in reference to what had already been said, of making the remarks which follow. But Tholuck, Reiche, Glockler, and many others, represent διὰ τοῦτο here as *illative;* although none of them seem to me to have satisfactorily shown *how* the sequel is strictly a *logical deduction* from what precedes.

Although διὰ τοῦτο is not always employed in an *illative* sense, as some assert, (cf. Matt. xiii. 52. Mark xii. 24. Rom. xiii. 6; to which other doubtful passages might be added); still a minute and extensive review of this subject has brought me to the conviction, that διὰ τοῦτο here is employed in a kind of *illative* sense, although not in one which is strictly of *logical* illation. I do not view it as having relation in particular to ver. 11, but to what precedes this, and particularly to the great points brought to view and established from chap. iii. 28 to ver. 11, viz., the extent, the greatness, and the certainty of salvation by Christ. The connected course of thought seems to me to be this: 'The extent, the greatness, the certainty of salvation, I have now exhibited to you, *therefore* (διὰ τοῦτο) it is worthy of all reception, or *therefore* it is true, that *as by one man's sin*,' etc. Instead of repeating a simple deduction, the apostle makes out one accompanied by illustrations and remarks which serve very much to strengthen the impression that he intends to make. He who fully recognizes this last circumstance, will probably be relieved in his mind from the main part of the difficulty occasioned by the use of διὰ τοῦτο, in this connection.

On any other ground than this, substantially, I do not see how the *appropriateness* of διὰ τοῦτο can be made out. If we suppose that the *main* point in vers. 12 — 21, is to exhibit the relation of Adam to us, or the influence of his offence upon us, then it is quite impossible to make out in reality and propriety an *illative* sense of διὰ τοῦτο here. For the apostle has not anywhere previously discussed the subject of Adam's offence or influence. It is men's *own personal* sins which he has thus far represented as the cause of their guilt and danger before God. How then must his reasoning stand, on the ground which I am opposing? Simply thus: 'All men have brought themselves under the curse of the law by their sins. God is the common father of Jews and Gentiles, and has the same designs of pardoning mercy towards both, and has *promised* to bestow it; the death of Christ has assured the promised salvation; the riches of his grace are exceedingly great and wonderful; THEREFORE (διὰ τοῦτο) *as Adam by one offence ruined all men, so Christ by his obedience has procured salvation for all.*' That this is a fair statement of the course of thought will not be denied by any; and the last particular must be admitted by those whom I am now opposing. But how the *logical illation* is to be made out by them, if we subjoin the last particular in its present shape, is a problem that my powers of reasoning are not adequate to solve.

We must change the shape, then, of the last member of this series of propositions, and say: '*therefore, i. e.*, because of the arguments produced and reasons already given to show the extent, the greatness, and the certainty of salvation by Christ—*therefore*, it is true, that, etc.; or *therefore* we must admit, that as Adam introduced sin and misery into the world in such a way that they became universal, and certain, and abounding, so Christ has become the author of salvation universal, certain, and abounding, or great.' The main object of course is the latter one, and it is for the very purpose of heightening the intensity of the picture given of this, that the antithesis and similitude of Adam's case is introduced.

As, ὥσπερ, of course introduces a comparison; ὥσπερ standing before the *protasis*, which seems to extend through the verse. The *apodosis* appears to be wanting here. The form of the sentence completed would be: Ὥσπερ κ. τ. λ.—οὕτως καὶ κ. τ. λ. This *apodosis* is supplied, however, in different ways, or is differently constructed, by different critics.

(*a*) Διὰ τοῦτο [τὴν καταλλαγὴν ἐλάβομεν], ὥσπερ δι' ἑνὸς κ. τ. λ.; making ὥσπερ κ. τ. λ. itself an *apodosis* instead of a protasis. So Coccerus, Elsner, Koppe, Cramer, Rosenmüller, Stolz, and some others.

(*b*) By inverting καὶ οὕτως, and writing it οὕτως καὶ κ. τ. λ.; and so making the rest of the verse which follows, to be the *apodosis* of the sentence. So Le Clerc, Wolf, Homberg, and others.

(*c*) Καὶ διὰ τῆς ἁμαρτίας κ. τ. λ. is made the beginning of the *apodosis* by Erasmus and Beza; which of course they must translate thus: *so also by sin*, etc.

(*d*) Calvin, Gomer, Tholuck, Schmid, and some others, find the *apodosis* in verse 14, viz., ὅς ἐστι τύπος τοῦ μέλλοντος.

(*e*) Others find it concealed in verse 15; and some make it out from the whole of the sequel after verse 12.

But all these methods come short of fully and definitely exhibiting the *contrast* here, which the apostle designs to make between the one man (Adam) who sinned, and Christ; which contrast appears fully and plainly in verses 18, 19. With the majority of interpreters, therefore, I hesitate not to regard verses 13 — 17 as substantially a parenthesis (thrown in to illustrate a sentiment brought to view in the protasis, verse 12); and I find a full apodosis only in verses 18, 19, where the sentiment of verse 12 is virtually resumed and repeated, and where the apodosis regularly follows, after an οὕτω καί. (I admit, however, that ὅς ἐστι τύπος τοῦ μέλλοντος in verse 14 conveys a general sentiment, which may make a kind of apodosis in the way of hint.) In this manner, and only in this, can I find the real antithesis or comparison as fully made out, which the apostle designs to make. This method of writing, too, where the protasis is suspended for the sake of explanations thrown in, is altogether consonant with the usual method of the apostle Paul; see introduction and cf. Rom. i. 3 — 7. ii. 6 — 16. Eph. ii. 1 — 5. iii. 1 — 13. 1 Tim. i. 3, 4. Rom. ix. 10, seq. Rom. ix. 22, seq. Rom. viii. 3. Heb. iv. 6 — 9. v. 6 — 10. v. 10. vii. 1. ix. 7 — 12. All that is necessary to be noted is, that the apodosis in verses 18, 19, is given in language that takes its hue from the intermediate parenthesis of verses 13 — 17. The simple apodosis independently of this would be: οὕτω καὶ διὰ ἑνὸς δικαιοσύνη εἰς κόσμον εἰσῆλθε, καὶ εἰς πάντας ἀνθρώπους διῆλθε.

By one man, δι' ἑνὸς ἀνθρώπου, *i. e.*, by Adam, as appears from verse 14; comp. 1 Cor. xv. 21, 22, 45. The apostle cannot design that this should be strictly construed; for he himself has told us, that "Adam was not deceived; but the *woman*, being deceived, was in the transgression." (1 Tim. ii. 14. 2 Cor. xi. 3), *i. e.*, Eve first transgressed; which, moreover, Paul assigns as a reason why she should not usurp authority and have precedence in the church. In the like way the son of Sirach represents Eve as the first transgressor, xxv. 24. Then why is not Eve mentioned here? Either the apostle, in making mention of Adam, trusted that his readers would spontaneously call to mind the primitive pair, the woman being comprehended along with the man; or he designed merely to compare the origin itself and extent of sin and misery (without particularizing the manner), with the origin and extent of the deliverance from them as wrought by Christ. In respect to the first of these suppositions, the rule *a potiori nomen fit* seems to be applicable to the sentiment of it. Adam is named as the constituted superior, who was first formed and made lord of the inferior creation. Nor can any importance be here attached to the fact itself, that *two* were concerned in the primitive transgression: "they twain were one flesh;" they were one also in guilt, *i. e.*, they were both partakers of the same criminality. The object of investigation is not the exact *manner* in which the first transgression came to be committed, but; What influence had the primitive sin, in which Adam was the most conspicuous, responsible, and important actor, on the race of men, as to introducing and occasioning sin and misery? Besides, had Adam refused to unite with his wife in her transgression, the consequences must inevitably have been altogether different from what they have now been. His act, then, *completed* the mischief which was begun by Eve; and so the apostle names him here as the cause of all the evils which followed; not, however, implying that he considered Eve as less blameworthy than Adam, or more inexcusable, to which 1 Tim. ii. 14 is directly opposed. But *congruity* in respect to the comparison which he is to make, probably led to this manner of representation, *i. e.*, the comparing of the one *man* (*i. e.*, the first Adam) with one *man* (*i. e.*, the second Adam). How would it strike readers, if Eve had been here substituted for Adam? And this suggestion leads, at once, to a perception of what *congruity* demands in the case before us.

As to διὰ in this phrase, it designates, as often elsewhere, the *causa principalis*, not the mere secondary, instrumental, or occasional cause. In the Sept. and New Test., such a usage is beyond all doubt a frequent one, as any good lexicon will show.

Sin, ἡ ἁμαρτία. *The sin*, in English, would mean something different from the Greek here, although the article is prefixed to the word. Whenever anything is named which is generic in its nature, but *unique* or single in its kind, the Greeks usually prefix the article to it; *e. g.*, ὁ φιλόσοφος, ἡ ἀρετή, ἡ ἀλήθεια, τὸ ἀγαθόν, ἡ δικαιοσύνη, etc. In such cases, ἡ δικαιοσύνη (for example) as an entire *genus*, is *unique*, *i. e.*, it differs from all other qualities of moral beings; and so it has the article prefixed in order to denote this. But still, δικαιοσύνη may at another time be regarded by the mind as a genus comprehending *several subordinate species*, such as commutative justice, penal justice, integrity, etc.; in which case the article would naturally be omitted. Agreeably to these principles, ἡ ἁμαρτία here appears with the article, because it appears in its simple *generic* nature, *i. e.*, as single or monadic. That it is generic here, *i. e.*, that it comprehends both sinful actions and affections, seems to be clear from the nature of the case, and from what follows. If Adam was created so as to be upright, and was purely holy until his fall, then sin commenced with his fall; sin of any kind; sin either in *affection* or *action*. That such a *generic* meaning must here be given to ἡ ἁμαρτία, is evident, from the simple fact, that Adam's desire of the forbidden fruit inordinately indulged, was a sin of the *affections*, and his actually eating it was a sin of external action.*

Bretschneider remarks (Dogmat. II. 48, ed. 3), that the article is used before ἁμαρτία in the verse before us, because it designates *vitiositas*, but not *peccata actualia*. But surely the sequel here will not justify his remark; for the ἡ ἁμαρτία of Adam is called (verse 14) his παράβασις; in verses 15, 17, and 18, his παράπτωμα; in verse 19, his παρακοή; all of which implies *peccatum actuale*, viz., the unlawful desiring and eating of the forbidden fruit.

The simple scriptural idea of ἁμαρτία is ἀνομία, i. e., lawlessness, violation of law. *To miss the mark, to err, to fail,* is the primitive meaning of ἁμαρτάνω; and ἁμαρτία always has reference to some rule or law which is violated by it; as the apostolic definition of it by ἀνομία clearly shows. At all events nothing but sin as an *act* can be here designated; for Adam's sin was such. He had no previous *vitiositas;* and if *vitiositas* had been a part of the *original* constitution of man, Adam surely could not have been the *author* of this. The meaning must be, as afterwards asserted, that sin commenced with Adam's παράβασις or παράπτωμα or παρακοή, neither of which is *vitiositas* but *vitium*.

Into the world, εἰς τὸν κόσμον, i. e., among men, into the world of human beings; comp. Matt. xxvi. 13. 2 Pet. ii. 5. iii. 6. Matt. xiii. 38. John. i. 10. iii. 16, 17. xvi. 33. 2 Cor. i. 12. Comp. also ἔρχεσθαι εἰς τὸν κόσμον, John vi. 14. ix. 39. xi. 27. xii. 46. Heb. x. 5. 2 John ii. 7. That the right explanation of κόσμος is given above, is confirmed by verse 18, where εἰς πάντας ἀνθρώπους is a substitute for it, and one of equivalent report.

Entered into, invaded,† εἰσῆλθε. The first entrance or the commencement of sin is here designated; as is plain from the sequel, where διῆλθε is used to designate the further and universal progress of sin. Compare Wisd. ii. 24, φθόνῳ δὲ διαβόλου θάνατος εἰσῆλθεν εἰς τὸν κόσμον; and also xiv. 14.

And by sin, καὶ διὰ τῆς ἁμαρτίας, i. e., through the instrumentality of sin; or rather, *by reason of sin, in consequence of sin*, on

---

* De Wette says: *sin*, ἁμαρτία, is here a *power* ruling over men (verse 21 and 3. 9), partly as a *principle* existing and developing itself in all (7: 8); and partly as a *state*, as it is represented in 1. 17—3 21. It cannot be restricted to *original sin* (Calvin), *the habit* of sinning (Olshausen), *the propensity* to sin (Rothe), or *to sin impersonated*, as in 7· 8 seq.

† *Entered into the world*, i e as De Wette says, not *merely, esse coepit*, primum commissa est (Reiche, Meyer, et al), i e that which was before something merely possible, now began its real existence. But there is the accompanying idea of diffusion, i e. sin entered into, gained access, to the world, κόσμος, to men, to human beings.

account of sin; διά being usually employed in this sense, when put before the Genitive.

Death, θάνατος. But what death? That of the body, or of the soul, or of both? In other words: Is *temporal* evil only here meant, or *eternal,* or both?

The answer must be sought for, first of all, in the *usus loquendi* of the author himself. In the context we have his own explanation of θάνατος. In verse 15, *death,* (ἀπέθανον) stands opposed to χάρις τοῦ Θεοῦ καὶ ἡ δωρεὰ ἐν χάριτι. In verse 17, it stands opposed to τὴν περισσείαν τῆς χάριτος καὶ τῆς δωρεᾶς τῆς δικαιοσύνης. In verse 21, it stands opposed to ζωὴν αἰώνιον. In chapter vi. 23, θάνατος is directly contrasted with ζωὴ αἰώνιος. That θάνατος, then, by the *usus loquendi* of Paul, does sometimes mean *a death* which is the *opposite* of *eternal life* or happiness, is here made certain.

In the like sense, *i. e.,* as used to designate *the penalty of sin,* the reader may find θάνατος in other writings of Paul; viz. in Rom. i. 32. vi. 21. vi. 16. vii. 5. vii. 10. vii. 13. vii. 24. viii. 2. viii. 6. 2 Cor. ii. 16. vii. 10. 2 Tim. i. 10. Heb. ii. 14. Nor is this peculiar to Paul alone, for it agrees with that of other sacred writers in the New Testament; *e. g.,* John viii. 51. v. 24. James i. 15. 1 John iii. 14. Rev. ii. 11. xx. 6. xx. 14.

In like manner we find the word *death* to be used in the Old Testament; *e. g.,* Deut. xxx. 15. Jer. xxi. 8 (comp. Sirach xv. 7). Prov. v. 5. viii. 36. xi. 19. xii. 28. Ezek. xxxiii. 11. And in the same way the verb *to die* is employed; *e. g.,* by Paul, Rom. viii. 13; by John vi. 50. xi. 26. viii. 21. So in the Old Testament; *e. g.,* Ezek. xviii. 4, 17, 20, 21, 24, 28, 32, Prov. xv. 10. Ezek. xxxiii. 8, 11. 13, 14, 15. Must not this be the sense, also, in Gen. ii. 17. iii. 3, 4?

It is clear that in many of these cases it is quite impossible to limit the words *death, die,* to the dissolution of the body, or temporal death. *E. g.,* John viii. 51, 'If any man shall keep my saying, *he shall never see death.*' John v 24. 'He that heareth my words ... *is passed from death unto life.*' John xi. 26, 'Whosoever ... believeth in me, *shall never die.*' Ezek. xviii. 28, 'He ... that turneth away from his transgressions ... shall surely live, *he shall not die;*' and so in many of the other passages quoted. The biblical usage is very definitely and specifically set forth in Deut. xxx. 5; 'See, I have set before thee this day, LIFE and GOOD, and DEATH and EVIL.' *Life* is the image of all good, and therefore is employed to express it; *death* is the consummation of all evil, and so it is used as a strong expression in order to designate every kind of evil, whether temporal or eternal.

The *usus loquendi*, then, doubtless *permits* θάνατος to be construed as designating the *penalty of sin*, yea the *whole* penalty. The only question is: Whether θάνατος is employed in this sense in the passage before us?

The antithesis in verses 15, 17, 21, and vi. 23, as produced above, would seem to go far toward a final settlement of this question. Indeed, there is no *philological* escape from the conclusion, that *death* in the sense of *penalty for sin*, must be regarded as the meaning of the writer here.

Is there anything now in *the nature of the case*, which goes to show that death should here have a *limited* meaning given to it, or (in other words) that it should be construed as meaning only *the death of the body*?

What then is the nature of the case? It is this, viz., that as condemnation [κατάκριμα] came upon all men by the offence of one man (Adam), so by the obedience of one (Christ), all men have access to δικαίωσις εἰς ζωήν, verse 18. Now as ζωή is here plainly the antithesis of θάνατος [κατάκριμα], we have only to inquire what must be the meaning of ζωή in order to obtain that of θάνατος. But in respect to this there can be no doubt. Ζωή means the blessings or happiness procured by a Saviour's death, *i. e.*, it designates all the holiness and happiness which this introduces. But certainly these blessings are not limited to *the resurrection of the body*. I do not deny that such a resurrection is a blessing to the righteous; see 1 Cor. xv. I would rather say however, that the resurrection is something preparatory to the bestowment of blessings. But it must be remembered, that the wicked will be raised from the dead as truly as the righteous; yet surely no one will count this a *blessing* to them. It is only a preparation for augmented misery.

It cannot be, then, that the simple resurrection from the dead, in itself considered, should be called δικαίωσις ζωῆς, and therefore a state of temporal death is not a direct and full antithesis to life, *i. e.*, in the sense given to this word by the apostle, temporal death is not principally the evil from which it is the main object of Christ to deliver us; for resurrection from this is a *good* or an *evil*, just as the case may be in regard to the moral character of him who is the subject of such resurrection.

It is unnecessary to enquire whether Christ delivers from the *suffering itself* of temporal death, since all men without distinction, are mortal and die. One thing, however, should be said in reference to this; which is, that 'the sting of death' is taken away as to believers, through the hopes inspired by a Saviour's blood; and that in this way the evil is greatly mitigated in respect to those who have true hope in Christ.

Once more; the penalty of *all* sin is *evil, i. e.,* evil as to both body and soul. "The soul that sinneth shall die." Evil to the *body* those of course will admit, who hold that temporal death is here meant. Evil to the *soul* they must also admit; for how is it possible that any one should sin, without defiling, polluting, and rendering unhappy the soul? The primary elements of the *moral* universe must be changed, before this can take place. It is impossible in the case of Adam, or in any other case, that sin should be committed without injury to the *soul.* It would follow with certainty, then, that if Adam's first sin was a *real* sin, and *a fortiori* if it was one of the greatest of all sins (as we surely have much reason to conclude when we consider its consequences), then death in its *extensive* sense must have been the penalty attached to it. What reason can be given, why other sins less than his are punishable with *death* in the enlarged sense of this word, and yet that the sin of Adam was not punishable in the like way? Was he not even the more culpable, who fell from a state of entire holiness?

Finally, the apostle, when he comes to point out the dissimilitude between Adam's offence and its consequences, and the obedience of Christ and its consequences (as he does in verses 15 — 17), opposes the κατάκριμα occasioned by Adam to the δικαίωμα effected by Christ, verse 16; and the θάνατος introduced by the former, to the βασιλεύειν ἐν ζωῇ accomplished by the latter, verse 17. Now as δικαίωμα is not, in its more important sense, a deliverance from temporal death merely, nor *the reigning in life* merely a deliverance from mortality; so *temporal death,* although included (see 1 Cor. xv. 22) cannot with any good appearance of reason, be understood here as the only and essential meaning of θάνατος.

And thus, καὶ οὕτως, *i. e., and so,* or *and in like manner.* The exact idea that the writer means to express by these words, we shall be better able to understand, when we have examined the remaining words of the verse.

BECAUSE THAT *all have sinned,* ἐφ᾽ ᾧ πάντες ἥμαρτον. Another method of rendering this has often been urged, viz., IN WHOM *all have sinned.* So the Vulgate; and so, in conformity to this, Augustine, Beza, Calixtus, E. Schmidt, Calovius, et alii. But the objections to translating ἐφ᾽ ᾧ by *in quo, in whom,* are weighty; for, (1) If ᾧ be made masc., there is no antecedent for it within any probable limits. Ἀνθρώπου lies too far back; and θάνατος would make no tolerable sense; for what meaning could be conveyed, by saying, 'in *which death* all have sinned?' (2) Not ἐπὶ ᾧ, (ἐφ᾽ ᾧ), but ἐν ᾧ would be the proper expression for *in whom.* So Thomas Magister and Phavorinus: ἐφ᾽ ᾧ, ἀντὶ τοῦ διότι. Comp. 2 Cor. v. 4, ἐφ' ᾧ οὐ θέλομεν. (3) The assertion ἐφ' ᾧ πάντες ἥμαρτον, is dwelt upon and explained in verses 13, 14; and in these verses, men's own *personal* sins appear to be spoken of (as we shall hereafter see), not those of another which are laid to their charge ; and if this explanation be admitted, then ἐφ' ᾧ cannot here mean *in whom*. (4) If ἐφ' ᾧ could be properly taken as equivalent to ἐν ᾧ, (and ἐπί and ἐν are beyond all doubt sometimes commuted as to sense in the New Test.), yet the whole phrase, viz., ἁμαρτάνειν ἐπί τινι, meaning *to sin in some one* or *by one*, is so far as I know, without any example to support it. If the apostle had designed to express such an unusual idea, would he not of course have shunned all ambiguity of phraseology, and made the form of his expression so definite that no doubt could remain? As it is, we must follow the usual laws of interpretation ; and there can be no doubt that we are authorized by these to translate ἐφ' ᾧ, *because, for that,* etc. Thus in the examples adduced by Phavorinus : ἐφ' ᾧ τὴν κλοπὴν ἐργάσω, BECAUSE *thou hast committed theft;* ἐφ' οἷς [plur.] τὸν νόμον οὐ τηρεῖς, BECAUSE *thou dost not obey the law.* So in the example of Thomas Magister : ἐφ' ᾧ Γεννάδιον ἔγραφεν, BECAUSE *he has given a sketch of Gennadius.* So Marcus Aurelius says : ἐφ' οἷς ὁρᾶτέ με διακείμενον, BECAUSE *ye see me determined,* in Herod. 1. 4. Theophilus (ad Autol. 2) says : ἐφ' ᾧ οὐκ ἴσχυσε θανατῶσαι αὐτούς, BECAUSE *he could not kill them ;* Plutarch (de Pyth. extr.) ἐφ' οἷς ἐγενόμην . . . . πρόθυμος, BECAUSE *I was ready.* In fact, ἐφ' ᾧ is a well known elliptical phrase, employed in the same sense as ἐν τούτῳ ὅτι, or our English *in that, because.* And in this rendering agree Theodoret, Photius, Pelagius, Erasmus, Luther, Calvin, Pet. Martyr, our Eng. Version, Gerhard, Piscator, Paræus, Buddæus, Raphel, Wetstein, Carpzov. Koppe, Flatt, Schott, Vatablus, Schmid, Steudel, Tholuck, Ruckert, Reiche, and many others.

Other translations of ἐφ' ᾧ have also been defended; *per eum* (Grotius); *propter quem* (Elsner); *secundum quem* (Photius, Œcumenius, Bretsch.); *cum quo* (Cocceius); but it is enough to say of these, that if Paul had meant to express such a sense, we can hardly suppose that he would not have employed διά, or σύν, or μετά, or κατά, instead of using ἐπί. Even *post quem* has been proposed as a version of ἐφ' ᾧ, *i. e.,* AFTER *whom*. But what would be the sense of Paul's saying, that Adam's posterity sinned *after* he did ? Did his readers need to be told this? Others, as Homberg, Venema, Schmid, and Glockler, render ἐφ' ᾧ UNTO *which,* viz., unto which death or punishment; thus making ἐπί to mark the *end* or *consequence* to which sinning came. In the classics we do indeed find νοσεῖν ἐπὶ θανάτῳ, *to be sick* UNTO *death*

(Ælian), and δῆσαι ἐπὶ θανάτῳ, *to bind* UNTO *death* (Herod.), and other like phrases. But a conclusive objection against this interpretation is, that the apostle has just said, and more strongly said, the very thing that this interpretation makes him to say over again. Besides, to understand the apostle here as saying that *all have sinned* UNTO *death*, would seem to imply, that they might have sinned to a certain extent without incurring such a penalty. Different from this is the case where another apostle says, "there is a sin unto death;" for he is there discussing the subject of an *unpardonable* sin.

Finally: to render ἐφ' ᾧ, *on account of which, for the sake of which*, would be little short of nonsense; for how could the apostle say, that all men sinned *for the sake of* bringing death upon themselves?

When Origen, Ambrose, Jerome, Augustine, and some other fathers, adopt the sense of *in quo*, this appears to be the result of their *theology* rather than of their philology. Augustine has given us the explanation of his views: "Fuerunt enim omnes *ratione seminis* in lumbis Adam quando damnatus est: et ideo sine illis damnatus non est, [Heb. VII. 9, 10]; contra Jul. Pelag. V. 12. And again: "In Adam omnes tunc peccaverunt, quando in ejus natura, illâ insitâ vi quâ eos gignere poterat, adhuc *omnes ille unus fuerunt*," De pecc. Merit. et Rem. III. 7. The same *unity* with Adam has Pres. Edwards labored to establish in Part IV. chapter 3 of his work on Original Sin; where he has argued, that the *unity* of each individual of the human race with Adam their common ancestor may as well be asserted, as the unity of any individual with himself at different points of time; unity in both cases being merely a matter of "sovereign and arbitrary appointment." The schoolmen have speculated *ad nauseam* on this subject.

All have sinned, πάντες ἥμαρτον. But how? In their *own proper persons*? Or in Adam? Or is it merely the meaning of ἥμαρτον here, that all men *are treated* as sinners?

This last opinion Storr maintains; and he appeals to Gen. xliv. 32, וְהָטָאתִי *then I will bear the blame, i. e.*, I will be *treated* as a sinner, as he construes it. But the meaning is, 'I will consent to be regarded as a sinner by my father.' He also refers to Job ix. 29, אם ארשע; which however does not support the appeal. Grotius also appeals to Gen. xxxi. 27, and Job vi. 24 (?) for the like purpose; but without ground. And although, if an exigency of the passage demanded it, ἥμαρτον might be rendered, *are treated as sinners* (comp. 1 K. i. 21, where, however, the meaning is 'I and my son shall be sinners in the view of the reigning prince'); yet no such exigency occurs here, as vers. 13,

14, show; for in these (which are plainly built upon the latter part of verse 12), the writer labors to show that men are themselves *actual* sinners; as we shall see in the sequel. Besides, it is a good rule of interpretation, never to depart from the *usual* sense of words unless there is an imperious reason for it; and ἁμαρτάνω does not usually, if ever, mean *to be treated as a sinner*.

But the second method of explanation, viz., 'that *all men have sinned* IN *Adam*, cannot be adopted here, because it is founded merely in the mode of expression, *i. e.*, in the phrase ἐφ᾽ ᾧ. The reasons for rejecting this opinion have already been stated above. It can be admitted only in case of *philological* necessity, which does not occur here. There remains, therefore, only the first plain and simple method of interpretation, viz., all men have sinned in their own persons; all men have themselves incurred the guilt of sin, and so subjected themselves to its penalty; or at least, all men are themselves sinners, and so are liable to death. The word ἥμαρτον contains in itself an *active* sense throughout; and must therefore imply *sin in an active sense*. Accordingly, the word ἁμαρτάνω has neither passive nor middle voice; which is a striking evidence that the word is, from its very nature, susceptible of only an active sense. Besides, in the case before us the *Aorist* is employed; which, as Ruckert and Reiche have well observed, designates what was matter of *fact*, not mere state or condition. The connection strongly impresses the same idea. The sin of Adam, mentioned in the first clause of the verse, was one of fact, deed, action. not of state or condition; and the implication is, that πάντες have sinned as he did, although not against the same law, or precept, verse 14. Moreover, the assertion of universal sinfulness has an evident reference to the apostle's previous declaration and conclusion, in iii. 19 — 23. All his proof in chaps. i.— iii. of universal sin, consists in appeal to *facts, i. e.*, to sins actually committed.

Some of the most respectable commentators, it is true, regard πάντες ἥμαρτον as meaning that all have sinned in Adam, or at least, that through him they have become sinners; and they appeal to verse 17 — 19 in support of this sentiment. And it must be confessed, that there is no more ground for objection to the *sentiment* which the expression thus construed would convey, than there is to the sentiment in verse 17 — 19. But still there are philological difficulties involved in such an exegesis, which I see no way of satisfactorily removing. Verses 13 and 14 seem plainly to recognize such sin as that of which men are *personally* and *actually* guilty; yea a sin different in some important respects from that of Adam's first transgression, ... ἐπὶ τοὺς μὴ ἁμαρτήσαντας ἐπὶ τῷ ὁμοιώματι τῆς παραβάσεως Ἀδάμ.

This is a sin moreover, on account of which "death reigned over them." But if this sin were the very sin of Adam imputed to them, and not their own actual sin; if it were merely his sin propagated to them (as the usual sentiment respecting original sin is); then how could it be that death came upon them, although they had *not* sinned after the likeness of Adam's transgression? So far from this must it be, that Adam's sin is their very sin, and the very ground here alleged by the apostle why death reigns over them.

This consideration, united with the principle that the ordinary meaning of ἥμαρτον should be received, unless there is a solid reason for departing from it; and all this added to the consideration that verses 13, 14 are clearly epexegetical of the latter part of verse 12; seem to make it unavoidable that πάντες ἥμαρτον should be here construed, *all have sinned in their own persons* or *actually*.

Calvin, Edwards, Flatt, Tholuck, and others, explain the phrase in question by referring to verse 19; and some of them allege as a ground of this, that the design of the apostle requires us so to understand πάντες ἥμαρτον here, because he is evidently intent upon representing the evils which Adam occasioned. But because verse 19 asserts an influence of Adam upon the sinfulness of men, it does not follow that the same sentiment must therefore be of course affirmed in verse 12; certainly not that it should be directly asserted in the same manner. It appears quite probable, I readily concede, that Paul, in making the declarations contained in verse 12, had in his own mind a view of the connection between the first offence of Adam and the sinfulness of his posterity. It is quite probable, indeed, that καὶ οὕτως implies this; which (with Erasmus, Tholuck, and others) we might construe, *et ita factum est*, i. e., *and so it happened*, or *and thus it was brought about*, viz., brought about that all men became sinners, and thus fell under sentence of death; in other words, Adam's offence was the occasion of, or brought, sin and condemnation upon all men; yet it seems clear, that no more is here *explicitly* and *directly* asserted, than that all men are themselves actual sinners, and therefore come under condemnation. But in the preceding ἁμαρτία εἰς τὸν κόσμον εἰσῆλθε, and in the καὶ οὕτως . . . . διῆλθε, I think we may without any forced construction, nay that we must, discover an *indirect* intimation of what is directly asserted in verses 17—19, viz., that *the first offence of Adam was connected with the sin and misery of his posterity, and in some sense or other causal of it*. At the outset, then, Paul may have had this sentiment in his mind; yet in verse 12 he seems to intimate it only in the expressions just cited. Construed in this way, the sense of the verse would be as follows: 'By means of Adam's first offence sin and death invaded the world of mankind; and having thus invaded it, they have been marching through it (διῆλθε) and carrying on their conquests ever since; all men have become sinners, all have come under condemnation.'

While the clause before us, then, simply *asserts* the fact that all have become sinners and have therefore come under condemnation, it may be regarded as intimating, by implication, that the whole of what has come upon men stands connected with the introduction by Adam of sin and death into the world. I cannot, therefore, agree with those commentators, who find in our verse *no* intimation of such a connection of all men with Adam; less still can I assent to those, who find in it no charge at all upon Adam's posterity of *actual* sin *in propriâ personâ*.

The objection has been made, that by construing the clause before us as having respect to *actual* sin, *infants* must be included among *actual* sinners; which is not true. But how can any more difficulty arise from saying that *all are sinners* here, than from the apostle's saying the very same thing so often in the previous part of his epistle, *e. g.*, iii. 9 — 18, 19, 23? Of course the writer of such declarations must be understood to designate such as are capable of being sinners. That the apostle had his eye on the case of *infants*, in particular, anywhere in this whole paragraph, may be justly regarded as doubtful; particularly when we take in to account the implication in reference to the state of infants in Rom. ix. 11.

Are such commands and declarations as these: "He that believeth not, shall be damned; Except ye repent, ye shall all perish; Without faith it is impossible to please God; He that cometh to God must believe that he is, and that he is the rewarder of those who diligently seek him; Make to yourselves a new heart, for why will you die," and numerous others, to be applied to *infants* and *idiots*? Are we not, on every rational ground of interpretation, just as much entitled to say that the Saviour purposely consigns over to damnation all infants because they do not and cannot believe? To *believe* what we do not understand, is out of the question; and that infants and idiots should understand the gospel method of salvation, is equally so. By general consent, then, we omit to include infants and idiots in the threatening, "He that believeth not shall be damned." We suppose this is applicable to those only, who are physiologically and psychologically *capable* of understanding and believing. Let us be consistent. When the apostle speaks of those who have sinned and come under the penalty of death, he must mean those who were capable of sin in the *actual* sense; *i. e.*, he must mean so, if the word ἥμαρτον characterizes such. And that it does, has, as it seems to me, been already shown above.

Again; should it be objected, that the parallel between the effects of Adam's sin and the grace of Christ would lose its meaning, in case we suppose that men's own *actual* sins are designated in the passage before us; my answer would be, that this is by no means the case, if Adam be regarded as the original cause of introducing sin into the world, and his offence as in some way the cause or occasion of all the offences that followed. Indeed this is the only ground on which a *true* parallelism can be maintained. Does the grace of Christ save any sinner who does not *repent* and *believe?* Surely not. Then of course the grace of Christ is not the only thing requisite to the salvation of sinners. There must be *some act of their own*, as well as the provisions which grace has made, in order that they should be saved. Must there not then be something on the part of the sinner himself as well as on the part of Adam, to complete his full and final destruction? Must there not be a true and real πάντες ἥμαρτον? This argument, then, although so often and so strenuously urged, would seem to be a kind of *felo de se*. The very nature of the parallelism before us would seem to demand a different conclusion, and in some respects one opposite to that which is often drawn.

Once more; the evils occasioned by Adam surely are not, as many suppose, limited by the apostle, and by the nature of the case are not to be limited, to that part only of suffering which comes upon our race by reason of *original* sin (as it is called), whatever this sin may be. Verse 14 speaks of 'death as reigning over those *who had* NOT *sinned after the similitude of Adam's transgression;*' and of course it speaks of sin committed by Adam's posterity, different from that of Adam; and verse 16 speaks of the *many* offences which the free gift of Christ takes away or causes to be pardoned, in distinction from the *one* offence only of Adam that is concerned with our sin and condemnation. It follows of course, and we are thus assured, that the apostle does not limit himself to the *one* offence of Adam and its consequences in the alleged way of *imputation*, when he exhibits the contrast between Adam and Christ. Why should he do so? If *actual* sin in any way proceeds from, is connected with, or is occasioned by, the sin of Adam; then does it follow, that actual sin should enter into the contrast presented by the apostle, between the sin and misery occasioned by the first Adam, and the justification and happiness introduced by the second.

On the whole, then, there seems to be no valid reason why we may not construe πάντες ἥμαρτον, as I have done above.

Let us now return to the interpretation of καὶ οὕτως. Does it mean: "*And in like manner* with Adam did his posterity sin, and like him come under sentence of death? Or is this the meaning: 'As death followed sin in the case of Adam, so did it in the case of his posterity?' Or does the apostle intend to say, 'Since Adam introduced sin and misery into the world, his sin has been imputed to all his posterity, and all of them have been subjected to death thereby?' Not the first; because verse 14 tells us that death came on many of Adam's posterity, who had NOT sinned in the manner that he did, *i. e.*, against a revealed and express law. Not the third; for the reasons already given above, reasons why we must accede to the idea, that πάντες ἥμαρτον here means *actual sin in propriâ personâ*. Shall we conclude then, that the meaning of καὶ οὕτως must be substantially what is implied in the *second* of the above questions, viz., 'As sin entered the world, and death was inseparably connected with it, so death has passed through the world, and come upon all men, because it was inseparably connected with the sin which all men have committed?' Even this statement does not appear to me to convey the whole truth. The whole verse seems to contain an intimation, as has already been stated above, that both the *sins* of men and their *condemnation* stand connected, in some way or other, with the first offence by Adam. Καὶ οὕτως then must mean: 'And the matter being thus,' or 'circumstances being such,' viz., Adam having thus introduced sin and death, 'it passed on through all his race,' *i. e.*, all have sinned, and all have come under condemnation in these circumstances. If we look at verses 18, 19, we shall surely find that the *introduction* of sin and death was considered by Paul as having some important connection with the diffusion of them in after ages. Καὶ οὕτως then may mean here, *et hac conditione, et ita factum est, et rebus sic constitutis.*

CHAP. V. 13, 14.

The apostle having thus declared that sin and death were introduced into the world by one man, and had become universal, in order to complete the comparison which he designs, and which is intimated by ὥσπερ at the beginning of verse 12, he would have naturally filled out the sentence by adding, at the end of this verse, οὕτως καὶ δι' ἑνὸς ἀνθρώπου ἡ ζωὴ εἰς τὸν κόσμον [εἰς πάντας ἀνθρώπους] εἰσῆλθε, comp. verses 17, 18. But he suspends his *apodosis* here, for the sake of elucidating and confirming what he had already said. This he does by taking a case in respect to which one might be disposed to think that it would be difficult to prove that men are sinners, viz., (ἁμαρτία ἦν ἐν κόσμῳ) before the giving of the Mosaic law; although they are not themselves prone to acknowledge their guilt in such circumstances, or they make but little account of it. Yet it is a fact that they were sinners, and that death therefore prevailed over them all, even all who had not sinned against revealed law as Adam did.

(13) *Until the law*, ἄχρι νόμου; *i. e.*, the law of Moses, as verse 14 plainly leads us to construe it. Some commentators (Origen, Chrysostom, Erasmus, Coppe, and others) construe ἄχρι νόμου not as designating the *commencement* of the Mosaic economy, but as extending *through the whole period of it*. In defence of such an interpretation, we are referred to ἄχρι in Acts iii. 21, and its synonyme ἕως ἄν in Acts ii. 35. Gen. xxviii. 15, etc. That these words are sometimes employed in such a manner as not to indicate a cessation of anything that is, or is done, at the time which is mentioned in connection with ἄχρι or ἕως, is true. In other words, the *terminus ad quem* does not limit the thing affirmed *universally;* it only expresses a limit for a certain purpose. For example: in Acts iii. 21 it is said, that 'the heavens must receive Jesus ἄχρι χρόνων ἀποκαταστάσεως πάντων, *until the restoration of all things;* by which is not meant, that he is no longer to dwell in heaven, but that he will certainly dwell there until the time specified. But whatever may be true in regard to the possible meaning of ἄχρι in some cases, verse 14 clearly shows that here it means only *until* the commencement of the laws of Moses, *i. e.*, the time when these laws were given.

'But was sin in the world no longer than until that period? Did it cease when the law was introduced? This would be a direct contradiction of verse 20, and of many other passages.' The answer is brief. It is no part of the apostle's object, to aver that sin did not exist *after* this period; but to declare that it existed *before* it. What he had already said, once and again, necessarily involved the idea, that where law was there sin was. But he had also said, that "where there is no law, there is no transgression," iv. 15. Now some of his readers might suggest, that: 'Since you say that where there is no law, there is no transgression, how then were men sinners *before the law was given?* To this question, I suppose the apostle to answer in our verse. 'Sin was in the world until the law of Moses, *i. e.*, men were sinners between the time of Adam and Moses, for death reigned during all this period,' verse 13. In other words; it is not necessary that there should be a law *expressly* revealed, in order that men should be sinners; for "the heathen who have no law, are a law unto themselves," ii. 14.

That ἁμαρτία here means something different from *original* sin, or *imputed* sin, seems to be clear from the reference which the apostle tacitly makes to a law of nature that had been *transgressed*. A *revealed* law there was not for men in general, antecedently to the time of Moses; yet men were sinners. How? By sinning against the law "written on their hearts" (ii. 15); and sinning in despite of the penalty of death, i. 32. But if such was their sin, it was *actual* sin, not merely *imputed* guilt.*

Some, however, state the apostle's reasoning here in the following manner: viz., 'Men's own sins were not imputed to them on the ground of their transgressing any law, until the law of Moses was given; yet they were counted sinners (ἁμαρτία ἦν ἐν κόσμῳ); consequently, it must have been by reason of Adam's sin being imputed to them, inasmuch as their own offences were not imputed.'

Although this mode of exegesis is supported by names of high respectability, I cannot accede to it for the following reasons: 1. To aver that men's *own* sins were not imputed to them by God (so they construe ἁμαρτία δὲ οὐκ ἐλλογεῖται μὴ ὄντος νόμου), is directly to contradict the whole tenor of the Old Testament history and declarations; and also what Paul has, in the most explicit manner, asserted in the preceding part of his epistle. As evidence in favor of the first assertion I appeal to the case of Cain; of the antediluvians who perished in the flood; of Sodom and Gomorrah; and to all the declarations of divine displeasure made against the *actual thoughts* and *deeds* of the wicked, not against their *original* or *imputed* sin. In respect to the second, I appeal to the whole of what Paul has said in Rom. i. 19—32. ii. 12, 14, 15. iii. 9, 19, 23, 25. All these charges are made against *actual* sins; and it is impossible to suppose that the apostle means here to say, that those who are ἄνομοι (without revelation), are, or ever have been, counted by God as being without sin, actual sin; for both ἄνομοι and ἔννομοι, according to Paul, are ALL UNDER SIN, *under* ACTUAL *sin*. To admit the contrary, would be to overturn the very foundation the apostle had taken so much pains to lay, in chapters i.—iii., in order to make the conclusion entirely evident and unavoidable, that all men need gratuitous justification.

2. To aver that men's sins are not imputed to them, when they do not live under a revealed law, would be to contradict what the immediate context itself must be considered as asserting. Who are those that have *not* sinned after the manner of Adam? The answer of those whom I am now opposing, is: 'They are those, who have only *original* sin or *imputed* sin charged to their account.' But then I find great difficulty in this answer. By

* So Alford says · "There was sin in the world, men sinned, see Gen 6 5—13, committed actual sin, not men were accounted sinners because of Adam's sin; the apostle reminds us of the historical fact that there was sin in the world during this period."

the supposition of many who make it, Adam's first sin does become really and truly that of all his posterity, inasmuch as it is propagated to them in the way of natural generation. Yea, Augustine, Pres. Edwards, and many others, maintain a real *physical* unity of Adam with all his posterity; and hence they derive to all his posterity a participation in his sin. But if his sin be theirs in any proper sense, *i. e.*, be really theirs by such a unity as is asserted; or even if it be theirs by mere imputation without this; then how is it that the sin of the ἄνομοι is (as Paul asserts) NOT like that of Adam? How can it be unlike it, when it is the very same; either the very same in reality (as Augustine and his followers hold), or the very same *putatively*, as others suppose? But,

3. There is another difficulty. How can the sins of Adam be asserted to be imputed to all his posterity, and yet their own personal sins be not at all reckoned? By the exegesis of those whose opinion I am now endeavoring to controvert, Paul is made to say, that God did not count to men their own personal and actual sins, *i. e.*, to those who lived before the Mosaic law. By a parity of reason, then, the Gentiles at all times and everywhere, who are ἄνομοι, are freed from the imputation of their own transgressions; which would directly contradict the declarations of Paul.

From this conclusion, however, Schott and Tholuck, do in some measure revolt, and say that to οὐκ ἐλλογεῖτο must be assigned only a *comparative* sense; that although the *guilt* of men who sinned against the law of nature, was not taken away absolutely, yet their *accountability* for it was in a good measure superseded. To illustrate this, Tholuck refers us to ἀνοχῇ in Rom. iii. 26, and to ὑπεριδὼν ὁ Θεός in Acts xvii. 30. Both of these instances, however, relate to *deferring* punishment, not to a remission of accountability; comp. 2 Pet. iii. 8, 9. Such a remission of punishment would directly contradict what Paul has fully and strongly asserted, in Rom. ii. 6—16.

And to what purpose is it to say, that men who were ἄνομοι, were in a *comparative* sense not accountable to God for their own personal sins? This can mean neither more nor less, than that they were accountable in some degree, although not as highly so as those who were ἔννομοι. But accountability being admitted (how can it be denied after reading Rom. ii. 6—16?), then the argument is marred which those whom I am opposing deduce from the verses in question. They make these verses to say, that 'the ἄνομοι are not accountable for their own sins; but inasmuch as they are still *treated* as sinners, it must be because of *imputed* sin only.' But while we admit accountability *in some degree* for the sins of the ἄνομοι, it forecloses such an argument from the passage; for it leaves it fully liable to the following construction, viz., 'Although men were held less accountable and criminal, who lived before the Mosaic law, than those who lived under this law, yet that they were still sinners, and were regarded as such, is true; for all were subjected to death.' That they were sinners in their own person, or actual offenders in a way different from that of Adam, is clear from what is said in ver. 14 respecting them. How then can Adam's sin be here asserted to be theirs, and, by implication, to be the only sin for which death came upon them?

In such an interpretation, moreover, as that which I am now considering, a very different sense is given to ἐλλογεῖτο from that which it will here consistently bear; as we shall see in the sequel.

Reiche states the argument thus: 'Positive punishment (like death) can be inflicted only for breach of positive law. Now no positive law threatening death, except in the case of Adam, was given before the Mosaic law. Therefore all men who died during this interval, must have died by reason of punishment threatened to Adam being extended to them.' And in consonance with this view he construes vers. 13, 14, in general; although he seems to me far from maintaining consistency. To this statement we may easily reply: (1) The major proposition directly contradicts what the apostle has said in Rom. i. 32. ii. 14, 15. iii. 19. The apostle plainly makes no other difference between Jew and Gentile, than what is made by the respective degree of light which each enjoyed. The Jew is the *more* guilty, because he enjoyed better advantages and abused them. But all, both Jew and Gentile, he pronounces to be ἄξιοι θανάτου and ὑπόδικοι τῷ Θεῷ. How then can we assume that death is *not* threatened to any, except in consequence of a *positive*, *i. e.*, a revealed law? It is the very opposite of the apostle's argument and of his explicit and repeated declarations. In Rom. v. 14, moreover, Paul directly asserts that the penalty of death was incurred by those who had *not* sinned in the manner of Adam, *i. e.*, against express and positive precept. But Reiche makes the apostle here to mean, that they suffered on account of Adam's transgression and not their own; although he had just before strongly contended that πάντες ἥμαρτον must have an *active* sense, and mean that all had voluntarily and in fact sinned. (2) The minor proposition is equally untrue, in respect to its real and essential meaning; for of what importance is it, whether the law was *positive* or *natural*, so long as the declarations in Rom. i. 32. ii. 14, 15. iii. 19, and the like remain? How shall we admit positions which the apostle himself expressly contradicts? (3) It follows, of course, that the conclusion from such premises must be erroneous, viz., 'That all men from Adam to Moses, died merely because of the penalty threatened to Adam, and not by reason of their own sins.' The reader will observe, that I do not here deny that in *some* sense the doctrine of this conclusion may be true ; but only that in the sense alleged it cannot possibly be made out satisfactorily from such premises. Of course the exegesis of vers. 13, 14 by Reiche, which is made in general to conform to such views, must be very questionable.

Whilst Reiche earnestly remonstrates against the sentiment of Tholuck here, viz., that 'death came upon men living between Adam and Moses, because of the *vitiositas* of which they partook, and which they derived from Adam ;' how much does he relieve the difficulty, by making death come upon all men without any other reason than that it does come? According to him, Adam set it in motion, and it kept on, from the momentum which he gave it, down to the time of Moses, irrespective of sin either original or actual?

The very limitation of the period, viz., *from Adam to Moses*, is an objection to the exegesis, which represents the apostle as laboring to show, not that men *sinned* and therefore perished (as he had just asserted in verse 12), but that they perished merely because of their relation to Adam, either in consequence of *propagated vitiosity*, or else without any specific assignable reason, as Reiche avers. Why should the apostle stop within these narrow limits? The Mosaic Law was given to only about three millions out of six or seven hundred millions of our race, and from that time down to the present moment, has immeasurably the greater portion of the human race been destitute of any *revelation*. How does their case differ at all from that of those between Adam and Moses? And if not, why should the apostle confine his assertion merely to those between Adam and Moses ? If his object be the *general* one supposed by the commentators in question, no good reason can be given for such a procedure. Besides, such a method of illustration makes verses 13, 14, inapposite, in case we allow that πάντες ἥμαρτον means, that all men did of themselves sin. The γάρ at the beginning of verse 14 shows, that what follows is designed to illustrate and confirm what had just been asserted ; and this is *not* that all men die because of inherited vitiosity, but *because all have sinned.* How then could Reiche, with any consistency, strenuously defend this latter sentiment, and yet interpret verses 13, 14 as he has done ?

I must regard the apostle then as designing, in verses 14, 15, to illustrate and confirm the proposition that 'all men have sinned and perished,' by the introduction of a case that might be deemed doubtful, or called in question by some of his readers. If he could show that no valid objection could be made to this, he of course might take it for granted that no objection would be made to the plainer parts of his position. And I regard him as referring to the period between Adam and Moses, because it presented an obvious and striking case adapted to his purpose. But if his object was to establish the proposition, that all men without revelation have died because of *inherited corruption*, or died merely because Adam introduced a fatal disease (as Reiche maintains), why should he make such a limitation, or indeed, any limitation at all? We may well ask also: 'Do not those who have a revelation stand in the same relation to Adam and as really partake of *original* sin as others? And if so, what can be the object of Paul in *limiting* his remarks to those who lived between Adam and Moses, since the connection between *imputed* sin and death is uniformly the same, if it exist at all, in all ages, nations, and circumstances? There was no more reason, surely, for Paul's readers to doubt of imputed sin between Adam and Moses, than there was to doubt of it between Moses and Paul; nay, in some respects there was less, inasmuch as the evils suffered during the former period were very great, and yet the *actual* sins were less, because there was less light. Yet, if the more usual exegesis be true, the apostle has selected the former period as the very one about which he expected there would be the most doubt. Can this be so? The nature of the case would seem to decide in the negative.

But suppose now the question to be, as I have stated, whether men can sin and perish without law (a question very naturally raised after Paul's declaration in iv. 15); then the period which Paul has selected for his purpose, is altogether apposite and striking. For this very reason we may well suppose he chose it. On every side difficulties start up against the other view — difficulties philological and theological — difficulties arising from incongruity, ineptness, and contradiction of previously avowed sentiment and the nature of accountability. That the sinning of men had a connection with the offence of Adam, and that this was in some way the cause or occasion of their sinning, is what (as I have before stated) I do not doubt the apostle here admits. But as he has asserted in verse 12 that *death passed on all*, BECAUSE ALL SINNED, so here he confirms what he has said; as the γάρ plainly shows.

It has been asked why the apostle here asserts again what he had so often asserted before, viz., that all men are sinners. The answer is easy. The subject here comes up in a new light, viz., the connection between *death* and *sin*. That death is *universal,* cannot be denied; at least this is certain in regard to the death of the body; and that the apostle has this part of the penalty against sin here particularly in view, will hardly be doubted. Yet this does not, by any means, oblige us to suppose that other parts of the penalty are designedly excluded, because this plain and palpable part of it is here specifically made prominent. If then death is universal, does it not follow that the cause of it, *i. e.*, sin, is universal too? Of course the argument relates to all who can and do sin, and thus come under the penalty in question. Thus both the guilt and misery of our race are here brought into the account, and placed in opposition to the grace and salvation of the gospel; and thus the contrast designed to be made by the whole representation is greatly heightened. But on the supposition that no proper sin of Adam's posterity, or that only *imputed* sin is here in question; then surely it follows that Christ delivers us from no sin, or from only imputed sin and the death which that brings; at least nothing further can here be made out from the words of the apostle. Yet in verse 16 Paul asserts, that our deliverance is from πολλῶν παραπτωμάτων; which disproves entirely that mode of exegesis, which confines ἁμαρτία here to *imputed* sin or to mere *vitiositas*.

I have only to add that the supposition of men's own personal sins *not* being reckoned to them, while they are considered as perishing forever by the mere imputation of another's sin, is a position so revolting with respect to the justice, and goodness, and impartiality of the sovereign Judge, " who will render to every man according to his *works*," that it requires most ample and satisfactory evidence and argument to support it.

The phrase ἄχρι νόμου ἁμαρτία ἦν ἐν κόσμῳ, appears then, to be only an affirmation respecting a particular class of men (whom some might think it difficult to prove to be sinners) of something which in the preceding clause had been affirmed of *all men*, πάντες ἥμαρτον. It is designed to show that even that class of men are sinners, whom one might be prone to exempt from such a charge; and especially so, after what the apostle had just said in iv. 15. Any other mode of expounding this makes the γάρ irrelative and out of place, when it is once admitted that πάντες ἥμαρτον affirms the proper sin of Adam's posterity. And to construe vers. 13, 14 as having relation only to *imputed* sin, comes virtually to the representation of Christ's death as a salvation only from *imputed* sin; which would amount to a virtual contradiction of verse 16.

Although sin is not made account of where there is no law, ἁμαρτία δὲ . . . . νόμου. Perplexity and difficulty have arisen here from construing ἐλλογεῖται as though it were connected with Θεός, as the agent by whom the *counting* or *imputing* is to be done.* The difficulties of such an interpretation have already been stated, in the considerations presented above. Bretschneider (Dogmatik. II. 49. edit. 3) seems to have suggested the true solution of the phraseology; " Ἐλλογεῖται is not *imputatur a Deo*, but *refertur ab hominibus ad peccata, i. e., habetur, agnoscitur peccatum.*" The like views did Calvin and Luther entertain relative to the expression. The former says, that 'men do not count themselves as sinners, and are not alarmed for their guilt, unless the law first excites and quickens their consciences.' So Luther renders ἐλλογεῖται by *achten, to regard, to have respect to.* To the like purpose Heumann, Camerarius, Photius (in Œcumenius), Schoettgen, Koppe. The words of Photius deserve to be recited. " When [the apostle] says ἐφ' ᾧ πάντες ἥμαρτον, lest some one should reply and ask: ' How then could men sin where there was no law? For thou thyself hast said above, that *where there is no law there is no transgression;* and if no transgression, then surely no sin. How then could death pass upon all men, *because all have sinned?* Lest therefore some one might make such an objection, Paul anticipates and solves the doubt, and says ὅτι ἦν καὶ πρὸ τοῦ νόμου; for sin was *committed*, and what is committed must have an existence." To which remarks of Photius, Œcumenius after citing them adds: " See the exactness of the apostle. That we might not think ourselves to be wronged because we die on account of another, he says ἁμαρτία ἦν ἐν κόσμῳ although it was disregarded (εἰ καὶ μὴ ἐλογίζετο); therefore we die not only because of Adam, but also because of sin." Surely when ἐλλογεῖται is rendered, *habetur, imputatur* [ut peccatum] *ab hominibus*, this is no more a departure from the meaning of ἐλλογεῖται, than

---

* It may well be questioned whether De Wette, Tholuck and Olshausen are not substantially right in the meaning which they give to ἐλλογεῖται here. Both the significance of the word and its connection would seem to imply two parties. Paul is not treating at all of the extent of human consciousness. The word, it should seem, must in any case be used in a modified sense, and the only question is whether the idea, if it is translated "*reckoned*," is or is not Pauline, or at least consistent with other passages of Scripture. It should be noticed that *transgression*, παράβασις, of *law*, or a *positive precept* is specially brought to view here in the sin of Adam and the sins of his posterity after the promulgation of the Mosaic Law. But those who lived between Adam and Moses were differently situated, and their sins were not formally *accounted as transgression*. So Paul says in Acts 17: 30: "The times of this ignorance God winked at," etc. See also 7 13 and 2: 11. These and other passages show that although sin was punishable when there was no law, yet the law brought out into distinct and prominent manifestation individual transgressions which were formally "reckoned" against the transgressor.

to render it *imputatur a Deo*. Whether Θεός or ἄνθρωποι is to be understood here, must be decided of course by the nature of the sentiment. And as to ἐλλογεῖται, why should attributing to it the sense of *regarding, accounting, esteeming*, etc., be called strange? inasmuch as this word accords as to both sense and origin altogether with λογίζομαι, which often occurs with such a meaning; *e. g.*, Acts xix. 27. Rom. ii. 26. vi. 11. viii. 36. ix. 8. xiv. 14. 1 Cor. iv. 1. 2 Cor. x. 2. xi. 5, et sæpe. So חָשַׁב, Gen. xxxi. 15. 1 Sam. i. 13. Job xli. 27 (19). The ellipsis after ἐλλογεῖται may be supplied by εἰς ἁμαρτίαν or ὡς ἁμαρτία, both methods of construction being common after λογίζομαι, as any one may see by consulting the above instances. That ἐλλογέω occurs (Philem. ver. 18) in the sense of *impute*, is no valid reason why it should have that particular meaning in the verse before us. But even in Phil. verse 18, the sense is altogether good when we translate τοῦτό μοι ἐλλόγει, *reckon that to me*, or *put that to my account;* which conveys exactly the idea intended, viz., that the writer would be responsible for the wrong done by Onesimus.

That the sentiment derived from such an exegesis as that which I have adopted, is not foreign to the writings of Paul, is quite clear from comparing Rom. vii. 7 — 11 and iii. 20. In the former of these passages, the law is represented as greatly exciting and aggravating the unholy desires of the carnal heart by its restraints and disclosures; so that "without the law sin is death," *i. e.*, it is little estimated and felt. In the latter, Paul declares that "by the law is the knowledge of sin." How well this accords with ἁμαρτία δὲ οὐκ ἐλλογεῖται μὴ ὄντος νόμου, needs hardly to be suggested.

I admit that a *modified* sense of the expression is to be regarded as the true one, viz., that it is not to be considered so absolute as to convey the idea that *no* sense of sin existed among the heathen in any measure; for this would contradict fact, and contradict what Paul says in chap. ii. 14, 15. But then the modification is of just the same nature as is to be received in respect to Rom. vii. 7 — 11, iii. 20, and also of John xv. 22 — 24, where the Saviour says, that if he had not come and spoken to the Jews, "they would not have had sin." But the sense of ἐλλογεῖτο, as maintained by Tholuck and others, *i. e.*, a modified sense in respect to the account which God makes of sin, does not answer the purpose at all for which it is intended by them. If God made *any* account of men's own sins before the law, then *imputed* sin is not the only thing for which men die. Of course the argument that they labor to establish, is given up. The assertion considered as absolute, viz., that God made no account at all of men's own sins, who were not under the law, is contradicted by all the preceding part of the epistle.

Pres. Edwards has given the verse before us a peculiar turn: "For *before* the law of Moses was given, mankind were all looked upon by the great Judge as sinners, by corruption, and guilt derived from Adam's violation of the original law of works; which shows that the original universal rule of righteousness is not the law of Moses; for if so, there would have been no sin imputed before that was given, because sin is not imputed where there is no law," (*Orig. Sin*, p. 275. Worces. edit.) Thus the main design of the apostle is to show, that the Jews could not claim their law as the only criterion of right and wrong; and in order to do this, Paul shows that men were condemned on account of *imputed* sin, before the giving of the law. But this makes a forced construction and also introduces a subject of consideration that the apostle seems for the present to have dismissed from his mind, viz., the confident and boastful reliance of the Jews on their law. And besides, in order to make out the interpretation of Edwards, it must also be shown that the apostle here asserts the existence of another law antecedent to that of Moses, to which men were accountable. This he had done in chap. ii. 14, 15; but here it is not to his purpose to repeat it. He says merely, that men were sinners antecedently to the law of Moses, although in a state of nature they made but little account of sin; they were sinners, notwithstanding they made light of it; and they incurred the sentence of death, although they had not, like Adam, sinned against a revealed and express law.

(14) *Yet* or *nevertheless death reigned from Adam unto Moses*, ἀλλ' ἐβασίλευσεν Μοϋσέως. Ἀλλά, *tamen, attamen* — *Reigned*, ἐβασίλευσε, *i. e., was predominant*, exercised uncontrolled sway or power, held universal dominion among men. But what death? The same, I would answer, as before; but still, I should be disposed to believe, as has been remarked above, that he had in his eye here a particular part of what is comprehended under the generic term *death ;* in other words, that temporal death was the special object to which he here adverts. For temporal death is a *palpable* part of the execution of the sentence, so palpable that all must admit it; and to some such undeniable evidence the writer seems to appeal. I do not look upon this sense of θάνατος here as a departure from the preceding one, in any important respect; for should it be construed as referring to a *palpable* part of the death threatened, this, by its relations to the other parts of the same, involves or implies them also. So Tholuck, Comp. p. 187. 2 edit.

Even over those who had not sinned after the similitude of Adam's transgression, καὶ ἐπὶ . . . . Ἀδάμ. A part of the text itself is here a matter of dispute. Some Latin Codices, also Origen, Cyril, Rufin, Tertullian, Victorinus, Sedulius, and Ambrosiaster, omit the μή here. Semler, Mill, and some others, have done the same. But nearly all the Greek manuscripts (three only, and these *a secunda manu*, excepted), the Syriac version, the Vulgate, and many of the most conspicuous Greek and Latin fathers, *e. g.*, Chrysostom, Theodoret, Theophylus, Irenæus, Jerome, Ambrose, Augustine, and others, insert it. The weight of authority on the side of inserting it seems, therefore, to be quite conclusive. Moreover, there is internal evidence of its genuineness. Toellner, Koppe, and Schott, have well remarked, that the use of καί here before ἁμαρτήσαντας, intimates that something unusual or unexpected was designed on the part of the writer. Accordingly while one would expect to find him saying simply (which would apparently make a much more facile and seemingly unexceptionable sense) ἐβασίλευσε . . . ἐπὶ τοὺς ἁμαρτήσαντας, we find him saying, ἐβασίλευσε . . . καὶ ἐπὶ τοὺς μὴ ἁμαρτήσαντας. Besides all this, the proof that *all have sinned* requires μή; otherwise, those who had no *positive* precepts might, in the minds of some, be exempted. But now, those who have sinned like Adam, *i. e.*, against *positive* precept, and those who have sinned against the *internal* law, make up the *all men*.

The phrase ἐπὶ τῷ ὁμοιώματι is like the Hebrew לִבְנַה (*confidenter*); *i. e.*, a noun with a preposition is employed instead of an adverb. So the Hebrew כִּדְמוּת בְּנֵי אָדָם, Dan. x. 16, is rendered in the Septuagint ὡς ὁμοίωσις υἱοῦ ἀνθρώπου. In all respects ἐπὶ τῷ ὁμοιώματι is equivalent to ὁμοίως; so that ὁμοίως τῷ Ἀδὰμ παραβάντι would express the sense; as would ὥσπερ Ἀδὰμ παρέβη. Comp. ὁποίωμα in Rom. i. 23. viii. 3. Phil. ii. 7.

As to the sense of the passage; by mentioning those who lived before the law of Moses as *not* having sinned after the manner of Adam there is a plain implication that those who lived under the law did sin after the manner, or *in the likeness* of Adam. But the *likeness* in question did not consist in this, that the very *same* precepts were given to them and were transgressed by them; it consisted plainly in the fact that they, like Adam, had *positive* or *revealed* precepts as the rule of duty. Consequently those who sinned, but yet did not sin in the like way (and such are described in vers. 13, 14), must have sinned without positive revealed precepts. Such are described also in ii. 14, 15.

Origen, Augustine, Melancthon, Beza, Pres. Edwards, and others, have construed the clause μὴ ἁμαρτήσαντας κ. τ. λ., as having respect to *infants* only. But Calvin rejects this interpretation: "Malo . . . interpretari de iis qui sine lege peccaverunt." Nevertheless he thinks infants may be included. But the ground of this is, that he construes πάντες ἥμαρτον and ἁμαρτία ἦν ἐν κόσμῳ as referring to the sinning of all men in and by Adam. The remark of J. A. Turretin is directly to the point: "Ex scopo apostoli serieque sermonis patet, hic agi etiam de *adultis* omnibus qui ab Adamo usque ad Mosem vixerunt. Etenim si de solis infantibus ageretur, cur intra id spatium se contineret, quod inter Adamum et Mosem fuit? Nam infantium omnium, et ante et post legem, eadem est ratio." Accordingly, the interpretation of Augustine is generally rejected, so far as I know, by distinguished critics of all parties at the present day.

I am aware that it has been sometimes alleged, in regard to μὴ ἁμαρτήσαντας κ. τ. λ., that the *dissimilitude* here affirmed consists in the fact that Adam was an *actual* sinner, and others (to whom reference is here made) sinners *only by imputation*. But such an interpretation has been shown above to be inconsistent with the tenor of the passage, and with the declarations of the Old and New Testament in relation to this subject. Any attempt to establish such an interpretation must surely fail. For if such an imputation be made out, by virtue of the *unity* of Adam's posterity with himself (and this is the ground on which it is asserted), then it would follow, of course, that their sin, is NOT *different* from his, but the *very same;* for if they were *in* him, and sinned *in* and *with* him, surely their sin is not *different from*, but the *same with* his; which is what the apostle here denies. Or if his sin is merely imputed to them without their actually participating in it, then, in the first place, how can it be said of them that they "all sinned?" And secondly, if it be said that they sinned *in*, *by*, and *through* Adam, then, so far as their sin is concerned, how does it differ from his? There is but one act of sin but the guilt of it is divided among countless millions; or, if this statement be rejected, then the alternative must be taken, viz., that the guilt of it is multiplied and repeated as often as there are individuals belonging to the human race. In either case there remains only the actual sin of Adam, and so far as this belongs to his posterity in any sense, either real or putative, so far the sin is not different from that of Adam, but the same. It is only when we construe the passage as referring to men's own *personal* sins, that the difficulty can be removed.

Who is a type of him that was to come, ὅς ἐστι τύπος τοῦ μέλλοντος. Τύπος signifies, (1) in its original and most literal acceptation, *an impress, a note* or *mark* made by impression, sculpture, beating, etc.; inasmuch as it comes from τέτυπα the second Perf. of τύπτω. In this sense it is employed in John xx. 25. Hence, (2) It means *example, pattern, model;* as in Acts vii. 44. Heb. viii. 5. Ex. xxv. 40 (where the Hebrew has תַּבְנִית). (3) It means *example, model,* in a good sense; *e. g*., Phil. iii. 17. 1 Thess. i. 7.

2 Thess. iii. 9. 1 Tim. iv. 12. Tit. ii. 7. 1 Pet. v. 3; but sometimes an example for the sake of warning, not of imitation, as in 1 Cor. x. 6, comp. verse 11. (4) It means *image, something which is a resemblance* of some other thing supposed or real; as in Acts vii. 43. Amos v. 26 (Heb. צלם). In this last sense, *i. e.*, that of *image* or *resemblance*, not in a physical sense but in a *causal* one (if I may so speak), is Adam called a τύπος of Christ. The appropriate scriptural sense of *type* is, a person or thing, which by special appointment or design of an overruling Providence, is intended to symbolize, or present a likeness of some other and future person or thing. So the word τύπος here implies that by special divine arrangement and appointment, Adam was made in particular respects to present an antithetic image of what Christ was to be.

That Christ is meant by τοῦ μέλλοντος, is clear from verse 15, seq., where he is by name brought into comparison with Adam. The ellipsis after μέλλοντος, *i. e.*, the noun with which this participle agrees by implication, seems to be 'Αδάμ, viz., *the second Adam* or ἔσχατος 'Αδάμ, as he is called in 1 Cor. xv. 45.

But in what sense, *i. e.*, how far, is the first Adam here considered as an image of the second. A question of no small importance, since by the answer to it, our views of the general meaning of verses 12 — 19 must be, in no small measure, regulated. But an answer in detail, would occupy too much space here; I therefore refer the reader to Excursus IV. for the illustration, and support of the following sentiments:

I. The τύπος asserted of Adam, in respect to Christ, is *not* to be taken in the widest and fullest sense here. For, (1) In many cases, a τύπος in the Old Testament is of the *same* nature with the ἀντιτύπος in the New Testament. But here, the whole is most plainly *antithetic ;* on the one hand are the evils done and occasioned, and on the other are the good done and the blessings procured. (2) The *degree* or *measure* of the evils occasioned by Adam, is not the point of τύπος in respect to Christ; for this measure is declared to be far exceeded by the blessings which Christ has procured; " grace superabounds." " *Many* offences are forgiven," verse 16. (3) It is not the *person* of Adam as such, which is compared with the *person* of Christ. It is *the* ACTS *of each* and the CONSEQUENCES *of what each has done*, that are the objects of a comparison by the apostle; it is the παρακοή or παράπτωμα and κατάκριμα of Adam, and the effects of the same, which are compared with the ὑπακοή and δικοίωμα of Christ and the effects of these. (4) *One* sin of one individual, viz., Adam, was the occasion of *evil* to all men; while, on the other hand, *many* sins are forgiven on account of one individual, viz., the Lord Jesus Christ.

II. The actual and principal point of *similitude* between Adam and Christ is, that each individual respectively, was the cause or occasion, in consequence of what he did, of greatly affecting the whole human race ; although in an opposite way. Adam introduced sin and misery into the world ; and in consequence of this all men are, even without their own concurrence, subjected to many evils here; *they are born entirely destitute of a disposition to holiness ; and this condition and their circumstances render it certain that they will sin, and will always sin* IN ALL THEIR ACTS OF A MORAL NATURE, *until their hearts are renewed by the Spirit of God;* and of course, all men are born in a state in which they are greatly exposed to the second death, or death in the highest sense of the term, and in which this death will certainly come upon them, unless there be an interposition of mercy through Christ. On the other hand ; Christ introduced righteousness or justification, and all the blessings spiritual and temporal which are connected with a probationary state under a dispensation of grace and with the pardoning mercy of God. A multitude of blessings, such as the day and means of grace, the common bounties of Providence, the forbearance of God to punish, the calls and warnings of mercy, the proffers of pardon, etc., are procured by Christ for all men without exception, and without any act of concurrence on their part ; while the higher blessings of grace, actual pardon and everlasting life, are indeed proffered to all, but are actually bestowed only upon those who repent and believe. The *extent* of the influence of Adam, is therefore a proper τύπος of that of Christ. Each of these individuals, by what he did, affected our whole race without any concurrence of theirs, to a certain degree ; the one has placed them in a condition, in which they actually suffer many evils, and in which, by their own voluntary acts, they are peculiarly exposed to the most awful of all evils; the other has actually bestowed many and important blessings on all without exception, and proffers to all the opportunity to secure the greatest of all blessings. Here then is antithetic τύπος of the like *extent*, in both cases.

The *superabounding* of gospel grace, which is insisted on so emphatically in vers. 15—17, consists (as is stated in ver. 16) in the fact, that the death of Christ procures pardon for the numerous offences which we commit (πολλῶν παραπτωμάτων), *i. e.*, the death of Christ had respect to a multitude of offences ; while the effects of Adam's sin have respect only to one offence, viz., that of eating the forbidden fruit. In other words ; the death of Christ as a remedy, is far more powerful and efficacious than the sin of Adam was as a means of corruption and misery. See further explanations in Excursus IV. Calvin, Tholuck, and others, regard the expression, ὅς ἐστι τύπος τοῦ μέλλοντος, as the *apodosis* of verse 12; see remarks on that verse above.

CHAP. V. 15—17.

The general object of these three verses is to magnify the greatness of gospel grace, by contrasting it with the evils occasioned by Adam's sin (verse 15), to show that while all men are sufferers on account of Adam, it is only to that degree in which *one* sin could affect them, while, on the other hand, the free gift of Christ extends to the pardoning of a *multitude* of offences (verse 16) Nor is pardon of many offences all which the gospel achieves, for if Adam's offence did bring death on all his posterity, or subject them all to more or less of evil, then it is surely more credible still, that the grace of Christ will bestow blessings on all, and especially that it will perfect the work of pardon, and secure the blessings of eternal life to all who have obtained it (v 17) There is then plainly a *gradation* of sentiment in these three verses In verse 15 we have the general idea that grace abounds beyond any evil brought upon us by Adam. In verse 16 it is specifically declared, that the evil inflicted is only such as corresponds to *one* offence, while the good bestowed consists in pardon extended to *many* offences In verse 17 we have the assurance, that pardon shall be crowned with everlasting life. All these points of *dissimilitude* or antithesis illustrate and enforce the idea of the *greatness*, the *certainty*, and the *extent* of gospel blessings, and of course dispel any apprehension that the reader might have from the mention of τύπος, that *equality* or similitude in all respects was intended to be asserted, in regard to the respective influence of Adam and Christ. In pointing out the particulars of dissimilitude and inequality, the apostle has limited the signification of τύπος, and at the same time, he strengthens the idea in the preceding context, and helps to confirm the faith and hope of the believer. The sentiment which attributes to the grace of Christ *good* which is far *greater* than the evil occasioned by Adam's offence, lies upon the very face of verses 15—17, and should never be overlooked. What we should be in ourselves. as the fall of Adam has left us, is one thing, what our condition now is, through the grace of Christ, is another and very different one When we maintain, then, that our present state, depraved and ruined as in itself it is, *is more eligible as to securing final salvation*, than that of Adam was while on his first probation, let it not be said that we deny or extenuate the evil consequences of the fall By no means, but let this be said, viz., that after the example of Paul we represent grace as *superabounding* over all the evils introduced by the apostasy.

One point more deserves special notice here Paul points out in these verses, as has been observed, the principal features of *dissimilitude* or *inequality* between the type and antitype. If now it be true, as some confidently maintain, that *the many* on whom blessings are bestowed, means only the *elect* in Christ; and *the many* who suffer on account of Adam's sin, means *all mankind without exception*, then how can we suppose that the apostle would have here neglected to mention this οὐχ ὡς, *i e*, this point of dissimilitude ? A point surely of not less magnitude, interest, or importance, than any one which he has mentioned So far is he, however, from pointing out such a prominent feature of *dissimilitude*, that he has apparently taken a course directly the reverse of this, and such a one as could scarcely fail to mislead more or less of his readers, provided his design be in reality that which is alleged Does he name the mass of men who are injuriously affected by the sin of Adam οἱ πολλοί in verse 15 ? In the very same verse he calls those on whom Christ bestows favors τοὺς πολλούς. Does he again call the first class (in verse 18) πάντες ἄνθρωποι ? In the same verse he names the second class πάντες ἄνθρωποι. Does he again call the first class οἱ πολλοί, in verse 19 ? The very same designation he there again applies to the second. No common principle of philology, then, whatever our theological systems may demand, can of itself justify us in making an immeasurable distinction here as to *numbers*, while the apostle (whose specific object here is to point out the *dissimilitudes* of the two cases), has not given us any intimation by the language which he employs, that such a distinction is here intended to be designated by him. In a word, had Paul meant what some ascribe to him here, how could he do otherwise than say something like this 'And *not* us the *number* affected by the sin of Adam, is the number affected by the grace of Christ, for all men without exception, were condemned through the sin of Adam, while the elect only were the subject of blessings through the grace of Christ? But then, if he had thus spoken, his assertion would amount to a declaration that *sin superabounds over grace*, directly contrary to what he is laboring to establish, viz., *the superabounding of grace over sin*. Can anything be plainer, then, than that the sentiment here attributed to Paul, viz, *universality* of meaning as to οἱ πολλοί in the first case, and *partial extent only* in the second, is incongruous with the evident design of the writer?

The difficulty that seems to arise in respect to *universal* salvation, by the natural exposition of Paul's language, is only apparent not real. It is only when, on the one hand, we view all mankind as absolutely and unconditionally given over to the *whole extent* of the penalty of death on account of Adam, instead of considering them as actually incurring a part, and as exposed to and in imminent danger of the whole, and then on the other, regard Christ as having actually bestowed eternal life on all thus exposed, instead of having bestowed more or less of the blessings procured by him on all, and eternal life only on all who actually believe, it is only in such a case, I say, that anything of consequence can be made out to favor the doctrine of *universal* salvation. But no rules of interpretation oblige us to embrace such an exegesis. *The* NATURE *of gospel-grace*, as contrasted with the evil effects of Adam's sin, is the grand theme. Why is not the great object of the writer answered, when he has shown, that all men have gained more by the grace of the gospel, than they have lost by the offence of Adam? Or why, because the writer particularizes (as usual) some of the highest blessings and evils on both sides, should all inferior blessings and evils be excluded from his meaning? When it is an actual fact that the grace of Christ does confer many important favors on all men without exception, why should we, why need we, limit the declarations of the apostle to only a small part of men? The interpretation which I defend has the manifest advantage, as it seems to me, of comporting with *fact*, as well as with the philology of the passage. It is no more true that all men suffer the whole of *everlasting* death, than it is that all men obtain the whole of *everlasting* life. But all suffer more or less of the sentence, in the first case, they enjoy more or less of the blessings in the second. Beyond this, all are in imminent peril, in the first case; to all salvation is proffered in the second. Why are not the demands of the passage answered, when the *nature* of the two things is fully and respectively disclosed? But in case we resort to what *actually happens*, we may then advance to a certain extent, both as to evil inflicted and good bestowed. If we look beyond, and take a general survey of the *nature* of each dispensation, we find that the pit is open on the one hand, and heaven on the other. It depends now on the choice of men, whether they will advance to the right or the left. The universality, the greatness, the certainty of gospel-salvation to all who will accept the proffered good, *i e*, *the true nature and principle of all this*, is altogether and strikingly illustrated and confirmed by the passage before us.

It belongs to those who defend the *limitation* of οἱ πολλοί in regard to blessings, to show how the great point which the apostle urges throughout the passage before us, viz, the *superabounding* of grace, is made out by him on the ground which they assume. Thus they have a right to insist on, who are of the opinion that οἱ πολλοί must mean the same in both cases. If the former should say, 'It is made out as to the *elect*, then the question will be whether the elect are the *predominant* party, the great mass? I do not undertake to say that they will not eventually be so. but when the apostle wrote (and even down to the present time), all might say as Jesus did,

'Strait is the gate and narrow the way, and *few* there be that find it' Besides, if a *superabounding* of grace over sin as to the elect *only*, is here the question, then, to be consistent, only the elect can be taken in the counterpart, *i e*, the apostle must be supposed to speak only of the elect here as injured by the sin of Adam And thus, difficult as it would be to render it probable, would be a more eligible and *consistent* interpretation than the other. How can the two respective members of a comparison or similitude, or (if one pleases) dissimilitude or antithesis, be so immeasurably disproportionate as its exegesis that I have been examining makes them? Even if we can get no satisfaction from this passage, without assuming such premises, I do not see how we can bring ourselves to assume them Whenever the mind is thus forced upon conclusions contrary to the nature of the language, and against the tenor of the surrounding context and the apparent aim of the writer, it must after all remain in a wavering, uncertain, conjectural state It is much better to give up the expectation of finding the true sense, than thus to do violence to the laws of interpretation.

One remark more should be made. This is, that the *superabounding* of the grace now in question, is its superabounding over the evils occasioned by Adam's fall. It goes far beyond these It embraces the πολλὰ παραπτώματα of men, verse 16 It exceeds even the sins that are committed under the law (verse 20), great and grievous as they are

(15 *Offence*, παράπτωμα, *i. e.*, *the fall*, the *first* sin of Adam. That only *one* sin, and this altogether peculiar as to its effects, is here taken into view by the apostle, seems clear from verses 16, 17, 18. — *Favor*, χάρισμα, *i. e.*, *benefit, good bestowed* on us or *done* for us

For if, εἰ γάρ, does not imply *uncertainty* here, but *concession*. The shape of the argument stands thus : 'Granting (as we must do) that the many [all] die [come under sentence of death] through Adam or by means of him ; much more must we allow,' etc. The Indic. here stands in both the protasis and apodosis, (ἀπέθανον — ἐπερίσσευσε), and the protasis is assumed as being *conceded ;* New Test. Gramm. § 129. 3. *a.* Γάρ is here obviously γάρ *confirmantis*, — Ἑνός refers of course to Ἀδάμ.

The many died, οἱ πολλοὶ ἀπέθανον, *i. e.*, all men came under sentence of death. Πολλοί here is exchanged in verse 18 for πάντας ἀνθρώπους; this therefore is doubtless the meaning of οἱ πολλοί. The reason why the apostle employs this word seems plainly to be, because he had just said τοῦ ἑνός, of which οἱ πολλοί is the direct *antithesis*, and as such would designate all men in distinction from Adam. In regard to ἀπέθανον, see remarks on θάνατος under verse 12. I would merely remark, that if θάνατος means, as I have there stated it to mean, *evil of any kind* in this world or in the next, then it is true that Adam did by his offence cause θάνατος to come on all without exception, inasmuch as all his race are born destitute of a disposition to holiness, and in such a state that their natural passions, whenever they come to act as moral agents, will lead them to sin. All too are the heirs of more or less suffering. It is true, then, that *all* suffer on Adam's account; that all are brought under more or less of the sentence of death; in a word, that οἱ πολλοὶ ἀπέθανον; but still it does not follow that all, without distinction and without any voluntary act of their own, are equally exposed to θάνατος in its fullest and highest and most awful sense, more than that it follows that all men partake of the χάρισμα of Christ in its highest sense, without any act of their own, *i. e.*, without repentance and faith; see Comm. on verse 4, and Excursus iv.

It certainly is not necessary to suppose, that those who never had any knowledge of duty, and never arrived at a state in which they were capable of moral agency; in a word, that infants and idiots — are liable to the same θάνατος in *all* respects, as those who have πολλὰ παραπτώματα (verse 16) of their own to answer for. It is enough for the apostle's purpose, that all, even without any act or concurrence of their own, do in some degree partake both of the evil and the good, while the good ἐπερίσσευσε, at the same time, all by their own acts may either bring on themselves θάνατος in its ultimate and highest sense on the one hand, or by penitence and faith they may obtain ζωή in its highest sense on the other.

Much more, πολλῷ μᾶλλον; in sense just what the old logicians call an *a fortiori* in argument. — *The grace of God and the gift which is by grace*, ἡ χάρις τοῦ Θεοῦ καὶ ἡ δωρεὰ ἐν χάριτι, some regard as a Hendiadys, and that the meaning is *the gracious gift of God*, viz., that gift which the gospel proffers, or those blessings which Christ has procured. But viewing the design of the writer as I do, I prefer to construe each clause separately. Χάρις τοῦ Θεοῦ should, in this way of interpretation, be regarded as designating the favors which God bestows on all men without distinction for Christ's sake, and without any act on their part which is the condition of their being bestowed. See the same distinction made by the phraseology of verse 17 — τὴν περισσείαν τῆς χάριτος, καὶ τῆς δωρεᾶς δικαιοσύνης. — Ἡ δωρεὰ ἐν χάριτι, if I am right in the suggestion above, must mean the special blessings which are actually bestowed on some, through Christ, or on account of what he has done and suffered, and which are proffered to all. While all without distinction participate in some of the blessings which Christ has procured, and which are in their full extent freely proffered to all, yet those who believe and actually receive pardon, do in this way become *de facto* participators of these further blessings in their highest sense. If any one should incline to interpret χάρις τοῦ Θεοῦ and ἡ δωρεὰ ἐν χάριτι κ. τ. λ. as a repetition of the idea for the sake of *intensity*, he should even in this case, refer χάρις Θεοῦ to the gracious or benevolent feeling or intention of the divine mind, and ἡ δωρεὰ κ. τ. λ. to this design as developed in the actual execution of such intention

Which is of one man Jesus Christ, τῇ τοῦ ἑνὸς . . . . Χριστοῦ. Τῇ has χάριτι for its antecedent. The Genitive τοῦ ἑνὸς κ. τ. λ. might be taken as Gen. *objecti*, *i. e.*, as indicating the favor bestowed on Christ, *i. e.*, of which he was the recipient; but the object of assertion here seems to be to designate the grace of which Christ is the cause or author, Gen. *auctoris*. Paul has just said χάρις Θεοῦ, where Θεοῦ plainly denotes the author; and here it is more probable, that τοῦ ἑνὸς κ. τ. λ. is Gen. *auctoris*, *i. e.*, it signifies here, that the blessings bestowed upon men come by or through Christ, as their *immediate* cause or author. Such is the economy of the gospel, that we may ascribe all its blessings to God, and call them χάρις Θεοῦ; we may also, with equal correctness, say, that Christ is the author or bestower of all the peculiar blessings of gospel grace. "Of his fulness have we all received, even grace for grace," John i. 16.

Hath abounded toward the many, εἰς τοὺς πολλοὺς ἐπερίσσευσε. Τοὺς πολλοὺς with the article, has a different meaning from πολλοὺς without it; just as οἱ πολλοί, in the preceding clause, differs from πολλοί. The latter would signify *many* in distinction from a *few*; but οἱ πολλοί signifies *the many*, *i. e.*, the mass of men, as we say in English; or in German, *die Gesammtheit der Menschen*; in Hebrew, כָּל־אָדָם. Rightly has Augustine said (on verse 19): Ἁμαρτωλοὶ κατεστάθησαν ο ἱ π ο λ λ ο ί, *multi* constituti sunt peccatores, *i. e.*, *omnes*, qui revera sunt *multi*. So in verse 18, the synonyme is πάντας ἀνθρώπους. Indeed the laws of language here seem to place the meaning as thus given beyond the reach of fair controversy. When the apostle wished, as he did here (certainly in the first clause of verse 15), to divide all men into two classes, if the ὁ εἷς be put in the one, then οἱ πολλοί must designate the other. Πάντες would not here answer his purpose, for this would make but one class, which would of course include the ὁ εἷς; for the opposition of πάντες is οὐδείς, *no one, none*. Moreover πολλοί (without the article) would not answer his purpose; for this is in opposition to *some*, not to *one*. Just so in the second member of ver. 15, where Christ (*the one*) is put in opposition to, or in distinction from, οἱ πολλοί, *i. e.*, all others besides himself. If it be asked, How then could the apostle employ πάντας ἀνθρώπους in verse 18? The answer is easy. In verse 18 there is no antithesis of ὁ εἷς, *one person*, but only of ἓν παράπτωμα; which of course leaves the apostle at liberty to exchange οἱ πολλοί for πάντες.

The reader will observe, that the statement made in this verse is simple declaration; a declaration, however, in which the appeal is tacitly made to that sense of the divine goodness, which the apostle seems to have taken for granted, dwelt in the breast of all his readers. 'If it be true,' says he, 'that the sin of Adam occasioned so much evil; then surely we may regard it as true, that the goodness of God has abounded so as to counterbalance it.' He needed no argument to make his readers inclined to receive this. Let us count in what manner we please, if we make a right estimate, the blessings of the gospel will be found to be more than sufficient to counterbalance the mischiefs of the fall; and this must be true, even when we take into view the full extent of those mischiefs; see Excursus iv.

(16) *Yea*, Καί, *imo, immo*; or it may well be rendered *moreover* or *again*. The preceding verse exhibits the diverse nature or kind of influence upon men, through Adam and Christ respectively. The one *condemns* or *destroys;* the other *forgives* and *saves*. The present verse exhibits a diversity of influence in another respect, viz., as to the *degree* in which it exists or is exercised. On the one side is the mischievous influence of *one* offence only; on the other is forgiveness extended to *many* offences. The comparison begins with the general assertion of *dissimilarity* (οὐχ ὡς) as in verse 15, and then continues with a γάρ *causal* as before. After οὐχ ὡς, we should mentally insert κατάκριμα in order to fill out the ellipsis; as is clear from the next clause, viz., τὸ μὲν γάρ κρῖμα εἰς κατάκριμα. Comp. οὐχ ὡς, τὸ παράπτωμα, in verse 15.

Several important Codices read instead of ἁμαρτήσαντος, ἁμαρτήματος, viz., D., E., F., G., Cant., Germ., Bœrn., Harl.; also the Syriac, Vulgate, and old Latin versions, with Theodoret (not uniformly), Aug., Rufin. Pelag., Ambrosiast., Sedul., which Griesbach has received into the text. But the present reading has a decided weight of evidence in its favor; and it is attended with no serious difficulty. One need only insert κατάκριμα after ὡς, and the comparison is obvious; and that this should be done is plain, as has already been hinted, fiom the clause immediately following, viz., τὸ μὲν γὰρ κρῖμα κ. τ. λ. The whole would then read thus, 'Moreover [the condemnation] on account of one who sinned, is not like the free gift; for the sentence by reason of *one* [offence] was unto condemnation [was a condemning sentence]; but the free gift [pardon] is of *many* offences unto justification, *i. e.*, is a sentence of acquittal from condemnation for many offences.'

After δώρημα we must supply ἐγένετο or ἐξῆλθε.— Τὸ μὲν γὰρ κρῖμα ἐξ ἑνός, i. e., ἐξ ἑνὸς [παραπτώματος]; for the antithesis, χάρισμα ἐκ πολλῶν παραπτωμάτων, shows very clearly that παραπτώματος is to be supplied after ἑνός. It is clear throughout this passage (verses 12—19), that τὸ παράπτωμα, ἡ παράβασις, ἡ παρακοή, all have a specific relation to Adam's *first* sin. Equally clear is it, that 1 Tim. ii. 14. 2 Cor. xi. 3. 1 Cor. xv. 21, 22, favor this opinion. And in the verse before us, ἐξ ἑνός [παραπτώματος] is plainly and directly opposed to πολλῶν παραπτωμάτων. But how could this be, unless Paul considered the *first* offence of Adam, and (I may say) this only, as having occasioned the evils which he here contrasts with the blessings bestowed by Christ? It must be granted, indeed, that this was a peculiar dispensation of the Most High, one which displayed his sovereignty in a special manner. But so was the dispensation of grace. It was *the one act of obedience unto death*, by which Christ procured justification (δικαίωμα) for us. All the obedience of his life did, no doubt, contribute to the perfection of his character, and thus fitted him to become an *acceptable* propitiatory sacrifice; but his *obedience unto the death of the cross*, was the grand act by which our salvation was ensured; comp. Phil. ii. 8. Matt. xxvi. 39, 42. John x 18. Heb. x. 7 — 10. In this respect, therefore, the *obedience* of the second Adam may be compared with the *disobedience* of the first; and so, indeed, does the apostle make the comparison in verse 19.

The word κρίμα, as here employed, probably has reference to the formal threatening recorded in Gen. ii. 17, in accordance with which *sentence* was passed upon Adam. This sentence was [ἐγένετο] εἰς κατάκριμα of his posterity, all of whom were subjected to evil, *i. e.*, to death, on his account. Κρίμα then has reference to *him*, and κατάκριμα to his posterity, as they are here employed. The words are often synonymous; and are substantially so here; but the two forms are used for the sake of variety and distinctness.

Free gift, χάρισμα, is here the opposite of κρίμα or κατάκριμα, i. e., *forgiveness* or the bestowment of favors on the one side, and *condemnation* or infliction of evil on the other. The preposition ἐκ is not strictly accommodated to the connection with χάρισμα, for the simple Genitive would be more exact, according to the usual mode of expression. Its use here seems to have been occasioned by its use in the preceding clause, viz., in ἐξ ἑνός, where it is employed in the sense of *propter, because of, on account of*, as in John iv. 6. Acts xxviii. 3. Rev viii. 13. xvi. 10, 11. Sept. Gen. xvi. 5. al.; see Bretsch. Lex. ἐκ, 2. d. But there ἐκ seems to denote the *occasional* cause, *i. e.*, forgiveness could not be exercised unless there existed offence or sin. In this sense χάρισμα proceeds from offences. The πολλῶν is introduced to qualify παραπτωμάτων, but does not alter the nature of the construction. The use of ἐκ in these two different relations and shades of sense, is a kind of *paronomasia*.

Many offences, πολλῶν παραπτωμάτων, not *sins of many*, for that would require the article, viz., τῶν πολλῶν παραπτωμάτων. — Δικαίωμα differs from χάρισμα, only as the *act* differs from the *intention*. Χάρισμα is favor as exhibited in the gracious intention of him who forgives. Δικαίωμα is actual pardon or gratuitous justification. For δικαίωμα, Cod. D., Clar., Æth. have δικαίωμα ζωῆς, which is favored by δικαίωσιν ζωῆς in verse 18, and seems to be by no means an improbable reading.

The verse thus interpreted shows the ground of the περισσεία — *the abounding* of the grace of the gospel — over the κατάκριμα occasioned by the sin of Adam. This *abounding* was generically asserted, or rather *implied*, in verse 15, but not particularly explained. *Here* it is particularized. Whatever were the evils brought upon the posterity of Adam by his fall, they were only such as *one* offence occasioned. But, on the other hand, the blessings procured by Christ are not merely commensurate with these evils, they extend not only to counterbalancing the consequences of the fall, but also to the removing of the consequences of the πολλὰ παραπτώματα of men.

It is quite evident, that whether the κατάκριμα in question be considered as the loss of the righteousness of man's original state, and the being born in a condition in which it is certain that our passions will get the better of our reason and bring us under condemnation; or whether it be considered as matter of fact, that the sin of Adam causes all men to be born with a disposition which is in itself positive sin, and thus necessarily brings us into condemnation; it is still true, in either case, that the evil inflicted or suffered is of such a nature as to lead to, or to prepare the way for κατάκριμα, *condemnation*, i. e., θάνατος; see remarks on the 15th verse and Excursus V.

(17) Verse 17 does not seem to be designed as a confirmation of the leading idea in verse 16, which is, the contrast between the evils occasioned by *one* sin, and the good bestowed by the forgiveness of *many* sins. The reigning idea here is, that if God inflicted so much evil as the consequence of the one sin of one man, *a fortiori* he will secure the greater good where his grace *abounds* through one; the same idea, for substance, is in verse 15; where, indeed, the very same hypothetical form of assertion (εἰ γάρ κ. τ. λ.) is used, and the same nouns (χάρις and δωρεά) are employed. There we have χάρις καὶ δωρεὰ . . . . ἐπερίσσευσε, and here we have τὴν περισσείαν τῆς χάριτος καὶ δωρεᾶς . . . . λαμβάνοντες, which is altogether equivalent. The expressions in verse 17 are *more intensive*, e. g., verse 15 οἱ πολλοὶ ἀπέθανον, but in verse 17 ὁ θάνατος ἐβασίλευσε; in verse 15 χάρις καὶ δωρεὰ . . . εἰς τοὺς πολλοὺς ἐπερίσσευσε; in verse 17 οἱ λαμβάνοντες περρισσείαν . . . ἐν ζωῇ βασιλεύσουσι, and the whole verse seems to be introduced for

the sake of putting *emphasis* upon the reigning idea of the whole passage, viz., the abounding of grace over sin. In this view the reader may connect it with the οὐχ ὡς τὸ παράπτωμα οὕτως τὸ χάρισμα of verse 15, or better with the equivalent expression at the commencement of verse 16. The general idea that runs through the three verses is, *the abounding of grace over sin.* Verse 15 declares that we may naturally expect this, viz., from the well-known character of God (for such seems to be the writer's view); verse 16 shows that it must be so because *many* sins are forgiven by grace, while *one* sin comes into the account as the cause of the evils in question. Verse 17 then repeats the main idea in language more strong and specific than had before been used. The γάρ seems therefore to be referrible to an οὕτως ἐστί, or something of the like nature here in the apostle's mind, in reference to the *greatness* and the *certainty* of the salvation bestowed through Christ, which he has so strongly insisted on in verses 1—11 of the present chapter. As if he would say, 'Salvation is sure and certain; our hope will not make us ashamed or disappoint us (verse 5); we may rejoice confidently in God as our covenant God (verse 11); *for, because,* (γάρ), it is certain that if sin has done great mischief in bringing all into a state of condemnation, grace will do much more good as dispensed through Jesus Christ.' Or if the reader is not satisfied with the *causal* relation as thus indicated, because he may deem it too remote, we may state it thus: 'The dissimilarities between the nature and operations of the sin of Adam and the beneficence of Christ, are not only great in some important respects, but they are such as lead us to believe with the greater certainty that salvation is secure. This is so; FOR *if by the offence of one,* etc.'

The attentive reader will not fail to observe, that the *conclusion* drawn in this verse (for such it is when considered in a logical point of view), is apparently drawn in part from premises indirectly asserted or implied, and in part from the nature of the case, which the writer might presume would be understood and assented to by all his readers. What is indirectly asserted, is, that there is περισσεία τῆς χάριτος καὶ τῇ δωρεᾶς τῆς δικαιοσύνης. The consequence of this is, the bestowment of life in Christ. Then, moreover, the idea that is brought to view in verse 15, viz., that we may well expect from the nature of the case and the character of God, that the effects of the beneficence of Christ will predominate over the effects of Adam's sin, seems to be here conjoined with the sentiment assumed respecting the *abundance* of grace. The 17th verse, then, is properly an *enthymeme, i. e.,* a syllogism whose form is not fully made out.

The phrase διὰ τοῦ ἑνός may be regarded as *emphatic.* The

apostle had already said, τῷ τοῦ ἑνὸς παραπτώματι; and when he says again, ἐβασίλευσε διὰ τοῦ ἑνός, he renders emphatic two things, viz., the predominance of death, and the fact that this predominance was occasioned by *one* individual, viz., Adam.

Much more, etc., πολλῷ . . . . Χριστοῦ. It seems evident to me that πολλῷ μᾶλλον here should be referred to the *greater credibility* that the happiness of the pardoned will be secure, and not that it should be taken as Tholuck and others maintain, as qualifying βασιλεύσουσι. In verse 15, the same words may qualify ἐπερίσσευσε, and so they are construed by some; and here they may be construed with βασιλεύσουσι; but in both cases the most simple and obvious method is to construe them as referring to the *greater credibility* of super-abounding grace. They stand too far from the respective verbs, to be *naturally* joined with them. On the phrases τὴν περισσείαν τῆς χάριτος and τῆς δωρεᾶς τῆς δικαιοσύνης, see remarks on verse 15. I would merely add here, that some of those who think that there is no ground for any distinction of meaning between the two phrases, adopt the exegesis here which represents Christ as the author of blessings *only to the elect.* But the laws of philology and interpretation, and indeed the fact itself, are opposed to it. Others make actual redemption co-extensive with the human race, which the context and innumerable declarations in various parts of the Scriptures contradict. Yet, on the ground, that a simple and essential *principle* merely of the gospel dispensation is here stated, both of the expressions employed *may* be regarded as equivalent, without any serious difficulty; for then the declaration is, that '*the gospel, taken as a system of grace in opposition to the evils of sin*, PROFFERS *blessings far more abundant than the evils which the sin of Adam has introduced. It proffers abundant pardon and eternal glory.*' And in this case, *the reigning in life* would seem to indicate a higher measure of happiness than men would have attained, had they continued obedient under a system of mere law. Respecting this we can only say: ' O the depth of the riches of gospel-grace.' With men this may be unexpected and even improbable; but— 'God will be *greatly* glorified in his Son.'

Tholuck refers δικαιοσύνη here to internal sanctification, or to the life of God in the soul of man, *i. e.*, subjective holiness. But it seems to me quite clear, that δικαιοσύνη conveys the same meaning here as δικαιωθέντες in verses 1, 9. Certainly this makes the antithesis to the state of condemnation, designated by ὁ θάνατος ἐβασίλευσε in the preceding clause.

Shall reign, etc., βασιλεύσουσι ἐν ζωῇ. It is well known that ζωή is the common word to indicate *happiness*, and therefore it needs not to be here proved. That *to reign* means *to be exalted* to an elevated and glorious condition, the reader may see by comparing Rev. ii. 26, 27. iii. 21. Matt. xix. 28. Luke xxii. 30. 1 Cor. vi. 2. 2 Tim. ii. 11, 12. Rev. xx. 4. Dan. vii. 22. Ps. xlix. 14. Ex. xix. 6, comp. 1 Pet. ii. 9.

CHAP. V. 18, 19.

WE have already seen, that verse 12 contains a *protasis* without a corresponding *apodosis* We have also seen, that ὅς ἐστι τύπος τοῦ μέλλοντος (verse 14) may be regarded as comprising in the way of hint, but not formally, a kind of *apodosis* No sooner was τύπος τοῦ μέλλοντος uttered by the apostle, than he turns from the main object of his discourse, to guard his readers against misconstruing τύπος, by carrying too far the resemblance which it indicates, 15—17 This being completed, he now proceeds fully to exhibit his *apodosis* or main conclusion, in verses 18, 19. But these verses are not a simple resumption of the subject as left unfinished in verse 12, for the manner of expression in them is built upon what is said or declared in the intermediate verses This will be made evident in the explanation of the phraseology.

(18) *Wherefore, as by the offence of one* [sentence came] *upon all men unto condemnation,* ἄρα οὖν . . . . κατάκριμα. Ἄρα and ἄρα οὖν are commonly *illative*, according to New Testament usage; *e. g.*, Matt. vii. 20. Gal. iv. 31. Rom. vii. 3, 25. viii. 12. ix. 16, 18. xiv. 12 : 19 et alibi. So it may be here. The apostle had already averred, that Adam was τύπος τοῦ μέλλοντος; and had shown, that the mischiefs resulting to our race from the fall of Adam, were more than repaired by the grace of Christ. Ἄρα οὖν, then, would by no means be inapposite. It is as much as to say: 'Matters being as I have already declared, it follows or results from them, that the comparison begun in verse 12 will hold, viz., that as all have been introduced to sin and death by Adam, so righteousness and life are provided for all by Christ. While ἄρα οὖν may be admitted then (as Tholuck urges), to be *illative*, this does not hinder these words from standing at the head of a sentence which is in substance a resumption of what had been said in verse 12, although the form of it is *illative* in respect to what had been said in the intermediate verses.

That δι' ἑνὸς παραπτώματος means *by the offence of one* [*man*], has been strenuously argued by some, from the antithesis δι' ἑνὸς δικαιώματος; which (as they aver) cannot mean anything but *the righteousness of one* (not *one righteousness*). But the idiom of the whole passage is opposed to this interpretation. For such a designation Paul uses the phraseology : τῷ τοῦ ἑνὸς παραπτώματι; see verse 15, and the same again in verse 17. In verse 16, where he employs ἑνός without the article, he uses a participle (ἁμαρτήσαντος) with it, in order to prevent mistake; while in the antithetic part, he employs ἀνθρώπον (verse 15), and I. Χριστοῦ (verse 17), so as effectually to guard against any misconception of his meaning by the general reader. Not so here. How then can we well avoid the conclusion, that δι' ἑνὸς παραπτώματος means *by one offence ;* and so, that δι' ἑνὸς δικαιώματος must mean *by one righteousness*. The latter expression appears somewhat unusual or strange, but Paul's love of antithesis occasions, in not a few instances, unusual expressions, which carry out a kind of paronomasia and render the diction on the whole more striking. All difficulty about δικαίωμα here however, is removed by verse 19, where ὑπακοή is employed in its stead. Both words refer, no doubt, more specifically to his great act of "obedience unto death," on account of which God highly exalted the Saviour and gave him the fruits of his obedience, viz., sinners justified and accepted. Δικαίωμα, here taken as the antithesis of παράπτωμα, must mean the obedient fulfilling of what was required of Christ as our substitute. Κρῖμα is implied after παραπτώματος, as suggested by Calvin.

The phrase εἰς πάντας ἀνθρώπους is twice employed in this verse, instead of the οἱ πολλοί used in the preceding verse and in verse 19. The reason of this seems to be, that the ἑνός here employed does not designate one *man*, but one *offence*, one *righteousness* or act of obedience. If ἑνός here meant one *man*, then οἱ πολλοί must have been employed as the natural antithesis of it ; for πάντας would include that one, and πολλοί would not. It should be noted also, that if the apostle had designed here to designate only the *elect* by πάντας ἀνθρώπους in the second case, he could hardly have avoided subjoining to πάντας some other word than ἀνθρώπους, which is the very word he had already employed in the antithetic member of the sentence, and which the reader would naturally and indeed spontaneously understand in the same way in both cases. Where else in all the Bible is πάντες ἄνθρωποι employed as the designation of *the elect only?* How can we feel ourselves at liberty here, then, to construe it in a manner contrary to the plain and obvious sense of the words as usually employed, and contrary to the very nature and object of the antithesis in this case? So Calvin did not construe this passage: "Communem omnium gratiam facit, *quia omnibus exposita est, non quod ad omnes extendatur re ipsâ;* nam etsi passus est Christus PRO PECCATIS TOTIUS MUNDI, *atque* OMNIBUS INDIFFERENTER *Dei benignitate offeratur;* non tamen omnes apprehendunt." It is true that in his early work entitled *Institutiones,* he sometimes exhibited sentiments which appear to differ from these, but no words can more exactly express what I suppose the apostle to mean, than those of Calvin above; for it is manifest, that he here considers the object of Paul to be a statement of what the gospel-plan of salvation is, considered as it is in its own proper nature, and not as giving the simple history of what has actually taken place in all respects. On the one hand is a state of imminent exposure to everlasting death, together with many other actual evils; on the other hand is free access for all to everlasting life, with the bestowment of many actual blessings. Could Calvin, if he were consistent with himself, view the subject in any other light than this? Does matter of *fact* justify us in extending it beyond this, if the parallel of the two cases is to be made out?

So [the free gift came] *upon all men unto justification of life*, οὕτω καὶ . . . . ζωῆς. That χάρισμα is here to be supplied, is manifest from the nature of the case, from the elliptical state of the phrase, and from a comparison with the latter clause of verse 16. Οὕτω καὶ is the sign of the *apodosis*, which stands in antithesis both to verse 12, and to the first clause in the present verse, which is in substance a resumption or repetition of that verse.

Justification of life, δικαίωσιν ζωῆς, means that justification which is connected with eternal life or happiness. So Calvin; and so the nature of the case requires. It is plain that δικαίωμα in verse 16, δικαιοσύνη in verse 17, and δικαίωσις here, are all used in accordance with the practice of the New Test. writers, substantially in the same sense, for the sake of avoiding uniformity of diction. On the other hand, the one δικαίωμα ascribed to Christ in the preceding phrase, must mean either his " obedience unto death," or his *incarnation* as preparatory and essential to this; comp. Heb. x. 5—10.

(19) Most interpreters have considered this verse to be little, if anything, more than a repetition of verse 18. So Theophylact, Œcumenius, Semler, and even Tholuck, Ruckert, and Rosenmüller. Still, the γάρ at the beginning of the verse shows, that the writer meant to assign some reason or ground for what he had just asserted in the preceding verse, either in the way of explanation or confirmation. Verse 18 *asserts fully*, having both a protasis and an apodosis, what verse 12 begins to assert but leaves unfinished, viz., that as by the offence of Adam all men were brought into a state of condemnation, so by the δικαίωμα of Christ all were brought into a state of justification. In verse 19, the apostle adds the ground or reason why all men have come into a state of condemnation and of justification, viz., because they have become sinners through the disobedience of Adam on the one hand, and righteous through the obedience of Christ on

the other; *i. e.*, the disobedience of Adam was a cause or ground why all men became sinners and therefore came into a state of condemnation, and the obedience of Christ is in like manner a cause or ground why all are come into a state of justification. The course of thought in vers. 18, 19 is substantially the same as that in verse 12, with the exception that what is there merely *hinted*, is here fully and explicitly declared. There the sentiment is, that by the offence of one man sin entered the world and death followed, and followed so as to extend itself over all the human family, inasmuch as all became sinners, ἐφ' ᾧ πάντες ἥμαρτον. There too, as we have seen above, the καὶ οὕτως intimates, that the entrance of sin and death into the world being brought about by the offence of Adam, the spread also of these was in some way connected with or occasioned by this offence. But in vers. 18, 19, these thoughts are fully and explicitly unfolded; for verse 18 declares explicitly that condemnation and justification are connected with or occasioned by the offence of Adam and the righteousness of Christ, and verse 19 shows that the ground or reason of this is, that on the one hand men are made sinners by the disobedience of Adam, and on the other are made righteous through the obedience of Christ. The apodosis is merely *implied* in verse 12, and not at all expressed; but ἁμαρτωλοὶ κατεστάθησαν οἱ πολλοί of verse 19, is evidently intended by the apostle to correspond with the ἐφ' ᾧ πάντες ἥμαρτον in ver. 12. What is added in verse 19, to the former statement is, that '*by the disobedience of one man*, the many became sinners;' a thing not explicitly declared but merely hinted in the καὶ οὕτως of verse 12.

It is allowed by nearly all commentators, that verses 18, 19 resume and complete the statement begun at verse 12. If then, as seems to be quite clear, ἐφ' ᾧ πάντες ἥμαρτον in verse 12 and ἁμαρτωλοὶ κατεστάθησαν οἱ πολλοί in verse 19 correspond, it is plain that in the latter case *actual sinners* are denoted as well as *actual sin* in the former case. The fact, that Adam's sin was a cause or ground of men's becoming sinners in reality (not putatively so), and that Christ's obedience was a ground of men's becoming righteous, *i. e.*, of their being justified in reality (not merely in a putative or fictitious manner), constitutes the substance of the declaration in verse 19; and all this is a fuller and more explicit declaration of the sentiment implied in verse 12, while at the same time it stands related to verse 18 as assigning a ground or reason of the condemnation and justification there asserted.

That παρακοή here is the same as παράβασις in verse 14, and as παράπτωμα in verses 15, 17, 18, needs hardly to be mentioned.

In all of these cases the reference is specifically to the first offence of Adam and to that only. See on verse 16 above.

Everything peculiar in this verse depends, as will readily be seen, on ἁμαρτωλοί, δίκαιοι, and καθίστημι. In what sense then does scriptural usage entitle us to take the first of these words? In all other places except this, I cannot hesitate for a moment to say, it is taken as designating *a sinner in heart and life*, or (in other words) an actual sinner. The very form and limitations of the verb ἁμαρτάνω, which has only an *active* voice, confirm this idea. If ἁμαρτωλός is ever employed in order to designate those who are *guilty*, in the sense of *being obnoxious to punishment;* like the word *guilty* itself, in such cases, it implies at the same time moral turpitude and ill desert as the ground of this obnoxiousness. To designate one who has merely the susceptibility of receiving impressions that will lead him to sin (Adam had this before his fall); or one who has (as we say) merely an original disposition to sin, *i. e.*, such a disposition as is native and not superinduced; or one who is beset with temptations to sin, and is in great danger from them; to designate one who is simply exposed to evil, or is merely unhappy or wretched; the word ἁμαρτωλός is never used elsewhere in the Scriptures. Why then should we introduce a new sense of the word here? In ver. 12, when the apostle had said, that 'by one man sin entered the world, and death by sin, *and so death passed upon all men*,' he meant by these last words (as we have seen above), that his readers should understand him to hint, that the passing of death upon all men had some connection with Adam's offence. But still he subjoins immediately, as the specific and immediate reason or ground of this death, ἐφ' ᾧ πάντες ἥμαρτον. Why not recognize the same connection and the same sentiment here? Adam's sin was a *cause* or *ground* why all men are constituted sinners; yet Adam's sin is not affirmed to be their sin; they are not said to be ἐν αὐτῷ ἁμαρτωλοί, nor τῇ ἁμαρτίᾳ αὐτοῦ ἁμαρτωλοί, nor yet τῷ κατακρίματι αὐτοῦ καταδεδικασμένοι; but they are ἁμαρτωλοί in, by, and for themselves. A ground or cause of this, was Adam's offence. But natural evil, and disadvantage, and degeneracy of nature is one thing, and *sin*, is another. A man's *sin* is and must be his *own act*, either internal or external, or both; and for men to be ἁμαρτωλοί, they must be actively and voluntarily so. Another man's sin can no more be mine, than his soul can be mine; no more than his consciousness, will, affections, or disposition, can be mine. To impute them to me, then, must be to impute to me what in fact does not belong to me, what never did, and what never can. The candid advocates of imputation in its highest sense, concede this. But how much progress do we make in the knowledge of *things*, and in the explanation of important *principles* in theology, when we affirm that God counts that as existing which does not in reality exist, and which is in itself an impossibility?

To avoid the difficulty of such imputation (which indeed such men as Calvin, and Edwards, and Stapfer pointedly rejected) some, *e. g.*, Edwards and others, have assumed an absolute unity or oneness of Adam and all his posterity. But this method of explanation is fraught with difficulties both physiological and moral. It is physiologically untrue. A separate consciousness, will, affections, desires, etc., make separate beings; or else there is but one being material or immaterial, in the universe. Consciousness contradicts this theory. Individual *accountability* renders it incredible. If Adam and his posterity are indeed all *one*, then all their sins are just as much his, as his is theirs; and his penitence is as much theirs, as his offences. Or is it true, that God, a being of boundless benevolence and love of holiness, has made such a world that nothing but sin can be propagated in it?

The simple statement of fact seems to be, after all, that God has such an utter aversion to sin, that he has testified his displeasure by an appalling exhibition of the woful consequences to which it leads. Sin is a violation of the order and harmony of the universe, and consequently productive of evil, because it disturbs those laws and tendencies all of which are in themselves productive of good. The greatest mischief of all is, that sin, in this way, brings suffering and sorrow upon the innocent as well as the guilty. But in this very way, too, the odious and abominable nature of sin is most fully and completely exhibited. The earth cursed for man's sake; the brute creation subjected to innumerable evils on his account; the posterity of Adam born heirs of suffering, and despoiled of the disposition to obedience which our primitive ancestors possessed; are all striking and melancholy evidences of the evil of sin. But for the evils to which Adam's posterity are subjected and exposed, God has provided a remedy; or rather, he has prepared the way for redemption from them. The two things, therefore, now go together, viz., the exhibition of the dreadful effects of sin on the one hand, and of abounding mercy and benevolence on the other. The constitution of the universe, by which sin was made to appear so dreadful in its bitter fruits, is doubtless ordained to serve great and wise purposes, sooner or later, in the scheme of the divine moral government and discipline. Nor is the case of Adam's sin the only one, and altogether singular in its kind. The same *principle* in the constitution of the world everywhere develops itself. Parents by their vices ruin their children; wicked men corrupt their neighborhood; bad rulers affect whole nations with evil, the innocent as well as the guilty. Nothing can be more untrue, than that the mischiefs occasioned by sin light only upon the guilty. The horrible evil of sin is, that according to the constitution of the universe, it often involves the innocent as well as the guilty in its consequences. Nor could "the exceeding sinfulness of sin" be fully displayed and held forth in its odious light to the abhorrence of all benevolent beings, unless such were the case. Still, after all is attributed to the first sin which belongs to it, it would be difficult to see how Adam's first offence differed from other sins, as to the consequences which it superinduced, excepting that his condition and his relations to the *whole* human race differed greatly from those of any of his posterity. The consequences of his sin, therefore, were peculiar and awfully deleterious.

It is then one thing to be made a *sufferer* on account of the sin of others, and another thing to be *constituted a sinner* by something that he has done. So far as it respects the manner in which Adam's sin has affected us, both of these consequences have flowed from it. This leads us to consider next the word,

Κατεστάθησαν. The primary and literal sense of this word, as *actively* used, seems to be *to lay down*, *put down*, *deposit;* as its composition (κατά and ἵστημι) would plainly denote. In a secondary sense, the word means *to establish, ordain, settle, decree, constitute,* etc., *to cause* that any person or thing should be this or that, possess this or that quality, or fill this or that place or office, etc. It has also *neuter* or *intransitive* meanings, e. g., *to subsist, to be extant, to be established, to stand firm* or *unmoved,* but they would be quite inappropriate to the passage before us, and are therefore plainly out of question. The form κατεστάθησαν is *passive* Aor. 1; which tense, although frequently employed, in the sense of the *middle* voice (see New Test. Gramm. § 61. 4), where there is no Aorist middle, yet as here there is a middle Aor. 1, it must be regarded as *passive,* and passive as to some of its *transitive* meanings. We come then to the conclusion, that κατεστάθησαν must mean *were constituted, were made to be, were caused to be;* for standing in connection as it does with παρακοή as designating a *cause* or *means,* it would hardly seem susceptible of any of the other transitive meanings which the verb καθίστημι has. Reiche has labored, with much learning, to prove that καθίστημι may mean *to show, exhibit, publicly demonstrate anything to be* this or that; and that the Pass. voice may of course mean *to be shown,* etc. *Classic* examples of this usage are not at hand, excepting αἴτιον καθιστάνειν (to show cause) as employed by Lucian. But in

Hellenistic Greek he thinks this to be more common: *e. g.*, 3 Macc. iii. 5, where however the neuter sense *(became permanently)*, is better than the one he proposes, and indeed the only one that can well be given to καθειστήκεισαν, because the tense is Pluperfect. So in Josephus, (Ant. VI. 5, 6,) τὸν Θεὸν αὐτοῖς εὐμενῆ καταστῆσαι may mean *to render the Divinity propitious to them*, not (as Reiche proposes) *exhibit* him as propitious. We can not therefore regard κατεστάθησαν here as equivalent to ἐφανερώθησαν, and render it *declarati sunt esse*, with Koppe, C. Flatt, and Reiche. Nor can we, with Grotius, Limborch, Whitby, Storr, Suskind, Flatt, and others, render κατεστάθησαν, *were treated* as sinners; for the apostle has told us in verse 12 that death has passed upon all men ἐφ' ᾧ πάντες ἥμαρτον; and how, moreover, could a just and unerring God treat men as sinners unless they were so? See Comm. on εἰς κατακρίμα in preceding verses.

By the obedience, διὰ ὑπακοῆς, equivalent to δι' ἑνὸς δικαιώματος in verse 18. See the remarks under this verse, and also on ver. 16; and compare the passages in Matt. xxvi. 39, 42. John x. 18. Phil. ii. 8. Heb. x. 7 — 10. But although I can scarcely entertain a doubt that the *obedience* of Christ, in this connection of thought, means in particular his obedience in assuming our nature and his suffering an expiatory death in it, yet I would not exclude the idea that the *active* (as well as passive) obedience of his whole life did contribute, yea was necessary, to the perfection of his character as a Mediator and a great High Priest who should make atonement for us. Without such an obedience, he would have needed an atonement for himself, instead of being able to make it for others. But in respect to the specific allegation, that 'Christ's obedience (ὑπακοή) is *imputed* to us;' this Paul does not here nor elsewhere say, nor any other sacred writer. This is a phraseology superinduced upon the Bible, many years since the Reformation, from human systems and methods of explanation; and not one which is taken from the Scriptures and transferred into Symbols. *In all the Bible there occurs* NOT *such a declaration, as that one man's sin or righteousness is* IMPUTED *to another.* The *thing* for substance aimed at, by many who employ such phraseology, is doubtless a doctrine of the Bible, viz., that the obedience of Christ, above all his obedience unto death, did contribute to constitute him an all-glorious and all-sufficient Mediator. As to the rest, *that God* FOR CHRIST'S SAKE *forgives sinners, not imputing their trespasses to them*, is the very sum and substance of what is appropriately called THE GOSPEL, and all which can be exegetically made out from the simple interpretation of the Scriptures. For in what part of the Bible is it said that *Christ obeyed for us?* Or where, that *his obedience is imputed to us?* And yet, that *on our account* or *in our behalf*, he obeyed and suffered, I deem to be a great and fundamental doctrine of the gospel.

The many shall be made righteous, δίκαιοι κατασταθήσονται οἱ πολλοί. Is δίκαιος to be taken in an *active*, or *passive* sense? That is, does it mean one who is *pious, fearing* God and *obeying* his commands, *justus, probus;* or does it mean *justificatus*, a *justified* person, one forgiven or delivered from the curse of the law? In all cases excepting the present one and ὁ δίκαιος ἐκ πίστεως, I think it must be conceded that δίκαιος is employed in the *active* sense; that is, it means either one who obeys the whole law, *i. e.*, it has a *legal* sense, or else it means one who obeys in such a manner as proves him to be a sanctified, holy, devout person, *i. e.*, it has an *evangelical* sense. As to the case of δίκαιος ἐκ πίστεως, I do not see any good reason for departing from the common *usus loquendi* in respect to δίκαιος; for the declaration amounts simply to this, viz., that a man is pious, holy, of an obedient spirit, through faith, or in the way of exercising faith in the Lord Jesus, and has thus been graciously sanctified, so that he now fears God and keeps his commandments in a Christian sense. I doubt on several accounts, whether here, we can translate or explain δίκαιος by the word *justified;* for this would merely designate a *passive* sense, and be descriptive of what Christ has done for sinners, without exhibiting the active sense in which they are *holy* or *obedient*, δίκαιοι. Δικαιωθείς, δικαιωθέντες is employed by Paul, when he wishes to designate simply the *passive* idea; *e. g.*, Rom. v. 1, al. Δίκαιοι, moreover, must have an *active* sense here, in order to make out the antithesis to ἁμαρτωλοί, which clearly bears only an *active* sense, if the *usus loquendi* may decide this point; at least it does so wherever else it is employed.

How then is the *obedience* of Christ to make many *just* or *righteous?* In the like manner, we may answer, as the disobedience of Adam made many sinners, *i. e.*, was a cause or ground of their becoming sinners. Christ, by what he has done and suffered, has opened a new and living way of access to God, in which sinners may hope for pardon, and grace to become humble and obedient, *i. e.*, to become δίκαιοι, or δίκαιοι ἐκ πίστεως. But in this case, abundant as the provision is which he has made for sinners, yet penitence and faith are a *conditio sine qua non* to the bestowment of the higher blessings of the gospel. And so in the opposite case; some voluntary act of sin, which is properly one's own, would seem to be necessary in order to make sure the final and eternal damnation of any one of Adam's posterity. Before this they are indeed in a *damnable* state, *i. e.*, in imminent hazard

of damnation (if I may so express it); and it is also true, that
before repentance and faith sinners are in a state of peculiar
probation, and in a *salvable* state, *i. e.*, a state in which they may
be saved.

The reader will note, that the future tense ($κατασταθήσονται$)
is employed in this apodosis. This corresponds to the sentiment
implied in the $δικαίωσιν$ $ζωῆς$ of verse 18. The affirmation of
Paul then is, that the efficacy of Christ's obedience will bring *the
many* to be righteous, holy, or devoted in heart and life to the
service of God. If this were already done in the sense in which
he expected it to be done, and in the sense which the idea of *imputed* righteousness would render necessary, why should he here
employ the *future* tense? The fact that he does so, appears to
afford evidence that the whole paragraph is intended to disclose
the virtue and efficacy of the two dispensations, under the first
and second Adam, rather than to detail *facts* merely as such, or
to give us a simple *historical* picture. Thus considered, there is
no difficulty as to any of the apostle's declarations. What he
declares concerning the influence of Adam's offence, discloses
what would be the certain result of that, if all men were left to
themselves in the condition into which that offence brought them;
while what he declares respecting the obedience of Christ, discloses to us the true nature of gospel grace, its all-sufficiency, the
certainty of its accomplishing its ends, and its adaptedness to the
wants and woes of all our race. The apodosis here, then, is not
so much a narration of mere historical occurrences in this case,
as it is a declaration of the nature of that which Christ's obedience
is adapted to accomplish. Or may it and must it be construed
(the tense being *future*) of the millennial day of glory — the
future and universal prevalence of the Christian religion? This
would seem to be rather a forced construction, and that the
$δίκαιοι$ here described are those which the work of Christ will be
efficient in constituting, either in this world, or in the next, or in
both. $Δίκαιοι$ those are called, who at the last day appear before
the throne of the final Judge, and meet with acceptance through
the mercy of a Saviour; see Matt. xxv. 37; where the appellation is doubtless given, in reference to the character which they
sustain as the subjects of sanctifying grace. The meaning
of Paul seems therefore to be, that as Adam's offence had been
the cause of ruining the many, the obedience of Christ should be
the cause why the many should be justified. In a word, as
actual suffering and a dangerous and ruinous condition are the
lot of all through Adam; so, on the other hand, a state of renewed and peculiar probation, attended with many privileges
and blessings, even such as exceed all that were lost by the fall,

with the proffer of eternal life and glory, is procured for our guilty race by the Lord Jesus Christ. For further remarks, see Excursus on Rom. v. 19.

CHAP. V. 20, 21.

In verses 12—19, respecting the evils occasioned by Adam and the blessings procured by Christ, nothing was said of any good achieved by the Jewish dispensation. It is very natural to suppose that the Jew, ever jealous for the honor of the Mosaic economy, would feel a strong objection to the representation which attributes deliverance from these evils wholly to Christ and his gospel, without regard to the law Verses 20, 21, seem designed to answer such an objection ' As to the Mosaic law, it was so far from delivering men from sin and its fearful consequences, that the result of it was just the contrary, viz , the abounding of sin, or at least the more conspicuous and striking exhibition of it.' Both of these sentiments, indeed, we may suppose to be included in the assertion made in verse 20 The same idea is more fully developed in Rom vii 5 — 13

Moreover in verses 20 21, the apostle plainly designs to show, that the gospel, instead of being superseded by the law in any important respect, was rendered (so to speak) the more necessary The law, instead of diminishing the sins of men, did, on account of their abusing it (Rom vii 11), render them more guilty, and consequently it increased their need of a new dispensation of pardoning mercy And such is the rich provision for mercy under this new dispensation, that not only the sins which men committed before the law of Moses was published (verses 13, 14) may be forgiven but even the more aggravated guilt which they incur who sin against the precepts of revelation, may be pardoned Considered in the point of view now presented, the verses under consideration are pregnant with highly important meaning

(20) *Revelation*, νόμος, *i. e., the Mosaic law*.— Παρεισῆλθεν is rendered by some, *came in unawares ;* but this makes no tolerable sense here, and moreover it contradicts fact, for the law was introduced with awful pomp and solemnity; Ex. xx. Gal. iii. 19. Heb. xii. 18—21, 26. We must therefore translate : *supervened, came in the way of addition, præterea introiit* (as Beza renders it); *i. e.*, it supervened upon the state which preceded Moses, when men were living without a revelation.* The word παρεισέρχομαι is employed in both significations in the classics ; and Philo uses the word παρεισῆλθεν, in the same sense as εἰσῆλθεν (see Bretsch. Lex.); but I regard the second meaning above given to the word, as the best in this passage.

"Ἵνα is said by some to be not *causal*, *i. e.*, not introducing a reason or cause *why* the law came in, *in order that*, etc., but *ecbatic* (ἐκβατικός), *i. e.*, showing the effect or consequence ; so

* Meyer says. *came in addition, supervened* to sin, ἁμαρτία, which had already made its entrance into the world.

that we may translate; *the law supervened* SO THAT *offences abounded.**

The *telic* sense of ἵνα, however, might be retained in the verse under examination, by construing πλεονάσῃ as we do ἐπερίσσευσεν in iii. 2, which there means *may appear to abound, may exhibit or display its abounding* (like the Piel and Hiphil conjugations of Hebrew verbs); and in the like way is περισσεύσῃ used in 2 Cor. iv. 15. In this way the sense will be: 'The law came in order that sin might be abundantly exhibited, or that a full display of sin might be made;' according with Rom. vii. 13, comp. vii. 5 — 12. iii. 12. In this way it is construed by Tholuck, Flatt, and others; and it scarcely needs to be said, that the end or design of the law itself was not the *increase* of sin, but the *restraint* of it. My objection, however, to the explanation of these interpreters is, that verse 21 evidently demands a sense of πλεονάσῃ different from that which they give. If we say: 'The law entered in order that the odious nature of sin might be more fully and plainly exposed and known;' then what shall we make of verse 21? It must be this: 'Where sin was more fully displayed, grace superabounded,' viz., above the display. But clearly the apostle does not mean to say this, (for what can be the meaning of such a declaration?) but that where sin *actually abounded*, there grace *actually superabounded*.

We must return then to the *ecbatic* use of ἵνα here, which Chrysostom has proposed. The meaning of the verse may be thus given: 'The Mosaic law which was introduced, instead of diminishing the guilt and sins of men, served only to increase them; for although in itself holy, and just, and good, yet being abused and resisted by the evil passions of men, it was made the occasion of increasing their guilt, because the light which it shed on them, both aggravated their offences and rendered them more conspicuous.' Chap. vii. 5 — 13, as before suggested, is a full and satisfactory comment on these sentiments. Turretin, Reiche, Glockler, Barnes, and others have for substance adopted the same explanation.

(21) *But where sin abounded, grace did superabound;* i. e., the pardoning mercy of the gospel has triumphed even over the sins of the Jews, which were greatly aggravated by reason of the light they enjoyed.

So that as sin reigned by death, ἵνα ὥσπερ κ. τ. λ., i. e., brought sentence of death or condemnation upon all men, *in like manner also grace might reign by justification unto eternal life, through*

* Alford and others consider ἵνα here is telic, *in order that*. Alford says: "no possible objection can be taken to this statement by those who view the law as a preparation for Christ."

Christ Jesus our Lord, i. e., grace might reign or have an influence widely extended, in the bestowment of justification or pardoning mercy, which confers eternal life or happiness on all men who will accept it, through Jesus Christ our Lord.—After δικαιοσύνης here, one must supply τῆς οὔσης *(which is)* εἰς ζωὴν αἰώνιον. In this verse, ἐν τῷ θανάτῳ is the Dative of *means* or *manner ;** and it stands in antithesis with διὰ δικαιοσύνης εἰς ζωὴν αἰώνιον. Of course δικαιοσύνης does not here mean *righteousness* in the sense of holiness or conformity to the divine law, but in the sense of *justification*, i. e., *God's righteousness,* viz., that which he gives or bestows; in the like sense as δικαίωμα, δικαιοσύνης, and δικαίωσιν, in vers. 16—18 above. The meaning is, that as sin exercised its sway over men in occasioning their condemnation (θάνατον), so grace, which superabounds, has exercised its sway in procuring a remission of the sentence of condemnation, and bestowing that justification which is connected with eternal life. Turretin wrongly makes δικαιοσύνης here mean both *justification* and *sanctification.* For the antithesis of δικαιοσύνη, viz., θάνατος, does not mean both *sin* and *condemnation* at the same time.

The reader will remark, also, that as θάνατος is the direct antithesis of ζωὴ αἰώνιος here, so it must mean more than temporal death merely ; nay, more than any limited term of misery in a future world ; unless, indeed, it can be shown that the happiness of the righteous is *limited.* But this none will attempt to show. How then can the misery of the wicked be shown to be *temporary?* That θάνατος is here employed in the same sense as in verses 12—19, impresses itself, as it seems to me, spontaneously on the mind of every reader not misled by *a priori* reasonings.

It should also be noted, that ὑπερεπερίσσευσεν ἡ χάρις of course cannot be applied to the *number* of its subjects here; for how could grace *superabound* in this respect, when *all* men were sinners? It plainly has reference, therefore, to *abounding sin* which existed after the law was introduced. What the apostle means to affirm, is, that however much sin was aggravated under this new order of things, yet such was the greatness of gospel grace that it triumphed even over this aggravated guilt. In other words, the salvation of the gospel is so ample, that it may be extended to all men however depraved and deserving of punishment they may be; and those who are under the law and have transgressed it, do of all men most need the salvation of the gospel.

* It may be better to take ἐν τῷ θανάτῳ as denoting the sphere or kingdom in which the dominion of sin was specially held, or "that in and by which the reign was exercised and shown." See Meyer and Alford.

CHAP. VI.—VIII.

WHEN the apostle (chap. i.—ii.) had shown the guilt of all men, both Jews and Gentiles, and that none could escape the wrath to come except by the mercy of God through Christ, he represents the Jew as objecting to such a sentiment, on the ground that the fidelity of God, in respect to the promise made to Abraham and *his seed* would be called in question by it. To this the apostle replies, that no such objection could be made; for God is to be regarded as faithful to his promises, even if all men are thereby convicted of being unfaithful to their engagements. The faithfulness of God is in fact the more conspicuous, when he treats those who have sinned, and who continue impenitent, according to their real desert.

The Jew, however, not satisfied with this, objects that there would in this way be encouragement for men to sin, inasmuch as the divine glory would be the more conspicuous, in consequence of the display of pardoning mercy. But this objection the apostle repels, with strong language of disapprobation, iii. 5—8. He does not, however, proceed to canvass it, because he has other things which he is desirous to say, before he enters particularly into the consideration of such an objection.

These he exhibits in chap. iii. 9, to v. 21. After all which he here says, and especially after such an exhibition of *superabounding grace* as is made in chap. v. 12—21, it is natural to expect that the Jew would renew, at least in his own mind, the same objection as before, and this, with more appearance of reason than he then had. Accordingly, we find the apostle representing him as immediately objecting to the views of gospel grace which he had expressed, in the following words. "Shall we continue, then, in sin, that grace may abound?" Chaps. vi. vii. viii. are designed to canvass the great subject which this objection brings forward, and fully to illustrate it. The course of thought appears to be as follows:

1. The very profession and nature of the Christian religion are directly opposed to continuance in sin, for he who is "baptized into the death of Christ," if sincere in his professions, must renounce sin and mortify his carnal appetites, vi. 2—11.

2. The remainder of chap. vi. forms a peculiar argument, if I may so call it, with respect to the subject under the apostle's consideration, viz., whether a dispensation of grace allows its subjects to sin. Verses 12, 13, are an *exhortation* to guard against sin; which is occasioned by the preceding considerations that the writer has proffered. But in verse 14 Paul places his subject in a new attitude. He had before shown that Christianity, from its very nature, stands opposed to sin, and implies the subduing and mortifying of all evil passions and desires. He now ventures to suggest, not only that there is no good ground for the allegation of the objector, viz., that the doctrine of grace would encourage men to continue in sin, but that this very doctrine furnishes powerful motives, yea, more powerful ones than those which a dispensation of law furnishes, to excite men to the practice of holiness. He begins by saying, that 'sin will not have dominion over Christians, for they are not under law, but under grace.' This is as much as to say, that if they were still under the law (in the sense here meant) sin would have dominion over them; but inasmuch as they are under grace, this will not be the case. The subject thus introduced is one of vast magnitude and importance. If it be true, that *a system of grace is the only one which now proffers adequate means of* SANCTIFICATION *as well as pardon*, then is the importance of the gospel rendered doubly conspicuous. This is what the apostle intimates in verse 14, and what he goes on through the remainder of chapter vi., and also through chapters vii. viii. to confirm and illustrate.

The first illustration of the power of gospel grace to subdue sin, is drawn from the relation which the Christian sustains toward the gospel or χάρις. He has become *the servant of grace*, consequently, he must yield it his obedience; and by becoming the servant of grace, he has renounced his subjection to sin, consequently, he must act in a manner that accords with the relation which he sustains, i. e., he should live in a holy manner, verses 16—20. And thus the Christian must be led to act, also, on the ground that the consequences of obeying sin and of obeying grace are so unspeakably different and important, verses 21—23. This, however, is negative argument; if I may so speak. I mean, that it does not *directly* prove what is intimated in verse 14, viz., the superiority of grace to law in influencing us to lead a holy life. But it proves, that even in those respects in which the law might seem to claim a high pre-eminence, it has none. The gospel confers as high obligation and threatens as high penalties. In both respects it is opposed to sin, its obligations are directly contrary to sin; its consequences are just the reverse of those which follow sin. In all these respects, then, we may truly affirm of the gospel as much as could be affirmed of the law.

3. All this prepares the way to accomplish the subsequent part of the apostle's design; which is to show that *the law* (in the sense to which Jewish legalists adhered to it) *is virtually and substantially renounced*, by giving ourselves to Christ in the way of the gospel, vii. 1—4. This is an important point, and a great advance toward the attainment of the apostle's design. He then goes on (vii.) to assert and prove that the law, instead of being an effectual means of sanctifying men and making them truly holy, is in reality the occasion of their plunging into deeper guilt; while grace produces just the contrary effect. See further in the preliminary remarks to these several passages in this chapter. Secondly, he removes the objections which one might naturally raise against the law on such a ground, vii. 13—25.

4. He next shows that grace operates upon men in a manner different from that of law, viii. 1—11.

5. In the remainder of chapter viii., he insists on the duties and privileges that result from such a state of grace.

If the reader will now look back, for a moment, he will see a regular series of thought, all pertaining to the same great subject, from the commencement of chap. vi. to the end of chap. viii. To the apostle's plan of justification by grace alone, the natural and most formidable objection at first view would be, that such a doctrine would lay no restraint upon sin, but rather encourage it. Already had he adverted to this objection, in chap. iii. 5—8. But with chap. vi. the formal discussion of the subject which is introduced by it commences. The simple outlines of the argument and illustrations are, (1) The very profession and nature of Christianity imply a renunciation of sin, vi. 1—11. (2) The gospel lays more effectual constraint upon us to abstain from sin than the law can do, vi. 14; for, (a) By becoming servants of it, we must yield our obedience to it, vi. 16—20. (b) It sets before us the highest possible rewards, and renders them attainable, vi. 21—23. (3) We renounce our *legality*, i. e., our dependence on the law as the effectual means of sanctification, when we become affianced to Christ. We sustain a new relation in consequence of this, and are laid under new obligations which are of a more forcible nature, vii. 1—4. (4) The law, instead of restraining and subduing our sins, is even the occasion of their being aggravated, of plunging us into deeper condemnation, vii. 5—11, yet this is not chargeable upon the nature of the law, which in itself is holy and just and good, but on our evil passions which abuse it, while our consciences testify to the excellence and purity of the law itself, vii. 12—25. Consequently *sanctification*, as well as justification, can be expected not from the law, but only from a dispensation of grace. (5) Such is the *actual* effect of grace, it subdues and mortifies the principles of sin within us, and affords us the effectual guidance and aid of the Spirit of God in the discharge of our duty, viii. 1—11. Consequently, (6) The obligation to live in a holy manner may now be urged on Christians with the hope of success, for they have aid which is adequate for every time of need; yea, which will make them to triumph over all the troubles, and sorrows, and trials of life, and to persevere even unto the end in the way of holiness and truth, viii. 12—39.

This partial repetition of the course of thought in chapters vi.—viii., I have made merely for the sake of being explicitly understood. The attainment of correct views in regard to this course, is a *sine qua non* to a right exegesis of the whole. The particular parts form one harmonious whole; all resolve themselves, at last, into the simple design of showing not only that the grace of the gospel is not justly liable to the charge of encouraging sin, but that *it does in fact proffer to sinners the only hopeful and effectual means of* SANCTIFICATION, *as well as* JUSTIFICATION; yea, that it assures them of these means being effectual even to the end, so that their hopes can never be disappointed

If the reader has still any doubt, whether I have correctly stated the general outlines of the apostle's design and argument, let him look back on chaps. I. — IV , and see that the great discussion concerning gratuitous justification is there terminated; as is evident from chap. v , which is designed to point out the sequel or consequences of such justification. Let him look at the nature of the subject proposed by the question in vi 1, and the arguments and illustrations which follow Let him duly consider the assertion in vi 14, with the sequel in verses 15 — 20. Let him then see, in verses 21 — 23, that καρπός εἰς ἁγιασμόν is still before the writer's mind. In passing to vii 1 — 3, 4, let him note, that verse 4 sums up the object of all by ἵνα καρποφορήσωμεν τῷ Θεῷ. In reading verses 5, 6, he must observe, that the law is set forth as being even the occasion of aggravating our carnal desires, instead of mortifying and subduing them: all of which shows the insufficiency of it as a means of sanctification. Verses 7 — 11 only expand and enforce this idea; while verses 12 — 23 defend it from abuse Chap. viii opens as if the subject of justification were a prominent object of the writer's attention; but verses 2 — 4 show that this is only in consequence of justification being connected with sanctification The special object of God's sending his Son, as considered in verses 3, 4, is κατακρίνειν τὴν ἁμαρτίαν ἐν τῇ σαρκί, and ἵνα τὸ δικαίωμα τοῦ νόμου πληρωθῇ ἐν ἡμῖν. And so the sequel shows that *sanctifying* grace subdues sin, and secures filial obedience. Hence, in verses 12 — 17, the exhortation subjoined to the preceding context is, that Christians " should not live κατὰ σάρκα." And finally, it is the sanctified, filial, obedient spirit, inspired by the gospel and given by the Spirit of God in connection with it, which supports us under all sorrows and trials, and will end in complete and everlasting triumph On the face of all this course of thought, then, there lies what has already been attributed to it.

There is another circumstance still, which affords no small ground for confirming what has been stated above In chap. v., the apostle, after having finished his discussion with regard to the subject of justification by grace, goes on to declare the happy fruits of this, viz , cheering support under all the sorrows of life, and assurance of final happiness in the kingdom of glory, through the redemption of Christ. Just so in chap viii. 14 — 39. When Paul has completed the discussion of his second grand theme, viz., *the sanctifying nature of gospel grace*, he goes on to show, first, how it triumphs over sufferings and sorrows, inspiring a joyful hope; and, secondly, that it will assuredly bring the believer, at last, safe to glory. The parallelism, as to the general course of thought, is so exact between chaps. v. and viii 14 — 39, that no one can help perceiving it. There is then good ground to believe, from this circumstance, in addition to the other evidence produced above, that the apostle had, in his own view, here completed a second prominent topic of discussion, just as, at the end of chap. IV , he had completed his first one. The rest of his epistle is employed in canvassing various objections raised by Judaizing opponents, and in delivering various precepts and exhortations suited to the condition of the church at Rome.

(1) *What shall we say then?* τί οὖν ἐροῦμεν; words of the objector; viz., 'What shall be said, now, as to such a sentiment as that just uttered, viz., that *where sin abounded, grace did superabound?* May we not say: 'Let us continue in sin, that grace may abound?' The meaning of the question is: 'Since God is glorified in the abounding of his grace ; and since this abounds in proportion to the sin which is committed; then why should we

not go on to sin, as the glory of God will in this way be made to abound?

Shall we continue? ἐπιμενοῦμεν; But all the uncial Codd., many Codd. minusc., Copt., Codd. Lat., Damasc., Augustine; and after these, Grotius, Hammond, Wetstein, Griesbach, Lachmann, Reiche, prefer ἐπιμένωμεν (Subj.) which would mean, *must* or *should we continue*, etc.? The latter seems to be the preferable reading.

(2) *Dead to sin*, ἀπεθάνομεν τῇ ἁμαρτίᾳ, means, to renounce sin, to become, as it were, insensible to its exciting power or influence (as a dead person is incapable of sensibility); or, as Chrysostom well expresses it, μήκετι ὑπακούειν [τῇ ἁμαρτίᾳ], ἀλλὰ μένειν ἀκίνητον ὥσπερ τὸν νεκρόν. Comp. Gal. ii. 19. 1 Pet. ii. 24. Rom. vii. 4. The Greek and Latin writers employed the like phraseology; *e. g.*, τέθνηκέ μοι (Libanius); *mortuus tibi sum*, Plautus. So of the antithetic expression; *e. g.*, ἐμοὶ ζῆν (Alciphr.); ζῆν τῇ γαστρί (Diony. Halic.). In all such cases, a sense of such a nature as that given above was attached to this phraseology.

How shall we any longer live in it? πῶς ἔτι ζήσομεν ἐν αὐτῷ; *i. e.*, how shall we who have renounced sin, and profess to be insensible to its influence, any more continue to practise it, or to be influenced by it? The Fut. tense here expresses not simply what is declarative but what has relation to *duty*, viz., what *can* or *ought* to be done; N. Test. Gramm. § 125. Note 5.

The objector asks (verse 1), *whether we should continue in sin*, he means, beyond all doubt: 'May we go on to sin? May we then still continue the practice of it?' To this question the apostle answers in the negative; and this negative he expresses by the phrase ἀπεθάνομεν τῇ ἁμαρτίᾳ. *To become dead to sin* must mean, 'to refrain from the practice of sin, no longer to continue in it, no more to be guided or influenced by it,' *i. e.*, it is just the opposite of ζήσομεν ἐν αὐτῇ, to continue in the practice of it, or to find pleasure in it. That such is the condition of true Christians, the apostle now proceeds to show, in suggesting what is implied by the very nature of a Christian profession with its initiatory rites.

(3) *That as many*, etc., ὅσοι ἐβαπτίσθημεν, κ. τ. λ. The sense of this depends on the meaning of the formula βαπτίζειν εἰς τίνα — or βαπτίζειν εἰς τὸ ὄνομα τίνος. *(a)* In regard to βαπτίζειν εἰς τὸ ὄνομα the noun ὄνομα is, no doubt, to be regarded as *expletive*; as בש in Hebrew often is. So in the Jewish formula of baptizing proselytes, if the proselyte was a servant, the master, at his baptism, made a declaration whether he intended to make the servant free as a proselyte, or to have him still remain a servant. This

declaration was made thus: טְבַל לְשֵׁם בֶּן חוֹרִין, *he is baptized into the name of a freeman;* or טְבַל לְשֵׁם עֶבֶד, *he is baptized into the name of a servant.* So Matt. xxviii. 19, *baptized* εἰς τὸ ὄνομα τοῦ Πατρὸς, καὶ τοῦ Υἱοῦ, καὶ τοῦ Πνεύματος Ἁγίου; which is the same as *baptized* εἰς τὸν Πατέρα, καὶ τὸν Υἱὸν, καί τὸ Πνεῦμά τὸ Ἅγιον. Accordingly we find ὄνομα omitted in our text, as also in 1 Cor. x. 2. Gal. iii. 27; it is used, however, in Acts viii. 16. xix. 5. 1 Cor. i. 13, 15.

(b) The sense of the *whole* formula is more difficult to be ascertained. Most commentators, after Vitringa (Obs. Sac. III. 22), explain εἰς as meaning INTO *the acknowledgment of;* with an implication of affiance, subjection, discipleship, etc. But the formula in 1 Cor. xii. 13, πάντες εἰς ἓν σῶμα ἐβαπτίσθημεν, seems not to accord with such an explanation. Here εἰς plainly designates *participation,* and the meaning of the phrase is, that by baptism we come to belong to *one* body, to participate in one body, to be members of one body. In like manner we may say: By baptism we come to belong (in a special and peculiar sense), to Father, Son, and Holy Ghost. So the apostle speaks of being baptized into (and so of belonging to) Moses, 1 Cor. x. 2; to Paul, 1 Cor. i. 13. In this way all the passages of this nature may be construed alike, and the sense in all will be good. The idea is, for substance, that 'by baptism we become consecrated to any person or thing, appropriated (as it were) to any person or thing, so as to belong to him or to it, in a manner peculiar and involving a special relation, and consequent special duties and obligations.'

Thus the passage under examination would mean: 'As many of us as have become devoted to Christ by baptism; or as many of us as have been consecrated to Christ by baptism, or have been laid under peculiar obligations, or have taken upon us a peculiar relation to him, by being baptized.' The word ὅσοι is employed by the Greeks to designate the meaning *whoever,* etc., *i. e.,* all without any exception.

We have been baptized into his death, εἰς τὸν θάνατον αὐτοῦ ἐβαπτίσθημεν, *i. e.,* we have, as it were, been made partakers of his death by baptism; we have come under a special relation to his death; we have engaged to die *unto* sin as he died *for* it; we have a certain communion or participation in death to sin; comp. Rom. vi. 6. Gal. ii. 19. *The being baptized into his death,* therefore, is an internal, moral, spiritual thing; of which the external rite of baptism is only a symbol; for the relation symbolized by baptism is in its own nature *spiritual* and *moral. The participation in the death of Christ,* of which Paul here speaks, is surely something more than what is external; it is therefore of a *moral* or *spiritual* nature, of which the external rite can be regarded only as a symbol.

(4) *We have been buried with him, then, by baptism into his death,* συνετάφημεν οὖν κ. τ. λ., *i. e.*, we are (by being baptized into his death) buried as he was, συν ἐτάφημεν; where συν means *like, in like manner with;* comp. verse 6 ; also Rom. viii. 17. Col. iii. 1, where any other sense of συν is out of question ; 2 Tim. vii. 11, to which the same remark will apply.

Most commentators have maintained, that συνετάφημεν has here a necessary reference to the mode of *literal* baptism, which, they say, was by *immersion;* and this, they think, affords ground for the employment of the image used by the apostle, because *immersion* under water may be compared to *burial* under the earth. As my own conviction is not, after protracted and repeated examinations, accordant here with that of commentators in general, I feel constrained briefly to state my reasons for it.

The first is, that in the verse before us there is a plain *antithesis;* one so plain that it is impossible to overlook it. If now συνετάφημεν is to be interpreted in a *physical* way, *i. e.*, as meaning burial in the water in a physical sense, why is there no corresponding *physical* reference in the opposite part of the antithesis or comparison? The *resurrection* here spoken of is entirely *moral* and *spiritual,* for it is one which Christians have already experienced during their present life; as may be fully seen by comparing vers. 5—11, below. I take it for granted, that after ἡμεῖς in verse 4, ἐγερθέντες is implied; since the nature of the comparison, the preceding ὡς ἐγέρθη Χριστός, and also verse 5, make this entirely plain.

In Col. ii. 12 (which is altogether parallel with the verse under examination), we shall find more conclusive reason still, to argue as above respecting the nature of the *antithesis* presented. "We have been buried with him [Christ] by *baptism.*" What now is the *opposite* of this? What is the kind of *resurrection* from this grave in which Christians have been buried? The apostle tells us: "We have risen with him [Christ], by faith wrought by the power of God [τῆς ἐνεργείας τοῦ Θεοῦ], who raised him [Christ] from the dead." Here, then, there is a *resurrection by faith,* i. e., a *spiritual* and *moral* one. Why then should we look for a *physical* meaning in the antithesis? If then one part of the antithesis is manifestly to be construed in a manner entirely *moral* or *spiritual,* why should we not construe the other in like manner, provided it is susceptible of such an interpretation, as it plainly is here? Do not the laws of interpretation forbid us to understand συνετάφημεν as designating a *literal* burial under water?

(b) Nothing can be plainer, than that the word συνετάφημεν here, is equivalent in sense to the word ἀπεθάνομεν in verse 8; and is adopted merely for the sake of rendering more striking the image of a *resurrection*, which the apostle applies in the other part of the antithesis. 'A resurrection *from the grave,*' is a natural phrase when one is speaking with respect to the subject of a *resurrection;* see John v. 28, 29; comp. Dan. xii. 2. This statement is most plainly in accordance with the context, both here and in Col. ii. 12. For here the apostle goes on in the very next verse (as is usual with him), to present the same idea in a different costume. Verse 5 (which is a mere epexegesis of verse 4) says, *If we have been homogeneous* (σύμφυτοι, *i. e.,* like, of the same kind) *with Christ* IN HIS DEATH, *then shall we be in his resurrection.* The same idea and explanation is repeated in ver. 8 — ἀπεθάνομεν — συζήσομεν; and the whole is summarily explained in verse 11; *So reckon ye yourselves to be* νεκροὺς μὲν τῇ ἁμαρτίᾳ ζῶντας δὲ τῷ Θεῷ. Exactly in the same manner has the apostle gone on to explain συνταφέντες in Col. ii. 12. In verse 13 he adds, " *You* νεκρούς *in your offences* .... συνεζωοποίησε, *has he* [God] *made alive with him* [Christ], *having forgiven us all our offences.*"

There can be no real ground for question, then, that by συνετάφημεν, in both cases, is meant for substance neither more nor less than by ἀπεθάνομεν, νεκροί, etc. The epexegesis, added in both cases seems to make this quite plain. The reason why συνετάφημεν is used, seems to be, that the language employed may be a full antithesis of the word *resurrection*, which is used in the corresponding part of the comparison. "You who were *buried* with Christ," gives energy to the expression. A *dead body* would indicate that life had departed; but a body *dead* and *buried*, would indicate more thoroughly the entire removal of it.

(c) But my principal difficulty in respect to the usual exegesis of συνετάφημεν is, that the image or figure of *immersion, baptism,* is, so far as I know, nowhere else in Scripture employed as a symbol of *burial* in the grave. Nor can I think that it is a very natural symbol of burial. The obvious import of washing with water, or immersing in water, is, that it is symbolical of purity, cleansing, purification. But how will this aptly signify *burying* in the grave, the place of corruption, loathsomeness, and destruction?

(d) Last, the reader can scarcely fail to remark, that the comparison, as continued by the apostle through verses 5 — 9, is built wholly upon the idea of a *death* like to that of Christ, and not of a *burial.* The *unity* of the allegory or continued figure would be destroyed, then, by supposing that the principal circumstance in the mind of the apostle was the *burial* and not the death of Christ.

For these reasons it seems clear that the apostle had only a *moral* and *spiritual* burial, as he had only a *moral* and *spiritual* resurrection in view, in the corresponding part of the antithesis. Indeed, what else but a *moral* burying can be meant, when the apostle goes on to say, *We are buried with him* [not by baptism only, but] *by baptism* INTO HIS DEATH? Of course it will not be contended, that a literal *physical* burying is here meant, but only a *moral* one. And although the words *into his death*, are not inserted in Col. ii. 12 ; yet as the following verse there shows, they are implied. In fact, it is plain that reference is here made to *baptism*, because, when that rite was performed, the Christian promised to renounce sin, and to mortify all his evil desires, and thus to die unto sin that he might live unto God. I cannot see, therefore, that there is any more necessary reference here to the *modus* of baptism, than there is to the *modus* of the resurrection. The one may as well be maintained as the other.

If any one should say : 'I admit that *burial with Christ* has only a *moral* sense ; but then the language in which this idea is conveyed (συνετάφημεν), is evidently borrowed from the custom of immersion ;' In reply to this, I must refer him to the considerations under *(c)* above. The possibility of the usage I admit; but to show that the image is natural and obvious, and that it is a part of Scripture usage elsewhere, is what seems to be necessary in order to produce entire satisfaction to the mind of a philological inquirer. At any rate, I cannot at present think the case to be clear enough to entitle any one to employ this passage with confidence, in a contest respecting the mode of baptism. In this general view of the subject I find Reiche to concur.

In order that, ἵνα, *to the intent that ;* which may refer to the intention of mind in the individual who took baptism on himself, or the end which the nature of the case required to be kept in view. — *Glorious presence,* διὰ τῆς δόξης (= בְּכָבוֹד) *i. e.,* glorious display of power, might, or majesty. The Hebrew עֹז, *might, power,* is sometimes rendered δόξα by the Seventy ; *e. g.,* Psalm lxviii. 35 (lxvii. 34). Is. xii. 2. The idea really conveyed by διὰ τῆς δόξης here, can be satisfactorily explained, however, only by a reference to the Hebrew כָּבוֹד, which was employed to designate *the divine presence* as being attended with a supernatural *brightness* or *splendor.* In the same sense שְׁכִינָה was employed by the Rabbinic writers ; comp. Matt. xxviii. 3. Luke xxiv. 4, which seem to disclose that to which διὰ τῆς δόξης here refers. Διά here, *by,* or *through ;* where it signifies *on account of, for the sake of*, as an end or object, it has the Accusative after it. Compare, as to sentiment, Col. ii. 12. Eph. i. 19.

With ἡμεῖς, ἐγερθέντες, plainly must be supplied in order to make good the comparison commenced with ἠγέρθη above.— *We*, [being raised from the dead] *should live a new life*, ἐν καινότητι τῆς ζωῆς περιπατήσωμεν; *i. e.*, as we have been made like unto Christ in his death, so must we also in his resurrection, *i. e.*, we must, like him, live a new life after our resurrection. Καινότητι τῆς ζωῆς I regard as a Hebraistic form, in which the *first* noun supplies the place of the adjective. See Heb. Gramm. § 440. *b*. See further in verse 11.

The comparison here is not one in all respects of *like with like*. Christ died FOR *sin*, *i. e.*, on account of it, in order to make expiation for it; the believer dies TO *sin*, that is, he mortifies and subdues it, he becomes more or less insensible to its influence, or at least he successfully resists it. Christ had no sin of his own to mortify; the believer's *dying* consists in the mortification of his own sins. Even so it is with the resurrection. Christ rose *physically* from the dead; the believer, in the present life, rises *spiritually* from a state of moral death. Christ lived physically and naturally a new life; the believer lives spiritually and morally a new life.

On the whole, this is one of those cases of comparison, which, not affording strict analogies throughout, can be brought to bear only in a *general* way, and will not stand the test of being urged into particulars. It were easy to bring many instances of the like nature from the Scriptures; but the attentive reader will of course observe them. Turretin, in speaking of verse 4, says truly and forcibly: "Non tam est argumentum directum . . . quam vivida atque elegans hujus argumenti illustratio, et quasi pictura pro more orientalium hominum ac specialiter Judæorum, qui ejusmodi figuris atque emblematibus plurimum delectabantur."

(5) *If we have become homogeneous*, εἰ γὰρ σύμφυτοι γεγόναμεν. So σύμφυτοι must be explained, if philology is to be our guide. Σύμφυτος and συμφύης appear to be synonymous; and both mean *grown up together*, *sprung up together*, and so (secondarily) *intimately connected together*, *cognate*, etc. Of the whole grain, growing together in one field, the Greeks would say, It is σύμφυτος. The evident meaning here is for substance the same as ὅμοιος, *like*, *homogeneous*, *i. e.*, participating in, or intimately connected with, as to something. Therefore we may render, *If we have become connected* or *homogeneous by a likeness in respect to his death*, τοῦ θανάτου being the Gen. *objecti*, *i. e.*, the object in respect to which we have become like to Christ; or we may

translate: *if we have become cognate in the likeness of his death,* the latter clause showing that in respect to which we have become cognate. The meaning is: If we have become dead to sin, as he died for sin; then shall we in like manner live a new life, when risen from our [moral] death, as he lived a new one after his resurrection.' The translation *planted* is wrong, as φύω does not mean *to plant*, but *to grow, spring up, become nascent*, etc.; and the nature of the imagery here employed is obscured by such a version.

We have become and still are, γεγόναμεν; the Perfect often has, as here, a *continuative* sense, New Test. Gramm. § 125. Note 3. *a*. The reader will observe, that the sentence is conditional (εἰ γάρ); but as the Indic. Perf. is here used in the protasis, and the Ind. Fut. in the apodosis, it is what is called a *simple* or *absolute* conditional proposition, in which the condition stated in the protasis is taken for granted, and the apodosis is then stated as designating a thing that is necessarily consequent; New Test. Gramm. § 129. *a*.

Then surely, ἀλλὰ καί. Ἀλλά is *concessive*, *i. e.*, it implies that what precedes it is conceded; and here it may stand in *hypothetical* sentences like the present, where deductions are made; although in mere simple conclusions of a logical nature, ἀλλά is not employed. The real fact seems to be, that this formula implies an οὐ μόνον δέ before it, or some declaration which involves what amounts to this. So here, 'If . . . [then not so only] . . . *but also*,' etc. The Fut. ἐσόμεθα may be regarded here as expressive of *obligation ;* for so the Fut. is not unfrequently employed; *e. g.*, Matt. iv. 10. Luke iii. 10, 12, 14. Judg. xiii. 13, 14 (Sept.) Deut. vi. 5 (Sept.) Matt. xxii. 37, 39. Lev. xix. 17, 18 (Heb. and Sept.); New Test. Gramm. § 125. Note 5. *a*. That the apostle does not mean here to argue merely that Christians should at some future period become alive to God, is clear from verse 11 ; he means to inculcate the sentiment, that from and after their spiritual resurrection they are bound to be so. Τῆς ἀναστάσεως depends on ὁμοιώματι implied. We should naturally expect the article τῷ before τῆς ἀναστάσεως ; but it is often omitted in such cases; see New Test. Gramm. § 92. 1. *b*.

(6) *Knowing this*, τοῦτο γινώσκοντες, *i. e.*, we acknowledge, concede, or consider as established, thus much, viz., what is immediately mentioned in the sequel. It is equivalent to γινώσκομεν γάρ.

Our old man, ὁ παλαιὸς ἡμῶν ἄνθρωπος, a phrase of Jewish origin, no doubt. Thus in the Talmud it is said of proselytes, that "they became as little children," (Jemavoth. fol. 62. 1;) and they are also called *a new creation* בְּרִיאָה חֲרָשָׁה. This serves to show, that when our Saviour spoke to Nicodemus of the necessity of being born again, and when Paul spake of him who is in Christ as being *a new creature* (καινὴ κτίσις), there is no probability that the language employed by them was unusual or strange among the Jews. The παλαιὸς ἄνθρωπος here seems plainly to mean *the internal man, i. e.*, the sinful desires and propensities which belong to us in a natural or unrenewed state. The epithet παλαιός (old) is given, as designating something in opposition to the new spiritual man which is put on in Christ Jesus.

Is crucified, συνεσταυρώθη, as he [Christ] *was*, literally, *is crucified with him*. On the *comparative* meaning of συν in composition, see on συνετάφημεν under verse 4. Meaning: 'The sinful desires and propensities of the natural man are mortified and subdued in the Christian, so that they will no longer have a predominant influence over his conduct.' Not improbably the apostle, in choosing the word συνεσταυρώθη here, might have an allusion in his mind to the painful and protracted struggle which every Christian must go through, in subduing his carnal desires. Certainly, the word is very significant, when viewed in this light. Cf. Gal. ii. 20.

Might be deprived of efficiency, καταργηθῇ, *i. e.*, might be deprived of sinful vigor, power, life; might be rendered inefficacious as to sin, or be disabled from causing sin any more.

Τὸ σῶμα τῆς ἁμαρτίας, (*locus vexatus*), is explained by Hammond, Schœttgen, Glass, Tholuck, and others, by referring it to the Hebrew idiom; in which עֶצֶם and גּוּף (*substance* and *body*) are often employed either in a kind of superfluous manner, or (which is the more usual fact) in order to add *intensity* to the expression. Explained in this manner the whole runs thus: 'Our old man, *i. e.*, our carnal or natural man, is crucified as Christ was, in order that the substance or essence of our sinful passions might be destroyed.'

A more simple method still of interpreting τὸ σῶμα τῆς ἁμαρτίας, is that followed by many of the fathers, and not a few distinguished modern interpreters. Theodoret says: τὸ σῶμα τῆς ἁμαρτίας, περιφραστικῶς, αὕτη ἡ ἁμαρτία, *i. e.*, periphrastically used for *sin itself*. So Œcumenius. The reason why σῶμα is employed seems to be, that the apostle wishes to carry through the metaphor that he had begun, by speaking of *the crucifixion of our old man*. A *body* only can be literally crucified. Sin is personified, and represented as a monster with a body. Comp. the same figure of speech again in Col. ii. 11.

Beza, Semler, Bohme, Bretschneider, Wahl, Tholuck, Ruckert, and some others, retain the *literal* sense of σῶμα, and construe ἁμαρτίας as qualifying it = sinful body, *i. e.*, body practising sin, or causing sin, source of sin, etc. Such was the sense which I formerly gave it. And although this seems to be a justifiable meaning, if we compare Rom. vi. 12. viii. 13. vii. 23 — 25; yet I now view the meaning given above as the more simple and obvious. Reiche contends strongly, that Paul *never* teaches the doctrine that the body is the seat or cause of sin; which, he moreover avers, must be metaphysically untrue. But I am not able to make any important distinction between σάρξ and σῶμα as used by him in respect to things of a moral nature; and that Paul everywhere uses σάρξ as characterizing *carnal* passions and desires, admits of no doubt. Moreover, how can we refuse to concede, that ἐπιθυμίαις αὐτοῦ (sc. σώματος) in Rom. vi. 12, σώματος τοῦ θανάτου in Rom. vii. 24, and πράξεις τοῦ σώματος in Rom. viii. 13, afford evidence that σῶμα may be employed in the same way as σάρξ? Nor can I see why it may not be true, that our bodies, by their appetites and passions, may be the cause or means of our sinning as well and as truly as that the external world may be so. Sin, in a strict sense, is doubtless an act of the spirit or soul only; but the exciting cause need not be spiritual; and the body is often the instrument of acting out sin. The sense of *totality, entirety*, τὸ πᾶν, has also been given to σῶμα here; but very ineptly. Carpzov renders it *slave;* and he appeals to similar usage among the Greeks, e. g., in Rev. xviii. 13. But there seems no good reason why the word here should bear such a sense.

That we should no more be servants to sin, τοῦ μηκέτι δουλεύειν ἡμᾶς τῇ ἁμαρτίᾳ. Τοῦ . . . δουλεύειν, instead of ὥστε δουλεύειν; for in this latter way the Greeks usually express themselves. There are, indeed, examples of such a use of τοῦ before the Infinitive, even in classic Greek authors; see Buttmann's Gr. Gramm. § 127. *b.* Anm. 1. But the *frequency* of this usage in the New Testament and Septuagint in the sense of *that, in order that*, which must be assigned to τοῦ in some of these cases, seems to have its basis in the use of ל before the Infinitive in Hebrew, where it may signify either *design, object*, or *end, event, consequence.* See N. Test. Gramm. § 138. 8. *a.* Winer's Gramm. § 45. 4. — Τῇ ἁμαρτίᾳ is still personified here. The meaning of the apostle is, that we should no longer obey our passions and appetites which lead us to sin.

(7) This verse may be regarded as a kind of general maxim or truth, in regard to all such as die physically or naturally. The object of the writer is, to draw a comparison between the effects of *natural* death and those of *spiritual* death; the first causes men to cease from all actions, and of course from their transgressions; and by analogy we may conclude that the second, which is a *death unto*

sin, will do as much. The maxim, in its *physical* sense, was probably *proverbial* among the Jews. Thus in the Talmud, it is said: "When a man dies, he is freed from the commands," *Tract. Nidda*. Now what is said by the common proverb adduced by the apostle, in a *physical* respect (and correctly said in the sense intended to be conveyed), the apostle means to intimate will apply, in a *spiritual* respect, to one who is *spiritually* dead as to sin, *i. e.*, he must become free from its influence. His great object is to illustrate and enforce this point. The γάρ with which the proverb is introduced, is *γάρ illustrantis vel confirmantis*.

We may understand δεδικαίωται, in the sense already intimated above, viz., *freed, delivered from*. Nothing is more common in the writings of Paul than the use of δικαιόω in the sense of *acquitting, freeing*, viz., from the sentence or penalty of the law, etc. But here the idea seems to be more general, and is equivalent to that conveyed by ἐλευθερόω, which is substituted in its room in verse 18 below. Comp. 1 Pet. iv. 1, ὁ παθὼν ἐν σαρκὶ, πέπαυται ἁμαρτίας. In Sirach xxvi. 29, we read: οὐ δικαιωθήσεται κάπηλος ἀπὸ ἁμαρτίας, *a peddler will not be free from sin*, meaning that in the course of his business he will almost of course be led to contract guilt.

Thus explained, verse 6 asserts the fact, that in case the old man is crucified, Christians can no more be engaged in the service of sin. Verse 7 enforces this declaration by a simile drawn from natural or physical death; viz., as he who is physically dead ceases from all action, and therefore from sin, so he who is dead to sin (for this apodosis is implied) ceases from the practice of it. What is said *literally* of the one literal death, is said *morally* or *spiritually* of the other death which is of a moral nature. It hardly needs to be added here, that when the apostle speaks of natural death as freeing us from sin, he means from sinning here, in our present state and condition. What may be the condition of the soul in a future world, is not here an object either of inquiry or of assertion.

A more simple interpretation and construction is preferred by some, thus: ὁ ἀποθανὼν [τῇ ἁμαρτίᾳ] δεδικαίωται κ. τ. λ.; supplying ἁμαρτίᾳ from verse 2, and from what is implied in συνεσταυρώθη and καταργηθῇ in verse 6. If [with Chrysostom] we understand δεδικαίωται here as equivalent to ἀπήλλακται (is freed), this mode of exegesis may be admitted. The reasoning then would stand thus: "We know that our old man must be put to death, in order that the power of sin may be destroyed, so that we may no longer be in subjection to it; for he who dies in this manner, *i. e.*, dies unto sin by crucifying the old man, will be freed of course from the power of sin.' This is not mere *tautology* (as it has been called) but only appealing to the fact, that crucifying sin so as to become dead to it, must from the nature of the case free us from slavishly obeying it. In any way of construing the passage, ἁμαρτία must here mean sin in its active sense, as personified and exercising power. It cannot mean *penalty of sin;* for that is not here the subject of discussion.

(8) In order to understand the nicer shades of the apostle's discourse here, we must re-survey the course of thought in verses 5 — 7 : ' We are dead with Christ, and we shall live with him [in the sense explained above]; for if we are made like him in the first respect, then we must be in the second. That such must be the case, follows from the fact that our *old man* is crucified, and we are thus freed from the power of sin and can no longer serve it. Vers. 5 — 7 are therefore merely an illustration or confirmation of verse 4; and accordingly εἰ γάρ and ὁ γάρ, the usual signs of clauses added for such a purpose, here make their appearance. But verse 8 commences with εἰ δέ. Δέ here, as not unfrequently, is employed as a *continuative* of the discourse ; and particularly where the theme before introduced is resumed, and something added by way of illustration or confirmation; in which case we may call it δέ *resumptionis.* Here the apostle resumes the sentiment of verse 4 (Turretin and Tholuck say of verse 5, overlooking the γάρ confirmantis of verse 5), for the sake of adding a new circumstance by way of establishing his position, viz., that as Christ died but once and thenceforth lives for ever a new life, so the believer dies once for all to sin when he truly dies to it; consequently he must ever after live a new life, and no more practise sin as he once did.

If now we are dead, etc., εἰ δέ ἀποθάνομεν κ. τ. λ.; *i. e.,* if we die unto sin, as he died for it; for so verses 4, 5 seq. lead us of course to interpret this.— *We shall live with him,* συζήσομεν αὐτῷ, or rather *like him we also shall live.* See remarks on σύν in composition in verse 4. Origen, Chrysostom, Theodoret, Grotius, Heumann, Semler, Flatt, and others, have contended that συζήσομεν refers to *future glory* in another world; and Reiche contends strongly for this exegesis. But the latter part of verses 4, 5, 11, are conclusive against it. The simple sentiment is as before, viz , that ' as Christ died and rose again, so the Christian (in a moral sense) dies and rises again; as Christ lives a new life, so does he.' If it be objected that this is *repetition* or *tautology,* the answer is, that the sentiment of the preceding verses is indeed *resumed* here, but it it is for the purpose of adding a new circumstance as evidence of what had been affirmed, viz., that Christ died once for all, and so the Christian must die once for all to sin, *i. e.,* he can no more resume the practice of it.

(9) Εἰδότες ὅτι is employed here in the same way as τοῦτο γινώσκοντες in verse 6, and for the same purpose, viz., as prefatory to the introduction of matter that was confessedly obvious and true. This form of speech is equivalent to saying : 'What I have now asserted must be true, inasmuch as you know this or that to be true from which my position is a plain and necessary deduction.'

Dies no more, οὐκέτι ἀποθνήσκει, *i. e.*, will never more die. The whole force of the illustration hangs on these two words; for in these consists the *additional* matter which the apostle introduces.— *Death has no more dominion over him*, θάνατος .... κυριεύει; a repetition of the preceding thought in different language, in order to give it intensity. It is as much as to say, 'Christ will die no more, for death has no longer any power over him.' As to the sentiment here and in verse 10, comp. Heb. ix. 25 — 28. x. 11 — 14. One is strongly tempted to believe, that the same hand traced all these passages, from the peculiar shade of sentiment which is found in them. They mutually illustrate and confirm each other.

(10) *For in that he died, he died once for all*, or *only once on account of sin*, ὃ γὰρ .... ἐφάπαξ. The construction of ὅ (neuter pronoun here) is rather unusual in the New Testament; comp. also Gal. ii. 20. For its use in the classics, see Matth. Gramm. II. 894. Like the corresponding Latin *quod* thus placed, it means *in respect to this*, viz., in respect to that which is immediately subjoined; which here is ἀπέθανε. The sense ὅ thus *absolutely* used is the same as καθ' ὅ.*—Γάρ is used to confirm the preceding affirmation.

He died to sin, τῇ ἁμαρτίᾳ ἀπέθανεν. But "he who knew no sin," could not die to sin in the sense that sinful men do. The *Dativus causæ vel occasionis, on account of*, etc., is not unfrequent, (see N. T. Gramm. § 106. 5), and might be applied to the expression before us, in case it stood alone. But then we could not well interpret ζῇ τῷ Θεῷ which follows, in like manner. The Dative, seems rather designed to express an object to which the action of the verb stands related; *i. e.*, the *dying* expressed by ἀπέθανεν bears a relation to τῇ ἁμαρτίᾳ. This is designated by the Dative of this noun. But what the kind of relation is, the Dative does not of itself designate. This must be gathered from the context, or from the nature of the case. And here the sense requires us to construe Christ's dying to sin, as meaning that he died in order to diminish its power or influence (*Dat. incommodi*

---

* It is perhaps better here to make the relative pronoun ὅ the direct object of the verb: *for what* [i. e. *the death which*] *he died*, etc. See Philippi, Meyer, and others.

as the grammarians express themselves in such a case).—'Εφάπαξ, lit. *for once;* but the meaning is, as we say in English, *once for all;* comp. Heb. ix. 12. x. 10.

But in respect to his living, he lives to God, ὃ δὲ ζῇ, ζῇ τῷ Θεῷ. As this clause is an antithesis of the former, so the Dative here is an antithesis of the one there employed; for here it is a species of the *Dativus commodi* (as grammarians call it), the meaning being evidently that 'Christ lives to the honor and glory of God.' This indeed he always did; but not in that high and peculiar sense which is meant in reference to his state of exaltation. For such a sense of the Dative, and in a like case, comp. Rom. xiv. 6 — 8. See also 2 Cor. v. 13. Matt. iii. 16. Luke i. 55. xii. 21. The case in Luke xx. 38, πάντες γὰρ αὐτῷ ζῶσιν, resembles the present one in form, but not in sense, inasmuch as αὐτῷ (sc. Θεῷ) appears to mean *by him.* The ὃ (neuter pronoun) is construed here as in the first clause of the verse.

(11) Now follows the comparison of the *members* with the *head.* Οὕτω καὶ . . . . Θεῷ, *in like manner you also must count yourselves dead to sin, but alive to God.* For the sense of νεκροὺς τῇ ἁμαρτίᾳ, see on verse 2 above.— Ζῶντας τῷ Θεῷ, has here a meaning like to that in the preceding verse. Comp. Eph. ii. 5. Col. iii. 1. Eph. iii. 20.

The principal difficulties in respect to verses 1 — 11, are (1) That the comparison in verses 10, 11, between Christ and believers, will not hold in the *same* sense. But on this I have already remarked under verse 4. (2) That Christ *lived to God,* in the sense here supposed to be asserted, *before* his resurrection as well as *after* it. How then, it is asked, 'can the apostle be supposed to assert what would imply that it was only *after* his resurrection that he lived to God?' The answer to this is virtually exhibited in the context. The apostle has said that *Christ died to sin once for all; death has no more dominion over him.* Now as his living to God is placed in antithesis to this, the necessary implication is, that he lives to him in such a way as to have no more concern with suffering and sorrow on account of sin, he lives to him in a state that is new, and the happiness of which is not interrupted by sin. In like manner believers are to become dead to sin, *i. e.*, to be unaffected by its solicitations, and to be alive to God, *i. e.*, devoted in heart and life to the honor and glory of God, or to live in a state in which God (and not sin) shall be the chief object of all their regard. All this is to be attained ἐν Χ. 'Ιησοῦ, *through Jesus Christ,* for this is the only name given under heaven among men, whereby we can attain to such a happy condition. Or the sense may be, and from the well known idiom of Paul, probably is: 'you, being in Christ Jesus, *i. e.*, "by virtue of your union with him" must count yourselves as living to God, etc.' — Τῷ Κυρίῳ ἡμῶν is considered by Knapp, Griesbach, and Koppe, as being spurious. It matters nothing to the sense of the passage in general, whether it be received or rejected.

(12) *Therefore*, οὖν, *i. e.*, all this being true which I have said, it follows that sin ought not to reign, etc. — *Reign, predominate, have rule*, βασιλευέτω; see on verse 17. — *In your mortal body*, τῷ θνητῷ ὑμῶν σώματι. The word θνητῷ has given occasion here to a variety of exegeses. The reason why the apostle calls the body θνητόν, *mortal, exposed to death*, seems to be, that he may present in an impressive manner the sin and folly of permitting the lusts and passions of a *frail, perishable* body, to have dominion over the soul. The ground why he speaks of the body as the seat of reigning sin, is that its passions and lusts have great influence in leading men to sin. It is evident that σῶμα θνητόν here is equivalent to ἑαυτούς in verse 13, and to ὑμῶν in verses 14, 16; excepting that the representation is, as has been suggested, rendered more impressive by this designation. Σῶμα is often employed in Greek, as a designation of the *whole person*, e. g., γυναικῶν καὶ παίδων σώματα, Jos. Antiq. XI. 3. 10; so κατὰ σῶμα, *man by man;* and so the Latin *corpus*. But in the passage before us I cannot doubt that the apostle means to designate the *body* as the seat of carnal passions and lusts. Comp. with the sentiment here, Rom. vii. 5, 23, 24. viii. 3, 6, 7. See also the remarks on τὸ σῶμα τῆς ἁμαρτίας, verse 6 above.

Εἰς τὸ ὑπακούειν . . . . αὐτοῦ, *i. e.*, let sin not have such predominance as to yield obedience to its dictates. There seems to be a tacit acknowledgment in the form of this expression, that sinful appetites are not *extinguished* in the believer; he must keep them in subjection, but he does not wholly extinguish them. Fact accords with this. The enemy is taken captive, but not absolutely slain.

The text varies in the latter part of this verse; the Receptus reading αὐτῷ ἐν ταῖς ἐπιθυμίαις αὐτοῦ; which is wholly omitted in Clar., Germ., Ambros., Faustin.; rejected by Griesbach, Koppe, and Tholuck; and suspected by Vater and Flatt. Ταῖς ἐπιθυμίαις αὐτοῦ is supported by many MSS., versions, and fathers, and received by Bengel, Knapp, Lachmann, and others. Αὐτῇ simply, in the place of this, is supported by several MSS., D., E., F., G., Clar., and some of the fathers, and admitted by Mill. There are some other varieties of reading; *e. g.*, αὐτῷ, αὐτοῦ, αὐτήν, ἐν αὐτῇ, and αὐτῆς. Reiche thinks the whole clause was *originally* omitted, and that the varieties have arisen from efforts to supply a seeming deficiency by conjecture. It is a mere question of lower criticism. The sense is not materially varied by any of the readings.

(13) *Proffer*, παριστάνετε, *give up, devote*. Μέλη means literally, *the members of the body;* which, however, here designate the *whole man*. This verse, then, is only a virtual repetition of the preceding one, in different language and for the sake of intensity. — Ὅπλα here, as Reiche thinks, should be rendered (as usual) *armor;* because *sin* is represented as a king, and compelling us to his service. But idea of *contest* is not the predominating one here; and therefore ὅπλα may more appropriately be rendered *instruments*. The article is omitted before it, although in apposition with τὰ μέλη; see New Test. Gramm § 89. 6. Or it may be construed as following εἶναι understood. — Τῇ ἁμαρτίᾳ connects with μὴ παριστάνετε, *give not up to sin, i. e.*, to sinful lust or desire, or to the service of sin, *your members as instruments of iniquity, i. e.*, as instruments of doing that which is sinful.

Τῷ Θεῷ being arranged immediately after παραστήσατε here, shows that τῇ ἁμαρτίᾳ in the clause above is to be construed in like manner. — Ὡς ἐκ νεκρῶν ζῶντας, *as alive from the dead, i. e.*, as raised from the dead; comp. Eph. ii. 1, 5. The ground of this figurative language is easily discovered in verses 3—11. That *moral* life and death are here meant, the reader scarcely needs to be reminded.

[*Give up*] *to God your members as instruments of righteousness*, καὶ τὰ μέλη [παραστήσατε] . . . . τῷ Θεῷ; viz., as instruments of doing that which is lawful and right. Τῷ Θεῷ is construed here by Tholuck, and others, as a *Dativus commodi*, in the following manner, viz., *for God, i. e.*, for the glory and honor of God. But analogy with the preceding clause seems plainly to require the construction which I have given in the translation above.

(14) *For sin shall not have dominion over us*, ἁμαρτία γὰρ . . . . κυριεύσει. The apostle here assigns a reasonable and proper ground of the commands given in verses 12, 13. If it be true that Christians are *under grace*, and that therefore they will be enabled to subdue sin, then is this a good reason why they are exhorted and commanded to do so. That the sense of the verse is *prediction, promise* (and not simply command or obligation), I must believe with the great body of commentators, *e. g.*, Origen, Chrysostom, Augustine, Theodoret, Melancthon, Erasmus, Calvin, Tholuck, Ruckert, Reiche, etc. It was as true *under the law* as it is *under grace*, that men were obligated not to sin; and therefore an expression of mere obligation here seems to be fairly out of question. Although the Fut. tense may express *obligation* as

well as *predict*, yet it never can express mere *physical* possibility
Prediction is here the only consistent sense for it.

For ye are not under law but under grace, οὐ γάρ ἐστε . . . .
χάριν ; *i. e.*, 'Ye are not under a *legal* dispensation, but a *gracious*
one.' This general proposition in which the apostle asserts the
incompetency of the law to furnish the requisite means for the
sanctification of the sinner in his present condition, is explained
by the remainder of this chapter and by chapters vii. viii. See
in particular vii. 1 — 5, 9 — 11. viii. 3, 4.

Some commentators contend that ὑπὸ νόμον refers only to the
ceremonial law, but this gives to this passage a frigid and inept
sense. Where, in all the sequel down to the end of chap. viii. is
there anything which reminds us that the discussion here has
relation merely to the ceremonial law? The law discussed in
chap. vii. 5 — 25 is not only "holy and just and good," but it is
the internal moral law, the νόμος τοῦ νοός (verse 23), it is a νόμος
πνευματικός (verse 14). 'But how can it be true, that Christians
are not *under the law*? The Saviour did not come to abolish the
moral law ; nay, he came that it might be fulfilled (Matt. v. 17,
18). Can it then be said that we are not under the moral law?'
My answer is, that this is not said. The expressions of such a
nature as the one under examination, are of course to be understood
according to the circumstances and intention of the writer.
Paul had to do with Jewish *legalists*, whose doctrine was, that
salvation was attainable by legal obedience, not in theory only,
but in an actual and practical way, and that the law, by its precepts,
its restraints, and its penalties, was an adequate and effectual
means of sanctification. The first part of this scheme the
apostle has overthrown in chaps. i. — iv. ; the last part he is now
employed in overthrowing. — How he does this the reader may
see, by reperusing the illustration of the general course of thought
prefixed to the present chapter.

The apostle asserts in this verse that Christians are not under
the law, as an actual, effectual, adequate means of justification or
sanctification ; and if they are so, their case is utterly hopeless ;
for ruin must inevitably ensue. This is all that he means as appears
from the sequel of his remarks (vi. 15 — viii. 39). What
can be plainer, than that the moral law as *precept*, is altogether
approved and recognized by him? See chap. vii. 12 — 14.
Nay, so far is the apostle from pleading for abolition or repeal of
moral precept, that he asserts directly (viii. 3, 4), that the gospel
is designed to secure obedience to these precepts ; which the law
itself was unable to do. It is then from the law viewed in this
light, and this only, viz., as inadequate to effect the sanctification
and secure the obedience of sinners, that the apostle here declares
us to be free.

Let no one, then, abuse this declaration, by imagining that it in any measure affords ground to believe, that Christians are freed from obligation to obey the precepts of the *moral* law. What is the divine law but a transcript of the divine will? And are not Christians to be conformed to this? Is not all the law summed up in these two declarations: "Thou shalt love the Lord with all thine heart; and thy neighbor as thyself!" And are Christians absolved from loving God and their neighbor? If not, then this part of the subject stands unembarrassed by anything which the apostle has said in our text or context.

I will only suggest in addition, that ὑπὸ χάριν implies that Christians are placed in a condition or under a dispensation of which *grace* is the prominent feature; grace to sanctify as well as renew the heart; grace to purify the evil affections; grace to forgive offences though often repeated, and thus to save from despair, and to excite to new efforts of obedience. Viewed in this light, there is abundant reason for asserting, that Christians, under a system of grace, will much more effectually throw off the dominion of sin, than they would do if under a mere law dispensation.

(15) *What then? Shall we sin, because we are not under the law but under grace?* Τί οὖν . . . . χάριν; The first impression made by the declaration of the apostle, we might easily suppose, would lead the legalist to such questions as these. 'Is not the law,' he would ask, 'holy? Does it not *forbid* all sin? And does not grace *forgive* sin? How then can grace *restrain* sin?' That is, why may we not sin, if we are under grace merely, and not under the law? But this question the apostle follows with a μὴ γένοιτο; and he then goes on to illustrate and confirm the important truth which he had uttered in verse 14. Comp. verse 1.

(16) *Know ye not?* Οὐκ οἴδατε; *i. e.*, I take it for granted that ye know and believe. This and the like expressions, the apostle often employs as a preface to matter which he knows is well understood, and to which he expects assent will be given by those whom he addresses; see τοῦτο γινώσκοντες verse 6, and εἰδότες verse 9.

That to whomsoever ye give up yourselves as servants bound to obey, ye are the servants of him whom ye obey, ὅτι ᾧ . . . . ὑπακούετε. Δούλους εἰς ὑπακοήν means *servants unto obedience, i. e.*, servants bound to obey, devoted to obedience; εἰς before the Accusative denotes purpose, object, intention, obligation. Δοῦλοί ἐστε, *i. e.*, when you have once given up yourselves to any one as δούλους εἰς ὑπακοήν, you are no longer your own masters or at your own disposal; you have put yourselves within the power and at the disposal of another master. If the reader will call to mind the extent of a master's power over his slave or servant in the days of Paul, he will perceive the unusual strength of the expressions here.

Whether of sin unto death, or of obedience unto justification, ἤτοι ἁμαρτίας . . . . δικαιοσύνην; *i. e.*, ye are servants when once ye have given yourselves up either to sin or to righteousness. If ye give up yourselves as servants of sin, then you must expect the consequences to be death; for the "wages of sin is death," verse 23. Once devoted to sin, and continuing to be so, you cannot avoid the end of it, which is death. But if you are the servants of that *obedience which is unto justification, i. e.*, which is connected with justification, which ends in it, then you may expect eternal life (ζωὴν αἰώνιον, verse 22). The argument intended to be urged by these representations is, that when the Christian has once given himself up as the servant of grace he will of course, if sincere, yield obedience to its dictates; and these are such as will lead εἰς δικαιοσύνην, *to justification*. This meaning seems plain both from the antithesis of εἰς θάνατον, and the very explicit epexegesis of the whole in verses 21, 22, where ζωὴν αἰώνιον is substituted for δικαιοσύνην in verse 16. There is, indeed, a little doubt about the *genuineness* of the reading, inasmuch as Codd. D., E., the Syriac version, and two or three Codd. minusc. omit εἰς θάνατον; yet, on the whole, no substantial doubt remains that it should be retained. The sentiment is 'Fearful as the consequences of sin are, when you are its servants you must follow its dictates. But on the other hand, the obedience which you yield to grace, is a joyful, glorious service, ending in eternal life.' How any one can maintain that nothing more than *physical* death with its terrors is meant, when it is placed in opposition to δικαιοσύνη here and to ζωὴν αἰώνιον in verse 22, I am unable to see. Θάνατον means *condemnation or sentence of death;* and δικαιοσύνην, *acquittal, justification, sentence of acquittal,* not *holiness;* compare verse 22.

(17) *But thanks be unto God that ye were the servants of sin, but have become obedient from the heart to that model of doctrine in which ye have been instructed,* χάρις δὲ . . . . διδαχῆς. Such is the literal translation. But the nature of the case is sufficient to show, that the apostle's thanks to God are not designed to have a special bearing on ἦτε δοῦλοι τῆς ἁμαρτίας. In view of the *whole* case, viz., that they once were the servants of sin, but now are devoted to Christian obedience, Paul thanks God, as well he might, for 'there is joy in heaven over one sinner that repenteth.' The meaning of ἦτε here plainly is, that 'ye once were but no longer are,' *i. e.*, that having once been so they have ceased to be so. Thus in Latin: Fuit Ilium; fuimus Troes.

It has been proposed here to render ὅτι *although;* but, first, there is no adequate authority for such a translation; secondly, the present construction of the sentence requires ὅτι as *rationem reddens* in respect to χάρις τῷ Θεῷ; and the δέ (but) after ὑπηκούσατε indicates that ὅτι in the preceding clause retains its usual sense. The true solution of the difficulty consists in taking the whole phrase together; for then a meaning is conveyed, which might well excite the mind of the apostle to gratitude.

But ye have heartily or *sincerely become obedient,* ὑπηκούσατε δὲ ἐκ καρδίας. The apostle means to express his cheering confidence in the reality of their devotedness to the cause of Christ, which they professed to love; and this seems to me to be all that he here means to express. Tholuck says, however, that ὑπηκούσατε joined with ἐκ καρδίας, 'is designed to render conspicuous the idea of the free will with which the sinner first came to Jesus and received pardon. Was it true, then, that Jesus first sought the sinner, or the sinner him? Do we "love him because he first loved us;" or is it the reverse? That the sinner was "willing," I doubt not; but that he was "made willing in the day of God's power," seems to be equally plain. Does not " God work in us both to will and to do?"

Εἰς ὅν . . . . διδαχῆς. Ὑπακούω may govern the Accusative as well as the Dative; see examples of the Accusative in Prov. xxix. 12. Deut. xxi. 18. It may also govern the Genitive; *e. g.*, Deut. xxi. 20. xxvi. 14, 17, et al. sæpe. The Dative after it, however, is most common. We may then construe thus: ὑπηκούσατε τύπον διδαχῆς . . . . εἰς ὅν παραδόθητε. Εἰς with the Accusative very frequently follows παραδίδωμι, although the simple Dative is the most usual. But here the Dative would not give the sense — *into which ye have been initiated* or *in respect to which ye have been instructed.*

A second way of solving the grammatical construction, is by *attraction.* The noun, as often, is *attracted* to the case of the pronoun, so that τύπον is written for τύπῳ, which would be the more usual construction after ὑπακούω. Tholuck, and others, seem to prefer the rather forced construction here, ὑπηκούσατε εἰς τύπον ὅς παρεδόθη ὑμῖν. That ὑπηκούσατε, in the second clause here, corresponds to ἦτε δοῦλοι in the first, is plain. The apostle might have used ἐδουλώθητε in the room of it; but ὑπηκούσατε corresponds better to the phraseology of the preceding verse.

Model of doctrine, τύπον διδαχῆς; τύπος, *model, form, example,* etc. Comp. Rom. ii. 20, μόρφωσις τῆς γνώσεως; 2 Tim. i. 13, ὑποτύπωσις ὑγιαινόντων λόγων. So in the classics; *e. g.*, Jambl. Vita Pythag. c. 16. He had τῆς παιδεύσεως ὁ τύπος, τοιοῦτος, *such a model of instruction,* etc.; Ib. c. 23: τὸν τύπον τῆς διδασκαλίας.

Some render τύπον here *impression;* a sense which might receive some countenance from ἔμφυτον λόγον in James i. 21, but which, however, cannot be maintained as Pauline, after weighing the examples in Rom. ii. 20. 2 Tim. i. 13.—Ἐκ καρδίας means *willingly, heartily, sincerely.* Παρεδόθητε refers to the fact that they had been taught of God, or taught of the apostles. I see no good reason, however, why the idea may not include both, and so generally designate all the right teaching which they had received.

(18) *Being freed from sin*, ἐλευθερωθέντες .... ἁμαρτίας, *i. e.,* from a state of bondage to sin, from being the servants of sin. This was effected, when they "passed from death unto life," from "the bondage of Satan to enjoy the liberty of the children of God." Then it was also, that they became the Lord's; they became so ἐκ καρδίας. Being "bought with a price," they held themselves, in their new state, to be under obligation to "glorify God with their bodies and with their spirits which are his;" which is expressed by ἐδουλώθητε τῇ δικαιοσύνῃ.—The δέ in this verse is *continuative, i. e.,* it means *then* or *morover.*

Verses 17—20 are not designed to advance the argument of the apostle, but merely to deepen the impression on the minds of his readers. He intends to show them, that they have a personal interest in what he says, and indeed that they are themselves examples of what he is declaring. Verse 18 may indeed be viewed as an appeal *ad hominem:* 'Ye, brethren, are no more the servants of sin; how then can you any longer continue to obey its dictates? Ye have become the servants of righteousness; and of course you must obey its dictates, *i. e.,* live a life of holiness.'

(19) Ἀνθρώπινον λέγω seems to be equivalent to κατ᾽ ἄνθρωπον λέγω, iii. 5; *i. e., I speak as men are accustomed to speak*, viz., I use such language as they usually employ in regard to the affairs of common life. So classic Greek authors say: ἀνθρωπίνως λέγω or ἀνθρωπείως λέγω; see Aristoph. Ranæ, 1090. Vespæ, 1174. Strato in Athenæus, Deipnos. Tom. III. lib. IX. 29. So also the Latins; as Petronius, Satyr. c. 50, Sæpius poetice quam *humane* locutus es. Cicero, de Divinat. II. 64, *hominum more dicere.* The apostle means to say, that in speaking of the subject under consideration, he uses language borrowed from common life, which may be easily understood. The reason of this he now proceeds to assign. I consider the declaration in ἀνθρώπινον λέγω as referring to what precedes and also to what follows.

Because of the weakness of your flesh, διὰ τὴν .... ὑμῶν. Τῆς σαρκὸς ὑμῶν may, like the Hebrew בָּשָׂר, be used by way of periphrasis, merely to indicate *your own selves.* Or ἀσθένειαν may be used here (as ἀσθενῶν is in Romans v. 6) for *moral weakness*. So Beza and others; but this is an improbable sense; for the apostle does not here speak in the tone of *chiding*. The expression in 1 Cor. iii. 1, seems to afford aid sufficient to make the matter plain: "I could not speak to you as πνευματικοῖς but as σαρκικοῖς;" which latter word is immediately explained by the epexegetical clause, ὡς νηπίοις ἐν Χριστῷ. So here the apostle adapts himself to the ἀσθένεια τῆς σαρκός, the feeble or infantile state of spiritual knowledge among the Romans; by making use of the familiar phraseology which the context exhibits. In giving this construction to ἀσθένειαν τῆς σαρκός ὑμῶν, we must regard τῆς σαρκός as Gen. *causæ* vel *auctoris ;* so that the sense is: 'The weakness which the flesh or carnal part occasions, viz., the inability to comprehend language of a higher and more difficult nature, which had been occasioned by their fleshly passions and appetites.

For as ye have given up your members to be the servants of impurity and iniquity, for the sake of iniquity, ὥσπερ γάρ . . . . ἀνομίαν. The simple ground of γάρ is to be found in the implied sentiment: 'Ye must now be the servants of righteousness, *for as*, etc.' That is, 'Ye must be servants of righteousness, if you would act consistently; for when you served sin you engaged actively in its service, and so it must be when you serve righteousness.' Τὰ μέλη ὑμῶν is equivalent to σῶμα θνητόν in verse 12. It is resuming the diction of verse 13. The ground of the usage is, that *our members* are the instruments actually employed either in the service of sin or righteousness. They are our instrumental agents.— Δοῦλα is here an adjective, δοῦλος -η -ον, comp. Wisd. xv. 7.— Τῇ ἀκαθαρσίᾳ καί τῇ ἀνομίᾳ, Dat. *commodi*, at least a species of it.— *For the purpose of iniquity*, εἰς τὴν ἀνομίαν, *i. e.*, of doing iniquity, of committing sin. *So now give up your members to be the servants of righteousness, for the sake of holiness*, οὕτω νῦν . . . . ἁγιασμόν.— Εἰς ἁγιασμόν stands here without the article, although we have in the antithesis εἰς τ ὴ ν ἀνομίαν. But this is one of those cases of the use of abstract nouns where the article may be inserted or omitted without any important difference of meaning; see New Test. Gramm. § 89. 2.

(20) *For when ye were the servants of sin ye were free in respect to righteousness*, ὅτε γὰρ . . . . δικαιοσύνῃ. The connection and object of this verse are somewhat difficult. Tholuck says that γάρ points to verse 22, in respect to the reward of Christians; but this is a liberty with γάρ which it would be no easy task to justify. I must connect it with what *precedes*, in this case, not with what follows. What says the apostle? 'As you once served sin, so now you must serve holiness. [Your present relation admits of no other conclusion]; *for* when you served sin, you

deemed yourselves free from all obligation to righteousness, [so now, serving holiness, count yourselves free from all obligation to sin].' I cannot see in what other way ὅτε γὰρ κ. τ. λ. is here connected. There is, indeed, an *anacoluthon* in this case; but how often Paul admits this into his epistles, the distinguishing reader of them needs not to be informed.

Some render ἐλεύθεροι here, *destituti*; but this is a sense which it would be difficult to vindicate, and which is unnecessary. When the apostle says, that they, being the servants of sin, were ἐλεύθεροι τῇ δικαιοσύνῃ, he can not mean that in fact they were free from all obligation to holiness (for this can never be true of any moral being whatever); he must mean, then, that in their own estimation, or according to the tenor of their own reasonings, they were absolved from obligation to pursue holiness; or he means, that in *fact* they lived as those who are absolved from obligation to holiness. I understand him here to be making an appeal *ad hominem*, as in the preceding verse, and to say in effect: 'Since you formerly, when in the service of sin, counted yourselves free from the dominion of holiness; so now, as the servants of righteousness, count yourselves free from all obligation to obey sin.' The Dative here (τῇ δικαιοσύνῃ) designates *in relation to, in respect to*. See New Test. Gramm. § 106. 1; and comp. 1 Cor. xiv. 20. Acts vii. 51. xx. 22. 1 Cor. vii. 34. Heb. v. 11.

(21) *What fruit, moreover, had ye then, in respect to those things* [of which] *ye are now ashamed?* Τίνα οὖν .... ἐπαισχύνεσθε, There are various ways of pointing and constructing this sentence. Some put the interrogation point after τότε, and make the answer to be: 'Such fruit as ye are now ashamed of.' So Koppe; with whom Flatt and Tholuck agree.* I prefer the division of Knapp, who points as above. Οὖν, "*orationi continuandæ inservit*." There seems to me plainly to be a *transition* in the discourse here to another topic, viz., from the topic of *obligation* of which the writer had been speaking, to that of *consequence*, *i. e.*, either penalty or reward. This makes the second point of comparison, between being under the law and under grace. The *end* or *event* of the two states is unspeakably different. The writer, however, assumes the position here, that while under the law men will continue to sin, and thus bring death upon themselves. It is only in the sequel (chap. vii. 5—25), that he fully illustrates the reason or ground of this.

What reward had ye? Καρπὸν εἴχετε κ. τ. λ. Comp. Rom. i.

---

* Most of the critical editors, as Lachmann, Griesbach, Hahn, etc., and modern commentators, prefer the pointing τίνα οὖν καρπὸν εἴχετε τότε, ἐφ' οἷς, κ. τ. λ., *what fruit then had ye at that time? in things in which*, etc.

13. xv. 28. Heb. xii. 11. Ἔχειν καρπόν has a different meaning from φέρειν καρπόν. To make the construction full, ἐκείνων must be understood before ἐφ᾽ οἷς. Such an ellipsis is very frequent; see Bretschn. Lex. ὅς, c. β. Ἐπαισχύνομαι usually governs the Accusative, but is here constructed with ἐπί after it.

For the end of those things is death, τὸ γὰρ τέλος ἐκείνων θάνατος; viz., of such things as they formerly practised, but are now ashamed of. Τέλος retains here a sense which is very common, viz., the *consequence, final event, fata ultima, exitus rei*. Γάρ *confirmantis;* as if the writer had said: 'What solid good could result from your former course of life, *since* the end of this course must be death?' For the sense of θάνατος, see chap. v. 12.

(22) *But now, being freed from sin, and having become servants to God, ye have your fruit in respect to holiness*, Νυνὶ δὲ . . . . ἁγιασμόν. The preceding context explains ἐλευθερωθέντες . . . . Θεῷ. Ἔχετε τὸν καρπόν must mean the same as in verse 21, viz., *you have your benefit or reward.*—Εἰς . . . . ἁγιασμόν, *in respect to holiness* or *sanctification;* not (with Flatt and others) *unto holiness, i. e.*, the consequence is, that ye are holy. This is not the writer's object here, for *serving God* implies that holiness already exists. It is the *fruits, i. e.*, the consequences of serving God, which Paul here brings into view; for nothing else would make out the antithesis to the preceding verse; a circumstance overlooked by many commentators. I understand the apostle as saying: 'You already enjoy important benefits, in respect to a holy course of life; and you hope for more important benefits still, viz., ζωὴν αἰώνιον.'

And the end [is to possess] *eternal life*, τὸ δὲ . . . . αἰώνιον. The reader will observe, that the Acc. (ζωὴν αἰώνιον) renders it necessary here to supply some verb in order to complete the construction; and some verb which is different from that in verse 21 (ἐστί), where θάνατος is in the Nom. The sentence may be filled out in two ways; viz., (1) Τὸ δὲ τέλος [ἔχειν or ἕξειν] ζωὴν αἰώνιον. (2) Τὸ δὲ τέλος [ἕξει] ζωὴν αἰώνιον. The sense is the same in both cases. In the latter case, ζωὴν αἰώνιον is put in apposition with τὸ τέλος, and is explanatory of it. In the former case, the construction is thus: 'The end or event will be, that you shall obtain everlasting happiness.' One or the other of these constructions, the context and the form of the words compel us to adopt. The antithesis between ζωὴν αἰώνιον and θάνατος has been previously alluded to. How can the latter be temporal only? What comparison would this make, between the two members of the antithesis?

(23) Such consequences must follow from the established rules of the divine government, respecting the fruits of sin and of holiness.

For the reward (wages) *of sin is death,* τὰ γὰρ .... θάνατος ; comp. on Rom. v. 12.— Γάρ *confirmantis;* for what is said in the sequel confirms verses 21, 22.— Ὀψώνια, properly the *rations of soldiers, i. e.,* their wages, which at first were paid in grain, meat, fruit, etc., but afterwards in money. Observe that the apostle employs this term in order to designate something which was really the *proper due* of sin, viz., for the service of it; as the wages which a soldier earns by his hard military service, are properly his due. But on the other hand the reward of Christians is all of *grace*, not of *debt;* and so it is designated in the sequel by χάρισμα. *Through Jesus Christ,* ἐν Χριστῷ Ἰησοῦ τῷ Κυρίῳ ἡμῶν, *i. e.,* through the redemption or atonement of Christ, iii. 23—26. v. 1, 8, 11, 17—19, 21.

CHAP. VII. 1—4.

All the difficulty in these verses seems to arise from an exertion to make the illustration too exact and carry it out in all the little particulars. The object of the comparison is to illustrate the relation of the Christian to the law as modified by the death of Christ. As the wife is liberated from the law of her husband by his death, so the Christian is freed, by the death of Christ, from the law as a means of salvation, and brought under the dominion of another, even him who was raised from the dead. The seeming discrepancies in the comparison, viz, that the liberated person is the survivor in one case, and the deceased in the other is of no importance, since the comparison is plainly not to be extended to these minor particulars.

These verses may be considered an *illustration* of what the apostle had avowed in vi 14 " *For we are not under law but under grace* * The simple basis of the whole comparison I understand thus ' Brethren, you are aware that death, in all cases, dissolves the relation which exists between an individual and a law by which he was personally bound. For example: the conjugal law ceases to be in force, by the death of one of the parties So it is in the case of Christians. They not only die to sin, i e , renounce it, when they are baptized into the death of Christ, vi 2—11, but they also die to the law at the same time, i e , they renounce all their hopes and expectations of being sanctified by the law, so that sin will no more have dominion over them They do, by the very fact of becoming real Christians, profess to receive Christ as their "wisdom, and justification and sanctification (ἁγιασμός) and redemption," 1 Cor i 30.

If we consider, for a moment, the true nature of the apostle's assertion, no alarm need be felt as to the tendency of his sentiments For what is it which he affirms in chap. vi 14? It is, that " sin shall *not have dominion* over Christians, because they are not under the law but under grace " The *dominion* or *power* which sin is to have over Christians, is then the subject of his inquiry and of his assertions. So indeed the preceding context teaches; and so the subsequent context also. That

* Meyer and others connect this with the last verse of the preceding chapter · The gift of God is eternal life, etc. This you cannot doubt since you are not ignorant, etc. But the connection seems more natural with verse 14, the remaining verses of chap vi. being an answer to verse 15. And yet the way is prepared by the preceding verses, especially 22 and 23, for the introduction of the illustration in vii. 1—4.

ROMANS VII. 1. 231

we are *not under the law*, then, must of course mean, in this connection, that we are not under it as an efficacious or successful means of deliverance from the power of sin, for thus it has never been, and cannot be, as chap vii 5—25 most fully shows. Christians are dead to the law, then, in this respect, viz , they renounce all hope of deliverance from the power of sin, through the law It convinces, and condemns, and keeps up a continual struggle in the sinner's breast by awakening his conscience, but does not deliver, vn 14—25, comp vni 3, 4 Consequently the true penitent, coming to feel its impotence as the means of delivering from the power of sin renounces all hope of deliverance in this way, and gives himself up to Christ, as his *sanctification*, as well as his wisdom, justification, and redemption

Now what is there in all this, which infringes on the obligation of moral precept contained in the law? Surely nothing "The law is holy, and just, and good, " it is all summed up in the requisition, ' to love God with all our heart, and our neighbor as ourselves ' Will any one assert that Paul contends against this, after all that he has said in chaps vi —viii , relative to the Christian's obligation to renounce sin and live a holy life? Nothing can be further from his intention The only question that needs to be solved, in order to remove all difficulty is. In what sense does Paul say that we are *dead to the law* ? This I have endeavored to answer, by making the apostle his own expositor The sum of the answer is, that as Christians renounce the law as an effectual means of *justification* (chaps. i —iii), so they must renounce it as an effectual means of *sanctification*. Christ is our only hope in this respect, as well as in the other The grace of the gospel is the only effectual means by which we can hope successfully to resist sin and persevere in holiness I appeal to chap vin 3, 4 for an exhibition of the sum of this sentiment, and to the whole of chaps. vi —viii , and also to the experience and feelings of every truly enlightened and humble Christian on earth, — in confirmation of the same sentiment.

(1) *Know ye not*, ἢ ἀγνοεῖτε; in sense the same as οὐκ οἴδατε in vi. 16; which see. Ἤ, *num*, *an*, merely a sign of interrogation. Here, as in vi. 16, the writer means to say, that they well know, or that they will readily acknowledge, viz., that which he is about to state. — Γινώσκουσι .... λαλῶ, *for I address those who are acquainted with the law*, viz., the Mosaic law. The apostle may mean here, that he addresses especially the Jewish part of the Church at Rome, or it may be implied, that the whole church had some acquaintance with the Old Testament Scriptures, which is not improbable, as the Old Testament was everywhere and continually appealed to by the primitive teachers of Christianity, and was moreover extant in the Greek language which was very generally understood at Rome. However, I should consider it to be most probable, that he is here particularly addressing the Hebrew Christians. The article is here omitted before γινώσκουσι, but it is not unfrequently omitted in such cases ; N. Test Gramm. § 144.

That the law exercises control over a man as long as he lives, ὅτι ὁ νόμος .... ζῇ. The apostle means the Mosaic law here; but what he says is equally true of other laws of a permanent nature. — Κυριεύει, *performs the office of* κύριος, i. e., *controls*, *is valid in respect to*. Not improbably the choice of this word was dictated by the τῷ κυρίῳ of the preceding verse. It is as much as to say, that so long as we are affianced to the law, the law is our κύριος, and not Christ.— Τοῦ ἀνθρώπου, THE *man*, *i. e.*, the man who lives under it, not any man in general, but only one who holds such a relation. Some interpreters here take ἀνθρώπου in the same sense as ἀνδρός, i. e., *husband*. But the *usus loquendi* is against this and the proposition is evidently of a *general* nature, in respect to such individuals as lived under the Mosaic law.— ζῇ is rendered by Flatt and others, IT *lives*, viz., the law. But first, if the man dies, the law still lives as to others; it becomes inefficacious as to him, only by means of *his* death. It cannot die in any other way. Then it would be mere tautology; The law is in force (κυριεύει), as long as it is in force (ζῇ)! Is this the manner of Paul? Besides, the ἀνὴρ ζῶν and ἀποθανῶν of verses 2, 3, clearly show, that in verse 1 ἄνθρωπος is the Nominative to ζῇ.

(2) *For the married woman is bound to her husband by the law, so long as he liveth,* ἡ γὰρ . . . νόμῳ.— Ὕπανδρος, a very expressive word, classical as well as Hellenistic, and like the Hebrew תַּחַת אִישָׁהּ, Num. v. 29. In the East, ὕπανδρος denotes a higher degree of disparity between husband and wife, than is admitted in the western world.— Δέδεται νόμῳ has a force also here, which commentators have generally overlooked. Under the Mosaic economy, the husband could divorce the wife almost at pleasure; but where is the precept giving the like liberty to the wife? This would have been contrary to the genius of eastern manners and customs. This seems to be the reason why the apostle has chosen the *woman*, in this case, in order to exhibit an example of obligation while the life of the parties continues.— Γάρ *illustrantis;* and it might, as to sense, be well translated *for example.* The instance in verses 2, 3, seems to me very plainly to be a mere illustration of the general principle in verse 1.

But if her husband die, she ceases to be under the conjugal law, ἐὰν δέ . . . ἀνδρός.— Κατήργηται when followed by ἀπό (as in the present case), means *to cease to belong to any one, to cease to be subject to his control;* comp. verse 6 below, and Gal. v. 4. In the next verse we find ἐλευθέρα ἐστὶν ἀπὸ τοῦ νόμου— κατήργηται ἀπὸ τοῦ νόμου in this. So the Hebrew בְּעַל מִן is used.— Τοῦ ἀνδρός, Gen. *of relation*, viz., the law which related to her husband *i. e.*, the conjugal law which gave him power and right as a husband.

(3) *Therefore if she marry another, during her husband's life, she shall be called an adulteress,* ἄρα οὖν . . . ἑτέρῳ; *i. e.*, it follows from the nature of her obligation, that she cannot be united with another man while her husband is living. *So then,* ἄρα οὖν; an intensive form of particles designating *conclusion.*— Χρηματίσει, *she shall bear the name of, she shall receive the appellation of.* This usage

of the word belongs to later classics; in which the verb puts the name called into the Nominative after it; ἐχρημάτιζε βασιλεύς, Diod. Sic. XX. 54.

So that she shall not be, τοῦ μὴ εἶναι αὐτήν. The classic Greek would usually express this by ὥστε μὴ εἶναι αὐτήν. But for the infinitive with τοῦ in the Septuagint and in the New Testament; see note and references, chap. vi. 6.

(4) The true sense here indicated by ὥστε, seems to be *thus*, or *so that;* i. e., these things being so, you also have become dead to the law, in order that you might be affianced to Christ, etc. In other words; allowing that a new connection may be lawfully formed, after the death of one of the parties in the conjugal union, it follows that you, who have become dead to the law, *i. e.*, wholly renounced it as an adequate means of sanctification, may be affianced solely to Christ, etc.— Καὶ ὑμεῖς, *you also, i. e.*, you, as well as the woman, having become dead to the law may be affianced to another.

To the law, τῷ νόμῳ, the Dative of *specification;* New Test. Gramm. § 106. 1. The declaration that *they had become dead to the law,* is new in respect to *form.* Dead to sin the apostle has asserted them to be, in chap. vi.; he has also asserted that they are not ὑπὸ νόμον, vi. 14. But that they were *dead* to the law, is a new expression, and the phrase διὰ τοῦ σώματος τοῦ Χριστοῦ is subjoined in explanation of it. He must of course mean the body of Christ as crucified, as having suffered in order to redeem us from the curse of the law; comp. Heb. x. 5 — 10. Col. i. 22. ii. 14. 1 Pet. ii. 24. Eph. ii. 15, which are decisive in respect to the meaning of σῶμα Χριστοῦ here. As Christ, by his death, is made unto us "righteousness and *sanctification*, and redemption;" so it is his death which has opened such new prospects for perishing sinners that they are enabled to look away from the law, and to renounce it as an effectual means of sanctification. Hence the apostle says: "Ye have become dead to the law, by the body of Christ."

In order that ye should be [affianced] *to another, who has risen from the dead,* εἰς τὸ γενέσθαι . . . ἐγερθέντι; *i. e.*, Christ has called you away from your vain hopes and expectations respecting what the law could accomplish as to purifying and saving you, and admitted you to participate in the blessed fruits of his death, viz., the gift of a sanctifying Spirit. But although by his *death* you are freed from the relation in which you once stood to the law as a means of sanctification, yet you are not affianced to him as being *dead,* but as being *risen from the dead,* as a conqueror who has burst the bars of death, and ascended to glory at the right hand of God the Father.

So that we may bring forth fruit to God, ἵνα ..... Θεῷ; *i. e.*, such fruit as God will accept. Θεῷ, Dat. *commodi*. The reader will observe, that the last circumstance noted here is the climax of the figurative language used by the apostle. First, there is an annulling of a former marriage contract by the death of one of the parties; next, there is a new union; and lastly the fruits of this, and also the object of it, are designated. *To bring forth fruit for God* or *unto God*, is to live a holy life, to yield obedience unto his precepts, to act in such a manner as to do honor to him. This is not intended as *argument* in a strict sense, but *illustration*. The similarity between the two cases presented, rests partly on the nature of them, and partly on his own declarations. The case in regard to husband and wife, he takes it for granted his readers will admit; the similarity of the Christian's case to this, rests in part on his own declaration or authority. Does this never supply the place of *formal* argument? Or are we to concede no *authority* to the apostle as to the determination of matters in religion? It is too true, alas, that some do not appear to make any concessions of this nature.

CHAP. VII. 5, 6.

The objector might here reply "What you say implies that it is only in our new state of alliance to Christ, that we can *bring forth fruit to God;* and that, while under the law, no fruit but such as is of a contrary nature can be produced." The apostle now comes out with his last, highest, and boldest assertion concerning the law, as to its efficacy with respect to the point under consideration, viz., its efficacy to sanctify the hearts of sinners. The course of thought seems to be in substance as follows: 'I have said that you must be freed from the law and united to Christ, in order that you may bring forth fruit to God This is true; for the law is so far from accomplishing the great end of subduing and sanctifying the hearts of sinners, that it occasions just the opposite effect, *v. e*, it is the occasion of their becoming more deeply involved in guilt, and of bringing them into more aggravated condemnation. It is the occasion of their *bringing forth fruit unto death*, and not unto God. But when we are freed from all reliance upon it as a means of subduing and sanctifying us, and with a becoming sense of our guilt and helplessness have betaken ourselves to Christ, and relied on him only as our "sanctification and redemption," then we are enabled to serve God with a new spirit, and not in the old way of only a literal and external obedience It should be noted, that verse 5 here is the theme of discussion through vers. 7 — 25 in the sequel, while verse 6 (the antithesis of verse 5) constitutes the theme of chap. viii 1 — 11, which is in all important respects the antithesis of vii. 7 — 25. See remarks at the beginning of the chapter, and also Excursus VII.

(5) *For when we were in the flesh*, ὅτε γὰρ ... σαρκί; *i. e.*, when we were in our natural or carnal state. That such is the meaning of this expression, and that it is not to be *literally* taken here, is clear from the *usus loquendi*, and from the nature of the

case. From the first; because they who are *in the flesh*, as contrasted with τοῖς ἐν Χριστῷ Ἰησοῦ, in chap. viii. 1—11, where vers. 7—9 put beyond all question what ἐν σαρκὶ εἶναι means. From the second; because the contrast in vers. 5, 6, is between the character which those whom the apostle addresses sustained *before* they became affianced to Christ, and that which they sustained *after* they were affianced to him. Of course ἐν σαρκὶ εἶναι must mean *to be in a natural or unregenerate state, i. e.*, in that state in which men not yet united to Christ are.

Our sinful passions which were by the law, τὰ παθήματα .... νόμου; *i. e.*, our sinful passions which were occasioned by the law, verse 11.— Τῶν ἁμαρτιῶν, Gen. of *attribute*, our passions which lead us to sin, our sinful passions..— Τὰ διὰ τοῦ νόμου [sc. ὄντα or γεγονότα], *which were by the law;* not, as Chrysostom and Carpzov, τὰ διὰ τοῦ νόμου [φαινόμενα or γνωστά], *which were shown* or *disclosed by the law*; and not as Locke (Comm. on Romans), *that remained in us under the law*, who construes διὰ νόμου as διά *conditionis*, viz., we being in a law state. To both of these methods of commentary verse 12 is an unanswerable objection, as it is the author's commentary upon his own words. Moreover, Mr. Locke's translation would require ἡμεῖς διὰ τοῦ νόμου ὄντες, instead of τὰ [παθήματα] διὰ τοῦ νόμου.

Put forth their energy in our members, to bring forth fruit unto death, ἐνεργεῖτο .... θανάτῳ. Ἐνεργεῖτο, *wrought, vim suam exserebat*, in the Middle voice.— Ἐν τοῖς μέλεσιν ἡμῶν, the same in sense as σῶμα θνητόν in vi. 12, as may be seen by comparing verse 23 below. Μέλη is used as an equivalent for σῶμα, because the *members* of the body are its efficient agents in doing anything.

Such was the influence of our *sinful passions*, τὰ διὰ τοῦ νόμου, that the consequences were fatal. Our fruit was *unto death, i. e.*, was such as turned to the account of death, such as brought us under its power or subjected us to it. The Dat. τῷ θανάτῳ is a kind of Dat. *commodi;* as expressed in the paraphrase above. Θάνατος is here used in the way of personification, and put in antithesis to Θεῷ in verse 4.

(6) Thus much, then, for the influence of the law upon us in our natural state. It was utterly unable to effect our renewal and sanctification; nay, it did but aggravate our guilt and condemnation, instead of delivering us from them. It is only in our new state and under our new affiance, that we are enabled to bring forth fruit of a different kind.

But now being freed from the law, νυνὶ δὲ .... νόμου; *i. e.*, no longer placing our reliance on it as a means of subduing and sanctifying our sinful natures. For the sense of κατηργήθημεν, compare κατήργηται ἀπὸ τοῦ νόμου in verse 2 above. The reading ἀποθανόντες has been controverted, but both external and internal evidence are quite conclusive in its favor. The sentiment of it is exactly the same, as that of ἐθανατώθητε τῷ νόμῳ in verse 4 above. Here the *first* person plural is used,—and there the *second;* but this changes not the nature of the sentiment. The full construction here would seem to be: ἀποθανόντες [ἐκείνῳ] ἐν ᾧ κατειχόμεθα. A goodly number of authorities, viz., D., E., F., G., Vulg., It., Codd. apud Rufin., read τοῦ θανάτου here instead of ἀποθανόντες. R. Simon and Reiche prefer this reading.—The verb κατέχω means *to hold back, to retain, to hold firmly,* etc. Here κατειχόμεθα must mean, the holding as it were in a state of bondage, from which the gospel frees. Ἐν ᾧ, *i. e., ἐν ᾧ νόμῳ*. The sense of the whole may be made more facile by a different arrangement: *but now being dead* [to the law], *we are freed from the law by which we were held in bondage.*

So that we now serve [God] *in a new and spiritual manner,* etc., ὥστε ... γράμματος. That Θεῷ is to be understood after δουλεύειν, seems certain from the nature of the antithesis, and from comparing vers. 4, 5.— Πνεύματος I take to be the Gen. of *attribute* or *explanation*. Ἐν καινότητι πνεύματος, *in a newness of a spiritual kind, i. e.,* in a new and spiritual manner. So παλαιότητι γράμματος designates the former method of *literal external obedience,* which the Jews endeavored to render to the law while ἐν σαρκί. There was no heart in it. *God is a Spirit;* and he must be worshipped ἐν πνεύματι. But this command is obeyed, only when there is a "new heart and a right spirit" in men; and this is not until they become affianced to Christ. "The law," says Calvin, "puts a check upon our external actions; but it does not in the least restrain the fury of our concupiscence."

CHAP. VII. 7—12.

The legalist would naturally indignantly repel the declaration of the apostle, viz, τὰ παθήματα τῶν ἁμαρτιῶν τὰ διὰ τοῦ νόμου. 'What' then,' he would say, 'are we to believe that the holy and perfect law of God is not only incompetent to sanctify us, but that it is even the occasion of our becoming greater sinners. Can it be? is the law sin?'

To this objection the apostle now replies; and replies in such a way as to show, that while he fully maintains his ground, viz, that the law is the occasion of greatly aggravating our guilt and condemnation, still the fault lies in us, and not in the law; for this is altogether worthy of approbation and obedience, because it is "holy, just, and good." This is at once a delicate and difficult part of the apostle's discourse, and it is managed with great skill and effect.

(7) *What shall we say then? Is the law sin?* τί οὖν .... ἁμαρτία;

Language of the objector, in opposition to what the apostle has said in verse 5.—Ἁμαρτία, from the necessity of the case must here mean, *the cause of sin.* So Mic. i. 5, "What is the *transgression* of Jacob? Is it not Samaria?" *i. e.*, what is the cause of Jacob's transgression, etc.? Eph. ii. 16, "having slain the *enmity* thereby," *i. e.*, the cause of enmity. To give ἁμαρτία a different sense here, would be inept.

Μὴ γένοιτο is the answer of the apostle. He plainly means by it wholly to deny the charge involved in the previous question, in the sense in which the legalist supposed the charge might be made, viz., that the law was the efficient cause or the sinful cause of our sin, and that our guilt might be justly put to the account of the law. But he does not mean to deny, that there is a sense in which the law is connected with our sins, and that it is the occasion of their being aggravated, rather than the efficient means of our being sanctified. Ἀλλά intimates, that the apostle allows of some exceptions to the universal sense of μὴ γένοιτο. It is frequently employed, as here, after negative assertions, in order to indicate that there is some limitation or qualification of them to be made. The course of thought runs thus: 'The law is not the sinful or efficient cause of sin, in the sense that you suppose; but still there is a sense in which the law is the occasion of sin.' What this is, the writer goes on to describe.

I had not known sin except by the law, τὴν ἁμαρτίαν . . . . νόμῳ. By what law? As a general proposition, it would be true as to the law of nature or of revelation. "Where there is no law, there is no transgression," Rom. iv. 15. When the apostle (Rom. i.—ii.) speaks of the Gentiles as sinners, he makes them offenders against the law of nature written upon their hearts, Rom. ii. 14, 15; and when he convicts the Jews of guilt, he represents them as offending against revelation. What is said in the verse before us, if understood in a *general* way, might be explained and defended, then, on general principles. But plainly this is not the object of the writer here. He is controverting the *legalists*. And who were they? *Jews*, not Gentiles; at least, they usually were not Gentiles. It is the *Jewish* law, then, to which he here adverts.

But in what sense would he *not have known sin, except by the law*? Surely the Gentiles were sinners, who had no revelation; as he has abundantly shown in chaps. i. ii. This consideration leads us of course to say, that the meaning of *known* (ἔγνων) is a *qualified* and *comparative* one, in the present passage. The meaning must be that he would not have known sin in any such manner and measure as he then actually did, had it not been for the law. The explanation subjoined in verse 8, appears to leave no room to doubt this exegesis. The simple explanation of the whole seems to be this: 'Unless the law had put restraint upon sinning, I should never have known how great my wickedness is, or how much propensity to evil I have. The restraints of the law galled my evil passions, and they broke out with redoubled violence; and in this way I have come, from bitter experience, to know much more of the nature and extent of my sinfulness. I should never have known to what extent I was capable of going, had not the restraints of the law brought me to a full development of myself. I was excited by the check which they put upon me; and I acted out myself in such a manner as I never should have otherwise done; and in this way I have come to know my sinfulness, through the law.

In this compound sense of fuller development and (through this) of more complete means of knowledge, does the apostle appear to affirm that he has acquired a knowledge of sin by the law. Verses 7 and 8 taken together (and so they should be), can leave no room to doubt, that it is not merely the instruction which the law gives concerning the nature of sin, which the apostle aims here to describe; but a knowledge which is acquired (as described in verse 8), by an experimental acquaintance with sin; which had been heightened to so great a degree by the restraints of law, as to place the subject of it in such a condition as to practical knowledge with regard to his own sinfulness, as nothing else could have brought about. On any other ground of exegesis, the connection between verses 7 and 8 must be virtually broken up.

For I had not known even lust, unless the law had said: Thou shalt not lust, τήν τε γὰρ . . . . ἐπιθυμήσεις. Γάρ *confirmantis* here. The second clause is an assertion of the same general nature with the first, excepting merely that it is in emphasis more intense. Ἐπιθυμίαν means here, *unlawful* or *sinful desire* in general, *i. e.*, desire of what would be in any way injurious to our neighbor. The reference in the mind of the writer appears plainly to have been to Ex. xxix. 14, לא תחמד etc.; which is well rendered: *Thou shalt not covet, i. e.*, shalt not inordinately desire; but which is rendered in Greek by οὐκ ἐπιθυμήσεις, *thou shalt not desire inordinately, thou shalt not lust after* or *covet*. We have no English noun that corresponds well to the *generic* sense of the verb *covet;* for *covetousness* means *a greedy appetite for wealth;* and *lust* means (at least as now employed), *impure desire*. We must then paraphrase ἐπιθυμίαν, and render it *inordinate desire, forbidden desire*. The word, it is true, sometimes means *unlawful sensual desire;* but plainly it is not here limited to a meaning so circumscribed. The reference to Ex. xx. 14, as well as the nature of the case, forbids this supposition.

Τέ, when employed alone (as here), is used to join those things which in their own nature are united and naturally follow each other; or those which, for some other reasons, must be associated together. It does not like καί connect coordinate but subordinate clauses. It is accordingly employed in clauses annexed (as here) for the sake of illustration or confirmation. Ἐπιθυμία, in the sense which it here has, is a *species* under the *genus* ἁμαρτία. The general principle is illustrated, then, by this particular sin which the law inhibits. The genius of our language does not permit us to translate τέ here, without doing injury to the mode of expression, if not to the sense. In Greek it affords a sign to the reader, that he is to connect the clause in which it stands with the preceding one.

That the whole is here to be understood in a *comparative* sense, is a clear case. If no revelation had ever been given to the Jews, then, like the Gentiles, they would have had the law of nature to guide and check them, Rom. ii. 14, 15. In the *absolute* sense, then, the apostle cannot be supposed to speak. The writer means: 'I had not so known sin as I now know it, except by the law.' A complete and full illustration and vindication of such a comparative sense, may be found in John xv. 22 — 24; which the reader is desired attentively to consult.

(8) This verse explains *how* the law has been the occasion of promoting the knowledge of sin, in the sense which the writer here means to convey. *But sin, taking occasion by the commandment, wrought out in me all manner of inordinate desire,* ἀφορμὴν δὲ . . . . ἐπιθυμίαν.— Κατειργάσατο, *wrought out;* it is more than εἰργάσατο, and means *more fully to complete, develop,* or *accomplish.*— Ἁμαρτία is here *personified.* It cannot mean simply *sinful desires* or *affections;* for these are affirmed to be the *effect* of its influence or operation. Nor can it be what is called *actual* sin; for this again is the *effect* of its operations. It would seem, therefore, that the *personification* of sin in this case must answer to the ἐγὼ σαρκικός and πεπραμένος ὑπὸ τὴν ἁμαρτίαν of verse 14 seq.; in other words, that it stands for the *carnal man,* as such, who is opposed to the divine law, and who is roused by its prohibitions and threatenings to more active engagement in the commission of sin. Accordingly, while ἁμαρτία is employed in the way of personification = ἐγὼ σαρκικός in verses 8 — 13, and in the sequel ἐγὼ σαρκικός, for the most part takes its place. It is in fact the *carnal I* which rouses up the passions, and which is the cause of all the evil that follows. And if the whole passage relates to the experience of *Christians* (as some suppose), even then it is the remains of the *carnal I* in them, which occasions all

the evil. But how or why did sin take occasion by the commandment to produce all manner of inordinate desires? The apostle does not definitely answer this question, but leaves it to be supplied, as a matter of course, by his readers. What then is the principle in human nature, which he seems to consider so obvious as to need no mention? It is the one, I answer, to which I have already more than once adverted; viz., that opposition to the desires and passions of unsanctified men, inflames them and renders them more intense and unyielding. So most of the commentators. Calvin: Neque inflctor quum acrius a lege exstimuletur caro ad concupiscendum. — Per legem instigatur cupiditas nostra, ut in majorem ebulliat insaniam. — Vitiosa hominum natura, cujus perversitas ac libido, quo magis justitiæ repagulis coërceretur, eo furiosius erumpit (in verse 5). Chrysostom: *When we covet anything, and are hindered from obtaining it, the flame of our inordinate desire is the more augmented.* So Erasmus and others. A most striking and melancholy example in point is, that prohibition and penalty were not sufficient, even in paradise, to prevent our first parents from ruining themselves and all their posterity.

The very heathen fully acknowledge the principle in question; so plainly is it a part of our nature. Thus Cato (Liv. xxxiv. 4) says of *luxury*, Non mota, tolerabilior esset quam erit nunc; ipsis vinculis, sicut fera bestia, irritata deinde emissa. Seneca: Parricidæ cum lege cœperunt, de Clem. I. 23. Horace: Audax omnia perpeti, gens humana ruit per vetitum nefas, Carm. I. 3. Ovid: Nitimur in vetitum semper cupimusque negata, Amor. III. 4. To the like purpose is Prov. ix. 17: Stolen waters are sweet, and bread eaten in secret is pleasure. Now as this is an obvious principle of a corrupt natural state, and will account for the fact which the apostle has asserted in the text, we may adopt the conclusion that it lies at the ground of his assertion. Ἁμαρτία, therefore, as here employed in the way of personification, designates the ἐγὼ σαρκικός.

Observe the strength of the expression, διὰ τῆς ἐντολῆς .... ἐπιθυμίαν; as much as to say, 'Sin, *i. e.*, my disposition to sin, did not simply produce ἐπιθυμίαν, *i. e., some* inordinate desire that would lead to the commission of evil — but πᾶσαν ἐπιθυμίαν, *every kind* of inordinate desire, a great variety of evil passions.' To account for this, we must resort to the principle already stated. It should be noted here, also, that in this way it was, that the law became the occasion of his obtaining a knowledge of sin, which he would otherwise never have acquired. So the sequel intimates:

For without the law sin is dead, χωρὶς γὰρ νόμου ἁμαρτία νεκρά;

i. e., comparatively sluggish and inoperative ; comp. James ii. 17, 26, πίστις νεκρά. Χωρὶς νόμου is equivalent to μὴ ὄντος νόμου, *i. e.*, there being no law. That such must be the sense, the preceding declaration shows; the amount of which is, that 'sin did by the commandment produce all kinds of inordinate desire in him.' Now if this be correct, then sin, without such commandment, *i. e.*, without such an occasion of producing πᾶσαν ἐπιθυμίαν, would be comparatively inoperative. For the *comparative* sense of the whole passage the reader is again referred to John xv. 22 — 24. That the apostle could not mean to be understood in the *absolute* sense, is plain from chap. i. ii., where the Gentiles are charged with sin, who nevertheless are without the particular law here spoken of, *i. e.*, without a revelation. In the *absolute* sense, the time never has been, and never can be, when men are *without the law*. "The heathen, who have no [written] law, are a law unto themselves." No individual, at any period of his life when he is capable of moral action, can be said to be without law in the *absolute* sense ; for the law always exists, independently of this or that individual. The meaning of Paul, then, according to the views which he himself inculcates, must be this, viz., that before an individual has any particular and definite views of the nature and extent of the divine law as to its prohibitions and penalties. When these first come home to his mind with power, then it is that he, through enmity and opposition to them, plunges deeper than ever into sin, and becomes at the same time more consciously guilty.

It is singular that some commentators represent ἁμαρτία in this verse as meaning *actual sin*, and not a disposition to sin or *vitiositas*. Actual sin, they say, produces sinful desires; and these again produce sinful actions in their full development; and thus comes the train of evils which the apostle here adverts to. But whence the *mother* sin ? we may well ask ; and this of course is a question which renders the whole of this theory quite improbable. It is true, beyond all doubt, that sins of action do beget various lusts, and nearly always do this ; and these in their turn develop themselves in action. But the apostle is speaking here of something in us which is roused up by the law to produce *inordinate desires*, which then bring forth death. Now what is that *originally*, if it be not the native disposition that we have to be excited by sinful objects, and to oppose holy ones; and which we, since the fall of Adam, possess in a measure that is sure to triumph over all the restraints of the divine law, and of reason and conscience, which testify in its favor, and remonstrate against our evil passions ? I must believe, with the great mass of commentators, that ἁμαρτία here is a personification of the disposition. The theory of Reiche and Glockler, in this case, seems to me to involve a real ὕστερον πρότερον.

(9) *For I was alive once, without the law*, ἐγὼ δὲ ἔζων . . . ποτέ. The δέ here introduces an additional *explanation:* "accuratius definit," Bretschn. Lex.; and it may be rendered *moreover, besides*. It might be rendered *for*, inasmuch as the connection in which it stands often entitles us so to render it (see Passow's Lex.); yet here it does not seem to be *subordinate* to the last clause in verse 8, but *co-ordinate*. The last clause in verse 8 asserts, that *sin is dead without the law*, while verse 9 declares that when the law came, sin developed itself with power; with which declaration it also connects other additional circumstances.

The ἐγώ here must of course mean *another self* different from the one which ἁμαρτία designates in the verse above. I hesitate, however, whether we should here construe it as designating merely *self, i. e.*, I myself as a person or individual, taken in the usual sense and without reference to another and different. self; or whether the ὁ ἔσω ἄνθρωπος (verse 22) should be here regarded as constituting the ἐγώ. On the whole I incline to the former, for two reasons; (1) Because the antithetic ἐγώ seems not to be introduced until verse 14 seq. (2) What is said in the sequel of the verse would seem rather to belong to the whole person; to the man as man, than merely to the ὁ ἔσω ἄνθρωπος in the limited sense in which Paul uses this phrase in the sequel.

Ἔζων is plainly used here in a *comparative* and figurative sense; and seems to be suggested by the preceding νεκρά, to which ἔζων of course is the direct antithesis. To find out the full meaning of this antithesis, then, we must revert to ἁμαρτία νεκρά. This, we have seen, must be taken in the *comparative* sense, viz., as indicating the comparatively inactive power and influence of sin, before an individual has a definite apprehension of the prohibitions and penalties of the divine law. Ἔζων, then, characterizes the state of the man, as opposite to that which is affirmed of ἁμαρτία. Now as sin is declared in the condition supposed, to be comparatively inoperative or dead, so the man himself is comparatively without sin, or (in other words) alive; just as when our Saviour says of the Jews, ' If I had not come and spoken to them, *they had not had sin.*' To say that sin is *dead*, and to say that the man is *alive*, evidently means for substance one and the same thing. So the apostle immediately asserts, that as soon as sin *gathered new life* (ἀνέζησεν) the man died (ἐγὼ ἀπέθανον). Now what was this *death*, except to come under the active and predominating power and penalty of sin? What then must be the *life*, (ἔζων), in this case, but to be free from such a state? But then — the whole is beyond all doubt to be taken in a *compara-*

tive sense. For what is the apostle laboring to prove? Not that a man must be under the Jewish or revealed law (for that is the law here designated), in order that he should be a sinner; for how could this agree with chaps. i. ii., where he labors to convict the Gentiles of sin? He is laboring here to show, that the law, instead of sanctifying and saving men, is, through their abuse of it, the means of plunging them deeper in guilt. In other words; the Jewish law, to which so many are prone to look as the means of safety and sanctification, does actually serve, under the present circumstances and condition of men, to render them more guilty than they would otherwise have been. Of course then the ἔζων here can mean nothing more nor less than that before an individual has a distinct and vivid perception of the nature and spirituality and extent of the divine law, he is less active and desperate in his sin and guilt than after he comes to such a knowledge. And thus explained, all is easy, natural, and coherent. The reader cannot fail to observe, also. how exactly this sentiment parallelizes with that in chap. iii. 20, where Paul declares, that "the law entered so that sin would or should abound." It is the *un*abounding state of it, then, which is described in our text by ἐγὼ ἔζων.

According to Barnes, Calvin, Augustine, and others, ἔζων here means: 'I deemed myself alive once,' *i. e.*, before I understood the spirituality and extent of the law. But this exegesis is attended with insuperable difficulties. For example: 'I once deemed myself spiritually alive; but when I came under conviction by the law, a sense of sin revived and I was brought to deem myself spiritually dead (so far all seems well); 'and the commandment which was designed to give life, proved to be deadly (εἰς θάνατον) to me;' it was deadly to me, because it brought me under real and true conviction as to my desperate spiritual condition! Is this then the way in which the law of God proves *fatal* to the sinner, viz., by convincing him of the true and deadly nature of sin? Others understand ἔζων here in the simple sense of *degere vitam, to exist* or *be* for any length of time. But the nature of the antithetic language here does not seem to permit this; for in the sequel ἀπέθανον is plainly opposed to ἔζων here; but ἀπέθανον cannot be the antithesis of ἔζων taken in the sense of *vitam degebam*, for then ἀπέθανον must mean *physical* death; which surely is not the sense of it here.

What period is designated by χωρὶς νόμου? Augustine, Origen, Ernesti, Morus, and others, understand it of the period of *infancy;* Luther, Ammon, and others, the period before he was taught by Gamaliel; Theodoret supposes he alludes to his pre-existence in Adam! Calvin and Beza seem plainly to have hit nearest to the point; "Intellige legem venisse, cum ab eo cœpit intelligi." It seems plain, that Paul must mean some application of the law to himself in a new manner, or in a way different from any which he had before experienced. *When* this was, he does not say. We may suppose it to be in childhood, or in riper years. The principle is the same. Whenever the law of God was pressed on his mind and conscience with such a weight and power that he could not dismiss attention to its demands, then began his active and increased opposition to it. Before this, sin was comparatively dead. Now it revived in all its strength, and brought him into deeper guilt and more aggravated condemnation.

The δέ after ἐλθούσης is *discretive*, introducing the antithesis of the preceding clause.—Ἁμαρτία ἀνέζησε, *sin revived* or *flourished*. Ἀναζάω means *to gather new life, to show additional vigor;* and such is clearly the sense here, as it does not mean merely a *renewal* of a life which had before existed. The expression itself is plainly one which the writer uses as equivalent to ἁμαρτία . . . . κατειργάσατο ἐν ἐμοὶ πᾶσαν ἐπιθυμίαν, in the preceding verse. As there 'all manner of inordinate desire is said to have been wrought διὰ τῆς ἐντολῆς,' so here the consequence of ἐλθούσης τῆς ἐντολῆς, is, that *sin becomes more vigorous*.

(10) *But I died*, ἐγὼ δέ ἀπέθανον. The δέ may be here regarded as discretive, *i. e.*, = *but*, since ἀπέθανον is the antithesis of ἀνέζησε; yet perhaps it simply introduces a thought additional to the one which precedes.—Ἀπέθανον, *I died, i. e.*, I fell under sentence of death or came into a state of death; for "the soul that sinneth shall die," "the wages of sin is death." So plainly the next clause explains it, where the death incurred is placed in opposition to the life which obedience to the whole law would ensure. But then there is plainly an intensive sense to be attached here to the word ἀπέθανον; just as there is to the word ἀνέζησε. The apostle means to say (as verse 8 shows), that sin put forth fresh vigor when the commandment came; consequently he incurred *aggravated* guilt; and aggravated condemnation must necessarily follow. It also lies on the face of the whole, that the writer designs to convey the idea, that the law, instead of affording sanctification and deliverance from sin, is the occasion of aggravating both guilt and condemnation. So he had intimated in vi. 14; and so he here proves the fact to be.

And the commandment which was designed [to bestow] *life, the same was found to be unto death*, καὶ εὑρέθη . . . . εἰς θάνατον. This clause is evidently added for the sake of intensity and variety of expression — an epexegesis of ἀπέθανον, with the addition of a new circumstance. In saying ἐντολὴ εἰς ζωήν, there was a reference in the mind of the writer to such passages of the Old Testament as the following: "My statutes . . . which if a man do he shall even live by them," Ezek. xx. 11, 13, 21. Lev. xviii. 5, et alibi. Μοί is, in point of sense, to be construed after θάνατον, and is a Dat. *incommodi;* comp. verse 13, and see N. Test. Gramm. § 104. 2. Note 1.

(11) A repetition of the sentiment in verses 8, 9, with some characteristic of the manner in which sin performed its deadly work. — *For sin taking occasion by the commandment deceived me, and by it slew me,* ἡ γὰρ .... ἀπέκτεινε. Γάρ *confirmantis;* for the sequel shows how the commandment came εἰς θάνατον to him. In respect to ἀφορμὴν λαβοῦσα, see verse 18. The *occasion* afforded, was the circumstance that the law restrained evil passions; which, in a graceless state of the heart, aggravates opposition to it. — Διὰ τῆς ἐντολῆς must mean, through the law as an *occasional* instrument or cause; not by it as the *efficient* cause of sin, which the sequel denies the law to be. — Ἐξηπάτησέ με seems to mean the deceit which our sinful passions practise upon us, by leading us to regard all restraint of them as unreasonable and oppressive, and to feel that we are in the right when we resist such restraint. The consequences of such a feeling will be, to obey our passions and not the law. Of course *we are slain* by such deceit; it leads us to plunge into ruin. — Δι' αὐτῆς must mean δι' ἐντολῆς. In what sense sin slays through the commandment, has been once and again stated.

(12) *So that the law is holy, and the commandment holy and just and good,* ὥστε ὁ μὲν . . . ἀγαθή. The true force of ὥστε seems to be *so that, i. e.,* things being as I have said, it follows, that, etc. In consequence of such a connection, ὥστε may be rendered *wherefore, therefore;* for it is, in the classics, not unfrequently employed as an *intensive* particle of conclusion. — Μέν is difficult of grammatical solution here. Taken as the usual sign of *protasis,* where is the *apodosis?* Καὶ ἡ ἐντολὴ κ. τ. λ. will not make one, for it is merely epexegetical of ὁ νόμος ἅγιος. In the Greek classics, μέν is often employed without any subsequent apodosis *expressed,* but it is not so used probably unless one is *implied.* What then is the implied apodosis here? We may perhaps supply it from verse 13; and if so, it would seem to be this: ἁμαρτία δέ ἐστιν ἡ κατεργαζομένη θάνατον διὰ τοῦ ἀγαθοῦ νόμου. Ruckert makes the implied apodosis to be, ὁ δὲ Ἰουδαῖος κακὸς καὶ ἄδικος.

The present is not a regular *logical* deduction from the preceding verses. The writer means to say, that the view which he has taken of the case is such, on the whole, that the excellence and purity of the law stand entirely unimpeached. The law is indeed the *occasion*, but it is the *innocent* occasion, of sin. It is the evil passions which convert what in its own nature tends to life, into an instrument of death. The reason of repeating both νόμος and ἐντολή here, seems to be, that both had been employed in the preceding illustration; see verses 7—10. If there be any difference between the two words, it must be this, viz., that νόμος is the generic appellation of the divine law, תּוֹרָה; while ἐντολή corresponds to חֹק, *i. e.*, any particular precept. As used by the writer, however, no difference seems to be here intended. Ἁγία means *holy, free from all moral defect, free from sin, opposed to sin*. Δικαία, *agreeable to* δίκη, *i. e.*, promoting justice and punishing sin. Ἀγαθή, *good* in its object and end, tending to secure the ends of benevolence. The most appropriate to the apostle's purpose here of all the qualities which he mentions, is that of *holiness*. Hence, ὁ νόμος ἅγιος and ἡ ἐντολὴ ἁγία.

The vindication of the character of the law as thus stated, which makes it the occasion of the aggravation of our guilt instead of delivering us from it, follows. But before we proceed to consider this, we must endeavor to solve some questions which naturally arise here.

The reader has doubtless perceived, that I suppose the apostle to be here speaking of himself when in a *legal* state or under the law, and before he was spiritually united to Christ. This I must, on the whole, believe to be the case. In support of this view many reasons may be offered; but some of them I defer to the close of the chapter. It is sufficient for my present purpose to state, verses 7—11 plainly appear to be a defence and confirmation of the obnoxious expression (obnoxious to the legalist) contained in verse 5. It is this verse, surely, which gives occasion to the objection expressed at the beginning of verse 7; and it is of course the same, therefore, which is the theme of verses 7—11. But on looking back to verse 5, we find ἦμεν ἐν τῇ σαρκί to be the condition of the person, on whom the law of God produced the unhappy effect stated in the sequel. Indeed the case of itself determines this; for surely the law of God is not the object of the *believer's* hatred, nor does it enkindle his passions and aggravate his offences; it reproves, restrains, moderates, subdues, his evil affections and desires. To prove this, would be as superfluous as to prove that the renewed heart loves and approves of holiness. It is surely none but an *unsanctified* heart which can make such a use of the law of God as is stated in verses 7—11.

Moreover, insuperable difficulties attend the usual exegesis (in modern times and among a certain class of writers) of this passage. *E. g.*, verses 9, 10, are thus explained: 'I thought myself alive, *i. e.*, holy or good, before I was brought under conviction by the law; but when this conviction took place, a penitential sense of sin became strong and active; I was then fully persuaded that I deserved condemnation (ἐγὼ δὲ ἀπέθανον); and I found that instead of keeping the commandment, I had only brought myself under its penalty. Now all this would do well, in itself considered; the sentiment is evangelical and correct. But the difficulty in obtaining this sentiment from the passage before us, is, (1) That one must violate the *usus loquendi*. (2) He must bring contradiction and inextricable difficulty into the context. (3) He must make the writer assert what is irrelevant to his present purpose.

First, to construe ἁμαρτία ἀνέζησεν as meaning *a penitential sense of sin revived* or *become strong*, has no parallel in Scripture. Ἁμαρτία cannot be shown ever to mean *penitential sense of sin*. As little too can ἔζων be shown to mean, *I thought myself alive, i. e.*, righteous. Both renderings are discrepant from all *usus loquendi*.

Secondly, if we take this meaning of ἁμαρτία, viz., *penitential sense of sin*, and carry it on through verse 11, which is indissolubly connected with verse 10, (as a comparison of verses 7, 8, and the γάρ in verse 11, show,) it will make a sense utterly inadmissible. *E. g.*, 'A penitential sense of sin (ἁμαρτία) taking occasion by the law, *deceived me and slew me!*' Sorrow for sin neither *deceives* nor *slays*, but just the opposite. Yet such a carrying forward of the sense given to ἁμαρτία in verse 10, is fairly inevitable, unless one renounces the principles by which a writer's thoughts are connected together.

Thirdly, such a sentiment as is given to verse 10, although true in itself, is irrelevant to the writer's purpose here. His object is to show that he has not rashly said, τὰ παθήματα τῶν ἁμαρτιῶν τὰ διὰ τοῦ νόμου, verse 5. How will it prove this, if he declares merely that the law undoes the false hopes of the sinner, and brings him under true conviction? This would seem, at least, to be proving just the opposite of what he designs to show. Nor will it help the matter in the least, if you suppose him to be speaking of the experience of Christians; for surely it would not illustrate the declaration, that the law is the occasion of our evil passions being aggravated, to assert that Christians are convinced of sin by it, and brought to true penitence.

I must proceed, therefore, in explaining the remainder of the chapter, on the ground that a person in a *law-state*, and not in a state of grace, is described. To some of the reasons for this method of interpretation I have just adverted; and others will come up in the course of my exposition. But for a more ample exposition and defence of this exegesis, see Excursus vii.

Does the apostle by employing the *first person singular*, throughout verses 7 — 25, mean to designate himself specially and peculiarly, or does he include others with himself? Others certainly are included, understand him as you please. If he speaks of himself while under the law, he means by a parity of reasoning to include all others who are in the same condition. If he speaks of himself as a Christian, he means in the same manner to include all other Christians, who of course must have similar experience. So that Ambrose very appropriately and truly says: Sub suâ personâ quasi generalem causam agit. The use sometimes of the plural and sometimes of the singular number, favors this supposition; comp. verses 5, 7, 14, seq. and viii. 1, seq. The apostle often employs the first person singular, where he is discussing general principles; *e. g.*, 1 Cor. vi. 12. x. 23, 29, 30. xiii. 11 — 13; Gal. ii. 18, et al. sæpe. That it is not unusual for the apostles to include themselves, even where they are saying things which convey sharp reproof, is also true; *e. g.*, James iii. 1, 2, 9. Comp. 1 Cor. iv. 6, where he explicitly asserts such a principle. Even Reiche, who represents the ἐγὼ σαρκικός as the commonwealth of the Jews under the law, and the *better I* as the ideal Jew without sin, is still obliged to concede that Paul uses μετασχηματισμός here, *i. e.*, that he appropriates to himself what belongs to others, or represents them in his own person.

CHAP. VII. 13—25.

The apostle proceeds in these verses to exhibit the fact that the law can in no way be involved in the charge of being the efficient cause of sin, for it stands in direct and perpetual opposition to all the sinful desires of men in an unsanctified and carnal state. That it is holy and just and good, is evinced by the fact, that the conscience and moral sense spontaneously take sides with it or approve of its precepts. Yet, notwithstanding all this, such is the force of sinful desires and lusts, that they triumph over the precepts of the law, and lead the unsanctified man to continual opposition and transgression. Even against the voice of reason and conscience, *i e.*, of an internal moral nature, as well as against the divine precepts, does carnal desire prevail, we yield the *moral self* to the power of the *carnal self*, and plunge deep into ruin, while the voice of God's law is thundering in our ears, and the voice of our own consciences is loudly remonstrating against our conduct. Who can refrain, now, from perceiving that all this is much to the purpose of the apostle, whose object it is to show, that to be *under grace*, (and not under the law) affords the only hope for the sinner? Accordingly, in chap viii. 1—17, he shows that the opposite of all which he has been before describing takes place in the regenerate, and that a filial spirit subdues carnal affections, overcomes the world, and enables Christians *to walk ac-*

cording to the spirit, nothing of which is accomplished, while men are in the condition described in vii 14—25

Now to what special end of the apostle would it be here subservient, if we suppose him to be describing *a state of grace* in chap vii? How does the contest in the breast of Christians against sin, prove the inefficacy of the *law* to sanctify them? For to prove such an inefficacy, it must be admitted, is the general object of the present discourse. The fact is, that such a statement would prove too much It would show that *grace* is wanting in efficacy, as well as the *law*, for the Christian, being a subject of grace, and still keeping up such a contest, one might of course be tempted to say, 'It appears, then, that grace is no more competent than law, to subdue sin and sanctify the heart' And indeed why might he not say this, if the ground of those who construe all this of the *regenerate* man be correct? For what is the real state of the whole matter as represented by the apostle? It is, that in every contest here between the flesh and the spirit (the moral man), the former comes off victorious. And can this be a *regenerate* state? Is this " the victory which is of God, and overcometh the world?" "He that is born of God sinneth not," those that love his law " do no iniquity," he that loveth Christ " keepeth his commandments," *i e*, an habitual and voluntary offender such a one is not, he gives not himself up to any course of sin; it is his habitual study and effort to subdue his passions, and obey the commandments of God. But what of all this is there, in the case which the apostle represents in vii 14—25? Read now chap. viii 1—17, and then ask, Is the man described in vii 14—25, who yields in every instance to the assault of his passions, and suffers them continually to triumph over law, conscience, and every other consideration, such a man or the same man as is described in viii 1—17? In this latter passage the man is described, " who walks NOT after the flesh but after the Spirit" Can this then be the same man who does walk after the flesh, and always does thus, even when the voice of God and conscience is thundering in his ears, and his own internal moral nature is warning him against the course he pursues? Impossible. Light and darkness are not more diverse than these two cases.

(13) *Has then that which is good become death to me?* τὸ οὖν ἀγαθὸν .... θάνατος; *i. e.*, 'You call the commandment ἀγαθή, *kind, beneficent, productive of happiness;* how can that which is beneficent, be fatal to me? Is this not a contradiction?' The answer is, μὴ γένοιτο! *i. e.*, it is not true that the ἐντολὴ ἀγαθή was of itself fatal or deadly to you, ἀλλὰ ἡ ἁμαρτία, *but sin* [was death to you]; for that σοι γέγονε θάνατος is implied after ἁμαρτία, is very plain from the nature of the sentence. — 'Ἀλλά here, as often elsewhere, stands before a clause designed to give a true account of a thing in opposition to an erroneous one. — Γέγονε is wanting in F., G.; and in A., B., C., D., E., ἐγένετο stands in its room. The sense is the same in all the cases, and *hermeneutically* the reading is a matter of indifference.

So that sin might exhibit itself as causing death to me by that which is good, ἵνα φανῇ .... θάνατον. — Φανῇ is 2 Aor. pass. Subj., but is employed (as the Aorists pass. often are) in the sense of the Middle voice. The meaning is; 'Sin became the cause of death to me, by leading me to abuse the law which was altogether good; and so it exhibited, in a true light, its own deadly and odious nature.' The μοί here and the ἐμοί above are the Dative *incommodi*.

So that sin, through the commandment, might be exceedingly sinful, ἵνα γένηται . . . . ἐντολῆς; *i. e.*, so that sin, by abuse of the commandment which was good, and by making it the occasion of death to the sinner, and by its opposition to a commandment in its own nature holy and just and good, might thus appear to be exceedingly aggravated and detestable. The *heinousness* of sin, not the increase as to quantity, is here characterized. For καθ' ὑπερβολήν, used adverbially instead of ὑπερβαλλόντως, comp. 1 Cor. xii. 31. 2 Cor. i. 8. iv. 17. I take the two phrases in these verses beginning with ἵνα, to be *co-ordinate;* and both of them I regard as suspended on ἀλλὰ ἡ ἁμαρτία [θάνατος γέγονε]. One of the phrases declares that sin developed itself according to its true nature, by perverting the holy law of God; the other, that the exceedingly odious nature of it was thus made the more manifest.

(14) Οἴδαμεν γάρ some critics divide thus: οἶδα μὲν γάρ. But the general usage of Paul is against this; for in appeals of this nature he generally uses the *plural* number and not the singular. — Γάρ *illustrantis et confirmantis* for the sequel is designed to illustrate and confirm what he has said in respect to the law and sin, in verse 13.

The law is spiritual, ὁ νόμος πνευματικός ἐστι, *i. e.*, the law enjoins those things which are agreeable to the nature and mind of the Spirit. *Flesh* and *spirit* are often opposed to each other in a variety of senses; viz., (1) As *flesh* is weak and perishable (Gen. vi. 3. Ps. lxxviii. 39. lvi. 4. Jer. xvii. 5. Is. xl. 6), so *spirit* (רוּחַ, πνεῦμα), the animating and invigorating principle, is sometimes placed in opposition to it with the meaning of strength and permanence; *e. g.*, Is. xxxi. 3. But, (2) The most common usage in the New Testament is the *tropical* one; where σάρξ is viewed as the seat of carnal desires and affections, and is often employed to designate them, sometimes simply, and sometimes with φρόνημα added to it; while πνεῦμα, when employed in the way of antithesis to it, means *a new and holy disposition*, which is τὶ πνευματικόν, *i. e.*, something produced by the influence of the Spirit of God and guided by this influence. Hence Christians are πνευματικοί and unsanctified men are σαρκικοί, because the former are under the influence of the Spirit, and the latter are guided by their carnal appetites and desires. All this is quite plain, when one reads Rom. viii. 1 — 17, where the antithesis is fully and explicitly stated.

To say then that the *law* is πνευματικός, is to affirm that its nature is *pneumatic*, *i. e.*, agreeable to the mind or will of the Spirit. The antithesis therefore is plain, viz., ἐγὼ δὲ σαρκικός εἰμι, *but I am carnal, i. e.*, I am under the influence of carnal desires and affections. Even such desires as do not spring directly from the flesh, are sometimes named *carnal;* and this, it would seem, because most of our sinful propensities are in some way connected with the flesh, and those which are not, are similar in regard to their moral character. For example; in Gal. v. 19 — 22, the apostle names *hatred, envy, anger,* etc., as ἔργα σαρκός; and so in Rom. viii. 5 — 9, κατὰ σάρκα εἶναι or περιπατεῖν, includes every kind of vicious conduct. And in the passage before us, σαρκικός εἰμι is explained by a clause which the writer immediately adds; viz.

Sold under sin, πεπραμένος ὑπὸ τὴν ἁμαρτίαν, *i. e.,* the bond slave of sin δοῦλος τῆς ἁμαρτίας; for so the sequel shows him to be, inasmuch as he obeys sin in every case, whatever opposition is made to it on the part of conscience or the divine law. The language is borrowed from the practice of selling captives, who have been taken in war, as slaves. They were viewed as having forfeited their lives; and so they were sold into a state of the most absolute despotism. In allusion to this, the apostle represents the person who is still under the law, and therefore unredeemed, as being the bond slave of sin. Stronger language than this he could not employ; and it will be important, in the sequel, to look back on this expression in order to solve some of the doubts which may arise from ὃ μισῶ, ὃ οὐ θέλω ἐγώ, τὸ θελεῖν παράκειταί μοι, συνήδομαι τῷ νόμῳ τοῦ Θεοῦ, etc. Let the reader who wishes to consult the writer's own exposition of σαρκικός, carefully compare chap. viii. 5 — 9. The law then is good, for it is πνευματικός, *i. e.,* agreeable to the dictates of the Spirit. It is not this, therefore, which is the efficient cause of men's sins; it is that they are σαρκικοί, devoted to the desires of the flesh, following the dictates of its desires.

(15) That the law does sustain such a character, must be well known to the sinner himself. His own reason and conscience take sides with the law and approve of its precepts. Yet still so *carnally inclined* is he, that he listens not to these, but acts directly against them. In other words, he is actually the slave of sin. Γάρ in this verse would seem to have direct relation to the declaration just repeated. Observe the tenor of it: 'He does that which he dislikes, he is as it were forced by his slavish condition to do that which is hateful to his better self.' In this way, the idea that he is πεπραμένος ὑπὸ τὴν ἁμαρτίαν, because very prominent.

In order to express the sentiment which he intends to convey in the most striking manner, the apostle divides the person thus in bondage into *two selves* (if I may thus speak), viz., the νοῦς or ὁ ἔσω ἄνθρωπος (verses 22, 23), and the σῶμα, σάρξ, or carnal part of his nature. In the latter dwell the passions and affections which sway the ἄνθρωπος σαρκικός; in the former is still a portion of the image of God (James iii. 9; 1 Cor. xi. 7), which discerns and cannot but approve the holy and perfect law of God that is merely a transcript of his own nature; cf. Rom. ii. 14, 15. That the unregenerate have reason and conscience, which approve and must approve the divine law, shows nothing more than that they are *rational* and *moral* beings with faculties adapted to a state of moral probation, and that they are made in the image of God so far as a rational and moral nature is concerned; *i. e.*, they are *men*, and not brutes. The faculty to discern what is good, the power to approve of it, is in itself no more holy or sinful, than the faculty of ratiocination is, or of seeing or hearing. Nothing can be more unfounded, than the supposition that *moral good* is put to the account of the sinner, merely because one assigns to him reason to discern its nature and conscience to approve it. Without these he could not be a rational and moral being. They are mere *pura naturalia*, to speak in the language of the old theology.

The reader need not be in any degree alarmed, then, for the doctrine of human depravity, when he finds the sinner here represented as seeing something of the nature of the divine law and testifying in its favor. It is on such ground as this, that the ways of God toward men may be vindicated; for allowing it to be true, that our physical nature is the peculiarly exciting cause of most of our sins, we may still ask: 'Is there not an ἔσω ἄνθρωπος which opposes all inordinate desires, and warns us to avoid sin and cleave to duty?' And on this ground it is, that God regards the heathen as being without excuse; as is clear from Rom. i. ii., especially ii. 14, 15.

For that which I do, I disapprove, ὃ γὰρ . . . . γινώσκω. Κατεργάζομαι means more than the simple ἐργάζομαι; it designates the *habitual doing* or *practising* of anything. — Οὐ γινώσκω is rendered by Chrysostom, Theodoret, Tholuck, and others, *I know not, i. e.*, my mind is so darkened by sin that I do not perceive the true nature of what I am doing; but the explanation which Paul immediately subjoins seems to forbid this exegesis, viz., οὐ γὰρ ὃ θέλω, κ. τ. λ.* Besides, the very height of the criminality here depicted is, that the sin is against light, and knowledge, and conscience. On the other hand, that γινώσκω in Greek, as well

---

* There is little difficulty in understanding this word literally *I know not*. A reason is given here for the preceding declaration "sold under sin," and the language is conformed to it. I am the slave of sin, *for in my customary actions, I proceed blindly not intelligently, as a slave who acts in accordance with the will of another.*

as the Hebrew יָדַע, not unfrequently means *to know* in the sense of *acknowledging* or *approving* may be seen in the lexicons; see Matt. vii. 23 xxv. 12. Luke xiii. 27. Ps. i. 6. Hos. viii. 4. That *knowledge* speculatively considered is not here meant, *i. e.*, that οὐ γινώσκω does not mean *I am ignorant, insciens sum*, is clear from the sequel, where the apostle speaks of his neglecting to do that *which he wills*. Now what he *wills*, must be an object of *perception* with him; so that οὐ γινώσκω cannot be understood of mere intellectual ignorance.

For not that which I approve, do I perform, οὐ γὰρ ὃ θέλω, τοῦτο πράσσω. Γάρ *confirmantis, i. e.*, the clause of the sentence that follows, confirms the preceding statement. First, we have a general declaration. *What I do, I disapprove*. Next follows a specific one which illustrates and confirms it: *Not that which I approve do I perform, but I do that which I hate*. If there be anything paradoxical here (and the first view of the case may seem to present a paradox), it is occasioned entirely by the plan of the writer to represent the two contrary selves in one and the same person. Κατεργάζομαι belongs to the *carnal* self, and γινώσκω to the νοῦς or ἔσω ἄνθρωπος; and thus in succession it is the conscience and reason, *i. e.*, the internal moral man, which disapproves (οὐ θέλω) and hates (μισῶ), while the carnal man *practises* (πράσσω, ποιῶ) the thing· which is disapproved and hated.

All speculative metaphysical questions would here be entirely out of place. One might ask: 'Is it true, then, that a man does what he is unwilling to do, and hates to do? This would be not only to represent him as acting against predominant motives, but as a machine who could not follow his own inclination.' And on the ground of some systems of metaphysical philosophy, the whole would indeed be an unaccountable affair, as it is here represented by the apostle; although such philosophy is not unfrequently insisted on, and urged as being all-important in theology. But still the apostle might make the appeal, for his own triumphant vindication, to the breast of every man on earth, where the moral warfare has been carried on as he describes it, between conscience and passion. And a most exact and striking picture it is too. The demonstration of its correctness is *internal*, in the very consciousness of the soul; it depends not on metaphysics or ratiocination. It is not true, indeed, that a man does that which *on the whole* he is unwilling to do; nor is this what the apostle means to affirm. But it is true, that men often do what reason and conscience disapprove; and which he here expresses in the strong language of οὐ θέλω and μισῶ, *i. e.*, it is the ἔσω ἄνθρωπος of whom this is predicated. These words, in a contrast like the present, are not to be urged to the highest point of possible meaning. So, for example, μισῶ may mean not *positive* hatred, but a *not loving* or merely a *comparatively* not loving, *i. e.*, a less loving; for so the examples in Matt. vi. 24, Luke xvi. 13. xiv. 26, as compared with Matt. x. 37. That θέλω and μισῶ, then, can both be affirmed of the conscience enlightened by the divine law (comp. verse 9), when they are understood in this qualified sense (and on any ground of exegesis a qualified sense is absolutely necessary), is sufficiently manifest. Any one who undertakes to urge the sense of words employed in such a contrast as is here presented, to the highest meaning of which they are capable, must involve himself at least in difficulties that are absolutely inextricable.

There is a striking passage in Xenophon (Cyrop. VI. 1), in which Araspes the Persian says, by way of excusing his treasonable designs: " Certainly I must have two souls . . . . for plainly it is not one and the same which is both evil and good, nor which loves honorable and base conduct, and at the same time wishes to do a thing and not to do it. Plainly then there are two souls; and when the good one prevails, then it does good; and when the evil one predominates, then it does evil." So Euripides, Medea, 1077, 8:

Μανθάνω μὲν, οἷα δρᾶν μέλλω κακά·
Θύμος δὲ κρείσσων τῶν ἐμῶν βουλευμάτων.

I know, indeed, that such things as I am about to do, are evil; but my mind is better than my inclinations.

The same poet (as quoted by Clemens Alex. Strom. II. 15):

Λέληθεν οὐδὲν τῶνδε μ᾽ ὧν σὺ νουθητεῖς·
Γνώμην δ᾽ ἔχοντά μ᾽ ἡ φύσις βιάζεται.

I have forgotten none of the things respecting which you have admonished me; but although I have a desire to do them, nature forces me another way.

To the same purpose, and in a manner very much like that of Paul, Epictetus says (Enchirid. II. 26). Ὁ ἁμαρτάνων, ὃ μὲν θέλει οὐ ποιεῖ· καὶ ὃ μὴ θέλει, ποιεῖ. So Plautus, (Trinummus, Act. IV. Scen. 2, verse 31): Scibam ut esse me decerct, facere non quibam miser; *I knew that it was becoming, but, me miserable! I could not do it.* See also Seneca (Ep. III.) and Hippol. verse 604. Lactantius also represents a heathen as saying: Volo equidem non peccare, sed vincor; indutus enim sum carne fragili. Itaque ducor incertus, et pecco non quia volo, sed quia cogor.

These quotations (for which I am indebted to Prof. Tholuck) show how clear and distinct the impression is upon the human mind, in all countries, that there is a struggle in the breast between conscience and carnal inclination. They also show how much alike men, enlightened or unenlightened by revelation, express themselves in relation to the struggle in question. They answer still another purpose, viz., to show that language of this nature is used and is to be understood in the *popular* sense, and in this only.

(16) *If then I do that which I do not approve, I consent to the law as good*, εἰ δὲ .... καλός; *i. e.*, if my reason and conscience disapprove that which I do, then my *inward* man bears testimony in favor of the law, gives assent to the goodness of it. Δέ "orationi continuandæ inservit." Σύμφημι, lit. *to speak with, to confess, to acknowledge*. The appeal here in favor of the law is very strong; for even those who habitually violate it, are represented as testifying in its favor. In one point of view, this is stronger testimony than that of Christians; for if the real enemies themselves of the law feel obliged to confess its excellence, we may well expect that the friends of the law will do the same; as indeed they of course do. The reader will notice, that when the apostle says that *he does that which he disapproves*, he represents the ἔσω ἄνθρωπος, in thus disapproving, as giving its testimony in favor (σύμφημι) of what the law decides. It is not then the *physiological* exercise of the will here which is designated by θέλω (for this of course determines the outward actions); but it is the *approbation* of the reason and conscience, *i. e.*, of the internal man, which is meant.

(17) *But now it is no longer I who do this, but sin which dwells in me*, νυνὶ δὲ .... ἁμαρτία. Νυνί is properly a particle of time, but often employed (like *now* in English) as a mere *continuative* of argument. It is as much as to say: 'In these or in such circumstances, the case being as represented, then it follows,' etc. Δέ *discretive*, "accuratius definit." The apostle means to guard against the possibility of confounding the *two selves*, which he has here introduced, and to aver strongly that the *internal* man does not participate in approving the course which the carnal passions pursue, but takes sides with the divine law, and continues to give its assent to its sanctions, even amid all the predominant opposition of the carnal self. Two consequences then plainly follow from the principle asserted in verse 15; viz., first, that the internal man assents to the goodness of the divine law; secondly, that it is not reason and conscience which of themselves unperverted lead men to sin, but their own carnal desires. The latter sentiment is fully and strongly asserted in verse 17.

Ἐγώ therefore is the moral self, the νοῦς or ἔσω ἄνθρωπος here; while ἡ ἁμαρτία (here personified) means, the sinful passions and affections of men, or the disposition to indulge them. The distinction here made between the higher moral self of *reason* and *conscience*, and the lower one of *carnal passions* and *appetites*, is very striking. In like manner Seneca says: Mens cujusque is est quisque, non ea figura quæ digito monstrari potest; *the* MIND *of a man is* HIMSELF, *not that part which may be pointed out with one's finger*, *i. e.*, not the body. So Augustine: Magis ego in eo quod in me approbabam, quam in eo quod in me improbabam, Confess. VIII. 5. The higher moral self has the better claim to the title of ἐγώ.

There is some difficulty of rather a serious nature here, as to the ἐν ἐμοί in which sin dwells or reigns or is predominant. It is not the first, the ἄνθρωπος σαρκικός, some one may say; 'for to suppose this, would be to suppose that the apostle represents sin as dwelling in itself; for what is sin here but the *carnal* man?— Not the second; for the ἔσω ἄνθρωπος is opposed to sin and takes sides with the divine law, as the whole passage abundantly testifies.' 'The ἐμοί then,' he might say, 'must here *designate the whole person*, and be employed in its usual sense. This seems plausible, at first view, but as the apostle has *personified* sin here, the mode of expression must be in accordance with this figure of speech. For the moment, sin is spoken of as a *separate* agent, and as dwelling and acting in the man who obeys its dictates. But it is in the carnal man, *i. e.*, the carnal self in this case, that it dwells. The ἔσω ἄνθρωπος disapproves and condemns what the other self, in which sin dwells, approves and practises. It is plainly a popular and allegorical, not a metaphysical, mode of representation.—But more must be said in respect to the difficulty before us, in explaining the next verse.

(18) *For I know*, etc., οἶδα γὰρ . . . . ἀγαθόν. The γάρ introduces a confirmation of the declaration that he has just made, viz., that *indwelling sin* leads him to thwart the promptings of reason and conscience and the commands of God's holy law. This is clear from the conclusion drawn in verse 20. The intervening matter, then, is designed to illustrate and confirm the position just mentioned. First of all, therefore, he avers that he is conscious (οἶδα) that no *good thing* dwells in him, *i. e.*, in his carnal part.—Ἀγαθόν, without the article, means *any good thing*, *i. e.*, anything *morally* good, or inclining to moral good; for not *natural* but moral good and evil are here the subject of consideration. That σαρκί μου must mean *the carnal man*, and not mere flesh and blood, is evident enough from the nature of the case, and from verse 5, where ἐν τῇ σαρκί surely does not mean flesh *physiologically* considered.

For to will is present with me, τὸ γάρ θέλειν, παράκειταί μοι, *i. e.*, is in my power, is accessible to me, is in readiness, is what I can readily and easily come at or accomplish. The γάρ here is again *causal, i. e.*, it introduces a reason or proof of the fact, that no good dwells in the *carnal* man, and that he is conscious of this; for experience tells him, that while the inner man, the reason and conscience approves of and consents to that which is good, the carnal man has no power or inclination or readiness to accomplish it. As to οὐχ εὑρίσκω, *I do not find*, it is plainly an elliptical expression.— Οὐχ εὑρίσκω [παρακείμενόν μοι], *i. e.*, I do not find it in my power. But not metaphysical nicety of expression is here intended. The writer evidently means to say, that the carnal part is altogether the predominant self; just in the same manner as he says, that "the natural man receiveth not the things of the Spirit of God . . . . neither *can he know* them." So again : "The carnal mind is enmity against God, and is not subject to the law of God nor indeed *can it be*," Rom. viii. 7. As σαρκικός, *i. e.*, as swayed and directed by carnal desires and affections, the sinner finds no power to do good. The assertion of the apostle does not respect the ability of men in a mere psychological or physiological point of view, with simple reference to the powers and attributes of their nature as men ; but it respects them as σαρκικοί, as ἐν σαρκί, and as acting agreeably to this predominating part of themselves. So long as they are in this state of servitude, and under such masters, they cannot serve another master. But this does not decide that they have no power, in any sense of this word, to quit the service of a bad master, and go over to a good one.

(19) *For the good which I approve,* etc., οὐ γὰρ ὃ θέλω κ. τ. λ. This verse is for substance a repetition of verse 15 ; still it is not a mere repetition, for the form is varied; since here we have ἀγαθόν and κακόν, and the sentence commences with a γάρ *confirmantis,* and it appears to be designed to confirm the preceding declaration. The proof that my reason and conscience approve that which is good, and that I find myself unable or indisposed to effect it, is this: that I in fact leave undone the good which I approve, and do the evil which I disapprove.

(20) Εἰ δὲ κ. τ. λ. Here δέ marks the *continuation* of the discourse, while it is *discretive* as to the matter to be added. In effect this verse is a conclusion drawn from the matter suggested in verses 18, 19, serving to confirm the position in verse 17 ; for a part of verse 19 is repeated here, and also the latter part of the sentence in verse 17. The form is *hypothetical;* which is a favorite mode of Paul in making out conclusions. The amount of it is thus : 'If what I have said in verses 18, 19, be true [and

clearly it is], then what I have affirmed in verse 17 must be true.' The phrase οὐ θέλω is related, as before, to the *internal* moral man; and τοῦτο ποιῶ to the *carnal* man. So the οὐκέτι ἐγὼ κατεργάζομαι refers to the former, and the ἐν ἐμοί to the latter.

(21) Next follows a general deduction from the preceding representations, of which ἄρα, *then, therefore*, is the sign.

Only two methods of explanation seem to me worth discussing here. (*a*) 'I find τὸν νόμον, *a law* or *constitution*, viz., of my nature, that when I would do good, evil is near at hand.' So Calvin, Venema, Limborch, Michaelis, Bolten, Ammon, etc. It is charged as a difficulty upon this mode of interpretation, that the article in τὸν νόμον cannot well be accounted for; for νόμον in verse 23 has it not. But this objection has little weight, for νόμος in verse 21 is surely a *particular* and *specific* νόμος; but in verse 23, τὸν ἕτερον νόμον (*i. e.*, adding the article) would give a sense which the writer does not intend, for he means here only to say that there is another law, *i. e.*, some other law, in opposition to *the law of his mind*. Ἐν τοῖς μέλεσι does indeed specificate the νόμος in question; but in such a case the article may be either inserted or omitted. A comparison moreover of verse 21 with verse 23 seems to render it quite plain, that τὸν νόμον in the former is the same as the ἕτερον νόμον in the latter. I take the meaning of the writer to be, that he finds it to be a *custom* or *law* with him, resulting from his carnal nature, that when his reason and conscience decide in favor of doing good, evil comes in and prevents it; *i. e.*, his carnal affections and desires interpose and hinder his doing good; in other words, he finds the doing of evil so habitual with himself, that he must regard it as a controlling law of his carnal nature.

(*b*) The second method puts a comma after ἄρα, and construes the intermediate clause thus: Ἐμοὶ τῷ θέλοντι ποιεῖν τὸν νόμον, [sc. ποιεῖν] τὸ καλόν; thus making τὸ καλόν a synonyme with τὸν νόμον, and supposing ποιεῖν to be virtually repeated before it. So Tholuck, Knapp, et al. This explanation is a possible one; but I can hardly bring myself to feel that it is probable. In sense it does not differ materially from the other; and therefore it offers no special inducement to adopt it. That νόμος in this case does not mean the *Mosaic law*, as some maintain, seems to me quite certain from the two different senses given to νόμος in verse 23.

Evil is at hand, evil is near or *in readiness,* ἐμοὶ τὸ κακὸν παράκειται. The meaning here is, as verse 23 shows, that evil stands ready to usurp the place of good, and does in fact usurp it. This last clause, beginning with ὅτι, etc., is epexegetical of τὸν νόμον.

(22) *For I delight in the law of God, as it respects the internal man*, συνήδομαι γὰρ . . . . ἄνθρωπον. The sentiment is, for substance, the same as in verses 15—17; but the costume in which it appears, is diverse. That the sentiment, moreover, is epexegetical of verse 21, is quite plain. Hence the γάρ *illustrantis* with which it is introduced. Συνήδομαι here corresponds to σύμφημι in verse 16; and ἔσω ἄνθρωπον, here, corresponds to ἐγώ in verse 17. If the strength of the expression συνήδομαι τῷ νόμῳ, is supposed to be inconsistent with an unregenerate state, it may well be asked, whether the expression in verse 14, on the other side, is not still stronger. The truth is, in a contrast like this, where the mind of the writer is wrought up to a high pitch of feeling, the mere *forms* of expression cannot in themselves go very far toward establishing any principle of doctrine. It is *to the object at which the writer is aiming*, that we must look; and this object has been already brought to view. But if any one insists on urging the *form* of expression, let him first construe verse 14 by the rule which he himself here adopts; and then compare Mark vi. 20 ἡδέως αὐτοῦ ἤκουε, *i. e.*, Herod heard John ἡδέως; John v. 35. Matt. xiii. 20. John ii. 23—25. Acts viii. 13, comp. verse 20—23, Isa. lviii. 2, where it is said of the wicked, that "they delight to know my ways," and "they take delight in approaching to God." Comp. also 1 K. xxi. 27—29. 1 John iii. 9. Ps. cxix. 3. Many other passages of the like tenor could be adduced, in order to show that a *qualified* sense is to be put on such expressions. Above all, John xv. 22—24. Matt. vi. 24. Luke xvi. 13 and xiv. 26, show that very strong expressions of this kind are to be modified according to the nature of the case which is under consideration.

In accordance with such examples, and with the whole context, I cannot hesitate to say, that verse 22 only expresses in a more intense form and with more feeling, what is simply expressed in verse 16, σύμφημι τῷ νόμῳ. The approbation, complacency (so to speak), which reason and conscience yield to the divine law as holy and good, is strongly expressed indeed; but not more so than in the cases to which the reader is referred above, and about the exegesis of which there can be no disagreement. In fact the very next verse shows that the apostle cannot here be understood to mean the pleasure which a regenerate and filial spirit takes in the divine law; for this, as chap. viii. 1—17 most clearly shows, would lead the person who might possess it to "walk after the Spirit" and not "after the flesh;" while here, the very individual who "delights in the law of God after the inner man," is at the same time represented as being under the actual dominion of the law of sin and death, and led to destruction by it. Is this the real state of a child of God? Comp. viii. 9—14.

(23) *But I perceive another law in my members, warring against the law of my mind*, βλέπω δὲ . . . . μου. Δέ *adversative* or *disjunctive ; i. e.*, notwithstanding my reason and conscience strongly approve of the divine law, yet I do not obey it; for there is another law directly opposed to it, viz., the law dictated by my carnal passions and desires. — Νόμος must of course mean not *law* in the sense of *precepts*, but *a predominating tendency, i. e.*, it has a figurative or secondary sense, kindred to the meaning which we often give it, in speaking of *the laws of nature, the laws of fluids*, etc. Μέλεσι is only another designation of σῶμα, σάρξ, or ἄνθρωπος σαρκικός; comp. verse 5. The ground of employing νόμος, in this case, is paronomasia; for it stands as the offset to another kind of νόμος mentioned in the preceding clause — As to νοός (Gen. of νοῦς), it evidently means the same thing as the ἔσω ἄνθρωπος above. — This law not only *wars against* the law of the inner man, but actually overcomes it — αἰχμαλωτίζοντά με . . . . μου, lit. *making me a captive to the law of sin which is in my members, i. e.*, reducing me to entire subjection unto, placing me altogether at the disposal of, the law of sin or carnal self. Αἰχμαλωτίζοντα comes from αἰχμή *a spear* and ἁλόω *to take, seize upon*, and belongs to the later Greek. Captives taken in war were put to death, or kept or sold as slaves, at the pleasure of the victor. The meaning therefore is, that the law of sin had entire rule or control, notwithstanding the *inner man* decided against it. And can such be the *habitual* state of any real Christian ?

If the reader is in any measure perplexed with the question, How could the *other law* in his members bring him into captivity to the law of sin, when the law of sin, *i. e.*, a predominating sinful propensity is the very thing designated by both expressions? The obvious answer is, that here, as in verses 17, 20, sin is *personified*, and the carnal man is represented as being ruled over or subdued and made captive by it. The difficulty is merely of a rhetorical nature, and belongs only to the *mode* of representation.

(24) *Wretched man that I am ! Who shall deliver me from the body which occasions this death* or *condemnation ?* ταλαίπωρος . . . . τούτου. No wonder that the sinner, whose conscience has been awakened by the law of God, and who has been brought by bitter experience to see that all which reason and conscience do for him proves ineffectual as to the actual control of his lusts and passions — no wonder that he should be constrained, in view of the dreadful condemnation which seems to await him, to exclaim, "Wretched man that I am !" Well may he express a wish, too, for deliverance from the predominating power of his

bodily carnal lusts and inclinations; which, in spite of all the remonstrances that his awakened conscience makes, continue to expose him to the curse of the divine law, yea to its aggravated penalty.

The body of this death, τοῦ σώματος τοῦ θανάτου τούτου is construed by some as being equivalent to σῶμα θνητόν, *i. e., frail, dying body.* The sentiment would then be: 'Oh, that I might die, or be liberated from this mortal body!' This would, in the connection here presented, be the language of despair; like that of Job when in deep distress, iii. 3 — 11. x. 18. But although this is a *possible,* it does not seem to be the probable sense, as the comparison of it with chap. viii. 2 shows. Σῶμα I understand here (so not unfrequently elsewhere) as equivalent to σάρξ, *i. e.,* as designating the seat of *carnal* desires. In such a sense σάρξ stands opposed to πνεῦμα, in John iii. 6. Rom. viii. 9, 5, 6. Θανάτου is the Genitive of *effect,* as grammarians say, *i. e.,* it is a Genitive which marks or designates the effect produced by σῶμα; and this latter word designates the agent, viz., *carnal desire* in natural men, which leads to death or condemnation; comp. viii. 6. Comp. verse 13, where ἁμαρτία is said to *work death ;* which *sin* is only a personification of the carnal appetites, and dwells in the carnal man; see verses 17, 20, and comp. verse 18. So here it is intimated of the body, which is the abode of this ἁμαρτία, that it is the cause of death.

(25) *I thank God, through Jesus Christ, our Lord,* εὐχαριστῶ . . . . ἡμῶν,* viz., that there is deliverance; an exclamation from sympathy for the guilty and wretched sufferer, who had just been described. It should be read as in a *parenthesis,* inasmuch as it breaks in altogether upon the thread of discourse, and is simply an anticipation of what is about to follow in chap. viii.

Wherefore I the same person serve with the mind the law of God, but with the flesh the law of sin, ἄρα οὖν . . . . ἁμαρτίας. A summary of the whole preceding representation, as ἄρα οὖν denotes, in respect to the contest which he had been describing. The sum of all is: ' While my *mind, i. e.,* reason and conscience, takes part with the law of God and approves its sanctions, my carnal part obtains the actual predominance, and brings me into a state of condemnation and ruin.' Why should the apostle prefer νοῦς here and in verse 23, to πνεῦμα the natural and usual antithesis of σάρξ ? The obvious answer seems to be, that he especially designs to characterize the intellectual, rational, and moral ἐγώ of man, as being that part of him which approves the

---

* The text here is very doubtful. Lachmann, Alford and others prefer the reading χάρις τῷ Θεῷ διὰ 'Ιησοῦ, etc. The idea is nearly the same, whichever text we adopt.

law of God. — Αὐτὸς ἐγώ, *I myself;* so designated here, as it would seem, in order to distinguish the ἐγώ now introduced (*self* in the usual and comprehensive sense), from the ἐγώ *carnal* and *internal* which he had all along been employing, *i. e.*, the *two selves* which he had been representing. The ἐγὼ αὐτός, then is the same person (as we say), who has, while in a law-state, two minds or inclinations in him. I do not perceive any need of the difficulties which some commentators have made here.

But what follows from all this? Just what the writer set out to prove, viz., (1) That the law of God, which has reason and conscience on its side, is not to be accused as being the efficient cause of sin; but that the indulgence of the sinner's own evil passions is the direct cause of his guilt and misery. (2) That the law, with all its holiness and justice, and goodness, and even with reason and conscience on its side, is unable to control the person who is yet under it, and is destitute of the grace of the gospel. From all this follows the grand deduction which the apostle intends to make, viz., that we must be "under grace," in order to subdue our sinful passions and desires. In other words: "Christ is our ἁγιασμός, as well as our δικαιοσύνη."

And now, at the close of this whole representation we may well ask; What stronger proof could the apostle produce, than that which he has brought forward, in order to show that the law is ineffectual as the means of subduing the power of sin and of sanctifying sinners? The law with all its terrors and strictness, even when reason and conscience are on its side, cannot deliver ἐκ τοῦ σώματος τοῦ θανάτου τούτο. On the contrary, its very restraints are the occasion of the sinner's guilt being aggravated, because his passions are excited by them to more vehement opposition. Does not all this fully and satisfactorily establish the assertion implied in verse 5, τὰ παθήματα τῶν ἁμαρτιῶν τὰ διὰ τοῦ νόμου? And yet, with what admirable caution and prudence is the whole of this nice and difficult discussion conducted? The law stands fully vindicated. Even the sinner himself, who abuses it to his own aggravated guilt and ruin, is obliged to concede that it is holy, and just, and good. But with all its excellence and glory, with all its promises and threatenings, it never did and never can redeem one soul from death, nor "hide a multitude of sins." Christ is, after all, our only and all-sufficient Saviour; his is "the only name given under heaven among men whereby we can be saved." He is "our wisdom, our *justification,* our *sanctification,* and our redemption." What then becomes of all the vain and selfish hopes of the legalist? The apostle has scattered them to the winds, and showed that 'no man can come unto the Father, except by the Son.'

That there is, after all, adequate help for the poor perishing sinner, the apostle next proceeds to show. What the law could not accomplish, Christ has effected. That control over the carnal passions and desires, which no legal penalties and no remonstrances of reason and conscience would give to him, the grace of the Holy Spirit given through the gospel, does impart. No longer does he live to the flesh; no more does sin have a habitual and supreme control over him. Such is the happy state to which the perishing sinner comes, by being brought ὑπὸ χάριν; and this, he has abundant assurance, will be a permanent state, *i. e.*, his 'grace will be crowned with glory.' Such is the theme of the next chapter. For additional hints respecting the grounds on which chap. vii. 5 — 25 has been interpreted, as having respect to a person who is *under the law* and *not under grace*, see the *Excursus* upon this chapter.

CHAP. VIII. 1—11.

In the preceding chapter (verses 7—25), the apostle has illustrated and enforced the proposition made in chap. vii 5, viz., that while in a carnal state, our sinful passions are not only exercised, but that they are even rendered more vigorous or energetic by reason of the restraints which the divine law puts upon them; and consequently, that they 'bring forth fruit unto death.' The law, then, being thus abused by our unholy inclinations and desires, and made the occasion of increasing our sin, and enhancing our condemnation, can never be the means of our salvation or deliverance from that very penalty which itself pronounces on all transgressors

The present chapter exhibits the *antithesis* of all this. It is a commentary upon vii. 6, or at least an enlargement and illustration of the sentiment there exhibited. As verse 6 there is the antithesis of verse 5; so here viii 1—11 is the antithesis of vii. 7—25

(1) *Now then*, ἄρα νῦν, *i. e.*, now agreeably to this, or in accordance with what has been said. Ἄρα is here, as usually, *illative*, at least in part. But it does not stand connected with the next preceding sentence. The reader must go back beyond the illustration in vii. 7 — 25, to vii. 6, and vii. 4, in order to find the connection of the ἄρα νῦν here.* The course of the sentiment is thus: 'Since ye have been absolved from your legal state, *i. e.*, since ye have quit your hope of being sanctified and saved by the law, and have become united to Christ in order that

---

* Meyer, Alford, and others, refer this directly to the 25th verse: I myself with my mind serve, etc. There is then, *now* no condemnation, i e. because *with your mind*, and that mind *dwelt in and led by the spirit of Christ*, you serve, delight in the law of God. But it seems far more natural to refer it to the general idea in the previous discussion · since you are not under law, but under grace, there is *now*, etc.

you may bring forth fruit unto God and serve him in newness of spirit, there is no condemnation to you in your present state.' This of course implies that there would have been condemnation to them, had they remained under the law.

No condemnation, οὐδὲν . . . . κατάκριμα, here means, of course, *no condemnation* which is to be carried into execution, *no penalty* actually to be inflicted. The gospel condemns all sin either in believers or others, with even more strictness than the law (see Matt. v.); but under it a way of pardon is provided, by which the condemned may obtain remission of the penalty that they have incurred.

The subject of condemnation is suggested here by the previous exclamation : Τίς με ῥύσεται ἐκ τοῦ σώματος τοῦ θανάτου τούτου; Besides, sin and condemnation are inseparably connected; and hence it is, that in verse 2 the apostle speaks of "deliverance from sin and death" by the power and grace of the gospel. The subject of *death* or *condemnation* is, however, merely *secondary* here; for chaps. i. — v. fully treat of this. It is *sanctification*, and not justification which, as has been repeatedly remarked, is the main subject of discussion here. This is made quite plain by verse 3, seq.

To those who are in Christ, τοῖς ἐν Χριστῷ Ἰησοῦ, *i. e.,* those who are truly and spiritually united to Christ; comp. 2 Cor. v. 17. Rom. xvi. 7 — 11. Phil. i. 1. 1 Cor. i. 2. So Erasmus : Qui in Christo insiti sunt. The ground of this idiom, is the *spiritual* union which exists between the Head of the church and its members; comp. Eph. v. 30. 1 Cor. vi. 15. xii. 27. Eph. iv. 15, 16 John xvii. 11, 21, 23. xiv. 20. 1 John iv. 13. iii. 24.

The phrase, μὴ κατὰ . . . . πνεῦμα, is marked by Knapp as spurious, and is omitted by Mill, Semler, Bengel, Griesbach, Vater, Lachmann, and Ruckert. It is omitted in manuscripts C., D., F., G.; also in many versions and fathers. Only the last clause, however, *i. e.,* ἀλλὰ κατα πνεῦμα, is omitted in manuscripts A., B.; also in the Vulgate, Syriac, and Armenian versions; likewise in Basil, Chrysostom, and many of the fathers. It is a matter of little or no importance whether the words are received or rejected, either in whole or in part, so far as the sense of the whole passage is concerned. The very same words occur again in verse 4; and accordingly many critics have supposed that they are not genuine here. But we may as well attempt to prove the spuriousness of verse 4 by assuming that it is a mere repetition of this, as the spuriousness of this by assuming it to be a repetition of verse 4. The *external* evidence only makes the genuineness of it doubtful. The sense is : 'Who do not live in such a manner as to gratify the desires of the flesh, but walk in such a manner as accords with tne desires which the spirit imparts,' and the whole clause is epexegetical, and added in order to characterize *those who are in Christ Jesus.*

(2) The word νόμος here will be best understood by referring back to vii. 21, 23, 25, where, in νόμον, ἕτερον νόμον, and νόμῳ ἁμαρτίας, the word means *dictate* (as we say), *dominatio, jussum, præceptum.* As νόμος ἁμαρτίας means *dictate of sin,* so νόμος Πνεύματος (the opposite of νόμος ἁμαρτίας) must mean *dictate of the Spirit, i. e., the law of the new man, which results from the influences of the spirit, who imparts life in Christ Jesus, or true Christian life.*

Of the Spirit of life in Christ Jesus, πνεύματος τῆς ζωῆς ἐν Χριστῷ Ἰησοῦ, *i. e.,* of the Spirit which imparts true, quickening, Christian influence or a Christian disposition; comp. as to the influences of the Spirit, verses 9, 11 below; also 1 Cor. ii. 10, 12. xii. 4, 7, 11, 13. Something different from the natural powers or the natural conscience of men is meant, as is plain, from comparing this with what is asserted of the natural conscience in vii. 15 — 25; when the inefficacy of the natural conscience to control the passions and to free the sinner from the condemning sentence of God's holy law is conspicuous. Ζωῆς is *abstract* for *concrete,* designating quality and holding the place of an adjective; *i. e., life-giving, quickening.* Ἐν Χριστῷ Ἰησοῦ means the same as in verse 1. The sentiment then is this: 'The dictate of or the inclination imparted by the Spirit, who quickens those that once were dead in trespasses and sins, and gives them the predominant inclination to live in Christ."

This influence of the Spirit, Paul goes on to say, *frees from the law of sin and* [from] *death.* Here (as this is the antithesis of the former clause of the verse), *the law of sin* means *the dictate* [jussum or impetus] *of sin,* which leads to death or condemnation. To suppose ἀπό to be repeated or implied before τοῦ θανάτου, seems to be the most correct method of explaining the phrases; yet, if any one prefers, he may construe it thus: 'The law, viz., impetus, which leads to sin and condemnation.' The apostle does not mean to say, that Christians who are under the influences of 'the Spirit of life in Christ Jesus,' are perfectly sinless, but that they are freed from the *predominating* power of sinful inclination, such as is described in the preceding chapter, verses 7 — 23, and such as subjects them to the penalty of the divine law. More than this need not be attached to his words; and more than this cannot properly be attached to them, when the antithesis in the preceding chapter is taken into the account, or when facts themselves are regarded.

(3) *For that which the law could not effect,* or *that which was*

impossible for the law, τὸ γὰρ ἀδύνατον τοῦ νόμου,* viz., that which the law of works could not effect or accomplish. What that is, is designated by the sequel, viz., the subjugation of sin or the sinful affections and lusts of men, the slaying of the *carnal* man. This, as the preceding chapter abundantly shows, could not be effected by the law; which served rather to irritate and rouse up the carnal man than to subjugate and destroy him. Γάρ is prefixed to a clause introduced for the sake of illustration or confirmation.

Because it was weak through the flesh, ἐν ᾧ ἠσθένει διὰ τῆς σαρκός, *i. e.,* because, through the strength of our carnal inclinations and desires, it was unable to regulate our lives so that we should be perfect or entirely free from sin; comp. vii. 14 — 25. Σάρξ here, as often elsewhere, designates carnal appetites or inclinations.

What the law of works could not effect, ὁ Θεὸς . . . . ἁμαρτίας, *God sending his own Son in the likeness of our sinful flesh, i. e.,* God sending his Son, with a body, or having a nature, like that of corrupt and sinful men [did accomplish]. Ἐποίησε, therefore, or some verb of an equivalent meaning, should doubtless be supplied. Others translate thus: 'As to the impossibility of the law,' etc. But the idea in this case seems to be left in an imperfect state. The simple meaning is: 'What the law could not accomplish, God by the mission of his Son did accomplish.' As to ὁμοιώματι σαρκὸς ἁμαρτίας, comp. John. i. 14. Rom. i. 3. Heb. ii. 14, 17. iv. 15. Phil. ii. 7. Gal. iv. 4. 1 John iv. 2, 3. 1 Tim. iii. 16. The phrase ἐν ὁμοιώματι does not mean, as the Docetæ construed it, merely an *apparent* likeness of human nature and not a real one; for in Heb. ii. 17, Christ is said ὁμοιωθῆναι κατὰ πάντα, in respect to his brethren, *i. e.,* men. That Jesus possessed a nature *really* and *truly* like our own, is established beyond all doubt by the passage above quoted, and others of the like tenor. No less certain is it that he did not on that account become a sinner; see Heb. iv. 15. 2 Cor. v. 21. Heb. vii. 26. The idea therefore in the expression before us, is, that Christ took on him such a *physical* nature as sinful men possess, with all the powers, faculties, and susceptibilities of soul and body, which belong to human nature. Accordingly the apostle represents him as having the *sympathies* of our nature, and as feeling the power of temptation in like manner with us, although without sin; Heb. iv. 15. It is not *susceptibility* of being excited by sinful objects, then,

* According to some, τὸ . . . ἀδύνατον is in the nominative, and in apposition with the clause κατέκρινε, κ. τ. λ. The idea is *that which is impossible for the law,* God condemned in the flesh, i e this last, the condemning, etc., is what is impossible for the law to accomplish

which makes men sinners, but it is the *yielding* to this excitement. This Jesus did not.

The phrase καὶ περὶ ἁμαρτίας may be equivalent to καὶ προσφορᾷ περὶ ἁμαρτίας, *and by an offering for sin.* The *elliptical* phrase, περὶ ἁμαρτίας, is frequently used instead of the entire one; comp. Heb. x. 18, with x. 8, 6. Lev. iv. 3. Num. viii. 8. Ps. xxxix. 6 (Sept.) There can be no serious difficulty in regard to such an ellipsis. Moreover, that ἁμαρτία alone is sometimes used for *sin-offering* (חַטָּאת), seems to be altogether probable from 2 Cor. v. 21, ἁμαρτίαν ἐποίησε; also from Heb, ix. 28, χωρὶς ἁμαρτίας. In this way περὶ ἁμαρτίας would be construed as designating the way or means by which Christ condemned or destroyed sin, viz., by giving himself an *offering for sin*, and so procuring sanctifying grace for sinners.

But although I adopted this interpretation in the former edition of this work, it seems better to take περί in some of its more usual meanings; *in respect to, on account of, for the sake of, for, concerning, respecting, because of, about,* etc. In significations so multiform and generic as these, it is easy to perceive that the latitude in which περί is used must be very great. In connection with *expiations, sacrifices,* etc., it often has the meanings: *for, on account of, because of,* which have a direct bearing on the present case, *e. g.,* Mark i. 44, 'Offer what is commanded, περὶ τοῦ καθαρισμοῦ,' *i. e., for the sake of* accomplishing or effecting the requisite legal purification; so also in Luke v. 14. In Luke ii. 27: περὶ αὐτοῦ, *in his behalf, on his account, for him.*' So in Heb. v. 3, ' offerings περὶ τοῦ λαοῦ, *for the people, i. e.,* in their behalf.' But when ἁμαρτία follows περί, there must of necessity be a different shade of sense. Thus in Heb. x. 18 προσφορὰ περὶ ἁμαρτίας, Heb. x. 26 θυσία περὶ ἁμαρτιῶν, Heb. x. 6, 8 περὶ ἁμαρτίας (elliptically for προσφορὰ περὶ ἁμαρτίας, comp. v. 18), 1 Peter iii. 18 περὶ ἁμαρτίας ἔπαθε, 1 John ii. 2. iv. 10 ἱλασμὸς περὶ τῶν ἁμαρτιῶν, it must be understood that the sacrifice was *occasioned by* sin, and that it is offered *in relation to* sin, *i. e.,* in order to make atonement for it. So I would construe περὶ ἁμαρτίας in the verse before us. It is connected with πέμψας τὸν ἑαυτοῦ Υἱόν, and the apostle makes two affirmations, viz., (*a*) God sent his Son in the likeness of men, *i. e.,* with the nature of those whom he was to redeem. (*b*) God sent him καὶ περὶ ἁμαρτίας, *also on account of sin, i. e.,* to make atonement for it, to prevent its evil effects. The change of prepositions, (ἐν being first employed and then περί); and the consequent change of construction, is not unusual in the writings of Paul. Περὶ ἁμαρτίας here, seems plainly to be chosen for the sake of the paronomasia, with ὁμοιώματι σαρκὸς ἁμαρτίας. And for a like reason, and in reference to the two last words of this clause, he says immediately afterwards, κατέκρινε τὴν ἁμαρτίαν ἐν τῇ σαρκί, i. e., the sin already mentioned (the article is used here before ἁμαρτίαν), and the sin which has its seat in the flesh, i. e., in our carnal passions and appetites, τῷ σαρκί (also with the article). The whole phraseology is *paronomasiac* in a peculiar degree.

Condemned sin in the flesh, κατέκρινε .... σαρκί, i. e., (as many explain) condemned the sin which fleshly appetites occasion. The word κατέκρινε has occasioned much difficulty among critics. The reason why it is employed here, seems to be, that the writer had just used κατάκριμα in verse 1. The antithesis stands thus: 'There is now no κατάκριμα for Christians; but there is a κατάκριμα of their carnal appetites and desires;' i. e., Christians are indeed delivered from the penalty of death, but their sinful lusts are condemned to death or slain, in consequence of the provision made by Jesus Christ for their deliverance. In such a paronomasiac use of words, we are not to feel obliged to remain by the mere literal and usual meaning, but to give the latitude which the nature of the connection requires. The meaning of the apostle evidently is, that instead of being condemned themselves, Christians experience, through the grace of Christ, the condemnation of the sin within them which works their ruin. This very same idea is insisted on in different language at large in chap. vi. 2 — 11, where the *old man* is represented as *crucified, mortified*, etc. The expected consequence of κατέκρινε ἁμαρτίαν here is plainly that Christians should yield obedience to the divine precepts; ἵνα τὸ δικαίωμα κ. τ. λ., verse 4. And so according to chap. vi. 11 seq., he whose *old man is crucified* lives henceforth to God. Such of course is the consequence of the carnal affections *being put to death*, or (to use the language of our text) *condemned*, i. e., to death, (κατέκρινε not ἔκρινε). All this is effected by the mission of Christ, who came to save his people from the *power* as well as from the penalty of sin.

The words ἐν σαρκί here may be joined with ἁμαρτίαν, and so indicate what Paul has so often declared in the preceding context, viz., that sin is occasioned by *fleshly* appetites and desires; and so the majority of expositors understand it. In such a case τὴν ἐν σαρκί would be the usual and full mode of expression; but the article may be omitted; see New Test. Gram. § 92. *b*. But ἐν σαρκί may be joined in sense with κατέκρινε, and so indicate the manner or means in or by which Christ condemned sin, viz., by assuming our fleshly nature (ἐν ὁμοιώματι σαρκὸς ἁμαρτίας). Many prefer this construction as the more apposite and congruous. Either sense is good, and allowed by the idiom of the apostle.

The course of thought, which is somewhat obscured by the arrangement of the words, may be made plain to the reader by a somewhat different position of some parts of the sentence. *E. g.*, 'God sent his own Son, in the likeness of men and on account of their sins, and destroyed the power of sin in their carnal nature, (which the law could not possibly effect because it was deprived of its energy through the strength of the carnal affections), in order that the precepts of the law which demands holiness of life, might be obeyed by those who walk according to the dictates of his spirit.'

(4) *The precepts of the law*, τὸ δικαίωμα τοῦ νόμου. So in the Septuagint δικαίωμα is used to translate חֹק, מִשְׁפָּט, and מִצְוָה. Πληρωθῇ ἐν ἡμῖν, *might be accomplished or done by us;* viz., that we, who are influenced and guided by the Spirit, might be obedient to divine precepts requiring holiness of life, and no longer devoted to the lusts of the flesh.

Here then we have a view of the end which is accomplished by the death of Christ; viz., the sanctification of believers. This is one of the passages, which shows the whole drift of the discourse in chap. vii. and viii. 1 — 11. Ἐν ἡμῖν may be rendered *by us*, but better, *in us*, so as to designate the internal spiritual influence of the death of Christ upon believers, inasmuch as it causes a conformity of spirit or heart to him. Some understand this verse as having respect to an *imputed* and *vicarious* fulfilling of the law, or the imputation of Christ's obedience to believers. But the context shows plainly, that *actual* sanctification, the mortification or death of sin, is here the subject of discussion.

(5) *For they who are in a carnal state, have regard to carnal things*, οἱ γὰρ . . . . φρονοῦσιν. Γάρ *illustrantis*. Κατὰ σάρκα is here used, because the same phrase stands in the preceding verse. Εἶναι κατὰ σάρκα, *to be according to the flesh*, does not differ in sense from εἶναι σαρκικοί, or from ἐν σαρκὶ εἶναι, when taken in the figurative sense. The meaning plainly is, 'to act in accordance with carnal desires and affections.'

But they who are in a spiritual state, have regard to spiritual things, οἱ δὲ . . . πνεύματος. Comp. verses 2 and 9 — 11. Οἱ κατὰ πνεῦμα being the antithesis of οἱ κατὰ σάρκα, is easily understood.

(6) *For the carnal mind is death*, τὸ γὰρ . . . θάνατος. Γάρ *illustrantis* again, where we might naturally expect δέ. However, I take verse 6 to be co-ordinate with verse 5, and the γάρ here to indicate an illustration of what is said in verse 4. So Ruckert. The connection seems to be thus: 'The precepts of the law are obeyed by those who walk not after the flesh, but after the Spirit; but carnal men will not give heed to spiritual things,

and their pursuits lead to death; while eternal happiness, is the consequence or fruit of a *spiritual mind, i. e.*, a mind conformed to the dictates of the Spirit.' This is not *direct* confirmation of what is asserted in verse 4, but is an illustration of the condition there described, by showing its connections and results, and also those of the opposite condition. Φρόνημα σαρκός means a mind or will conformed to carnal passions and appetites.

(7) Next follows the ground or reason why this is and will be so, *because the carnal mind is enmity toward God,* διότι . . . . εἰς Θεόν, *i. e.*, is inimical to God, or (in plain terms) hates him, dislikes his precepts, his character, and his ways. So the sequel, τῷ γὰρ κ. τ. λ. The abstract noun ἔχθρα, is here used for the adjective ἐχθρά, *inimical, unfriendly.* The proof that the sentiment just uttered is correct, follows in the next clause.

For it is not subject to the law of God, nor indeed can be, τῷ γὰρ . . . . δύναται; *i. e.*, it does not obey the precepts of God's law, nor can it obey them. The very nature of a carnal mind consists in gratifying *carnal* and *sinful* desires, viz., those desires which the law of God prohibits. Of course this mind or disposition, so far as it prevails, leads to the very opposite of subjection to God's law, *i. e.*, leads to disobedience. From its very nature this cannot be otherwise; for when it is otherwise, the mind is no longer carnal.

Upon this passage the advocates of metaphysical reasoning with respect to *ability* in men have speculated, and disputed not a little. What is the *cannot?* One Answers: It is *a will not;* another, that it is to be literally understood, without any abatement. So Luther, *de Servo Arbitrio;* and so many others. That the phrase stands in the way of Pelagianism, and indeed of all *unqualified* assertions of ability in the carnal man; at least, that it may be easily and naturally so construed, it is not difficult to see. Still what the natural and physiological powers of the sinner are, is not here the subject of discussion. Thus much the writer appears to say, and no more, viz., that the φρόνημα σαρκός is not subject to God's law, and cannot be subject to it. And is not this plainly and obviously true? So far as φρόνημα σαρκός goes, it is directly the opposite of subjection in its very nature. "How," says Augustine (and much to the point), "can snow be warmed? For when it is melted and becomes warm, it is no longer snow." And so it is with the carnal mind. Just so long as it exists, and in just such proportion as it exists, it is and will be enmity against God and disobey his law. But whether the sinner who cherishes this φρόνημα σαρκός is not actuated by other principles also, and urged by other motives, and possessed of ability, arising from other sources, to turn from his evil ways, does not seem to be satisfactorily determined by this expression. What Chrysostom says, deserves very serious attention: "He does not affirm that the bad man cannot become a good one; but that, while he continues to be bad, he cannot possibly obey God. When converted, however, it is easy to be good and to obey God."

(8) *Those then who are in the flesh, cannot please God*, οἱ δὲ . . . . δύνανται. The particle δέ is *continuative* here; comp. its use in Rom. viii. 28. Mark xvi. 8. Acts xxiii. 13. Rom. iii. 22. 1 Cor. x. 11. xv. 56. James ii. 15. Οἱ δὲ ἐν σαρκὶ κ. τ. λ. resumes the sentiment contained in τὸ φρόνημα τῆς σαρκὸς ἔχθρα κ. τ. λ. and repeats it in another form. Moreover, this latter form has special reference to vii. 5, 18.

Those who are ἐν σαρκί, are those, "who are *not* led by the Spirit of God," comp. verses 9, 13, 14; who follow fleshly desires and appetites. All men who are not regenerated or sanctified, who are in a natural state, are ἐν σαρκί, *carnal*, and therefore are influenced and guided by their carnal desires and affections; comp. John iii. 6. 1 Cor. ii. 14. Eph. ii. 1—3. Col. ii. 13. Consequently, as may well be supposed, Θεῷ ἀρέσαι οὐ δύνανται, *they cannot please God; i. e.*, while they live in such a state, and are led on by such carnal desires, they can do nothing which is pleasing to God. The οὐ δύνανται here is to be understood in the same way as the οὐ δύναται in the preceding verse.

(9) The opposite character is now brought into view, in order to render the sentiment more striking. *You, however, are not in the flesh but in the Spirit, provided the Spirit of God dwells in you*, ὑμεῖς δὲ . . . . ὑμῖν. The δέ here is *distinctive*. If the Spirit of God dwells in any one, he cannot be in a carnal state; for the Spirit dwells in and guides only those who are *the sons of God* (verse 14), and therefore his friends, verse 17. Such cannot be at enmity with God. The πνεῦμα Θεοῦ which is here mentioned, is the same as that to which the writer has all along referred. In the next verse it is called πνεῦμα Χριστοῦ. As to the *dwelling* of the Spirit in Christians, comp. 1 Cor. iii. 16, 17. vi. 19. 2 Cor. vi. 16; and with these texts comp. John xvii. 23. xiv. 23—26.

The Spirit of Christ, πνεῦμα Χριστοῦ, is either the Spirit which Christ imparts, or the Spirit which makes us like to Christ. The first should seem the more probable meaning, when we compare John xiv. 15—18, 26. xv. 26. It is remarkable that in this short paragraph (verses 9—11), πνεῦμα Χριστοῦ, Χριστός, and τὸ πνεῦμα τοῦ ἐγείραντος Ἰησοῦν (i. e., πνεῦμα Θεοῦ Πατρός), should be exchanged for each other, and plainly stand for one and the same thing. Is not this evidence, that the apostle saw and felt no inconsistency in speaking of Christ, and of the Spirit of God or of Christ, as *in some respects* distinct, and yet in others as constituting a unity of nature? There seems to me to be an entire simplicity in the mode in which Paul has treated this subject; a subject which has unhappily been made so complex and intricate, by the subtilties of the schools. The simple *facts*, without speculation or nice distinctions, that Christ and the Spirit are *divine*, are one in nature with God, and yet in some respect distinct from the Father, seem to be the basis of the apostle's language here and elsewhere; may the time soon come, when Christians shall also be content with simple facts relative to this great subject, without useless speculations.

Possesseth not, οὐκ ἔχει; *i. e.*, if the Spirit of Christ does not habitually dwell in and influence any one. — *He is not his*, οὐκ ἔστιν αὐτοῦ, *i. e.*, he is no Christian, he is not a true disciple or follower of Christ. The δέ at the beginning of the clause seems to be *continuative*, and therefore may be translated *now*. If any choose they may render it as adversative, *but*.

(10) *But if Christ be in you*, εἰ Χριστὸς ἐν ὑμῖν, *i. e.*, if he dwell in you by his Spirit, if ye have the Spirit of Christ, if ye are habitually influenced by him in your lives and conversation. The δέ here is plainly *adversative*.

The body indeed is mortified on account of sin, but the spirit lives on account of righteousness, τὸ μὲν σῶμα . . . . δικαιοσύνη. There are three methods in which this passage has been interpreted.

One class of interpreters explain it thus: 'The body is dead *in respect to sin, i. e.*, sin has no more power to excite its evil appetites and desires. The soul has, moreover, the principle of spiritual life; and he who raised up Jesus will also give to your bodies [viz., at the resurrection], a new principle of spiritual life or animation.' So for substance, Origen, Theodoret, Clarius, Grotius, Raphel, Taylor, Melancthon, Bucer, and others.

The objection to this is, that it renders it necessary to construe διά before the Accusative as meaning *in respect to, in reference to;* which can hardly be admitted. Moreover it destroys the antithesis in verse 10. It renders quite insipid, also, the antithesis between σῶμα νεκρόν in verse 10, and ζωοποιήσει τὰ θνητὰ σώματα in verse 11.

Another method of interpreting the phrase in question is this: 'The body must die [physically] because of sin; but the spiritual part lives and even the body itself will be made to live at the period of the resurrection, *i. e.*, it will be raised up and become like Christ's own glorious body.' So Tholuck, Flatt, Calvin,

Augustine, Beza, and others. Thus it would foreclose an objection which would arise in the mind of some reader, who might ask: 'Are *all* the consequences of sin, then, removed by the death of Christ?' To this the apostle may be viewed as replying in the verse before us: 'No, not absolutely and entirely all. Natural death still remains. But a glorious resurrection will follow this; so that in the end all its consequences will be done away.' But there are weighty objections against this mode of interpretation. If νεκρόν is to be understood in its *literal* sense, then of course the following ζωή must be understood literally also; and what sense would it make to say, that 'the soul has *natural life* because of righteousness,' when all know that the wicked are as immortal as the righteous? But if νεκρόν means *dead* in the sense of having our carnal passions *mortified*, then ζωή would of course designate the peace and happiness of the soul or spirit.

With Chrysostom, Erasmus, and others, I understand σῶμα νεκρόν in verse 10, as not indicating [physical] death; nor yet as meaning *death* in the sense of being *dead in trespasses and sins*, *i. e.*, destitute of spiritual life, or in a state of death or condemnation; but as used in the same sense as θάνατος in vi. 4, 5; as expressing an idea exactly kindred with συνεσταυρώθη and καταργηθῇ τὸ σῶμα τῆς ἁμαρτίας, in vi. 6; the same with ἀποθανῶν in vi. 7; ἀποθάνωμεν in vi. 8; and νεκρούς in vi. 11. That the writer did connect vin. 10, 11, in his own mind with vi. 4 — 13, appears quite plain from his diction and general course of thought. In vi. 12 he calls the body θνητόν, just as in viii. 11; and in the former passage he evidently means to designate by it a corporeal, material, perishable body; which is also the sense, for substance, in viii. 11.

But all the words above mentioned, in chap. vi., serve merely to characterize what we call *the mortification* [the putting to death] *of the body, i. e.*, the subduing and mortifying our carnal desires and affections, which are cherished by or originate from the body. So I understand νεκρόν here (as I do νεκρούς in vi. 11), to designate, viz., a state in which *the old man is crucified*, in which the carnal desires of the body are mortified and subdued. This exegesis has, at least, plain analogy on its side. Interpreted in this way the sentiment of the whole passage would run thus: 'If the Spirit of Christ dwells in any one, his body is indeed dead on account of sin, *i. e.*, the old man is crucified, or he undergoes mortification as to his bodily and sinful appetites; but his *spirit* is rendered *happy on account of righteousness, i. e.*, because of conformity to the requisitions of the gospel. Yea, if the Spirit of him who raised up Jesus from the dead dwells in any man, that same Spirit will quicken, *i. e.*, impart life to, his mortal body;' in other words, he will not suffer it to remain a mere σῶμα νεκρόν, but make it an instrument of righteousness (vi. 12, 13, 19), and give it a power of being subservient to the glory of God.

By degrees the Christian "brings under his body," and keeps it in subjection. At first it is, as it were *crucifying the old man;* but in the sequel, the grace of God makes conquest easy and even delightful. It is such a quickening of our bodies, a converting of them into "instruments of righteousness," to which the apostle seems to me here to refer. It seems to be conclusive in regard to this exegesis, that the apostle here describes the Spirit which "quickens the bodies" of Christians, as being the Spirit which *dwells in them*, ἐνοικοῦν ἐν ὑμῖν. For where is the resurrection of our physical bodies, at the last day, attributed to the *sanctifying* Spirit in believers? Very different is the statement in Col. ii. 12, 13. Eph. i. 19, 20. ii. 5, 6. Rom. vi. 4. It is, then, the Spirit who dwells in believers that is to quicken them in the sense which is here meant; and what can this be, except the one designated in vi. 12, 13, 19?

Verse 13 seems clearly to indicate that the present passage is to be understood as above explained; for there, τὰς πράξεις τοῦ σώματος θανατοῦτε appears plainly to convey the same meaning as σῶμα νεκρόν. The object of the writer, as I apprehend it, is to show Christians, that although mortification and self-denial must be practised in order to subjugate carnal desires, yet even here they may expect relief in due time. Victory repeated becomes easier. The enemy often vanquished, becomes weaker. The Spirit of Christ, in fine, brings the believer at last fully and freely to dedicate all that he has and is to the service of his Lord and Master; so that no discouragement should be felt, because the way is at first rough and difficult. It is a path which conducts to life.

(11) Εἰ δὲ τὸ . . . . ὑμῖν. *The Spirit of him who raised up Jesus from the dead*, is the Spirit of God the Father, or the Spirit of God; comp. verse 9, also Col. ii. 12, 13. Eph. i. 19, 20. ii. 5, 6. Rom. vi. 4. Εἰ δέ, *if also, if moreover;* δέ here is a *continuative*. Ζωοποιήσει, *will give life to, will animate, i. e.*, will make them active instruments. Διὰ τὸ ἐνοικοῦν . . . . ὑμῖν, *i. e.*, the same Spirit who dwells in you, will enable you to quicken the θνητὸν σῶμα or σῶμα θανάτου, which now occasions so much pain and mortification, and to make it a willing instrument of righteousness. Can all the promise that is made to Christians here be, that their bodies shall be raised up at the last day? If so, the inference might be, that the wicked will not be raised up;

which we know to be contrary to the doctrine of Paul and other New Testament writers. Such an exegesis should seem to reduce the whole passage to comparative insignificance, or else make it speak that which is contradictory to Christian doctrine.

The MSS. A., B., C. (which has αὐτῷ for αὐτοῦ) 12 Codd. minusc., and many of the fathers, exhibit the common reading here, viz., διὰ τοῦ ἐνοικοῦντος αὐτοῦ πνεύματος; while διὰ τὸ ἐνοικοῦν αὐτῷ πνεῦμα is the reading of D., E., F., G., the majority MSS. minusc., Syr., Erp., Sahid., Vul., Ital., Origen, Ephiph., Phot., Chrys., (usually,) Method., Theod., Maxim., Theoph., Œcum., Iren., Tertul., Hilar., Ruf., Sedulius. This seems to be altogether the best supported, and is preferred by Erasmus, Stephens, Mill, Bengel, Griesbach, Knapp, Koppe, and many recent critics. The internal probability is strong against the Genitive; for διά with the Gen. would denote the agent by whom the change in the bodies of Christians is to be made; whereas that agent has been already named, viz., ὁ ἐγείρας τὸν Χριστόν. The reading διὰ τὸ . . . πνεῦμα, in the Accus., of course obliges us to translate, BECAUSE OF *the Spirit which dwelleth in you.* In this way the last clause assigns a reason or ground why he who raised up Jesus from the dead, will quicken his true followers; it is because he has given them his Spirit; and having done thus much for them, he will complete the work which he has begun.

The analogy of the course of thought and diction in chap. vi., removes all serious difficulty in the interpretation here. There Christians are represented as *dead* to sin; their old man as *crucified;* and, as Christ was raised from the dead by the glorious power of the Father, so are they quickened in like manner, in order that *they may live unto God.* If therefore it should be said (as it has been), that 'inasmuch as the raising of Christ from the dead was an act of *physical* power (so to speak), in like manner the raising up of believers here must be regarded in the same light; the obvious answer is, that Paul goes through an extended comparison of the like nature in chap. vi., where the death of Christ and his resurrection are all along taken in the natural and *physiological* sense, while the death of believers and their resurrection are taken throughout in a *moral* sense. Indeed, after all which the apostle has said in chap. vi. in relation to this subject, I think there should be strong and plain reasons given for a *physiological* sense of his words here, before we can adopt it. It is contrary to his own analogy, and inapposite to his present purpose.

It has been objected: (1) that σώματα (plural) cannot be employed in the same *figurative* sense as σάρξ.' But why not? Σάρξ is not used in the plural, merely because it has no plural. Σῶμα in the singular is clearly exchanged with σάρξ (see verse 13); and σώματα in the plural as applied not to one but to *all* believers, is altogether appropriate. (2) ' Θνητός has only a physiological sense.' This is in general true, but it is manifestly employed here as the mere substitute for νεκρόν in verse 10; and this latter word confessedly has very often a figurative or *moral* sense. (3) ' Ζωοποιήσει must have a *future* meaning; but believers are *already* quickened in a moral sense.' The answer to this is, they are indeed alive as to the spirit and temper of the mind; but the process of sanctification, until all the bodily appetites are thoroughly subdued and mortified, is usually a long one, and the apostle might well employ ζωοποιήσει. Other objections have been answered for substance above.*

CHAP. VIII. 12—17.

In the preceding verses, the apostle has consummated his argument to prove that Christians, who are under grace, are the only persons who possess means adequate and ample of living devoted to the service of God, and of renouncing sin and mortifying all their sinful desires. What those under the law could not do, God, sending his Son on account of sin, and pouring out his Spirit, and giving a filial and obedient temper of mind, has accomplished. The mind is thus filled with desires of conformity to Christ, and even the body, the seat of carnal appetites and sinful desires, will be so quickened as to become an instrument of righteousness.

And what now follows? Just that which we should expect from an apotle so zealous of good works as Paul, and so grateful for the blessings of redemption, viz., an animated exhortation to live in a manner accordant with Christian obligation, and a view of the consequences which will ensue from the believer's being united to Christ.

(12) *Therefore, brethren, we are not under obligation to the flesh, to live in a carnal manner,* ἄρα οὖν . . . . ζῆν; *i. e.,* since

---

* If the apostle had referred merely to the resurrection of the body here, ἐγείρει might and probably would have been employed. But still is not that included in the complex idea? So Alford says: "The higher phase of the ζωοποιεῖν takes place in the *spirit* of man; and even of that which takes place in the body, there are two branches — one the quickening of it from being a tool of unrighteousness unto death [eternal], — the other the quickening it out of death [physical] to be a new and glorified body. And the καί joined with θνητά signifies that the working of the πνεῦμα ζωοποιοῦν shall not stop at the purely spiritual resurrection, nor at that of the body from dead works to serve the living God, but shall extend *even to the building up the spiritual body in the future new and glorious life.*" The implication that has been supposed here, that if there is a reference to physical resurrection, the wicked will not be raised, is entirely groundless; for it is only *the good*, that come into the account, and the resurrection that awaits them as participating, in a sense, with the resurrection of Christ.

the Spirit is given to us, and we have such privileges, we must not obey the lusts of the flesh. The expression is negative in form but affirmative in meaning. The writer means that we are bound not to obey the dictates of carnal appetites and desires. — Τοῦ . . . ζῆν shows the object of obligation: 'We are under no obligation — *to live*, etc.' For the use of τοῦ with the Inf., see N. Test. Gramm. § 138. 8.

(13) *For if ye live in a carnal manner, ye shall die*, εἰ γὰρ . . . . ἀποθνήσκειν; *i. e.*, if ye live carnally, ye shall come under the penalty of the divine law, which threatens death to the soul that sins. See on θάνατος, in chap. v. 12. Reiche, who all along understands θάνατος as designating *temporal* death, necessarily concedes that here it must have a *more extended* sense,' for if the death of the body only is threatened, then there is no distinction between those who live in a carnal manner, and those who do not, which would deprive the apostle's words of all meaning.

But if through the Spirit ye mortify the deeds of the body, ye shall live, εἰ δὲ . . . . ζήσεσθε; *i. e.*, if, yielding to the influence of the Spirit which dwelleth in you, ye crucify the old man with his lusts, if you suppress those deeds to which your carnal affections would lead, then ye shall live, *i. e.*, enjoy the spiritual blessedness which the gospel promises to the obedient. The exchange of σῶμα for σάρξ, in the phrase τὰς πράξεις τοῦ σώματος is plain. D., E., F., G., and many of the fathers read σαρκός for σώματος; which only shows that they understood both in the same sense here. The efforts of some to show that σῶμα means ' body as a composite organization,' and σάρξ, ' body as an animated, active, and excitable substance,' are here to no purpose; nor indeed is this in conformity with *Pauline* usage.

(14) The γάρ here introduces an *illustration* or *confirmation* of the declaration just made: that those who mortify their sinful appetites and desires, *shall live, i. e.*, such persons are led by the Spirit of God, and consequently must be the children of God; and if so, he will give them the portion which belongs to children, viz., the heavenly inheritance. *For so many as are led by the Spirit of God, they are the sons of God*, ὅσοι γάρ . . . . Θεοῦ. A *special* divine influence is here implied in ἄγονται; for if nothing but the simple means of moral suasion by objective truth is employed in guiding the children of God, how do they differ from others who enjoy the same means? If you say: 'The difference is that the former *obey* the suasion, while the latter *resist* it;' I answer: The fact is true; but then it does not reach the point of difficulty. How comes the one to *obey* the suasion, and the other to *resist* it!. What is the *first* occasion of this? If you say:

'A corrupt nature leads the impenitent to resist;' then I ask: Had not the regenerate the like corrupt nature before their change? What then is the *efficient* cause why one obeys and the other disobeys? The passage before us ascribes it to the influence of the Spirit of God. The idea here seems to be: that *those only* who are led by, *are under the controlling influence* of, the Spirit, are the *sons* of God. The inference is a necessary one, (and in accordance with our every day observation and experience,) that all men are not "the sons of God, in the sense here indicated, as not being under the controlling influence of his Spirit. *Sons of God*, υἱοὶ Θεοῦ, a term of endearment; comp. Matt. v. 9, 45. Luke vi. 35. xx. 36. Rom. viii. 19. 2 Cor. vi. 18. Gal. iii. 26. iv. 6, 7, et alib. comp. Hosea xi. 1. Ex. iv. 22, 23. See also the remarks of υἱοῦ αὐτοῦ in Rom. i. 3, with the Excursus.

(15) *For ye have not received a servile spirit, that ye should again be afraid*, οὐ γάρ . . . . . . εἰς φόβον; *i. e.*, ye have not the spirit of slaves, who fear and tremble before the dreaded severity of a master; in other words, ye are not, through fear of condemnation or death, all your life time ἔνοχοι δουλείας, Heb. ii. 15. Γάρ *illustrantis et confirmantis;* for the object of the writer is, to show that they are *sons* and not slaves. The phrases πνεῦμα δουλείας, and πνεῦμα υἱοθεσίας indicate such a spirit as slavery is wont to produce, *i. e.*, such a temper or disposition of mind as is appropriate to it; and such a spirit or temper of mind as belongs to affectionate children.

But ye have received a filial spirit, by which we cry: Abba, Father! ἀλλὰ . . . . ὁ πατήρ! That is, instead of the timid and cowering spirit of *slaves*, who tremble before their masters, we are endowed with the spirit of *children*, so that we may approach God with affection and confidence. The word Ἀββᾶ is the Chaldee אבא, sc. πατήρ! Augustine and Calvin think that, the design of using both Ἀββᾶ and ὁ πατήρ here, is to show that both Jews and Greeks, each in their own respective language, would call on God as a Father. But the same idiom is exhibited in Gal. iv. 6, and Mark xiv. 36, where, at least, such a distinction is out of question. If ὁ πατήρ here be designed for anything more than a translation of Ἀββᾶ, we may suppose the repetition to be designed for expressing intensity of child-like feeling, (as *my father, dear father,*) for this naturally prompts to a repetition of the name of a parent. So Theodoret. Ὁ πατήρ is the Nom. used instead of the Vocative; New Test. Gramm. § 21. N. 3.

(16) *The same Spirit testifies to our minds that we are the children of God*, αὐτὸ τὸ πνεῦμα . . . Θεοῦ; *i. e.*, as many inter-

pret this passage: this filial, confiding, affectionate spirit, $\pi\nu\epsilon\hat{\upsilon}\mu\alpha$ υἱοθεσίας, imparted by the Spirit of God who dwells in us, affords satisfactory evidence to our minds that we are the children of God. $\Sigma\upsilon\mu\mu\alpha\rho\tau\upsilon\rho\epsilon\hat{\iota}$ here $= \mu\alpha\rho\tau\upsilon\rho\epsilon\omega$; so $\sigma\upsilon\mu\mu\alpha\rho\tau\upsilon\rho\epsilon\omega$ is employed also in Rom. ii. 15. ix. 1, al. The sentiment of the passage thus construed would be, that the affectionate spirit which the children of God possess, is an evidence to their minds of their standing in a filial relation to him. $T\hat{\omega}\ \pi\nu\epsilon\upsilon\mu\alpha\tau\iota\ \eta\mu\hat{\omega}\nu$ means, *to our minds, animis nostris*.

On the whole, however, I am persuaded that αὐτὸ τὸ πνεῦμα is the same as πνεῦμα Θεοῦ in ver. 14, *i. e., the spirit of God*. And if the question be urged, as it is natural that it should be: "How then does the Spirit bear witness to our minds or souls, that we are the children of God?" The answer is, by imparting the *spirit of adoption* or a *filial spirit* to us. It is this, then, which affords the evidence to our minds of being in a state of *filiation*, *i. e.*, of bearing the relation to God of spiritual children. And as this spirit comes from the Spirit of God, so he may be said in this case *to bear witness*, because he is the author of that spirit which affords the evidence of our *filiation*.

That the world deny any such testimony in the hearts of believers, and that they look on it with scorn or treat it with derision, proves only that they are unacquainted with it; not that it is an illusion. It was a sensible and true remark of the French philosipher, Hemsterhuys, in regard to certain sensations which he was discussing: "Those who are so unhappy as never to have had such sensations, either through weakness of the natural organ, or because they have never cultivated them, will not comprehend me." Œuvres, I. p. 208. So Paul, elsewhere, expresses himself still more strongly: "The natural man receiveth not the things of the Spirit of God, for they are foolishness to him," 1 Cor. ii. 14.

(17) *But if children*, etc., Εἰ δὲ τέκνα καὶ κληρονόμοι, *i. e.*, if we sustain the relation of sons, then shall we be treated as such, *i. e.*, we shall be *heirs*. With τέκνα, ἐσμέν, and with κληρονόμοι, ἐσόμεθα are to be supplied. Κληρονόμοι Θεοῦ, *heirs of God*, means, possessors of that inheritance which God bestows. Δέ *continuative*.— Συγκληρονόμοι Χριστοῦ, *joint heirs with Christ;* *i. e.*, as Christ endured sufferings and was advanced to glory, in like manner shall we also be advanced to glory. We shall be made like him, be united to him, be with him in possession of the heavenly inheritance. For the manner in which Christ obtained this heritage, see and comp. Phil. ii. 8, 9. Heb. ii. 9, 10, v. 7—9; and for the comparison of believers to Christ, see 2 Tim. ii. 11, 12. Heb. xii. 2. Rev. iii. 21. John xvii. 22—24. These

texts sufficiently explain the sequel of the verse, εἴπερ κ. τ. λ. which may be rendered: "In case we suffer as he did, [in the cause of truth], in order that we may be glorified with him."

CHAP. VIII. 18—25.

THESE verses constitute one of those passages which the critics call *loci vexatissimi*. The *general* object of the passage, however, is plain. In ver. 18 the apostle asserts, that *the sufferings of the present life are not to be regarded in comparison with the glory to be revealed*, i e , future glory is great beyond all comparison or expression. Such is the proposition to be illustrated or confirmed. And the apostle proceeds in the following manner: 'Now that such a glory is to be revealed, (i e., there is a world of surpassing glory beyond the grave), the whole condition of mankind, in the present world, abundantly proves. Frail and perishable nature serves to show that no stable source of happiness can be found on earth In the midst of the sufferings and sorrows to which men are here exposed, they look forward to another and better world, where happiness without alloy and without end may be enjoyed Even the Christian, with all his hopes and joys, is compelled by sufferings and sorrows to sigh and groan, and to expect a state of real and permanent enjoyment only in heaven; so that he can only say that he is *saved* because he hopes or expects salvation in another and better world.'

The practical conclusion from all this the apostle now proceeds to draw, viz , 'that Christians, in the midst of sufferings and trials, ought not to faint or be discouraged, inasmuch as a glory to be revealed is in prospect, which should make them regard their present temporary sufferings as altogether unworthy to be accounted of.'

(18) Λογίζομαι here means *I count, reckon, regard, estimate*. The classical Greek writers employed this word rather in the sense of *computing or reckoning*, e. g., a sum of numbers, or of *estimating* a conclusion drawn from premises by the act of reasoning.

It is difficult at first sight to account for the γάρ here.* I construe in this simple manner, viz., 'We shall be glorified with Christ, *i. e.*, obtain great and eternal glory, *for* (γάρ) all the sufferings and sorrows of the present state are only temporary. All things do, and must, work together for good to those who love God.'

Παθήματα τοῦ νῦν καιροῦ means suffering such as Christians were then called to endure, or sufferings such as all men are exposed to endure in the present life. The latter seems to be

---

*It should seem to introduce the inducements which the apostle felt there were "to suffer here, εἴπερ συμπάσκομεν, κ. τ. λ." v. 17. viz., that we may attain to that state of final blessedness which Christ has prepared for his followers. v. 18—25.

the preferable sense; because the reasoning of the apostle, in the context, has respect to the whole period of our present life down to its close, when a glorious reward succeeds a life of sorrow. The Genitive here, as often elsewhere, is the *Genitivus temporis*, *i. e.*, it marks the time belonging to the noun which precedes it. See N. Test. Gramm. § 99. 1. *h.*

Not worthy, οὐκ ἄξια, *insignificant, unworthy to be compared with*, (πρός). So the preposition πρός is sometimes used; *e. g.*, Ecclus. xxv. 19, Joseph. cont. Apion. II. 22. When we have suitable regard to future glory we make but little account, in comparison, of the sufferings of the present time.

The phrase τὴν μέλλουσαν δόξαν ἀποκαλυφθῆναι is equivalent to ἀποκαλυφθησομένην. The Greek could use the simple future; or, instead of it, as here, the verb μέλλω and the Infinitive. The employment of μέλλουσαν here indicates the confident expectation not only of future glory, but of its *speedy* revelation. Μέλλω is employed by the Greeks to designate a *proximate* future. The word δόξα, which here signifies *future happiness*, signifies in classic writers, *opinion, fame, reputation,* etc. But the New Testament meaning of δόξα is borrowed from the Hebrew כָּבוֹד or הָדָר, *splendor, magnificence, excellence*. The idea of δόξα in the presence of God, seems to be founded upon being there in the *light* or *splendor* of his presence. Hence light is used so often in the Bible as the image of happiness. Hence too we may see something of the plenary meaning which δόξα has, when used to describe a state of future happiness. In the present world, "eye hath not seen;" but when another world bursts upon the vision of Christians, after death shall have rent away the veil of mortality, there 'in God's light they will see light;' there too they shall enjoy "*everlasting* light, for God will be their glory."

(19) The particle γάρ is here prefixed to a clause added by way of confirming the sentiment of the preceding assertion. The apostle in ver. 18 has introduced, as an object of attention, *the glory which is to be revealed*. That there is such a glory he now proceeds to show, or at least to adduce reasons why Christians should confidently expect it.

Earnest expectation, ἀποκαραδοκία, the German *Ahndung*. The etymology favors this meaning; for the word comes from ἀπό (prep.), κάρα *head*, and δοκεύω *to observe, look after*. The Etymologicum Magnum explains it by τῇ κεφαλῇ προβλέπειν, *to thrust forward the head and see, i. e.*, to look with anxiety or eagerness; like the Hebrew הִתְחוֹלֵל. The same sense the word has in Phil. i. 20.

Very much of the difficulty of the passage before us turns on the meaning of the word κτίσις. We will, first, consider its

282 ROMANS VIII. 19.

meaning in the other passages of the New Testament, where it is found, and then compare it with the corresponding Hebrew words; and secondly examine some of the various meanings which have been assigned to the word in this place, and endeavor to vindicate the preferable sense.

I. The meanings of κτίσις, in all the other passages of the New Testament where it is found, excepting the one before us, may be distributed into two classes; viz:

1. It means *the act of creation, creating.* In such a sense it is generally conceded that it is employed in Mark x. 6, xiii. 19. Rom. i. 20. 2 Pet. iii. 4. Yet all of these passages might be referred to No. 2, as the sense would be equally good. But this first sense is the *proper* and *primary* meaning of the word, according to the ending -σις, in which words derived from verbs commonly denote the *act* of doing anything, *nomina actionis.* So frequently in the Greek classics, *making, constructing, creating,* etc. But in the New Testament the meaning is for the most part different from this.

2. It means *creature, created thing, any product of creating power, creation* as an existing thing. Such a deflexion from the primary meaning of a word is very common, not only in the Greek, but in all other languages; the *abstract* (nomen actionis) passing, as grammarians say, into the *concrete* sense; *i. e.,* the word which denoted action, being also used to denote the consequences or effects of that action. So here, κτίσις (*the act of creating*), is more commonly employed in the New Testament to signify the effects of this action, viz., *a thing created, res creata.* But this second signification may either be *generic,* or employed to designate any of the several *species* of meanings that constitute a part of the generic whole.

(*a*) In its generic sense it means *created things, creation, any created thing,* in Rom. i. 25. viii. 39. Col. i. 15. Heb. iv. 13. Rev. iii. 14, perhaps also in Mark x. 6. xiii. 19. Rom. i. 20. and 2 Pet. iii. 4. In a sense very nearly allied to this, it is used in Heb. ix. 11. to designate the *material* creation as such, in distinction from the *spiritual* one. This distinction, however, results rather from the exigency of the passage, and it seems to be made here rather by the word ταύτης than from the force of κτίσις.

(*b*) In a specific sense it means the *rational creation, man, men, the world of mankind.* Thus in Mark xvi. 15, 'Go preach the gospel πάσῃ τῇ κτίσει *to all men, to every man.*' Col. i. 23, 'which [gospel] has been preached ἐν πάσῃ τῇ κτίσει *among all nations.*' 1 Pet. ii, 19, 'Be subject, then, πάσῃ ἀνθρωπίνῃ κτίσει, *to every man, to every human being,* for the Lord's sake, *i. e.,* out of rega d to the Lord Christ. The exportation immediately subjoined explains this, viz., εἴτε βασιλεῖ, ὡς ὑπερέχοντι· εἴτε ἡγεμόσιν, ὡς δι' αὐτοῦ κ. τ. λ.: 'be subject to every man placed in authority, whether he be a king who has preeminence, or a governor appointed,' etc.

(*c*) In a more specific and limited sense still, it designates the *new rational creation, those who are created anew in Christ Jesus, Christians*. So in 2 Cor. v. 17, 'If any one be in Christ, he is καινὴ κτίσις, *a new creature*.' Gal. vi. 15, 'In Christ Jesus neither circumcision nor uncircumcision avails anything, but καινὴ κτίσις.' This, however, may mean *a new act of creating*, *i. e.*, the power of the Spirit in renovating the soul. But in both of these cases, the *special* meaning it must be confessed, depends rather on καινή than upon κτίσις.

These are all the cases in which κτίσις occurs in the New Testament, excepting those in the passage under examination. From these we gather the conclusion that the *usus loquendi* allows us to assign to κτίσις either of the three meanings ranked under No. 2, *i. e.*, it may be interpreted as meaning *things created;* the *natural creation, i. e., men* or *mankind,* or *Christians* who are a new *spiritual* creation; yet this last meaning is plainly uncertain, unless some qualifying word (*e. g.*, καινή) is joined with κτίσις.

I have only to add here, as a confirmation of the above meanings assigned to κτίσις (which however are not altogether peculiar to the New Testament, see Judith ix. 12. xi. 14. Wisd. ii. 6. xvi. 24. xix. 6), that the Chaldee and the Rabbinic Hebrew coincide with the usage just exhibited. The words in these languages which correspond to κτίσις, are בְּרִיָה, בְּרִיאָה, בְּרִיתָא, בִּרְיָא, which all mean *creatio, creatura, res creata, i. e.,* the act of creating, and the thing created, just in the same way as κτίσις does. Moreover, in Rabbinic Hebrew the plural form בְּרִיוֹת sometimes means *homines, men,* specially *the heathen*. All this, we see, corresponds with and explains the New Testament use of κτίσις. In regard to the last particular of all, viz., that בְּרִיוֹת sometimes means the heathen, by way of degradation or contempt; it is singular that we have adopted, into vulgar English, the very same meaning of the word *creature*, and applied it in a derogatory sense to human beings; *e. g.*, 'the creature refused to obey.'

Which of these meanings, now, shall be applied to κτίσις in the passage before us?

The following interpretations have been given to it. These are, 1. The Angels. 2. The souls (the animating principle) of the planetary worlds. 3. Adam and Eve, because they were the immediate work of creative power. 4. The souls of believers, in distinction from their bodies. 5. The bodies of believers, *i. e.*, their dead bodies, in distinction from their souls. 6. Christians in general. 7. Christians in particular, *i. e.*, either Jewish Christians, or Gentile Christians. 8. Unconverted men in general. 9. Unconverted men in particular, *i. e.*, either unconverted Jews or unconverted heathen. 10. The material creation, inanimate and animate, exclusive of rational beings. 11. The rational creation or men in general, mankind.

All these supposed meanings I have canvassed in an exegesis of vers. 18—25, printed in the Biblical Repository, Vol. I. pp. 363, seq. I deem the first five too improbable to need discussion here; and therefore proceed with the others.

The *sixth* and *seventh* opinions may be both ranked under one head, viz., that of Christians. Can κτίσις, then, here mean Christians, either in general or in particular? (*a*) The *usus loquendi* is wanting, to render this probable. The word κτίσις in 2 Cor. v. 17 and Gal. vi. 15, does not, as I have already remarked, of itself mean Christians. In both these cases it is connected with καινή. (*b*) In vers. 19, 21, the word κτίσις seems to designate those who are distinguished from the children of God, and who belong not to such as are now entitled to their privileges. But I do not consider this argument to be decisive; for the expressions in vers. 19, 21, are not much unlike that in verse 23, where Christians are represented as groaning within themselves and waiting for their filiation (υἱοθεσίαν) *i. e.*, for the consequences of it, viz., the redemption of their bodies from their present frail, painful, and dying state.

(*c*) A more conclusive argument is deducible from the form of ver. 23, where αὐτοὶ τὴν ἀπαρχὴν τοῦ Πνεύματος ἔχοντες seems plainly to mean *Christians*, as I shall in the sequel endeavor to show. Conceding this then, it is quite plain that κτίσις in the preceding verses cannot mean *Christians*, because the class of men designated in verse 23, is very clearly distinguished from the preceding class in vers. 19—21, who are there designated by κτίσις.

On the same ground, viz., that κτίσις cannot be regarded as meaning Christians in general, it must be excluded from meaning Christians in particular, *i. e.*, either Jewish Christians or Gentile Christians. How are these to be distinguished from "those who had the first fruits of the Spirit?" Even supposing that ἀπαρχή means here *special miraculous gifts*, (as some believe), *Jewish* Christians surely, above all others, possessed these; and if we look into the first epistle to the Corinthians, we find there a graphic account of the special gifts of the Spirit, which leaves no room to doubt that they were distributed to Gentile as well as to Jewish Christians. Still stronger is the argument, if we suppose (as I shall endeavor hereafter to show that we must suppose), ἀπαρχήν here to mean *the prelibation, the foretaste, the earnest* of future glory, which is common to all Christians. For as those who have this ἀπαρχήν, are here plainly and explicitly distinguished from those denominated κτίσις above; so, if these are Christians in general (as they clearly seem to be), it follows that κτίσις above is not used to designate either Christians in general, or Jewish or Gentile Christians in particular.

The *eighth* and *ninth* opinions may also be classed under one head. These are, that κτίσις means either unconverted men in general as such, or unconverted men in particular, viz., Jews or Gentiles. In regard to the specific meaning here assigned to κτίσις, I cannot see any tolerable ground of support for it. Why should either unconverted Jews or Gentiles be represented as peculiarly exposed to a frail and dying state? Surely there is no good reason for any distinction here, as all are equally exposed to the miseries of life.

More probable is the interpretation, which assigns to κτίσις the meaning of *unconverted men in general*. In this case it is easy to make a plain and evident distinction between κτίσις in vers. 19—22, and οἱ τὴν ἀπαρχὴν τοῦ πνεύματος ἔχοντες in ver. 23. I think this to be substantially the right meaning. But I would not assign to it the signification simply of *unconverted* men. I apprehend the meaning to be the same as in Mark xvi. 15. Col. i. 23. 1 Pet. ii. 13, *i, e., man, men, mankind in general.* But of this, and of the objections urged against it, I shall say more in the sequel.

On the whole, then, we have reduced our multiplex interpretations down to two, viz., *the material creation in general* animate and inanimate, and *the rational creation* or *mankind in general.* Critics of high rank and great abilities are divided between these two interpretations.

The first of these two meanings, that of *the material creation, the world in general,* or *the universe* exclusive of rational beings, has had many defenders both in ancient and modern times. Chrysostom, Theodoret, Theophylact, Œcumenius, Jerome, Ambrose, Luther, Koppe, Doddridge, Flatt, Tholuck, Reiche, and a multitude of others have been its advocates. Flatt, Tholuck, and Reiche, in their recent commentaries, have collected all which has been said in its favor, besides advancing some things peculiar to themselves. What they have brought forward deserves a serious examination.

That κτίσις *might be* employed to indicate the natural creation around us, consisting of things animate and inanimate, is philologically certain from the *usus loquendi* of the word, as seen under No. 2, *a*, above. But *is* it so employed in the passage before us? I have satisfied my own mind that κτίσις means here, as in Mark xvi. 15. Col. i. 23 (and for substance in 1 Pet. ii. 13), *mankind in general, gens humana*, in distinction from, but not in opposition to, Christians as such. See further proofs, etc., in EXCURSUS, viii.

Expects, or *waits for, the revelation of the sons of God*, τὴν ἀποκάλυψιν τῶν υἱῶν τοῦ Θεοῦ ἀπεκδέχεται; *i. e.*, the period when the sons of God in their ultimate state, and endowed with all their honors and privileges, shall be fully disclosed. This will be at the general judgment; when the Father who seeth in secret will reward them openly. Here they are in obscurity; the world knoweth them not. They are like to the seven thousand of old who had not bowed the knee to Baal, but who were unknown even to the prophet Elijah. However, it will not always be so. The day is coming when they will shine forth as the sun in his strength and as the stars for ever and ever, in the kingdom of their God and Father. See also Excursus.

(20) *For the creature*, τῇ γὰρ ματαιότητι ἡ κτίσις ὑπετάγη, *i. e.*, mankind, *was subjected to a frail and dying state*. That ματαιότης here has the sense thus assigned to it, is clear from the epexegesis of it in ver. 21, viz., δουλεία τῆς φθορᾶς, which is there used instead of repeating ματαιότης. Such as wish for further confirmation as to this sense of the word, may consult in the Sept. Ps. lxi. 9. xxxviii. 5. Ecc i. 2, 14. As the Hebrew הֶבֶל *vanity*, to which ματαιότης in the Septuagint corresponds, sometimes designates *an idol;* so some commentators have here interpreted ματαιότης, *idolatry;* the idea then is, mankind became subjected to idolatry, or the natural world was employed as the object of idolatry. So Tertullian, Luther, Marck, Baumgarten and others. Consequently they interpreted the succeeding clause, *not voluntarily, but through him who subjected it*, as having reference either to Satan, or to Adam as concerned in the original fall of man. But δουλεία τῆς φθορᾶς (ver. 21) seems to remove all probability from this interpretation of ματαιότης; and of course ὑποτάξαντα can be applied only to God the Creator of man. Compare Gen. iii. 17—19.

Not voluntarily, but by him who put it in subjection, οὐχ ἑκοῦσα ἀλλὰ διὰ τὸν ὑποτάξαντα, *i. e.*, to a frail and dying state. The creature did not voluntarily choose its present condition of sorrow and pain; but God the Creator has by his sovereign will, by the arrangements of his holy providence, placed man in this frail and dying state. It seems quite probable that Paul here referred in his own mind to the effects of the *fall*, as described in v. 12, seq. This state of ματαιότης was not original, but superinduced by sin. The use of the Aorist, ὑπετάγη seems to indicate some specific fact which happened in past time. Had the apostle's design been merely *general*, i. e., merely to indicate that *man has been and is frail*, he would most naturally have employed ὑποτέτακται, Perf. passive. But still, this frail condition is a state of *hope*. So we are assured in the next verse. Διὰ τὸν ὑποτάξαντα is adduced by some to show that διά may be understood of an *efficient* cause, although employed with the *Accusative*. That we may thus render διά by *per*, Germ. *durch*, i. e., *through, by means of*, many critics contend, and most concede.

(21) *In hope*, ἐπ' ἐλπίδι. Here the Dative designates the state or condition in which the κτίσις is, although subjected to ματαιότητι. It is a state in which a hope of deliverance can be indulged; not a state of despair. Ἐπ' ἐλπίδι may be connected either with ὑπετάγη or ὑποτάξαντα. Is it not doing violence to the word κτίσις, to construe it here as meaning *natural world*, and then to predicate of it ἑκοῦσα and ἐπ' ἐλπίδι? It would be an example of prosopopœia, which I believe even the most animated poetical parts of the Scriptures no where present.

But what is the hope in which the creature is permitted to indulge? It is, ὅτι καὶ αὐτὴ ἡ κτίσις ἐλευθερωθήσεται ἀπὸ τῆς δουλείας φθορᾶς, *that this very same creature*, viz., the one which is subjected to a frail and dying state, *shall be freed from the bondage of a perishing condition*. Φθορά comes from φθείρω, *to corrupt, to destroy*. Here it plainly means a *state of corruption*, i. e., a frail and dying state. Such a state the apostle calls δουλεία, *bondage*; first, because the creature was *not willingly* subjected to it; secondly, because it is not only a state of pain and misery, but it places us at the disposal of masters, who inflict upon us suffering and sorrow while we cannot resist or control them. The word ἐλευθερωθήσεται is fitly chosen as the antithetic correlative of δουλεία.

[And shall be introduced, καὶ εἰσαχθήσεται] *into the glorious liberty of the children of God*, εἰς τὴν ἐλευθερίαν τῆς δόξης τῶν τέκνων τοῦ Θεοῦ. Εἰς, put before the Accusative here, shows the state unto which the creature is to attain, by being delivered from the bondage of a frail and dying state. The phrase, however, is elliptical, and some verb is implied, as indicated above. Δόξα, by an idiom very common throughout the Scriptures, is used in this place as an adjective qualifying the preceding noun. In what sense men in general may be said to hope for this state, has been already explained above. If there be any objection to predicate this of *men* in general, is there not a still stronger one to predicating it of the *natural* world?

Verses 20, 21, thus explained, render a reason why the creature looks with ἀποκαραδοκία to another and better state; which is, because men are born with an instinctive and unquenchable thirst for happiness, and cannot find what they desire in this frail and perishing condition. This explains the reason why γάρ is prefixed to ver. 20; "γάρ orationi rationem reddenti præfigitur."

(22) *For we know that every creature,* οἴδαμεν γὰρ . . . . ἄχρι τοῦ νῦν, *i. e.*, the whole human race, *has sighed and sorrowed together until the present time.* In other words, it has been the lot of man, from the beginning down to the present time, to be subject to a frail and dying state, which has cost much sighing and sorrow. The idea in οἴδαμεν is, *no one can have any doubt, we are well assured, i. e.*, it is taken for granted that the thing to which it refers is well and familiarly known to all. But suppose, now, that the *natural* world is here represented as sighing and sorrowing, from the beginning of the world down to the time then present, and this because it waited for its renovation, which will take place only at the end of the world, or after the general resurrection; was this a thing so *familiar* to all, that the apostle could appeal to it by saying οἴδαμεν? I cannot but think that the advocates themselves of this interpretation must hesitate here. Γάρ is prefixed to a clause which confirms what the writer has said, in verse 21, of our frail and dying state. The immediate antecedent clause may be supplied thus: 'I say *bondage of a perishing state*, for (γάρ) the whole creation exhibits abundant evidence of this. The verbs συστενάζει and συνωδίνει denote the *mutual* and universal sighing and sorrowing of mankind. No one part is exempt; there is a *mutual* correspondence between them all in regard to the subject in question. The verbs στενάζω and ὠδίνω are appropriate, especially the latter, to the sighs and pains of a travailing woman. The language is therefore exceedingly appropriate to the apostle's purpose, inasmuch as it not only indicates a great degree of sorrow and distress, but that this is indicative of a new birth, *i. e.*, a new state of things, or (in other words) that a change for the better is to be looked for. The prep. σύν, here joined with these two verbs, serves to indicate a mutual participation on all sides in the sorrows mentioned.

(23) *Yet not only so, but we ourselves, who have the first fruits of the Spirit, even we groan within ourselves ; i. e.*, not only have mankind in all ages, down to the present hour, been in a frail and suffering state, but even we, who, as having within us an earnest of future glory and a pledge that we are the children of God, and are to receive the inheritance of his beloved, might naturally be supposed to be exempted from the common lot of sinful men, are in distress and sigh for deliverance from it.

Some interpret the phrase καὶ αὐτοὶ τὴν ἀπαρχὴν τοῦ πνεύματος ἔχοντες, of *special* and *supernatural* gifts, limiting it to the apostles only; while others explain it in the like way, but extend it to all Christians who were endowed with such gifts. Others regard ἀπαρχή as meaning *gift* or *present* merely, in a general way; while most interpret it as meaning the *earnest*, or *first fruits*, or *pledge*, of that which is afterward to be given in a more complete manner. I can find but one meaning of it throughout the New Testament; and this is, *that which is first of its kind*, or *that which is first in order of time*, πρῶτος. It is applied both to persons and things, in a sense compounded of both of these, viz., *first in respect to kind and time also; e. g.*, Rom. xvi. 5. 1 Cor. xvi. 15. James i. 18. 1 Cor. xv. 20, 23. Rev. xiv. 4. In this last passage it may have, it is said, the general sense of *sacrifice* or *offering*, inasmuch as the Septuagint puts it for the Hebrew תְרוּמָה; but on the whole the other sense is preferable. I take the meaning of the writer in Rev. xiv. 4 to be, that the persons there named may be considered in a light resembling that of the ἀπαρχή in ancient times, as the first-fruits of a glorious Christian harvest.

Ἀπαρχή, then, = the Hebrew רֵאשִׁית, for which it so often stands; *caput, princeps, first in its kind, first in point of time*, etc. Comp. רֵאשִׁית in Gen. xlix. 3. Prov. viii. 22. Lev. ii. 12. xxiii. 10. Deut. xviii. 4. xxvi. 10. xxxiii. 21. Num. xxiv. 20. Amos vi. 6. In the passage before us, all the Greek fathers appear to have attached the same meaning to ἀπαπχή, viz., that of *first fruits*, in the sense of *earnest, pledge, foretaste*, of joys to come. The apostle represents Christians as the habitation of God by his Spirit, Eph, ii. 22, comp. 1 Cor. iii. 16. vi. 19; the Spirit of God dwells in them, 1 John iii. 24. iv. 13; and this Spirit, thus conferred on them, is the ἀῤῥαβών, *the pledge* of future glory, 2 Cor. v. 5. Eph. i. 14. What hinders, then, that we should understand ἀπαρχή as meaning *foretaste* or *first fruits* of future glory which the Spirit who dwells in Christians imparts? The *usus loquendi* of the word does not seem to admit of any other exegesis, and this gives a meaning entirely congruous with the nature and design of the passage. Cf. Keil, Opusc. p. 294 seq. If this be correct then it follows that the ἀπαρχή here spoken of is common to all true Christians; and that the interpretation which limits this verse to the apostles, or to a few of the primitive Christians endowed with miraculous gifts, has no stable foundation.

That Christians were subject to sorrows, which even the earnest of future glory did not exempt them from, needs not to be proved. See 2 Cor. v. 2, 3. 1. Cor. xv. 19. That they longed and sighed for deliverance, followed from their very nature. But there is a peculiar energy and delicacy in the expression which marks the consequences of their sufferings; *we* GROAN *within ourselves*, *i. e.*, internally, not externally. We suppress the rising sigh; we bow with submission to the will of God which afflicts us; we receive his chastisement as children; our frail nature feels it, and we sigh or groan inwardly; but no mourning word escapes us; we suppress the outward demonstrations of pain, lest we should even seem to complain. Is this imaginary on my part? Or did the writer mean to convey what I have attributed to him? So much at least we can say, viz., that such a sentiment was worthy of Paul, and of all Christians who suffered with him. It is worthy of being carried into practice at the present hour; it commends itself to the conscience of every one who thoroughly believes in the holy, just, and benevolent providence of God.

Waiting for [our] *adoption* or *filiation*, υἱοθεσίαν ἀπεκδεχόμενοι. There is a twofold *filiation* spoken of in the New Testament. The first is, that which takes place when believers are born again, John i. 12, 13. iii. 3—5. Rom. viii. 14, 15 represents believers as possessing πνεῦμα υἱοθεσίας; see also 1 John iii. 1, 2. But there is another and higher sense in which believers are to become the children of God, viz., they are to be so, when they shall be perfected in the world of glory, when they become "the children of the resurrection," when they are made "like to the angels," Luke xx. 36. Their first adoption or filiation is secret, in regard to the world; their second is the ἀποκάλυψις τῶν υἱῶν τοῦ Θεοῦ, when "he who seeth in secret shall reward them openly;" The clause τὴν ἀπολύτρωσιν τοῦ σώματος ἡμῶν, *the redemption of our body, i. e.*, its redemption from a state of frailty, disease, and death is epexegetical. This body is, at the resurrection, to be like to Christ's glorious body, Phil. iii. 21; it is to be a σῶμα πνευματικόν, 1 Cor. xv. 44; this mortal is to put on immortality, this σῶμα φθαρτόν is to become a σῶμα ἄφθαρτον, 1 Cor. xv. 53, 54. Such is the ἀπολύτρωσις of this frail and dying body, which believers now inhabit. Comp. ἀπολύτρωσις in Luke xxi. 28. Eph. i. 14. iv. 30. Heb. xi. 35. The reader will note that the expression ἀπολύτρωσιν τοῦ σώματος here is equivalent to the ἀποκάλυψιν τῶν υἱῶν τοῦ Θεοῦ in ver. 19, and to the ἐλευθερίαν τῶν τέκνων τοῦ Θεοῦ in ver. 21; and therefore serves to show what those expressions mean in the connection in which they stand.

Christians, then, in their present state, must long and wait for their second and final adoption or filiation. They must wait with confidence; yea, with assurance: "for he who cometh will come, and will not tarry." But let them not regard the present world as their home. It is not the Canaan in which they are to rest. They must "seek a city which hath foundations, whose builder and maker is God." Then the agitated breast, the heaving sigh, the groaning within, will no more annoy or distress them. Let not the child of God complain, then, that his final reward is not anticipated and distributed to him here in the present world, while he is in a state of trial. He must wait until he comes to the goal, before he can wear the crown of him who has been a victor in the race. He must defer his expected laurels until his combat is over. Then he shall receive a crown of glory that fadeth not away.

(24) That the Christian cannot expect a full reward here, the apostle goes on most explicitly to declare. *For we are saved in hope*, τῇ γὰρ ἐλπίδι ἐσώθημεν, *i. e.*, we have obtained salvation, but a part of it is only in hope ; we have attained a condition in which we indulge the hope of a glory that is yet future. This is all which can be rationally expected or accomplished in the present life. As he had said in the preceding verse, Christians are here in the attitude of *waiting* for their filiation. Verse 24 is designed to confirm this; hence the γάρ at the beginning of it. The reader should observe that the Aor. ἐσώθημεν is qualified in its sense by τῇ ἐλπίδι. *We are saved* or *have attained to a state of salvation*, says the apostle, yet it is not fully and completely so, but is so, τῇ ἐλπίδι, *i. e.*, it is a salvation of which *hope* is at present a leading constituent.

Now hope which is seen, is no longer hope, ἐλπὶς δὲ . . . . . ἐλπίς, *i. e.*, the object of hope (ἐλπίς in the first instance here means this) is no longer such, when one attains the actual possession of it. Δέ introduces a clause which is designed to continue and illustrate what precedes. *For what one sees, how does he still hope for it*, ὃ γὰρ . . . . ἐλπίζει. That is, what a man has actually attained or come to the enjoyment of, how can he be said to look forward to with *hope* or anticipation? *Γάρ rationem rei dictæ reddit.*

(25) *But if we hope for that which we do not enjoy, then we patiently wait for it*, εἰ δὲ . . . . ἀπεκδεχόμεθα. That is, if it be true, as all will concede, that in the present life we attain not to our final reward, but can be called *the heirs of salvation* only because we have obtained a well-grounded hope of it; if it be so that we cannot rationally expect an exemption from trials and troubles here, but must take our part in them with all around us; if it be true, also, that a great and glorious reward is reserved in heaven for all who endure patiently until the end of their probation (and that this is true, the very nature that God has given to men, which is here so imperfectly developed, and which therefore points to a state of greater perfection, satisfactorily shows); then it becomes Christians to endure with all patience and meekness

the trials and sufferings of the present life. Time is short; eternity is long. Our sufferings are comparatively slight and momentary. Who can place them beside that glory "which eye hath not seen, nor ear heard, and of which it hath not entered into the heart of man to conceive," and which is to endure as long as the God who bestows it, and yet make any serious account of them? *Christian brethren*, says the apostle, *let us patiently wait the appointed time of our deliverance*. The διά before ὑπομενῆς stands before a noun marking the state or condition of those of whom it is said, ἀπεκδεχόμεθα.

CHAP. VIII. 26—27.

IN this our weak and suffering condition, we are greatly aided by the Spirit who dwells in us; so that even when we are so much perplexed and distressed that we know not what to ask for or what to say in our prayers, our internal sighs which are not uttered by words, and which arise from his influence on our souls, are noticed and understood by the Searcher of hearts, whose ears will be open to them Such is the course of thought in these verses; the natural inference from it is: 'Christians, be not discouraged, even in your deepest distresses He who sees in secret, counts every groan, hears every sigh, and will be a very present help in time of need '

(26) *In like manner*, i. e., *in the very same way*, ὡσαύτως. Some critics render ὡσαύτως by *præterea, uberdiess*, i. e., *moreover, besides*. This would do well, if philology would allow it. It seems, however, to be rather making a new meaning for the word than explaining the usual one. The true answer to the question, 'Like to what?' seems to be this; 'In like manner as hope supports, strengthens, cheers us, and renders us patient, so do the influences of the Spirit aid us, in all our distresses. Ὡσαύτως δὲ καί, *and in like manner also*, or *and in like manner moreover*.

The Spirit, τὸ πνεῦμα. But what Spirit? Our own mind? A filial spirit? Or the Spirit of God? Each of these methods of exegesis has been defended. I was formerly inclined to regard the second meaning as the most probable; principally on account of the 27th verse. It is natural to ask: Does not the phrase ὁ ἐρευνῶν τὰς καρδίας, designate him who knows the secrets of the *human* breast? And as this same Searcher of hearts is said to know φρόνημα τοῦ πνεύματος, i. e., *the mind* or *will of the spirit*, does not this mean the same thing as τὰρ καρδίας, and therefore designate the *human* mind? One may also ask: Where in all the Scriptures is the Spirit of God represented as *making intercession* (ἐντυγχάνει) for the saints. These difficulties have led many to construe πνεῦμα throughout the passage as meaning πνεῦμα υἱοθεσίας, comp. ver. 15. But this explanation is doubtful, especially when we compare πνεῦμα in verses 2, 4, 5, 6, 9, 11, 13, 14, 23, where it clearly and certainly means the Spirit of God or of Christ. The probability is, therefore, that the writer here uses πνεῦμα in the like sense. The Spirit which sanctifies Christians, which subdues their fleshly appetites, which gives them a filial temper, which bestows a foretaste of future glory,— this same Spirit aids Christians in all their sufferings and sorrows; and consequently they ought to endure them with patience. It cannot be denied that *intensity* of meaning is given to the whole passage by this exegesis.

Helps, συναντιλαμβάνεται; but in the Greek σύν augments the signification, so that one might translate, *greatly assists, affords much help*. The σύν in composition not only denotes *con, with, together with*, etc., but also marks the *completeness* or *entirety* of an action ; *e. g.*, συμπληρόω, *to fill entirely full;* cf. also συνάγνυμι, συμπατέω, συντέμνω, etc. *Our infirmities*, ἀσθενείαις ἡμῶν, seems to mean our frail, infirm, afflicted, troubled state; and this accords entirely with the context. A., B., C., D., many Codd. minusc., with many versions and fathers, read τῇ ἀσθενείᾳ, in the Dat. singular. Indeed the weight of authority seems to be in favor of this reading.

For we know not that which we should pray for as we ought, τὸ γάρ . . . οὐκ οἴδαμεν κ. τ. λ.; *i. e.*, in our perplexities, weaknesses, ignorance and distresses, we are often at a loss what would be best for us, or most agreeable to the will of God respecting us. Καθὸ δεῖ, *as we ought, i. e.*, the object for which we should pray, in accordance with duty, κατὰ τὸ θέλημα τοῦ Θεοῦ (comp. 1 John v. 14), or in a becoming manner, is frequently unknown to us. Καθὸ δεῖ belongs to or qualifies προσευξώμεθα. In this state, *the same Spirit*, αὐτὸ τὸ Πνεῦμα, the same who sanctifies us, dwells in us, and helps our infirmities, *earnestly intercedes for us,* ὑπερεντυγχάνει ὑπὲρ ἡμῶν; where ὑπέρ in composition with the verb augments the force of it, which I have endeavored to express.

Prayer or supplication, however, made by the Spirit, *i. e.*, by the Spirit of God as such and by himself, is not here intended. So the sequel clearly shows; viz., *the Spirit makes intercession for us,* στεναγμοῖς ἀλαλήτοις, *in sighs* or *groans which are unutterable, i. e.*, the full meaning of which cannot be spoken in words. Or ἀλαλήτοις may mean, *that which is not uttered*, that which is internal, *i. e.*, suppressed sighs; for *verbals* in -τός may have either a *passive* meaning, as in this case, or they may designate what *may* or *can be done*; New Test. Gramm. § 82. Note 1 Either sense is good; the Spirit then intercedes for the saints, by exciting within them such longings for conformity to God, for deliverance from evil, and for the enjoyment of future blessedness, that no language can adequately express them. What is thus done in the souls of believers through the influence of the Spirit, is here attributed to him; *i. e.*, he is said to do what they do under his special influence. In accordance with the idiom of the sacred writers, that is often attributed to God, which human agents perform under his oversight, government, or aid. In accordance with such a sentiment, Fenelon, in his Essay entitled, *Que l' Esprit de Dieu enseigne en dedans*, says in a very striking manner: "The Spirit of God is the soul of our soul." So Augustine, with equal correctness and concinnity: " Non Spiritus Sanctus in semetipso apud semetipsum in illa Trinitate gemit; sed *in nobis gemit, quia gemere nos facit* (Tract. VI. in Johan. § 2); that is, the Divine Spirit does not groan or intercede in and by himself, as God and belonging to the Trinity; but he intercedes by his influence upon us, and by leading us to aspirations which language cannot express;" a sentiment equally true and striking.

(27) *The Searcher of hearts*, ὁ δὲ ἐρευνῶν τὰς καρδίας, a common appellation of God, who is *omniscient;* comp. vii. 9 (10). Jer. xi. 20. Acts 1. 14 — *Knoweth the desire of the Spirit* or *the mind of the Spirit*, οἶδε τὸ φρόνημα τοῦ Πνεύματος, *i. e.*, what is sought after, willed, or desired, when these στεναγμοὶ ἀλάλητοι excited by him arise. In other words: " *The Searcher of hearts* does not need that desires should be clothed or expressed in language, in order perfectly to understand them and to listen to them." It is not the *mind* of the Spirit of God, in himself considered and as belonging to the Godhead, but as disclosed ἐν στεναγμοῖς ἀλαλήτοις τῶν ἁγίων, that the writer means to designate. In this way, there is no difficulty in applying πνεῦμα to the Spirit of God. The sense is, that God knows the mind or desire of the saints, which is prompted or excited by his Spirit.

That he intercedes for saints agreeably to the will of God, ὅτι κατὰ .... ἁγίων. Ὅτι must be translated *because*, but the sense is better if we construe the clause ὅτι κ. τ. λ. as *explicative* of the preceding assertion. Paul frequently adds explicative clauses which begin with ὅτι, *e. g.*, 1 Cor. iii. 20 al. Meaning: 'God knows what the unutterable sighs mean which the Spirit excites in the bosoms of his saints; he knows, that aided by his Spirit they make intercession κατὰ Θεόν, i. e., καθὸ δεῖ. Κατὰ Θεόν, then, must mean not *to God*, which would require πρὸς Θεόν, but *secundem Deum*, *i. e.*, κατὰ τὸ θέλημα τοῦ Θεοῦ, comp. 1 John

v. 14., and for this sense of κατά, cf. Rom. viii. 4. 2 Cor. xi. 17. Rom. ii. 2. Luke ii. 22, 24, 27, 29, et al. sæpe. With the word ἁγίων here, employed as a *noun*, we might naturally expect the article. But where particular emphasis or specification is not intended, the article may be omitted; N. Test. Gramm. § 90. 4. Note 1.

The Christian who reads this passage with a spirit that responds to the sentiment which it discloses, cannot avoid lifting up his soul to God with overflowing gratitude for his mercies. Here we are " poor, and wretched, and miserable, and blind, and naked," and in want of all things; we are crushed before the moth; " we all do fade as a leaf, and the wind taketh us away;" we are often in distress, in darkness, in perplexity, in straits from which we can see no escape; even in far the greater number of cases we know not what will be for our ultimate and highest good, and so " know not what we should pray for *as we ought;* but then, the Spirit of the living God is present with all the true followers of the Saviour; he excites desires in their souls for liberation from sin and present evil, and for heavenly blessedness and holiness greater than words can express. The consequences or designs of present trials and sufferings are often too uncertain for us even to venture on making a definite request with regard to them; because we do not know whether relief from them is best or not. The humble Christian, who feels his need of chastisement, will very often be brought to such a state. Then what a high and precious privilege it is, that our " unutterable sighs " should be heard and understood by Him who searches our hearts! Who can read this without emotion? Such are the blessings purchased for sinners by redeeming blood! Such the consolations which flow from the throne of God for a groaning and dying world!

CHAP. VIII. 28—39.

To crown the whole, the apostle now goes on to assure those to whom he is writing, that *all things*, i e., all the sufferings and sorrows and trials of the present life, will prove to be instruments, in the hand of a wise and powerful God and merciful Redeemer, of promoting the final and greatest happiness and glory of all true saints. The purposes of God in respect to the saints are certain, and nothing can ever separate them from the care and kindness and affection of the Saviour who has redeemed them. Christians have, therefore, no reason to despond or to be discouraged, while suffering the evils and trials of life

(28) *We know, moreover,* οἴδαμεν δέ. Δέ *orationi continuandæ inservit.* What follows here, is in addition to what is like in kind

or relating to the same subject in the preceding context. *All sufferings, sorrows, trials*, etc., *shall coöperate*, πάντα συνεργεῖ, *i. e.*, mutually contribute or each contribute, *for the good*, for the final and highest good, *of those who love God*. Augustine and some other fathers suppose sin to be here included in the πάντα. But plainly this was not here in the apostle's mind.

To those who are called according to his purpose or design, τοῖς . . . . οὖσιν. Κλητοῖς, in the New Testament, is used *twice* in the sense of *invited, bidden*, viz.. Matt. xx. 16, xxii. 14. In all other cases it = ἔκλεκτος, and means not only such as have been *invited*, but such as have *accepted* the invitation, the *true Christian; e. g.*, 1 Cor. i. 2, 24. Jude v. 1. Rom. i. 6. Rev. xvii. 14. So in the verse before us, the persons designated are those *who love God*. Κατὰ πρόθεσιν, those who are called or chosen *in conformity with the purpose* [of God]. This πρόθεσις is κατ' ἐκλογήν, Romans ix. 11, *i. e.*, free, without any merit or desert on the part of the sinner, or of obligation (strictly speaking) on the part of God; it is the πρόθεσις of him who worketh all things after the counsels of his own will, and hath before ordained that Christians should have a heavenly inheritance, Eph. i. 11 : it is a πρόθεσις τῶν αἰώνων, an *eternal purpose*, Eph. iii. 11; or it is a πρόθεσις . . . . πρὸ χρόνων αἰωνίων, *a purpose before the ancient ages, i. e.*, before the world began, 2 Tim. i. 9. That the *purpose of God* is here meant, and not the purpose or will of man, as many have maintained, is rendered entirely clear by the sequel, verse 29, seq. See the *Excursus* on this passage.

(29) *For those whom he foreknew*, ὅτι οὓς προέγνω. The course of thought seems to be thus : 'All things must work together for good to Christians—to such as are called to the privileges of a filial relation, and were chosen before the world began, to be conformed to the image of God and to be advanced to a state of glory. The everlasting love and purpose of God cannot be disappointed.' Ὅτι κ. τ. λ. introduces the reasons why it is certain that all things will work together for the good of true Christians. Προέγνω, *foreknew*, or *before decreed* or *constituted* or *determined*, (viz., as κλητοί, *elect, saints, chosen*, see on ver. 28), a word so endlessly disputed, that it would seem to have been too often forgotten, that the object and argument of an expositor should be *philological*, not *theological*, *i. e.*, he should seek for what the apostle *does say*, not for what he may conjecture he ought to say.

Πρό (in composition) gives to the verb the additional signification of *previous time, formerly*. What then does γινώσκω mean? It means (1) *To know* in any manner generally ; *to know* by the aid of any of the bodily senses, by hearing, etc., or by experience, trial; Lat. *cognoscere, sentire*. (2) *To be acquainted with, to perceive so as fully to apprehend, to take knowledge of, to make one's self acquainted with.* (3) *To recognize one as a known friend, a familiar acquaintance;* Matt. vii. 23. Mark vii. 24. 1 Cor. viii. 3. Gal. iv. 9. 2 Tim. ii. 19. Heb. xiii. 23. To the same purpose is the corresponding Hebrew יָדַע employed, *i. e.,* it means, *to regard with affection, to treat with favor;* e. g., it is said of God in respect to the saints, Ps. i. 6. cxliv. 3. Amos iii. 2. Nah. i. 7; of men in respect to God, Hos. viii. 2. Ps. xxxvi. 11. ix. 11. Job. xviii. 21. The first and second classes of meaning above given are so common, and so easily confirmed by any of the lexicons, that I have deemed it superfluous to adduce examples. Προέγνω then *may* mean, *he before loved. he before regarded with affection, he before looked on with favor.* In this sense many have here understood the word; *e. g.,* Origen, Erasmus, Calvin, Mosheim, Baumgarten, E. Schmidius, and generally the Arminians.

On the other hand; Theophylact, Œcumenius, Ambrose, Augustine, Bucer, Balduin, Hunnius, Calovius, Heumann, and others, have construed προέγνω here as meaning *he foreknew*, understood in the literal and primary sense of the word; *i. e.,* say the Lutheran commentators in general: 'God foreknew that the κλητοί would freely believe.' In the same way many at the present day construe this text. But the question on which all turns, as to this interpretation, is: Does the apostle here represent the calling, and justification, and glorification of the κλητοί, as the result of God's love to them, or of their love to him? That is, did God bring them by his Spirit into a state of grace *because they loved him first* or before they were brought into this state, or did he *by his mercy* bring them into this state so that they might love him? This question is finally and fully settled by such texts as 1 John iv. 10, 19, John xv. 16, Rom. v. 6—10. Jer. xxxi. 3. 2 Tim. i. 9, οὐ κατὰ τὰ ἔργα ἡμῶν—ἀλλὰ κατὰ πρόθεσιν καὶ χάριν τὴν δοθεῖσαν . . . . πρὸ χρόνων αἰωνίων. It is settled by the nature of the case. The Spirit of God "breathes on the valley of *dry bones;*" he "quickens those who are *dead* in trespasses and sins;" he "calls the *dead* to life;" he "creates anew in Christ Jesus;" sinners are "born of the Spirit;" and it is in this way, and in this only, that they come to love God; for "the carnal mind is enmity against God, and is not subject to his law, nor indeed can be;" and that "which is born of the flesh is flesh." It is God who first loves us (1 John iv. 10, 19), before we come to love him. There is no setting aside declarations so plain, so full, so often repeated as these. It must necessarily be true that God foresees and perfectly knows all the voluntary love and obedience which his children will ever exhibit; and it is equally certain that he has before determined to reward these in proportion to their desert. But this cannot be the *ground* of his causing them, when they are his enemies, and dead in trespasses and sins, to become συμμόρφους τῆς εἰκόνος τοῦ Υἱοῦ αὐτοῦ. It must for ever remain true, that we are brought "to love him because he *first* loved us."

Of those who embrace the sentiment respecting προέγνω given in No. 3 above, some say that God *before loved* his saints, *because he foresaw their character and good works*; others, that *out of his mere good pleasure he set his love upon them*. In the latter way, Calvin, Beza, the Westminster Catechism, and most of the Calvinistic writings take it. But our text, it should be observed, assigns neither the one reason nor the other; it states the *simple fact*, and no more. No conclusive objections of a philological nature can be urged against adopting the sense of *before loving* or *regarding with affection;* because the like sense of the verbs γινώσκω and יָדַע is common. It is only when the *reason* for doing this is forced upon us, as being disclosed in the text itself, that I should object to such an exegesis.

With Tholuck, however, I prefer a sense of προέγνω, different from any yet mentioned; and this merely from the philology of the passage. It is well known in respect to γινώσκω, that it sometimes means *volo, constituo mecum, I will, I wish, I determine with myself, I resolve,* or *determine,* or *decide.* So Rom. vii. 15. Josephus: ὁ Θεὸς ἔγνω τιμωρίσασθαι αὐτούς, *God hath determined to punish them,* Antiq. I. 2; comp. also Antiq. II. 4, 5 and III. 12. 3. Psalt. Sal. xvii. 47: ἣν ἔγνω ὁ Θεὸς ἀναστῆσαι, *which God hath determined to establish.* In like manner Plutarch; ἔγνω φυγεῖν ἀποδημία τὴν ὑπόνοιαν, *he determined to avoid suspicion by going abroad,* Lyc. c. 3. Polybius: ἔγνωσαν διὰ μάχης κρίνειν τὰ πράγματα, *they have determined to decide matters by appeal to arms,* V. 82. So often in Esop's Fables.

That προγινώσκω may have the like sense, is clear from 1 Pet. i. 20; where προεγνωσμένου πρὸ καταβολῆς κόσμου (said of Christ) means plainly *before decreed, before constituted* or *determined.* In the like sense (as many think) it is used in Rom. xi. 2, *God hath not cast away his people,* ὃν προέγνω, whom *he chose* to be his, or *constituted* his, viz., before the foundation of the world; comp. 1 Pet. i. 20. Eph. iii. 11. 2 Tim. i. 9. And in accordance with this πρόγνωσις is used; *e. g.,* Acts ii. 24, where it is the equivalent of ὡρισμένη, βουλή. So also in 1 Pet. i. 2; and it is the same as πρόθεσις, in 2 Tim. i. 9. Eph. iii. 11.

In this view of the subject, ὃν προέγνω is to be regarded as a *resumption* of the idea expressed by κατὰ πρόθεσιν κλητοῖς in ver. 23, *i. e.,* those who by his purpose were κλητοί, those whom προέγνω, *i. e.*, whom *he had before resolved* or *determined* should be his κλητοί — those προώρισε κ. τ. λ. That πρό in composition here means *before* the foundation of the world, may be seen by comparing 1 Pet. i. 20. 2 Tim. i. 9. Eph. iii. 11.

The objections to this view lie equally against translating προέγνω, *he foreknew*, or *he loved before*. If God did actually *foreknow* who were to be his κλητοί, then it was not *uncertain* whether they would be or not. If he LOVED them *before* the foundation of the world, then it must have been that he did *foreknow* that they would be his κλητοί, and this again makes the same *certainty*. If he *determined* before the foundation of the world that they should be his κλητοί, then again the same *certainty* existed, and no more. Nay even if we could abstract God and his purposes from the whole, and suppose the order of the universe to move on without him in its constituted way, the same certainty would still have existed. I do not see, therefore, in what way we can avoid the conclusion, that *certainty* must exist, by the divine purpose and counsel, in regard to the κλητοί — a certainty not merely that they will be saved, provided they believe and obey and persevere in so doing, but a certainty that the κατὰ πρόθεσιν κλητοί will be brought to believe and obey and persevere, and will therefore obtain salvation; for such is the manifest tenor of the whole passage.

Still, all those of any party in theology who draw directly from προέγνω the conclusion that God *fore-ordained* or *chose* or *loved*, out of his *mere good pleasure*, on the one hand ; or from his foresight of *faith* and *good works* on the other ; deduce from the text what is not in it, for it says neither the one nor the other. It avers merely that the κατὰ πρόθεσιν κλητοί were *foreknown*, or *fore-loved*, or *fore-determined*. The *certainty* of future glory to all the κλητοί Θεοῦ is what the writer means to affirm; and to affirm it *by showing that it is a part of the everlasting purposes of God.*

He also fore-ordained, καί προώρισε, predestinated, decreed *before*, viz., before the foundation of the world. So, clearly, the word is used in Acts iv. 28. 1 Cor. ii. 7, expressly πρὸ τῶν αἰώνων. I take the πρό in composition with the several verbs here, to have the same meaning as in πρὸ τῶν αἰώνων. It does not mean simply that God determined or decreed this or that *before* men individually came into existence, but *before the world began*. Eph. i. 5, 11. The idea that the *decree* here has respect merely to the *external privileges* of the gospel, and not to *eternal salvation*, is directly contradicted by 1 Cor. ii. 7 — εἰς δόξαν ἡμῶν; by Eph. i. 5 — εἰς υἱοθεσίαν διὰ Ἰησοῦ Χριστοῦ . . . ἐν ᾧ ἔχομεν τὴν ἀπολύτρωσιν . . . and verse 11, ἐν ᾧ ἐ κ λ η ρ ώ θ η μ ε ν, προορισθέντες κατὰ πρόθεσιν κ. τ. λ. The whole tenor of the passage before us also clearly contradicts this; for here the subject is *final* and *future glory*, not merely present opportunities and external advantages for acquiring Christian knowledge. The only remaining passage where the word is used (Acts iv. 28), employs it in an entirely different connection, but with the plain sense of *before decreed.* The sense of the whole is: 'Those who are κλητοί according to the purpose of God, those whom he determined from everlasting to save, he did at the same time *predestinate to be conformed to the image,* etc.'

To be of the like form with the image of his own Son, συμμόρφους . . . αὐτοῦ, *i. e.,* to be like him, to resemble him in a moral respect. God has not then (as is often objected to the doctrine of predestination) decreed that men should be saved whether they be sinful or holy, *i. e.,* without any regard to the character which they may have; but he has determined that all who are conducted to glory, must resemble *in a moral respect* him who leads them to glory, *i. e.,* the great Captain of their salvation. Philology requires that συμμόρφους should be made the *predicate* acc., as indicating the character *which God designed they should sustain,* and = συμμόρφους εἶναι.

That he [the Son] *should be the first-born among many brethren,* εἰς τό εἶναι . . . ἀδελφοῖς, *i. e.,* that the Saviour should, in his office as Lord of all and Head over all things for his church, still sustain a *fraternal* relation to those whose leader he is, they being made to resemble him by being made partakers of the like qualities or affections; comp. Heb. ii. 11 — 18. The apostle does not say here, whether believers are to resemble the Saviour in their moral qualities, their sufferings, or their glorification. But nothing forbids our extending the idea to all these particulars; and the context invites us to do so. For the sense of πρωτότοκος, comp. Ps. lxxxix. 27, (28). Ex. iv. 22. Heb. i. 6, Col. i. 15.

(30) *And whom he fore-ordained or predestinated,* οὓς δὲ προώρισε, viz., to be conformed to the image of his Son. In other words, whom he before determined to regenerate and sanctify, to purify from sin, and to make holy in some measure as the Saviour is holy.

The same did he also call, τούτους καὶ ἐκάλεσε. Is this the so-named *effectual calling;* or does it mean nothing more than the *external* invitation of the gospel, the moral suasion of it addressed to the heart and understanding of sinners? That καλέω is sometimes employed in the latter sense is clear from such passages as Matt. ix. 13. Mark ii. 17. Luke v. 32. But it is usually applied to *effectual calling, i. e.,* such a calling as ensures acceptance, election. In such a way κλῆσις and κλητός are, beyond all doubt, commonly applied. So here ἐκάλεσε manifestly means such *a calling* as proceeds from the πρόθεσις, from the *fore-knowledge* and from the *predetermination* of God in respect to the objects of it, and which is followed by justification or pardon of sin and final glory.

The same he also justified, τούτους καὶ ἐδικαίωσεν, *i. e.*, pardoned, acquitted, absolved from the penalty of the divine law, accepted and treated as righteous.— *And those whom he justified, the same he also glorified*, οὓς δὲ . . . . ἐδόξασε; the work begun in accordance with his everlasting love and purpose, he carries through and consummates by bestowing endless glory in heaven upon the κατὰ πρόθεσιν κλητοί.

Can then the mere *external* invitations and privileges of the gospel be here meant? Is it indeed true, that *all* to whom these are extended are κλητοί in the higher sense here meant? Such texts as John xv. 22 — 24. ix. 41. iii. 19. Heb. ii. 1 — 3. iii. 18, 19, vi. 4 — 6. x. 26 — 30. Mark xvi. 16, and verses 1 — 11 above decide the question whether all who hear the gospel will be saved. If now all who enjoy the external privileges of the gospel are not κλητοί or κεκλημένοι in the sense of the present passage, then must it be true, that such only as are *conformed to the image of Christ* will be saved. See EXCURSUS on this passage.

It should be noted also that Paul uses the Aorist here in all cases; as well in respect to future glorification (ἐδόξασε) as in regard to predestination and justification. This is altogether in the manner of the Hebrew prophets, who usually speak of future events that are certain, as events which have already past. The obvious solution of this is that in the knowledge and purpose of God, things future are like those which are past as to the certainty that they will take place. The use of the Aorist indicates the certainty of the writer's mind in regard to such things.

(31) *What shall we say in respect to these things*, τί . . . ταῦτα, *i. e.*, what shall we say now in reference to the facts and principles which I have just mentioned, viz., the purposes of God in respect to the κλητοί, and the manner in which he deals with them? The sequel answers this question; the sum of which is that, 'such being the purposes of God, none of the sorrows or troubles of life, yea, none of the spiritual enemies and opposers of the children of God will be able to disappoint or frustrate their hopes.' *If God be on our side*, εἰ ὁ Θεὸς . . . ἡμῶν, *i. e.*, espouse our cause, who can contend with success against him?

(32) *Even he who spared not his own son*, ὃς γέ κ. τ. λ. Γέ quidem, German *eben*; γὲ . . . . vim verbi auget, *i. e.*, intensiva est." *His own*, ἰδίου, *i. e., his genuine*, in opposition to or in dis-

tinction from υἱοῦ Θετοῦ, *an adopted son*, for such *believers* are; *e. g.*, Abraham prepared to offer up *his own* son as a sacrifice instead of selecting a supposititious or adopted heir. *Son* being evidently used here as μονογενής in Luke i. 35, not for the divine Logos as such, but for the Messiah clothed with our nature; as the sequel plainly shows.

He spared not, οὐκ ἐφείσατο, *i. e.*, he did not withhold; a λιτότης as in v. 12 above, equivalent to ἐχαρίσατο, *he gave.* So the sequel; *but gave him up for us all*, ἀλλ᾿ .... αὐτόν, *i. e.*, gave him up to suffering and death, devoted him to be a sacrifice for our sins; comp. John iii. 16. Luke xxii. 19. Gal. i. 4. The word παρέδωκεν is stronger than ἔδωκε, which is used in these cited passages. It means *delivered over*, viz., to death. Πάντων is plainly the same here as ἡμεῖς, *i. e.*, all Christians.

How [can it be] *that with him he will not also bestow all things upon us?* πῶς οὐχί .... χαρίσεται. That is: 'How can we possibly suppose, that, after having bestowed the greatest of all gifts upon us, viz., his own Son, he will refuse to bestow those gifts which are smaller and less costly?'

Tholuck says that "the apostle has here assured Christians that nothing shall hurt them unless they injure themselves." And again: "If the Calvinistic idea [of perseverance] had been intended to be conveyed [by the apostle] he must also have said, that neither *apostasy* nor *sin* would, under any circumstances, have rendered their *calling* uncertain or disappointed it." That this may be rendered uncertain, he thinks is shown by 2 Pet. i. 10.

But if exhortations, commands and threatenings of a most awful nature, addressed to Christians, are to be considered as implying an uncertainty whether the work which God has begun in Christians will be completed; then the Bible is indeed full of proof that they may fall away and finally perish; for it is filled with passages of such a nature. Above all does the epistle to the Hebrews abound in them. But while it is impossible to deny this, or even to deny that if Christians were left to themselves they would fall away every day and hour of their lives, one may still, without any just cause of reproach, be permitted to believe with the apostle, that "*whom God calls he justifies and glorifies;*" he may believe, with the same apostle, that "if Christ died for us while we were yet sinners, while we were ἀσθενεῖς καὶ ἀσεβεῖς, MUCH MORE, being justified [*i. e.*, obtaining pardon through his blood], shall we be saved from wrath," Rom. v. 6 — 10. How can we then put a construction so frigid on this most animated and energetic passage which is now before us? 'The purposes of God,' says the apostle, 'will not be disappointed in bringing his elect to glory." Why? "Because, since God hath given us his own Son — the greatest possible gift — to redeem them from sin, therefore, their redemption remaineth not uncertain, but will be accomplished." This reasoning we can see and feel. But how is it with the exegesis of Tholuck? " God will save you from the power of *external* causes of disappointment, if you only take care yourselves of the *internal* ones." Indeed! But I have great difficulty in finding the consolation or assurance which I need in such a declaration as this. It is offering me only a single drop of water, when I am ready to faint with thirst, and need a copious draught. Ten thousand thousand enemies *without* are not half so strong as the one *within;* and if God's gift of his own Son has not secured *sanctifying* and *restraining* grace for his children, which shall enable them to "crucify the old man with his lusts and to put on the new man," then is the work not only incomplete, but it will most certainly fail of being finally accomplished. The world and the devil would have little influence over us, indeed, were our hearts altogether right toward God; and certain it is, that all other combats are mere skirmishes, compared with the warfare that is going on within us by reason of our *internal* enemy, *i e.*, a corrupt heart. But did not Christ die to redeem us from the dangers of this most powerful of all enemies, as well as from other dangers? If not, then we may abandon all hopes which the gospel inspires, and give ourselves up, after all, for lost. But no, NO! This exegesis does not meet the object which the apostle has in view. It is and must be true, that "if when we were enemies we were reconciled to God by the death of his Son, MUCH MORE, being reconciled, *we shall be saved by his life.*" Rom. v. 10.

But all this purpose (which belongs only to the counsels and mercy of God) does not hinder Paul, nor any other sacred writer, from reproving, warning and threatening Christians, just as if they were liable, every day and hour of their lives, to fall away and to lose the glorious reward of the saints. *In themselves considered* they are liable to this; and God employs the very means in question in order to preserve them against apostasy. Thus, while we admit that the promises of Christ will not fail, nor the efficacy of atoning blood be frustrated; while we believe that "where God has begun a good work, he will *carry it into execution.* (ἐπιτελέσει) until the day of Jesus Christ" (Phil. i. 6); we admit in the fullest manner the importance and duty of warning, reproving, exhorting, and threatening Christians, just as we should do were there no direct assurances that "whom God calls he justifies, and whom he justifies he glorifies." We admit all this, because the sacred writers evidently admit it, and write constantly in a manner that accords with this admission.

(33) *Who shall bring an accusation against the elect of God?* Τίς . . . . . . Θεοῦ, That is: "Who shall prefer an accusation against them of crimes that would occasion their condemnation, when they come before the tribunal of God?" Ἐκλεκτῶν, Heb. נִבְחָר, בָּחִיר, בָּחוּר, *chosen, dear, beloved, precious;* comp. 1 Pet. ii. 9; Luke xxiii. 35. 1 Pet. i. 1. Matt. xxiv. 22, 31. Mark xiii. 20. Luke xviii. 7. Col. iii. 12. Tit. i. 1. Rev. xvii. 14; also Matt. xx. 16. xxii. 14 (where ἐκλεκτοί is used in distinction from κλητοί). That ἐκλεκτῶν, however, here means something more than merely ἀγαπητοί, may be seen from comparing ver. 28 above — κατὰ πρόθεσιν . . . κλητοί and Pet. i. 1, 2, ἐκλεκτοῖς . . . κατὰ πρόγνωσιν Θεοῦ Πατρός.

It is God who justifieth, Θεὸς ὁ δικαιῶν. So I prefer to render and to point it, viz., by making this phrase answer to the preceding question. So Luther, Tholuck, our English version, and most commentators. On the other hand, Augustine, Erasmus, Locke, Schottgen, Griesbach, Knapp, Reiche, and others, put an interrogation point after δικαιῶν, and likewise after all the succeeding clauses; with diminished emphasis, as it seems to me, and certainly with no great probability; for how can we well suppose that *seventeen* successive questions are here put, without any answer or intervening matter? as Dr. Knapp's and Griesbach's pointing represents them to be. Θεὸς ὁ δικαιῶν means, *it is God who acquits, pardons, forgives* the sins τῶν ἐκλεκτῶν. Now as God is the supreme and final judge, how can any accusation against them occasion their condemnation?

(34) *Who shall condemn or be the condemner?* Τίς ὁ κατακρίνων; *i. e.*, who shall pass sentence of condemnation? God acquits; can any one besides him condemn? No; Christ has prevented all condemnation by his death: Χριστὸς ὁ ἀποθανών, *i. e.*, his death having made expiation for the sins of believers, no sentence of condemnation can now be passed. I construe Χριστὸς ὁ ἀποθανών as an answer to the preceding question; so Tholuck and Flatt.

Yea rather, who is also risen, who moreover is at the right hand of God, and maketh intercession for us. Μᾶλλον δὲ . . . . ἡμῶν, *i. e.*, Christ not only died to make atonement for our sins, but he is risen from the dead, and is exalted to the throne of Majesty in the heavens, in order that he may complete the glorious work which he began by his death. In regard to the phrase ἐν δεξιᾷ τοῦ Θεοῦ, see Comm. on Heb. i. 3. — Ἐντυγχάνει conveys the general sense of *aiding, assisting, managing one's concerns for his advantage*, etc.; comp. Heb. vii. 25. ix. 24. 1 John ii. 1. In construing the passage in this way, one must remove the interrogation points after the respective clauses, and substitute a comma after the first and second, and a period after the third.

(35) *Who shall separate us from the love of Christ?* Τίς . . . . Χριστοῦ; *i. e.*, from that love which he cherishes for us. Calvin remarks on τίς here (instead of τί), that the apostle uses τίς because he considers all creatures and trials here as so many *athletæ*, striving against the efforts of Christians. Θλίψις, ἢ στενοχωρία ἢ διωγμός; *i. e.*, shall *vexation* from without, or *anxiety* from within, or *persecution* by the enemies of the Christian religion, effect a separation from the love of Christ? Θλίψις is strictly applicable to any strait or pressure which comes from *circumstances*, *i. e.*, from external causes; στενοχωρία (lit. *narrowness of place*) is applied more especially to *anxiety of mind;* διωγμός obviously designates distresses arising from the rage and malice of persecutors. All three words together express intensely the general idea of trouble or distress. Bodily sufferings and dangers next follow; to which Christians, who live in periods of persecution, must of course be peculiarly exposed. *Famine* and *nakedness* are the natural result of being driven from home, and made to wander in deserts and desolate places. *Peril* and *sword* are necessarily connected with the bitter hostility of persecution.

(36) The quotation here from Ps. xliv. 23 (Sept. xliii. 22), is applied to the state of Christians in the apostle's times, as it was originally to those whom the Psalmist describes; in other words, the apostle describes the state of suffering Christians, by the terms which were employed in ancient days to describe the suffering people of God. — Ὅλην τὴν ἡμέραν, כָּל־הַיּוֹם, *continually unremittingly*.

We are counted, i. e., we are reckoned, regarded, dealt with, *as sheep for the slaughter;* Ἐλογίσθημεν ὡς πρόβατα σφαγῆς, or we are killed as *slaughter-sheep, i. e.*, unremittingly and without mercy.

(37) *But still*, ἀλλά, *i. e.*, notwithstanding these severe pressures and trials. — *In all these,* Ἐν τούτοις πᾶσιν, viz., all these sufferings and sorrows. *We are more than conquerors;* Ὑπερνικῶμεν an intensive and powerful expression, used with great appropriateness and significancy here. Διὰ . . . . ἡμᾶς, *i. e.*, through Christ who loved us, viz., in consequence of the strength and courage which he imparts: comp. Phil. iv. 13.

(38) The γάρ here stands as a *reason* for the assertion that we are *more than conquerors.* "It must be so," says Paul, "*for* nothing can separate us from the love of Christ." Θάνατος . . . . ζωή; *death*, may naturally refer to *a violent death* by the hands of persecutors, and Ζωή, to *life* on condition of recanting a profes-

sion of the Christian religion. If any one, however, choose to give
the words a more extensive meaning, and to regard them as equivalent to saying, that there is nothing in death itself or in life,
which will separate, etc., there can be no valid objection to this.

Neither angels, nor principalities, nor powers; Οὔτε ἄγγελοι,
οὔτε ἀρχαὶ . . . . οὔτε δυνάμεις. The separation of δυνάμεις here
from ἀρχαί, by an intervening clause, although it produces difficulty
in interpretation, does in fact exist in the best manuscripts, and
in the Coptic, Armenian, and Syriac versions. So we are
obliged, as critics, to receive it as it stands, and to interpret it in
the best manner we can.

Is δυνάμεις here intended by the writer to designate *an order
of angels*, either good or bad? Many suppose so, because we
find words of the same and the like kind, elsewhere ranged together to designate such classes or orders; *e. g*, Eph. i. 21, . . .
ἀρχῆς καὶ ἐξουσίας δυνάμεως. Col. i. 16, εἴτε θρόνοι, εἴτε κυριότητες,
εἴτε ἀρχαί, εἴτε ἐξουσίαι, 1 Pet. iii. 22, ἀγγέλων, καὶ ἐξουσιῶν, καὶ
δυνάμεων. The Seventy often render צָבָא, (*exercitus*) by δύναμις.
And this seems to give us a key to the meaning of the word, when
it is applied to the angels. In the passages just cited, different
ranks or *orders* of angels would seem to be designated. Is the
use of the word thus here in accordance with the Jewish *usus
loquendi*?

So far as we can gather, from the Old Testament and from the
Rabbins, what this usage was, we may answer in the affirmative.
Thus in Dan. xii. 1, Michael is called *the great* prince. In
Isaiah vi. 1, seq., the Seraphim are represented, as *presence-
angels* (so to speak) of Jehovah. In Matt. xviii. 10, the guar-
dian-angels of little children are also represented by our Saviour
as *the presence-angels* of Jehovah. And with regard to the
Rabbins, it is well known that they made a great many different
orders of angels; *e. g*., בְּנֵי הָאֱלֹהִים, שְׂרָפִים אָפְנִים, שְׁרָשִׁים, כְּרוּבִים,
תַּרְשִׁישִׁים הַשְׁמַלִּים, גִּנְאָנִים; and also מְלָכִים שָׂרִים and כִּסְאִים, *i. e*.,
κυριότητες, ἀρχαί, and θρόνοι.

From all this it appears, that *angels, and principalities, and
powers* correspond somewhat exactly to the Jewish orders of
angels as occasionally reckoned ; and that, so far as the *possibility* of meaning is here concerned, there lies no difficulty in the
way of applying these three words to angels. Nay, we may advance still farther, and say that in respect to ἀρχαί at least, it is
quite improbable that it should have been intended to designate
magistrates of any kind. Ἄγγελοι and ἀρχαί may very naturally
be taken as designating *angels* and *archangels ;* comp. Jude
verse 9. 1 Thess. iv. 16. Dan. x. 13. xii. 1. If we understand
here these two great divisions of angels it will be in accordance

with the *usus loquendi* of the Old Testament. The fact that ἄγγελοι and ἀρχαί are joined by juxta-position, renders it probable that they belong to the same category of meaning; for so words of this class are commonly employed.

But allowing this, are *good* or *evil* angels here meant? That evil angels were also distributed by the Jews into classes, is as clear as that good angels were classified; *e. g.*, Eph. vi. 12. 1 Cor. xv. 24. Col. ii. 15, where they are called ἀρχαί καὶ ἐξουσίαι, and in 2 Pet. ii. 4. they are also called ἄγγελοι. Moreover Satan is styled ὁ ἄρχων, Matt. ix. 34. xii. 24. John xii. 31. xiv. 30. xvi. 11. Eph. ii. 2, which implies *precedence, i. e.*, rank among evil angels. The passage in Eph. vi. 12 seems to be most direct to our purpose, where the apostle represents Christians as in violent contest πρὸς τὰς ἀρχας καὶ πρὸς τὰς ἐξουσίας. So in the verse before us, I understand the apostle as averring, that neither *angels* nor *archangels* with whom we are contesting, *i. e*, neither the inferior evil spirits, nor Satan himself, (or it may be, Satan and others of similar rank), shall be able, by all their assaults and machinations, to separate true Christians from the love of their Saviour. Tholuck supposes the *good angels* to be meant here; but how can those "who are sent forth to minister to such as are the heirs of salvation" (Heb. i. 14), be well supposed to be the *opposers* and *enemies* of Christians?*
Accordingly, with Flatt, I understand ἄγγελοι and ἀρχαί of *evil spirits*

Δυνάμεις not to be associated in meaning with ἄγγελοι and ἀρχαί, because it is not associated with them by juxta-position; for it has juxta-position in all other instances where it means *angels*. I must interpret it, therefore, as designating *magistrates, civil powers*, viz., persecuting kings and princes. That δύναμις means *auctoritas, imperium*, is beyond all doubt; see Luke iv. 36. Acts iv. 7. 1 Cor. v. 4. Rev. xiii. 2; also Rev. iv. 11. v. 12. vii. 12. xii. 10. And that the *abstract* sense may become *concrete, i. e.*, that δύναμις may designate those *persons* who are clothed with civil power, is clear from 1 Cor. xv. 24. Eph. i. 21, as also from comparing its synonyme ἐξουσία, in Rom. xiii. 1—4.

Neither the present nor the future; οὔτε ἐνεστῶτα οὔτε μέλλοντα, *i. e.*, neither any objects of the present time nor of the future. The apostle, after having mentioned particular things in the preceding context, here comes to the generic ideas of *time*, including of course all occurrences that take place in it; and in the next

---

* Can there be any greater objection to the implied supposition, for rhetorical effect, of the possibility of this kind of influence from good angels, than in Gal. i 8 "But though .... an angel from heaven preach any other gospel," etc. ?

clause he seems to predicate that of *space* or *place*, which he here asserts of time.

(39) *Neither height nor depth*, οὔτε ὕψωμα οὔτε βάθος. A great variety of explanations have been given to these words; *e. g.*, Origen: 'Evil spirits in the air and in hades.' Ambrose: 'Neither high and haughty speculation [in doctrine] nor deep sins.' Augustine: 'Idle curiosity about things above us and below us.' Melancthon: 'Heretical speculation of the learned, and gross superstition of the vulgar, etc.' So likewise: 'Honor and dishonor,' 'high place and low place,' 'happiness and misery,' 'the elevation of Christians on the cross, and the submersion of them in the sea,' have all had their advocates. The meaning *happiness or misery, honor or dishonor*, is a possible one; but the animated and glowing spirit of the whole passage naturally leads the mind to expect something more elevated than this. Ὕψος may mean *heaven*; so מָרוֹם, and so ὕψος in Luke i. 78. Eph. iv. 8. As to βάθος, it has been taken to mean *the earth*, and Eph. iv. 9 is appealed to as sustaining this interpretation. But Ps. cxxxix. 15, תַּחְתִּיּוֹת אָרֶץ, *the lower parts of the earth*, τὰ βάθη τῆς γῆς (comp. Eph. iv. 9), would be a more apposite appeal, inasmuch as here the meaning plainly is, *earth* or *secret recesses of the earth*. On the whole, however, βάθος (as the antithesis of ὕψωμα) would more appropriately designate *the under-world*, שְׁאוֹל, ᾅδης, ἄβυσσος. Thus understood, the sentiment of the apostle ends in a climax; viz., neither heaven nor hell, *i. e.*, neither the world above, nor the world below, οὔτε τις κτίσις ἑτέρα, *nor any other created thing*. The whole summed up together, and understood after the Hebrew manner of speaking stands thus: 'The universe shall not be able to separate Christians from the love of Jesus, who died for them;' heaven above and Sheol below, and other created things constituting, in the language of Scripture, *the universe*. I prefer, however, the simple meaning *above* and *below*, *i. e.*, no time and no space can separate us, etc.; or no period of time and no place can occasion the disappointment of our hopes.

This is, indeed, "an anchor sure and steadfast, entering into that within the vail;" A BLESSED, CHEERING, GLORIOUS HOPE, WHICH ONLY THE GOSPEL AND ATONING BLOOD CAN INSPIRE.

CHAP. IX. 1—33.

WITH the eighth chapter concludes what may be termed strictly the *doctrinal* part of our epistle. What follows is either by way of forestalling or of removing objections, or of justifying what has been said (chapters IX —XI.), or else in the way of practical exhortation and caution (12—16). In different parts of the epistle, the apostle had already advanced sentiments on the subject of salvation by grace— a salvation proffered on the same terms to Gentile and Jew— which he knew would be very obnoxious to many of his kinsmen, not excepting some who professed to be converts to the Christian religion. In chapters ii and iii he had formally shown that the Jews were not only in a state of condemnation by the divine law, but even more guilty than the Gentiles, and this because they had enjoyed greater religious privileges. At the close of chap. iii he had plainly and explicitly declared, that God is the God of the Gentiles as really and truly as of the Jews, and had labored to show (chap 14), that such was the principle or doctrine which is taught in the Old Testament Scriptures themselves. "The seed of Abraham," in the highest, and noblest, and only really important sense of the phrase, means his *spiritual seed*, which comprises all who imitate the faith of Abraham, and like him believe implicitly in the divine declarations. In chap v. the apostle had implicitly justified the extension of the gospel privileges and blessings to all men indiscriminately, inasmuch as all were affected by the fall of Adam, their common progenitor. Then in chapters vi —viii he had shown that Christ and his grace are the only effectual ground of our *sanctification* as well as justification, that all objection to the scheme of grace on the ground that it will encourage sin, not only is destitute of foundation, but that the sinner has no hope of resisting sin with success, but through the grace of the gospel, and, finally, that the *sanctification* of believers will, as certainly as their justification, issue in their *salvation*.

But how could the Jew, accustomed to pride himself in his descent from Abraham, to regard God as his peculiar and covenant God, and to expect acceptance in consequence of his lineage and of the peculiar favors which had been shown to the Hebrew nation— how could he receive with approbation a doctrine, which not only went to prostrate all the hopes that he had cherished of pre-eminence in this world, and of happiness in the world to come, and to place the very heathen on a level with himself, but which even advanced still farther, and made him more guilty than the heathen, and consequently involved him in higher condemnation, because he had sinned against peculiar light and love? Nay, the very privileges, which had been the ground of his greatest confidence that he must be regarded with divine approbation and entitled to the favor of God, had become, according to the representation of the apostle, the occasion of his peculiar and aggravated condemnation.

The apostle accordingly expected that his countrymen would accuse him of having become alienated from his kinsmen after the flesh, and partial to the Gentiles, since he was an apostle to them. To counteract this feeling, he evidently wrote the chapter now before us. He begins this by a most solemn profession or declaration of his sincere and ardent affection for his own nation. He protests against the idea, that in declaring God to be the God of the Gentiles, as well as the Jews, he has therefore abjured every kind of pre-eminence to his own people. He allows that they have enjoyed special and distinguished *external* privileges, above all, that the Messiah himself has come from the midst of them, verses 2—5. He then proceeds to show that God in selecting the heirs of his grace where he pleases, i e , making the Gentiles the κατὰ πρόθεσιν κλητοί as well as Jews, had violated no promise. His word οὐκ ἐκπέπτωκε (ver. 6), i. e , his promise made to Abraham and *his seed* is not frustrated or annulled, as the Jewish Scriptures themselves do testify. Abraham, for example, had several children; but in Isaac only was his seed called, verses 7—9. To Isaac two sons were born, Esau and Jacob; yet Esau was rejected and Jacob received, and the decision respecting this was made even before they were born, verses 10—14. God's declaration to Moses, and his dealing with Pharaoh, exhibit the same truth in a striking manner, verses 15—18. All objection to this on the ground of partiality or injustice, is without any good support ; since the sovereign Lord of the universe has a perfect right to dispose of his own as seems good in his sight, verses 19, 20. He does injustice to none; for those whom he passes by are left to the course of justice and equity, verses 21—23 The Hebrew

Scriptures have not only displayed, in this way, God's sovereignty in his dealings with his people, but they also contain express declarations that the Gentiles shall be brought into the church and become the children of God, verses 24 — 26. Equally certain is it that they predict the unbelief and rejection of the natural descendants of Abraham, verses 27 — 29. Finally, the apostle sums up the whole matter in discussion, by declaring that 'the Gentiles are admitted to the gospel privilege of justification by faith, but that the Jews in general remain in a state of unbelief and rejection, because Christ crucified is to them a stumbling-block, and none but believers on him can be saved,' verses 30 — 33.

It is in this way that the apostle justifies what he had already advanced respecting the Jews and Gentiles, and in particular what he had said, in the eighth chapter, in reference to the bestowment of blessings upon the κατὰ πρόθεσιν κλητοί. 'God has always,' he would say, 'dealt in the same manner by his people.' The Old Testament is full of the same doctrine, or of facts which illustrate and confirm it. It contains predictions concerning the very things of which the Jews now complain.'

The question in the eighth chapter is not one of *external* privileges or advantages; it is one of *calling, justification,* and *glorification.* It is one which respects the everlasting and inseparable love of Christ. Defence, therefore, of the sentiments inculcated in respect to these topics, occupies the ninth chapter. In itself it contains not the great doctrine in question, that is, it does not *directly* reveal or inculcate it. The *examples* of God's sovereignty produced in it are of various kinds, some of them having respect to temporal advantages or disadvantages, and some to both spiritual and temporal. But the *principle* illustrated and confirmed by all these is the main and all-important question, and the principle is that which is avowed in the eighth chapter, viz., that the κατὰ πρόθεσιν κλητοί are the certain heirs of *future glory*. It is the eighth chapter, then, which is the key of the ninth; and without keeping this in view one may look in vain for the object of the various examples and illustrations which the ninth chapter exhibits. In a word, the apostle shows in the ninth chapter, 'that *God in calling, justifying and glorifying,* οὓς προέγνω, *does only what he has a perfect right to do,* what is analogous to examples of his dealings as exhibited by the Jewish Scriptures, and what accords with the doctrines and predictions which they contain. In this way, and in this only, can we fully see the scope, object, and connection of the ninth chapter.

CHAP. IX. 1 — 5.

(1) First of all the apostle makes the most solemn and glowing assurances of his affectionate regard for his own nation, in order to prevent the apprehension that any alienation from the Jews had caused him to believe and teach as he had done respecting the Gentiles.

I speak the truth in Christ. Ἀλήθειαν . . . Χριστῷ. Most interpreters regard ἐν Χριστῷ as the formula of an oath: and they appeal to the Hebrew form of an oath, which prefixes ב (ἐν) to the object or person by whom any one swears. So also ἐν in the

New Testament, e. g., Matt. v. 34—36. Rev. x. 6. So Dan. xii. 7. (in Theodotion's Greek version). But this interpretation is very doubtful. Compare for example, ἐν Κυρίῳ in Eph. iv. 17, where it follows μαρτυροῦμαι, and where the formula of an oath is out of question. It is only solemn declaration, such as Christ or the Spirit of Christ prompts or suggests. In like manner we have χαρὰ ἐν Χριστῷ, ἀγάπη ἐν Χριστῷ, κ. τ. λ., where an oath is out of all question. Indeed the phrase ἐν Κυρίῳ, ἐν Χριστῷ, etc., occurs so often, that abundant analogies are at hand to justify the exegesis which is given to ἐν Χριστῷ, here, when we construe it as meaning *agreeably to what becomes one who is in Christ*, or *who belongs to him;* i. e., as a Christian, or one who is spiritually united to Christ, I speak the truth, etc. Οὐ ψεύδομαι repeats the affirmation and strengthens it by *litotes*. Comp. John i. 21. Eph. iv. 25. 1 Sam. iii. 18, for the form of the expression; 1 Tim. ii. 7, for the like words.

My conscience bearing me witness, in the Holy Spirit, συμμαρτυρούσης . . . . ἁγίῳ. Dr. Knapp and some other critics incorrectly join οὐ ψεύδομαι with ἐν Πνεύματι ἁγίῳ, making the latter phrase a part of the formula of an oath. The repetition of an oath here would be unnatural and excessive; besides that no example elsewhere of Christians swearing by the Holy Ghost can be produced. Conscience is the voice of God in man; or at least the faculty on which the influence of the Spirit of God seems to be specially exerted. It was a conscience moved and enlightened by this Spirit, which, the apostle here solemnly declares, testified his affectionate regard for the Jewish nation; ἐν Πνεύματι ἁγίῳ, meaning, I who am moved *by the Holy Spirit*, or am *in the Spirit;* comp. Rev. i. 10, ἐγενόμην ἐν πνεύματι.

(2) *That I have great sorrow and continual anguish in my heart*, ὅτι . . . . μου. For the like expressions of sympathy and affection, comp. 1 Cor. i. 4. Phil. i. 3, 4. Eph. i. 16. 1 Thes. i. 2. Rom. i. 9, 10. Philem. ver. 4. 2 Tim. i. 3, 4. 2 Cor. xi. 29. xii. 15.

(3) Nearly every word in this verse has been the subject of different and contested exegesis. *For I myself could wish*, ηὐχόμην γὰρ αὐτὸς. Compare Acts xxv. 22, ἐβουλόμην, *I could wish;* Gal. iv. 20, ἤθελον, *I could desire*. But why not translate, *I did wish, i. e.,* when I was an unconverted Jew I did wish? Because (1) The apostle designs to show his *present* love to the Jews. Who questioned this strong attachment to them, when he persecuted Stephen and others before his conversion? Or to what purpose could it be now to exhibit this, when his love to them since he became a Christian is the only thing that is called in question? Then (2) Neither the present εὔχομαι, nor the

Optative εὐχοίμην, would accurately express what the apostle means here. Εὔχομαι (Ind. present) would mean, *I wish* by way of direct and positive affirmation, and with the implication that the thing wished might take place; εὐχοίμην (Opt.) *I am wishing with desire*, implying the *possibility* that the thing wished for would take place. On the other hand, ηὐχόμην as here employed, (*I could wish*) implies, that whatever his desires may be, after all the thing wished for is impossible or it cannot take place; which is doubtless the very shade of thought that the writer would design to express. See New Test. Gramm. § 136. Note 1. (b). If the apostle had designed here merely to describe what he once felt or desired, *i. e.*, before his conversion, he would of course have employed the *Aorist* of narration, and not the Imperfect. See upon this use of the Imperf. with ἄν, especially Robinson's Buttmann, § 139. R. 12. b., who says, that by rule, the Imperfect Tense with ἄν is used when the reference is to the present time, "to signify that *in consequence of the impossibility or non-fulfilment of certain conditions*, some action or thing in like manner cannot or could not be fulfilled."

To be an anathema, ἀνάθεμα εἶναι, i. e., *to be devoted to destruction*, or *to be excommunicated*. In *classical* Greek ἀνάθεμα and ἀνάθημα are synonymous; just as εὔρεμα and εὔρημα were, and also ἐπίθεμα and ἐπίθημα, etc. (1) The proper and original meaning of ἀνάθεμα or ἀνάθημα, was *a setting out* or *setting up* of anything consecrated to the gods, in their temples, such as tripods, images, statues, inscriptions, etc. The *exposure* of such things in the temples, in any way, whether they hung up, stood up, or lay down, was ἀνάθεμα; the action of exposing them, or the exposure itself, was called ἀνάθεμα. Hence, (2) *The thing itself exposed, the thing consecrated* or *devoted* to the gods, was by a very common principle of language called ἀνάθεμα. Then (3) As any thing devoted or consecrated to the gods was irrevocably given up to them, and was no more subject to common use; so when any *living* thing, beast or man, became an ἀνάθεμα, it was of course to be slain in sacrifice, and offered to the gods mostly as a piacular victim. In like manner, under the Levitical law, every חֵרֶם or ἀνάθεμα devoted to God, was incapable of redemption. See Lev. xxvii. 28, 29, comp. Judg. xi. 30, 31 and 39; which, however, is the only instance on record in the Scriptures of a *human* ἀνάθεμα, and which at all events is not encouraged by the laws of Moses. And in consequence of such a custom or law, cities, edifices, and their inhabitants, which were devoted to *excision* or *entire destruction*, were called חֵרֶם, *i. e.*, ἀνάθεμα as the Seventy have rendered it. So Jericho was חֵרֶם, Josh. vi. 17, comp. verse 21; and so the cities of the Canaanites that were *utterly destroyed* by Israel, were named חָרְמָה, *destruction*. Any thing in fact, whether man, beast, or any species of property or ornament, *which was to be utterly destroyed*, was called חרם (ἀνάθεμα) by the Hebrews; see Lev. xxvii. 28, 29. Deut. xiii. 15—17, and comp. 1 Kings xx. 42. Is. xxxiv. 5. Zech. xiv. 11. The Greek words ἀναθεματίζω and ἀνατίθημι correspond, in the like manner, to the Heb. החרים (Hiph. of חָרַם), and mean *to pronounce to be an* ἀνάθεμα, *to give up as an* ἀνάθεμα, *i. e.*, to set apart or deliver over to destruction.

Some suppose that natural death or sufferings in the present world, are here referred to. Then ἀπὸ τοῦ Χριστοῦ means *by Christ;* in which case the whole sentiment would seem to be: 'I could wish to suffer temporal death inflicted by Christ, provided this would exempt my countrymen from it.' But the apostle is not here discussing the subject of the Jews' *temporal* punishment or excision, but of their excision from the blessings of a future world by reason of their unbelief; comp. ix. 25—33. A mere willingness to suffer physical dissolution to avert this, is unworthy to be put into the mouth of the apostle. It is a חֵרֶם of a far different kind, that he would consent to take upon himself, could they be saved by it. That ἀνάθεμα may be used to signify the *second* death, is clear from 1 Cor. xvi. 22. Ἀπὸ τοῦ Χριστοῦ may however, mean *by Christ; i. e.*, it is equivalent to ὑπὸ τοῦ Χριστοῦ. So clearly ἀπό is often employed; *e. g.*, Mark viii. 31. Luke ix. 22. xvii. 25. Matt. xi. 19. Luke xii. 58. Acts ii, 22. x. 17. et sæpe. Still, as the idea of being an *anathema* involves the idea of separation or banishment from Christ, ἀπό may be rendered *from*, without any important variation of the sense.

On account of or *in the room of my brethren, my kinsmen after the flesh,* ὑπὲρ τῶν . . . . . . σάρκα, *i. e.*, for the sake of my natural brethren; my kinsmen by natural descent or generation, *i. e.*, the Jews.

Tholuck gives a little different turn to the passage, but the same sense in substance. He compares ἀνάθεμα to חרם in the later Heb.; which was used to denote *excommunication*, separation from the Jewish community or קָהָל. The Rabbins make *three* gradations of excommunication, which they call, (*a*) נדוי *seclusion*, which lasted a month, and obliged a man to keep four ells distant from all his household. (*b*) The חֵרֶם, which forbade all intercourse, action, eating, drinking, etc., with any one, and all approach on the part of the excommunicated person to the synagogue. (*c*) The שַׁמָּתָא (from שמה, *excludere*), which designated utter exclusion on the part of God and man, and the being given up to destruction. For a tremendous example of the Rabbinic חֵרֶם see Buxtorf, Lex. Rabb. p. 828. In this way, ἀνάθεμα ἀπὸ τοῦ Χριστοῦ would mean, *one banished, cut off, separated from Christ;* which would involve, however, all the consequences that are involved in the preceding exegesis. But on the whole, as the preceding sense is most consonant with Scriptural and classical usage, I should give it the preference. The sentiment then is: 'Such is my love for my kinsmen after the flesh, that were it possible, I would devote myself to the destruction which threatens them, could they but escape by such means.

The objections urged against this sentiment seem to be of little weight. It is asked: 'How could the apostle be willing to be for ever cast off and separated from Christ? How could he be willing to become a sinner and to be miserable forever?' I answer, (1) The possibility that such could or would be the case, is not at all implied in what he says; no more than the possibility that "an angel from heaven should preach another gospel," is implied by what is said in Gal. i. 8. (2) Even supposing the actual possibility of the exchange in question was believed by the apostle, it would not imply that in itself he was willing to be a sinner, or to be forever miserable. When the apostle says that Christ *was made a* CURSE *for us*, does he mean to say that Christ took on him the temper of mind which they have who are accursed? "Quid mirum," says Origen, "si, cum Dominus pro servis maledictum sit factum, servus pro fratribus anathema fiat?" It would imply merely, then, that Paul would be willing, in case he could save the whole nation, to take on himself the *miseries* to which they were hastening. And a sentiment like this, is surely capable of a rational and sober defence. If benevolence would lead Paul to undergo any assignable degree of suffering, in the present life, in order to promote the everlasting welfare of the Jewish nation; would not the like benevolence lead him to undergo any assignable degree of misery in a future world for the same purpose, provided such a purpose could be answered by it? Who can draw the line where benevolence would stop short; except it be, where the evil suffered was to be equal to the good accomplished, or even greater? Could Paul have the genuine spirit of his Lord and Master, unless he could truly say what he has said in the passage before us? But, (3) The inference that Paul "was willing to be damned," or that Christians must come to such a state of willingness, is made without any ground from the verse in question. If Paul's being cast off by the Saviour could occasion the reception and salvation of the whole Jewish people, this apostle expresses his readiness to submit to it. But as such a thing was impossible; and as he really knew it to be so; all that we can well suppose the passage teaches, is, that the apostle possessed such a feeling of benevolence toward the Jewish nation, that he was ready to do or suffer anything whatever, provided their salvation might be secured by it. In other words, this is a high and glowing expression, of his strong affection, springing from an excited state of feeling, which the use of common language could not at all satisfy. Such expressions are still very common in the East. The Arabians, for example, very commonly, in order to testify strong affection, say, *let my soul be a ransom for thee.* So Maimonides (Sanhed. fol. 18. 1), in explaining the Talmudic expression חֲרִינִי כַפָּרָתָךְ, *see I am thy ransom* states, that this was a common expression of strong affection.

(4) *Israelites,* Ἰσραηλῖται, *i. e.,* who bear this honorable or far-famed name; comp. Gen. xxxii. 28. John i. 47, 2 Cor. xi. 22. Phil. iii. 5. This however is only an *external* privilege; for they are not all Israelites in truth, who are of Israelitish descent, Rom. ix. 6. comp. iii. 28, 29.

Whose is the sonship, ὧν ἡ υἱοθεσία, *i. e.,* the relation of sons or children; comp. Ex. iv. 22, 23. Deut. xxxii. 5, 6, xiv. 1. Hos. xi. 1. The meaning is, that Israel stood in a special relation to God, and was treated with distinguished and peculiar affection. This last circumstance forms what is the special ground of the υἱοθεσία. This υἱοθεσία was however *external,* and consisted with the Jewish nation's being in a very imperfect state; comp. Gal. iv. 1—3. 2 Cor. iii. 6—18. For a sonship of a much higher nature than this, comp. Gal. iv. 4—7. Rom. viii. 14—17.

Δόξα may have the sense here of *glory,* and be joined with υἱοθεσία in the way of Hendiadys or as explicative, so that the meaning would be for substance *glorious adoption* or *sonship, i. e,* one which is worthy of praise, etc. And this method Tholuck prefers. But the epithet δόξα appears to be too strong for a mere external υἱοθεσία; and besides all the other nouns which precede and follow stand single. On this account I must prefer giving to δόξα the sense of כָּבוֹד, and regard it here as designating the visible splendor which was the symbol of Jehovah's presence, and which was peculiarly manifested in the *sanctum sanctorum* of the temple; comp. Ex. xxv. 22. xl. 34, 35. Lev. ix. 6. Ezek. i. 28. iii. 23. viii. 4. It is true, indeed, that in all these passages we have כְּבוֹד יְהוָֹה (δόξα Θεοῦ), and not simply כָּבוֹד. But the Targum, which employs שְׁכִנְתָּא יְהוָֹה for כָּבוֹד, יְהוָֹה also employs שְׁכִנְתָּא (Shechinah) *alone* in the same sense. Paul then may have here used δόξα elliptically, in a corresponding manner. Beza, Turretin, Vitringa, Ruckert, Reiche, and others, agree with me in this interpretation. The sentiment then is: 'To the Israelites belonged the *visible splendor* or *glory,* which was indicative of the immediate presence of Jehovah.'

Covenants, Διαθῆκαι, *i. e.,* those made at different times with Abraham, Jacob, Moses, etc.—*Legislation,* νομοθεσία, or *system of laws,* viz., the Mosaic legislation or laws ; as to the distinguished privilege of these, comp. Deut. iv. 5 — 8. Ps. cxlvii. 19, 20. Rom. ii. 18, 19.— *Service,* λατρεία, צְבוּרָה, *rites* of the temple, priesthood, etc. — *The promises,* ἐπαγγελίαι, viz., those which had respect to the Messiah : comp. Gal. iii. 16. Rom. xv. 8. Heb. xi. 17.

(5) *Whose are the fathers,* ὧν οἱ πατέρες, *i. e.,* whose progenitors were the fathers, Abraham, etc., to whom so many promises (ἐπαγγελίαι) were made, and who are so distinguished in sacred history. *From whom* [descended] *Christ, in respect to the flesh,* ἐξ ὧν . . . σάρκα, *i. e.,* in respect to his human or inferior nature, or so far as he was man ; comp. Rom. i. 3 and ὁμοίωμα σαρκός in viii. 3. But if he had no other nature, why should such a distinction as is implied by κατὰ σάρκα, be here designated ? Would a sacred writer say of David, for example, that he was descended from Abraham κατὰ σάρκα ? Would it not imply that κατὰ πνεῦμα he was not descended from Abraham ? But here, the other nature of Christ appears to be designated by the succeeding phrase ὁ ὢν ἐπὶ πάντων Θεός.

Who is God over all, blessed forever, Amen? ὁ ὢν . . . ἀμήν. Ὁ ὢν is equivalent to or the same as ὅς ἐστι, *who is ;* for so the article followed by a participle is often employed in the Greek language ; see John i. 18. iii. 13, xii. 17. 2 Cor. xi. 31, ὁ Θεὸς . . . ὁ ὢν εὐλογητός κ. τ. λ.—᾽Επὶ πάντων, being placed here between the article ὁ and the noun Θεός to which this article belongs, is of course an *adjective* as to meaning, and designates the idea of *supreme.* Some indeed have understood ἐπὶ πάντων as meaning ἐπὶ πάντων πατέρων ; but this is plainly a forced and frigid exegesis. In Hebrew, אֱלֹהֵי צְבָאוֹת and שַׁדַּי are epithets of Jehovah, the supreme God ; and to these παντοκράτωρ in the Septuagint corresponds ; *e. g.,* 2 Sam. v. 10. 1 Chron. xi. 9. Jer. v. 14. Amos iii. 13. Zech. i 3, seq., et alibi. So in the Apocalypse παντοκράτωρ often appears as an epithet of Jehovah, *e. g.,* Rev. i. 8. iv. 8. xi. 17. xv. 3, etc. Now παντοκράτωρ is for substance the equivalent of ἐπὶ πάντων as to meaning ; so that ὁ ἐπί πάντων Θεός must be altogether equivalent to ὁ Θεός ὁ παντοκράτωρ.

Blessed, εὐλογητός is equivalent to the Hebrew בָּרוּךְ. The Jewish Rabbins from time immemorial have been accustomed, whenever the name of God is mentioned, to add בָּרוּךְ הוּא, *blessed is he.* So Paul here, after calling Christ ὁ ὢν ἐπί πάντων Θεός, adds εὐλογητὸς εἰς τοὺς αἰῶνας, *i. e.,* בָּרוּךְ לְעוֹלָם וָעֶד. Compare now the same appellation given to God in Mark xiv. 61. Whether an ascription of divine honour to Christ is intended by applying to him here the word εὐλογητός, the reader may satisfy himself by comparing the use of this word in 2 Cor. i. 3. xi. 31. Eph. i. 3. 1 Pet. i. 3. Luke i. 68. That divine honor is ascribed to Christ by the heavenly hosts (and the same too which is rendered to the Father), appears from Rev. v. 13, 14. Nor can it be objected that it is contrary to the usage of Paul, to name Christ Θεός; for so he is called in Tit. i. 3, and *the great God* in Tit. ii. 13; moreover he is represented as ἴσα Θεῷ in Phil. ii. 6; and as Θεός in John i. 1; not to mention the controverted but seemingly well authenticated reading (Θεός) in 1 Tim iii. 16. Nor is it any objection to this, that in 1 Cor. xv. 24—28, the apostle represents the Son as renouncing or laying aside his supremacy or dominion, at the final consummation of all things; for the office of the Messiah, and *the dominion of the Messiah, as such*, must of course cease, when all the objects of that office and that dominion shall have been fully accomplished. In reference to this kind of dominion, Christ is called Κύριος in 1 Cor. viii. 6; and it is such a dominion which is represented as bestowed on him in Phil. ii. 9—11. Col. i. 17, 18. Heb. i. 3. ii. 5—9. viii. 1.

Neither the grammatical arrangement of the text, then, nor the sentiments of the apostle elsewhere, require us, or (may I not say?) permit us, to give a different interpretation to the words of the verse in question. Nor do any various readings of the verse occur, which are of any authority at all. It has been conjectured, indeed, that we should read ὧν ὁ κ. τ. λ., i e., *whose is the God over all*, etc ; so Whitby, Crellius, Taylor, and others. But not to say, that taking such liberties with the text is fairly out of question, it will be enough to compare the sentiment which the passage thus modified would give, with Rom. iii. 29, 30. This then is one of the cases, in which Paul has directly asserted Christ to be *supreme God,* and has accordingly rendered to him the sacred doxology.*

The efforts to evade this conclusion have been many and strenuous. The interpretations which have resulted from them may be divided into two classes, viz : —

I. Those which put a full period after σάρκα, and make the remainder of the verse a doxology to God the Father So Erasmus, in the enlarged edition of his notes; so Enjeddin, Whiston,

---

* Alford says of the rendering given above that "it is not only that most agreeable to the usage of the Ap but *the only one admissible by the rules of grammar and arrangement.* It also admirably suits the context· for, having enumerated the historic advantages of the Jewish people, he concludes by stating one which ranks far higher than all, — that from them sprang, according to the flesh He who is God over all, blessed forever."

Semler, Glöckler, and others; this of course, we might expect from Reiche, who is apparently a high Arian. But (*a*) It was long ago noted by Bengel (with whom Faustus Socinus also agrees, that in all classes of doxology, בָּרוּךְ in Hebrew and εὐλογητός in Greek *precede* the name of God who is blessed. So the laws of grammar beyond all doubt demand; for יְהוָֹה בָּרוּךְ would mean, *the blessed Jehovah, i. e.*, the blessed Jehovah does this or that; for both words (thus arranged) make out merely the *subject* of a sentence. On the contrary, בָּרוּךְ יְהוָֹה means *blessed is* or *blessed be Jehovah;* Jehovah being the *subject* of the sentence, and בָּרוּךְ the *predicate*. So, more than *thirty* times, the words בָּרוּךְ in Hebrew and εὐλογητός in Greek are placed in the Old Testament, and so all the examples in the New Testament. Only *one* can I find in all the Bible, that differs from this; and this is Ps. lxvii. 19 (Sept.), where however the repetition of εὐλογητός is plainly an error of the scribes, as it has no corresponding repetition in the Hebrew, and is against all analogy. Even Eichhorn (Einleit. ins. A. T. § 320) concedes that the reading in the Sept. is a doubtful one. (*b*) Construed in this way, ὤν is entirely useless and destitute of meaning, and the addition of it is altogether unaccountable. The natural and simple order of the text would be ; Εὐλογητὸς ὁ ἐπὶ πάντων Θεὸς κ. τ. λ. (*c*) In this mode of interpretation there is no antithesis to κατὰ σάρκα, which plainly requires one ; as the natural inquiry is: If Christ be descended from David only κατὰ σάρκα, what is he as to his higher nature? Comp. Rom. i. 1, 3.

II. Another class of critics viz., Locke, Clark, Justi, Ammon, and others, put a full period after πάντων, and then make a doxology of the sequel. In this way the difficulty last suggested with regard to the interpretation No. I, is in a measure removed, as a kind of antithesis is made out by ὁ ὢν ἐπὶ πάντων, sc. πάντων πατέρων, *i. e.*, Christ in his human nature was a descendant of David, but still was a personage of exalted dignity, being elevated above all the Jewish fathers, who are objects of so much encomium in sacred history and of so much veneration among the Jewish people. But still there are weighty objections against this mode of pointing and explaining the text; for (*a*) The difficulty in regard to the *position* of εὐλογητός, is the same here as has been already described above, under No. I. *a*. (*b*) In such a case the noun Θεός must have the article, as being the *subject* of the sentence, and in its own nature customarily requiring it. So uniformly in the Sept. and in the New Testament, where Θεός is the subject of a doxology made by εὐλογητός it takes the article; *e. g.*, Gen. ix. 26. xiv. 20. xxiv. 27. 1 Sam. xxv. 32. 2 Sam. xviii. 28. 1 K. i. 48. v. 7. viii. 15. 2 Chron. ii. 12. vi 4. Ez. vii.

46. Ps. xvii. 50. xl. 14. lxv. 19. lxvii. 20, 38. lxxi. 19. cv. 47. cxliii. 1. Dan. iii. 29. Luke i. 68. 2 Cor. i. 3. Eph. i. 3. 1 Pet. i. 3 In regard to Κύριος, the usage of the Sept varies; *e. g*, 1 Sam xxv. 39, εὐλογητός ὁ Κύριος, according to the usage of Θεός; but in other passages the article is omitted, *e. g.*, Ex. xviii. 10. Ruth iv. 14. Ps. cxxiii. 5. cxxxiv. 21. But no instance of the like variation can I find, in respect to Θεός. The example in our text must stand *alone*, if it be one, of Θεός in a doxology with εὐλογητός, and yet without the article. (*c*) To break off a sentence with ὁ ὢν ἐπὶ πάντων, seems at least to make it very abrupt and incomplete. To what can πάντων refer, in such a connection, except to the *fathers ?* And to say that the Messiah was exalted above the Jewish patriarchs, although it might be saying something, would not seem to be saying very much, considering the efficacy which Paul had been ascribing to his love and sufferings, and death, and the greatness which he had ascribed to his power. (*d*) There is something incongruous in a doxology here to God the Father; which even Crellius himself suggests (Artemon. Init. Evang. Johan.) The apostle is here expressing the deepest and most unfeigned regret of his soul, that notwithstanding the exalted and peculiar privileges of the Jewish nation, they had by their unbelief forfeited them. all, and made themselves obnoxious to a most terrible condemnation. To break out into a doxology here, would be (as Flatt suggests) like saying : 'These special privileges have, by being abused, contributed greatly to enhance the guilt and punishment of the Jewish nation; God be thanked that he has given them such privileges !' It is a duty, indeed, to be grateful for blessings which are bestowed; but— all in its proper place. Doxologies are not appropriate to paragraphs, which give an account of mercies abused and deep guilt contracted. (*e*) Besides all this, the abruptness of a doxology here, which could contain no reference to God as mentioned in the preceding context (for he is not there mentioned), is plain and striking: and also, as Nosselt, Flatt, Koppe, and Ewald have observed, it would be without example. Comp. Rom. i. 25. xi. 36.

The remark of Eckermann and Justi, that εὐλογητός is required to stand *before* Θεός in a doxology, only when this doxology stands at the *beginning* of a sentence, is not true in point of fact ; *e. g.*, Gen. xiv. 20, where καί shows that εὐλογητός is not at the *beginning* of a sentence ; 2 Sam. xxii. 47. Ps. xvii. 46. lxvii. 35. In the last case, one might contend and say, that εὐλογητός begins a *new* sentence; but then where does it not, on the same ground ? The burden of proof lies on those, who assert that εὐλογητός need *not* be *prefixed* except it stand at the *beginning* of a sentence ; yet where are the instances in which it is not prefixed? The only one (except an instance of a manifestly corrupt text, Ps. lxvii. 19), is the very verse before us. To assume the principle in question, then, is to take for granted the very point in dispute.

The remark of Doderlein, that ἀμήν necessarily implies an *Optative* doxology (sc. εὐλογητὸς ε ἴ η Θεός), is disproved by Rom. i. 25, where ὅς ἐ σ τ ι ν εὐλογητὸς . . . . ἀμήν, are the words of Paul, *i. e.*, the apostle speaks in the *Indicative* mode, and not in the Optative. The same is the case in 1 Pet. iv. 11, ᾧ [sc. Θεῷ vel Χριστῷ] ἐ σ τ ι ν ἡ δόξα κ. τ. λ. And in other cases where no verb is supplied, *e. g.*, Rom. xiv. 27. Gal. i. 5. 1 Tim. i. 17. vi. 16. 2 Tim. iv. 18, etc., it is not by any means certain (as the above explicit instances of *Indicative* usage show), that the Optative εἴη, rather than the Indicative ἐστί, is to be supplied. Nor does the remark of Erasmus, that in some of the manuscripts of Cyprian, Hilary, and Chrysostom, *Deus* or Θεός is wanting in the citations of Rom. ix. 5, prove anything; for these are evidently omissions of copyists, since all the best manuscripts of these fathers insert *Deus* or Θεός.

Grotius is still more unsuccessful, in asserting that the Syriac version (the *Peschito*), omits Θεός; for this version has words translated *Deus super omnia*. Stolz, in his celebrated German version, has left out Θεός; whether on the authority of Grotius as above, or because he thought it a disagreeable appendage to the text, does not appear. After all these proposed changes, however, of punctuation, of the order of the text, and of the substance of it, the text, as it now stands, remains in reality untouched by any criticism which can have any considerable weight with men of ingenuous and candid minds. That those who deny the divinity of Christ should be solicitous to avoid the force of this text, is not unnatural; for while it remains in the records of the New Testament, it stands an irrefragable evidence of what Paul believed, asserted, and taught, relative to this subject. The only way in which any avoiding of its force is practicable, seems to be, to assert that ὁ ὢν ἐπὶ πάντων Θεός is meant to designate merely *the supremacy of Christ as Mediator*, in which capacity he is *quasi Deus*, and in the like capacity is styled אלהים in Ps. xlv. In pursuing this course, more probability than is now exhibited in the various evasions that I have above noticed, and also more ingenuousness, might be shown. But still, the general and spontaneous feeling of an unprejudiced reader must always be (at least so it seems to me), that *God over all* means SUPREME GOD, and that εὐλογητὸς εἰς τοὺς αἰῶνας, ἀμήν, can be applied only to him who is *truly* divine. A Θεὸς δεύτερος, in a real and veritable sense, seems to oppose the fundamental principle of the Scriptures.

Rückert and Usteri, the first in his Commentary, and the second in his *Lehrbegriff Pauli*, both acknowledge that there is no avoiding the usual exegesis of this text on the common principles of philology. Both of them doubt or impugn the *divinity* of Christ; yet they yield to the laws of grammar and philology here. But both assert that this is a ἅπαξ λεγόμενον on the part of Paul (which I would by no means admit), and Usteri says, that "he cannot divest himself of the suspicion, that there must be some error in the text or in the interpretation." But Reiche is made of sterner stuff. He yields nothing to the laws of grammar, or to the position of εὐλογητός, etc.: he makes a period at σάρκα and constructs the rest as a *doxology*. Both proceed upon the ground, so far as their *feeling* of objection is concerned, that Christ is only a *derived* God, and therefore cannot have *supreme* divinity ascribed to him. This is indeed a legitimate inference from the Nicene creed; but still it is not what the Nicene fathers meant to teach in a direct way. *Real* divinity, although not *supreme* divinity, they undoubtedly meant to ascribe to Christ.

(6) *It is not so that, etc.*, οὐχ οἷον δέ. (1) Οἷον may be taken adverbially, as ὡς or ὥσπερ to which it is very often equivalent (see Passow on οἷος, No. 6); and then we may translate: *It is not so that*, etc.; just as we translate μὴ ὡς ὅτι, 2 Thess. ii. 2. (2) Οἷον in classic Greek often implies a preceding τοῖον. The whole phrase would be: οὐ τοῖον δέ ἐστι or λέγω οἷον ὅτι κ τ. λ.; *i. e.*, "it is no such thing as that, etc.;" in which case we may render: There is no such thing as that, etc.; ἐκπέπτωκεν κ. τ. λ. The former method is most simple, perhaps, but not the most probable; for οἷον used *adverbially* is generally employed in a merely *comparative* way. The meaning is: "But what I have said in respect to the defection of Israel, does not at all imply that the promises of God are sure and certain." Δέ, *but*, continuative and adversative.

It is not true, as has been alleged, that οἷόν τε must always have the infinitive after it. Οἷός τε with an Infinitive has indeed the meaning *possibile est*, etc.; but it is often employed *without* an Infinitive, in the sense of *so as, such as, like;* and even without an Infinitive, it sometimes means *possible;* see Passow on οἷος No. 2. *e.* No. 3. *c.* Still it is doubtful whether οἷον δέ is employed in the sense of οἷόν τε, *possible*. Consequently I must prefer the rendering given above.

Promise or *word*, Λόγος in the sense of *something promised;* often so in English, *e. g. he has given his word.*—Ἐκπέπτωκεν, *failed, been frustrated, irritum factum est.* So the Hebrew נָפַל, which corresponds in sense with ἐκπέπτωκε; *e. g.*, in Josh. xxi. 45. 1 K. viii. 56. 2 K. x. 10.

For not all who are of Israel, are Israel; οὐ γὰρ . . . Ἰσραὴλ, *i. e.*, not all the natural descendants of Abraham, are Israelites in the true, spiritual, scriptural sense of the word. The Talmud (Tract. Sanhed. cap. 11) expresses the feelings and views of the Jews, relative to their claims of preeminence: כל־ישראל יש חלק לעולם הבא, *i. e*, *all Israel have their portion in the world to come*. But such claims are rejected by our text and the sequel; as well as by Rom. iii. John viii. 39. Matt. iii. 9, Gal. iii. 9, 28, 29. Γάρ here introduces a reason why the promise has not been broken ; and that is, that all the natural descendants of Abraham are not, as such, the heirs of the promise.

(7) *Natural descendants,* σπέρμα — *children,* Τέκνα, here in the higher *spiritual* sense, like that of Ἰσραὴλ above in the second instance. — *But,* "*in Isaac shall thy seed be called;*" Ἀλλ' ἐν Ἰσαὰκ . . . . σπέρμα; *i e.*, (as most explain it) in the person of Isaac, thy seed, viz., thy descendants who are to stand in a covenant relation to me, shall be chosen or selected. But a more probable and efficient sense is given by taking κληθήσονται as in iv 17 ; and then the meaning will be: "In Isaac or through Isaac shall thy seed (the seed here promised), be called into being." Καλέω, used like the Hebrew קרא, means *to call out of nothing into being;* as Rom. iv. 17 shows. After ἀλλά and before ἐν κ. τ. λ. either οὕτως ἐῤῥήθη or ἐῤῥήθη, is implied. — As to τέκνα, these are, in the next verse, called τὰ τέκνα τῆς ἐπαγγελίας. In verse 5 above, ἐπαγγελίαι (ברית) are reckoned among the *external* privileges which the Israelites enjoyed. But even these, only a *part* of Abraham's natural descendants enjoyed. Ishmael, Abraham's eldest son, was excluded from the covenant relation ; and so were Abraham's six sons by Keturah, Gen. xxv. 1 — 5.

Ἐπαγγελίας in verse 8, however, refers to the promises in Gen. xv. 4, 5. xvii. 15, 16, 19, 21 (see verse 9). Isaac was in a special sense the son of promise ; and his natural descendants, therefore, may be styled τέκνα τῆς ἐπαγγελίας.

(8) *That is,* τοῦτ' ἔστιν, *i. e.*, which signifies, which means. But does Paul intend to say, that the explanation which follows exhibits the sense of the original promise? Or does he mean to intimate merely, that he gives to the subject under consideration a meaning *analogous* to that ancient promise? That it is capable of a satisfactory explanation on the former ground, may be shown from the considerations suggested in the sequel. — *The natural descendants* [of Abraham] *are not the children of God.* Θεοῦ. Τὰ τέκνα τῆς σαρκός plainly means *physical* or *natural descendants*, children in the first and literal sense. But the sense of τέκνα τοῦ Θεοῦ is not so obvious. Is it here used to des-

ignate the children of God in the highest *spiritual* sense of this term? I think not; for it is Isaac and his descendants as such, who are here contradistinguished from Ishmael and the other six sons of Abraham and their descendants. The point here insisted on is, that *natural* descent from Abraham did not of itself entitle any one to the high *spiritual* privileges of the gospel; that the Jew had no more right than the Gentile, to expect any peculiar favor to himself merely on such a ground. But how does the apostle illustrate and confirm this principle? By showing that in ancient times, the promise of a numerous seed who should stand in a covenant relation to God, and enjoy peculiar external privileges on this account, was not made to the natural descendants of Abraham as such, but only to those natural descendants who would spring from Isaac the son of peculiar promise. In other words, Ishmael and the sons of Abraham by Keturah, had no share in the covenant-engagements made with the promised seed.

The deduction from all this is, that God does not dispense his blessings or favors according to claims grounded on mere natural descent or external privileges, but according to his own infinite wisdom and pleasure. The best of reasons he doubtless has; but these reasons God has kept to himself: he has not revealed them to us. When this is the case, the apostle speaks of him as acting κατὰ τὴν πρόθεσιν αὐτοῦ — κατὰ τὴν ὡρσιμένην βουλὴν καὶ πρόγνωσιν αὐτοῦ, etc. But nothing can be farther from truth, than to suppose that a Being of infinite wisdom and goodness ever acts *arbitrarily*.

That τέκνα τοῦ Θεοῦ may mean, "the children of promise in respect to the external privileges and blessings of the ancient covenant or dispensation," and not the highest spiritual blessings, is clear from the manner in which τέκνα (בָּנִים) is applied to the whole body of Israelites, in Deut. xxxii. 5, 6. xiv. 1. Hos. xi. 1. Ex. iv. 22, 23. So τὰ τέκνα τῆς ἐπαγγελίας designates those on whom the promised blessings were bestowed, which are mentioned above in verses 4, 5; or else those who were the descendants of Isaac, himself a τέκνον τῆς ἐπαγγελίας. In the same manner σπέρμα at the close of the verse, is to be understood, *i. e.*, as equivalent to τέκνα Θεοῦ in the sense just explained, or as זֶרַע in Gen. xvii. 8. Θεοῦ is omitted in F. G. 37. 67 ex emend. 70. Matt. *c. k.*, Chrysostom. Probably the copyists were stumbled with the appellation τέκνα Θεοῦ as applied to the posterity of Isaac in general. But the texts cited above show that they need not have been; for the meaning of τέκνα Θεοῦ is, such children as God according to the special promise to Abraham would raise up for his posterity, who should enjoy covenant privileges.

Another view of this whole subject may be taken. We may suppose Paul by τοῦτ᾽ ἔστιν to mean, that the promise concerning Isaac was typical of a future and spiritual seed, to be chosen on like principles. In other words, as not all the *literal* posterity of Abraham were selected to be heirs of the special covenant-promise made to the patriarch, but only Isaac was selected, so it is in respect to the new covenant. God does not select merely the *literal* seed of Abraham, but he chooses a *spiritual* seed of *the father of the faithful* to be the heirs of gospel blessings. In a word, *selection, choice*, was a *principle* of action in respect to the patriarch's posterity; choice or selection is still equally visible in dispensing the blessings of the new covenant. In this way Paul would be understood as saying, by τοῦτ᾽ ἔστιν, that the ancient promise was as much as to say or equivalent to saying what follows, which contains an exhibition of the same principle.

The amount of the whole in either way of explanation, is that Paul, in order to illustrate and defend God's proceedings in respect to bestowing spiritual blessings of the highest kind, adduces examples from the Old Test. Scriptures, where the *principle* concerned is exactly the same as that which is concerned with the calling and glorifying of the κλητοί, viz., where the blessings bestowed are not conferred on the ground of being a natural descendant of Abraham, nor on the ground of merit or desert, but κατὰ πρόθεσιν Θεοῦ. Now certainly God can be no more unjust in great things than in small ones; and if he was not unjust in selecting the objects of his temporal favors κατὰ πρόθεσιν αὐτοῦ, why should we regard him as unjust in selecting the objects of his highest spiritual favors in the same way; that is, not according to *claim* or *merit* on the part of men (for these things belong not to them), but according to reasons, good and sufficient ones, known only to himself? Such as are inclined to feel that this would be wrong on the part of God, and that it is in any measure proper for us to complain of this, will do well to read the sequel of this chapter with a candid, humble, inquiring mind.

(9) *For this was the word of the promise: "According to this time will I come, and Sarah shall have a son,"* ἐπαγγελίας γὰρ . . . υἱός, Gen. xviii. 10, 14. This shows who the children of the promise were, that are described in the preceding verse, viz., the descendants of Isaac the son thus promised. Hence the γάρ at the beginning of the verse.

According to this time, κατὰ τὸν καιρὸν τοῦτον. In Hebrew the whole phrase runs thus: שׁוּב אָשׁוּב אֵלֶיךָ כָּעֵת חַיָּה, *I will surely return* or *come back to thee, when the time shall be renewed*, Gen. xviii. 10. The word חַיָּה seems to be simply an adjective, as the text now stands, and to mean *living again*, in the sense of being *renewed*. So Saadias, Tremellius, Rosenmüller, Gesenius, Winer, and Tholuck; comp. Gen. xvii. 21 and xviii. 14, מוֹעֵד. The Sept. reads in this last case, εἰς τὸν καιρὸν τοῦτον ἀναστρέψω πρὸς σὲ εἰς ὥρας. What is meant by εἰς ὥρας, unless it be *exactly, at the very hour,* I am unable to conjecture. In regard to τοῦτον (which seems to be put for חָיָה), one almost spontaneously falls upon the conjecture, that the Sept. and Paul must have read חָזָה in Gen. xviii. 10, 14, instead of חָיָה; which is by no means improbable, considering that the ancient manuscripts were destitute of vowel points, and that the two words היה and חזה are so nearly alike. Fritsche and others compare פְּעַת חַיָּה with the ζῶν χρόνος of Sophocles (Trach. 3. 1159) where καὶ πάρων νῦν is added (as they aver) in the way of explanation. Thus construed the sense would be *present time, i. e.,* when this time shall be again present. Reiche, Meyer, Alford and others accept this explanation as satisfactory, but Tholuck opposes it. Ζῶν χρόνος appears to mean *flourishing age.* — I would suggest another interpretation still, viz., *as at life-giving time;* in which case the meaning would be, that God would again add ess her as a mother who gives life to, *i. e.,* bears children. Comp. the sense of חיה and ζάω, in the lexicons.

(10) The apostle having thus shown that the promised seed was not *all* but only a *select* part of the natural descendants of Abraham, he now goes on to show that not only did God make a distinction κατὰ πρόθεσιν αὐτοῦ among the natural descendants of Abraham, but that even among the descendants of him who was "the Son of promise," he made a like distinction; and this too, in a case where the respective merit or desert of the parties could not possibly be the ground of distinction. Thus Jacob the younger son of Isaac was chosen as the object of favor, and Esau the elder son, who according to the custom of the patriarchs had higher rights, was rejected. This choice was made too, before the children were born, *i. e.,* before they could have done either good or evil, before they could have possessed any merit or demerit. Consequently the πρόθεσις of God was according to his ἐκλογή and not ἐξ ἔργων or on the ground of merit.

To the reasoning in the preceding verses the Jews might reply: 'As to Ishmael, he was only the son of a bond-woman, and therefore had no good title to be an heir of promise; and as to the sons of Keturah, they were much younger than Isaac, who of course was entitled to the rights of primogeniture. On these grounds we may suppose the preference was given to Isaac.' In order to foreclose every thing of this nature, the apostle now produces an example of ἡ κατ' ἐκλογὴν πρόθεσις. This effectually accomplishes his object. Esau was not only the son of Rebecca, the lawful, proper, and only wife of Isaac, but he was the *elder* son, and therefore entitled by usage to the rights of primogeniture. Yet notwithstanding all this, Jacob was preferred to him, and was chosen as the τέκνον τῆς ἐπαγγελίας.

The bearing which all this has on the main subject of the apostle, is plain, and is specially confirmatory of 8: 28—39. 'If God did, κατ' ἐκλογήν, make such distinctions among the legitimate and proper children of Isaac, the *son of promise*, then the same God may choose, call, justify, and glorify those who are κλητοί in respect to the heavenly inheritance. If it is not unjust or improper, in one case, to distribute favors κατὰ πρόθεσιν αὐτοῦ, then it is not in another.'

And not only, οὐ μόνον δέ; an elliptical expression in itself, which has been filled out in different ways by different critics. The most natural supplement seems to be τοῦτο. Then the sentiment is: 'Not only was such the case with Abraham, but also in respect to Rebecca, etc.' The use of οὐ μόνον δέ denotes advance to more cogent reasons still. Οὐ μόνον δέ, καὶ ἀλλά means, *but not only* is that true which I have already said, *but also*, etc. Some critics, and some versions, make the supplement after μόνον δέ to be thus: 'Not only did Sarah obtain a special promise respecting her son, but Rebecca also." This is allowable; but the other mode seems to me more facile and more fraught with meaning.

Ῥεβέκκα forms here a kind of *anacoluthon*, *i. e.*, the beginning of a sentence, the construction of which is afterwards changed, or (in other words) the sentence is not finished in the same manner in which it was begun. Here the natural grammatical construction would be, οὐ μόνον δὲ [τοῦτο,] ἀλλὰ καὶ Ῥεβέκκᾳ, ἐξ ἑνὸς κοίτην ἐχούσῃ . . ἐρρήθη . . . ὅτι κ. τ. λ. Instead however of Ῥεβέκκᾳ (Dat.), we have in the text Ῥεβέκκα (Nom.) with which ἔχουσα agrees. But the construction thus begun in the Nominative, is not carried through. Instead of associating the Nom. Ῥεβέκκα with some following verb of which it might be the subject, the verb ἐρρήθη is afterwards employed, and the Dative required by it is made by a pronoun referring to Ῥεβέκκα, viz., by αὐτῇ. This construction is frequent in Hebrew, where what is called the Nom. absolute is employed, whilst a pronoun referring to it, is put in the case in which the verb or the nature of the sentence requires it to stand. Comp. Acts vii. 40, ὁ Μωυσῆς οὗτος . . . τί γέγονεν αὐτῷ.

Ἐξ ἑνὸς κοίτην ἔχουσα, *accipiens semen unius viri*. Literally κοίτην means *cubile, bed;* figuratively however it is employed to designate *concubitus;* compare the Hebrew זרע שִׁכְבַת, *concubitus seminis,* (Gesen. *effusio* seminis), Lev. xv. 16, 32. xviii. 20, 23. xxii. 4. In Lev. xviii. 23. שִׁכְבָה alone is employed to designate the same idea. A clear case of such a usage, is in Num. v. 20 (Sept.). Κοίτην ἔχουσα, *conceiving.* — Ἐξ ἑνός, *by one,* viz. Isaac; which last word immediately follows in the context.

(11) Γάρ *illustrantis.* — Γεννηθέντων, sc. παίδων, which the mind spontaneously supplies, by recurring back to ἐξ ἑνός κοίτην ἔχουσα. The whole phrase in the verse is a construction with the Genitive absolute; which is a species of *anacoluthon;* see N. T. Gramm. § 102.

Neither having done anything good or evil, μηδὲ .... κακόν; a very important declaration in respect to its bearing on some of the controverted questions about hereditary depravity or original sin. It appears that when the words related in the next verse were spoken to Rebecca, the children in her womb had arrived to such a state or growth as that life and motion in them were perceived by the mother, Gen. xxv. 22, 23, *i. e.,* to the age of some five months, comp. Luke i. 24. At this period, then, the apostle declares that they *had done neither good nor evil, i. e.,* they had as yet no positive moral character or (in other words) that there was as yet no development of their moral powers. And with the principle here developed, the tenor of other texts, as well as every man's consciousness, agrees; *e. g.,* Is. vii. 15, 16, comp. viii. 4. Deut. i. 39. Jonah iv. 11. That some knowledge of law and its obligations should exist in order that positive sin can be committed, seems to be clearly decided by Rom. iv. 15, and to be plainly implied by James iv. 17. John ix. 41. 1 John iii. 4. But *when* children do arrive at such a growth of moral nature that they begin positively to sin, the Scripture does not seem to have decided. The poetic and intensive expressions in Ps. li. 5, when compared with Ps. lviii. 3, will hardly establish the doctrine which many have supposed it to establish. Gen. viii. 21 decides no more, than that men begin *very early* to commit sin; and John iii. 6. Eph. ii. 3, and other texts of a like nature, decide only that men in a *natural* state, *i. e.,* in an unregenerate or unsanctified state, are children of wrath and carnal; which must be true, since they actually need regeneration.

The apostle, however, has here told us *when sinning had* NOT *begun,* in respect to Jacob and Esau. That they possessed *powers* or *faculties,* even in the womb, which were afterwards employed in committing sin when they were more fully developed, is undoubtedly true. But the *power* or *faculty* of sinning is one thing; the commission of sin another. Adam in paradise, before his fall, certainly possessed a susceptibility of excitement to sin, and the power or faculty of sinning, (else how could he have been tempted and sinned as he did?) yet he was not guilty of sin because he *possessed* them, but for the *abuse* of them. It is not therefore the power or susceptibility which the Creator has given us, which makes us sinners; it is the abuse of them. But the fallen posterity of Adam possess a susceptibility of sin in a much greater degree, so that before regeneration, all their moral *acts* are sinful. Yet the apostle has decided in our text, that such acts do not take place before birth. Excitability in respect to forbidden objects must be yielded to before it becomes actual sin; or rather, the sin itself is in the yielding, and not in the original disposition which God himself has given us. Disposition to sin, so far as it is created by our indulgence in it, may fairly be put to our account and reckoned as sin. But to count that as sin, which the Maker of heaven and earth himself gave us, before all voluntary moral action, involves consequences that are of fearful aspect. See further remarks in Excursus vi. on Rom. v. 11—19.

It should be noted that ἤ here is less in accordance with the usual idiom than μηδέ (New Test. Grammar § 151. 2); which the Text. Recept. has. It is, however, well supported by authority.

That the purpose of God according to election might stand, not of works, but of him that calleth, ἵνα .... ἐκ καλοῦντος. Ἡ κατ' ἐκλογὴν πρόθεσις means, *a purpose which proceeds from one's own free choice*, one to which he is moved by *internal*, and not merely by *external* causes or motives. It means here, a purpose which God did not entertain because he was moved to it by any thing which Jacob or Esau had done, or would do (οὐκ ἐξ ἔργων), but for reasons which he has not disclosed, and which pertain merely to himself. But let the reader beware, how he represents or even imagines these reasons to be *arbitrary* or *ungrounded*. This would be to represent the divine conduct as utterly inconsistent with infinite wisdom and goodness.

Not of works, οὐκ ἐξ ἔργων, *i. e.*, not because of merit, not because of obedience, yielded to the law of works, *i. e.*, the law requiring good works. —*But of him that calleth*, ἀλλ' ἐκ καλοῦντος; *i. e.*, the admission of the one to privileges, and the rejection of the other from them, proceed not from their personal desert, but from him who *calls*, *i. e.*, chooses or selects men to be the objects of his special favor for reasons within himself. That such is the sentiment here, seems very plain; for the apostle has just asserted, that the decision of God in respect to the future condition and privileges of Jacob and Esau, was made before they were born, and before they had done either good or evil; and that it was so made, in order that God's κατ' ἐκλογὴν πρόθεσις *might be stable*, μένη, Heb. יָקוּם׃.

(12) But what is the thing decided in this case? *The elder shall serve the younger*, ὁ μείζων . . . . ἐλάσσονι; or rather *the first-born shall serve the younger*, *i. e.*, he who by right of primogeniture would take the precedence, he shall in fact be inferior or take the lower place. The *precedence* then of Jacob is established by this declaration.

(13) *Jacob have I loved, and Esau have I hated*, τὸν . . . . ἐμίσησα, *i. e.*, on Jacob have I bestowed privileges and blessings, such as are the proofs of affection; I have treated him as one treats a friend whom he loves; but from Esau have I withheld these privileges and blessings, and therefore treated him as one is wont to treat those whom he dislikes; comp. Mal. i. 2, 3, from which the quotation here is made, and where the prophet adds to the last clause ('Ησαῦ ἐμίσησα) the following words, *and laid his mountains and his heritage waste*. That the whole refers to the bestowment and the withholding of *temporal blessings*, is clear not only from this passage, but from comparing Gen. xxv. 23. 27—29, 37—40. As to ἐμίσησα, its meaning here is rather *privative* than *positive*. When the Hebrews compared a stronger affection with a weaker one, they call the first *love* and the other *hatred;* comp. Gen. xxix. 30, 31. Deut. xxi. 15. Prov. xiii. 24. Matt. vi. 24. Luke xiv. 26 comp. with Matt. x. 37. Glass. Rhet. Sac. lib. III. tr. 3. can. 19.

After all, this does not answer the question: What is the ultimate object of the apostle in making his appeal to such an instance of κατ' ἐκλογὴν πρόθεσις? Must not this answer be, that he does so in order to justify and support what he had said in chap. viii. 28—39? And surely what he has there said does not relate merely to *temporal* condition or privileges, but to *effectual calling*, to *justifying* and *glorifying*. All however which is decided is, that God, in either case, does not bestow his blessings on the ground of merit, (for how can any sinner be blessed on such a ground?) but for reasons known only to himself, and which are *ab intra*, not *ab extra*.

Those who contend against this sentiment, contend against what is every day exhibited before their eyes. Why was this man born white, and that one black? Why is this child born and nurtured in the bosom of a pious family, and that one in the midst of robbers and murderers? The children had done neither " good nor evil," when their lot was decided. This no one can deny. Then, in the next place, is not their eternal condition connected with their means of grace, their pious nurture, their present condition and associations in life? And who placed them in their present condition? All nature, as well as the Bible, proclaims this doctrine of *divine sovereignty*. Yet with all this, the Bible plainly recognizes the *freedom* of men, and attributes to themselves their own destruction. The world say that there is contradiction here; but if there be, the naturalist has as really to contend with its difficulties as the advocate for revelation. However, there can in reality be no contradiction or absurdity in two things which are *both true*. All the difficulty lies in our ignorance of the *manner* in which predestination and free agency can be reconciled. When will men learn, that their ignorance is not the measure of truth! See farther in Excursus X.

Finally, I remark, that those who refer the preferences given to Jacob over Esau so exclusively to temporal blessings and privileges, as to maintain that the sentiment of the whole passage can prove at the most merely that such privileges and blessings are granted to Christians, and nothing more, by the election of God, would do well to read over again the first five verses of this chapter, where Jews, in the possession of all these privileges, are counted as reprobates and as exposed to the anathema of the Lord Jesus Christ. Does the *election* of God then amount to nothing more, than to leave men after all to perish who are his chosen saints?

(14) *What shall we say, then?* τί οὖν ἐροῦμεν; language which Paul puts into the mouth of the objecting Jew. *Is there unrighteousness before God!* μὴ ἀδικία παρὰ τῷ Θεῷ; a very natural question for one whose mind is perplexed and offended with the doctrine of divine sovereignty, and the dispensation of favors on the part of God κατὰ πρόθεσιν αὐτοῦ. From the time of the apostle down to the present hour, the same questions have been repeated and the same difficulties felt. That some of those who have maintained the doctrine of divine sovereignty, have, at times given occasion for the charge of making *predestination* amount to *fate* or *destiny*, and κατ' ἐκλογὴν πρόθεσις to amount to *arbitrary* decision — is what I feel unable to deny. In some treatises on *reprobation*, enough that stands exposed to such, or a similar charge, may be found. But to argue from such expressions as τὸν Ἐσαῦ ἐμίσησα, an actual hatred, like that which men cherish towards one another, would be a great abuse indeed of the sound principles of exegesis. On the same ground one might prove that it is our duty actually and positively to hate father, mother, wife, etc.; and that we cannot be Christians without so doing, if he should urge the literal meaning of Luke xiv. 26, and other texts of the same tenor. God cannot hate *more humano* any

thing which he has made, much less man who is made in his own image. Rom. v. 8—10. John iii. 16, 17. Tit. iii. 4, 5. Wisdom of Solomon xi. 24. But still, God may and does hate sin; he may and will punish it; he may treat sinners therefore as if he hated them, *i. e.*, he may inflict evil or suffering upon them. In the future world, he never does this but in consequence of actual guilt, and in proportion to that guilt; but in the present world, trouble and sorrow may be brought on men as the instruments of trying them, of purifying them, of humbling them, and this without being proportioned by the simple principles of *retribution;* for sufferings and trials here are not always in the way of simple retribution. In all this God acts κατὰ πρόθεσιν αὑτοῦ; yet not in an *arbitrary* manner, and without any good reason, but still, in a manner which we, in our ignorance, cannot explain. But surely our want of knowledge cannot establish against him a charge of injustice.

(15) That God does dispense his favors without being moved thereto by any *merit* on the part of him who receives them, is clearly established, and is designed to be confirmed by the quotation which Paul makes from the Old Testament, Ex. xxxiii. 19 — *Μὴ γένοιτο .... οἰκτείρω, not at all; for he saith to Moses: "I will have mercy on whomsoever I will have mercy; and I will show compassion to whomsoever I will show compassion."* In other words: 'As none of the human race have merited my approbation and reward, as none are entitled to them on the ground of merit, I may properly and do bestow my favors where and when I please.' Is there any injustice, ἀδικία, here? Out of a hundred criminals who have all deserved death, may not a wise and benevolent government, for reasons entirely within itself, choose some as the objects of pardon, while others are given up to the punishment which the law enjoins? I am fully aware of the opposition made by the natural heart to such a proceeding on the part of God; but I am not aware how the fact that God does this can be *reasonably* denied, nor how injustice can with any propriety be charged upon him because he does it.

(16) *Consequently, i. e., it follows, therefore* [that ἐκλογή is not obtained] *by him that willeth, or him that runneth, but through the mercy of God,* ἄρα οὖν .... Θεοῦ. That ἐκλογή is here to be supplied, may be seen by looking back to verse 11. The sense is given substantially by the supplying of ἐκλογή, but perhaps the ellipsis is more natural from the quotation preceding: *The favor of God,* God's compassion is not of, in the power of him that willeth, etc., but of God who exercises the compassion. The Gen. θέλοντος, κ. τ. λ., is the Gen. of *agent* or *cause*. — Θέλοντος indicates *desire, wishing,* etc., and probably has reference

to the wish of Abraham in Gen. xvii. 18. xxi. 11. Τρέχοντος may possibly refer to Esau's *haste* to prepare food for Isaac; see Gen. xxvii. 1 seq. It is often used to designate Christian efforts, as in 1 Cor. ix. 24, 26. Heb. xii. 1. Phil. ii. 16. iii. 14. Gal. ii. 2, etc. 'Ελεοῦντος refers to the quotation Paul had just made. The sentiment of the whole is, that God bestows his favors not because they are first merited or acquired by strong desire or of strenuous action, but because he has mercy on those who are the objects of his favor. *Of him that runneth.* The language may be supposed to be figurative and drawn rather from the running in the race, cf. 1 Cor. ix. 24 seq. Hence the idea is the same for substance as given above: God's favor is not bestowed in *consequence* of previous desire and exertion. This does not imply that let men merit ever so much, *i. e.*, desire salvation ever so much, or labor for it ever so strenuously, all this will be of no account with God; and that he will bestow mercy in a manner merely arbitrary, and irrespectively of all works or character on the part of the sinner. *Before* sinners are made the objects of his special mercy, they are "dead in trespasses and sins;" they are "by nature children of wrath and disobedience;" "what is born of the flesh is flesh;" "the carnal mind is enmity against God, is not subject to his law, nor indeed can be;" consequently, the case here supposed (of *previous* merit and effort) never exists. It is God's mercy which *first* disposes sinners *to will and to do* (Phil. ii. 13. Eph. ii. 1. Rom. v. 6—10); and it is accordingly impossible that his mercy can be bestowed *in consequence of* their previous merits.

All this, however, does not disprove the doctrine that good works will be rewarded; which is certainly and plainly a Scripture doctrine. But what are *good* works? Those which are done *before* conversion, or *after* it? Surely the latter. But in respect to the reward of Christians for *evangelical* good works, the apostle is not here speaking. What he says has respect to the *fore-knowing, fore-ordaining, calling, justifying,* and *glorifying,* mentioned in viii. 29, seq. All this is not on the ground of merit, but of pure gratuity; and consequently it is τοῦ ἐλεοῦντος Θεοῦ. The fact that good works themselves are rewarded, is itself a part of this pure system or plan of grace; for it is only the works of those who are sanctified, which are reputed good in the scripture sense, *i. e*, holy, acceptable to God; and even the best of these are imperfect, so that they could not claim any reward on their own account and on principles of legal merit. The law allows of no imperfection. It requires us "to love God with *all* the heart, and our neighbor as ourselves." Now as no man on earth has ever done this (Jesus only excepted), so no man has ever been in a condition to advance a *claim to reward on the ground of law*, in any age or country of the world. Consequently, the fact that the good works of saints are rewarded, is a matter of *gratuity* and not of legal claim. But still, this is not what the apostle is here discussing; and consequently what he says is not to be regarded as at all interfering with or contradicting what he says on the subject of the reward of good works in other parts of his writings.

It may be proper to remark, that so plain is the sentiment above exhibited by the words of the apostle here, that some critics very far removed from belief in the doctrines of the Reformation, have felt compelled to acknowledge that Paul has here advanced the doctrine of election or decrees. So Ammon, Ruckert, Usteri, and others.

(17) The preceding verse, although comprising a sentiment which is very disagreeable to the natural heart and to the pride of unsanctified men, is still more easily acquiesced in than the one now before us, which has been the theme of great contention, and the occasion of not a little unguarded and hazardous assertion. Let us first investigate the language.

For the Scripture saith to Pharaoh, λέγει γὰρ ἡ γραφὴ τῷ Φαραώ, instead of the formula *for God saith to Pharaoh*. So Gal. iii. 8, 22. iv. 30. What the Scripture says, God says, for πᾶσα ἡ γραφὴ θεόπνευστος, *i. e.*, it is *the word of God*. So the Rabbins frequently exchange the two formulas of quotation, הַשֵּׁם אָמַר, *the Name* [*God*] *says*, and הַכָּתוּב אָמַר, *the Scripture says;* both of which are designated by the abbreviations אָא. The γάρ here stands before a quotation which is designed to confirm the doctrine of the divine sovereignty.

For this very purpose have I roused thee up, that I might exhibit my power. Ὅτι εἰς . . . δύναμίν μου. Paul has departed from the Septuagint version, which runs thus: ἕνεκεν τοῦτο διετηρήθης, ἵνα ἐνδείξωμαι ἐν σοι τήν ἰσχύν μου, substituting ἐξήγειρα for διετηρήθης ὅπως for ἵνα, and δύναμιν for ἰσχύν; *i. e.*, he makes a translation of his own, which on the whole, was better adapted to the purpose of his argument and equally, not more, accordant with the original Hebrew than that of the LXX. We must not therefore take διετηρήθης for a commentary on ἐξήγειρα here, inasmuch as the apostle has rejected this verb and preferred another, for the sake (as it would seem) of a nearer accordance with the meaning of the original Hebrew in this passage. What then is the sense of ἐξεγείρω, as employed in Hellenistic Greek? In the Septuagint it is used some *seventy* times. In none of these cases does it mean *to create, to produce, to raise up*, in the sense of *bringing into being*, etc.; so that those who construe ἐξήγειρά σε,

I have created thee or *brought thee into existence*, as Beza: Feci ut existeres, do that which is contrary to the Hellenistic *usus loquendi*. Augustine, Reiche, Calvin.

It is employed throughout in the sense of *arousing, exciting, rousing up, waking up, from*, etc., with slight variations in meaning, according to the connection and the adjuncts of the verb. Accordingly it is employed by the Septuagint to translate the Hebrew הקיץ, *to rouse up*, or *to wake up*, *i. e.*, from sleep, Ps. iii. 5. lxxii. 20. cxxxviii. 18. Jer. xxxi. 26. li. 39. Dan. xii. 2. In the like manner it stands for יקץ *to wake up* or *rouse up* from sleep; Gen. xxviii. 16. xli. 22. Judg. xvi. 15, 21. Ps. lxxvii. 71. With these meanings it is used intransitively. But the principal use of it is transitive; in which case it is employed to designate the idea of *rousing up* one's self to action, *exciting* or *rousing up* others to action, *exciting* or *rousing up* any thing, animate or inanimate, to do this or that; *e. g.*, Judges v. 12. Ps. vii. 7. xxxiv. 26. lvi. 11. lxxix. 3. cvii. 2. Cant. iv. 16. Jer. l. 41. Joel iii. 9. Zech. xiii. 7, etc.; and so in the like manner, forty-two times; see Trommii Concord. in verbum, No. 11. In all these cases it corresponds to the Hebrew עיר, הֵעִיר, etc. In *seven* other cases it corresponds to קום, when this word is used in a sense altogether synonymous with that of עור, *e. g.*, Num. x. 35. 2 Sam. xii. 11. 1 Kings xi. 14. Est. viii. 5. Ps. cxviii. 62. Hab. i. 6. Zech. xi. 16. Throughout all these, the idea is uniform, viz., that of *rousing, exciting, stirring up, rendering active, urging to activity*, in a word, in the sense of bringing out of a state of rest or inaction or inefficiency into a contrary state, *i. e.*, in the sense of *exciting*.

Twice only have the Seventy employed ἐξήγειρα, where the meaning might perhaps be thought doubtful. In Prov. xxv. 24, ἄνεμος . . ἐξεγείρει νέφη, *the wind raiseth up clouds*. The Hebrew verb is חוֹלֵל, *begetteth* or *bringeth forth*. But the sense of ἐξεγείρω here in the Septuagint, is plainly the usual one. So also in Ezek. xxi. 16. (Heb. xxi. 21), ἐξεγείρεται corresponds to מִצְרוּת (from יָצַר); but still it has the sense of *excite*, and this meaning corresponds substantially with the Hebrew, although not literally.

In the New Testament we have only one example besides that before us, where ἐξεγείρω is used, viz., 1 Cor. vi. 14, where it is clearly used to designate the action of *rousing* from the sleep of death, *raising* or *exciting* from a state of inaction or death.*

On the whole, then, the sense of the Greek word is altogether clear, and subject to no well grounded doubt. It means *to rouse*

---

* These uses are entirely in accordance with the signification of the word in the few cases where it is used in classical authors, where the meaning is to rouse up, as from sleep, death, etc.

up, to excite, to stir up, in any manner or for any purpose. But does the Hebrew word in Ex. ix. 16, which corresponds to ἐξήγειρα, admit of such a sense?

The Hebrew word is הֶעֱמַדְתִּי, Hiphil of עָמַד: which usually means (in Kal) *to stand, to stand fast, to continue standing, to stand up,* etc., Ex. ix. 28. Lev. xiii. 5. Dan. x. 17. In Hiphil (הֶעֱמִיד), it means *to make to stand, to place,* also *to keep standing, to persevere* or *continue in standing.* Tholuck and others have labored to show that הֶעֱמַדְתִּי has the *usual* Hiph. sense in Ex. ix. 16. That the Hebrew word *might* have such a sense, is sufficiently plain from 1 Kings xv. 4. 2 Chr. ix. 8. Prov. xxix. 4. 2 Chr. xxxv. 2 But although the Hebrew word הֶעֱמַדְתִּי might have the sense which Tholuck and others assign to it, yet the Greek word ἐξήγειρα, which Paul uses, can hardly, according to the *usus loquendi,* have such a sense put upon it.

Still has הֶעֱמִיד ever the sense of *exciting, arousing,* like the ἐξήγειρα of the apostle? If so, then we may presume the apostle chose this Greek word, in deliberate preference to the διετηρήθης of the Septuagint. Instances of this nature are clear. So in Neh. vi. 7, הֶעֱמַדְתָּ, *thou hast roused up* or *excited* the prophets, etc. So Dan. xi. 11, 13, וְהֶעֱמִיד *and he shall excite* or *rouse up* a great multitude, etc. We can have little reason, then, to doubt that the apostle had such a meaning of הֶעֱמַדְתִּי in view, when he rendered it ἐξήγειρα; for this *Greek* word is fairly susceptible of no other meaning. In accordance therefore with this result respecting the meaning of ἐξεγείρω, I have translated thus: *For this very purpose have I roused thee up.*

That I might show forth my power and declare my name in all the earth, ὅπως . . . . τῇ γῇ, *i. e., in all the land,* viz., of Egypt. The consequence of Pharaoh's conduct was, that the Hebrews were brought out of Egypt by signal divine interposition, exhibited in the various plagues inflicted on Egypt after the declaration recorded here, *i. e.,* the hail, the locust, etc., Ex. ix. 16, seq. Cf. also Ex. xv. 14 — 16. Such interpositions caused the power and glory of Jehovah to be known through all the land of Egypt. Or if *all the earth* be construed as having a still more extensive sense, one might justify this by observing, that the Scriptures themselves now diffused so widely through the world, the Koran read and revered by many millions, the Greek author Artapanus (Euseb. Præp. Evang. IX. 29), also Diodorus Siculus (Bibl. III. 39), and the Latin Trogus (Justin. Hist. XXXVI 2), all speak of the wonders which were done in Egypt, and the overthrow of Pharaoh there.

(18) *Therefore hath he mercy on whom he will have mercy, and whom he will he hardeneth,* ἄρα οὖν . . . . σκληρύνει. A con-

clusion of the apostle's, and not the words of the objector, as some have intimated. This is clear from what is immediately subjoined by Paul: Ἐρεῖς οὖν μοι, κ. τ. λ. On the nature and force of the conclusion here drawn, I have already remarked in commenting on verse 16. Rambach, Carpzov, and Ernesti have endeavored to show that σκληρύνει means here *to deal hardly with*. They appeal to 2 Chron. x. 4, and Job xxxix. 16 in order to confirm this; but in the first instance the sense is *to make hard, to render grievous ;* in the second, the Hebrew is הִקְשִׁיחַ and the Sept. ἀποσκληρύνω, and the sense harmonizes substantially with the obvious one in the verse before us. I see, therefore, no proper philological method of construing σκληρύνει, but in the way already intimated above.

(19) *Thou wilt say to me, then: Why doth he still find fault, for who resisteth his will?* Ἐρεῖς οὖν . . . . ἀνθέστηκε: "Whom he will, he hardeneth," says Paul. "Then why blame men for being hardened? How is this inconsistent with what God wills?" is the reply of the objector; and this contains a sentiment, which has been repeated from the time when Paul wrote his epistle, down to the present hour. Although the objection *seems* to be formidable at first view, yet it is specious ; for it does not follow, because God by his infinite goodness and almighty power will convert the wicked deeds of the sinner into means of promoting his own glory, that the sinner may not be called to an account and punished for the evil which he intended. Because a wise and benevolent government may convert the crime of some individuals into a means of furthering the public good, do not the criminals in question deserve punishment ? Supposing then that there is *a sense*, in which sin is made even the instrument of accomplishing the wise and holy purposes of God and the greatest good of his creatures, it does not follow, that the sinner who had malignant purposes in view is not deserving of punishment, nor that there is not an *important* sense in which he has *resisted* the will of God.

(20) *But rather,* μενοῦνγε, *at vero, verum enimvero.* This compound particle is found elsewhere in the New Testament only in Luke xi. 28 and Rom. x 18. Suidas explains it by τὸ ἀληθές, or μᾶλλον μὲν οὖν, i. e., *verily* or *the rather then.* Here the sense seems to be *then* or *but rather ;* and the construction or sense of the passage is thus: ' *Then i. e.*, in case you do thus say, I may *rather* say, *i. e.*, I have a still better right to say, Who art thou, etc. ? Σὺ τίς εἶ . . Θεῷ; *who art thou that repliest against God*, *i. e.*, who sayest something that charges him with acting wrongly or improperly ? The apostle, in answer to the objector, does not endeavor at all to explain *how* it is that God should *harden* sin-

ners, and yet sinners be guilty of their own ruin; he does not attempt any *metaphysical* conciliation of divine sovereignty and control with human freedom and moral responsibility; he takes it for granted that the facts which he had been stating were true, and could not be contradicted. He first remonstrates with the objector for his presumption, and continues this remonstrance, by quoting from the Old Testament and applying to the object before him passages, which serve strongly to confirm the right of the Creator on the one hand to dispose of his creatures, and the duty of his creatures on the other to bow in submission before him. Would it not be well for those who are to teach the doctrines of Paul, at the present time, to imitate his example in dealing with objectors?

Shall the thing formed say to him who formed it, why hast thou made me thus? μὴ ἐρεῖ .... οὕτως; A quotation *ad sensum* from the passage in Is. xlv. 9, and xxix. 16. The design of this quotation is, to stop the mouth of the objector who inquires: 'Why doth he find fault then, for who hath resisted his will?' The implication in this of wrong on the part of God, in bestowing blessings on some which he withholds from others, and in advancing some to glory while he leaves others to hardness of heart and to the punishment consequent upon it, the apostle meets by appeal to the language of the Scriptures, in regard to the sovereignty of God over the works of his hands: 'Has the creature a right to call in question the Creator, by whose power he was formed, and by whose goodness he is preserved and nurtured? Should he reproach his Creator, because he has endowed him with the nature which he possesses?' It is as much as to say: 'Even supposing that there was some ground for the objection which you make, I might reply in the language of Scripture and ask, whether it is proper and becoming for a creature to summon the Creator before his tribunal, and to pass sentence of condemnation upon him.' Viewed in this light, it is a kind of *argumentum ad hominem;* applicable indeed to all who make the like objection in the like spirit, but specially adapted to stop the mouth of the haughty and presumptuous Jew, who, in Paul's time, was indignant that God should be represented as making the Gentiles the objects of his special favor. In appealing, however, to the *sovereignty* of God the Creator, Paul does not assert or intimate that God is *arbitrary* in any of his dealings with his creatures, or that he ever makes any arrangement in respect to them without wise, and good, and sufficient reasons. For being infinitely holy, and wise, and just, and good, he cannot act without the best of reasons for acting; although, indeed, these reasons might not be given to us. It should be remarked here, also, that it is only when a proud and contumacious spirit lifts up itself, like that of the Jew in the context, that an appeal to a direct and sovereign right of God, is made by the sacred writers, in order to abash and repress such arrogant assumption.

(21) But one quotation does not satisfy the apostle's ardor to repress the objector. He makes a second one (*ad sensum* again, not *ad literam*) from Jer. xviii. 6, comp. ver. 4, which by another image inculcates the same sentiment as before. *Hath not the potter power over the clay, to make out of the same lump one vessel to honor and another to dishonor?* ἣ οὐκ ... ἀτιμίαν; *i. e.*, one vessel for a use which is deemed honorable, and another for one deemed dishonorable; comp. Jer. xviii. 4. 'Even so (the apostle would say) are all men in the hands of God, and at his disposal;' comp. Jer. xviii. 6. In other words: 'Who can call in question his right to dispose of us as it seems good in his sight? The Jew, however, regarded his nation as the φύραμα from which none but σκεύη τιμῆς could be formed. But the apostle shows him, that God could make, and had made, the Gentiles also a φύραμα from which the like vessels were formed. The same God also makes unbelievers among the Jews to be σκεύη ὀργῆς, as well as unbelievers among the Gentiles. He chooses the objects of his mercy or of his justice where he judges best, *not* arbitrarily, but still for reasons which are not revealed to us.

(22) It is evident to any one who will attentively read vers. 22—24, that the sense remains incomplete, *i. e.*, the sentence (or sentences) is unfinished; which form of writing the Greeks called ἀνακόλουθον. But what must be supplied in order to complete the sense of these verses, is not sufficiently plain to command the unanimous consent of interpeters. Without delaying to recite different opinions, I would merely say, that at the end of vers. 22—24, it seems to me plain the question in ver. 20 is to be repeated, viz. σὺ τίς εἶ, ὁ ἀνταποκρινόμενος τῷ Θεῷ; Whether you repeat this question at the end of ver 22, or here and also at the end of ver. 24, seems to be of little importance; for the sense in each case would be substantially the same. The sum of the sentiment thus explained is: 'If God, in order that he might exhibit his punitive justice and sovereign power, endures with much long-suffering the wickedness of the impenitent and rebellious who are worthy of divine indignation; and if he has determined to exhibit his rich grace toward the subjects of his mercy whom he has prepared for glory, even towards us ([ἐπὶ] ἡμᾶς) whom he has called (viii. 30), Gentiles as well as Jews; who art thou, that repliest against the divine proceedings in respect to all this?'

If then, or *if now*, εἰ δέ, *i. e.*, since God is the supreme Lord of all things, and all his creatures are at his disposal by a sovereign and entire right (verses 20, 21); *if now*, determining to display his punitive justice and power, he has endured, etc. Δέ is sometimes construed as *adversative* here to ver. 14; but it is better to regard it as the sign of an additional illustration or confirmation of the sentiments just advanced. The connection of thought seems to be this: 'If the sovereign Lord of all creatures, who may dispose of them as he pleases, does still endure with much long-suffering the wickedness of some of them, and by all this determines to display his punitive justice, who can justly find fault with his proceedings?'

Willing, θέλων, *i. e.*, *determining, designing, purposing.* It intimates, of course, that in 'enduring with much long-suffering the vessels of wrath fitted for destruction,.God had a purpose or design of displaying his indignation against sin, *i. e.*, his punitive justice and his power.' Can it be a *reasonable* subject of complaint, that he is determined, or that he purposes (θέλων), to bring good out of evil?

To manifest or *exhibit his indignation* or *displeasure*, ἐνδείξασθαι τὴν ὀργήν; in other words to display his punitive justice with respect to the wicked. Ὀργή is often employed to designate the idea of *punishment*, *i. e.*, the consequences of indignation or anger; *e. g.*, Rom. i. 18. iv. 15. xiii. 4, 5, al. So Demosthenes: οὐκ ἴσην τὴν ὀργὴν ὁ νόμος ἔταξε, κ. τ. λ.; Reiske, Demosthenes, p. 528. — *And to make known, publish, declare his power*, καὶ γνωρίσαι τὸ δυνατὸν αὐτοῦ; comp. δύναμις in verse 17, where *the power* of God has special reference to his miraculous interpositions in order to punish Pharaoh with the Egyptians, and to deliver the oppressed Hebrews. Δύνατον, therefore, in the connection in which it here stands, must be viewed as having a special relation to *the power of making retribution to sinners, the power of punitive justice.* But this must be understood in accordance with the nature of a being who is self-existent, immutable, and independent. *Men* are prone to revenge, from malignity and because of wounded pride; they are prone to display, because of vanity and vain glory. But can we imagine the ever blessed God, whose glory and happiness cannot in any measure be affected by the favor or opposition of any of his creatures, as exhibiting his punitive justice and power for the purposes of revenge or display? He must exhibit them only for the purposes of benevolence, *i. e.*, for the sake of doing good to the subjects of his moral government; who, while they are allured to virtue, on the one hand, by all the glories of the upper world, are deterred from sin, on the other, by the judgments that are inflicted on the disobedient and rebellious.

Endured, bore with, ἤνεγκε. The verb φέρω has generally the sense of *bearing* or *carrying away, i. e.,* of *bearing* accompanied by *motion* in some way or other. But it is also employed in the sense of *fear, patior, to endure, to suffer,* Heb. xiii. 13 ; or of *tolero, sustineo, to tolerate, to bear with,* as Heb. xii. 20 ; in the Sept. Gen. xxxvi. 7. Num. xi. 14. Deut. i. 12. In this last sense it is clearly used here, as the adjunct ἐν πολλῇ μακροθυμίᾳ shows. — Μακροθυμίᾳ, *long-suffering, longanimitas, i. e.,* forbearance to punish, delay to enforce the strict claims of justice. The apostle seems to have his eye here on the case of Pharaoh in particular, who, after he had nine times resisted the mandate of Heaven to let the Hebrews go, was still spared and preserved in life, although he had long before forfeited all claim to forbearance. Still Paul plainly would not limit the case to Pharaoh only. He would intimate that God, in like manner, now (*i. e.,* at the time when he was writing) displays his long-suffering, by forbearing to punish those who deserve it. And what was true then, in respect to this matter, has been so ever since, and is so at the present moment.

Vessels of wrath, Σκεύη ὀργῆς, means vessels in respect to which wrath should be displayed, *i. e.,* wicked men who deserve punishment. Σκεύη was probably suggested here by its use in the preceding verse, where he has spoken of *vessels fitted for honorable and dishonorable use.* The language thus literally employed there, is *figuratively* used here. So in Is. xiii. 5, the Persian army is called כְּלֵי זַעַם יְהוָה, σκεύη ὀργῆς Κυρίου; comp. Jer. l. 25. But in these examples, by σκεύη ὀργῆς is meant *instruments of executing the divine displeasure ;* while in our text the meaning is *passive,* viz., persons on whom it ought to be or will be executed. *Fitted for destruction,* κατηρτισμένα εἰς ἀπώλειαν, another *offendiculum criticorum.* Κατηρτισμένα *fitted ;* how or by whom, the text does not say ; whether *merely* by their own act, or whether there was some agency on the part of God ; it simply designates the *actual condition* of the σκεύη ὀργῆς. The *passive* participle in such a case may be applied to designate what one has done for himself ; *e. g.*, 2 Tim. ii. 21, ἐὰν οὖν τις ἐκκαθάρῃ ἑαυτὸν ἀπὸ τούτων, ἔσται σκεῦος εἰς τιμήν ... εἰς πᾶν ἔργον ἀγαθὸν ἡ τ ο ι μ α σ μ έ ν ο ν, where the *being prepared* for every good work is the consequence of the ἐκκαθάρῃ ἑαυτόν. So in 2 Tim. iii. 17, ἐξηρτισμένος denotes the *being prepared* or *fitted* for every good work, by the beneficial influence of the inspired Scriptures. But in our text, how can we avoid comparing κατηρτισμένα in ver. 22, with ἃ προητοίμασε in ver. 23 ? The two verses are counterparts and *antithetic ;* and accordingly we have σκεύη ὀργῆς, to which σκεύη ἐλέους corresponds, and so εἰς ἀπώλειαν and εἰς δόξαν. How can we help concluding, then, that κατηρτισμένα and ἃ προητοίμασε correspond in the way of antithesis.

The objections which can be made to such a sense of κατηρτισμένα here, viz., a sense which makes it to designate *some agency of arrangement on the part of God*, by or in consequence of which, or under which, the *vessels of wrath* become fitted for destruction, are in all respects just the same as can be brought against the ἐξήγειρα κ. τ. λ. of verse 17, which has been discussed above. The answer to the question, whether God is, *in any sense*, the author of sin in such a way as throws any of the guilt, or any portion of it, upon him, and removes or diminishes the criminality of the sinner, is settled and certain from the tenor of the whole Bible, as well as from passages direct and express; *e. g.*, James i. 12. But is it proper for God, as the sovereign of the universe, having placed his creatures, who are moral and free agents, in circumstances in which he certainly knows beforehand they will sin, to exhibit upon them his punitive justice and power? This question has been sufficiently discussed in the Commentary on verse 17. If any one is still stumbled at this, I must refer him to such texts as 1 Pet. ii. 8. 1 Thess. v. 9, *for God hath not appointed us to wrath*, οὐκ ἔθετο ἡ μ ᾶ ς κ. τ. λ., *i. e.*, the implication is, that he has appointed some others, but not *us* to punishment, etc. Jude ver. 4. Prov. xvi. 4. Add to these such as designate the antithesis to this meaning, viz., the appointment of some to life eternal; as in Acts xiii. 48. ii. 47. Eph. i. 4, 5, 11. 2 Tim. i. 9. Rom. viii. 29, 30. Eph. iii. 11, al. If now to all these he adds such texts as 2 Sam. xii. 11. xvi. 10. 1 Kings xxii. 22. Josh. xi. 20. Ps. cv. 25. 1 Kings xi. 23. 2 Sam. xxiv. 1. Ex. vii. 13. ix. 12. x. 1, 20, 27. xi. 10. xiv. 8. Rom. ix. 17, 18. Deut. ii. 30. Is. lxiii. 17. John xii. 40, he can no longer doubt that there is *some sense*, (as explained in verse 17), in which the sacred writers do declare that God is concerned with evil. In the same sense, and in no other, can we suppose God to be here concerned. At all events there can be nothing more difficult in the *fitting the vessels of wrath for destruction*, in this verse, than there is in all the texts just referred to; and especially in Prov. xvi. 4. Jude verse 4. 1 Peter ii. 8. 1 Thess. v. 8. If one text is explained away, many others meet us which are of the very same tenor; and some of them, at least, admit of no explaining away. Unless we deny an *omnipotent* and *omniscient* God, we cannot abate, in the least degree, from any of the difficulties which such texts make. The great problem is: *How* entire free agency and accountability c n consist with entire dependence, and with the fact that our Creator has designs to accomplish even by our very wickedness? As has been repeatedly said, this is plainly beyond the boundaries of human knowledge. In the meantime, as *sin is actually in the world,* and *men are actually accountable,*— would it be any relief to the difficulties of our question, to suppose God to be so impotent that he cannot bring good out of evil; or so deficient in foresight and wisdom, as to have made a plan for the world of intelligent moral beings, which is radically defective in regard to accomplishing the ends of benevolence, and which admits evil that was not foreseen, and which cannot be prevented, nor even turned to the accomplishment of good? I think every candid and sober man will answer it then in the negative. It is better, then, to let the subject rest where the Bible has placed it; where it is placed in our text, and in verse 17.

(23) Καὶ ἵνα γνωρίσῃ, an enallage of construction. Verse 22 begins with εἰ θέλων ... ἐνδείξασθαι ... καὶ γνωρίσαι, *i. e.,* with a particle followed by the Infinitive mood. The same construction continued would here require [εἰ θέλων] γ ν ω ρ ί σ α ι τὸν πλοῦτον κ. τ. λ. But instead of this, we have ἵνα γνωρίσῃ. This usage of the Subj. with ἵνα, instead of the Inf., is very frequent in the New Test.; see New Test. Gram. § 138. 12. In the same manner the apostle might have said, εἰ δὲ θέλων ὁ Θεὸς, ἵνα ἐνδείξῃ ... καὶ γνωρίσῃ ... ἤνεγκεν κ. τ. λ. Of these methods of expression, both equally good in respect to grammar, the apostle, deviating from a strictly regular construction, as often, has used the one in verse 22, and the other in verse 23. For the use of θέλω followed by ἵνα with the Sujunctive (like θέλων ... ἵνα γνωρίσῃ), as well as by the Infinitive, see examples in Matt. vii. 12. xx. 32 (where ἵνα is implied); xxvi. 17 id. xxvii. 17 id. Mark vi. 25. ix. 30. x. 51 (ἵνα implied), et sæpe. For the use of the *participle* of θέλω see 2 Cor. xi. 12, θελόντων ... ἵνα .... εὑρηθῶσι κ. τ. λ. The full construction here then is, [εἰ δὲ θέλων] ἵνα γνωρίσῃ κ. τ. λ.

His abundant glory, τὸν πλοῦτον τῆς δόξης, where the first noun stands as an adjective; com. Heb. Geb. Gramm. § 440. *b*. Σκεύη ἐλέους, *i. e*, vessels toward which his mercy was to be displayed; the same as the κλητοί of viii. 28, and the antithesis here of σκεύη ὀργῆς—*which he had before prepared;* ἃ προητοίμασε; comp. Acts xiii. 48. ii. 47. Eph. i. 4, 5, 11. 2 Tim. i. 9. Rom. viii. 28, 29, 30. Eph. iii. 11, et. al. — Δόξαν, *glory, i. e*, happiness, glory in heaven. — As to πλοῦτος, comp. Rom. ii. 4. Eph. i. 7, 18. ii. 7. Col. i. 27.

After δόξαν there is plainly something wanting, in order that the sentence may correspond with ἤνεγκε κ. τ. λ. in the verse above. The most appropriate verb to be supplied seems to be ἠλέησε, *had mercy upon,* it being suggested by the phrase σκεύη ἐλέους. But supplying this, we read thus: "[And if desiring] that he [God] might make known his rich grace toward the *vessels of mercy* which he had before prepared for glory, [he showed mercy to] us whom he called, etc." In this way all runs on smoothly; and although I have not seen this exegesis of the passage in any commentator, I cannot help thinking that it is the most easy and obvious one. Tholuck supplies ἐκάλεσε; but the οὓς καί seems to forbid this. And besides, ἐκάλεσε does not seem to complete the sense. Understood as above explained, the sentiment is plain, and the transition in verse 24 . . . οὓς καὶ κ. τ. λ., is facile.*

The same thing is accomplished in another way, viz., by supposing the ellipsis to be completed from the former part of verse 23 thus: "*God desiring that he might make known his rich grace toward the vessels of mercy which he had before prepared for glory,* [ἐγνώρισε τὸν πλοῦτον τῆς δόξης αὐτοῦ ἐπὶ] ἡμᾶς, οὓς καὶ ἐκάλεσε κ. τ. λ." This evidently comes for substance to the same thing as the exegesis given above; and the whole of the ellipsis is in this way supplied from the context immediately preceding. Ἐκάλεσε governs οὕς, and ἡμᾶς, is synonymous with σκεύη ἐλέους, or is in apposition with it, and therefore may take the same preposition (ἐπί) implied before it. The phrase connected stands thus (according to the last proposed method of filling up the ellipsis): *He made known his rich grace toward* or *unto us,* [ἐπὶ] ἡμᾶς. See v. 22 above.

Reiche proposes a very different construction; viz., to connect καὶ ἵνα κ. τ. λ. with the preceding ἤνεγκε; and then he connects the whole thus: "Endured with great longanimity, etc , and *this in order that* (καὶ ἵνα) he might make known the abundance of his glory in respect to the righteous, the chosen objects of his mercy, etc " He compares the sentiment with Rom. ii. 4. Acts xvii. 27 seq. But here the long-suffering is for the good of the individuals toward whom it is exercised, not for the sake of others ; so that the cases are not analogous. Nor am I aware of any direct analogy in the Scriptures. Besides, to render καὶ ἵνα as = καὶ τοῦτο, and thus to make the clause that follows exegetical or supplementary, is as great a deviation from grammatical propriety as the anacoluthon proposed in verse 22 After all, the main difficulty with his exegesis is, that it does not correspond to the sentiment of the preceding verse, where two classes are described, who are widely diverse in their character and destiny; and each of these is at God's disposal. The prominency of this sentiment is destroyed by the interpretation which he proposes.

* The sense is very well given here by Alford and others, who consider εἰ δέ as used to introduce an answer to the question of the objection in v. 19,

Προητοίμασε here seems to designate the determination in the divine mind to prepare the elect; for the *calling*, as a matter of *fact*, must of course precede the fact of preparation. What God intends to do, is here spoken of as done; a very common idiom of the Scriptures.

(24) *Even us also whom he called,* οὓς καὶ ἐκάλεσε ἡμᾶς, *i. e.*, Gentiles as well as Jews. Comp. iii. 29, 30. i. 16. ii. 9, 10 iv. 9, 12.

(25) *Even so,* or *to the same purpose he saith by Hosea.* Ὡς καὶ ... λέγει. Ἐν Ὡσηέ may mean *in Hosea, i. e.,* in the book of Hosea; just as ἐν Δαβίδ (Heb. iv. 7) may mean *in the book of David.* But in both cases, it is perhaps more probable that the meaning is *by Hosea, by David;* like the Hebrew בדויד בהושע.

I will call him who was not my people, my people; and her who was not beloved, beloved, καλέσω ...... ἠγαπημένην, *i. e.,* the Gentiles, who were deemed outcasts from God, and were strangers to the covenant of his promise, will I bring into a covenant relation with me, and number among my beloved family, I will make them "sons and daughters of the Lord Almighty." The object of the quotation is to support the assertion just made, that the *vessels of mercy* were chosen from the Gentiles as well as the Jews, without any respect of persons. The Hebrew of this passage runs thus: "I will love her who was not beloved; and I will say to her who was not my people, My people art thou," Hos. ii. 23 (25). The Sept renders it literally and in the same order: ἀγαπήσω τὴν οὐκ ἀγαπημένην κ. τ. λ. The apostle has changed the order of the words, and quotes *ad sensum,* not *ad literam*

(26) *And it shall come to pass in the place where it was said to them: Ye are not my people, there shall they be called the sons of the living God;* καὶ ἔσται .... ζῶντος; another quotation from Hos. i. 10. (ii. 1), to the same purpose as the preceding. In both cases the original Hebrew, to which the language here is conformed, has reference to the reception and restoration to favor of Israel, who had been rejected on account of their transgressions. The apostle here applies the same language to the receiving of the Gentiles, who had been "strangers to the covenant of promise, and aliens from the commonwealth of Israel." It is an accommodation of the words of the prophet, so as to express his own views on the present occasion; and, furthermore, the *principle* of God's dealing, which is disclosed in the

and equivalent to ἐὰν οὖν in John vi 62 and ἀλλ' εἰ in classical Greek: ' But what if God, willing to manifest his wrath, and make known his might, (that which he would do), endured much long-suffering, the vessels of wrath prepared for destruction, and (what if this took place) that he might make known the riches of his glory," etc.

original passages and applied to Israel is the same which is involved in the reception to favor of the Gentiles who had been *out-casts*.

(27) Thus much for the reception of the Gentiles. Next, as to the more difficult point of casting off the great body of the Jews. In order, however, to settle the question on this point in a satisfactory manner, the apostle appeals to the declarations of the Hebrew prophets themselves. *Isaiah moreover says, in respect to Israel,* Ἡσαΐας δὲ ... Ἰσραήλ. Δέ *continuative, exclaims,* κράζει, *speaks aloud* or *openly. Although* ἐάν, or *if;* Hebrew here, כי אם, *although* — Ὡς ἡ ἄμμος τῆς θαλάσσης, *i. e.,* so great that it cannot be reckoned, exceedingly great. Τὸ κατάλειμμα σωθήσεται, *a remnant* [only] *shall be saved.* Κατάλειμμα here, and the corresponding Hebrew שאר means *a small number, a residue only.* So the context obliges us to interpret the word, both here and in Is. x. 22 seq. from which it is quoted. The apostle's purpose is to show that the Hebrew prophets had foretold the same thing which he affirms, viz., that *only a remnant* of Israel is to be saved. The passage, in the original Hebrew, probably relates to the times of the Messiah; as may be seen by comparing Is. x. 20, 21. The meaning of verse 22 seems to be that only a small remnant of them [small compared with those who had perished] will return to the Lord, so as to be received by him.

(28) The phrase Λόγον .... γῆς, is quoted nearly *verbatim* from the Sept., Is. x. 22, 23, with the exception that γάρ is added by the apostle, to show that he continues quoting for the sake of confirmation. The original Hebrew runs somewhat differently: *destruction is decreed, it shall overflow in justice; yea, destruction is verily determined on; the Lord Jehovah will execute it in the midst of all the land.* The Sept. and the apostle both represent the *general* sense of the Hebrew, but do not follow the words. Λόγον συντελῶν means *accomplishing his word, i. e.,* his promise or threat of excision. Καὶ συντέμνων, *deciding, bringing to an end, executing,* viz., his λόγον, as before. — Ἐν δικαιοσύνῃ, carrying all this into execution so as to satisfy the demands *of justice.*

For [Jehovah] *will execute his word decreed,* ὅτι λόγον συντετμημένον ποιήσει, *i. e.,* his threatening determined on, or decisively made, decisively pronounced. — *On the land,* ἐπὶ τῆς γῆς, *i. e.,* of Israel.

The object of the whole is only to show, that God of old threatened to destroy great multitudes of Jews for contumacy; and that it is no strange thing now to say, that great numbers of them will perish.

(29) *Yea,* [it happens] *as Isaiah had before said.* καὶ ......
Ἡσαίας: καὶ *affirmantis, imo, immo;* for here it is equivalent to καὶ γίνεται. The object of this quotation is the same as that of the preceding, viz, to show that it is no new or strange thing, that a part, yea a large portion of Israel should be rejected or cut off on account of their apostasy or unbelief. Consequently καί was followed, in the mind of the writer (and of course it should be in the mind of the reader), by γίνεται or ἐγένετο, *i. e., it happens* or *has happened.* — Προείρηκε here does not mean *predicted* (as it does in some cases), but *had before said.* The apostle had just cited one passage from Isaiah, viz., x. 22, 23, and here he adds: "To the same purpose had Isaiah spoken in a *preceding* part of his prophecy," viz, in i 9. καὶ καθὼς προείρηκεν Ἡσαίας.

The Lord of Hosts, κύριος Σαβαώθ. The Hebrew name צְבָאוֹת is often added to the title יְהוָה or אֱלֹהִים (אֱלֹהֵי), and designates the Supreme Being as Lord of the hosts of heaven, *i. e*, of the angels, etc, in heaven. There does not appear to be any good reason for the opinion of Tholuck and others, that this title was first given to Jehovah because he was the *mighty defender* (גִּבּוֹר) of Israel; and afterwards because he was considered as the *Lord of the stars;* which are called the host of heaven. *The Lord of the heavenly hosts, i. e.,* the angels, יְהוָה צְבָאוֹת is more simple: and so Gesenius explains it in his lex.con; comp. Ps. lxviii. 17, where the "chariots of God are said to be twenty thousand, even thousands of angels," and "the Lord to be among them;" also Deut. xxxiii 2, where he is said to come with *myriads of his holy ones* (מֵרִבְבֹת קֹדֶשׁ); comp. 2 K. vi. 16, 17. Dan. vii. 10, "thousand of thousands ministered unto him, and ten thousand times ten thousand stood before him." I add only that the appellation צְבָאוֹת does not occur in the Pentateuch, nor in the book of Judges, and that it is most frequent in Isaiah, Jeremiah, Zechariah, and Malachi. The apostle appears to have retained the Hebrew word untranslated, because it is so retained in the Septuagint version of Is. i. 9, which he here quotes.

Σπέρμα here corresponds to the Hebrew שָׂרִיד, the literal meaning of which is not *seed,* but *remnant, i. e.,* that which is left or saved after a general overthrow or destruction. In Deut. iii. 3 and Is. i. 9, the Septuagint has σπέρμα for שָׂרִיד. Σπέρμα often means *posteri, posterity, those who come after one.* But I apprehend the ground of its usage in this case by the Seventy, is that σπέρμα (*what is sown, seed*) denotes what remains of grain, after the consumption for the year, until seed-time comes, which is then sown; so that, considered in this light, σπέρμα is equivalent to *residuum,* which is the sense of it here.

Ὡς Γόμορρα ἂν ὡμοιώθημεν=Γομόρρᾳ ἂν ὡμοιώθημεν. The Greeks could employ either construction; at least the Seventy have done so; see in Hos. iv. 6. Ezek. xxxii. 2, in which latter case both constructions are employed in the same sentence; λέον τι ἐθνῶν ὡμοιώθης σύ, καὶ ὡς δράκων ὁ ἐν τῇ θαλάσσῃ. The Hebrew is היה כ. *To be like Gomorrha*, is to be utterly destroyed as this city was. The sentiment therefore is: "Isaiah said concerning the Jews, that only a small remnant should be rescued from utter destruction."

It is true, that in Is. i. 9 the passage does not respect the *spiritual* but the *temporal* punishment of the Jews. But the ground of the apostle's reasoning here is *analogy*. His object is, as it all along through the chapter has been, to illustrate a *principle* of action. What God did at one time and in one respect, he may do at another time and in a different respect, *provided the* PRINCIPLE *concerned shall be the same*. And surely it is no more against his benevolence or his justice, to punish *spiritually* for transgressions of a spiritual nature, *i. e.*, for continued impenitence and unbelief, than it is to punish *temporally* for sins against himself. His promises to Abraham and his seed, *i. e.*, his *literal* descendants, are only and always *conditional*, either as to temporal or spiritual blessings. Of course the same *principle* of action applies to both, when God punishes. It is on this ground, then, that the apostle adduces instances of threatening *temporal* evil, in order to illustrate and confirm *spiritual* threats.

Overlooking this obvious principle of analogical reasoning, many commentators on Rom. ix. have very strenuously maintained, that all which is there said pertains only to the present world, and to things of a merely temporal nature, or at most only to the external privileges of religion; and all this, because the instances here produced are mostly of such a kind. But let any one look back first on chap. viii. 28—39, which most plainly gives rise to the whole discussion in chap. ix.; then contemplate the resumption of this theme in chap. ix. 6; and above all, let him view the summing up of the main object in chap. ix. 18—23, and then glance forward to verses 30—33; and it does seem to me, unless he has made up his mind to an *a priori* way before he comes to the study of the text, that he cannot entertain any doubt what the object of the writer is.

(30) Τί οὖν ἐροῦμεν; a preface or transition to a summary of what he had been inculcating in the preceding context. It is as much as to say: 'How then may all that has been said on the point under consideration be summed up? The answer follows:

That the Gentiles who did not seek after justification, have

obtained justification, and that justification which is by faith!*
ὅτι ... ἐκ πίστεως. That is, one principal thing which I have maintained, (when I have averred that the Gentiles have become the children of Abraham by faith, and are received in the place of the unbelieving Jews) is that those *who did not seek after justification, i. e.,* who were once estranged from God and his law, were enemies to all which is good, and utterly regardless of spiritual blessings — these have now obtained justification by faith, *i. e.*, they are admitted by the mercy of God, without any merit on their part, to participate in the blessings of the gospel, even in the justification which Christ has procured. Διώκω is frequently used, even in the classic authors, in a sense like ζητεῖν; and so in Hebrew רָדַף for בִּקֵּשׁ. Reiche, Olshausen, et al., suppose that ὅτι is here designed to continue the question; *i. e.,* [*Shall we say*] *that,* etc. But the διατί of verse 32 is opposed to this interpretation.

(31) *But Israel, who sought for a law of justification, have not attained to a law of justification,* Ἰσραὴλ .... οὐκ ἔφθασε. That is, Israel, who, confiding in their own merit and good works, betook themselves for justification to their supposed complete obedience to the divine law, have not found or attained to such a law as would justify them; in other words: They have failed in this way of obtaining acceptance or justification. The reason or ground of this is fully stated in Rom. i — iii. as explained in the Commentary above. The apostle proceeds briefly to state the ground of what he had just asserted.

(32) *Why? because* [they sought] *not by faith but by works of law,* διατί, ὅτι .... νόμου; *i. e.,* Israel did not seek for justification in a *gratuitous* way, but by legal, *i. e. meritorious* obedience. That ἐκ πίστεως, *by faith,* necessarily involved, in the mind of the writer, the idea of *gratuitous* justification, is certain from Rom. iv. 4, 5, and especially iv. 16. It is equally clear, from iii. 20 — 28, that ἐξ ἔργων νόμου means *meritorious* obedience, *i. e.,* such works that the reward consequent on perfect obedience can be claimed. Such a reward, the apostle maintains, it is now impossible for any one of the human race to obtain, "because all have sinned and come short of the glory of God." Now as the Jews were self-righteous and proud, they of course lacked that humility and sense of ill-desert which the gospel demands, and without which its salvation is not to be had. This pride and self-righteousness led them to reject the Saviour of lost sinners,

---

* *And that justification,* etc. The particle δέ here is strictly adversative, the contrasted clause being omitted. The idea is not that justification which comes from works, *but* that which is of faith. The use of δέ expresses one of those nice shades of meaning so common with the Greek particles.

and to refuse all trust or confidence in him. Here it was that they stumbled and fell, yea even to their own perdition; as the apostle goes on to say:

For they stumbled on the stone of stumbling, as it is written, προσέκοψαν γὰρ . . . γέγραπται. Γάρ here introduces a clause which assigns the *cause* or reason why Israel had not obtained δικαιοσύνην. Yet A., B., D., E., F., G.; Syr. utr., Copt., Arm., Vulg., Ital.; Cyr., Chrys., Ruf., Aug., Ambrosiast., Pel., omit the γάρ; and it is probably spurious. The connection is more facile without it. But supposing it to be genuine we may thus explain the text; to the question, διατί; *why?* viz., Why did not Israel obtain justification? the apostle answers, (1) 'Because they sought it by legal obedience and not by faith.' (2) As subordinate to this he says: 'They did not exercise faith because they were offended with the Messiah as he appeared among them; they were stumbled at his character and claims.'

(33) *Behold I lay in Zion a stone of stumbling and a rock of offence; but every one who believeth on him shall not be ashamed,* ἰδοὺ . . . καταισχυνθήσεται. A peculiar quotation, made up of Is. xxviii. 16, and viii. 14. The former passage runs thus: "Behold, I have laid in Zion a stone, a corner stone, tried, precious, a firm foundation; he who confides in it shall not be afraid." The latter passage thus: "And he shall be for a refuge, and for a stone of stumbling and a rock of offence to both houses of Israel." The *stone of stumbling and rock of offence* is taken from Is. viii. 14, while the rest of the verse is from Is. xxviii. 16.

The Jewish Rabbins, in citing the Scriptures, often combine passages that are of the same tenor; and I may add, this is done by writers every day, without any consciousness of doing violence to the Scriptures, or of using an improper liberty; see Surenhusius's Βίβλος Καταλλάγης, Par. V. p. 43. The fact that the apostle has done so, too, seems to be plain. The reader will observe, that in Is. xxviii. 16 the predicates of the *stone that was laid in Zion* are, that it is *tried, precious, a firm foundation;* but one of the predicates in Is. viii. 14 is, that it is *a stone of stumbling,* or *a rock of offence.* The apostle is describing the unbelief of the Jews, their rejection of the Messiah, and of course the *stone of stumbling* is best adapted to the description of their case.

Paul seems to cite both of these passages, as if they referred to the Messiah. That at least they were, in his view, capable of such an application in the way of analogy is certain. Tholuck and many others understand them in the former way. The Chaldee Targum, on Is. xxviii. 16, translates thus: "See, I place in Zion a King, a mighty and a powerful King;" meaning the Messiah. Also the Babylonish Talmud (Tract. Sanhedrin. fol.

38. 1), the book of Zohar, and Jarchi. Kimchi also speaks of such an interpretation being given. In the New Testament, if the reader will compare Matt. xxi. 42, 44. Luke xx. 17, 18, and 1 Pet. ii. 5—7, he will find that Ps. cxviii. 22 ("the stone which the builders refused is become the headstone of the corner,"), and Is. viii. 14 are joined together, on account of their resemblance and their reference to the same object. Peter has not only joined these two passages, but added a third, viz., Is. xxviii. 16, and referred them all to the Messiah. This casts light therefore, on the intermingling of texts by Paul in the passage under consideration.

It seems evident, too, from Luke ii. 34, that the pious part of the Jews, to say the least, were accustomed to give to Is. 8, 14, a *Messianic* interpretation; for thus does the aged Simeon, when he takes the child Jesus in his arms, and says: "This child is set for the fall and rise of many in Israel, a sign that shall be spoken against." So the Gemara (Tract. Sanhedrin) also interprets Is. viii. 14, of the Messiah. That the Messiah would be rejected by the Jews, is plainly enough predicated (as their own ancient Rabbies acknowledge) in Ps. xxii. Is. liii. Zech. xi. xii., etc. So the Bereshith Rabba (a mystical commentary on Genesis, written about A. D. 300, by Rabbi Bar Nachmani), says: "One will sing no song, until the Messiah shall be treated with scorn; as it is written" [in Ps. lxxxix. 52].

The objection against the Messianic interpretation of Is. viii. 14. xxviii. 16, viz., that 'circumstances then present are referred to, the threatening of present punishment uttered, and excitement to present hopes and confidence then proffered,' cannot weigh much against such an interpretation. The prospect of the *future* was then held out by the prophet to the wicked as a matter of *dread;* to the pious as a matter of *hope* and *joy.* Let us see, now, how this matter stood. The Jews looked forward to a great deliverer, to a period of great prosperity and glory in the days of their Messiah. What says the prophet? He says; 'The days of the Messiah himself shall bring no liberation of the *wicked* from evil. They shall be consolatory only to the *good;* for even the Messiah himself will be only *a stone of stumbling and a rock of offence* to the wicked.' This is both *prediction* and *preaching.* It threatens and consoles, while it discloses what is yet future. Who can venture to say, now, that the prophet could not, or did not, entertain such views as these, and speak in such a manner? After the interpretation of Christ himself and of his apostles, in such a way as to support this view, we may venture to embrace it without any hazard.

Οὐ καταισχυνθήσεται, in the Hebrew לֹא יָחִישׁ. Paul seems to have read (and so the Seventy also), לֹא יְבִישׁ or לֹא יְבוֹשׁ. The present Hebrew text, לֹא יָחִישׁ, means literally *he shall not make haste;* but a secondary and derived sense of the same verb, is *to be afraid, to be agitated with fear so as to betake one's self to flight.* In this latter sense, it comes in substance to the same meaning which καταισχυνθήσεται expresses, viz., that of disappointed expectation and hope, failure of obtaining security and happiness. " Non refert *verbum*, sed *res.*"

CHAP. X. 1—21.

THE apostle now proceeds again to testify (as he has done in chap. ix 1—5) his strong affection for his kinsmen after the flesh, and his ardent desires and prayers for their salvation Nothing can be more appropriate than the expression of so much kind and deeply interested feeling on his part, for the Jews, whom he is obliged to denounce and threaten, as he does, in the preceding chapter, because of their character and conduct It serves to show, that he does not do this in the spirit of revenge, or because he loves denunciation, but with a sorrowful heart and eyes full of tears, that his bowels yearn over them, and that he retains for them all the affection which he once had when acting with them; yea, even more, and that too of a higher and better nature

He had just said, that Israel was διώκων νόμον δικαιοσύνης . . . καὶ οὐκ ἔφθασε. Here he resumes the theme, and explains himself more at large He states the reason why they did not attain justification, verses 2, 3, and goes on to show, that Moses himself confirms the same ideas which he had disclosed to them relative to faith and works, verses 4—8 The sentiment that *belief in Christ is necessary for all,* both Jew and Greek, is still further confirmed by verses 9—12

The apostle next presents the Jew as objecting thus 'If we allow what you say as to the necessity of faith or belief in Christ, yet how are we to be blamed for rejecting him, in case he has never been preached or declared to us? verses 13—15.

To this the apostle answers (1) That not all who have heard the gospel, believe it; as Isaiah himself declares, verses 16, 17. (2) But further, the objection cannot be truly made, that the Jews have not heard the gospel, at least enjoyed the opportunity of hearing it, for one may apply to them, in this respect, the words of Ps. xix. 4, or the words of Moses, in Deut xxxii. 21; or of Isaiah, in lxv 1, 2, so that they are left without any just apology for their unbelief, verses 18—21.

(1) *The benevolent* or *kind desire of my heart,* ἡ μὲν εὐδοκία τῆς ἐμῆς καρδίας; *i. e.,* his sincere and hearty wish (as we say) is, etc. — Εἰς σωτηρίαν, *for salvation, i. e.,* for their salvation. Literally *my prayer to God for them* [is] *unto* or *in respect to salvation.* But εἰς is frequently used in the New Testament in the same sense as לְ in Hebrew; *e. g.,* Rom. xvi. 6, εἰς ἡμᾶς, *for us;* 1 Cor. viii. 6, εἰς αὐτόν, *for him, i. e.,* for his honor and glory; 2 Cor. viii. 6, εἰς ὑμᾶς, *for your advantage;* and so often. The phrase ὑπὲρ αὐτῶν [ἐστὶν] εἰς σωτηρίαν is altogether equivalent, then, to ἵνα σωθῶσι or ὑπὲρ τῆς σωτηρίας αὐτῶν. The reading

ὑπὲρ αὐτῶν which is sanctioned by A., B., D., F., G., is now generally admitted in critical editions, instead of the Receptus ὑπὲρ τοῦ Ἰσραήλ. The sense is the same. The same MSS. omit ἡ before πρός.

(2) *For I bear them witness*, μαρτυρῶ γὰρ αὐτοῖς. Γάρ *illustrantis*. The apostle means to say, that he retains a strong affection for the Jews, and prays sincerely and ardently for their salvation; and specially so, as they have much feeling and zeal in respect to the subject of religion.

That they have a zeal for God, ὅτι ζῆλον Θεοῦ ἔχουσι; Θεοῦ, the Genitive *of the object* after ζῆλον. So in John ii. 17, ὁ ζῆλος τοῦ οἴκου σου, *zeal for the honor of thine house;* comp. Ps. lxix. 10 (9), קִנְאַת בֵּיתְךָ, also Acts xxii. 3, and John xvi. 2; comp. Gal. i. 14. Acts xxi. 20. The idea is, that the Jews had much zeal for objects of a religious nature; that they possessed strong religious feelings and sympathies. Philo, Josephus, and the various writers of the New Testament, by the facts which they disclose, most abundantly confirm the correctness of this declaration. *But not according to knowledge*, ἀλλ᾽ οὐ κατ᾽ ἐπίγνωσιν, *i. e.*, not an intelligent, discriminating, enlightened zeal; not a zeal regulated by a proper understanding of what was really religious truth. They persecuted Christians, for example, unto death, and yet thought themselves to be doing service for God, λατρείαν Θεῷ, John xvi. 2. *Zeal without knowledge*, is superstitious, persecuting, hostile to the peace and happiness of the community; and *knowledge without zeal*, is cold, sceptical, unfeeling, such as devils may possess as well as men. An actual union of both is accomplished only by sincere piety; and a high degree of this union, only by ardent piety.

(3) *For being ignorant of that justification which is of God*, ἀγνοοῦντες γὰρ ... δικαιοσύνην. The Gen. Θεοῦ here designates the author of that which the preceding noun signifies. Τὴν τοῦ Θεοῦ δικαιοσύνην is that method of justification, viz., gratuitous or by faith, which God has established, appointed, or revealed in the gospel. It stands opposed, here, to τὴν ἰδίαν δικαιοσύνην, *i. e.*, justification on the ground of merit or by the works of law. Γάρ (*for*) causal, introduces proof of the assertion contained in ἀλλ᾽ οὐ κατ᾽ ἐπίγνωσιν. The apostle does not mean by ἀγνοοῦντες, to imply that the Jews had enjoyed no opportunity to become acquainted with the δικαιοσύνην Θεοῦ; for this would contradict what he says in the sequel, verse 18, seq.; but whatever their opportunities of knowledge had been, they were in fact still ignorant, and criminally ignorant, of the gospel method of justification.

And seeking to establish their own justification, καὶ τὴν ἰδίαν ...

στῆσαι. Στῆσαι means here *to render valid, to make good one's claims*. The inclination of the Jews, as is well known, to seek for and expect justification by their own merit, *i. e.*, in obedience to their laws, specially the ceremonial law, is here referred to by the apostle.

They have not submitted themselves, οὐκ ὑπετάγησαν; Second Aor. Pass., with the *reflexive* sense of the Middle voice. See Buttm. Gr. Gramm. § 123. 2; N. Test. Gramm. § 61. 4. But if we render οὐκ ὑπετάγησαν passively, *they have not been subjected*, the sense will be substantially the same. The idea in the verse is: 'Having no correct views of justification by grace, and being earnestly desirous of justification on the ground of their own merit, they reject the justification which God has proffered to them in the gospel.'

(4) *For Christ is the end of the law*, τέλος γὰρ νόμου Χριστός; *i. e*, believing in Christ, receiving him by faith, and thus attaining to δικαιοσύνη Θεοῦ, accomplishes the *end* or *object* which the law, *i. e.*, perfect obedience to the law, would accomplish. In this simple way, and consonant with the context, I would interpret this long agitated and much controverted text. Thus τέλος is frequently used to denote *exitus rei, the event, end, ultimate object* or *design of a thing;* Matt. xxvi. 58, ἰδεῖν τὸ τέλος, *to see the event, final end,* Rom. vi. 21, τὸ τέλος, *the end* or *final event* of those things, is death; 2 Cor. xi. 15, ὧν τὸ τέλος, *whose end, final state* or *condition, i. e.*, reward, shall be according to their works; Phil. iii. 19, ὧν τὸ τέλος, *whose end* or *final state,* shall be destruction; 1 Tim. i. 5, τὸ δὲ τέλος τῆς παραγγελίας, *now the ultimate end, object, design, of the commandment,* etc.; Heb. vi. 8, ἧς τὸ τέλος εἰς καῦσιν, *whose end* or *final reward is burning.* See also James v. 11. 1 Pet. i. 5, τὸ τέλος, *the end* or *event* of your faith, is the salvation of your souls; iv. 17. So in other Greek writings; *e. g.*, τὸ τέλος τοῦ πράγματος εἰς κακίαν ἄγει, Test XII. Patriarch. p. 689; τὸ τούτου τέλος ἐν Θεῷ ἦν, *the end* or *event of this matter was with the Divinity,* Demosth. 292. 22. So in the phrases, τέλος λαμβάνειν, παρέρχεσθαι εἰς τέλος, ἐκ τοῦ τέλους γνωρισθέντα, κ. τ. λ.

The *end* of the law, was the justification of men, *i. e.*, their advancement to happiness and glory in a future world. So the apostle himself states in the sequel: "The man that doeth these things shall live by them." But inasmuch as "all men have sinned and come short of the glory of God," so "no flesh can be justified by the deeds of the law;" *i. e.*, legal justification on the ground of merit is now impossible. But what the law cannot accomplish, Christ does accomplish; for through him the justification of sinners is brought about, which would otherwise be impossible. Christ then is *the end of the law*, *i. e.*, he accomplishes or brings about that which the law was designed to accomplish — the acceptance of men with God, and their admission to the happiness of the future world. That ver. 4 is only epexegetical of the last clause of the preceding verse, seems to me quite plain; and the γάρ intimates this.

But τέλος has been very differently construed; viz., (*a*) As meaning *end* in the sense of *ending* or *completion*. In this case νόμος means the *ceremonial law;* and the sentiment is: 'Christ has, by his coming, made an end of the ceremonial law.' But it is a sufficient objection to this interpretation, that it is wholly *irrelevant* to the subject now under discussion. (*b*) Christ is the τελείωσις or πλήρωμα of the Jewish law, *i. e.*, Christ perfectly fulfilled or obeyed it. But this explanation, although preferred by Origen, Pelagius, Ambrose, Melancthon, Calvin, etc., is not in accordance with the *usus loquendi* of the word τέλος. And moreover; to say that Christ obeyed the whole law, ritual, or moral, or both, is saying what indeed is true: but then it has no direct or visible bearing upon the subject immediately before the mind of the writer. There are *two* supposable ways of justification, one *wrong* way and one *right* one; this it is his object to show. Now the Jews, having chosen the wrong one, viz., their own works of law, *i. e.*, their own merits, have of course missed the right one, viz., that by faith in Christ. (*c*) Chrysostom, Theodoret, Beza, Bengel, Turretin, Heumann, Tholuck, etc., understand τέλος in the sense of *end, design, final object*. Tholuck explains it thus: viz., that the law teaches us our sinfulness and our need of a Saviour, and this was what it was designed to accomplish; and thus it leads us *in the end* to Christ, or to Christ as its *final end*. He finds an exact parallel in Gal. iii. 34: "the law is our παιδαγωγός to bring us to Christ." But why we should give the passage this turn here, I cannot see; for the writer has expressly told us in what respect he means that Christ was the *end of the law*, viz. εἰς δικαιοσύνην.

In respect to the justification of every believer, εἰς . . . πιστεύοντι. This designates, as I have before observed, the very respect in which Christ was τέλος νόμου. He is so to every *believer;* but not so to others, *i. e.*, not so while they remain unbelievers, although he is proffered to them as mighty and willing to save all who will come unto God through him. Παντί, κ. τ. λ., the Dative of the person *for* whom.

(5) Μωυσῆς γάρ κ. τ. λ. Here is γάρ *illustrantis* again; for the quotations which follow are plainly designed to illustrate the two different methods of justification which the apostle had just brought into view.—*Describeth, delineateth,* Γράφει; often used in

such a sense.—*Legal justification*, τὴν δικαιοσύνην τὴν ἐκ τοῦ νόμου, *i e.*, a justification which a man may claim as the proper reward of his own good deeds or obedience. The apostle makes this appeal to Moses, both to confirm and illustrate his own declarations, and to show also that he is inculcating no new doctrine. *That the man who doeth these things shall live by them*, ὅτι . . . . ἐν αὐτοῖς. Ὅτι is prefixed as here to a quotation=*viz.*, *namely*, or *as follows*. The Greek word itself seems in reality to be the neuter of ὅστις, ὅτι = ὁ τί, i. e., *this thing, videlicet*. Ποιήσας αὐτά, viz., the thing spoken of in the preceding context. The quotation is from Lev. xviii. 5, which has a reference to preceding ordinances and statutes recorded in Leviticus. Ζήσεται ἐν αὐτοῖς, he shall be rendered happy by them, *i. e.*, by obedience to such statutes, etc. Obedience, *i. e.*, entire obedience, shall render him happy, shall entitle him to the rewards that are proffered to the obedient. That the Jews understood something more than *happiness in the present life* by the וָחַי (ζήσεται) in Lev. xviii. 5, seems probable from the version of Onkelos: "He shall live in eternal life by them." So the Targum of Pseudo-Jonathan: "He shall live in eternal life, and have a part with the righteous."

(6) *But justification by faith speaketh thus*, ἡ δὲ . . . . λέγει. Δέ *but*, here in distinction from or in opposition to the preceding declaration. Δικαιοσύνη is here *personified*. The idea is: "One who preaches justification by faith, might say, etc.' *Say not in thine heart*, μὴ . . . . σου, *i. e.*, within thyself. To say *within one's self*, is to think, imagine, suppose. So the Greek φημί is sometimes used. Ἐν τῇ καρδίᾳ σου, בִּלְבָב where לֵב (*heart*) is used like נֶפֶשׁ (*soul*) for self; and so very often in the Hebrew language.

Who shall ascend to heaven? τίς . . . . οὐρανόν; etc. The whole appeal and method of reasoning is in an analogical way. Moses, in Deut. xxx 11, assigns as one reason why the Hebrew nation should be obedient, that the statutes of the Lord given them were plain and intelligible; they "were not hidden from them, neither were they afar off." In order to enforce this last thought the more effectually, he dwells upon it and illustrates it in several ways. "The commandment," says he, "is not in heaven, that thou shouldest say: Who shall go up for us to heaven and bring it to us that we may hear it and do it. Neither is it beyond the sea, that thou shouldest say: Who shall go over the sea for us and bring it to us, that we may hear and do it?" Nay, "The word is very nigh unto thee, in thy mouth and in thy heart, that thou mayest do it." Deut. xxx. 14. That is: 'The commandment is in language which thou dost speak, and is such as thou canst comprehend with thine understanding.' The whole may be summed up in one word, omitting all figurative expression; viz., *the commandment is plain and accessible*. You can have, therefore, no excuse for neglecting it. So *justification by faith in Christ* is an equally plain and intelligible doctrine. It is not shut up in mysterious language, nor concealed from the eyes of all but the *initiated*, like the heathen mysteries. It is not in the books of countries which lie beyond the impassable ocean; not in the mysterious book of God in heaven, and yet undisclosed; not in the world beneath, which no one can penetrate and return to disclose its secrets. It is brought before the mind and heart of every man; and thus he is without excuse for unbelief. It is the *general* nature of the imagery, in the main, which is significant to the purpose of the writer. Paul means simply to affirm, that if Moses could truly say that his law was intelligible and accessible, the doctrine of justification by faith in Christ is even still more so. *That is, to bring down Christ,* τοῦτ' ἔστι .... καταγάγειν. The τοῦτ' ἔστι here designates the reference which the apostle designs to make of the *sentiment* just quoted, viz., that he means to apply it to Christ, and not to the law of Moses.—Χριστὸν here means *Christ* in the sense of verse 4, where he is called τέλος νόμου . . εἰς δικαιοσύνην.

(7) *Who shall go down into the abyss*, τίς .... ἄβυσσον. In the Hebrew, Deut. xviii. 3, the phrase is לֹא מֵעֵבֶר לַיָּם הוּא *not beyond the sea is it*. The expression differs, but the general sense is the same as here. To go beyond the sea, which was considered as of boundless width (Job. xi. 9) and impassable, is employed by Moses as the image of what is difficult or impossible. In the same way Paul employs ἄβυσσον. No one returns from the *world beneath* שְׁאוֹל or תְּהוֹם; (for שְׁאוֹל and תְּהוֹם are occasionally synonymous, being the antithesis of שָׁמַיִם, see Gen. xlix. 25. Ps. cvii. 26. Sirac. xvi. 18. xxiv. 5, and comp. Ps. cxxxix. 8. Amos ix. 2. Matt. xi. 23. Here ἄβυσσον designates the שְׁאוֹל of the Hebrews, considered as the *abode of the dead;* as is evident from Χριστὸν ἐκ νεκρῶν ἀναγαγεῖν. For the general idea see v. 6.

The quotations before us are clear examples of the liberty which Paul takes, of accommodating the *spirit* of the Old Testament to the objects and truths of the Gospel, without any slavish subjection to the mere form of words.

(8) *What saith it?* ἀλλὰ τί λέγει; *i. e.*, what saith ἡ ἐκ πίστεως δικαιοσύνη? It saith: *The word is nigh to thee, in thy mouth and in thy heart,* ἐγγύς σου ... σου. Ῥῆμα here means ῥῆμα πίστεως, *i. e.*, the gospel, as the sequel shows; comp. 1 Tim. iv. 6. *In thy mouth*, in thine own language, *i. e.*, a subject of conversation and teaching. *In thy heart, i. e.*, a subject of meditation and

thought. Sentiment; 'The doctrine which I inculcate, is so far from being an obscure and inaccessible and forbidden mystery, that it is daily a subject of reflection and of conversation.' That the apostle means the doctrine of faith which he taught and preached, is clear from the following τοῦτ᾽ ἔστι . . . κηρύσσομεν.

(9) Ὅτι, *because, i. e.* say not in thine heart, etc., *because if thou shalt openly profess with thy mouth that Jesus is Lord,* ἐὰν ὁμολογήσῃς . . . . Ἰησοῦν. The verb ὁμολογέω means literally *eadem loqui, to speak what consents* or *agrees with something which others speak* or *maintain.* But it is frequently used to denote *speaking* or *professing openly, i. e.,* proclaiming openly one's belief in Christ, which was speaking in accordance with what other Christians had avowed. Ἐν τῷ στόματι, *by word of mouth,* in words, or by the use of language. Κύριον I take to be the *predicate* of the sentence in this case, *i. e.,* a true believer is to confess *that Jesus is Lord;* comp. Acts ii. 36. v. 31. Phil. ii. 9, 10, where the order of the words is Κύριος Ἰησοῦς Χριστός (the same as here), but where it is certain that Κύριος must be a *predicate,* viz., that Jesus Christ *is Lord.* The position of Κύριον before Ἰησοῦν, is for the sake of emphasis. *And shalt believe in thy heart that God hath raised him from the dead,* καὶ πιστεύσῃς . . . . νεκρῶν; *i. e.,* shalt sincerely, *ex animo,* believe that God has raised him from the dead, and exalted him to the throne of universal dominion. It is not the simple fact of a resurrection of Jesus' body from the tomb, which in the apostle's view is the great and distinguishing feature of Christian belief; it is the exaltation, glory, and saving power that are consequent on the resurrection, which he evidently connects with this event. So in Phil. ii. 8—11. So in Acts ii. 24, 31—33, where the whole connection is very explicit; comp. also Heb. ii. 9. 2 Cor. iv. 14. Acts xvii. 31. Rom. iv. 25. 1 Cor. xv. 17—20. *Thou shalt be saved,* σωθήσῃ, *i. e.,* a bold and open profession of the Christian faith, united with a sincere and hearty belief of it, will secure the salvation of him who makes such a profession; all which shows that the way of salvation is open and easy of access.

The reader will observe that the apostle has here followed the *order* of the quotations which he had made from the law of Moses (verse 8) in stating the conditions of salvation. Independently of this we might naturally expect that belief of the heart would be first mentioned, and then confession of the mouth, *i. e.,* by words; for this is the order of nature. And so, in the explanation immediately subjoined, the apostle does in fact arrange his declarations; viz.

(10) *For with the heart there is belief unto justification, and with the mouth confession is made unto salvation,* καρδίᾳ γὰρ . . . .

σωτηρίαν. Πιστεύεται and ὁμολογεῖται, if regarded as being in the Mid. voice, may be rendered in an active sense; but both may be taken *passively* and rendered as above; or we may translate: *Belief is exercised, confession is made,* etc. Our English version takes the first verb *actively,* and the last *passively ;* which does not seem to have been intended by the writer. Γάρ introduces a clause which confirms or gives emphasis and definiteness to the preceding sentiment. Εἰς δικαιοσύνην and εἰς σωτηρίαν mean, so that justification is attained and so that salvation is attained. Εἰς here, as often, stands before a noun designating the object or end to be obtained, and may be called *εἰς telicum.* The sentiment is the same for substance as in the preceding verse ; see Comm. on σωθήσῃ. The design of the apostle in repeating it is to strengthen the impression upon this point, which is important specially in the course of his argumentation.

(11) This verse is a still further confirmation of the first part of v. 10, bringing into view a text to which he had before made an appeal in chap. ix. 33. Πᾶς ὁ . . . καταισχυνθήσεται, *no one who believeth on him shall ever be disappointed ;* i. e., salvation is certain to every true believer. Πᾶς . . . οὐ I have put together, and rendered *no one.* If the οὐ in this case had been connected with πᾶς by position, and not with the verb, the meaning would then have been, as in English, *not every one, i. e.,* some but not all. See New Test. Gramm. § 116. 1. The form of the Greek is *Hebraistic.* The Hebrew had no method of saying *none,* except by using כֹּל (*every one*) with a negative לֹא (*not*). Καταισχυνθήσεται, יֵבוֹשׁ, *none shall be put to shame* by a failure of his hopes, *none shall be disappointed.*

(12) The word πᾶς, which the above quotation from Is. xxviii. 16 exhibits, gives occasion here for the apostle to bring into view a point which he had often insisted upon in the previous parts of his epistle, particularly in chaps. iii. iv., viz., that the salvation of the gospel is proffered to all men without distinction, and on the same terms; *for there is no difference between the Jew and the Greek,* or *there is no distinction of Jew and Greek,* οὐ γὰρ . . . Ἕλληνος. Τε καί is used here, as often elsewhere, between two members coupled together closely by the sentence, but diverse or antithetic in respect to meaning. Γάρ *illustrantis,* viz., illustrating the πᾶς of the preceding assertion. In fact, there is a singular succession here of clauses, arising one out of another, to all of which γάρ is prefixed. Thus in verse 10, καρδίᾳ γὰρ κ. τ. λ., assigns a ground or confirmation of the preceding declaration; verse 11, τέλει γὰρ κ. τ. λ., assigns a ground of confirmation, in respect to what had been advanced in verse 10, *i. e.,* it appeals to the Scriptures in confirmation of it; verse 12, οὐ γὰρ κ. τ. λ., is again a confirma-

tion of the declaration πᾶς . . . οὐ ἐπαισχυνθήσεται, and this last declaration is, in its turn, confirmed by two succeeding ones, viz., ὁ γὰρ αὐτὸς, κ. τ. λ., and πᾶς γὰρ ὅς, κ. τ. λ., the first of which contains a declaration of the apostle, and the second an appeal to the Scriptures confirming this declaration: so that here are no less than *five* clauses in immediate succession, all of which have a γάρ prefixed, and in the same sense throughout, *i. e.*, each γάρ stands in a clause which serves to confirm or illustrate the preceding assertion. This is altogether characteristic of the manner of Paul; see Introd.

For there is the same Lord of all, ὁ γὰρ . . . . πάντων; *i. e.*, the Jews and Gentiles have one common Lord and Master; comp. Rom. iii. 29, 30. iv. 16, 17.—Πλουτῶν . . . . αὐτόν, *abounding* [in goodness] *toward all who call upon him*. Πλουτῶν means *being rich, having abundance*, viz., of wealth. But here the connection shows, of course, that the apostle means *rich in spiritual blessings, abounding in spiritual favors* towards men.— Ἐπικαλουμένοις ἐπ᾽ αὐτόν like the Heb. קָרָא בְשֵׁם, means *making supplication to him, performing acts of devotion to him*. Πάντας here again shows, that the goodness of God is not limited to the Jewish nation, but equally proffered to all.

(13) This is confirmed again by another quotation which exhibits the same πᾶς. *For every one who calls on the name of the Lord, shall be saved,* πᾶς γὰρ . . . σωθήσεται. Here we have the full Hebrew form, viz., כָּל־אֲשֶׁר יִקְרָא בְשֵׁם יהוָה *every true worshipper of God;* ὄνομα being pleonastic, as in " the name of the God of Jacob defend thee," "the name of the Lord is a strong tower," etc. In the quotations in vers. 11 and 13, from Is. xxviii. 16 and Joel iii. 5 (ii. 32), it is true, that the sacred writers of the Old Testament had principally in view the confidence which is placed in God the Father, in seasons of danger and distress, and the promise that such confidence should not be in vain. But it is the *principle* of action which is the main question, and not the *special relation* of it in ancient times. Is the *principle* the same under the Christian dispensation as it was under the Jewish one, viz., that those who are exposed to danger and distress, and who put their trust in God shall obtain deliverance? This is true in a spiritual, as well as in a temporal respect, *i. e.*, there is undeniably a πλήρωσις to this promise under the gospel. Paul did not expect his readers to deny this; and consequently he has used the quotations with special reference to Christ; although the passages, in their *original* connection, do not seem to have had such a *special* reference. But in doing this, he has plainly authorized us to apply to Christ the same divine worship and honor, which the saints of ancient days

applied to Jehovah. For he must have known that his readers would of course see, that he applied the very same things to Christ, which the writers of the Old Testament referred to Jehovah; and consequently, that he considered him as entitled to the same honors and confidence. I see not any way in which we can make less out of the passage than this, viz., that all who believingly call upon the name of Christ shall be saved.*

(14) The apostle here anticipates an objection which he expected the Jew would make to his argument, which urges the necessity of calling on Christ in order to be saved: 'How shall one call on him, unless he is first a believer in him, *i. e.*, first persuaded that he is the proper object of religious invocation! And how shall he believe this, provided no declaration of it has been made to him! And how can such a declaration be made, unless by a messenger or preacher duly commissioned? For the Scripture itself bestows its encomium on such messengers, and thus impliedly recognizes the importance of them.' To all this the apostle gives an answer in the sequel, verse 16 seq.

It is a matter of indifference, whether (with Grotius) we suppose the apostle to introduce an objector as speaking here in the person of an unbelieving Jew, or whether (with Tholuck and most commentators) we suppose the apostle himself to utter the words in question. If we attribute them to the apostle, we must suppose him to be uttering what an objector would naturally say. Nor is it necessary to suppose, that all which comes from an objector is false. The speciousness of an objection consists in the claims of some part of it to be considered as true. The *reasoning* of the objector here is correct, if you allow him his premises; *i. e.*, it is true that men first believe on a Saviour, before they will call upon him, etc. But the main question here after all is, whether the fact assumed as a basis of all this reasoning, viz., that *the Jew had not heard the gospel*, is true. The apostle proceeds in the sequel to show that this is not the case; and therefore that the whole objection falls to the ground.

How then shall they call [on him] *in whom they have not believed?* πῶς οὖν . . . ἐπίστευσαν; *i. e*, how shall they pray to him, do religious homage to him, who is not the object of belief or confidence? Οὖν marks here a relation to the foregoing assertions. "It is used," says Passow, "in interrogative sentences, with reference to preceding assertions which are con-

---

* De Wette, Meyer, Alford and others agree with the above interpretation. Alford says κυρίου is "used here of Christ beyond a doubt, as the next verse shows. There is hardly a stronger proof, or one more irrefragable by those who deny the Godhead of our blessed Lord, of the unhesitating application to him by the apostle of the name and attributes of Jehovah."

ceded." So here, the objector (or Paul in his place) says, 'Conceding now that all who call on him shall be saved, yet how can men call on one of whom they have not heard, etc?' By saying this he aims to apologize for the unbelief of many Jews who still rejected the Saviour. Εἰς ὅν here must mean *the Lord Jesus Christ;* for surely he is the specific object of faith or belief, about which the apostle is here discoursing. *And how shall they believe* [on him] *of whom they have not heard;* πῶς δὲ πιστεύσουσιν [εἰς αὐτὸν] οὗ οὐκ ἤκουσαν; That is, before one can believe on a Saviour, he must have some knowledge of him; this Saviour must be proclaimed to him. Οὗ here is the Genitive governed by ἤκουσαν; "verba sensûs gaudent Genitivo." — Κηρύσσοντος, *a preacher,* is one who proclaims in public any matter, who publishes aloud; in the Hebrew מְבַשֵּׂר.

(15) *And how shall they preach, except they be sent?* πῶς δὲ ... ἀποσταλῶσι; *i. e.,* unless they are divinely commissioned; comp. Jer. xxiii. 21. *As it is written,* καθὼς γέγραπται. The connection of the sentiment here presents some difficulty. But the course of the thought seems to be this, viz., 'the importance of the heralds of salvation is implied in the high commendation which the Scripture bestows upon them.' This is indeed truly implied in the words quoted; for why should these heralds be spoken of with high and joyful commendation, if they are not important instruments in the salvation of men? So the speaker in this case, in making this quotation, illustrates what he has just suggested respecting the importance of the heralds of salvation.

How beautiful are the feet of those who publish salvation, who proclaim good tidings, ὡς ὡραῖοι ... τὰ ἀγαθά. The Septuagint translates thus: ὡς ὥρα ἐπὶ τῶν ὀρέων, ὡς πόδες εὐαγγελιζομένου ἀκοὴν εἰρήνης, ὡς εὐαγγελιζομένου ἀγαθά! So the Codex Vaticanus; and I suppose that after the latter ὡς the translator must have supplied in his own mind the word πόδες, in order to make out a sense which would be good. The Hebrew runs thus: "How beautiful on the mountains are the feet of him who proclaims glad tidings, who publishes peace, who makes proclamation of good!" Is. lii. 7. Paul, in translating, has abridged the original Hebrew.— Οἱ πόδες, *feet,* i. e., a part of the person taken for the whole; as often in Hebrew, and so in other languages; comp. Acts v. 9. The reason why οἱ πόδες is here chosen rather than any other part of the body to be the representative of the *person* would seem to be, that the *heralds* who proclaim any thing (מְבַשְּׂרִים), *travel* from place to place in order to discharge their duty. *Salvation,* εἰρήνην, שָׁלוֹם, good in its most extensive sense. — Εὐαγγελίζω means primarily, according to its etymology, *to publish good news.* But secondarily, it conveys only the general idea *to publish;* consequently it takes after it the Acc. of a noun indicating the thing published, as here εἰρήνην . . . τὰ ἀγαθά.

(16) *But all have not obeyed the gospel,* ἀλλ' οὐ πάντες . . . εὐαγγελίῳ; *i. e.*, notwithstanding what you say (ἀλλά concedes), still it is true, the apostle replies, that all to whom the gospel has been published have not become obedient to it. *For Isaiah saith, Lord, who hath believed our report?* Ἡσαίας . . . ἡμῶν; Is. liii. 1. That is, the prophet complains that the declarations made respecting the Messiah are not credited by those who hear them. Here then is an example of Jews who hear and believe not; and the same *thing* is asserted by Isaiah, which the apostle now asserts; so that he could not be accused of producing a new or strange charge.

(17) *Faith then comes by hearing, and hearing by the word of God,* ἄρα . . . Θεοῦ; *i. e.*, the very quotation you make concedes the principle, that the gospel must first be *published* before men can be taxed with criminality for unbelief; for Isaiah complains of those to whom it had been *published.* — Ἡ δὲ ἀκοὴ διὰ ῥήματος τοῦ Θεοῦ, *i. e.*, the word of God, the gospel, must first be proclaimed before it can be heard, understood, and believed. The verse I take to be the suggestion of the objector. He means to insist by it, that many of the Jews are not culpable for unbelief, inasmuch as they have not heard the gospel, and hearing it is necessary to the believing of it.

(18) The apostle admits the correctness of the principle, viz., that faith cometh by hearing; but he denies the fact which was implied in the statement of it, viz., that there was a part of the Jewish nation who had not heard, *i. e.*, who had not enjoyed the opportunity to hear. So the sequel: *but I reply: Have they not heard?* Ἀλλὰ λέγω . . . ἤκουσαν; Μενοῦνγε, *yes, verily;* compounded of μέν, οὖν, and γέ. Μενοῦν asserts, and γέ increases the intensity of the assertion. In the μὴ οὐκ before ἤκουσαν, the μή is the sign of interrogation, and οὐκ simply qualifies the verb; see New Test. Gramm. § 153. 5.

Their sound hath gone forth, etc., εἰς πᾶσαν . . . τὰ ῥήματα αὐτῶν, quoted from Ps. xix. 5, in the words of the Septuagint, which here follows the Hebrew. Ὁ φθόγγος αὐτῶν, in the original Psalm, means the voice or sound of the works of nature, which show or declare in all the earth that he who made them is God, and the God of glory. The apostle seems to use the words in this place simply as the vehicle of his own thoughts, as they were very convenient and appropriate. The expressions πᾶσαν τὴν γῆν and τὰ πέρατα τῆς οἰκουμένης, are common and figurative expressions to designate the idea of far and wide, what is unlimited in extent, etc. As originally employed by the Psalmist, they may be taken in their greatest latitude. As used by the apostle, they may be taken in the like latitude so far as the Jews are concerned; for it is of them, and them only, that he is here particularly speaking.

(19) *But I say,* ἀλλὰ λέγω, *i. e.,* I reply again in reference to the opportunity of the Jews to gain some knowledge of the gospel. *Doth not Israel know?* Μὴ Ἰσραὴλ οὐκ ἔγνω; *What* — is not said, and has been matter of much controversy. To me, however, it seems plain, that it is to be gathered from the subsequent context; if so, it is clear that the sentiment is: 'Doth not Israel know (as I have before said, verses 11, 12), that the Gentiles are to be received as well as the Jews, and the Jews to be cast off for unbelief?' The apostle now proceeds to quote passages of the Old Testament, which show that the ancient prophets have explicitly declared the same thing. Reiche construes the phrase thus: 'Has not [God] loved or acknowledged Israel?' Comp. Amos iii. 2. Hos. viii. 5. Rom. xi. 2. But I cannot regard this as congruous with the context. Meyer, Tholuck, De Wette and others, agree with the explanation above.

First, Moses saith, πρῶτος Μωϋσῆς λέγει. Πρῶτος I understand here as meaning *first in point* or *order of time,* like the Hebrew רִאשׁוֹן: comp. the Lex. under πρῶτος. *I will move you to jealousy by that which is no nation, I will excite you to indignation by a foolish people;* ἐγὼ . . . παροργιῶ ὑμᾶς; i. e., I will make you jealous, by receiving to favor those whom you regard as unworthy of the name of the people (ἔθνος, גּוֹי), viz., the Gentiles; I will render you indignant, by receiving to favor a *foolish people,* גּוֹי נָבָל. The Hebrew נָבָל designates one that is spiritually foolish, *i. e.,* a wicked, unbelieving person, who contemns God. "The *fool* (נָבָל) hath said in his heart: There is no God." "Fools (נְבָלִים) make a mock at sin." Consequently the epithet ἀσύνετος here designates a wicked or idolatrous people. The meaning of the whole is: 'I will receive to my favor the heathen whom you regard as despicable, and who are without God and without hope in the world.' In Deut. xxxii. 21 (from which these words are quoted), God complains of the Jews, that they had apostatized from him and gone after idols, and thus provoked his jealousy and indignation. Because they had so done, he declares that he will, at some future period, provoke them, and excite their jealousy, by receiving a heathen and idolatrous people in their stead. It is not necessary to suppose that Moses (in Deut. xxxii. 21) had in view the salvation of the Gentiles in gospel times. It is enough for the apostle's purpose, that the same *principle* is developed in the words of Moses, which is developed by the reception of the Gentiles into the Christian church in his time. Now as the Jews were jealous and angry because of this reception, so the apostle might appeal to the declarations of Moses, as an exhibition of the very same views and sentiments which he had been teaching.

(20) *But Isaiah comes out boldly and says,* Ἡσαΐας δὲ . . . λέγει. In ἀποτολμᾷ, the ἀπό, as often, augments the signification. *I was found by those who sought me not, I manifested myself to those who did not inquire after me,* εὑρέθην . . . . ἐπερωτῶσι; *i. e.*, the idolatrous Gentiles, who did not seek after God, have, through the gospel, been brought near to him, and he has, in Christ, disclosed himself to those who were before in utter ignorance of him and made no inquiries for him. The passage is quoted from Is. lxv. 1, נִדְרַשְׁתִּי לְלֹא שָׁאָלוּ נִמְצֵאתִי לְלֹא בִקְשֻׁנִי. The apostle follows the Seventy here in sense; but has reversed the order of the clauses. The more literal and exact shade of meaning in the Hebrew is: *I am sought after* [viz., as an object of religious inquiry and worship] *by those who have not* [hitherto] *asked after me, I am found by those who did not seek for me.*

Thus far the apostle quotes in respect to the reception of the Gentiles; but the rejection of the Jews for their unbelief; or at least their unbelief itself, which implies their consequent rejection, is now brought to view.

(21) *But unto Israel he saith: All the day long have I stretched out my hand to a disobedient and gainsaying people,* πρὸς δὲ . . . ἀντιλέγοντα. Ὅλην τὴν ἡμέραν, כָּל־הַיּוֹם, *continually, constantly, without intermission;* which implies long and persevering efforts on the part of God's messengers to the Jews, and peculiar hardness of heart and blindness of mind on their part. *To stretch out the hands*, is to address by way of inviting, beckoning, beseeching, warning; comp. Prov. i. 24.—Ἀπειθοῦντα characterizes *unbelief* in what is said by God's messengers; ἀντιλέγοντα, *contradiction,* or *gainsaying*.

Thus has the apostle shown once more, and in a way different from that which he took in chap. iv., that the Gentiles stand on an equal footing with the Jews, as to gospel privileges, and that God may, in perfect consistency with his ancient promises and declarations, cast off the Jews, when they persist in unbelief, and receive believing Gentiles as his people in their stead. The repulsive nature of this doctrine to the feelings of his proud and self-righteous countrymen, seems to be the reason why the apostle recurs to it so often, and enforces it by such repeated appeals to the Old Testament.

CHAP. XI. 1—36.

THE apostle having thus plainly asserted the rejection of the Jews, and the reception of the Gentiles into their place as the people of God, now proceeds to suggest various considerations which might serve to correct the wrong views that his countrymen would probably entertain in regard to the general declarations which he had just made. The Jew would very naturally ask (as Paul suggests in ver 1)· "Is it true, then, that God has actually cast his people away, to whom pertained the *adoption* and the *glory* and the *covenant*, and the *promises* ? Can this be consistent with the numerous promises which he made to Abraham, and which he often confirmed and repeated to his posterity ? "

The apostle proceeds in this chapter to answer these questions. He shows in verses 1—5, that now, as formerly in times of the greatest declension, God has still a remnant among his people who are true believers, *i. e* , belong to the spiritual seed of Abraham But this remnant are, as he has already maintained in chaps viii. ix , those whom the election of God according to his purposes of grace has made the subjects of his mercy, and who are not saved by their own merits, while the rest are given up to their own hardness of heart and blindness of mind, even as their own Scriptures have expressly foretold, verses 6—10 Yet it will not always remain thus. The whole of the nation will, at some future day, be brought within the pale of the Christian church Their present general unbelief is now the occasion of the gospel being preached to the Gentiles, and of the increase of the Christian church among them, so that even their rejection has been the occasion of blessings to others How much more then is to be hoped, from their general return to God' verses 11—15.

This return must take place The nation, from its origin, were consecrated to God, and they must yet return to him, for although some of its branches were broken off because of unbelief, and others were grafted in to supply their place, yet in due time they will be again received. The Gentiles, therefore, who have been grafted in, can have no reason to indulge in pride and boasting on account of this Nor ought they to demean themselves loftily towards the Jews, who were yet to be received back to the divine favor, and fully restored as the people of God, vers. 16—27. Although they are now enemies of the gospel, good comes to the Gentiles through this, and the promises made to their fathers of old are not forgotten, and will yet be fully carried into execution, vers 28, 29 Although now in a state of unbelief, they will obtain mercy in the like manner as the Gentiles have obtained it who were once in the same state. vers 30, 31 For God has showed both Gentiles and the Jews, that they were included in unbelief and justly subject to the condemning sentence of the law, and he has suffered them to come into such a state, that he might display, in the more signal manner, his mercy toward them, ver 32. The ways and judgments of God in his proceedings with Jews and Gentiles, are beyond the reach of human wisdom; they are deep and unfathomable mysteries, which can be fully searched out and known only by the Infinite Mind We can admire and adore, but never fathom the depths thereof, vers 33 – 36

Is there not then, something more in these awful mysteries, than what those admit or believe who strenuously reject the doctrine of election? On the ground which they maintain, I do not see why the mind of the apostle should be so deeply affected with the *mysterious* and *unsearchable* nature of the whole transaction. This is, indeed. a very obvious remark; but I must leave it to the reader, whether it has not an important bearing on the exegesis of chaps viii ix xi , and some other parts of this epistle I cannot help thinking that Paul had something more in his mind, than they have who read him in the manner stated — something different also from that which they admit.

(1) *I say then*, Δέγω οὖν, the words of an objector:* ' If this be

---

* Rather perhaps a false inference which might be made from what precedes, and introduced here in order to be refuted.

true which you affirm, then must it not follow, that God has rejected his chosen people?' *His own people*, τὸν λαὸν αὐτοῦ, *i. e.*, his own peculiar people, the Jews. And here the objector means by λαὸν αὐτοῦ, the *whole* of the nation, as the sequel, which exhibits the answer, evidently shows.

Paul replies that an *universal* rejection of the Jews was not meant to be affirmed by what he had said. He adduces himself as an exception to such a rejection, and a proof that it was not meant to be asserted by him — Καὶ γὰρ ἐγὼ κ. τ. λ., *for I myself* or *even I*. The καὶ in this case qualifies ἐγὼ as an *intensive* particle, which is best rendered as above. Ἰσραηλίτης, *i. e.*, a descendant of Israel. Ἐκ σπέρματος Ἀβραάμ is only a synonyme with the preceding expression for the purpose of amplification, or with particular reference to the same phrase which is often repeated in the Old Testament.—Φυλῆς Βενιαμίν, so he describes himself in Phil. iii. 5. It is merely a circumstance of particularity in description, which serves to make it more impressive.

(2) *God hath not cast away his people whom he foreknew*, οὐκ .... προέγνω, *i. e.*, whom he before determined or decided should be his people. In other words, he has not utterly rejected the Jewish people, whom he from the first ordained to be his people. See on προέγνω in chap. viii. 29, and compare ver. 29 below. The sentiment plainly is such as is developed in chap. viii. 28, by the οὓς προέγνω κ. τ. λ.; and the choice of language here, seems plainly to have reference to the words there employed. The sentiment is, that the οἱ κατὰ πρόθεσιν κλητοί among the Jews are by no means cast off.

Know ye not what the Scripture says in Elijah? ἢ οὐκ .... ἡ γραφή, *i. e.*, in that part or portion of it which is cited by the name of Elijah, because it contains his history. The division of the Hebrew Scriptures into chapters and verses was made by Hugo de Cardinalis in the twelfth century; and of the New Testament, by the famous printer and editor, Robert Stephens. Of course, reference to the Scriptures in ancient times was, as above, in a very different way from that now practised. So the Rabbins cite, in the Mishna; and so the Greek authors were accustomed to cite Homer; *e. g.*, ἐν τῷ τῶν νεῶν καταλόγῳ, *in the catalogue of the ships;* comp. Mark xii. 26, ἐπὶ τοῦ βάτου, *i. e.*, in the passage which gives an account of the burning bush. The ἢ is the mere sign of interrogation. Ὡς, *when;* so it often signifies. Ἐντυγχάνει .... κατὰ, means *to plead against, to make intercession against;* as ἐντυγχάνειν .... ὑπέρ means *to intercede for.*

(3) Κύριε .... μου, cited from 1 K. xix. 10, *ad sensum* and with contractions. The Hebrew text runs thus: "And he [Elijah] said, I am very jealous for Jehovah, the God of hosts;

for the children of Israel have forsaken thy covenant, they have destroyed thine altars, and killed thy prophets; and I only am left, and they seek my life to take it away." The prophet complains, in these words, of what he supposed to be the universal apostasy of Israel. Κατέσκαψαν, lit. *digged down;* for altars were usually made with stones and earth or turf, so that *digging down* characterizes the kind of effort necessary to destroy them — Τὴν ψυχήν, *natural* or *animated life;* often so in the Hebrew; comp. Matt. ii. 20. *To seek one's life, i. e.*, to seek to take away one's life, is a Hebraism.

(4) *Divine response,* χρηματισμός, from χρηματίζω, *to do public business, to give public responses, etc*. In the New Testament, it is applied only to the response or warning of the true God. — Ἐμαυτῷ, *Dativus commodi, for myself, i. e.*, for my service.— Ἑπτακισχιλίους ἄνδρας, the number *seven* is probably employed here in the way of a *round number, i. e.*, a definite instead of an indefinite number. So the Romans were wont to use *sexcenti;* and in like manner 70 and 40 are frequently used in the Scripture. The idea is: a very considerable number. *Bowed the knee,* ἔκαμψαν γόνυ, a part of the religious service rendered to idols; the attitude is indicative of reverence and supplication. Baal (בַּעַל) was the name of the principal god among the Canaanites, Carthaginians, Assyrians, and Babylonians. The Phenicians called him אֲדֹנִי (*Adoni*), and the Greeks Ἀδονίς. Τῇ Βάαλ, with the fem. article τῇ; and so also in the Sept., in Hos. ii. 8. Jer. ii. 8. xi. 13. xix. 5. Zeph. i. 4, also Tobit i. 5. To explain the fem. of the article (for *Baal* generally has the masc. article), Erasmus, Beza, and Grotius, suppose that ἡ εἰκών is understood, so that the full expression would be τῇ εἰκόνι Βάαλ. Others suppose that there was a female deity by the name of Baal, *i. e.,* the moon; like מֶלֶךְ and מַלְכַּת (Jer. xxxii. 35. xliv. 17, 18, 19, 25), which were symbols of the sun and moon. But the objection to this is, that in Jer. xxxii. 35, ἡ Βάαλ (fem.) is the same as ὁ Μολόχ (masc.). Others suppose that Baal was ἀνδρογύνης, *a hermaphrodite* divinity, and so might take either ὁ or ἡ; like the Latin *Deus Lunus* and *Dea Luna;* and this seems most probable, at least the Seventy seem to have been of this opinion. The *fem.* article may be applied in the way of contempt; just as Mohammed (Koran Sur. LIII.) speaks with contempt of the heathen Arabians, who had gods with fem. names; and so in Arabic, the name of an idol is *God* (in the fem.); and so the Rabbins call idol gods, אֱלֹהוֹת, *gods* (fem.).

(5) *In like manner, then, even at the present time, there is a remnant according to the election of grace,* οὕτως καὶ . . . . γέγονεν; *i. e.*, as in ancient times when it appeared to the prophet Elijah

as if apostasy was universal among his countrymen, there were not a few sincere worshippers of the true God, so at the present time, although the unbelief of the Jews appears to be nearly universal, yet God has a people among them, viz., all such as he has of his mercy chosen to everlasting life; comp. viii. 28, seq. ix. 15, 16, 23, 27. The οὖν introduces an inference from what precedes. Οὕτως οὖν means: 'Such then being the case,' or 'circumstances being as I have now related.'—Καί qualifies ἐν τῷ νῦν καιρῷ, according to the version..—*A remnant*, λεῖμμα, *i. e.* a small number, a part which though considerable in itself is small compared with another part. So here, the number of Jewish believers, although then considerable and important, was small compared with the whole number of unbelievers. Consequently λεῖμμα may be used to designate it; comp. ix. 27.—Κατ' ἐκλογὴν χάριτος *according to an election* which is not made on the ground of merit, but of *mercy*. God has not chosen Jewish believers unto salvation, because their obedience first made them the objects of his choice; but he chose them because he had mercy on them; comp. the texts cited above from Rom. ix., and the commentary on them.

(6) *But if it be of grace, then it is not at all of works*, εἰ δὲ . . . ἔργων; *i. e.*, if God's ἐκλογή, his choosing this λεῖμμα to salvation, be *gratuitous* on his part, it follows that it is not ἐξ ἔργων, *i. e.*, that it is not in any degree *meritorious*.—*Otherwise grace would be no longer grace*, ἐπεὶ ἡ . . . χαρίς; *i. e.*, if this were not so, then it would be improper to speak of *grace* in our salvation; for if men are chosen on account of any merit or desert, then *grace* is not the ground of their being chosen, but *merit;* which would contradict the very idea of grace. See Comm. on ix. 15, seq.

But if of works, then it is not at all of grace, otherwise work is no more work, εἰ δὲ . . . ἔργων; the mere converse of the preceding sentiment, and most probably a gloss from the margin. It is omitted in Codices A., B., C., D., E., F., G., 47, and in the Coptic, Armenian, Æthiopic, Vulgate and Italic versions; also in Chrysostom, Theodoret, Damascenus, Jerome, and generally in the Latin Fathers, Erasmus, Grotius, Wetstein, Griesbach, Tholuck, Flatt, and others, regard it as spurious. At all events, it adds nothing to the sentiment of the passage; but is merely the counterpart of the preceding sentiment.

(7) *What then*, τί οὖν; *i. e.*, what is the sum and substance of that which I have been saying? *That which Israel sought after he hath not obtained*, ὃ ἐπιζητεῖ . . . . ἐπέτυχε; *i. e.*, the justification which he sought to obtain by his own merit (comp. x. 3), he has not obtained. Τοῦτο is a more approved reading than τούτου;

although ἐπιτυγχάνω almost always governs the genitive in Greek, it occasionally takes the Accusative. See Herm. ad Viger, p. 760, and Kuhn. Gr. II. p. 26.

But the election, ἡ δὲ ἐκλογή, *i. e.*, the elect, the abstract, (as grammarians say) being put for the concrete, as is often the case, *e. g.*, Rom. ii. 26, 27, etc. The meaning is: 'Although the Jews, who have sought justification by their own merit, have altogether failed as to obtaining this end in this way; yet those who are called according to the gracious purpose of God (viii. 28), who are justified by his mercy through Christ Jesus, have obtained justification in a way which others rejected; and therefore they have not failed in the accomplishment of their object.'

And the rest, οἱ δὲ λοιποί, *i. e.*, the unbelieving part of the Jews, those who did not belong to the ἐκλογή—Ἐπωρώθησαν, *were blinded*. The word πωρός is equivalent to τυφλός; and the verb πωρόω (in the active voice) means *to make blind*, but in the passive, *to be blind, to become blind*, etc. It is applied in a secondary sense to the *mind;* and so the apostle here employs it. By itself it indicates *state* or *condition;* but does not necessarily indicate the cause or agent by which that state or condition is produced. Thus οἱ λοιποὶ ἐπωρώθησαν may mean merely, that the remainder (the unbelieving part of the Jews) were in a state of blindness. Still, it is capable of designating, and doubtless does here designate the idea, that *they were made blind* by the agency of another, *i. e.*, God. If there be difficulty in admitting this sentiment, there is no more than is contained in chap. ix. 17, 18; where see Commentary It should seem that the conclusion cannot be avoided, by any candid philologist, that the text does both there. and in this and the following verses, assert, that in some sense or other the agency of God is concerned with the *hardening* of sinners. In what sense, I have endeavored there to answer in a Scriptural manner. And especially in verse 8, is it possible to deny that an *agent* is designated who is in some way or other concerned with the ὀφθαλμοὺς τοῦ μὴ βλέπειν, *i. e.*, with the πώρωσις of Israel, unless we do away by violence the most obvious sense of the apostle's words. But the question whether it is asserted that *some* agency on the part of God is concerned with all this, and the question whether such an agency is concerned as makes God the *proper* author of men's moral blindness and sins, and interferes with the free agency and accountability of men for their own actions, is a very different one. About the latter the Bible leaves us no room to doubt: see James i. 13, 14.

(8) Καθὼς γέγραπται does not of necessity mean that what follows is strictly a *prediction*. It is a clear case that nothing can be decided from the *formula* of quotation; for very different

formulas precede one and the same text, quoted for one and the same purpose. *Sameness of principle* in the two cases which are brought into the comparison, is here denoted by καθώς; *i. e.*, as in ancient times God declares respecting Israel (Is. xxix. 10. Deut. xxix. 4), that he gives them the spirit of slumber, blind eyes, and deaf ears; so now, the same thing is true respecting unbelievers among the Jews; for *they are blinded*, ἐπωρώθησαν.

God hath given them a slumbering spirit, or *the spirit of deep sleep*, ἔδωκεν . . . κατανύξεως. The original Hebrew, כִּי־נָסַךְ עֲלֵיכֶם יְהוָֹה רוּחַ תַּרְדֵּמָה, the Seventy have rendered thus: Ὅτι πεπότικεν ὑμᾶς Κύριος πνεύματι κατανύξεως. But the apostle in rendering נָסַךְ, by ἔδωκε, has translated *ad sensum* not *ad verbum*. The Hebrew designates the specific idea of *pouring out* on the hardened Jews the spirit of profound sleep; while Paul, dropping the particular image which the Hebrew presents, retains only the generic idea of *communicating* such a spirit to them. It is plain, then, that in this case, as in many others, the apostle makes his own translation *de novo* from the Hebrew. *Eyes that see not, and ears that hear not, unto this day*, ὀφθαλμοὺς . . . . ἡμέρας. The original Hebrew in Deut. xxix. 4 runs thus. " For Jehovah hath not given you a heart to understand, nor eyes to see, nor ears to hear, unto this day." If this be the passage which Paul had in his mind, he quotes merely *ad sensum*. The Hebrew declares, that ' God has *not* given Israel seeing eyes and hearing ears;' the apostle says, that 'he has given them eyes that see not, and ears that hear not;' the passage in Hebrew is in the negative form as to the verb, and in the affirmative as to the rest of the sentence; while Paul's declaration is in the affirmative form as to the verb, and negative as to the rest of the sentence. Is the sense the same in both? To our ear this latter seems to indicate more *active* interposition on the part of God; but not so to the biblical writers, who, beyond all reasonable doubt, regarded these expressions as equivalent. It would be easy to prove this from a multitude of passages which assert *agency* on the part of God, when at the very same time the wicked (to whom this agency has respect) are represented as the cause of their own ruin, by their own voluntary sins. Comp. what is said in chap. ix. 17, 18, above.

Dr. Knapp (in his New Testament) and some other critics, suppose that Paul has quoted ὀφθαλμοὺς κ. τ. λ. from Is. vi. 10, and that ἕως τῆς σήμερον ἡμέρας belongs not to the *quotation*, but contains the apostle's own words; and so Dr. Knapp has marked it in his Testament, placing the closing member of the parenthesis which includes the quotation, after μὴ ἀκούειν, thus joining ἕως τῆς σήμερον ἡμέρας with οἱ λοιποὶ ἐπωρώθησαν. But this attributes an idiom to Paul, which he seems to have made a very unfrequent use of. Ἕως τῆς σήμερον ἡμέρας belongs to the Old Testament, to writers who chronicled earlier events and spoke of earlier times, which they occasionally compared with present events and times. Moses could well make use of the expression, in Deut. xxix. 4; Paul could use it, for he has once employed it (2 Cor. iii. 15 ἕως σήμερον), where it is exactly the expression which he there needed. But it is difficult to make it probable that these words are his in Rom. xi. 8.

(9) *David also says*, καὶ Δαυὶδ λέγει; *i. e.*, nor are these the only passages of Scripture which speak the same sentiment, or develop the same principle. David, your most renowned king, and the most favorite of all your sacred poets, also utters sentiments still more severe. *Let their table be a snare to take them, and an occasion of falling, and a recompense to them*, γενηθήτω .... αὐτοῖς, *i. e.*, let their season of enjoyment and refreshment, when they expect quietude and pleasure, and feel themselves to be safe, prove to be a season of chastisement and of danger and of righteous retribution. The quotation is from Ps. lxix. 23 (22). The Hebrew, according to its present vowels, runs thus: "Let their table before them be a snare; yea, a gin to those who feel themselves to be secure." The Septuagint (Ps. lxix. 22) has ἡ τράπεζα αὐτῶν ἐνώπιον αὐτῶν εἰς παγίδα καὶ εἰς ἀνταπόδοσιν καὶ εἰς σκάνδαλον; so that the apostle seems to have made a version somewhat changing the order, and also exchanging some of the words for others (putting ἀνταπόδομα for ἀνταπόδοσιν), and leaving out ἐνώπιον αὐτῶν. He has also added εἰς θήραν, in order, apparently, to give the sense of εἰς παγίδα; for εἰς θήραν means *that they may be taken*, or *that they may be destroyed*, as this would follow their being taken. As to εἰς ἀνταπόδομα (Sept. εἰς ἀνταπόδοσιν), it is clear that the apostle and the Seventy read the present Hebrew (לְשִׁלּוּמִים) with different vowels from those now employed, *i. e.*, they read it לְשִׁלּוּמִים or לְשִׁלּוּמִים, *for a recompense*. To this rendering and pointing no good objection can be made, as the Hebrew is clearly capable of it. The present Hebrew conveys a different sense. *For a net* or *gin*, εἰς σκάνδαλον, לְמוֹקֵשׁ. But the Seventy have frequently rendered this word by σκάνδαλον, which means anything whereby another stumbles and falls to his harm. The *generic* idea of מוֹקֵשׁ is retained in σκάνδαλον.

(10) *Let their eyes be darkened so that they cannot see, and their backs always be bowed down*, σκοτισθήτωσαν ... σύγκαμψον; *i. e.*, let them be in a defenceless and helpless state, bowed down with troubles and infirmities, and groping in the darkness of affliction. Instead of τὸν νῶτον αὐτῶν διαπαντὸς σύγκαμψον (Paul

and the Septuagint), the Hebrew is מָתְנֵיהֶם תָּמִיד הַמְעַד, *make thou their loins continually to shake*. Here again the apostle has taken the passage *ad sensum*. This expression, in Hebrew, designates the tossing of the body hither and thither on account of distress. In the like sense is *bowing down the back always* to be taken.

These repeated instances show that the apostle was more solicitous about the general sense and object of the Old Testament passages than he was about the costume or diction of them; a principle which he, guided as he was, was not in danger of abusing; one also which may be used to good purpose by us, in sacred criticism, but which needs to be very closely watched in order to guard it against abuse.

As to the general sentiment of this passage from Ps. lxix. 23, 24, it is undoubtedly to be classed with the somewhat numerous passages in the Psalms which contain the like imprecations. Great difficulty is found in such passages by many minds, inasmuch as they seem to be so opposed to the tenor of those passages in the New Testament which require us "to love our enemies, to bless those who curse us, to pray for those who despitefully use and persecute us." If indeed these passages in the Psalms are to be viewed as the mere utterance of *private* and *personal* wishes and feelings, it would be utterly impossible to reconcile them with the spirit of the gospel. David, as king and magistrate, might certainly wish the punishment of the seditious and rebellious: nay, it would be an imperious duty for him to punish them. Now was it lawful for him to pray that the same thing might be done, which it was his duty to do? Could he not express desires of this nature without the spirit of *revenge*? Cannot we wish the robber and the assassin to be apprehended and punished, yea with capital punishment, and this without being actuated by a spirit of vengeance and a thirst for blood? No reasonable man can deny that such wishes are not only consistent with benevolence, but prompted by it.

The apostle, in making this quotation, need not be supposed to intend anything more, than to produce an instance from the Psalms where the same *principle* is developed as is contained in the assertions which he had made; *i. e.*, the ancient Scriptures speak of a part of Israel as blind and deaf, as in deep distress and under heavy punishment because of their unbelief and disobedience. What happened in ancient times may take place again; it has in fact happened at the present time.

(11) *I say, then, have they stumbled so as to fall down?* λέγω οὖν ... πέσωσι; Language of the objector, who inquires with solicitude, whether such passages as Paul has quoted can be

meant to designate the final casting off of the Jews. Οὖν refers to what had been said in the preceding context. The *form* of the question: μή ἔπταισαν κ. τ. λ., is suggested by the use of the word σκάνδαλον in the quotation above.

So that they may fall down, ἵνα πέσωσι, *i. e.*, have the Jews stumbled so that there is no recovery for them, so that they must fall entirely down? The question being asked by μή, implies that he who puts it expects an answer in the negative.

Not at all; μὴ γένοιτο, *i. e.*, you must not understand me as at all maintaining their *final* and *utter* rejection and ruin. Fearful as their doom is, there are many circumstances respecting it which are worthy of the highest consideration. For in fact this very lapse of theirs, *i. e.*, their unbelief and rejection of the gospel, has been the direct occasion of its being preached to the Gentiles; comp. Matt. xxi. 43. viii. 11, 12. xxii. 1—14. — Παραπτώματι, *lapse, offence, stumbling,* in a moral sense. — Σωτηρία, the blessings of the gospel, the salvation which it proffers.

To provoke them to jealousy, εἰς τὸ παραζηλῶσαι αὐτούς, *i. e*, to excite the Jews to be jealous on account of the privileges and favors bestowed on the Gentiles through their belief, and to seek after the same blessings for themselves.

(12) *Now if their lapse has been the riches of the world, and their degradation the riches of the Gentiles,* εἰ δὲ . . . . ἔθνων. Δέ "orationi continuandae inservit." — Πλοῦτος κόσμου, if their lapse has been the occasion of spiritual riches to the world, *i. e.*, of spiritual blessings in abundance. — *Their diminution,* ἥττημα αὐτῶν, *i. e.*, their degradation, rejection, punishment, has occasioned abundance of spiritual blessings to the Gentiles. *How much more their fulness,* πόσῳ μᾶλλον . . . . αὐτῶν! Πλήρωμα, is here the antithesis of ἥττημα; and of course it signifies restoration to favor, a copiousness of blessings and good things, such as would follow a restoration. The sentiment of the whole is: "If now the degradation and punishment of the Jews for their unbelief has been the occasion of rich and numerous blessings to the Gentiles, then surely their restoration to favor, their full reception, will redound still more to the spiritual riches of the world." Some understand ἥττημα and πλήρωμα in a moral sense, *i. e.*, their depraved and criminal state, and their restored and justified state; but the construction given above is more simple and obvious; comp. verse 15, from which it is plain that ἥττημα here = ἀποβολή, *casting off,* and πλήρωμα (the antithesis of ἥττημα) = πρόσληψις, *the reception* to favor.

(13) *For I say this to you Gentiles,* ὑμῖν γὰρ . . . ἔθνεσι. Γάρ makes some difficulty here; and it is omitted in A., B., several Codices minusc , Syr., Copt. Damasc., which supply δέ, and thus make

the sense facile. But it is admissible. The simplest connection of it seems to be an implied sentiment, viz , " the πλήρωμα of the Jews will yet be accomplished; for I speak to you Gentiles in such a way that I may stir up the Jews and contribute to their salvation." In this case λέγω is connected in sense with εἴπως in ver. 14, and the intervening matter is considered as in a parenthesis. This is not the usual, but it seems to me the more easy and natural mode of exegesis. The apostle is very careful, as is evident from this, while he fully represents the unbelief and ἀποβολή of the Jews, not to give occasion to boasting or exultation on the part of the Gentiles.

Inasmuch as I am indeed an apostle of the Gentiles, I do honor to my office, ἐφ' ὅσον μὲν . . . . δοξάζω. Μέν *simplex, i. e.*, without the usual δέ or some equivalent particle following it. But it is omitted in D. E F. G. 80. al. 5. Clar. Boern , Ambrosiaster; probably because no δέ follows. Where μέν is *simplex*, it = the Latin *quidem, equidem, videlicet ;* but oftentimes cannot be rendered at all into English, nor conveniently into Latin. It may be called μέν *explicantis ;* though it also appears to have an affirmative and concessive force. The supposition of the writer who thus employs it is, that what he says will of course be conceded. *Office of the ministry,* Διακονίαν, *i. e.*, the apostolic office of Paul. Δοξάζω, *magni æstimo, honoro, honore afficio.*

(14) *If by any means I may excite to jealousy some of my kinsmen after the flesh, and save some of them,* εἴπως . . . . ἐξ αὐτῶν. Εἴπως, *si fieri potest, si quâ ratione.* — Τὴν σάρκα, *my flesh, i. e.*, my relatives, οἱ συγγενεῖς κατὰ σάρκα, comp. Rom. ix. 3. So the Hebrew בָּשָׂר often means; *e. g.*, Gen xxix. 14. Judg. ix. 2. 2 Sam. v. 1. Gen. xxxvii 27. Is. lviii. 7. The meaning of the apostle in the whole passage is : " I extol the blessings of you Gentiles, not to lift you up with pride, but in order to excite the attention of the Jews to the distinguished favors which you enjoy, and which they have lost by their unbelief."

(15) *For if the casting away of them be the reconciliation of the world, what shall the reception of them be but life from the dead?* Εἰ γὰρ . . . . ἐκ νεκρῶν ; if the rejection of the Jews on account of their unbelief, has been the occasion of reconciling many of the Gentile world to God, what shall the reception of them back to the divine favor be, but as it were a general [spiritual] resurrection ? Γάρ marks the *resuming* of what was dropped at verse 12 for the sake of further explanation. So Reiche, Meyer and others — Καταλλαγή is applied to the conciliation of the heathen to God, who by their wicked works had before been *enemies* to him and *strangers* to the covenant of his promise. — Κόσμου here, as often, stands for the heathen Gentile world.

Reception to favor, πρόσληψις, *i. e.*, admission to the family or church of Christ.

Life from the dead, ζωή ἐκ νεκρῶν some (most of the ancient commentators and some recent ones) have understood *literally, i. e.*, as indicating the resurrection of the body; meaning thereby, that when the Jews should be brought into the Christian church as a body, the end of time would soon follow. But the time of the reign of Christ on earth as described in the Apocalypse, and the interval of wickedness that will succeed, seem to forbid this exegesis; it has no *usus loquendi* in its favor, for the proper phrase would be ἀνάστασις ἐκ τῶν νεκρῶν. It is true that we have ζῶντες ἐκ νεκρῶν in Rom. vi. 13; but then it is plainly figurative, *i. e.*, it signifies a moral resurrection. I regard ζωὴ ἐκ νεκρῶν, then, as a tropical expression, used in a kind of proverbial way, or as a figure of speech designating something great, wonderful, surprising, like to what a general resurrection of the dead would be. So Turretin: *Quid erit admissio eorum, nisi quoddam genus resurrectionis;* altogether to the purpose. So the Arabians speak proverbially of great agitations and changes, as of a *resurrection*. See example in Tholuck's Commentary. In Ezek. xxxvii. 1—14, too, we have the moral renovation of the Jews designated at full length by the similitude of a *resurrection;* and in all probability the apostle had this passage in his mind; so that ζωὴ ἐκ νεκρῶν here is equivalent to saying: "What shall such a πρόσληψις of the Jews be, but a general resurrection of them, such as Ezekiel has described, *i. e.*, a great, general, and wonderful conversion of them to Christianity!"

(16) *If, moreover, the first fruits were holy, so shall the mass be*, εἰ δὲ . . . . φύραμα. Ἀπαρχή, like the Hebrew רֵאשִׁית, means the *firstlings* or *first-fruits* of any kind which were offered to God. The Hebrews called the *firstlings* of fruit and grain, in their natural state רֵאשִׁית בִּכּוּרִים; the *firstlings* of grain, etc., in a *prepared* state, רֵאשִׁית תְּרוּמוֹת. But the particular name given to the firstlings of *dough* or *kneaded meal*, was רֵאשִׁית עֲרִיסוֹת, Num. xv. 20, where the Septuagint renders, ἀπαρχὴ φυράματος; which is the same expression as occurs in the passage before us, φυράματος being implied after ἀπαρχή. The comparison here lies between the small part of the mass of dough, which was taken as the רֵאשִׁית הַתְּרוּמוֹת and offered up to God, and the greater part or mass of it which was left for the use of him who made the offering. After the רֵאשִׁית was offered, the whole mass became *sanctified* to lawful use, *i. e.*, was set apart for this purpose and consecrated to it. In like manner, the apostle would here say, is the whole mass of the Jewish nation yet to be set apart for God and consecrated to

him? The ἀπαρχή of this nation, *i. e.*, the ancient patriarchs and fathers of it (comp. ver. 28), were set apart for God in a peculiar manner; and consequently the *mass* of their descendants are yet to be consecrated to him. The whole is *illustration*, however, rather than argument.

And if the root is holy, so are the branches, καὶ εἰ . . . οἱ κλάδοι. The same idea is here expressed as in the former clause. A *root* bears some such proportion to the *branches* of a tree, as the *first-fruits* did to the whole *mass* of bread. So here, the root represents the fathers (ver. 28), and the κλάδοι their descendants. — The word ἅγιος in both cases means *consecrated to God, devoted to God, set apart for God*, or *set apart, consecrated to God, devoted to God, set apart for God*, or *set apart, consecrated*, viz., for the service of God. But it should be noted, that the apostle does not design to say, that the φύραμα and the κλάδοι *are* holy, *i. e.*, that they were so when he was writing. He predicts only that they *will be* so at some future period.

(17) *But if some of the branches were broken off*, εἰ δέ . . . . . ἐξεκλάσθησαν, *i. e*, if now some of the natural descendants of the ancient fathers have been cast off, because of unbelief (ver. 20). Δέ may be construed here as *continuative, jam*, German *nun;* but the *distinctive* sense seems to be the more facile one. *And thou being a wild ol've, wert grafted in their stead, and made partaker of the root and fatness of the olive*, σὺ δέ . . . . ἐγένου. The ἀργιέλαιος, it is said, was often grafted into the fruitful one when it began to decay, and thus not only brought forth fruit, but caused the decaying olive to revive and flourish. This fact is denied by Glockler and Reiche, but it is substantiated by Columella (de Re Rust V. 9) and Palladius (de Insit. XIV. 53), and also by several modern travellers. According to the usual course of nature among us, the fruit will be according to the original nature of the *graft*, and not according to the stock. How far this is actually the case in respect to *olive-trees*, seems not to be yet satisfactorily made out. Be the fact however as it may, it will not change the meaning of the apostle's supposition The image which he here employs is a very vivid one. The Gentiles had been grafted in upon the Jewish Church, and had caused this decayed tree to revive and flourish. But still the apostle means to hold in check any exultation of the Gentiles on account of this. He reminds them, that after all they are not the *stock* but only *grafts;* that the root and fatness of the good olive had been transferred to them, only because they have been grafted into it. Ἐν αὐτοῖς seems to be used in a *local* way, viz., *in the place of them*.

All this shows, moreover, that in the apostle's view, there has in reality been but one church; the ancient Jewish one being only the foundation, the Christian one the superstructure and completion of the building; a sentiment which accords throughout with the representations in the epistle to the Hebrews, where only a change in rites and forms is argued, not a change of the spiritual and essential nature of the church.

(18) *Exult not over the branches*, μὴ κατακαυχῶ τῶν κλάδων; *i. e.*, exult not that the Jewish branches have been broken off, and that thou hast been engrafted in their stead. Κατακαυχάομαι means *to exult* in one's own advantages or pre-eminence, in such a manner as to look down with contempt on others who do not possess them. *But if thou dost exult, thou dost not support the root, but the root thee,* εἰ δὲ κατακαυχᾶσαι . . . . σέ; *i. e.*, if thou art so inconsiderate and wanting in humility as to exult, there is no ground for such exultation; for after all, the Jewish church is the stock on which the Christian has been engrafted: it is the root from which the tree with its branches have sprung; and as thou art only a *branch*, thou canst not boast as if thou wert the *root*.

(19) *Thou wilt say then: The branches were broken off, that I might be grafted in:* ἐρεῖς οὖν . . . . ἐγκεντρισθῶ; *i. e.*, perhaps thou wilt reply: 'There is at least some ground for exultation, because the branches were broken off in order to make room for me to be grafted in; which proves that I was considered as of more importance than the branches.—Κλάδοι has the article οἱ in many copies; but A., C., E., 3., 7., 37., 46., 47., 54., Chrysostom, and Damascenus omit it; and so Dr. Knapp. If inserted, it would designate the specific branches before mentioned; if omitted, then κλάδοι will designate *branches, some branches*, in an indefinite way.

(20) *Be it so, they were broken off by reason of unbelief, and thou retainest thy standing by faith:* καλῶς . . . . ἕστηκας, *i. e*, be it as thou hast said, viz., that the branches were broken off so that thou mightest be grafted in, yet the original ground or moving cause of their being broken off was the unbelief of the Jews; and thou retainest thy present condition only on the ground of faith or belief in Christ. Shouldest thou deny him, as the Jews have done, thou wouldest also be broken off in like manner.— Καλῶς *bene*, approves of the sentiment which had just been uttered in some respect or other, but it does not necessarily approve of it in the full extent in which the speaker himself might have done. Here καλῶς partially concedes the sentiment just expressed, i. e., it concedes that the branches were broken off so that the wild olive might be grafted in, still it is asserted that the prompting cause of their being broken off, was not merely the desire of grafting in new ones, but their unbelief ἀπιστία. The Gentile, is

also reminded that he retains his present place and standing on the very same condition as that on which the Jews held theirs, viz., on condition of faith or belief, σὺ δὲ τῇ πίστει ἕστηκας. The Perfect of ἵστημι has a *neuter* sense, viz., *to stand*, and is used with present significance. *Be not high-minded, but fear*, μὴ . . . . φοβοῦ ; *i. e.*, carry yourself not haughtily as it respects the Jews who have been broken off; or rather, do not think too highly of your elevation to favor, but demean yourself as a humble believer, and one who has need to be continually on his guard, and to fear lest he may fall through unbelief and be broken off.

(21) *For if God did not spare the natural branches, then* [fear] *lest he will not spare thee,* εἰ γὰρ . . . . φείσεται ; *i. e.*, if God did not refrain from rejecting the Jews, when they became unbelievers, then surely he will not refrain from rejecting thee, in the like circumstances. The γάρ in this case introduces a cause or reason why the Gentile should fear. — Κατὰ φύσιν κλάδων means the branches which naturally belonged to the original stock, *i. e.*, the Jews, the natural descendants of the partriarchs to whom the promises of God were made. Before μήπως the verb φοβοῦ is of course to be understood. Instead of φείσεται some copies read φείσηται (Subj.); and after verbs of *fearing* (for φοβοῦ is here implied) the Subj. is the usual mood. It is also the usual mood after the particle μή. But in cases where it is supposed a thing actually exists or will exist, the Indic. mood is employed to indicate this. Here evidently the apostle believes that God would not spare Gentile unbelievers; and so the Indic. is the preferable mood; see N. Test. Gramm. §152. 4. Note 1.

(22) *Behold, then, the kindness and the severity of God,* ἰδὲ οὖν . . . Θεοῦ ; *i. e.*, consider, on the one hand, the distinguished kindness which God has manifested toward thee who believest; and on the other, the strict regard to justice and truth which he exhibits, in the punishment of the unbelieving Jews. So the sequel of the verse ; *severity toward those who have fallen away ; but kindness toward thee, provided thou dost maintain a state of integrity ; otherwise even thou shalt be cut off,* ἐπὶ μὲν . . . ἐκκοπήσῃ. Ἐὰν ἐπιμείνῃς τῇ χρηστότητι may be rendered, *if thou dost continue in a state of favor ;* so Tholuck and others ; and so in the translation. But we may attach an *intransitive* sense to χρηστότητι ; for the phrase may be taken as an antithesis to ἐπιμείνωσι τῇ ἀπιστίᾳ in the following verse, so that χρηστότητι may here designate the state or qualification of the individual concerned, *probity, uprightness*, and not the goodness of God toward him. Cf. this use of χρηστότης, צְדָקָה, in the Septuagint, Ps. xiii. 1, 3 (xiv. 1, 3). xxxvi. 3. cxviii. 56 (cxix. 66). The former sense, however, is to be preferred.

(23) The present rejection of the unbelieving Jews is by no means final and exclusive. *And they also, unless they persevere in unbelief, shall be grafted in; for God is able again to graft them in,* καὶ ἐκεῖνοι δὲ . . . . αὐτούς. That is: 'Inasmuch as *unbelief* was the ground of their rejection, so, when they shall abandon this and become believers, they will be again received to favor; for God is able to bring them back to his favor.' He speaks here only of what can be done; but in ver 24 seq., he speaks of what *will* be done. — Καὶ ἐκεῖνοι δέ, *and they also;* or, if any one prefers, *but even they.*

(24) That the Jews *will be* again received to favor, the apostle now proceeds to show. *For if thou wert cut off from the wild olive which was naturally wild, and wert grafted into the good olive which was contrary to thy nature,* εἰ γὰρ . . . καλλιέλαιον; *i. e.,* if thou wert introduced into a state of favor with God, from a state of enmity which was in all respects foreign to a state of favor. *How much more shall the natural* [branches] *be grafted into their own olive?* Πόσῳ μᾶλλον . . . ἐλαίᾳ. Argumentum a minori ad majus; viz., if God had mercy on Gentiles, who were out-casts from his favor and strangers to the covenant of his promise, shall he not have mercy on the people whom he has always distinguished as being peculiarly his own, by the bestowment of many important privileges and advantages upon them? Comp. Rom. ix. 1 — 5. The γάρ in this verse introduces a sentiment co-ordinate with that which follows γάρ in the preceding verse

(25) The apostle now proceeds more directly to assert the future reception of the Jews. *For I would not have you ignorant, brethren, of this mystery,* οὐ γὰρ . . . τοῦτο. Γάρ introduces a clause which is designed further to illustrate and confirm the assertion in ver 24, viz., that the Jews would again be grafted in. The form of expression, *I would not have you ignorant,* is a μείωσις,=*I am desirous that you should know.* Μυστήριον denotes anything which is *hidden, concealed, unknown.* The fact that the Jews would be converted, must have been unknown to human wisdom. It was against all appearances and probabilities at that time. *Lest ye should be wise in your own conceit,* ἵνα μὴ . . . φρόνιμοι; *i. e.,* lest you should be puffed up with a view of your own importance I am going to tell you more plainly still, that you are not the exclusive objects of God's favor. *That blindness has come upon Israel in part, until the fulness of the Gentiles shall come in,* ὅτι πώρωσις . . . εἰσέλθῃ. As to πώρωσις, comp. verses 8, 10 above; comp. also 1 Thess. ii. 15, 16. — Ἀπὸ μέρους, is a qualifying expression to be joined with τῷ Ἰσραὴλ γέγονεν, which saves the proposition from being a universal one; comp. verses

1 — 5 above. Paul means to say, that 'Israel is indeed in part blinded, and will continue to be so, until, etc., without designating what proportion of them continues in unbelief. It is a softened mode of expression, or (as rhetoricians say) *per charientismum*, i. e., κατὰ χάριν.

The πλήρωμα τῶν ἐθνῶν, I understand as meaning *great multitudes* or *a great multitude*, comp. John i. 16. Rom. xv. 29. Col. ii. 9. It cannot be denied that πλήρωμα sometimes means *fulfilling, completion, completing*, i. q., πλήρωσις; *e. g.*, Rom. xiii. 10, applied to the *law;* Gal. iv. 4. Eph. i. 10, applied to *time*. But such a meaning would hardly be congruous in the present instance. The *fulfilling* of a *law*, or of a limited *time*, is an easy and obvious expression, because there is no obvious limit to which the *filling up* or *fulfilling* is to extend; but what the limit would be in πλήρωμα τῶν ἐθνῶν it would be difficult to answer. It accordingly seems altogether more facile and congruous, to take πλήρωμα in the sense of *copia, great numbers, multitudes*. How great this number must be, the apostle does not say; much less that *all* the Gentiles must first be converted to Christianity, before the Jews can be brought into the pale of the church. Critics are not wanting, who strenuously contend for the meaning of *totality* in this case, and who aver that πλήρωμα can mean nothing less. So Reiche and Alford. But the usus loquendi of the word will not support this allegation. The subject must therefore remain as Paul has left it, *i. e.*, indefinite as to the extent of Gentile conversions before the time when the Jews will return. Of course Christians are not debarred, by this view, from hope in laboring and praying for the Jews at the present period, although as yet but comparatively a small part of the Gentiles have been converted to the Christian faith. It is true, even now, that there is *a great multitude* of Gentile converts. May we not hope that the time is near at hand, when there will be a πλήρωμα of them?

(26) *And so all Israel shall be saved*, καὶ οὕτω . . . σωθήσεται; *i. e.*, when the πλήρωμα of the Gentiles shall have been joined to the Lord, then his ancient covenant people shall also be reclaimed. Καὶ οὕτω means *and so, i. e.*, when it shall be so that the πλήρωμα of the Gentiles shall be brought in, then, etc. That καὶ οὕτω, may be used substantially in the same way as καὶ τότε (*and then*), see Acts vii. 8. xvii. 33. xx. 11. xxviii. 14 — Πᾶς here means *all*, in opposition to the ἀπὸ μέρους of the preceding verse. But whether this means strictly *every individual*, it would be difficult indeed to determine. *A deliverer shall come from Zion, and turn away ungodliness from Jacob*, ἥξει ἐκ . . . Ἰακώβ. This is apparently a citation from Is. lix. 20, where the Hebrew runs thus: "A deliverer for Zion shall come, and for those who for-

sake ungodliness in Jacob." The Septuagint reads ἕνεκεν Σιών, instead of ἐκ Σιών; but in other respects it conforms to the quotation of the apostle; which gives the *general* sense of the original, *i. e.*, deliverance for Zion is to be accomplished, and penitents of the house of Jacob are to be saved. It is a very striking instance of free quotation as to the *general* sense of a passage, while the *particular* costume of it is disregarded. That Isaiah, in lix. 20, had respect to the salvation of gospel times, the context seems to me very clearly to indicate. But if he had respect to temporal deliverance merely, there can be no difficulty in the apostle's using the words as the vehicle of conveying his own thoughts, with regard to spiritual deliverance.

(27) *And this is my covenant with them,* καὶ αὕτη . . . . διαθήκη. Now suppose that this is quoted from the next succeeding verse in Isaiah, viz., lix. 21, as it agrees verbatim with the Septuagint there. But here the question stops, according to this supposition, and the next succeeding clause, ὅταν ἀφέλωμαι τὰς ἁμαρτίας αὐτῶν, is taken from Is. xxvii. 9, where the words stand in the midst of a verse which has relation to the punishment of the Jews, and their consequent moral reformation. I should therefore prefer the supposition, that the apostle here quotes and abridges, Jer. xxxi. 33, 34 (the same passage which is quoted at length in Heb. viii. 8—12). There the words αὕτη ἡ διαθήκη μου occur in verse 33; and in verse 34, Jehovah is represented as saying: ἵλεως ἔσομαι ταῖς ἀδικίαις αὐτῶν, καὶ τῶν ἁμαρτιῶν αὐτῶν οὐ μνησθῶ ἔτι; so that nothing is easier than to suppose that the apostle quotes *ad sensum* these last passages, when he says ἀφέλωμαι τὰς ἁμαρτίας αὐτῶν. This last supposition is favored by the fact that the whole passage in Jeremiah most evidently refers to a new dispensation, to gospel-times; which would be altogether appropriate to the apostle's purpose, for the very point he is laboring to establish, is, that there will be a general conversion of the Jews to the Christian religion.

(28) This alienation of the Jews, although an evil, exceedingly great in itself, has been overruled for the accomplishment of very important purposes in respect to the salvation of the Gentiles. *In respect to the gospel, they have become enemies on your account,* κατὰ μὲν . . . . ὑμᾶς; *i. e.*, they have become ἐχθροὶ τοῦ Θεοῦ, have apostatized from him, or have been rejected by him, and are no longer treated as his friends. That Θεοῦ is implied after ἐχθροί, (and not εὐαγγελίου, nor μου as Theodoret, Luther, Grotius, Cameron, Baumgarten, and others, have supposed), is clear, by comparing with ἐχθροί its antithesis ἀγαπητοί; with which it is clear that Θεοῦ is implied. *On your account,* δι' ὑμᾶς, *i. e.*, to your advantage. In other words, the rejection of the gospel by the Jews

has been the occasion of its being more widely diffused among the Gentiles; so that, in this respect, the loss of the Jews has been the gain of the Gentiles. *But in respect to the election, they are beloved for their fathers' sake,* κατὰ δὲ . . . . πατέρας; *i. e.,* in so far as God chooses men to salvation κατὰ τὴν πρόθεσιν αὐτοῦ (viii. 28) and without being moved thereto by any merit on their part (xi. 5, 6), he will have special regard to the Jews, because of the many and precious promises which he made to their fathers. Some, as Tholuck, find here only an *election to external privileges.* But that the point in question is not the *external* privileges of Christianity merely, but the *spiritual* blessings of the gospel seems to me impossible to doubt, unless one is led to do so by other considerations than those of simple exegesis.

The apostle appears plainly to aver, that although God has mercy on whom he will have mercy (ix. 18); and although men do not become the heirs of eternal life by any merits of their own, but merely by the good pleasure of his grace (xi. 5, 6); yet in bestowing that grace, he may have regard to his promises made in ancient days to the distinguished patriarchs of the Jewish nation; he may have regard to his original design that the seed of Abraham by faith, and the seed which also were lineally descended from him, should be "as the stars of heaven for multitude." That salvation is *entirely* of free grace and not of merit, of course leaves it open for the sovereign Lord of all to choose the objects of his mercy where and when he pleases. That he always does this with good and adequate reason, yea the best of reasons, his own infinite wisdom and goodness are a sure and perfect pledge. But that men are always acquainted with these reasons, or that he has revealed them, is not asserted, and is not capable of being proved.

(29) God will not disappoint the hopes which he has excited, nor violate the promises which he has made. The blessings which he promised to bestow, and the calling of Abraham's posterity to be his spiritual seed, will surely not fail. *For the gifts and calling of God he will not repent of;* lit. *are not the subjects of repentance,* ἀμεταμέλητα . . . . Θεοῦ. The meaning is, that God will never repent of the promises which he made to the fathers, and therefore never change his purpose in regard to the bestowment of spiritual blessings upon their offspring. The γάρ here introduces the reason why the Jews are still ἀγαπητοί. Here again Tholuck urged by the fear of *gratia irresistibilis* construes κλῆσις of the *external* calling of the Jews. But the reader is desired merely to turn back and compare viii. 28—30 with this whole passage, and also verses 5—7 above. No other answer need be given to the objection against the sense here maintained.

Above all, when one compares the sequel, verses 30—36, with verses 28, 29, can he constrain himself to believe, that *external* privileges only are here the subject of the apostle's discussion? Could these excite in him such wonder, admiration, and gratitude, as he evidently expresses in verses 33—36? And is this the *obtaining of mercy*, of which verse 30 speaks? Let every unprejudiced reader examine and judge!

(30) *For as you were formerly disobedient to God, but have now obtained mercy through their unbelief,* Ὥσπερ γὰρ . . . . . ἀπειθείᾳ. This refers to the former heathenish and unbelieving state of the Gentiles, and to the fact that the Gospel was preached to them, and they became believers in consequence of the Jews having rejected it, in the sense before explained. Γάρ introduces a clause added for the sake of confirming the preceding declaration.

(31) *So they too have now become disobedient that they also may obtain mercy through the mercy shown to you,* οὕτω καὶ . . . ἐλεηθῶσι. Here are two cases presented, parallel in some respects, but differing in others. (1) The Jews reject the gospel, and occasion its being preached to the Gentiles, who thus become believers. (2) The Gentiles, by the blessing bestowed on them in consequence of their faith, provoke the Jews to jealousy, and occasion their seeking to be restored to their former place as the people of God; comp. verses 13, 14. The parallelism consists in this, viz., that each party occasions the blessings of salvation to come to the other, *i. e.*, each is (ἀφορμετικῶς) the cause of salvation to the other. The difference is, that the Jews give occasion to this by their *unbelief*, but the Gentiles by their *belief*, which provokes the Jews to jealousy, and leads them to seek after the privileges of the gospel. May the time speedily come, when the example of Christians will have a better tendency to excite such a jealousy among the Jews than it has ever yet done!

The position of ἵνα here is peculiar. We should expect to find it before τῷ ὑμετέρῳ; but comp. 1 Cor. ix. 15. 2 Cor. ii. 4. Gal. ii. 10.

(32) *For God hath included all in unbelief, so that he might have mercy on all,* συνέκλεισε . . . . ἐλεήσῃ; *i. e.*, God hath left both Jew and Gentile to fall into unbelief or disobedience, in order that the true nature of sin might fully appear, and that he might thus magnify the riches of his grace, in pardoning multiplied and aggravated transgressions; comp. Rom. v. 20, 21, where the same general sentiment is developed. The fathers in speaking of this subject compare sin to a fever, which before it reaches a certain height, does not so develop itself that the

physician applies its appropriate remedy. They also compare it to a tree, which is permitted to grow up to full height, and to spread forth all its branches and leaves, before it is felled. So when sin had reached its acme, the Redeemer appeared and struck the mortal blow. The γάρ introduces an additional reason to show that God will have mercy on all.

Συνέκλεισε seems to be the best illustrated by a reference to the Hebrew הִסְגִּיר לְ, הִסְגִּיר אֶל, הִסְגִּיר בְּיַד all of which (from סָגַר) mean *to deliver over to, to give up to the power of.* — The whole verse, and also chap. v. 20, 21, seems plainly to teach, that God had a special purpose to answer in giving man over to the power or dominion of sin and unbelief, viz., to expose the "exceeding sinfulness of sin," and to magnify the riches of his pardoning mercy. But if any insist that συνέκλεισε, is to be taken in a more *active* sense, they may compare it with Rom. v 20, and also with ix 18: σκληρύνει. Still such a sense does not seem to be necessary here.

(33) Here then, to say the least, is some deep and mysterious proceeding on the part of God, which the human mind cannot fathom, and which it should wonder at and adore. *O the boundless riches both of the wisdom and knowledge of God!* Ὦ βάθος ... Θεοῦ. Πλούτου literally means *riches*, but here, *abundance.* — Σοφίας, the *wisdom* of God, viz., the wisdom displayed in thus making the unbelief of the Jews subservient to the purpose of bringing salvation to the Gentiles, and also in finally bringing the Jews back to their filial relation, through the mercy granted to the Gentiles. Γνώσεως, boundless *knowledge;* for what less than Omniscience could foresee the effects to be thus produced, the good effects that would flow from present and apparent evil? Tholuck refers the whole simply to divine *compassion*, and says that "the words are *contra decretum absolutum* of Augustine." This may indeed be true, if Augustine meant what Tholuck supposes he did — *fatality.* This excellent critic seems to find frequent matter of difficulty in the assertions of Paul here; so strongly is he exercised with the fear of the *decretum absolutum* of Augustine and Calvin.

How unsearchable are his proceedings, and his ways past finding out! ὡς ... ὁδοὶ αὐτοῦ. Understanding all this as of course having a reference to the preceding declarations of the apostle, we must interpret it as meaning: "How entirely above our comprehension, that God should accomplish such ends by such means," viz. the salvation of the Gentiles in such a way, and then that of the Jews! — Κρίματα seems plainly to mean like the Hebrew מִשְׁפָּטִים, *ordinance, arrangement, proceeding:* or rather *decision, counsel, determination.* Here it is

ROMANS XI. 34—36. 385

for substance a synonyme with ὁδοί, which evidently has the like sense. The word ὁδοί which literally means *way* or *track* that one makes in going, gives occasion to the adjunctive ἀνεξεχνίαστοι, *whose footsteps cannot be traced*, *i. e.*, unsearchable, *viæ non vestigandæ*. What can be plainer, now, than that the declaration in verse 32 gives the immediate occasion to the exclamation in verse 33 ? But if this be so, then συνέκλεισε contributes its share to excite the apostle's feeling, as well as ἐλεήσῃ. Tholuck admits only the latter.

(34) *For who hath known the mind of the Lord, or who hath been his counsellor?* τίς γὰρ . . . ἐγένετο. Γάρ is placed here before a clause added in order to confirm the assertion, that the ways of God are unsearchable. The verse is a quotation from Is. xl. 13, *ad sensum*, and nearly in the words of the Seventy. The object is, to challenge the wisdom of created beings; for the call is made on them to show, if there be any such case, wherein any of them has contributed anything to enlighten or to guide the divine counsels. The question implies strong negation.

(35) *Or who hath first given him anything, and it will be repaid?* ἤ τίς . . . . αὐτῷ. The sentiment of this verse may be found in the Hebrew of Job xli. 3 (11), מִי הִקְדִּימַנִי וַאֲשַׁלֵּם, *who hath done me any service, that I may recompense him.* This the apostle has changed to the *third* person, instead of the first, so as to make it congruous with the preceding quotation. The Septuagint, "abit in omnia alia" here; so that the apostle (if indeed he here quotes at all, which seems somewhat doubtful), has given a new version to the Hebrew. This latter quotation (if it be one) is designed by the apostle to have a bearing on all *claims* to the divine favor, which can be preferred on the score of desert or of services rendered to God. How prone the Jews were to make such *claims* every reader of the New Testament must know. This sentence is designed strongly to affirm, that no one can make any just claims upon God for his favor, as no one by his services has laid him under any obligation. The Nominative to ἀνταποδοθήσεται is αὐτό understood, which would refer to τι implied after the preceding προέδωκε.

(36) On the contrary, instead of creatures laying God under any obligation to them, God is all and in all, *i. e.*, he is the source of all being and blessing, by him all things come into existence and are sustained and governed, and for him, for his glory and honor, they "are and were created." — *For of him, and by him, and for him, are all things,* ὅτι ἐξ . . . . πάντα. *Of him,* ἐξ αὐτοῦ, *i e.*, he is the *original* source, the eternal fountain whence all the streams of existence take their rise. *By him* δι' αὐτόν, he is not only the *original* source, but the *intermediate* cause of all things.

33

It is the exertion of his power that brings them into being, and preserves, directs, and controls them. *For him*, εἰς αὐτόν, for his honor, praise, glory; he is the sovereign Lord and possessor of all, and all exist because he wills it, and exist for the accomplishment of purposes which the Maker of all has in view. The sentence seems equivalent to saying, "God is the beginning, continuance, and end of all things."

This strong expression of wonder, reverence, and adoration, in regard to the unsearchable ways of God in his dealings with men; and an assertion of the highest intensity, respecting his sovereign right to control all things so as to accomplish his own designs, inasmuch as all spring from him, "live, and move, and have their being in him," and are for his glory, appropriately concludes this part of the Epistle. A doctrine truly humbling to the proud and towering hopes and claims of self-justifying men; a stumbling-block to haughty Jews, and foolishness to unhumbled Greeks. I scarcely know of anything in the whole Bible which strikes deeper at the root of human pride than vers. 33—36. But what emphasis can there be in these, if the apostle is discoursing merely on the *external* privileges of men? Every one must see without argument, that distinctions of a temporal nature are co-extensive with the human race. But when we come to the great question: Are distinctions of a *spiritual* nature made, *which are eternal in their consequences;* and made too according to the good pleasure of God, without any merit on the part of men? it is then we find ourselves to need all the argument and reasoning of the apostle, to bring us submissively to bow, and to contemplate the whole subject (as he does) with wonder and adoration. It is then, that God's claims to be considered the GREAT ALL IN ALL, must be advanced in such a way, that "the loftiness of man may be bowed down, and the haughtiness of man laid low, and Jehovah alone be exalted."

On the other hand, if God has for reasons not disclosed to us, and therefore in the way of what we call *the exercise of divine sovereignty*, rejected for a time the Jewish nation, and brought in the Gentiles; and if God, in his own due time, shall also again bring the Jewish nation into his church; and all this in such a way as entirely exceeds our comprehension, and which of course we are altogether unable to explain; then we may exclaim with the wondering apostle, *O the depth!* Then we may find overwhelming reason to believe, that *God is all in all*, that he is the beginning, middle, and end of all things, and that "for his glory they are and were created." We can sympathize, therefore, while cherishing such views, with all which the apostle has here said, and find abundant reason to cherish sentiments such as he has avowed.

But to prevent all mistake here, I repeat, before I close this subject, what I have once and again expressed in the preceding pages, viz., that *sovereignty* in God, does not imply what is *arbitrary*, nor that he does anything without the *best of reasons.* It only implies, that *those reasons are unknown to us.* While clouds and darkness are truly about him, in respect to our vision, justice and judgment are the habitation of his throne forever. Infinite wisdom and goodness can never act at all without reason, nor without the very best reason. It would be the extreme of folly to suppose that because God acts in a way which is mysterious, he acts in an arbitrary or oppressive manner. Is he under obligation to disclose all the grounds of his proceedings to us? Enough he has disclosed to satisfy us that he is wise and good. May there not be something left to exercise our filial confidence, and to give us (what does indeed well become us) a deep sense of our humble and imperfect condition? Shall we prescribe to God the terms of our moral discipline? If not, then let us be content, when his mysterious ways press upon our minds, and we feel straitened and in darkness, to say with the apostle: Ὦ βάθος πλούτου καὶ σοφίας καὶ γνώσεως Θεοῦ! And if our hearts are ever tempted to rise up against the distinctions which God has made, either in a temporal or spiritual respect, in the bestowment of his favors, let us bow them down to the dust, as well as silence and satisfy them, with the humbling, consoling, animating, glorious truth, that "of God, and through him, and for him, are all things!" To him, then, be the glory for ever and ever! Amen.

CHAP. XII. 1—21.

THE apostle having thus concluded what may be called the *argumentative* part of his epistle, now proceeds to the *hortatory* and *practical* part; which contains precepts both general and particular that were specially adapted to those whom he was addressing, and the spirit of which is applicable to all times and nations. The very solemn and earnest manner in which he inculcates the practical maxims that follow, shows how deeply he felt the importance of uniting Christian doctrine and duty; yea, how necessarily the reception of the former must lead to the latter. He begins with urging Christians to make an entire consecration of themselves to God, verses 1, 2, he urges upon his readers humility, although they possess the special gifts of the Spirit inasmuch as all the diversities of such gifts are possessed by those who are only parts of the spiritual body to which all Christians belong, verses 3—5; he enjoins upon each to make a wise and diligent improvement of the special gift or office bestowed on him, verses 6—8, and then gives, in the remainder of the chapter, a most striking and admirable series of Christian precepts, of which no equal, and no tolerable parallel, can be found in all the writings of the heathen world.

(1) *I entreat you, then, by the tender mercies of God*, παρακαλῶ οὖν ... Θεοῦ, *i. e.*, such being the case as I have now stated, such being the love and compassion exhibited towards sinners, and such the provision made for them, I entreat you on account of the tender mercies, etc. Οὖν has reference to all that precedes, and intimates that the writer is making a general deduction from it. — Οἰκτιρμῶν, in the *plural*, is an imitation of the Hebrew רַחֲמִים which has no singular. It means *kindness, benignity, compassion*, etc. Διά, *by, on account of;* comp. Rom. xv. 30. 1 Cor. i. 10. 2 Cor. x. 1.

To present your bodies a living sacrifice, holy, acceptable to God, which is your rational service, παραστῆσαι ... ὑμῶν. Παραστῆσαι is common in classic Greek, and is employed to designate the action of bringing and presenting to the divinity a sacrifice of any kind. — *Your bodies*, σώματα ὑμῶν, *i. e.*, yourselves. The word σώματα appears to be suggested by the practice of sacrificing the *bodies* of animals. Θυσίαν ζῶσαν, *a living sacrifice*, in distinction from that of beasts which were slain. The meaning appears to be, that the living active powers of their bodies were to be continually offered or devoted to God. But possibly the reference may be to the custom of the Levitical law, which forbade the offering to God of what was accidentally killed. The animal must be brought *alive* to the altar, and slain there. *Holy*, ἁγίαν, *i e*, תָמִים, *integer, without blemish*, or *defect;* for no other kind of sacrifice could be ἁγία, *i. e.*, consecrated to God. — Εὐάρεστον τῷ Θεῷ is an epexegesis of the preceding ἁγία. — *Your rational service*, τὴν λογικὴν λατρείαν ὑμῶν, viz., your spiritual offering or service, or that which is mental or belongs to reason (λόγος), in distinction from an *external service* or λατρεία σαρκική, such as the Jews offered and relied on for salvation.

(2) *And be not conformed to this world, but be ye transformed by the renewing of your mind*, καὶ μὴ ... νοὸς ὑμῶν. The *Codices* A., D., E., F, G., and many Codd. minusc. read συσχηματίζεσθαι and μεταμορφοῦσθαι, in the Infinitive; which would imply παρακαλῶ before them. The sense would be the same, in such a case, as the Imperative of the text before us makes. — *The present world*, τῷ αἰῶνι τούτῳ, *i. e.*, הָעוֹלָם הַזֶּה, according to the later usage of the word עוֹלָם among the Jews. The classic sense of αἰών, never coincides with this. See my *Exegetical Essay* on αἰών, αἰώνιος, etc., § 5. *By not conforming to the world* the apos-

tle means, the not adopting of its sinful customs and practices, whether of an external or internal nature Ἀλλὰ μεταμορφοῦσθε, *i. e.*, put on another form, person; exchange the μορφή of the world, for that of Christianity. Do this *by the renewing of your mind*, ἀνακαινώσει τοῦ νοὸς ὑμῶν, *i. e.*, by renovating the νοῦς παλαιός, by exchanging it for a νοῦς καινός such as the gospel inspires. In other words: 'Cherish no more a spirit devoted to the world and sinfully conforming to it; cultivate a new and different spirit, one devoted to God, one which will love and practise what is good and pleasing to God.

That ye may learn what the will of God is, that which is good and acceptable and perfect, εἰς τὸ δοκιμάζειν . . . τέλειον. Δοκιμάζω means (among other things) *to explore, to investigate, to search out,* בָּחַן; and this for the purpose of learning and knowing. The apostle means to say, that a *renewed mind* is essential to a successful inquiry after practical and experimental Christian truth, in its whole extent. "If any man will do his will, he shall know of the doctrine whether it be of God." Τὸ ἀγαθόν, κ. τ. λ., I regard as nouns, formed in the usual way, viz., by prefixing the article to the neuter gender of the adjective; for τό is of course implied before εὐάρεστον and τέλειον. So Flatt and Glöckler. — Εὐάρεστον means *acceptable* to God, τῷ Θεῷ being implied. — Τέλειον, that which is wanting in nothing, which has no defect, *integrum*. Others construe these adjectives as qualifying θέλημα. The whole verse, is an exhortation to spiritual-mindedness, in order that Christians may attain to a full knowledge of what their holy religion demands.

(3) Γάρ here stands before specific reasons given for a general principle urged in the preceding context. *By virtue of the* [apostolic] *office of grace* bestowed on me, διὰ τῆς χάριτος; comp. Rom. i. 5. xv. 15. Eph. iii. 2, 8. — *Among you*, ἐν ὑμῖν; so ἐν frequently means. *Not to over-estimate himself beyond what he ought to estimate,* μὴ . . . φρονεῖν. Παρά, as often in *comparative* declarations; *e. g.*, Luke xiii. 2. iii. 13. Rom. xiv. 5 Heb. i. 9. i. 4. iii. 3. — *But to make such an estimation as to act soberly,* ἀλλὰ . . . σωφρονεῖν, *i. e.*, to think modestly, prudently, in a rational way, of himself, not being puffed up with his own attainments and gifts; the same as σωφρόνως φρονεῖν. Notice the *paronomasia* in ὑπερ-φρονεῖν and σωφρονεῖν.

According to the measure of faith which God hath imparted to him, ἑκάστῳ ὡς . . . πίστεως, *i. e.*, according to the measure of Christian belief and knowledge which God has imparted. In other words: 'Let each one estimate his gifts by the principles which the gospel has revealed.' But Flatt and Tholuck understand πίστις here as equivalent to χάρισμα, i. e., πίστις = τὸ πεπιστευμένον, *quod creditum est, donum;* for which I can find no adequate and satisfactory proof or example. Nor can I perceive that the meaning which this exegesis would give to the passage, is a probable one. For the apostle is not exhorting men to prize their gifts according to the diverse nature of them; but he is exhorting all, whatever may be their gifts, to demean themselves modestly and humbly. All belong to *one body*, and no invidious distinctions are to be made. Consequently it is more congruous to explain μέτρον πίστεως as indicating the measure of Christian belief or faith, *i. e.*, of Christian knowledge which is the object of faith.

(4) To show that no one has any reason to set up himself as superior to others, the apostle now introduces the admirable comparison of the *body of Christ, i. e*, the church, with the human body. There are various members of the latter; and they are designed for different uses. But all belong to one and the same body; and each performs its own proper functions for the good of the whole. So it ought to be in the Christian church. — *Use*, πρᾶξιν, *opus, negotium, office.*

(5) *So we, being many, are one body in Christ, and are each members of others,* οὕτως ... μέλη; *i. e.*, there is but one church, one spiritual body, of which Christ is the head. To this we all belong. In this respect there is no pre-eminence. — Καθεῖς for καθ' ἕνα, properly a solecism; see also John viii. 9. Mark xiv. 19. 3 Macc. v. 34, and ἀνὰ εἷς Rev. xxi. 21.

(6) *And possessing gifts which are diverse, according to the grace bestowed upon us,* ἔχοντες ... διάφορα; *i. e.*, we, who are many in number, and yet one body in Christ, possess gifts which are diverse, according to the diversity of the operations of the Spirit, who bestows different gifts on different persons. Ἔχοντες agrees with ἡμεῖς understood, and is a continuation of the preceding sentence. It is plain that here is grammatically an *anacoluthon;* for no verb as an apodosis regularly follows the participial ἔχοντες, κ. τ. λ. The preceding context may supply an apodosis; and this may either be ἀλλήλων μέλη ἐσμέν, or πρᾶξιν ἔχῃ.

Whether prophecy, εἴτε προφετείαν, i. e., εἴτε [ἔχομεν or ἔχοντες] προφητείαν, the ellipsis of ἔχομεν or ἔχοντες being quite plain. Προφητείαν here = χάριν προφητείας, i. e., *the office* or *gift of prophecy*, the prophetic office, appears certain from the sequel. — Εἴτε serves to enumerate particular species, which belong to the genus χαρίσματα. But is προφητεία a public or a private office, and what were its appropriate duties?

Προφήτης, among the Greeks usually signified an *interpreter of the will of the gods*, etc. The general idea is: *an interpreter, one who explains* or *declares*, viz., what was before dark, or not understood, or not known. So the Greeks could say, προφήτης θεοῦ—ἱεροῦ—μάντεως—Μουσῶν, κ. τ. λ. Sometimes (but more rarely) προφήτης means, *one who himself foretells, one who predicts*, etc., and it is then equivalent to the Greek μάντις. But in general it differs from μάντις, inasmuch as the latter means a person who is himself under the divine *afflatus* in such a manner as to be bereaved of his own consciousness and reason, and merely to utter (as an instrument) what the inspiring divinity causes him to utter. This, which the μάντις himself is not supposed to understand and cannot explain, it was the office of the προφήτης to interpret. Thus Plato derives μάντις from μαίνομαι, *to rave, to be out of one's senses;* which indicates its peculiar meaning, in distinction from προφήτης, a designation of such persons only as are in possession of their reason.

Προφήτης in the New Testament, corresponds well with the Hebrew נביא, which means *an interpreter of the divine will generally*, and specially one who by divine inspiration foretells future events. Of this latter sense, which all admit, it is unnecessary to give any examples; but as to the former, the reader may consult for נביא, Judg. vi. 8. 2 Sam. vii 2. Ex. vii. 1, where Aaron is said to be a נביא to Moses, *i. e.*, the interpreter to the people of the plans and designs of Moses (comp. Exod. iv. 16. Jer. xv. 19) Deut. xviii. 18. For the like sense of προφήτης in the New Testament, comp. Matt. v. 12. x. 41. xi. 9. xiii. 17. John vii. 52. Acts vii. 48, 52. Rev. x. 7. xi. 10, 18. xviii. 24, 20. Comp. also the verb προφητεύω in Rev. x. 11. xi. 3. Luke i. 67. Acts ii. 17, 18. xix. 6. xxi. 9. 1 Cor. xi. 4, 5, xiii. 9. xiv. 1, 3, 4, 5, 24, 31, 39; and with these texts compare Joel ii. 28. Num. xi. 25, 27. 1 Sam. x. 5, 6, 10—13. xix. 20—24.

From all these passages it is put beyond a doubt, that *to prophesy* means not merely *to predict*, (which is rather the predominant signification of the word), but also *to preach* (as we say), *to warn, to threaten, to utter praise;* in short, to speak any thing by divine inspiration or afflatus. Προφητείαν in our text, therefore, does not necessarily refer to *those who predicted;* but it is probable, indeed it is almost certain, that it has a more general sense, referring to those who publicly uttered any thing by special divine aid or inspiration, which had respect to the subject of religion.

Such then, were προφῆται in the Christian church, *i. e.*, men endowed with a supernatural gift in regard to addressing the people, either for the purposes of instruction or of devotion. The apostle directs them to perform the duties of their office, *according to the proportion of faith*, or *according to the analogy of faith*, κατὰ τὴν ἀναλογίαν τῆς πίστεως. According to the first method of translating it, the sense would be: 'Let the prophets speak only as they have *faith* to do it:' *i. e.*, let them not go beyond the faith imparted to them. *Faith* here may mean *that which is the object of their belief, i. e.*, what is given to them in an extraordinary manner as the object of their belief. In such a case, the apostle means to say: 'Let not the prophets exceed what is entrusted to them. Let them keep within the bounds of their reason and consciousness, and not, like the heathen μάντεις, rave, or speak they know not what.' Comp. 1 Cor. xiv. 32, where the fact is made clear, that Paul considered the prophets as conscious, rational, voluntary, accountable agents, while in the exercise of their gifts And as to the solemn and conscientious discharge of the duty of a prophet, comp. Jer. xxiii. 25 — 40. Ezek. ii. 6 — 8. iii. 17 — 21. In this manner Chrysostom, Theodoret, Calvin, Tholuck, and many others, have understood the phrase under examination. Reiche, however, and others, construe ἀναλογίαν τῆς πίστεως as meaning the 'measure of faith,' *i. e.*, the degree or measure of actual belief which the prophet exercised, or of which he was the subject. At the same time, as ἀναλογίαν may signify *analogy, agreement* (for so it means in the classics), the sense may be: 'Prophesy in such a manner that what you say will accord with the doctrine of faith, viz., with that which the Scripture contains.' The former sense is the most congruous here, and therefore the most probable.

The construction is elliptical here. We may understand προφητεύωμεν before κατὰ τὴν ἀναλογίαν; or we may fill out the construction thus: πρᾶξιν ἔχῃ προφητεία; or again we may make κατὰ ... πίστεως coordinate with κατὰ χάριν κ. τ. λ., and supply ἔχοντες. But the comparison of the clause εἴτε προφητείαν κ. τ. λ. with the succeeding clauses, εἴτε διακονίαν ἐν τῇ διακονίᾳ κ. τ. λ., opposes this latter construction. *Grammatically* it is possible; *exegetically* it is quite improbable.

(7) *Whether ministry*, εἴτε διακονίαν, i. e., εἴτε [ἔχομεν] διακονίαν. Διάκονος, in a general sense, means *a servant, a waiter* of any one. But as the office of a servant is elevated by the station of his master, and the duties which the servant has to perform, the word is sometimes, (like the Hebrew עבד) used in a most honorable sense, as *servant of God, servant of Christ, servant* (minister) *of the gospel,* etc. In the passage before us, διακονία probably refers to the *official duty* of the διάκονοι in the Christian church, to whom was committed the care of alms for the poor, of providing for the sick, of preparing conveniences for public worship, etc., and generally, of watching over and taking care of the *external* matters of the church. In the primitive age of the church this office was very simple, having reference only

to the *alms* of the church. So the verb διακονέω very often means, *to supply one with food, to make ready* or *provide food* for any one, *e. g.*, Matt. iv. 11. Mark i 13. Luke x. 40. xii. 37. xvii. 8. John xii. 2; comp. Acts vi. But in subsequent ages, the office was extended to all the external and merely temporal relations of the church. So in the Jewish synagogue, the חזן, *inspector, overseer,* corresponded to διάκονος. Ἐν τῇ διακονίᾳ, i. e., ὦμεν or ἔστω; like ἐν τούτοις ἴσθι, 1 Tim. iv. 15, i. e., *sit totus in illis*, let him be wholly devoted to his ministration or service, let him be deeply engaged to perform its duties with fidelity and zeal. Εἴτε ὁ διδάσκων. Here the construction is varied, although there appears to be no special reason for it in the nature of the sentence. We should expect εἴτε διδασκαλίαν here, *i. e*, the Accusative case of the abstract noun; but in its stead we have a participial noun in the Nominative. Of course the verb ᾖ or ἐστί is understood here after ὁ διδάσκων.—Ἐν τῇ διδασκαλίᾳ, *i. e*, ἔστω as before.

That the office of *teacher* is here distinguished from προφήτης on the one hand, and from παρακαλῶν on the other, is plain. But in what this distinction consisted, it would be a difficult matter for us at the present time to say definitely. It would seem however that προφήτης indicated *one who taught by inspiration*, and only so far as inspiration prompted and enabled him to teach. In the strict sense of the word, it was an office created and sustained by miraculous gift. But διδάσκαλος appears to have been an ordinary stated teacher, one who was so by official station, and who taught, according to the degree of religious knowledge which he possessed.

(8) Εἴτε ὁ παρακαλῶν, i e, ὁ παρακαλῶν ᾖ.—Ἐν τῇ παρακλήσει, i e., ἔστω as before. But what is παρακαλῶν? The verb παρακαλέω means *to warn, to console*. Παρακαλῶν, then, would seem to indicate *an exhorter, i. e.*, one who urged to practical duties, who dwelt upon the threatenings and promises of the gospel, and so aided and completed the work which the διδάσκαλος had begun. How long the distinction which is here intimated, was kept up in the church, is not certain. In the original settlement of the churches in New England, many of them had two ministers, a διδάσκαλος and a παρακαλῶν, as here explained; based upon the supposition that these distinct offices were intended to be perpetual in the church. But why consistency would not lead, also, to the maintenance of all the other offices here named, it would be difficult to say,

He who is a distributer, ὁ μεταδιδούς, sc. ᾖ, *i. e.*, he who distributes the charities of the church, or of individuals in it.—Ἐν ἁπλότητι, *i. e.*, with a simple or single regard to the good of those for whom the charity was bestowed, without any selfish or sinister purposes of his own. But in what respect ὁ μεταδιδούς differed from the διάκονος above mentioned, we are now unable to ascertain with precision. It may be that the διάκονος was the *general overseer*, the collector and provider of alms; while the ὁ μετοδιδούς was the *actual distributer* of them among the needy. The reader should remark, that with ὁ μεταδιδούς the construction is again changed, inasmuch as the εἴτε is omitted; so that the strain of the sentiment becomes purely hortatory.

Let him who presides do it with diligent attention, ὁ προϊστάμενος ἐν σπουδῇ. A question may indeed be raised here, whether ὁ προϊστάμενος means *an office* in the church, or only a person to whom the care of some duty or business is committed. As ὁ προϊστάμενος stands connected here with a series of other words which express some *official* duty, most interpreters have been inclined to construe it as having respect to *office*, as I have above. Thus it seems plainly to be used in 1 Thess. v. 12, to designate one who holds the office of a *teacher;* and in 1 Tim. v. 17, it also seems to designate one who holds the office of *ruling* or *governing* in the church, as well as teaching. The context of this latter passage has indeed been regarded by some commentators, as showing that there were some προϊστάμενοι who held the double office of teacher and governor or ruler in the church, although, as some of them suppose, these offices would seem more usually to have been separate. In like manner, Justin Martyr speaks of a προεστώς τῶν ἀδελφῶν, who (it appears) is the presbyter of the church, Apolog. I. c. 67. But see Excursus XII. for a more extended discussion, and a somewhat different interpretation of this word, and indeed of the whole verse. *He who shows compassion,* [let him do it] *with cheerfulness,* ὁ ἐλεῶν ἐν ἱλαρότητι; comp. 2 Cor. ix 7.

(9) *Let benevolence be sincere,* ἡ ἀγάπη, ἀνυπόκριτος. I render ἀγάπη *benevolence* here, because it seems to indicate *kind feeling* toward men in general. The *love of the brethren* is specified in verse 10. The apostle here enjoins on Christians to cherish a sincere and real, not merely a pretended and apparent, feeling of kindness toward all men. Ἀποστυγοῦντες, *i. e.,* ἔστε, which would make the Imper.; and this the nature of the case evidently demands. So κολλώμενοι, sc. ἔστε. In the connection in which τὸ πονηρόν and τῷ ἀγαθῷ here stand, the meaning is limited to *malice* and *kindness.* So πονηρός means, even in the classics, *malicious, mischievous;* and ἀγαθός is the converse of this, *kind, benevolent.* These two phrases, therefore, are merely an epexegesis of ἀγάπη in the preceding clause.

(10) *In respect to brotherly love, kindly affectionate one toward another,* τῇ φιλαδελφίᾳ, εἰς ἀλλήλους φιλόστοργοι. Τῇ φιλαδεφίᾳ,

is the *Dative of relation: in respect to, in regard to.* So often in the New Testament; *e. g.*, νωθροὶ ταῖς ἀκοαῖς, Heb. v. 11; Gal. i. 22; so Matt. xi. 29. Heb. xii. 3. Eph. iv. 18, et sæpe alibi. Φιλόστοργοι means *affectionate*, in such a manner as one is toward his own near relative; στοργή means *natural affection. In respect to honor anticipating each other,* τῇ τιμῇ, ἀλλήλους προηγούμενοι; *i. e.,* let each one, in paying the proper tribute of respect to others, strive to anticipate his Christian brother. Προηγέομαι means *to take the lead, to go before, to set the example.* The meaning is, that so far from being averse to pay that respect which is due to others, each should strive to excel the other in the performance of this duty. Christianity, therefore, is so far from banishing all civility and good manners from society, that it enjoins the greatest attention to this subject.

(11) *As to diligence, not remiss,* τῇ σπουδῇ μὴ ὀκνηροί. Τῇ σπουδῇ *Dative of relation* as before. Σπουδῇ here seems to be taken in the *general* sense; and so the passage accords with Eccle. ix. 10: "Whatsoever thy hand findeth to do, do it with thy might." So the next phrase explains the whole expression, by presenting the antithesis of it, viz., τῷ πνεύματι ζέοντες, *ferventes animo, warmly engaged* (as we say), *fervid, active in serious earnest;* comp. Acts xviii. 25. Some apply τῷ πνεύματι here to the divine Spirit; but I think without any good reason. Τῷ Κυρίῳ δουλεύοντες (for which Griesbach reads τῷ καιρῷ δουλεύοντες), is supported by the more important testimony of external witnesses. Griesbach has rejected it on the ground, that 'the less usual reading is to be preferred;' a ground which, to say the least, has many slippery places. Knapp, Morus, Bengel, and Beza, preserve Κυρίῳ, and I think with good reason. I take the whole expression to mean, that all our *diligence* is to be consecrated to God, to be made subservient to the cause of Christ. That Κυρίῳ here means *the Lord Christ,* the *usus loquendi* of Paul leaves no good room to doubt. Inasmuch as δουλεύω governs the Dative, we need not insist here on the *Dative of relation.* But in fact, all of the Datives in this whole paragraph are of this nature; so that exactly rendered it would be, *as to* (or *in respect to*) *the Lord, obedient* or *engaged in his service.*

(12) *As to hope, joyful,* τῇ ἐλπίδι, χαίροντες; *i. e.,* rejoicing in the blessed hope of glory which the gospel inspires; and this, amid all the troubles and sorrows of life. *As to affliction, patiently enduring,* τῇ θλίψει, ὑπομένοντες; *i. e.,* since you are animated with a joyful hope, you may well be called upon to endure the troubles and sorrows of life with patience. *As to prayer, be persevering,* τῇ προσευχῇ, προσκαρτεροῦντες; *i. e.,* the way to maintain a joyful hope, and to be patient under afflictions, is to cherish the spirit of prayer and to live near to God.

(13) *In respect to the wants of the saints, be sympathetic,* ταῖς . . . κοινωνοῦντες; *i. e.*, feel these wants as if they were your own. With all these participles, ἔστε is implied. While Christians were to be kind towards all others, they were to be specially so towards their brethren of the church. Κοινωνέω in classic Greek has always an *intransitive* sense; and the instances in Gal. vi. 6, and Phil. iv. 5 hardly prove that a *transitive* sense should be given to it in the New Test., viz., *communicate, distribute.* To be a partaker, to share in, is the genuine meaning of the word; and from that we need not here depart. *Readily practising hospitality*, τὴν φιλοξενίαν διώκοντες. Here the construction is changed, and the Accusative after διώκοντες is employed. Comp. 1 Tim. v. 10. Heb. xiii. 2. 1 Pet. iv. 9. 3 John verses 5—8. This virtue was specially necessary in the primitive times, when Christian teachers had no regular support, and when the missionaries of the cross were laboring to diffuse the knowledge of salvation.

(14) *Bless those who persecute you, bless and curse not,* εὐλογεῖτε . . . . καταρᾶσθε; comp. Matt. v. 44. Luke vi. 28. That is, while your persecutors imprecate divine indignation upon you, do you pray that blessings may descend upon them.

(15) *Rejoice with those who rejoice, and weep with those who weep,* χαίρειν . . . . κλαιόντων; *i. e.*, sympathize with your fellow Christians both in joy and grief; show that you enter with feeling into the consideration of their joys and sorrows. The Infinitive χαίρειν, κλαίειν, stands (as frequently in the Greek classics) instead of the Imperative. Strictly speaking, δεῖ is understood in such cases, *q. d*, *you must rejoice—weep*, *etc.*

(16) *Mutually think the same thing,* τὸ αὐτὸ εἰς ἀλλήλους φρονοῦντες, sc. ἔστε, *i. e.*, be agreed in your opinions and views. Whether this relates to matters that concerned spiritual or temporal affairs, the words themselves do not show; but the nature of the case would seem to indicate, that the expression is designed to have a general bearing on all their concerns and articles of belief. Origen, and others, have interpreted the passage as meaning: 'Enter into each other's circumstances, in order to see how you would yourself feel;' and so it parallelizes with the preceding expression. But the *usus loquendi* of Paul does not seem to admit of this exposition; comp. 2 Cor. xiii. 11. Phil. ii. 2; comp. Rom. xv. 14. Εἰς ἀλλήλους is not, indeed, the usual mode of expression in the New Testament, but ἐν ἀλλήλοις; comp. Mark ix. 50. John xiii. 35. Rom. xv. 5. But the exchange of εἰς with the Accusative for ἐν with the Dative, in the New Testament (and indeed elsewhere), is very frequent.

Mind not high things, but be led away by humble ones, μὴ τὰ . . . συναπαγόμενοι. Such is the *literal* translation of the words. The sentiment is: 'Shun pride, and culivate humility. That ἀλλὰ τοῖς ταπείνοις κ. τ. λ., is the antithesis of τὰ ὑψηλὰ, κ. τ. λ., seems to me very obvious. Ταπείνοις is then in the *neuter* gender, to correspond to ὑψηλά. But some construe it as of the masculine gender, and represent the sentiment of the phrase to be: 'Suffer yourselves to be led away, viz., to the judgment-seat of magistrates, with the *despised* Christian.' Others: 'Suffer yourselves to be led away by the humble, *i. e.*, conform to them. This agrees in *sentiment* with the above exposition; but it has the disadvantage of sacrificing the direct antithesis of the words ὑψηλά and ταπείνοις.—Συναπάγομαι is commonly used in a *bad* sense, viz, to suffer one's self to be led away by temptation, etc.; see Gal ii. 13. 2 Pet. iii. 17; but here it must have a *generic* sense, and we must translate: 'Suffer yourselves to be influenced or led away by things that are despised,' viz., by the proud world; i. e, 'Readily undertake offices or duties that are humble and mean, in the estimation of the proud.' *Be not wise in your own conceit,* μὴ . . . ἑαυτοῖς; *i. e.*, do not, trusting in your own superior skill and understanding, refuse to confer with others or to harken to their suggestions; a caution intimately connected with the preceding.

(17) *Not rendering evil for evil,* μηδενὶ . . . ἀποδιδόντες; comp. 1 Pet. iii 9. Matt. v. 43—48. This is, no doubt, one of the most difficult of all the precepts which the gospel enjoins; I mean, one which most thwarts our natural inclinations and desires. "The natural man receiveth not the things of the Spirit." *Seek after that which is good in the sight of all men,* προνοούμενοι . . . ἀνθρώπων; *i. e.*, be studiously attentive to those duties, which are commended by all, and which all therefore admit to be of the highest obligation. The expression seems to be taken, with some abridgment, from Prov. iii. 4, καὶ τρονοοῦ καλὰ ἐνώπιον Κυρίου καὶ ἀνθρώπων.

(18) *If it be possible, so far as you are able, be at peace with all men,* εἰ δυνατον . . . εἰρηνεύοντες. The limitations εἰ δύνατον and τὸ ἐξ ὑμῶν, show that the apostle did not deem this possible in all cases; and beyond all question it is not. The world hate the truths of the gospel, and will be at enmity with those who boldly and faithfully urge them on their consciences. Apostles and martyrs did thus urge them; and their sufferings prove the truth of what has now been alleged —Τὸ ἐξ ὑμῶν, i. e., κατὰ τὸ ἐξ ὑμῶν. Ἐξ is used here in the sense of *belonging to.* The whole phrase means, 'in proportion to that which belongs to you,' *i. e.*, according to your ability; like the French *votre possible.*

(19) *Avenge not yourselves, beloved, but give place to* [divine] *indignation,* μὴ ἑαυτοὺς . . . . ὀργῇ. Such is one method of in-

terpreting this clause. Διδόναι τόπον means *to allow, to give place to* (as we say in English). So Eph. iv. 22, μὴ δίδοτε τόπον τῷ διαβόλῳ, *give no place to the devil;* and Luke xiv. 9, Δὸς τούτῳ τόπον, *resign your place to this person* or *make room for him.* Cf. also Josephus, Antiq. xvi. ii. § 6, Plutarch, De Ira cohibenda, chap. 14; and Marcus Antoninus Lib. iii. 6. The meaning above given to δότε τόπον τῇ ὀργῇ, thus according with the frequent sense of the phrase δοῦναι τόπον, seems to be favored by the quotation which immediately follows: Ἐμοί κ. τ. λ. This quotation would be wholly inapposite, if we suppose that ὀργῇ here means *the wrath of our enemy*, and δότε τόπον, to mean *go out of the way of, get out of the way of,* etc., as many have done. In Rabbinic Hebrew, it is true indeed, that נָתַן מָקוֹם (give place) means *to go out of the way of;* but we need not resort to Hebrew idiom here.

Another method of interpreting ὀργῇ is, to assign to it the meaning of *one's own indignation*, and then to construe δότε τόπον as meaning *spatium date* i. e., *put off, defer.* The sense of this would be good; and Wisd. xii. 20 would help to justify the *usus loquendi.* So also Livy (viii. 32) says: Iræ suæ spatium . . . . daret. So Seneca: Ira surda est et amens, dabimus illi spatium (de Ira, iii. 39); also Lactantius: Dedisset iræ suæ spatium (de Ira, 18). Construed in this way the passage would mean: 'Put off the execution of that to which your indignation would prompt, or defer the execution of your anger: for God will repay evil to your enemy in case he has done wrong. Retribution belongs rather to him than to you.' This sense, on the whole, seems to be better supported than the other above given. Nor is there any want of congruity with what follows.

Retribution is mine, I will make it, saith the Lord, ἐμοί . . . Κύριος; or *vengeance is mine, I will render it, saith the Lord.* The passage is taken from Deut. xxxii. 35, לִי נָקָם אֲשַׁלֵּם. Λέγει Κύριος are the apostle's own words, for they are not in the Hebrew. The meaning is: 'God will render righteous judgment or retribution for acts of wickedness; Christians are not to claim for themselves the doing of that which it is his sovereign prerogative to do.'

(20) *If thine enemy hunger, feed him; if he thirst,* etc., ἐὰν οὖν . . . αὐτόν. Food and drink here stand as a part for the whole, and signify our obligation to treat an enemy with beneficence or kindness. The meaning is: 'Do good to thine enemy, instead of evil; show him kindness, instead of taking revenge.'

For in so doing, thou shalt heap coals of fire on his head, τοῦτο γὰρ . . . αὐτοῦ. This is quoted from Prov. xxv. 21, 22. In Ps. xviii. 8, 12, 13, גֶּחָלִים, *coals of fire,* are emblematical of *consuming* or *destruction.* The Arabians say, *he roasted my heart,* or *he kindled a fire in my heart,* to designate the idea of *giving* or *inflicting pain* So in 4 Ezra xvi 54, "Coals of fire shall burn on the head of him who denies that he has sinned against God." There can be no well-grounded doubt, then, that *pain* is meant to be designated by this expression. But is it the pain of shame or contrition for misconduct, or that of *punishment?* More probably the former here; for so ver. 21 would almost necessarily lead us to conclude. It is a noble sentiment when thus understood. "Take not revenge," says the apostle: "overcome your adversary with kindness and beneficence. These will bring him to shame and sorrow for his misconduct."

(21) *Be not overcome by evil, but overcome evil with good,* μὴ νικῶ .... τὸ κακόν, *i. e.*, be not led to an indulgence of a spirit of revenge on account of injuries; but subdue the evil temper which leads to the infliction of injury, by beneficence and kindness.

CHAP. XIII. 1—14.

At the time when Paul wrote this epistle, the civil power was everywhere in the hands of heathen men, who were idolaters and polytheists, and consequently hostile to Christianity. In Palestine even, the power committed to the hands of the Jews was principally of an *ecclesiastical* nature, and the Romans uniformly reserved to themselves the right of confirming or reversing any sentence which should affect the life or liberty of their subjects. The Roman civil power, as such, had not yet begun to persecute Christians, or even to tolerate persecution in others, but the Roman magistrates could not but look with indignation or scorn on those who denied the *religio licita* of the empire, and who without hesitation condemned all religion but their own as false and injurious. There were some superstitious men, moreover, among these magistrates, and there were multitudes of superstitious priests, who were peculiarly hostile to Christianity, and who urged the common people, and magistrates also, to testify their displeasure against it. Gradually this feeling increased, until at last, under Nero, it burst forth like a volcano, and swept before its fiery streams all the disciples of Jesus who were within its reach

On the other hand, the Jews, before they were converted to Christianity, as the chosen people of God, considered themselves entitled to pre-eminence above the nations of the earth They looked down with scorn and hatred upon the גוֹיִם the worshippers of stocks and stones The idea that the Romans claimed the right to dispose of their persons and property was insufferable They fortified themselves in this opinion, by an appeal to Deut. xvii 15 "Thou shalt in anywise set him king over thee whom the Lord thy God shall choose, one from among thy brethren shalt thou set king over thee; thou mayest *not* set a stranger over thee, who is not thy brother " Willing subjection to the Romans, then, was in their view disobedience to this injunction of Moses. Hence nothing but the fear of immediate and summary punishment restrained them, for many years, from rising up against the Roman power in Palestine, and even in other countries where they were numerous they made no small tumult whenever occasion offered.

When individuals passed over from the Jewish community to that of the Christians, they could not, or did not, divest themselves at once of all these feelings and views. Christianity introduced them to a new citizenship, new rights, new privileges, new spiritual rulers, new fellow-citizens Could they then have any regard for heathen citizenship? It was natural to ask this question; and above all, it was easy to do so, since the heathen magistracy were well known to be hostile in their feeling toward Christians, and since Christians were required to yield up life rather than to obey the civil magistrate as to some things which God had forbidden.

It is easy to see, that while matters stood thus, there was great danger that private Christians, instigated by their own particular views of heathen superstitions and by a sense of duty in some cases where they were called upon to renounce obedience to the magistrate, would be exposed to judge wrongly, and go too far in justifying a principle of insubordination to the civil power Paul felt a deep solicitude in regard to this subject, which was evidently encompassed with many difficulties For on the one hand, it was clear that in some cases life itself was to be sacrificed rather than to obey the civil power ; and the apostle himself was a most eminent pattern of high and holy independence, in cases of this nature. On the other, private individuals, with all their prejudices and scorn of heathenism, might greatly abuse the proper liberty of a Christian, and extend it to things to which Christianity did not allow them to extend it.

That there was a disposition to do so among the Christians at Rome, seems evident from the tenor of chap. xiii. The cautions here are salutary for the church in all ages ; but they were peculiarly needed in the age of the apostles

Nothing can be plainer, than that the *subjection* urged in chap xiii cannot be extended to cases where the commission of a *moral evil* is demanded But with the exception of this, the principles here enjoined are altogether of such a nature as our holy religion demands. We certainly should not neglect any remedy for evils of a civil nature, which is proper We are bound to make use of the proper remedy, if in our power, by a regard to the public good But where the government is despotic and there is no remedy but rebellion, and this may be a hazardous and bloody measure, it is better to suffer than to excite tumult. So thought Paul, comp Tit iii. 1, and so did Peter teach, 1 Pet ii. 13, 17 But let not the advocates of despotic power urge subjection in cases where the gospel will not allow it, under cover of the general expressions here used Every precept of this nature is to be interpreted with a proper regard to the time and circumstances in which it was uttered What these were in the case before us, we have seen. What the example of the apostle and the Saviour himself was, we know. We know, too, that Christianity in its very nature is *love to God and man*, that it makes all men a *brotherhood;* it places them on the same ground as to rights and privileges; it pays real deference to *moral* worth, and to this only. It acknowledges no right in one to oppress another, admits of no " Jew or Greek, Barbarian or Scythian, bond or free, " for it teaches that "all are one in Jesus." It teaches true equality of rights, true spiritual and civil freedom. It does not, indeed, abolish all distinctions among men , nor does it abolish civil governments Far from this; but then it decides, in its very nature, that all governments, and all civil orders and distinctions, should be only for the public good It admits no *divine right* of one man to be lord over another, it is at open and eternal war with all the mere claims of birth, and pride, and oppression. The universal good, the equal rights, the peaceful state of man is the object at which it aims, and whatever is incompatible with these, is incompatible with the fundamental principles of the great " law of liberty and love "

But all this may be allowed (and contradicted it cannot be with reason), and yet it may be true at the same time, that Christians, situated as the Romans were in Paul s time, are required to yield peaceful submission to magistrates, whether Christian or heathen, in all things where the command of God does not directly forbid it. What the world ought to be, what it would be if all men were Christians indeed, is one thing ; what the world is, and what is the present duty of Christians in such circumstances, is another and different thing. In a word, the *spirit* of the precepts in Rom xiii is to be regarded as a rule for all ages and nations so long as circumstances shall be like those which then existed. And even when these circumstances alter, and magistrates become really Christian, it must then be true in a still more eminent degree, that quiet and peaceful obedience in all lawful things will be a duty.

(1) *Let every soul be subject to the supreme magistracies,* πᾶσα .... ὑποτασσέσθω. Πᾶσα ψυχή is Hebraism, like כָּל־נֶפֶשׁ, *every one, each one :* — Ὑπερεχούσαις means *preeminent, supreme ; i. e.,* in this case, the civil magistracy or power of civil rulers. *For there is no magistracy unless by divine permission; and the existing* [magistrates] *are of God's appointment,* οὐ γὰρ ...... εἰσίν. Γάρ stands before a reason why they should be subject to the civil magistracy. The apostle intends to reconcile Christians to the idea of civil obedience, on the ground that obeying the magistrate is in accordance with the command of God. All magistrates are by his permission; and even when they are oppressive, the Christian is bound to regard them (so he should regard other evils), as existing by divine permission, since "the powers that be are ordained of God;" and to bow submissive in all cases where direct disobedience to God is not demanded by them. Such a view of the subject is greatly adapted to satisfy the mind of a Christian, when he feels galled with the yoke of oppression.

(2) *So that he who resists the magistracy, resists the comandment of God,* ὥστε .... ἀνθέστηκεν. The reason of this is, that as God has required obedience to the magistrates (in the sense before stated), so he who refuses to yield this, is disobedient to the divine command. *And they who resist shall receive punishment for themselves,* οἱ δὲ ... λήψονται. Κρῖμα is often used in the sense of *punishment ; e. g.,* Rom. iii. 8. 1 Cor. xi. 29. Gal. v. 10. 1 Tim. v. 12, et alibi. — Ἑαυτοῖς, is here the *Dativus incommodi,* see N. Test. Grammar, § 104. 2. Note 1. The meaning is, that those who are seditious, *i. e.,* make resistance against the civil government, will be brought to punishment, and that deservedly.

(3) *For rulers are not a terror to good works, but to evil,* οἱ γὰρ .... κακῶν. This clause shows what sort of rulers Paul expected Christians to obey, and how far obedience was a duty, viz., such rulers as protect the good and repress the evil ; and while they do this, there can be no question as to the duty of obeying them. But suppose the reverse, *i. e.,* suppose that they protect evil-doing and forbid good works, then Paul's own conduct shows what other Christians ought to do. — Φόβος here is *abstract* for *concrete, i. e.,* φόβος for φοβεροί. *And wilt thou not fear the magistracy?* θέλεις δὲ .... ἐξουσίαν. That is, since the ruler is terrible to evil-doers wilt thou not be afraid to do evil ? *Do good, and thou shalt have praise for it,* τὸ ἀγαθόν .... αὐτῆς, *i. e.,*

yield obedience to the civil power, and you shall obtain from it the commendation of being a peaceful and obedient citizen.

(4) *For it is an instrument in the hands of God, to promote thy good*, Θεοῦ γάρ ... ἀγαθόν. That is, civil government is of divine appointment, and it is designed to be an instrument of good to those who do well. Σοὶ εἰς τὸ ἀγαθόν, *for thy good;* σοί, *Dativus commodi.* The γάρ stands before a reason or ground why they might expect praise, ἔπαινος, for doing well.

But if thou doest evil, fear, ἐὰν δὲ ... φοβοῦ; *i. e.,* if thou art refractory and disobedient to the civil magistracy, thou hast reason to fear the consequences. — *For he beareth the sword not in vain; but he is God's minister punishing the evil-doer,* οὐ γὰρ ... πράσσοντι. The sword is here the emblem of punishment. Θεοῦ διάκονος, *a minister* or *instrument* of God's appointment, or one whom his providence has raised up or permitted to exist. Ἔκδικος εἰς ὀργήν, *exercens judicium ad pœnam, judging, condemning to punishment.* Τῷ πράσσοντι, the Dative of "the person *to* or *for* whom anything is, or is done."

(5) *Therefore we ought to yield subjection not because of indignation only, but also for conscience' sake,* διὰ ... συνείδησιν; *i. e.,* we should do our duty not merely in order to shun the evils of a different course, but we ought to do it from a conscientious regard to the obligation under which we are.

(6) *On this very account also pay tribute* διὰ τοῦτο .... τελεῖτε. Διὰ τοῦτο, *i. e.,* for the sake of conscience, as well as to avoid civil penalties. Γάρ *illustrantis.* It is difficult to make out a proper *causal* meaning for γάρ in this case; because διὰ τοῦτο itself designates such a meaning. Why may we not consider διὰ τοῦτο γάρ as an *intensive* causal formula, not unlike ἐπειδήπερ, etc.? I have so rendered it, viz., *on this very account.* Καὶ, *also,* denoting not only an additional circumstance, but also being *affirmative,* καὶ φόρους τελεῖτε, *ye should also pay tribute,* or ye should pay tribute as well as yield obedience in other things. Τελεῖτε I take as in the Imperative.*

For they are ministers of God, who attend to this matter, λειτουργοὶ ... προσκαρτεροῦντες; *i. e.,* they are God's *ministers* or *instruments,* in the same sense as the magistracy above mentioned. God who has ordained that there should be civil magistracy, has also ordained, as a means of supporting it, that there should be *tribute, custom, taxes.* Let the Christian pay these cheerfully; and even when they are oppressive, let him submit on the same ground as he does to other evils, *i. e.,* until a proper and lawful remedy for the oppression can be found. Προσκαρτε-

---

* The Greek negative particle μή shows that it is not Indic. but Imperative.

ρουντες indicates habitual and persevering attention to any thing; as much as to say, Whose proper official business it is to attend to this matter.

(7) *Render to all men what is due*, ἀπόδοτε, κ. τ. λ., on the ground and spirit of such precepts. — Φόρον means properly *a tax* either on persons or on land; or rather, in the present case, both of these together. Τέλος answers to our present term *custom*, *i. e.*, a tax on goods, wares, merchandise, etc. In respect to φόβον, comp. verse 4, above. The meaning of the apostle is, that we should so stand in awe of those who wear the sword of civil justice, as to deter us from sedition and civil disobedience. Τιμή commonly means *the respect* which one pays to his equals in rank. But here it means the respect to be paid to the magistracy; comp. 1 Pet. ii. 17. τὸν βασιλέα τιμᾶτε. The construction τῷ τὸν φόρον is elliptical = τῷ τὸν φόρον [δεῖ ἀπαιτεῖν], or some equivalent expression; and so of τῷ τὸ τέλος.

(8) From these precepts with respect to rendering to magistrates what is due on the ground of our civil obligations, the apostle makes an easy transition to our duty in general with respect to the subject of debts: *Owe no man any thing, except to love one another*, μηδενὶ .. ἀγαπᾶν; *i. e.*, scrupulously pay off all debts of whatever nature, and to whomsoever they may be due; except, as I may say, the debt of love. An animated and very expressive description of the extent to which the obligation of *benevolence* reaches! A debt of this nature is not like a pecuniary one, which, by the payment of a certain sum, is fully and finally extinguished. The debt of love is only renewed by payments ever so ample. In its own nature it is inextinguishable; for, as Augustine says: Nec cum redditur amittitur, sed potius reddendo multiplicatur; Ep. 62, ad Cœlest. But some with less significance take ὀφείλετε in the Indic. and construe thus: 'Ye have no debt but that of love, etc.;' *i. e.*, true benevolence will lead you to a proper discharge of all your relative duties. *For he who loves another, fulfils the law*, ὁ γὰρ ἀγαπῶν . . . πεπλήρωκε. Γάρ *illustrantis*, *i. e.*, it introduces a clause designed to show that *the debt of love* is one which is always due But how does the apostle intend to illustrate this? The answer is, by showing that the law of God demands love to our neighbor, and this is admitted to be of perpetual obligation; consequently the duty which it demands, must also be perpetual.

(9) He proceeds to show, that the sum of the moral law is contained in the precept *to love our neighbor*. Γάρ introduces the proof, from the law, of the position which he had just laid down. The τό here is the article prefixed before a quotation or citation, introduced as such; comp. Luke ix. 46, τὸ, τίς ἂν εἴη μεί-

ζων αὐτῶν. See also Luke xxii. 2. Acts iv. 21. xxii. 30. xxvii. 4, 9. Luke i. 62. 1 Cor. iv. 6. Rom. viii. 26. 1 Thess. iv. 1. Mark ix. 23. Gal. iv. 25; see N. Test. Gramm. § 93. 9. Οὐ μοιχεύσεις κ. τ. λ. All these commands proceed from the law of love. By committing any one of the crimes here named, a man sins against the good of his neighbor, and therefore against the precept which requires him to love his neighbor as himself— Οὐ ψευδομαρτυρήσεις, is not important to the meaning, and is of very doubtful authority. — Καί εἴ τις is not meant to express a doubt whether there be any other commandment, but only this idea: 'Whatever other commandment there may be,' viz., respecting our *relative* duties.

In this *saying* or *declaration*, ἐν τούτῳ τῷ λόγῳ, i. e., in the declaration which follows. — Ἀγαπήσεις κ. τ. λ., seems to be quoted from Lev. xix. 18, וְאָהַבְתָּ לְרֵעֲךָ כָּמוֹךָ, *thou shalt love thy neighbor as thyself*. In this one sentence the apostle rightly affirms that the whole essence of the relative *moral* law is contained. Suppose now that every man on earth should really and truly and as highly regard his neighbor's happiness as his own; then all injustice, fraud, oppression, and injury of every kind, would at once cease, and a universal fulfilment of our obligation to others would be the consequence. — Πλησίον in itself an *adverb*, is here employed with the Article as a *noun* in the Acc. case. So the Greeks frequently employed adverbs. The pronoun ἑαυτόν is here referred to the *second* person singular. It may designate either the 1st, 2nd, or 3rd person, by the usage of both classic and N. Test. writers. See Lex. on ἑαυτοῦ.

(10) *Love worketh no ill to its neighbor; love then is the fulfilling of the law*, ἡ ἀγάπη . . . ἡ ἀγάπη. That is, he who loves his neighbor as himself, will designedly do him no harm or injury. Πλήρωμα seems here to be of the same meaning as πλήρωσις; and so in Gal. iv. 4. Eph. i. 10. So Philo de Abr. p. 387, πλήρωμα τοῦ χρόνον; so πλήρωσις τῶν ἡμέρων, Ezek. v. 2. Dan. x. 3. *The fulfilling of the law* is the filling up the measure of its requisitions; and here the fulfilling of the law which has respect to our relative duties; comp. Gal. v. 14. James ii. 8. Matt. xxii. 39, 40. 1 Tim. i. 5. What the apostle designs to teach is: 'Love, such as the law demands, will lead us always to seek our neighbor's good, and so to be always paying the debt of benevolence, yet never paying it off.'

(11) Καί τοῦτο, i e., καὶ τοῦτο ποιεῖτε, *do this*, viz., all of which he had been exhorting them to do. Καὶ τοῦτο is explained by Theodoret as meaning, καὶ μάλιστα; which gives the sense very well *Considering the time*, εἰδότες τόν καιρόν, or *taking cognizance of the time*, or (taking the participles as *causal*, which is often

the case, New Test. Gramm. § 140. 7) *since*, or *because ye know*, etc., comp ᾔδειν in Acts xxiii. 5. Καιρόν I understand to mean *the gospel-time* which had already come The apostle considers the commencement of this, which had already taken place, as the beginning of a glorious day, the dawning of the Sun of righteousness with healing in his beams. A state of sin and ignorance is a state of darkness; and out of such a state Christians are brought, that they may see the light; comp. Eph. v 8, 11. John iii. 19—21. 1 Pet. ii. 9. *That it is now time to awake out of sleep, for now is our salvation nearer than when we believed*, ὅτι ὥρα . . . . . ἐπιστεύσαμεν. That is, the commencement of the Christian dispensation, and the beginning of light in your own souls, call for corresponding efforts and activity. The image of awaking out of sleep is often used, in order to designate the rousing up from a state of comparative inaction, to one of strenuous effort; comp. Eph. v. 14. 1 Cor. xv. 34. 1 Thess. v. 6.

But what is the σωτηρία, which is nearer than when Christians at Rome first believed? Tholuck, and most of the late commentators in Germany, even those who are most strenuous defenders of the inspiration of the apostles suppose that they expected the speedy advent of Christ upon earth a second time, when the day of glory to the church would commence. Accordingly, they represent him as here and elsewhere exhorting Christians to be on the alert, constantly expecting the approach of such a day. In support of this view, Tholuck appeals to Phil. iv. 5. 1 Thess. v. 2, 6. Rev. xxii. 12. But how the words of the apostles, when thus construed, can be made consistent with themselves (not to speak of other difficulties arising from the consideration that they were inspired), is more than I am able to see. The very passage referred to, in the first epistle to the church at Thessalonica, was understood by the Thessalonians in the same manner as Tholuck and others understand it; but this interpretation was formally and strenuously corrected in 2 Thess. ii. Is it not enough that Paul has explained his own words? Who can safely venture to give them a meaning different from what he gives?—Then as to Rev. xxii. 12, how is it possible that the writer who had just made an end of predicting a long series of events that should happen before the *day of glory*, one of which is to occupy a *thousand* years, can be supposed to have believed that all this was to take place during that very generation in which he lived?

I only add here, that I cannot with my present views admit it. I must, therefore, refer σωτηρία to the *spiritual salvation* which believers were to experience, when transferred to the world of everlasting light and glory. And so construed, the exhortation of Paul amounts to this: 'Christian brethren, we have been brought out of darkness into marvellous light; let us act in a manner that corresponds with our condition. We are hastening to our retribution; every day brings us nearer to it; and in prospect of the reward which now almost appears in sight, as we approach the goal of human life, let us act with renewed effort as duty requires.' So Chrysostom.

(12) *The night is advanced, the day is at hand*, ἡ νὺξ .... ἤγγικε; a repetition of a part of the idea contained in the preceding verse. Νύξ, the time of ignorance and darkness in which they had once been, 'is now nearly gone,' *i. e*, they had now come as it were to the confines of eternal day, i. e, of a more perfect knowledge of divine things. It behooved them, therefore, to rouse up all their energies, and to act in a manner congruous with their condition and obligations. *Let us put away then the works of darkness, and put on the armor of light*, ἀποθώμεθα ... φωτός; *i. e.*, let us reject such things as we were accustomed to do while in a state of darkness; and let us arise to combat all our spiritual foes, by girding on the armor of light, that is, by living and acting in such a manner as becomes those who are the sons of light.

(13) *Let us walk in a becoming manner, as by day*, ὡς .... περιπατήσωμεν; *i. e*, let us live as it becomes those who enjoy the light, to whom the path of duty is made plain; so as to guard against reproach from those whose eyes are fixed upon us to watch our demeanor. Ἐν ἡμέρα, I take here to be the *Dat. conditionis, i. e.*, to designate the circumstance that they have now to act as those who have daylight to guide their actions. *Not in revelling and drunkenness, etc.*, μὴ κώμοις ... ζήλῳ. The apostle here mentions some of those sins which were most usually committed during the night season.

(14) *But put ye on the Lord Jesus Christ*, ἀλλ' .... Χριστόν, *i. e.*, imitate him; which is the usual sense of the Greek ἐνδύσασθαί τινα; or perhaps it here means, like the Hebrew לבשׁ, *to be filled with*, and so the idea is: Be filled with a Christian spirit, abound in it; "let Christ dwell in you richly." *And make no provision for the flesh, in respect to its lusts*, καὶ τῆς σαρκὸς ... ἐπιθυμίας. Τῆς σαρκὸς πρόνοιαν means *provision for the sake of the flesh, i. e.*, in order to gratify its lusts, as εἰς ἐπιθυμίας explains it. For the Genitive see New Test. Gramm. § 99. So Rom. viii. 32, πρόβατα σφαγῆς, *sheep destined for the slaughter;* comp. Phil. i. 22. John v. 29. vii. 35. Matt. iv. 15. x. 5. etc.

CHAP. XIV. 1—23.

The apostle having given precepts, for the sake of caution and restraint, to the Jewish part of the church at Rome, now turns to the Gentile part, and gives them some salutary cautions with respect to their treatment of their Jewish brethren. It should be remembered, that (holocausts excepted) only a part of the offerings of the flesh of slain beasts was consumed by fire; the rest was reserved for the priests or the offerer, and frequently came to the market for sale. Now a man who ate meats that had been obtained at the market, might eat that which had been offered to idols. The Jew from his abhorrence of idolatry shuddered at such a possibility and even the Christian Jew could not at once divest himself of the feeling, and sometimes even abstained from all flesh lest he should eat that which had been offered to idols.

Clement of Alexandria and Augustine, however, interpret the chapter before us as having reference only to scrupulousness about meat that had actually been offered to idols, and not meat in general. But ver. 2 seems to be opposed to this opinion. Accordingly, Chrysostom, Origen, Theodoret, Jerome, and most modern commentators suppose, that there is reference to all kinds of meat sold in the public markets. A comparison of the present chapter with 1 Cor viii, would seem to afford confirmation that the scruples in question (about the eating of meat) arose from the circumstance, that meats which had been presented at the temples of idols, often came into the markets for sale (1 Cor. x 25—28), and in consequence of this, it was so difficult to distinguish lawful meats from unlawful ones, that it was duty rather to forego the use of meats, than to incur the danger of eating those which were polluted.

Some critics, however, as Koppe and Eichhorn have maintained, that the Christians whom Paul has in view here, were those called by the Greek $\dot{\alpha}\sigma\kappa\bar{\eta}\tau\alpha\iota$, ascetics, i e, those who practised peculiar self-denial as to food and drink, and subjected themselves to various penances and mortifications of the flesh, in order that they might attain to a more pure and elevated state of devotion and piety That a sect of this kind, viz . the Essenes, existed among the Jews at this time, is well known from the testimonies of Philo and Josephus But besides the Essenes, there were others among the Jews who practised abstinence from meat Cf Vita Josephi, §§ 2, 3 There were also, among the Greeks, many Pythagoreans of the newly reviving school of this philosopher, who pursued a like course of life with regard to food. Similar to those classes of men, in respect to their mode of sustenance, are some Christians mentioned by Origen (cont Celsum, V. 48), who lived in his time So in *Canones Apostol.* (L) the like class of men is mentioned.

Still it does not seem probable that it was such ascetics that the apostle here intends to describe. Ascetics of this class in every country where they have made their appearance, have usually obtained for themselves great credit and influence, on the ground of their supposed extraordinary sanctity. As was very natural, they took to themselves great credit on this account, and looked down with pity or contempt on those, who declined to pursue the course of self-denial which they had adopted If the apostle were here addressing men of this class, he would attack their pride and vain glory, as he does very strenuously in Col ii 21—23. But instead of this, we find the ascetic party here to be the one which needs defending Whom the others look down upon with contempt or disrespect and are prone to treat with some degree of scorn or neglect on account of their weakness or superstition. It is more probable, then that the whole difficulty in question was one which arose from *Jewish* scruples about meats and drinks offered to idols, in which the Jewish Christians believed that they could not partake, except at the expense of associating themselves with the worshippers of idols and becoming polluted

This is satisfactorily confirmed by ver 5, which speaks of the distinction that these same persons made between days, out of respect to the laws of Moses and the customs of the Jews, comp Col ii 16 The Gentile part of the church would naturally feel no scruple in respect to such matters, and it would not be unnatural for them to look at first with wonder, and afterwards with disdain, on the scrupulousness of their Jewish brethren respecting such external ordinances. It is easy to see, that the peace of the church would thus become endangered. And in order to prevent this, the apostle throws his shield over his brethren in a weaker state of belief, and insists upon it that others shall deal very tenderly and affectionately with scruples of such a nature, and not condemn or despise those who entertained them. This he could insist on with the more urgency, because their scruples were of a conscientious and sober nature, and not mere whims of superstition. Accordingly the present chapter gives precepts and principles in regard to things of this nature, which must be of great value to the church of Christ, down to the end of time; and on this account, we can aver, in one sense, that we rejoice in the occasion which called forth the expression of such views and feelings on the part of Paul. The whole constitutes a rule of life in regard to weaker Christian brethren, and with regard to food, drink, manner of living, and observance of fasts and feasts of an extraordinary nature, which is a very important guide to scrupulous and tender consciences.

(1) *Him that is weak in his belief,* τὸν .... πίστει; *i. e.*, him who is not yet fully convinced or enlightened in regard to the true extent of Christian liberty. The article τῇ here may, as often, be taken as equivalent to the pronoun *his;* or it may be construed as referring to the Christian belief or persuasion. Πίστις does not here mean strictly *saving* faith, but *belief* or *persuasion* in the more general sense of the term; comp. 1 Cor. viii. 11, 12. *Receive with kindness,* προσλαμβάνεσθε, *admit to your society* or *friendship;* so the verb προσλαμβάνομαι is used in the New Testament. It means literally *to take to one's self;* and so it is applied to taking a companion, Acts xvii. 5; to receiving into one's house as a guest or a friend, Acts xviii. 26. xxviii. 2. Philem. vs. 12, 18. Hence, in a sense somewhat more general, *to receive kindly;* comp. Rom. xiv. 3. xv. 7. Calov objects here against his Lutheran brethren, for employing this text to prove that Calvinists should be treated with lenity. He says that 2 John verse 10, is the proper rule to be applied to them!

Not so as to make decisions in respect to his opinions, μὴ εἰς διακρίσεις διαλογισμῶν. Διακρίσεις literally signifies *distinctions, decisions, discriminations.* The meaning *doubts, scruples,* needs confirmation, and is unnecessary here. The word διαλογισμῶν means *thoughts, opinions, sentiments.* The main difficulty here is, to make out the verb that is implied after the μή. We may repeat προσλαμβάνεσθε, and then the sense will be: 'Do not receive him for the sake of making decisions, or so as to make decisions, of opinions or sentiments,' viz., opinions in respect to the subject mentioned in the sequel. Or we may simply supply ἔστω, and then the meaning will be: 'Let not this (viz, the reception spoken of) be such as will lead you to sit in judgment upon the opinions of those who are weak in the faith, in respect to the matter that follows.' The construction of the verse is very obscure. Another exegesis not uncommon is: 'Do not act in such a manner as will have a tendency to promote, rather than allay *scrupulous thoughts* (διακρίσεις διαλογισμῶν) about meats, days, etc.' This sense is a good one if it could be fairly made out that διακρίσεις means *scruples* or *doubts*. As the matter stands, the other sense accords best with philology.

(2) *Ὃς μὲν . . . ὁ δὲ ἀσθενῶν.* At first sight the reader may mistake these formulas for distinctive *antithetic* pronouns. But strictly ὃς μέν would require ὃς δέ with the verb instead of the participle in the antithetic part (see in ver. 5); in the same manner as the pronominal article ὁ μέν requires the antithetic correspondent to be ὁ δέ. So there is a slight *anacoluthon* here. The μέν with ὅς has simply a *discretive* power in respect to ὅς, which is sufficiently marked in our English *one*. The δέ in the next clause is adversative or antithetic as to the sentiment, and is to be translated *but*. Πάντα agrees with βρώματα understood, comp. verse 15, but βρῶμα is not confined merely to the sense of *meat;* it means *anything eatable, any food.* Φαγεῖν is the second Aorist here, as appears from the accent φάγω, though usually ranged, in the lexicons, under the root ἐσθίω.

But he who is weak eateth herbs, ὁ δὲ . . . ἐσθίει; i. e., ὁ ἀσθενῶν ἐν πίστει, comp. ver. 1, he who is scrupulous about distinction of meats, etc, refrains from meat sold in the markets lest he should eat that which is offered to idols. He prefers to live on *vegetables* (λάχανα), rather than subject himself to this danger. After ἐσθίει the word μόνον is implied.

(3) *Let not him who eateth, despise him who eateth not; nor him who eateth not, condemn him who eateth;* ὁ ἐσθίων . . . . κρινέτω. Κρίνειν, in the sense of *condemn*, is frequent in the New Testament. The sentiment is: 'He who is freed from any scruples about distinction of meats, should not exercise an uncharitable and condemning spirit towards him who entertains such scruples. The reason is subjoined:

For God has accepted him, ὁ Θεὸς . . προσελάβετο, *i. e.*, received him into his redeemed family, and admitted him to its privileges; comp. προσλαμβάνεσθε in ver. 1 — Αὐτόν in this case must be *generic*, as it includes both him who eateth, and him who eateth not.

(4) *Who art thou that condemnest the servant of another?* Σὺ τίς . . . οἰκέτην. That is, such a one as is favorably accepted of God, and is his servant and not yours, how can you claim the right of exercising severity towards him, in respect to his scruples of conscience? The pron. σύ, *thou*, is emphatic in position: *Thou* that condemnest, etc., *i. e*, who art thou, etc.

By [or to] *his own master he standeth or falleth,* τῷ ἰδίῳ . . . . πίπτει. The apostle says to those who were freed from scruples about food : 'Brethren, do not be severe in condemning those who differ from you in opinion with respect to this point. Yours is not the prerogative to judge in this case ; it is God who will acquit or condemn. Στήκω is not a *classical*, but later Greek word, from the Perfect ἕστηκα. Its meaning here is, *to stand fast* or *firm* in a secondary sense, *i. e.*, to hold good one's place at a time of trial, to remain firm and secure. So Psalm i. 5, "The ungodly shall not *stand* in judgment;" *i. e.*, shall not be able to remain firm and safe. So the opposite term (πίπτει) would also lead us to judge. *To fall*, means, in this case, *to be condemned, to be insecure, to be subjected to condemnation* or *punishment ;* exactly as we say in English, of a man on trial for crime and condemned, *he was cast at the trial, he failed*, ἔπεσε. The Dative τῷ ἰδίῳ κυρίῳ, is here the Dative of *relation ;* comp. xii. 10, seq. and New Test. Gramm 106. 1. The strict rendering *ad sensum* would be: *In relation to his own master he is subject to a sentence of condemnation or acquittal ;* for it is only his own master who can call him to an account. *And he shall be established, for God is able to establish him,* σταθήσεται . . . αὐτόν; *i. e*, he shall stand in the judgment of his conduct in reference to this matter, for God is able to acquit him, or God has the power and right of acquitting him, although you should condemn him.

(5) *One esteemeth one day more than another*, ὃς μὲν . . . ἡμέραν, *i. e*, he makes a distinction between days, regarding one as more sacred than another. Κρίνει here has a very different sense from that which it conveys in the preceding verse, and is employed in a kind of *paronomasiac* way; it means *estimates, regards, deems ;* comp. Acts xiii. 46. xvi. 15. xxvi. 8. Rom. iii. 7. 1 Cor. ii. 2. Joseph. Antiq. Jud. IV. 8, 2. κριθείητε εὐδαιμονέστατοι, *ye shall be deemed most fortunate.* Παρά, *more than, above.*

Another esteemeth every day, ὃς δὲ . . . ἡμέραν ; *i. e.,* makes no distinction between days, regards all days alike. The μέν and δέ joined with ὃς in the two clauses, serve merely the purpose of antithetic distinction as to the pronoun. *Let every one be fully persuaded in his own mind*, ἕκαστος . . . πληροφορείσθω ; *i. e.,* let each one act conscientiously in respect to this matter, according to the real persuasion or belief of his own mind.

Whether the apostle means to include the *Sabbath,* or rather the *Lord's day,* under what he says here of the special observance of particular days, has often been called in question. It is well known, that in the early ages of the church a distinction was made between *Sabbath* and *Lord's day.* The former was the Jewish weekly Sabbath, *i. e.,* the seventh day of the week. It embraced also the occasional fasts and feasts prescribed by the Mosaic law ; comp. Col. ii. 16. Gal. iv 10. Such was the Jewish use of the word שָׁבַת, σάββατον. But the early Christians, in order to distinguish this from the first day of the week, on which they held their religious assemblies of worship (1 Cor. xvi. 2. Acts xx. 7), called the first day ἡμέρα Κυρίου (*Lord's day*), Rev. i 10. Of this distinction there is clear evidence in the writings of the ecclesiastical fathers; and the passages above quoted seem to make it sufficiently evident.

There is nothing in the context which furnishes any certain clew to the meaning of ἡμέρα here. But if we may venture to compare it with Col. ii. 16 and Gal. iv. 10 (and the two passages seem manifestly to have relation to the same usages and prejudices in the church), then we may draw the conclusion pretty clearly, that ἡμέρα here relates to days which the scruples of Jewish Christians deemed sacred, and has no relation to the ἡμέρα Κυρίου which all agreed to keep holy.

(6) *He who regards the day, regards it to* [the honoring of] *the Lord; and he who regards not the day for* [the honoring of] *the Lord, he doth not regard it,* ὁ φρονῶν . . . οὐ φρονεῖ; that is, he who makes the distinction in question between days, does so because he believes that God has required it, and he keeps such days sacred in order to honor him; but he who does not make these distinctions, refrains from doing it because he thinks that duty to God requires him to refrain, inasmuch as God does not require these days to be kept holy. Ὁ μὴ φρονῶν . . . οὐ φρονεῖ is omitted in A., B., C., D., E., F., G ; 23., 57., 67. ; Æth, Copt., Vulg., Ital.; Ruf., Ambrosiast., Pel., Aug, Hieron.; and neglected by Erasmus and Mill. Still, the context seems so to require it, that it is now generally admitted. Κυρίῳ is the Dativus *commodi*.

Likewise he who eats, eats to [the honoring of] *the Lord, for he gives God thanks,* καὶ ὁ ἐσθίων . . . Θεῷ; *i. e.*, he who eats food without any scrupulous distinctions, does this with a regard to the commands of God, and is thankful to God for the blessings bestowed upon him, viz., the privilege of enjoying his food without the troublesome distinction of clean and unclean. Γάρ stands before the reason why he eats in honor of the Lord. *And he who eats not, for* [the honoring of] *the Lord he eats not, and gives God thanks,* καὶ ὁ μή ἐσθίων . . . Θεῷ. That is, he refrains from certain kinds of food, from a design to obey the commands of God; and for the light which is imparted to him (as he supposes) with respect to making such a distinction in food, he is grateful. Flatt thinks this should be turned thus: 'For the little which he does enjoy, he is thankful to God.' But then this little would be *what he eats;* whereas, he who does *not* eat, is here represented as thankful—for what? *The not eating* must be the answer; and this, in the sense above given.

(7) *For none of us lives to himself*, οὐδεὶς γάρ . . . ζῇ ; *i. e.*, none of us, who behaves himself as a Christian, can live only for his own pleasure, or to obey his own inclinations. The apostle seems here to take it for granted, that those who made distinctions between food, and those who did not, aimed to honor God by this, because they stood pledged to be entirely devoted to his service and glory — Ζῆν τινι *to live devoted to any person* or *thing*, to accommodate all our actions and desires to his wishes ; comp. Luke xx. 38. Rom. vi. 10, 11. Gal. ii. 19.—The γάρ at the beginning of the verse, introduces a general reason for what he had just affirmed. *And none of us dieth to himself,* καὶ οὐδεὶς ἑαυτῷ ἀποθνήσκει; *i. e.*, in life and death we are the Lord's, we are bound to glorify him in all that we do. That the phrase οὐδεὶς ἑαυτῷ ἀποθνήσκει means, we are the Lord's whether in life or in death, *i. e.*, in the state of the dead, viz., in the present and future world, seems clear from comparing verses 8, 9.

(8) *For whether we live, we live to the Lord, and whether we die, we die to the Lord,* ἐάν τε . . . ἀποθνήσκωμεν ; *i. e.*, whether in a state of life or death (comp. v. 9), we belong to the Lord, we are bound to glorify him The γάρ introduces a clause illustrating and confirming the preceding declaration.—The phrases ἐάν τε . . ἐάν τε show the mutual connection of both, and their relation in common to something else ; which here is τῷ κυρίῳ ζῆν or ἀποθνήσκειν respectively. The nicer shades of τέ . . . καί or (as here) τέ . . . τέ, it is impossible to imitate in our language. *Whether we live, then, or die, we are the Lord's,* ἐάν τε . . . ἐσμέν ; *i. e.*, whether we exist in the present world, or in another, viz., the world of the dead, we belong to the Lord, *i. e* , to Christ, as appears from v. 9. Christ is our Lord, both here and hereafter. And this being the case, all judgment must be committed to him.

(9) *For Christ both died and revived, for the very purpose that he might be Lord of the dead and the living,* εἰς τοῦτο γάρ . . . κυριεύῃ. There is much discrepancy of readings here. Καί before ἀπέθανε is rejected by many uncial and other MSS. and ancient versions : also by Griesbach, Lachmann, and Reiche. The word ἀνέστε, *rose*, in the *textus receptus*, in some ancient MSS., versions, and fathers, is rejected on good grounds. It seems to have come from the margin, where it was written as a gloss or explanation of ἔζησε. Ἔζησε has here the sense of *reviving, coming to life*, and not simply of living, compare Matt. ix. 18. John v. 25. xi. 25. Acts i. 3. xxv. 15, et alibi. In relation to the sentiment here expressed, viz., that Christ suffered and rose, or in other words, that he " took on him our nature, and became obedient unto death," in order that he might be Lord of all, the reader may compare Phil. ii. 5 — 11. John xvii. 4, 5. Heb. ii. 9, 10. xii. 2. *Universal dominion*

though not the principal object of Christ's death, was a fruit or consequence of it, and indeed one of the ends which the Saviour had in view, because it was necessary for the accomplishment of his benevolent purposes.—To be *Lord of the dead and of the living,* is that he should be supreme ruler over the present world and the world of spirits; for *the living* and *the dead* make up all the human race. — The supremacy of Christ, and his absolute property in all Christians, living or dead, is fully asserted and implied in vers. 6 — 9.

(10) *And thou, why dost thou condemn thy brother?* Σὺ δὲ . . . σου; Σύ is emphatic as in verse 4 above. Δὲ, *but* in this case; for the sentiment is adversative. Τί κρίνεις, why dost thou censure thy brother for his weak and scrupulous conscience? *Even thou, why dost thou despise thy brother?* Ἢ καὶ σὺ . . . σου. Καὶ σύ, emphatic. *To despise* here means *to regard with feelings of contempt* brethren who have scrupulous consciences, to look upon them as inferior.

For we must all stand before the judgment-seat of Christ, πάντες γὰρ . . . Χριστοῦ; *i. e.,* such a brother is not amenable to you in a matter of this nature; Christ the supreme judge of all is his judge. We must leave such matters to him; at the same time feeling that we are accountable for all that we do or say in respect to our Christian brethren.—Γάρ introduces a reason why we ought not to despise a Christian brother for his weak conscience, viz., the fact that he is accountable to Christ himself and not to us; as we also are accountable for our demeanor toward him.

(11) In the phrase γέγραπται γάρ, γάρ is prefixed to a clause introduced in order to confirm what immediately precedes. *As I live, saith the Lord, every knee shall bow to me, and every tongue shall confess to God,* ζῶ ἐγώ . . . . Θεῷ; *i. e.,* all shall acknowledge subjection to me, and give to me an account of their actions; or, all are accountable to God as their supreme and final judge. The passage is quoted *ad sensum* from Is. xlv. 23 (xlv. 23, 24 Sept.), where the Hebrew for ζῶ ἐγώ is בִּי נִשְׁבַּעְתִּי = חַי אָנִי, Sept. κατ' ἐμαυτοῦ ὀμνύω, *by myself do I swear.* So the apostle has translated *ad sensum,* not *ad verbum.*

12) That the doctrine of accountability to God is contained or implied in this passage from the Old Testament, Paul now proceeds to assert: *every one of us, therefore, must give an account respecting himself to God,* ἄρα οὖν . . . Θεῷ. For λόγος, in the sense here given, comp. Matt. xii. 36. Acts xix. 40. 1 Pet. iv. 5. Heb. xiii. 17. iv. 13. The apostle here reckons the appearing before the judgment-seat of Christ, as giving an account to God. So God is represented as judging the world by Christ, Acts xvii. 31. Rom. ii. 16. "Deus et Christus arctissime conjuncti sunt, ita ut quod de hoc dicitur, dicitur etiam de illo."

(13) *Let us then no longer judge one another*, μήκετι .. κρίνωμεν; *i. e.*, let us no longer, as we have done, judge and condemn those who make a distinction of meats, days, etc. Since we are all accountable to God for all that we do, let us no more thus expose ourselves to his displeasure.

But rather determine this not to put a stumbling block, or *an occasion of falling in the way of a brother*, ἀλλὰ τοῦτο ... σκάνδαλον. Κρίνατε, used by a kind of *paronomasia* here = *determine, decide*, is taken in a sense quite different from that of κρίνωμεν in the preceding clause. Κρίνατε τοῦτο means, *make* or *come to this determination;* comp. Acts xvi. 15. xx. 16. 1 Cor. vii. 37. et alibi. Τῷ ἀδελφῷ is *Dativus incommodi*, as the grammarians say: πρόσκομμα and σκάνδαλον are not materially different; both mean *an occasion* or *cause of stumbling*. Here they are to be understood, of course, in a *moral* sense ; and the use of both words seems designed merely to indicate *every kind of occasion for stumbling*.

(14) *I know and am persuaded by the Lord Jesus*, οἶδα .. Ἰησοῦ; *i. e.*, I know, and know for certainty because the Lord Jesus himself has taught me. Ἐν κυρίῳ *by the Lord*, for so ἐν may be construed before the Dative of cause or agent. Or it may be construed as designating Paul's relation *to* the Lord, *i. e., I being in the Lord, am persuaded*, etc. The last is the more analogical meaning.

That nothing is unclean of itself, ὅτι .. αὐτοῦ; *i. e*, no food or drink in its own nature, or as it is in itself, is unclean to the Christian. Δἰ αὐτοῦ, *by* or *in itself, on its own account*. For αὐτοῦ, Lachmann reads αὑτοῦ. The exchange of these words for each other in the New Test., is very frequent, owing often to the negligence of collators as to making the requisite distinction. *But to him who deemeth anything to be unclean, it is unclean*, εἰ μὴ ... κοινόν; *i. e.*, if a man believes any species of food or drink to be unlawful, and then partakes of it, he defiles himself, because he does that which he believes to be sinful.

(15) *Now if thy brother is grieved because of meat*, εἰ δὲ .... λυπεῖται. Δέ continuative, *now;* but it is a well authorized reading. — Διὰ βρῶμα, because thou eatest meat which he regards as unclean. *Thou walkest no longer according to what benevolence requires*, οὐκέτι ... περιπατεῖς; *i.e.*, thou dost violate the law of love, which would require thee to do unto others that which thou wouldest that others should do unto thee. But this thou dost not, when thou demeanest thyself in this manner.

Destroy not him by thy meat, for whom Christ died, μὴ .... ἀπέθανε. That ἀπόλλυε means *destroy*, seems plain from comparing 1 Cor. viii. 11 and verse 20 below. The word ἀπόλλυμι was sometimes employed by the Greeks in the sense of *cruciare, to torment, vex*; a sense which is possible here, but not probable. The meaning seems to be: 'Do not furnish an occasion of stumbling to thy brother, lest he fall and come into condemnation.'— Ὑπὲρ οὗ Χριστὸς ἀπέθανε seems to be added in order to show how very differently Christ himself acted and felt, with respect to Christians who are weak in faith; and thus to paint, in glowing colors, the criminality of those who refused to imitate his spirit.

(16) *Let not your good, then, be evil spoken of,* μὴ ... ἀγαθόν. Οὖν, *therefore, then, i. e.,* since such is the case, viz., that Christ died for sinners, and that you are under obligation to show the spirit of similar benevolence, toward your fellow Christians, you ought to demean yourselves in such a way, as that you will give no occasion for the religious liberty which you enjoy to be evil spoken of. That ἀγαθόν here means freedom from the yoke of bondage which the ceremonial law imposed, I cannot well doubt; and so Origen, Theodoret, Bengel, Clarius, and others, understood it. But Chrysostom, Theophylact, Erasmus, and others, less appropriately understood by ἀγαθόν, the Christian religion in general.

(17) *For the kingdom of God is not meat and drink, but righteousness, and peace, and joy in the Holy Ghost,* οὐ γὰρ ... ἁγίῳ. The γάρ here introduces a reason why Christians should not suffer their good to be evil spoken of. Ἡ βασιλεία τοῦ Θεοῦ here means, the *spiritual kingdom* of God or Christ; his reign within; his moral dominion over the hearts of men: in a word, true *Christianity*. This does not consist in refraining or not refraining from this or that food or drink; but in holy conformity to God, peaceful and gentle demeanor, and joy such as is imparted by the influences of the Holy Spirit. A truly admirable description of the nature of real Christianity! Εἰρήνη here means *peace*, in opposition to discord and contention among brethren.—Ἐν πνεύματι ἁγίῳ may be applied, as a qualification, to δικαιοσύνη and εἰρήνη as well as to χαρά; but I prefer the construction above given.

(18) *For he who serveth Christ in respect to these things, is acceptable to God, and approved by men,* ὁ γὰρ ... ἀνθρώποις. The γάρ here introduces a reason why peace and joy follow the practice of pure Christian principles. Ἐν τούτοις means the things before mentioned, in regard to meats and drinks and feast days, etc. Δόκιμος, *acceptus, gratus*; the apostle means, that men will speak well of such a demeanor as he had commended.

(19) *Therefore let us strive after peace and mutual edification,* ἄρα οὖν ... ἀλλήλους. Τὰ τῆς εἰρήνης ... τὰ τῆς οἰκοδομῆς, are, according to a very common usage of the Greek, a periphrasis for τὰ εἰρηνικά, etc., or for the simple εἰρήνη, οἰκοδομή.—Τῆς εἰς ἀλλήλους, i. e., τῆς οἰκοδομῆς εἰς ἀλλήλους. For the use of the article

before the adjectives see New Test. Gramm. § 92. 1. The object of this verse is, to charge the church at Rome to demean themselves in such a way, with regard to the matters in dispute which he had touched upon, as would promote the peace of the church and the edification of both parties.

(20) *Destroy not the work of God on account of food*, μὴ . . . Θεοῦ. Τὸ ἔργον τοῦ Θεοῦ may = οἰκοδομὴν Θεοῦ in 1 Cor. iii. 9, and οἰκοδομή . . . ἐν κυρίῳ, in Eph. ii. 21, and οἰκοδομὴν ἑαυτοῦ in Eph. iv. 16; *i. e.*, it may designate Christians, or a Christian. But possibly the writer may refer here to the internal work of *faith*, which is called ἔργον Θεοῦ in John vi. 29. Cf. 1 Cor. iii. 9. 1 Pet. ii. 5. That the renewal and sanctification of the heart is the special reason why Christians are called *God's building*, etc., is plain; but I see no reason why the sense here of ἔργον Θεοῦ may not be *concrete*, *i. e.*, taken as including the *persons* in whom such a work is carried on.— Κατάλυε is a verb accommodated to the figurative expression ἔργον Θεοῦ, and means *to pull down*, *to destroy*. The meaning is: 'Do not so demean thyself, in respect to this dispute about meats clean and unclean, as to cause thy weak brother to sin and to fall into condemnation.'

All [meats] *are clean*, πάντα μὲν καθαρά; *i. e.*, no distinction of food is to be made under the Christian dispensation. All distinctions of this nature made by the Levitical law are abolished. That πάντα agrees with βρώματα implied, is clear from ἕνεκα βρώματος of the preceding verse. Μέν in the protasis here has, as often, ἀλλά in the apodosis for its corresponding particle. *They are hurtful to the man who eats so as to occasion stumbling thereby*, ἀλλά . . . ἐσθίοντι. Ἀλλά, here concedes what is said in the preceding clause, but introduces a clause which limits or makes exception to this general principle. Διά, before a noun in the Genitive, often designates the manner in which a thing happens or is done; so, e. g., in Luke viii. 4, διά παραβολῆς, i. q., παραβολικῶς; Acts xv. 27. διὰ λόγου, *orally*; 2 Cor. x. 11, δι' ἐπιστολῶν, *in the way of writing*; Heb. xiii. 22, διὰ βραχέων, *briefly*, etc. Here the context seems to indicate that διὰ προσκόμματος designates *the giving of offence*, not *the taking of offence*; inasmuch as the apostle is plainly addressing those who were not weak in the faith, but believed that all meats were clean. Is κακόν here subject, or predicate? The most facile construction seems to be, to repeat βρῶμα mentally from the preceding part of the verse, and to arrange the sentence thus: ἀλλὰ κακόν [ἐστι βρῶμα] τῷ ἀνθρώπῳ κ. τ. λ. Or πᾶν may be understood as the subject of the sentence; or κακόν may be rendered as a noun = *bad* or *evil thing*, for so καλόν appears to be constructed in the next verse. The meaning of κακόν in this case is *spiritual*, not physical. The apostle means to say, that it is a *sin* when any one eats so as to give offence. The participle τῷ ἐσθίοντι seems to be equivalent to the Inf. mode ἐσθίειν; and it may be rendered here as expressing conditionality, *i. e.*, *if* or *provided that he eat*, etc. See N. Test. Gram. § 140. 8.

(21) *It is good not to eat fl sh, nor drink wine, nor* [to do anything] *whereby thy brother stumbleth*, or *has ground of offence*, or *is made weak*, καλὸν .. ἀσθενεῖ. Μηδὲ ἐν ᾧ is elliptical; the full expression would be, μηδὲ φαγεῖν ἢ πιεῖν τι ἐν ᾧ κ. τ. λ. The words ἢ σκανδαλίζεται ἢ ἀσθενεῖ, are omitted in Codd. A. C. 67, and in Syr. Arab. Copt. versions; also in Orig., Ruf., and Augustine. Mill and Koppe hold them to be a gloss or repetition of προσκόπτει; but Reiche contends against this. The sense of ἀσθενεῖ is *to render incompetent*, viz., incompetent to walk safely or securely.

(22) *Hast thou faith? keep it to thyself before God;* Σὺ ... Θεοῦ, *i. e.*, hast thou a belief that there is no difference in meats (which is truly the case), yet deem it sufficient, in respect to this point, to regulate by it thy conduct in private as seen only by the eye of God. Do not act this out in public, when you may give needless and injurious offence. The meaning of πίστιν see in ver. 1 of the present chapter. *Happy* [is he], *who does not condemn himself in respect to the thing which he allows*, μακάριος ... δοκιμάζει, *i. e.*, we may congratulate that man, who does not so use his Christian liberty in respect to food, as to bring on himself condemnation or blame by an abuse of it, or by making use of it in an imprudent and inconsiderate manner. Ἐν ᾧ in this case is an example of attraction which is of an elliptical nature. It stands for ἐν τούτῳ ὅ; which would complete the grammatical construction. See N. Test. Gram. § 113. Note 2.

(23) *But he who doubts is condemned if he eat, because it is not of faith*, ὁ δὲ ...... πίστεως; *i. e.*, he who doubts whether it is lawful for him to eat a particular kind of food, and yet eats it, is worthy of condemnation; because he does this against, or at least without the approval of his conscience. *And everything that is not of faith is sinful;* πᾶν δὲ .... ἐστί, *i. e.*, not only the eating, but the doing anything else against one's conscience or without an approving conscience, is deserving of condemnation. No man should indulge in any demeanor or conduct, the lawfulness of which he doubts. A truly excellent maxim in Christian morals, and one which, if duly heeded by Christians, would prevent many a bitter hour of darkness and contrition.

CHAP. XV. 1—33.

In the present chapter, Paul continues to exhort the Church at Rome to strive after unity and peace. He sets before them the self-denial of Christ, vers 3, 4. He beseeches God to give them the spirit of Christian unity and love, vers 5, 6. He exhorts them to a mutual kind reception of each other, ver 7. He shows that the reception of Gentiles into the Christian church, had been clearly and often predicted, vers 8—12, and prays God to fill them all with joy and peace, ver 13. He apologizes, as it were, for writing to the Church at Rome, by describing the nature of his office as an apostle to the Gentiles, the labors which he had performed while holding this office, and the affectionate desire which he had cherished of paying the church at Rome a visit, vers 14—24. He describes to them the plan of his future journeys and labors, expresses his hope of yet visiting them, and begs an affectionate interest in their prayers to God for him, vers 25—32. He then concludes with a benediction, ver 33.

(1) *We, however, who are strong, ought to bear with the infirmities of the weak*, ὀφείλομεν δὲ . . . . βαστάζειν. Δέ must, on the whole, be considered as *adversative* here. The course of thought seems to be thus: "He who eats in a state of doubt, commits a sin against his own conscience; *but* we, who have more enlightened views, ought to bear with his scruples, and not to demean ourselves so as to increase them." Δύνατοι, *the strong in faith*, *i. e*, those who had no scruples about meats and drinks, etc. — Ἀδυνάτων, those who were not δύνατοι, *i. e.*, who had scruples, etc. Βαστάζειν *to bear with, to endure patiently, to tolerate*; comp. Gal. vi. 2. Rev. ii. 2. *And not to please ourselves*, καὶ μὴ ἑαυτοῖς ἀρέσκειν, *i. e.*, not to act merely in such a way as would gratify our own views and inclinations. See the example of Paul, in 1 Cor. ix. 22.

(2) *Let each one of us please his neighbor in respect to that which is good unto* [his] *edification*, ἕκαστος . . . . οἰκοδομήν, *i. e.*, let us act in such a manner as to please our neighbor, so far as we may do so and do what is good ; let us act so as to edify him.

(3) *For Christ did not please himself*, καὶ γὰρ . . . . ἤρεσεν, *i. e.*, Christ did not have respect merely to his own pleasure or pain, convenience or inconvenience; but did that which was grateful and useful to others, although he exposed himself to great suffering in consequence of acting thus. Γάρ stands prefixed here to a reason why we ought to seek the good of others. *But as it is written, the reproaches of those who reproached thee have fallen upon me*, ἀλλὰ . . . ἐπ' ἐμέ. The passage is quoted from Ps. lxix. 10 (lxix. 9). The general sentiment is here accommodated to a particular case; *i. e.*, the same thing which this sentiment declares, was in fact exemplified in the treatment which Christ received; he suffered reproaches rather than desist from his beneficence towards others.

(4) *For whatsoever things were written in ancient times, were written for our instruction*, ὅσα γὰρ . . . προεγράφη. The connec-

tion of this verse with the preceding is somewhat difficult. The γάρ here gives a reason for an implied sentiment, viz., "This Scripture is appropriate, *for*, etc." Προεγράφη, lit. *were written before, i. e.*, in former days, in ancient times.

That through patience and the admonition of the Scriptures, we might obtain hope, ἵνα . . . ἔχωμεν. Ὑπομενῆς refers to a patient endurance of the troubles and sorrows, to which the doing of good may expose us; or to patient tolerance of the ignorance and prejudice of others. Some refer it to patient continuance in belief. But this is not so apposite:—παρακλήσεως seems here to mean *admonition* or *exhortation*; for it refers back to διδασκαλίαν, and if rendered *consolation* does not seem to be directly congruous with that word. The reference is to the exhortation virtually contained in the Scripture quoted, to persevere meekly and patiently in doing good. Patience of this nature will produce *hope*; comp. Rom. v. 3—5. He who perseveres in thus doing good, amid the evils which may come upon him, will be rewarded with "a hope that maketh not ashamed."

(5) *Now may the God of patience and admonition give mutual unity of sentiment to you, according to Christ Jesus,* ὁ δὲ Θεὸς . . . Ἰησοῦν. Ὁ Θεὸς τῆς ὑπομονῆς means God, who bestows patience, or, is the author of patience; just as *the God of grace,* is the God who bestows grace. So ὁ Θεὸς τῆς παρακλήσεως means, either God, who is the author of consolation, or, better, who is the author of exhortation or encouragement [viz. to persevere], excites or exhorts to acts of self-denial, to do those things which make for peace and for mutual Christian edification, although they may cost self-denial and mortification; which accords with the context above.—Δῴη is a later form of Opt. 2 Aor. for δοίη; see also 2 Tim. i. 16, 18. ii. 7, et al.

Κατὰ Χριστὸν Ἰησοῦν means, in accordance with the Spirit of Christ, or agreeably to what Christ or the Christian religion requires. The earnest supplication of the apostle, that the Romans may be led τὸ αὐτὸ φρονεῖν ἐν ἀλλήλοις, shows how mistaken those are who think that practical unity of sentiment among Christians is not desirable, even as to matters not essential to salvation; for surely the sentiment about distinction of meats was not essential in this sense. If now such unity in smaller matters was urged by the apostle, then of course he would urge it far more in things essential to salvation. The precepts of the apostle show, also, that Christians may differ about externals, and things of minor importance, without hazarding their salvation; although not without endangering in some degree the peace and welfare of the Church. Such is the imperfection of human nature, that difference of opinion is apt to produce dispute; and dispute of course is apt to lead, more or less, to alienation of feeling.

(6) *That with one accord and with one voice you may glorify God, even the Father of our Lord Jesus Christ,* ἵνα . . . Χριστοῦ. Ὁμοθυμαδόν, from ὁμός *conjunctus*, and θύμος *animus*, characterizes the union of mind or sentiment, which the apostle desires should pervade the Christian church. Ἐν ἑνὶ στόματι characterizes the harmony of the voices, in the song of praise which was to be sung by the church; *i. e.*, they should not sing *discordant* but *harmonious* notes. The meaning is not literal here, but figurative, viz., that with union in their praise to God they might offer him thanksgiving, that they might all accord in the same feeling and same worship. In καὶ πατέρα, καὶ, *even,* is, *explicative;* a very common use in the New Testament; comp. 1 Pet. i. 3. 2 Pet. i. 11. ii. 20. Phil. iv. 20. Eph i. 3. Col. iii. 17. In such cases, where καί *explicative* is followed by a noun in apposition with the preceding noun and limiting or defining it, the article is usually *omitted* before the second noun, as here before πατέρα; compare also, the examples cited above.

(7) *Therefore show kindness to each other, as Christ also hath showed kindness to you, unto the glory of God,* διὸ . . . . Θεοῦ, *i. e.*, in view of all that has been said, I beseech you to treat each other with brotherly kindness and affection, such as Christ has shown to you, in order that God may be glorified. Διό refers to all which had been before said of Christian kindness and forbearance. As to προσλαμβάνεσθε, comp. xiv. 3. Ὑμᾶς in the *textus receptus* is ἡμᾶς. This latter is removed, because the MSS. A. C. D. E. F. G., many Codd. minusc., and several versions and fathers, read ὑμᾶς.—Εἰς δόξαν Θεοῦ Tholuck interprets of *eternal happiness, i. e.,* the glory which God bestows. The phrase is capable of this meaning, comp. Heb. ii. 10. Rom. v. 2. 1 Pet. v. 4; but vers. 8, 9, require a different sense here, viz., since Christ hath kindly received you, in order that God may be glorified.

(8) Λέγω δέ κ. τ. λ. Δέ, as often, is added to a phrase or sentence, inserted for the sake of more full and entire explanation. The design, however, is not directly indicated by δέ, but by the nature of the case. The writer having asserted that Christ has kindly received us in order that God may be glorified, goes on now to add some things which serve to show, that Christ entered upon the duties of his mediatorial office in order to propagate the truth, and to bring Jew and Gentile nations to glorify God.

Jesus Christ was a minister of the circumcision, on account of the truth of God, Ἰησοῦν Χριστὸν . . . . Θεοῦ; *i. e*, that Jesus Christ was a minister of the Jews, that he served the cause of divine truth among the Jews, in order to promote its true interests. Ὑπέρ, *on account of, for the sake of. In order to confirm the promises made to the fathers*, εἰς τὸ . . . πατέρων, *i. e*, in order to carry into execution the promises made to the ancient fathers, viz., of spiritual blessing to be bestowed on their children.

(9) [I say] *also, that the Gentiles are to glorify God for his mercy* [in Christ], τὰ δὲ . . . Θεόν; *i. e*, the Gentiles as well as the Jews, are to be brought into the church, that God may be all and in all, and thus be glorified by all men. Δέ, i. e., λέγω δέ as above, *I add further*. — Δοξάσαι is constructed with λέγω implied, as the version shows. The present phrase discloses the meaning of εἰς δόξαν Θεοῦ in ver. 7. *On this account will I praise thee among the Gentiles, yea, to thy name will I sing praise*, διὰ τοῦτο . . . . ψαλῶ. The design of this quotation from Ps. xviii. 49, is to show, that the Gentiles as well as the people of Israel, would have the blessings of the gospel proffered to them, and be brought to glorify God. — Ἐξομολογήσομαι, *I will praise thee*, אוֹדְךָ. — Τῷ ὀνόματί σου, *to thy name, i. e.*, to thee, לְשִׁמְךָ.

(10) Καὶ πάλιν λέγει; viz., *rejoice ye Gentiles with his people*, in Deut. xxxii. 43. Εὐφράνθητε . . . . αὐτοῦ; Hebrew הַרְנִינוּ גוֹיִם עַמּוֹ. The design of the quotation is, to show that the Gentiles are spoken of in the Old Testament Scriptures, as destined to be brought into the church of God, or as being made to praise him.

(11) Καὶ πάλιν, viz., in Ps. cxvii. 1 (Sept. 116. 1). The sentiment is the same as before. The object in accumulating quotations, is additional confirmation of what the writer had advanced.

(12) Καὶ λέγει, viz., in Is. xi. 10. In the quotation the apostle omits בַּיּוֹם הַהוּא, *in that day*. Also, instead of the Hebrew אֲשֶׁר עֹמֵד לְנֵס עַמִּים *who shall stand as a banner of the nations* or *Gentiles*, the apostle has (with the Septuagint) καὶ ὁ ἀνιστάμενος ἄρχειν ἐθνῶν, *one shall arise to be a leader of the Gentiles; ad sensum*, but not *ad literam*, as the Hebrew vowels now are. But probably the apostle read עֹמֵד, and then his version is literal. For ἐλπιοῦσι, the Hebrew has יִדְרֹשׁוּ. The whole quotation, therefore, is *ad sensum* only. It is added to the others for the same purpose as before, viz., with the design of showing that the Gentiles should belong to the Christian church, so that God may be glorified by them. Thus far in confirmation of the latter clause of ver. 7. The apostle now quits this subject, and resumes his supplications in behalf of the church at Rome, which were interrupted by ver. 7, seq.

(13) *Now may the God of hope fill you with all joy and peace in believing*, ὁ δὲ Θεὸς . . . πιστεύειν; *i. e.*, may that God who is the author of all Christian hope (comp. ἐλπιοῦσιν in ver. 12), make your joy and peace, which result from faith in Christ,

greatly to abound. *So that ye may abound in hope through the power of the Holy Spirit*, εἰς τὸ ... ἁγίου, *i. e.*, so that having much joy and peace in believing, you may also have a lively Christian hope of future glory, through the influence of the Holy Spirit who dwells in you, and who gives the earnest of future glory, comp. Eph. i. 13, 14. Rom. viii. 23. with the notes upon it.

(14) Πέπεισμαι δέ; δέ "orationi continuandæ inservit," as in ver. 13 above, and often. Καὶ αὐτὸς ἐγώ, *even I myself*. Καί added to pronouns in this way, serves to make the expression more distinct and intense. Here it is as much as to say, 'Even I who have thus warned and cautioned you, am persuaded, etc.' *In respect to you*, περὶ ὑμῶν; *that you yourselves*, (καὶ αὐτοί) *are filled with kindness*, ὅτι ... ἀγαθωσύνης. Ἀγαθωσύνης I take here to refer to the kind feelings which the apostle hoped and believed the Roman Christians would cherish towards each other.

Abounding in all knowledge, and able to give mutual admonition, πεπληρωμένοι ... νουθετεῖν. The meaning is: "I am persuaded that ye possess in abundance, such a knowledge of Christian truths and principles, that ye will be able to give such advice and warning as you may mutually need."

(15) *I have written in part the more boldly to you, brethren, as one repeating admonition*, τολμηρότερον ... ὑμᾶς, *i. e*, I have written with more freedom than might have been expected from a stranger, when reminding you of the various things which I have urged upon you. Ἀπὸ μέρους means *in some parts of his epistle*, *i. e.*, as to some things. It seems to qualify ἔγραψα — Ἐπαναμιμνῄσκων, adding to or repeating admonition, or something in the way of reminiscence.

On account of the favor which was bestowed upon me by God, διὰ τὴν χάριν .... Θεοῦ; namely the honor of the apostolic office (comp. Rom. i. 5), which the sequel shows to be the meaning of χάριν here.

(16) *That I should be a minister of Jesus Christ to the Gentiles*, εἰς τὸ εἶναι .... ἔθνη. Because his office led him to preach the gospel to the Gentiles, and to exercise a spiritual watch over them, he had ventured to address the church at Rome with freedom.

Performing the office of a priest [in respect to] *the gospel of God*, ἱερουργοῦντα .... Θεοῦ, *i. e.*, acting a part in respect to the concerns of Christians not unlike that of a priest among the Jews. *That the offering of the Gentiles might be acceptable, being purified by the Holy Spirit*, ἵνα γένηται ... ἁγίῳ, *i. e.*, that the Gentiles may be offered to God, whom as their λειτουργὸς I present, inasmuch as they have been rendered clean, pure, by the sanctifying influence of the Holy Spirit on their hearts.

(17) *I have then cause for glorying through Jesus Christ as to those things which pertain to God*, ἔχω οὖν ... Θεόν, *i. e.*, being a minister of Jesus Christ to the Gentiles, I have cause for rejoicing, that he has strengthened me and given me success among them, in things pertaining to religion. Οὖν, *then, i. e.*, since God has bestowed such an office upon me. — Ἐν Χριστῷ Ἰησοῦ may mean *through the aid of Christ*. Paul had just averred that he was λειτουργὸς Ἰησοῦ Χριστοῦ; and as such he may be understood as here intimating that Christ had afforded him aid, so as to ensure him success in his employment. Ἐν often has the meaning of *by* or *through*, in the sense of *ope, auxilio alicujus, e. g.* "He casts out demons ἐν τῷ ἄρχοντι, *by the aid of* the prince of demons," Matt. ix. 34. In like manner, ἐν is used in John xvii. 10. Acts iv. 9. xv. 7. xvii. 28, 31, et sæpe alibi. But ἐν Χ. Ἰησοῦ may also mean, "I being in Christ Jesus, viz. as before described, have cause for glorying, etc."

(18) *For I will not presume to mention anything which Christ hath not wrought by me*, οὐ γὰρ ... ἐμοῦ, *i. e.*, I do not, in saying this, intend to claim any praise by exaggerating my success, or taking to myself credit for what I have not done or for what Christ has not done by me, *in order to bring the Gentiles to obey* the gospel, εἰς ὑπακοὴν ἐθνῶν. — Λόγῳ καὶ ἔργῳ means *by preaching and by other personal effort*. Γὰρ *explicantis*. The connection seems to be thus: I speak of the glorying in Christ which I may truly have; *for* I will not presume to appropriate to myself any praise for what I have not done, or rather, for what Christ has not done by me.

(19) *By the influence of signs and wonders*, ἐν δυνάμει ... τεράτων. In Hebrew, אתות ומופתים (usually conjoined) means *wonders, signs*, or *miracles* adapted to persuade or enforce belief in the power, providence, veracity, etc., of God. The union σήμεια καὶ τέρατα in the New Testament, is an imitation of this idiom. It may be rendered as a Hendiadys, and the latter noun made an adjective to qualify the former, agreeably to an idiom common both in the Old and New Testament. If rendered *signs and wonders*, then σημείων means *miraculous proofs* adapted to impress the mind with conviction, and τέρατα means *wonderful events* or *occurrences*, adapted to fill the mind with awe. Both together constitute a very strong designation of supernatural interposition and impressive evidence arising from it.

By the influence of the Holy Spirit, ἐν δυνάμει ..... ἁγίου, may be considered a subordinate clause referring to the signs and wonders performed by virtue of this influence; and so Chrysostom, Theodoret, Erasmus, and others have understood it. But it may better be taken as *coordinate* with δυνάμει σημείων καὶ τεράτων, meaning *the internal influences of the Spirit*, e. g., the gift of prophecy, the power of speaking in foreign languages, etc., and so Beza, Grotius, Tholuck, and others have explained it.

So that from Jerusalem and around, even to Illyricum, I have fully declared the gospel of Christ, ὥστε με . . . Χριστοῦ. Ὥστε με . . . . πεπληρωκέναι is the usual construction of the Infinitive with ὥστε. Πεπληρωκέναι many interpret as having here the sense of *diffusing, spreading abroad;* derived from the more common sense of *filling up*, because in order to *fill up*, a *diffusion* into all parts is necessary. In Acts v. 28, the verb is followed by a noun which designates *place*, and therefore retains the usual meaning. But a real parallel may be found in Col. i. 25, πληροῦν τὸν λόγον ; where the meaning seems to be *fully to declare, i. e.*, to accomplish or complete the declaration of the divine doctrine. The passages quoted by Reiche, from 3 K. i. 14 (Sept.) and 1 Macc. iv. 19, are inapposite; the first having another sense, and the latter depending on a contested reading. Paul gives to the phrase a meaning peculiar to himself; elsewhere it means to *fulfil*, in the sense of fulfilling a prophetic declaration, etc. Illyricum corresponds with the modern Croatia and Dalmatia; and was the extreme boundary of what might be called the Grecian population. The circle of Paul's preaching, then, as here described, reaches from the extreme north-west of the land of the Greeks, to Jerusalem and round about, *i. e.*, it comprehends all Greece in the widest sense of this term, Asia Minor, the Grecian islands, the country between Asia Minor and Jerusalem, and the region *around* Jerusalem, *i. e.*, Phenicia, Syria, and part of Arabia. Comp. Acts ix. 20. Gal. i. 16, 17.

(20) *And was strongly desirous to preach the gospel, not where Christ was named lest I should build on another's foundation*, οὕτω . . . οἰκοδομῶ. Φιλοτιμούμενον is to be constructed with μέ, taken from the preceding verse. The word literally signifies *to covet* or *desire as an honor, to regard as honorable*, hence the secondary sense, *to desire strongly, earnestly to wish for* or *to covet* Οὕτω must be regarded as qualifying εὐαγγελίζεσθαι. Its present position seems to be for the sake of emphasis. Its correspondent is καθώς in the next verse. I have endeavored to represent all this in the version and its punctuation ; but it is difficult to do it in a satisfactory manner. As οὕτω refers to the *manner* of preaching, so the apostle describes the first negatively, by οὐκ ὅπου, κ. τ. λ., then affirmatively by ἀλλὰ καθώς, κ. τ. λ.

(21) *But, as it is written : They shall see to whom no declaration was made respecting him, and they who have not heard shall understand*, ἀλλὰ . . . συνήσουσι. The quotation is from Is. lii.

15; a passage which seems to have respect to the Messiah's being made known to the heathen. The apostle quotes it here in order to illustrate and to justify the principle which he had avowed, viz., that of preaching the gospel where it was entirely unknown before. The quotation says as much as to declare, that the gospel shall be thus proclaimed. Ὄψονται and συνήσουσι are to be understood as designating *mental* vision and perception; for this is what the writer intends to designate.

(22) *Wherefore I was greatly hindered from coming to you*, διὸ καὶ . . . ὑμᾶς. Διό, *i. e.*, on account of his many and urgent calls to preach elsewhere. Καί is joined with ἐνεκοπτόμην τὰ πολλά as an *intensive*, *i. e.*, "sensum intendit, *augmentat*." The apostle does not simply say, that *he was often hindered* or *much hindered* ἐκοπτόμην τὰ πολλά, but καὶ ἐκοπτόμην τὰ πολλά, *I was altogether hindered*, i. e., I had such frequent and urgent calls elsewhere, that it was impossible for me to visit Rome as I desired to do.

(23) *But now, having no longer any place in these regions, and being desirous for many years to pay you a visit*, νυνὶ δὲ . . . ἐτῶν. Τόπον ἔχων, *i. e.*, having no longer any considerable place, where I have not proclaimed the gospel.

(24) *Whenever I may go into Spain, I hope, as I pass on, to see you*, ὡς ἐὰν . . . ὑμᾶς; *i. e.*, intending to visit Spain, he meant to take Rome in his way. Ἐάν appears here (as often in the New Test, Sept. and Apocr.), to stand for ἄν. Its use in such a way seems to belong to the later Greek. See Winer N. T. Gramm. p. 257. ed. 3. Here it qualifies the particle of time, ὡς. The Subj. mood which follows is designed to designate a *possible* or *probable* action. Had the Indic. been used (as D. E. F. G. exhibit it), then the meaning would be, that the apostle certainly expected, or was resolved to go. In the *textus receptus*, ἐλεύσομαι πρὸς ὑμᾶς follows Σπανίαν; which Griesbach and Knapp have rejected, as they are not found in Codd. A. C. D. E. F. G., nor in the Syriac, Arabic or Coptic versions, etc. Whether the apostle in fact, ever made a journey to Spain, is not certain. The tradition of the church affirms this; but not on sure grounds. In case we allow that he was imprisoned a second time at Rome, such a journey is not improbable.

And to be sent on my way thither by you, καὶ . . . ἐκεῖ. The apostle here refers to the usual custom of the churches, when the messengers of the gospel departed from them, of sending their elders, etc., to accompany them for some distance on their journey; comp. Acts xv. 3. xvii. 14, 15. xx. 38. xxi. 5. *When I am in part first satisfied with your company*, ἐὰν . . . ἐμπλησθῶ. Observe the delicacy of the expression. The apostle does not say ἐμπλησθῶ, *satisfied*, but ἀπὸ μέρους ἐμπλησθῶ, *partly satisfied*, as though he never could enjoy their society sufficiently to gratify all his desires.

(25) *But now I go to Jerusalem to supply the wants of the saints,* νυνὶ δέ . . . ἁγίοις. Διακονέω is often used in the New Testament, to designate the supplying with food and other comforts of life. 'At present,' says the apostle, 'I cannot visit you, as duty calls me in another direction.'

(26) *For it has seemed good to Macedonia and Achaia, to make some contribution for indigent Christians at Jerusalem,* εὐδόκησαν γὰρ . . . . Ἱερουσαλήμ. Κοινωνίαν, *contribution, collatio beneficiorum.* Comp. 1 Cor. xvi. 1—4. 2 Cor. viii. ix. Acts xxiv. 17.

(27) [I say] *it has seemed good, for they are truly their debtors,* εὐδόκησαν γὰρ . . . εἰσι. Γὰρ καὶ ὀφειλέται αὐτῶν εἰσι, assigns a reason why it seemed good. Καί is here an *intensive, truly, really.* Dr. Knapp, has pointed this verse so as to disturb the sense. The comma should not be after γάρ, but after εὐδόκησαν.

Γάρ assigns a reason why they are debtors. *If the Gentiles have shared in their spiritual things, they ought surely to aid them in temporal things.* Καί intensive, in καὶ ἐν τοῖς σαρκικοῖς.

(28) *Now when this duty shall have been discharged, and this fruit made sure to them, I shall pass through the midst of you into Spain,* τοῦτο . . . Σπανίαν. Καρπόν here means the *fruit* of the contribution in Macedonia and Achaia, the fruit which their benevolence had produced. Σφραγισάμενος, applied to an instrument in writing, means *to authenticate it, to make it valid,* i. e., sure to answer the purpose for which it was intended. So here, the apostle would not stop short in the performance of the duty with which he is entrusted as the almoner of the churches, until he had seen the actual distribution of their charity among the indigent saints at Jerusalem; a fidelity and an activity well worthy of all imitation.

(29) *I know, also, that when I come to you I shall come with the full blessing of the gospel of Christ,* οἶδα δὲ . . . ἐλεύσομαι. *With an abundant blessing,* ἐν κληρώματι εὐλογίας ; where the first of the two nouns constitutes the adjective ; comp. Heb. Gramm. § 440. *b.*

(30) *Moreover I beseech you, brethren, by the Lord Jesus Christ,* παρακαλῶ δὲ . . . Χριστοῦ. Δέ continuative. — Διὰ Ἰησοῦ Χριστοῦ, *for the sake of the Lord Jesus Christ,* i. e., out of love and regard for him. *And by the love of the Spirit,* καὶ διὰ . . πνεύματος ; i. e., by the affectionate Christian sympathy for the friends of Christ, which the Spirit has given you. *That ye strive together for me, in your prayers to God in my behalf,* συναγωνίσασθαι . . . θεόν; i. e., that you unite with me in my Christian warfare, helping me by your earnest supplications to God in my behalf.

(31) *That I may be delivered from unbelievers in Judea,* ἵνα . . . Ἰουδαίᾳ; *i. e.,* pray that I may be delivered from the enemies of the gospel in Judea, whither I am going: for I have reason to expect persecution and injury from them.

And that my service which is for Jerusalem may be acceptable to the saints, καὶ ἵνα . . . ἁγίοις. Διακονία means his service in carrying and distributing the contributions of the Greek churches. It seems rather singular, at first, that he should doubt whether such a charity would be agreeable to indigent churches at Jerusalem. But when we call to mind the violent prejudices of the Jewish Christians, who were zealots for the law of Moses, we may well suppose that some of them would hesitate to come under obligations to Paul, the great champion of opposite opinions, and also to the charity of *Gentile* Christians, who disregarded the laws of Moses with respect to ceremonial observances.

(32) *So that I may come to you with joy, if God will, and may be refreshed among you,* ἵνα ἐν . . . ὑμῖν. Ἵνα is here connected in sense with the ἵνα ῥυσθῶ, κ. τ. λ., of the preceding verse. The sense is, 'that being delivered, etc., he may come with joy to them, etc. — Διὰ θελήματος Θεοῦ, *Deo volente.*

(33) *Now the God of peace be with you all,* ὁ δὲ Θεὸς . . ὑμῶν ; *i. e.,* may God, the author of peace, who bestows happiness, true prosperity, שלום be with you, *i. e.,* aid you, and bless you. Ἀμήν in the *textus receptus,* is of suspicious authority, and is so noted by Dr. Knapp.

CHAP. XVI.

THE apostle concludes his epistle by various affectionate greetings and commendations. 1 — 16. After which he warns the church against those who make divisions and give offence among them. ϝ e , such as practise the contrary of that which he had been enjoining in the preceding part of his epistle, vers. 17, 18. He expresses his affectionate desire that they might be kind and simple-hearted, and his wish that the God of peace would give them the victory over the adversary of souls, the fomenter of discord among brethren, vers. 19, 20. He then expresses the salutations of several Christian friends and companions, who were with him, vers. 21—24, and concludes with a devout doxology, vers 25 — 27.

(1) *Now I commend to you Phebe our sister who is a deaconess of the church at Cenchrea,* συνίστημι δὲ . . . Κεγχρεαῖς. Δέ continuative. — Διάκονον, i. e., τὴν διάκονον, for the Greeks used both ὁ et ἡ διάκονος. It should be remembered, that in the East women were not permitted to mix in the society of men, as in the western world they are at present. They were kept secluded, for the most part, in a retired room or γυνάκειον, to which no stranger could have access. Consequently it became highly important for

the church to have αἱ διάκονοι as well as οἱ διάκονοι, in order that the former might look to females who were indigent or sick. Accordingly we find the female deacons more than once adverted to, in the epistle of Paul; comp. 1 Tim. iii. 11. v. 10. Tit. ii. 3. Pliny in his letter to Trajan (x. 97), no doubt refers to the αἱ διάκονοι in the following passage: Necessarium credidi, ex duabus ancillis quæ *ministræ* dicebantur, etc.

Cenchrea, κεγχρεαῖς, was the *eastern* port of Corinth; for Corinth itself lay not upon the sea, but had two harbors some four or five miles distant from the city, viz., Cenchrea on the east and Lechea on the west. It would seem that Phebe was about to sail from Cenchrea to Rome, when Paul wrote this epistle; and it is quite probable that it was sent by her to the church at Rome. The word Κεγχρεαί is used only in the plural, like Ἀθῆναι.

(2) *That ye may receive her in the Lord in a manner worthy of the saints,* ἵνα . . . ἀγίων. That the phrase ἐν κυρίῳ may mean *being in the Lord, i. e.,* being a member of his spiritual body cannot be doubted. See 1 Cor. xii. 27. Rom. xii. 5. 1 Cor. x. 17. Eph. i. 22, 23. iv. 12. v. 30. Col. i. 24. So the sentiment here may be: 'Receive Phebe who is a Christian, in such a manner as becomes Christians,' *i. e.,* with distinguished kindness and benevolence. But some refer ἐν κυρίῳ to the church at Rome, and interpret thus: 'Do ye, as united to Christ, receive her worthily of the saints.' There is nothing in the language or context which decides absolutely for the one or the other interpretation. I rather incline to the latter, from its appositeness here. 'Do ye, who are professed Christians, act worthily of your profession in this matter.'

And render her assistance in anything, where she may need it of you; for she herself has been a helper of many, and especially of me, καὶ παραστῆτε . . . ἐμοῦ. For the words παραστῆτε and προστάτις, see on προιστάμενος in chap. xii. 8. This hint shows what the office of a deaconess was, *i. e.*, what duties it led her to perform. A comparison of προστάτις here will serve to cast light on ὁ προϊστάμενος in Rom. xii. 8.

(3) *Prisca,* Πρίσκαν, the same as Πρίσκιλλα in Acts xviii. 2, 26. 1 Cor. xvi. 19. The latter is merely a *diminutive*, which was commonly applied to women in the way of courtesy or affection; as John says to Christians: "My *little* children." Both Priscilla and her husband Aquila are here called συνεργούς of the apostle. Ἐν Χριστῷ Ἰησοῦ, *i. e.*, in the Christian cause.

(4) *Who exposed their own neck for my life,* οἵτινες . . ὑπέθηκαν, *i. e*, who exposed their own neck to the sword, their own head to be cut off, in order to defend me from harm. — *And the church which is in their house,* καὶ τὴν . . . ἐκκλησίαν, *i. e.*, which habit-

ually convenes there. Aquila and Priscilla are spoken of, also, as having a church in their house while at Ephesus, 1 Cor. xvi. 19; from which some have drawn the conclusion, that only their family, which consisted of Christians, are meant by ἐκκλησίαν; a criticism which is destitute of support from the *usus loquendi* of the New Testament. On the contrary, nothing is more natural than the supposition, that these zealous advocates of the Christian cause, wherever they sojourned, were accustomed to hold assemblies at their own house, for the purpose of Christian worship and instruction. All the meetings of the primitive Christians must have been in this way, inasmuch as they had at first no churches or temples where they could convene.

(5) *Epainetus;* this and other names which follow down to ver. 15, designate persons otherwise unknown to us, but who, personally or otherwise, must have been known to the apostle. Ἀπαρχὴ τῆς Ἀσίας, one of the first who embraced Christianity under my preaching in *proconsular* Asia, *i. e.*, Asia Minor probably in the Roman sense of that word. — Εἰς Χριστόν, *in respect to Christ.*

(6, 7) It appears probable, that the persons here named had formerly been residents in Asia or Greece, where the apostle was acquainted with them, but that they had now removed to Rome. *Of note,* ἐπίσημοι; *i. e., well-known, highly esteemed, among the apostles,* ἐν τοῖς ἀποστόλοις. *Who became Christians even earlier than myself,* οἱ . . . Χριστῷ; where ἐν Χριστῷ can hardly be mistaken.

(9) Ἀγαπητόν μου ἐν Κυρίῳ, *i. e., my beloved fellow Christian.*

(10) *A tried and approved Christian,* τὸν δόκιμον ἐν Χριστῷ.— Τοὺς ἐκ τῶν Ἀριστοβούλου, i. e., τοὺς ὄντας ἐν Κυρίῳ ἐκ τῶν οἰκείων Ἀριστοβούλου; comp. the close of verse 11.

(13) *His mother and mine,* μητέρα αὐτοῦ καὶ ἐμοῦ; *i. e.,* his mother in a literal sense, and mine in a figurative one.

(16) *Salute each other with a holy kiss,* ἀσπάσασθε . . . ἁγίῳ; *i. e.,* greet each other after the affectionate manner of Christians; live together in the kind exchange of Christian salutations and tokens of friendship. This custom is extensively maintained, at present, on the continent of Europe, among Christian friends, and others also. In itself, it is like any *external* thing, not essential, but only a *res loci et temporis,* depending on the manners and customs of the time and place, like the wearing or not wearing of long hair at Corinth, etc. Αἱ ἐκκλησίαι πᾶσαι, *i. e.,* all the churches in the vicinity of the apostle, or those which he had recently visited. This shows the custom of the early Christian churches, as to sending expressions of brotherly affection for each other, although they were mutual strangers in respect to personal acquaintance.

(17) *To consider attentively*, σκοπεῖν, *to beware of.*—*Divisions*, διχοστασίας, viz., in the church among brethren. *Offences*, σκάνδαλα, *i. e*, those who are the occasion of others stumbling and falling, by their uncharitableness or their superstition. Παρά *contrary to, against;* comp. Rom. i. 26. xi. 24. Gal. i. 8, 9. Heb. xi. 11. *Stand off from them*, ἐκκλίνατε ἀπ' αὐτῶν, i. e., *avoid them, i. e*, give them no countenance or approbation.

(18) Τῷ κυρίῳ ἡμῶν Χριστῷ, *i. e.*, the Christian cause, or him who is the author of Christianity. *Their own appetite*, κοιλίᾳ, *i. e.*, they do not labor for the good of the Christian cause, but merely for their own private interests, merely to obtain a maintenance. The apostle seems, therefore, to refer here to certain teachers at Rome, at this time, who were the authors of division and offence there, and whose views extended no farther than the acquisition of a maintenance for themselves.

And by flattery and fair speeches beguile the minds of the simple, καὶ διὰ . . . ἀκάκων. Theophylact: χρηστολογία, κολακεία, i. e., *flattery*. Εὐλογίας is *eulogy, praise*. Καρδίας, *minds*, like the Hebrew לב. Ἀκάκων means those who are *destitute of suspicion, without guile, simple-hearted*.

(19) *For your obedient temper of mind is known among all* [the churches], ἡ γὰρ . . . ἀφίκετο, *i. e.*, the fame of your Christian temper, your readiness to obey the gospel, has been spread among all the churches. Γάρ seems here to refer to a clause readily supplied, *e. g.*, [I exhort you to do all this] γάρ, *because* I know that you will lend a listening ear. See Bretschn. Lex. on γάρ.

I rejoice, therefore in respect to you, χαίρω οὖν . . . ὑμῖν; *i. e*, since your obedient disposition has procured you such a good name in the churches, I rejoice. Τὸ ἐφ' ὑμῶν, *i. e., κατὰ τὸ ἐφ' ὑμῶν. And I wish you to be wise in respect to that which is good, but simple in regard to that which is evil*, θέλω δέ . . . κακόν. The idea is: I do not desire you Christians to use dexterity in order to accomplish selfish ends, like the false teachers among them; but to be willingly accounted *simple* or *simpletons*, in regard to doing evil.

(20) *May God, who is the author of peace*, θεὸς τῆς εἰρήνης, or who loves and approves it! Συντρίψει, Fut. for Optative, like the Heb. Future. Σατανᾶν, *Satan*, viz., the malignant accuser of the brethren, and who delights in exciting the evil-minded to discord and division. May God disappoint all his malignant purposes, and preserve your harmony and kindly affection. The language of this wish (συντρίψει) refers to the prediction in Gen. iii. 15.

Χάρις here means favor of every kind, like the שלום לכם of the Hebrews. — Ἀμήν seems to be spurious.

(21) Luke, and Jason, and Sosipater are classed together here as *relatives* of Paul. If this be Luke the Evangelist, which seems altogether probable, then it would appear that he must have been of Hebrew descent, at least in part; for Paul was "a Hebrew of the Hebrews," *i. e.*, of pure Hebrew descent. Nevertheless, as συγγενεῖς does not mark the *degree* of relation, we cannot argue from this expression with much confidence.

(22) Τέρτιος ὁ γράψας, *i. e.*, who was the amanuensis of Paul on the occasion of writing this epistle.

(23) *My host*, ὁ ξένος μου; *i. e.*, who has received me into his house, and showed me hospitality; and who shows an extensive hospitality to all Christians. *The treasurer of the city*, οἰκονόμος τῆς πόλεως. Κούαρτος shows the manner in which the Greeks represented the Latin *qu*, *Quartus*.

(25) The whole now concludes with a general ascription of praise. Τῷ δυναμένῳ, sc. ᾖ ἡ δόξα, as appears from the close of ver. 27. The sentence is suspended, after the usual manner of Paul, until he resumes it in μόνῳ σοφῷ θεῷ. *To establish*, στηρίξαι, viz., in the Christian faith and practice. *In accordance with the principles of the gospel which I preach*, agreeably to the principles of this, κατὰ τὸ εὐαγγέλιον μου. — *Even the Gospel of Jesus Christ*, καὶ τὸ κήρυγμα, *i. e.*, even the gospel of which Jesus is the author, or which has respect to him. Κήρυγμα is in apposition with εὐαγγέλιον; and the object of Paul is to show by the whole declaration, that the gospel which he preached was the true one.

According to the revelation of the mystery which was kept in silence during ancient ages, κατὰ ἀποκάλυψιν . . . . . σεσιγημένου; *i. e.*, agreeably to the gospel which was not fully revealed in ancient times, but is now brought to light; comp. 1 Cor. ii. 7. Eph. iii. 5, 9. Col. i. 23. This phrase is coordinate with κατὰ τὸ εὐαγγέλιον above, and is designed for more ample description.

(26) *But is now revealed by the Scriptures of the prophets*, φανερωθέντος δέ . . . προφητικῶν. The apostle first refers to the most ancient times before any revelation was given, as the χρόνοι αἰώνιοι, when the gospel remained as it were concealed; next he points us to the Messianic prophecies contained in the Old Testament. Paul generally represents the gospel as hidden from the ancients, but *now* revealed, *i. e.*, under the Christian dispensation; see Col. i. 26. Eph. iii. 5, 10, and comp. 1 Pet. i. 12. But in Rom. iii. 21. he says of the grace of the gospel, νυνὶ πεφανέρωται, and at the same time he adds, μαρτυρουμένη ὑπὸ τοῦ νόμου καὶ τῶν προφητῶν; which concurs with the present representation. Three things are predicated of the μυστήριον which he mentions in ver. 25; (1) That it was kept in a hidden or concealed state down to the time when the Old Testament dis-

pensation commenced. (2) That it was disclosed, *i.e.*, comparatively brought to light (φανερωθέντος) by the ancient Scriptures. (3) That it was fully published or made known (γνωρισθέντος) under the gospel dispensation. Φανερωθέντος νῦν here means the same in all essential respects as the μαρτυρουμένη ὑπό τοῦ νόμου καὶ τῶν προφητῶν of Rom. iii. 21. There is a concurrent testimony, declaration, or disclosure, by the ancient prophetic writings, which gives force to the new testimony under the gospel dispensation.

In the other passages to which reference is made above, the revelation of the gospel mysteries in later times in opposition to the silence of former days is only *comparative*, just as when the Saviour says, that "if he had not come and spoken to the Jews they had not had sin, but now they have no cloak for it;" and just as when Paul says, that "life and immortality are brought to light by the gospel." Surely when Abraham and the patriarchs "sought a better country, even a *heavenly* one," they must have had some notions of immortality. It may be altogether correct, then, that gospel truth, as disclosed by the prophets, made only a twilight compared with the noontide glories of the new dispensation, and so there was ample occasion for the comparative views which the apostle has disclosed in Col. i. 26. Eph. iii. 5, 10; at the same time it may be, and is equally true, that the gospel is in some degree disclosed (φανερωθείς) in the Old Testament prophets, and is testified to (μαρτυρουμένην) by them in their works, which are every day still read by Christians.

Τε before γραφῶν seems to give occasion to some difficulty, inasmuch as the clause in which τε stands has another *connective* (δέ), we cannot regard it in the simple light of a conjunction, by which φανερωθέντος, κ. τ. λ. is joined to the preceding clause. It must then, as it would seem, have a *relative* meaning, and imply another clause after it to which either a καί or a τε is appended. Accordingly, the Syr., Arab., (Erp.), and Æth. versions insert the *and* before κατ' ἐπιταγήν, κ. τ. λ. But as there is no room for critical doubt of the genuineness of the τε here, and as καί is destitute of other support than these versions, it is better to consider the passage as elliptical, and καί as omitted before κατ' ἐπιταγήν, it being necessarily implied by the presence of the τε in the preceding phrase. In this way κατ' ἐπιταγήν, κ. τ. λ. belongs to the last clause, and is to be connected (as it should be) with the part. γνωρισθέντος; so that the sense of the last clause is, that "the gospel, by the commandment of the eternal God, has been published to all nations, in order to lead them to the obedience which faith ensures."*

* There need not be any hesitation in taking δέ as adversative to the preceding clause, and then making τέ connect what follows to φανερωθέντος δὲ

(27) The apostle now *resumes* the doxology which he had begun in ver. 25 by τῷ δυναμένῳ, with μόνῳ, κ. τ. λ. The pronoun ᾧ here would seem to relate grammatically and most naturally to Jesus Christ. But in such a case, in order to complete the construction, Θεῷ must be joined with ἡ δόξα εἰς τοὺς αἰῶνας implied, or δόξα, or some equivalent word must be understood immediately after it. Following another mode of construction, we must refer ᾧ to Θεῷ, and either construe it as equivalent to αὐτῷ (which however wants precedent to confirm it); or we must take ᾧ in the *demonstrative* sense, viz., as employed for οὗτος or ὅδε (it often is so employed, Passow, Lex. ὅς, B), and translate it, "*to this one* be glory, etc." This, on the whole is the more facile way of construing it. The first mode of construction seems at least to be rather hard; yet the elliptical form of the whole paragraph detracts somewhat from the hardness of it, and makes it quite possible.

The *subscription*, like most of the others in the Pauline epistles, is adscititious. Chap. xvi. 1 doubtless gave occasion to it; and the matter of it is in all probability correct. But we cannot regard it as coming from the hand of Paul; for surely he did not need to inform the church at Rome, by a subscription, who it was that conveyed the epistle to them, when he had once commended the same individual to their hospitality. Moreover, competent external evidence of genuineness is wanting.

νῦν. Thus we may translate: But now revealed, and by the prophetic Scriptures, in accordance with the command of the eternal God, made known to all nations, etc.

EXCURSUS I.

On υἱὸς Θεοῦ in Rom. i. 4 (p. 17).

THE *generic* idea in the phrase υἱὸς Θεοῦ is that of a being formed in the image of God, *i. e.*, possessing by his gift a moral and intellectual nature like his own. The *original* idea of *υἱός*, is that of *derivation*. The *secondary* one (which is often employed), is that of *resemblance*. The third gradation of meaning is, that of being *regarded* or *treated as a son, occupying the place of a son,* viz., having distinguished gifts, favors, or blessings bestowed on any one. To one or the other of these classes of meaning, may all the instances be traced in which the phrase *son* or *sons of God* is applied, in the Old Testament or the New.

This phrase is applied (1) To *Adam*, as proceeding immediately from the hand of the Creator, Luke iii. 38. (2) To those who are *regenerated*, or born of the Spirit of God, John i. 12, 13; Rom viii. 15, 17; 1 John iii 1, 2, et sæpe alibi. Connected with this, is the usage of calling all *true worshippers* of God his *sons; e. g.*, Matt. v. 9, 45, Luke vi. 35, xx. 36; Rom. viii. 14, 19; 2 Cor. vi. 18; Gal. iii. 26; Heb. xii 6; Rev. xxi 7, et alibi. (3) The same appellation is sometimes given to *such as are treated with special kindness; e. g.*, Rom. ix. 26; Hos. i. 10, xi. 1; Deut xxxii. 5, 19; Isai. i. 2, xliii. 6, Jer. xxxi 9; 2 Cor. vi. 18. God, as the common father and benefactor of all men, good and bad, in reference to this relation, often calls himself a *father*, and styles them his children; "If I be a *father*, where is mine honor?" "I have nourished and brought up *children*, but they have rebelled against me." Moreover, as all men are made in his image, *i e.*, have an intellectual, rational, and moral nature like his own, on this account also they may be styled his children; but more especially does this apply to those who are *regenerated*, and in whom the image of God that had been in part defaced, is restored. (4) As bearing some resemblance to the Supreme Ruler of the universe in respect to authority, or as having office by his special favor, *kings* are sometimes named *sons of God; e g*, Ps. lxxxii. 6 (בְּנֵי עֶלְיוֹן). 2 Sam. vii 14. So in Homer διογενὴς βασιλεύς, Il lib. i. 279, ii 196 (5) *Angels* are called *sons of God*, for the like reason that men are, viz, because God is their creator and benefactor; and specially, because they bear a high resemblance to God; see Job i 6, ii. 1, xxxviii 7, Dan. iii. 25.

It is evident from inspecting these examples, that men and angels may be called *sons of God* for more than one reason; nay, that in some cases all the reasons for giving this appellation are united. *E. g*, a pious Israelite might be called a son of God, because God was his creator, because of the special favors and blessings bestowed upon him, *i. e*, because of his being treated as a son; because he was born again by the power of the Holy Spirit, and because he bore a special resemblance to his heavenly Father. For all or for any one of these reasons, it is obvious we might, agreeably to Scripture usage, call any one *a son* of God, who is truly pious. To note this is of no small importance in rightly estimating the force of ὁ υἱὸς τοῦ θεοῦ, as applied to Christ. We come now to consider this last phrase, as applied in this manner.

(*a*) It designates Jesus as conceived by the Virgin Mary, by the miraculous influence of the Holy Spirit, Luke i. 32 (comp. Luke iii. 38). Perhaps the same sense belongs to it in Mark i. 1. The words of the centurion in Matt xxvii 54, and Mark xv. 39, seem, in the mouth of a Roman, to have the like or similar sense

(*b*) It means *Jesus as the constituted king or Messiah. E. g*, Matt. xvi 16, xxvi 63; Mark xiv 61; Luke xxii 70; John i 49, xi. 27; and probably in Matt viii 29, xiv. 33; Mark iii 11, v. 7; Luke iv 41, viii. 28; John i. 34, vi 69, ix 35, x. 36; Acts ix. 20, xiii 33; Heb. v. 5 So the appellation *son* is given to him, by the ancient prophets who foretold his appearance, Ps ii 7, lxxxix 27. On the like ground, kings, as we have seen in No. 4, are called *sons of God,* Ps lxxxii 6; 2 Sam. vii. 14.

(*c*) The most common use of the phrase *Son of God* as applied to the Messiah, is, to designate the high and mysterious relation which subsisted between him and God the Father, by virtue of which he was, in his complex person as θεάνθρωπος, the ἀπαύγασμα τῆς δόξης καὶ χαρακτὴρ τῆς ὑποστάσεως τοῦ πατρός, Heb i. 3, the εἰκὼν τοῦ θεοῦ τοῦ ἀοράτου, Col. i. 15; the εἰκών τοῦ θεοῦ, 2 Cor. iv. 4. In this respect, ὁ υἱὸς τοῦ θεοῦ is rather a name of *nature* than of office, for it is predicated of the high and glorious εἰκών, *resemblance, similitude,* which the Son exhibits of the Father, he being the *radiance* (ἀπαύγασμα) of his glory; so that what Jesus said to Philip is true, viz, "He that hath seen me, hath seen the Father," John xiv. 9 "It hath pleased the Father that in him all fulness should dwell." Col i 19; even "all the fulness of the Godhead bodily, Col. ii. 9; and that high, yea, divine honor should be paid to him, Phil. ii 9—11; Rom. xiv 11 (comp v 9); Rev v 13, 14; John v. 23; Heb i 6. As *Son,* Christ is lord and heir of all things, Heb. i. 2, 3, 8. In particular, it would seem to be one design of the New Testament writers, in using the appellation *Son of God,* to convey the idea of a most intimate connection, love, and fellowship (so to speak) between him and the Father. Compare such texts as Matt xi 27; Luke x. 22; John i 14, 18; Heb i 5, seq.; Matt iii 17; Luke iii 22, ix. 35; Col i 19, 2 Pet i. 17; Matt xvii 5; Mark i 11, ix. 7; and also, with these the parables in Matt. xxi. 37, seq., xxii. 2, seq, Mark xii 6; Luke xx 13; also John viii 35, 36, and x 36 That God has given Christ the Spirit without measure, that he dwells in him σωματικῶς, that all counsels and secrets (so to speak) of the divine nature are perfectly known to him (John i 18; Matt xi 27; Luke x 22; John vi 46, vii 29, viii 19, xiv 9, 10, 11, 20, x. 15); seems to be suggested by the appellation *Son of God* as frequently bestowed; for so the texts referred to, and other like texts, would imply

EXCURSUS I. ON ROM. I. 4.

In a word, similitude, affection, confidence, and most intimate connection, seem to be designated by the appellation *son*, as applied to Christ In this sense it is most frequent in the New Testament, although with Paul, the idea of *Messianic dignity* or *elevation* is more commonly designated by Κύριος.

But while I am fully satisfied that the term *Son of God* is oftentimes applied to Christ as a name of *nature*, as well as of office; yet I am as fully satisfied, that it is not applied to him considered simply as *divine*, or simply as *Logos*. It designates the Θεάνθρωπος, *the God-man*, *i. e.*, the complex person of the Messiah, in distinction from his divine nature simply considered, or his *Logos* state or condition. The exceptions to this are only cases of such a nature, as show that the appellation *Son of God* became, by usage, a kind of proper name, which might be applied either to his human nature or to his divine one, as well as to his complex person. In just such a way proper names are commonly used; *e. g.*, *Abraham* usually and properly means, the complex person of this individual consisting of soul and body. But when I say, 'Abraham is dead,' I mean the physical part only of Abraham is so; and when I say, 'Abraham is alive,' I mean that his immortal part only is so. So in regard to the name *Son of God;* when I say, 'The Son of God was crucified,' I mean that his mortal part was so; when I say, 'God sent his Son, the Son came out from the Father, he had glory with the Father before the world was,' etc., I mean, in such cases, that the divine nature of the Son became incarnate, that ἑαυτὸν ἐκένωσε . . . ἑαυτὸν ἐταπείνωσε (Phil. ii 7, 8), taking upon him the likeness of our nature. But when I say, with John that "Jesus is the Son of God," and that "Jesus Christ has come in the flesh," I mean to designate his complex person, the Θεάνθρωπος, the Θεὸς ἐν σαρκὶ φανερωθείς, the λόγος σὰρξ γενόμενος, and this is the case with most of the examples of the phrase in the New Testament.

If it is affirmed that Christ is called *Son* as being *divine*, and in order to designate his originating from the Father in his *divine* nature; the objections are many and serious. I can only glance at a few of them.

(1) If *Son of God* necessarily implies, *ex vi termini*, that Christ as to his *divine nature* is *derived;* how shall we construe such texts as the following; viz, "What and if ye shall see the *Son of Man* ascend up *where he was before?*" John vi 62. "No man hath ascended to heaven, but *he that came down from heaven*, even *the Son of Man* who is in heaven," John iii. 13. Does *Son of Man* indicate (*ex vi termini*) the *divine* nature of Christ? This I suppose will not be affirmed; for plainly it indicates the Θεάνθρωπος, the Θεὸς ἐν σαρκὶ φανερωθείς, *i. e.*, it has of itself a necessary reference to the *incarnate* condition of the Saviour. Yet when employed as a *proper* name, we see by the texts above that it can be used to indicate the original and *divine* nature of the Messiah along with his human nature. If not, then these texts would prove that the *incarnate* nature of Christ existed in heaven before he came down from that place; a fiction which we may well rank with the supposed rapture of Christ into heaven, and his subsequent descent from heaven, as maintained by Socinus.

Now as these texts, when thus employed will not prove that the *human* nature of Christ had a prior existence in heaven; so neither will the other texts above cited prove that the appellation, *Son of God,* means the *divine* nature of Christ as begotten of God, merely because the Father is said to have loved him and to have sent him into the world. But,

(2) If the Son as *God* be *derived* or *begotten,* then it must follow, that as God he is neither *self-existent* nor *independent.* It is of no avail to say here, that his generation is *eternal,* and that the *method* of it is mysterious, superhuman, and unlike to that of any created substance; for one may very readily allow all this, and still ask, whether the word *generation* (let the *manner* of the thing be what it may) does not of necessity, and by the usage of every language, imply *derivation?* And whether *derivation* does not of necessity imply *dependence,* and therefore negative the idea of *self-existence?* This the ancient Fathers acknowledged almost with one voice, asserting that Christ is not αὐτόθεος but derived from the Father, and *begotten of his substance.* The Father only they regarded as self-existent; not deeming it compatible at all with the idea of *generation,* that the Son could vindicate to himself this attribute of divinity. So the Nicene Fathers in their symbol: θεὸς ἐκ θεοῦ, φῶς ἐκ φωτός. They did truly and really regard the Logos as an *emanation* from the Father; many of the fathers (most of the earlier ones), as an emanation from him which took place in time, or rather perhaps an emanation just before time began. Hence the familiar phrase among them, λόγος ἐνδιάθετος, *i. e*, the Logos *which was in God as his reason, wisdom,* or *understanding,* from eternity; and λόγος προφορικός, *i. e., Logos prophoric, uttered, developed,* viz., by words. This development many of them supposed was made, when God said, "Let there be light;" others supposed it to have been still earlier, viz., at the period when God formed the plan of the world, and thus gave development to his internal λόγος, by the operations of his wisdom and understanding.

The philosophy of the Fathers permitted them to believe in a divine nature *derived.* Of course they could maintain the generation of the Son as *Logos* without any difficulty. But that we can now admit a being to be *truly* God, and worship him as such, who as to his divine nature is *derived* and *dependent,* does seem to me quite impossible. The very elements of my own views (to say the least) respecting the divine nature must be changed, before I can admit such a proposition.

To say that the Son is *eternally begotten,* and yet is *self-existent* and *independent,* is merely to say that the word *begotten* does not imply *derivation;* it is to deny that the word has any such meaning, as all antiquity and common usage have always ascribed to it. It is, moreover, to give up the very doctrine which the ancient church strenuously maintained. Tholuck, who appears to maintain the views of the Nicene creed, says (on Rom ix. 5): " The Father is the original source of all being, 1 Cor. viii. 6; John v. 26; the Son is only the εἰκών of his being, Col i. 15; 2 Cor. iv. 4; Heb. i. 3. But as being the *image* of the divine Being, the Son is in no respect different from the Father, but fully expresses the Being of God. As the church is wont to say · The attribute of ἀγεννησία is possessed *only* by the Father."

" The Son is in *no respect* (in nichts) different from the Father, but fully (vollkommen, *perfectly*) resembles or expresses (ausdruckt) the being of God," and yet to the Son belongs not ἀγεννησία, *self-existence, independence,* but ἀγεννησία, belongs *exclusively* to the Father!" What is this more or less than to say. The Son is perfectly like the Father in all respects; and yet in regard to that very attribute, which beyond all others united makes God to be what he is, viz., true and very God, *i. e*, in respect to *self-existence* (and of course *independence*), the Son has no participation at all in this, but it belongs *exclusively* to the Father! In other words: "The Son is in *all respects* like the Father, with the simple exception that he is, in regard to the most essential of all his attributes, infinitely *unlike* him."

A mode of reasoning which involves such difficulties as these, should not be adopted without very imperious reasons. I know of no such reasons, unless they be drawn from the expression ὁ Υἱὸς τοῦ Θεοῦ understood in a *literal* sense, *i. e.*, so far literal as can be possible in respect to spiritual beings. Now that one spiritual being can produce another, in some way or other (of course not *more humano*), will not be denied. And if *Son* necessarily imports derivation in the *divine* nature of the Logos, along with this it necessarily imports *dependence;* in other words it necessarily denies *self-existence* and *independence*. If any one refuses to acknowledge this, then of course he must abandon the meaning of *generation*. No matter what the *modus* of generation may be, however mysterious or super-human; this makes no difference as to real *dependence*, in case the generation is real and actually matter of fact. But in case we insist on preserving the term *generation*, as applied to the divine nature of the Son, and yet aver that he is self-existent and independent, then the *diction* merely of the ancient fathers is preserved, while the *doctrine* which they maintained is clearly abandoned.

All such as cannot admit the *emanation* philosophy into their system of theology (the ancient Fathers did this), will not regard Christ as Θεὸς δεύτερος, but as ὁ ὢν ἐπὶ πάντων Θεὸς, εὐλογητὸς εἰς τοὺς αἰῶνας, ἀμήν. The Logos, "who created all things,' "by whom all things were created in heaven and earth," bears at least the *highest* stamp of DIVINITY UNDERIVED. Who is *self-existent* if not the CREATOR? And who is God *supreme*. if not ὁ ὢν ἐπὶ πάντων Θεός? If there be any higher assertions of Godhead respecting the Father than these, let those who ascribe self-existence only to him, point them out.

The most formidable objection to the Nicenian and Athanasian Creed is, that it makes such a statement respecting the doctrine of the Trinity, as destroys the idea of full and proper equality of the persons of the Godhead. The Son is made dependent on the Father; and the Spirit also dependent on the Father, according to the views and explanations of the Greek church, but according to the Latin one, dependent on, *i. e*, proceeding from, both the Father and Son. The Son then has not two capacities or faculties which the Father has, viz, that of begetting and causing procession, as the Greek church would have it; and the Spirit is in like manner wanting as to both of these capacities. According to the Latin church, the Spirit is also wanting as to one capacity which the Son has, viz, that of causing procession. Now if God is everywhere in the Bible recognized as supreme and only

God, because he is Creator of the world, and all competition of those called gods is treated with scorn, because they cannot compare with him here, then how immeasurably more exalted still must the Father be above the Son and Spirit, if he is the ground or cause of their being, the *fons et principium* of *Godhead* itself! Arianism itself has placed the Son and Spirit too near the Father, if there be such an immeasurable discrepance between them as there must be between being derived and dependent, and self-existent and independent.

This, however, is not the place to enlarge on this topic; and it is the less necessary, inasmuch as I have discussed the subject at length in an Essay in the Bib Repository, Nos. 18, 19, 1835, where I have commented on Schleiermacher's comparison of the Sabellian and Athanasian Creeds.

EXCURSUS II.

On Rom. iii. 28, λογιζόμεθα γὰρ δικαιοῦσθαι πίστει ἄνθρωπον χωρὶς ἔργων νόμου (p. 117).

It will be conceded at once, that before we pronounce sentence respecting the agreement or disagreement of Paul and James with respect to the doctrine of justification, it is necessary that we should understand the meaning of the words which they respectively employ, and the nature of the object which they respectively have in view.

First, then, *what does Paul assert?* He says that "a man is justified by *faith*," χωρὶς ἔργων νόμου. The inquiry is fundamental, therefore, What does he mean by ἔργων νόμου?

I answer: He means *works which the law requires, works which the law makes it duty to perform*. That the Gen. case after ἔργον is sometimes employed to express such a relation, there can be no room for doubt; e. g., John vi. 28, 29, ἔργα Θεοῦ works which God requires; John ix. 4, τὰ ἔργα τοῦ πέμψαντός με, the works required by him who sent me; Acts xxvi 20, μετανοίας ἔργα, works such as repentance demands; 1 Thess i. 3, τοῦ ἔργου τῆς πίστεως, the works which faith requires; and 2 Thess. i 11, ἔργον πίστεως, in the same sense.

In like manner, ἔργον νόμου and ἔργα νόμου mean *work* or *works which the law demands* So the phrase is plainly used in Rom. ii. 15; iii. 20, 28; ix. 32; Gal. ii. 16 (thrice); iii. 2, 5, 10. Sometimes νόμου is omitted, and ἔργον is used alone in the same sense, *breviloquentiæ causâ*; e. g, Rom. iv. 6, ix. 12; xi. 6 (thrice); Eph. ii. 9.

What works, then, does the law of God require? The answer is: It demands *perfect obedience*. "The soul that sinneth shall die." "Cursed is he who continueth not in *all things written in the book of the law*, to do them."

It is manifestly on this ground that Paul argues the impossibility of justification by works of law. In Rom. iii 19, when summing up his argument contained in the preceding part of the epistle, he says: "The whole world is guilty before God," i. e., all men are chargeable with the guilt of sin. What follows? The apostle tells us in ver. 20: διότι, κ. τ. λ., *Therefore by works of law no flesh can be justified before God.*

Must not this be true? If the law of God demands *perfect* obedience, and its penalty is attached to *every* sin, then one sin ruins the hopes of man and effectually debars him from justification before God, on the ground of merit or obedience.

The apostle Paul disputes with those who denied this, and who expected justification on the ground of their own meritorious obedience; comp ix. 30, 31; x. 3, also Gal ii. 16; iii 8—13; Rom. iv. 4, 5 To say, then, that *a man is not justified by works of law*, is (with him) the same as saying, that *he cannot be justified meritoriously*, i. e., on the ground of merit or obedience, Rom iv. 5. But as *faith* in Jesus Christ, who died to procure mercy for sinners so that they might be pardoned and accepted, does from its very nature involve the renunciation of claims to merit, and the casting of ourselves on him for *gratuitous* justification; so the apostle opposes the being *justified by faith* to the *being justified by works of law*, the former meaning (with him) *gratuitous* justification, the latter *meritorious.* Let the reader now carefully and diligently compare Rom. iv. 4, 5, 14—16; ix. 6; Gal. v 4; iii. 11, 12, and he can entertain no doubt of the correctness of this representation.

We have then before us the object of Paul, in declaring that a man is not justified by works of law. It is the same thing as to say, 'No one is accepted with God on the ground of merit or perfect obedience to the law, for no one has done all which the law requires.'

But does this involve the idea, that Paul maintains GOOD WORKS (ἔργα ἀγαθά) to be unnecessary for a Christian? Nothing could be farther from his intention. Are not his epistles filled with the most urgent exhortations to Christians, that they should be fruitful in *good* works? Compare now, for a moment, Rom ii. 7; 2 Cor. ix. 8; Eph ii. 10; Col. i 10; iii. 17; 1 Thess. v. 13; 2 Thess. ii 17; 1 Tim ii. 10; v. 10 (twice), v. 25, vi. 18; 2 Tim ii. 21; iii. 17; Tit. i 16; ii. 7, 14; iii 1, 8, 14, etc. Compare the strain of Paul's reasoning in Rom vi.—viii.; and then say, is it possible to doubt, for a moment, that Paul urged *good works* as strenuously as James, or as any other apostle?

Let the reader mark well, that ἔργα νόμου, and ἔργα ἀγαθά or ἔργον πίστεως (1 Thess. i. 3; 2 Thess. i. 11), are two very different things; different not so much in their own nature, strictly considered, as in the use which Paul makes of them in his writings. With him, ἔργα νόμου always designates the idea of *perfect* obedience, viz., doing all which the law requires. But ἔργα ἀγαθά or ἔργα πίστεως are the fruits of sanctification by the Spirit of God; the good works which Christians perform, and which are sincere, are therefore acceptable to God under a dispensation of grace, although they do not fulfil all the demands of the law. On the ground of the first, Paul earnestly contends, at length, in his epistles to the Romans and Galatians, that no one can be justified. The latter he everywhere treats as indispensable to the Christian character.

In a word, when Paul is contending with a *legalist*, *i. e.*, one who expected justification on the ground of his own merit, he avers that justification by *works of law* or perfect obedience, is impossible. But when he is addressing Christians, he tells them that *good works* are absolutely essential to the Christian character.

2. Come we then, in the second place, to inquire what is the meaning and object of the apostle James, in chap. II. 14—26

He commences by asking: "Of what avail is it, my brethren, if a man *say he have faith*, and have not works?" It is then with those who make *pretensions* to Christian faith, and mere pretensions, that the apostle has to do. This is clear from the closing verse in the paragraph: "For as the body without the spirit is dead, so faith without works is also dead."

The characters, then, which the apostle James has in view, are of a kind directly opposite to those with which St. Paul was concerned. James is disputing with *Antinomians*, viz., such persons as held that mere speculative belief or faith, unaccompanied by works, was all which the gospel demands. He tells them that this is not the case, and cannot be. He appeals to the examples of Abraham and Rahab, and asks, whether the faith which they possessed did not co-operate with works, when they were justified.

Observe now, that James does not once mention ἔργα νόμου. This is not the subject which he has in view. It is ἔργα πίστεως, and these only, of which he treats; comp. verses 17, 22, 26.

Mark again, that James does not at all maintain that faith is not essential to justification. He expressly admits that Abraham's faith co-operated with his works, and was perfected by them, ver. 22. Nay, he appeals to the very same passage of Scripture, in confirmation of this, which Paul appeals to in Rom. IV. 3, when establishing the doctrine of *gratuitous* justification. The *work* of Abraham which James mentions, is recorded in Gen. XXII.; and it took place some 30 years after the words were spoken to him, which are quoted in ver. 22. By this work (viz., of offering up his son), Abraham "perfected his faith," and "fulfilled the Scripture which says: Abraham believed God, and it was counted to him for righteousness," verses 22, 23. In other words,: 'The faith of Abraham was inseparable from good works. It shone out in the most conspicuous manner by them. And in like manner did the faith of Rahab exhibit itself.'

James, then, maintains that no man has any good claim to the faith of a Christian, who does not at the same time exhibit good works; *i. e.*, good works superadded to faith are necessary to justification.

Paul maintains that men are justified gratuitously, in opposition to legal or meritorious justification. Still he is so far from denying that Christian faith must produce good works, that he everywhere strenuously maintains the necessity of them. Where, then, is the contradiction?

Luther strangely thought that he found it; and he rejected the epistle of James from the canon of the New Testament on this ground, calling it *epistola straminea.* So did the Magdeburg Centuriators; and not a few recent commentators have alleged, that James contradicts what Paul teaches.

For a more ample discussion of the subject of this Excursus, the reader may consult the dissertation by Dr Knapp, Bib Repos. III, pp 189 seq.; and also the recent one by C. Fromann, Bib. Repos. IV., pp. 683 seq; where he will find references to various writings on this subject, and an examination of the arguments of those who hold that James intended to gainsay some of the declarations of Paul.

EXCURSUS III.

On θάνατος in Rom. v. 12 (pp. 157 seq.).

AMONG some of the older commentators, and even among some very distinguished recent and living ones, *e. g*, Flatt, Schott, Reiche, and others, the position has been strongly asserted, that θάνατος can here mean only *the death of the body* The arguments as summed up by Reiche are briefly these. (1) 'No explanation added to θάνατος leads us to suppose the literal and usual meaning is not to be here admitted' But in verses 15—19, an antithesis to θάνατος, or (what is of the same import) to κρίμα, κατάκριμα, etc, shows beyond all reasonable question that the *death* is such an one as is the opposite of *reigning in life* and of *justification unto life*. Can this be mere *temporal* death? (2) 'The connection leads us to construe θάνατος as meaning *temporal* death only.' And what is this? It is, that in ver. 10 θάνατος is used to designate the physical death of Christ Can Prof Reiche show us that θάνατος is capable of any other meaning, as applied to Christ? And because the apostle from necessity uses the term *literally* in one case, can he not employ it in a secondary or tropical sense in another? Especially cannot Paul be supposed to do this, who so often employs the same word in different senses, even in the same sentence? (3) 'Paul elsewhere considers physical death as a great evil or enemy, which Christ came to destroy. He appeals to Rom vi 21 in proof of this; an unfortunate appeal, inasmuch as the antithesis in ver. 22 is ζωὴ αἰώνιος; also to 2 Tim. i. 9 (which says nothing concerning the subject), also to 2 Cor. v. 1; 1 Cor. xv. 54, which relate to the resurrection. But what should lead Paul or others to suppose, that because Christ liberates the body from its death, he does not liberate the soul also from the death that has befallen it? Or how can the proof that Christ does one thing, prove that he does not perform another, provided it be not the opposite of the first? Or how can it be shown, that because θάνατος sometimes designates the death of the *body*, that it never designates the death of the *soul*? (4) 'The apostle speaks according to Jewish views merely; and the Jews held that *temporal* death was introduced by Adam.' The answer to this is, that the Jews of his time probably did believe that temporal death was connected with Adam's fall; as Wisd. i. 13, ii. 24; Sirac. xxv. 24, xli. 3, would seem to show. Yet to this hour, so far as the efforts of the learned are concerned, no uniform and consistent views among the Rabbins are made out. Vitringa (Observ. Sac. III. 8, 9), Susskind (Magaz. St. 13), Bartoloccius (Biblioth. Rabb. V. II. pp. 47 seq.), and others, have maintained that the Rabbins reject the common doctrine of connection with Adam and derivation of evil from him; while many others (as Tholuck, Reiche, and many quoted by them) endeavor to show that they held, either that our temporal death was occasioned by Adam's fall, or that our moral corruption and physical death both sprung from him; for both of these opinions are avowed among the Rabbins. But what has all this to do with the meaning of Paul? He might assert what was generally believed by the Jews of his day in relation to the point in question, or he might contradict what they believed. In his epistle he has often done both, in respect to many points. He must be left, then, to be explained by himself, and by the general nature of the Scriptural idiom; which does not here decide for *temporal* death only. (5) 'The exegesis which explains θάνατος as meaning *all evil* of every kind, mixes the figurative and literal together, and therefore is improbable.' Then ζωή, which means (in its secondary sense) *happiness*, and implies *continued life* at the same time, is improperly used; and every word whose *tropical* sense is enlarged beyond its literal one while it is built upon it, is wrongly employed. How far can we proceed in the interpretation of Scripture on such a ground as this?

Such are the arguments by which the usual exegesis is assailed. Let us see what is said by the assailants, in answer to arguments adduced upon the other side of the question. (a) 'Physical death is not removed by Christ; it is still universal.' To this Reiche answers, that 'it is not indeed removed; but it will be at the resurrection; and it will be abolished even here, at Christ's second coming [viz., to reign on earth].' That is, the mischiefs of temporal death will in some way be repaired; but those mischiefs are not prevented. Is this all then that verses 15—19 mean? (b) '*Eternal life* in ver. 21 is the antithesis of θάνατος, which therefore must mean something besides the death of the body.' To this Reiche replies, that *eternal life* is merely the reunion hereafter of body and soul, and their continued existence. If it be urged that *happiness* is meant by *life*, then, he says, we may reply, that the blessings procured by Christ are much greater than the mischief occasioned by Adam, which was mere temporal death; see verses 15, 16. But on this I would remark, that the excess of the blessings as specificated by the apostle, has reference to the evils occasioned by *one* sin, and to the forgiveness extended to *many*; which is a different view of the subject from that which Reiche gives. (c) Finally θάνατος δεύτερος in Apoc. ii. 11, al., is disposed of by Reiche, by saying, that 'it may mean (according to the Rabbins) a second actual death of the body after the first resurrection; or if it does not mean this, we cannot conclude from the mode of expression (θάνατος δεύτερος) what simple θάνατος must mean.' But to me it seems the reverse. The writer of the Apocalypse, in order to remove all doubt respecting his meaning, when he mentions θάνατος as the reward of sin, adds δεύτερος for this very purpose.

I am well aware that the passage in 1 Cor. xv. 22, "For as in Adam all die, so in Christ shall all be made alive," has often been adduced, in order to show that θάνατος in the passage before us means only the death of the body. But with Toellner and Koppe I may venture to say, that because, in discussing the subject of the resurrection (the resurrection of Christians only,) the apostle represents Adam as having introduced the death of the body, it does not follow, that in another epistle, when treating of quite a different topic, and intending to show the *full extent* of the benefits procured by the death of Christ, he could not employ θάνατος in its most extensive latitude. Above all, this does not follow, when it is quite certain, that in the context of this last named epistle, and elsewhere, Paul does beyond all doubt employ θάνατος in its most enlarged sense. It lies, moreover, on the face of the whole antithesis which he makes in verses 12—19, that his object is to exalt the δικαίωμα of Christ, by showing the greatness of the κατάκριμα from which he delivers us, and which was occasioned by Adam. But how is this object effected in any important measure, in case θάνατος means no more than the dissolution of our mortal bodies ? a thing, by the way, from which none are at all delivered.'

On the whole, I regard the case as one which scarcely admits of a doubt on the ground of philology, or of the first principles of theology. When Adam sinned, *death* was threatened. Now is the death of *the body* the only penalty of sin ? If not, then more was meant than this; and the most rational exegesis seems to be that which we are so often obliged elsewhere to adopt, viz., that *evil of every kind* was threatened. In regard to the θάνατος which came upon the posterity of Adam, it was of the same nature; it was fully inflicted, or rather the penalty fully attached, where they *actually* sinned, as ver. 12 itself shows; and even where they did not *actually* sin, there was subjection still to death in as high a measure as the nature of the case admitted.

Another difficulty in respect to the present subject deserves notice before we leave it. It is suggested by the following statement: 'If the miseries of the present life and the death of the body be a part of the penalty threatened to Adam, then the subject is implicated in difficulties like to those which have been already suggested; for if these be a part of the *penalty* of sin, how can that penalty be contrasted with the deliverance which Christ has effected, inasmuch as he has not effected a deliverance from the evils just named ? Must not the miseries of the present life, then, and physical death, be wholly *excluded* from the penalty originally threatened ?'

Some have been led to exclude them by this or the like train of reasoning; and especially because, as our context abundantly asserts, the blessings procured by Christ do greatly exceed the evils occasioned by Adam's sin. Such being the case, they conclude that the death of Christ must of course remove the *very same* evils, in all respects, which were threatened in the original penalty; and as temporal evils and the death of the body still remain, and are universal, they cannot admit that they were included in the death threatened to Adam.

But in reply to this I would remark, that it does by no means follow that even those who become the subjects of redemption are to suffer *none* of the evils threatened against sin. The question, What would be the best means of training up men, who should be always sinless on earth, for the glory of the heavenly world? is something quite different from the question, How are *sinners* to be disciplined, in order that they may become fitted, and best fitted, for the happiness of heaven? A part of the discipline of the latter, (infinite wisdom has so decided it) must now necessarily be *suffering* and *trial;* and as included in this, we may also include the death of the body. Paul himself has told us, in the very chapter under consideration, that the children of God have reason to rejoice in afflictions, inasmuch as they result in patience, approbation, and hope, verses 3, 4 ; and again he says, that " our momentary [temporal] afflictions work out for us a far more exceeding and eternal weight of glory," 2 Cor. iv. 17 , and again, that " all things will work together for good, to those who love God," Rom. viii. 28   So far as bodily suffering is concerned, for the time being, Christians may suffer as severely as others ; and oftentimes they may be the subjects of severe mental as well as bodily sorrows , *but all this finally promotes their spiritual benefit*   Here then is the immense difference which Christ has made, between the effect of their sufferings and that of the suffering of the wicked.   So far as misery in the present life is concerned, Christians may indeed undergo and do suffer some portion of that which the penalty of the law threatens ; they are truly made to taste how bitter a thing it is to have sinned against God, and how dreadful the consequences of sin would be, if they should be subjected to them all But still, this lesson is by divine mercy made highly salutary, both in weaning them from sin, and in preparing them for glory.   To repeat the words of the apostle · " All things work together for their good."   In a word, although a portion of the penalty of sin (in the modified way just described), is the necessary result in every case of having sinned ; yet as Christ redeems us from immeasurably the greater part of the penalty, and makes that part of it which Christians do suffer, subservient to their own good ; above all, since he saves us from every evil which appropriately belongs to the *second* death, no valid objection can be made against the declaration, that the blessings which the Redeemer procures, do not only exceed the evils introduced by the offence of Adam and consequent upon it, but also that the salvation which he has wrought is an effectual antidote against the curse of the law. Even the small part of this which the believer (as having once been a sinner) must necessarily undergo, *i. e.*, the evils which in the present life he must suffer, is, as we have seen, converted into a means of spiritual good to him. This is sufficient then to justify the assertion, that *Christ has redeemed us from the curse of the law.*   It is not necessary, that all and every particular of this curse should be included in such an assertion ; it is enough that the very sufferings which Christians undergo, *i. e.* so much of the curse as they do suffer, prove at last to be only '' blessings in disguise "

But if *temporal* death merely constitutes the *whole* of the threatening to

Adam, or the main part of it, then has the death of Christ failed to accomplish the end which Paul asserts it to have accomplished, inasmuch as all men without distinction are still subjected to it. Viewing this death, however, as only a very subordinate and inferior part of the evil threatened to our first parents; and reflecting that even this is made the occasion of discipline, which ends in good; we may without any serious embarrassment maintain with Paul, that the death of Christ has been the cause of blessings which greatly superabound over the miseries occasioned by the fall.

The deeply interesting nature of the subject, the difficulties attending it, and the efforts of numerous commentators, among whom are some highly respected ones, to establish that interpretation of θάνατος which assigns to it the meaning of *temporal death only*, are my apology for dwelling so long on the topics which this word suggests.

EXCURSUS IV.

On τύπος τοῦ μέλλοντος in Rom v 14 (pp. 178—180.)

In making additional remarks upon τύπος, I observe, (1) That the comparison, from its very nature and design, is in the way of CONTRAST. *Adam was the cause of sin and death; Christ, of righteousness and life:* these are the simple elements of the contrast. The apostle himself indicates that he does not mean a type of something *the same in kind*, but an *antithetic* type, or one in the way of contrast; by immediately subjoining ἀλλ' οὐχ ὡς τὸ παράπτωμα, κ. τ. λ

(2) The same *measure* or *degree* of influence in bringing *evil* upon men, is not to be attributed to the first Adam, as is to be attributed to the second in respect to bringing *grace* and *salvation;* ἡ χάρις ... ἐπερίσσευσε—τὸ κρίμα ἐξ ἑνὸς [παραπτώματος] εἰς κατάκριμα, τὸ δὲ χάρισμα ἐκ πολλῶν παραπτωμάτων εἰς δικαίωμα; and this last sentiment is virtually repeated again in ver. 17. Nothing can be clearer than this makes it, that the blessings of redemption *predominate* over the mischiefs occasioned by the fall, yea, *greatly* superabound. The measure or degree then of mischief and of benefit, are not what constitutes the τύπος in the case under consideration.

(3) Is it then, as I have stated in the commentary (p. 179), the *extent* of the evil on the one side, and of the good on the other, which is a point of resemblance? That is, does the apostle insist that the mischiefs of the fall on the one side, and the blessings of redemption on the other, pertain in any sense to our *whole* race without exception? A deeply interesting question, and one on which hang some very important deductions. In answer to it, I would observe,

(*a*) That all Adam's race do suffer more or less evil in consequence of the fall. This point has been sufficiently discussed in the commentary, p. 178, seq. and below p. 450.

(*b*) As the counterpart of this, it may with equal truth be said, that *the blessings procured by Christ affect all the human race without exception, in some important respects.* References under (*a*) above.

(*c*) But it is important also to note that there are spiritual blessings, *i. e. actual* pardon and justification, which do not come upon all men without distinction, but only on those who believe. These blessings are indeed proffered to all; they are open to all; they are accessible to all. But they are not actually conferred on all; they are not actually possessed and enjoyed, except by *believers;* for *he who believeth shall be saved, and he who believeth not shall be damned.* It is necessary, then, in order to become an actual partaker of these blessings, to *believe, i. e.*, the acts of penitence and faith, acts which are *our own*, are the conditions of enjoying these highest blessings of the gospel, conditions without which they cannot be enjoyed.

And now—the other part of the contrast; which will not, perhaps, be so easily conceded by many of my readers. Does the *ultimate* and highest part of the sentence of death, the *second* death, *i. e.* future misery, which was threatened to Adam, actually come on all his posterity without any act of their own, without any real and personal concurrence with the sin of their ancestor? So the apostle does not say; for he says that "death passed through upon all men, *because that all have sinned; i. e.* (as we have seen above), in their own persons. But you will say that the apostle affirms, in ver. 19, that "by the *disobedience* of Adam the many, *i. e.*, all, were constituted sinners." I grant this; I believe fully what this passage affirms. But to say that Adam's disobedience was an occasion or ground or instrumental cause of all men's becoming sinners (which I must verily believe is the meaning of this declaration), and that it was thus an evil to them all; and to say that his disobedience was *personally* theirs, or was reckoned or imputed as being personally theirs; is saying two very different things. I see no way in which this last assertion can be made out by philology.

Besides; how utterly unlike, in this last case, would be the points of comparison? It is plain that none can enjoy the *higher* blessings procured by Christ without the personal and voluntary acts of repentance and faith; does it not seem equally true, now, that none will actually suffer the higher penalties of the curse threatened to Adam, without their own voluntary transgression? If this be not the true state of the case, how can the *superabounding* of grace, asserted so repeatedly in verses 15—17, be in any way defended? If we say that sentence of eternal perdition, in its *highest* sense, comes actually upon all men by the offence of Adam; and this without any act on their part, or even any voluntary concurrence in their present state and condition of existence; then, in order to make grace *superabound* over all this, how can we avoid the conclusion, that justification in its highest sense comes upon all men without their concurrence?

I am aware, indeed, that many commentators have considered Adam as being here produced by the apostle as the representative of *all* the human race, and Christ as the representative of only the *elect ;* see the discussion on this point, p. 183 seq. Nor is there any need of resorting to this construction, if we take into view the suggestions above, viz, that on the one hand blessings are proffered to all, blessings much greater than the evils occasioned by the fall, which blessings still can be actually enjoyed only through repentance and faith; while on the other hand, eternal death is before all, *i. e.*, all are exposed to it from their condition and circumstances, but some personal act, *i. e*, some actual sin, must precede it. I see not well how to escape from this conclusion, unless we give up a part of the *superabounding* of the grace of the gospel, or else take the position that Christ is here presented as merely the head of the elect. But how can the first be given up, when the apostle so often asserts it? And how can the last be received, without doing violence to the laws of interpretation, and to the nature of the contrast presented?

It must be particularly noted, that the *superabounding* of the grace of the gospel appertains not to the number of its *subjects*, but to the number of offences forgiven by it, *i e.*, the actual *greatness of evil* removed by it; for the evils of Adam's fall extend to *all* his race without exception, and how can the grace of Christ extend to *more* than all? This makes it clear, that the superabounding has reference to the forgiveness of the *many* offences which men commit, and which expose them to far greater evils than the *one* offence of Adam does; as it is asserted by the apostle in ver. 16.

There is one other point, also, which should not be omitted in this reference to the superabounding of the grace of the gospel. This is, that the gospel *places all men under a dispensation of grace*, where penitent sinners can be pardoned and accepted; while a dispensation of law (such was that under which Adam was first placed), subjects them to its penalty without reprieve, for the first offence which they commit. It cannot escape notice, then, that we are now, notwithstanding the numerous and dreadful evils occasioned by the fall, under a far more favorable dispensation in respect to an opportunity for *making sure* our final happiness, than we should have been by **being** placed in the original condition of Adam. Pres. Edwards has taken **great** pains in his book on Original Sin (p. 324 seq), to justify God's deal-**ings** with Adam's posterity, in charging Adam's sin upon them, by endeavoring to show that mankind had a most favorable trial in Adam, and one which was much more likely in the nature of things to result in their good, **than** if each had stood upon his own trial. Now if there be any foundation for this, and indeed if we simply admit that each in a state of innocence must **have** been tried as Adam was, then the fact that he fell, and the conclusion **thence** to be deduced by analogy that they would fall, seems to render it pretty **certain**, that the whole of our race would have been involved in a final and irretrievable ruin by being placed under a law dispensation, as Adam first was. Grace *superabounds*, then, above the evils of the fall, in that Adam lost for men only an innocent *legal* state—one in which men were on trial, and from which they might fall; while Christ has procured for them *a dispensation of grace*, under which many and aggravated offences are no bar to the salvation of the penitent.

I speak of a *legal* state in which men were to be on trial, because I am not able to find any good reason, to support the idea, that if Adam had obeyed, all his posterity would have been born in a state not only of perfect, but of *confirmed* holiness. Where is one sentence in all the book of God which declares this? And how is any argument to be obtained from analogy? The angels have had their trial, and some of them "kept not their first estate." The first human pair had their trial, when directly from the hands of their Maker; and they fell. But supposing they had not fallen, is there any ground to expect that their posterity would have been born in a condition *better* than that in which the first pair were created? As far as we know any thing of the history of rational beings, so far it is clear, that it is an indispensable rule of divine moral government, that *all should be subject to a state of trial*. If then the views of Pres. Edwards and others in relation to this subject are unsupported either by the Scriptures or by analogy, how can we admit them? It is not enough to appeal to symbols and to systems of divinity in such a case; nor to argue *ad verecundiam*, by reciting the names of such as have patronized a view of the subject like that which has now been examined. We must have Scripture, and argument drawn from it, and then we will cheerfully yield our assent.

I return from this partial digression, however, and observe that if, as stated in the commentary, the τύπος of the apostle is to be understood as having reference merely to evils and blessings that come on all Adam's posterity *without* any concurrence or voluntary act of their own, we may find sufficient here to answer the demands of a τύπος. But if any insist that the meaning shall be regarded as having respect to the *highest* penalty on the one hand, and the *highest* blessings on the other; then, in order to make out a real and true parallel, we must include the free and voluntary concurrence of each individual, who sins and suffers for himself or on his own account, or repents and believes for himself so as to receive the highest blessings which Christ bestows. I do not object to extending the τύπος in this way, provided it be understood when thus extended, not of penalty in the higher sense as *actually* inflicted, nor of blessings in the higher sense as *actually* bestowed, but of *exposedness* to penalty on the one hand, and *exposedness* (sit venia verbo comparationis causâ) to blessings on the other. How can anything more than this be made out? That everlasting death will *actually* be inflicted on all of Adam's race, of course will not be assumed; and as little can it be made out, that everlasting life will actually be bestowed on all.

The subject, properly considered, will afford relief to the mind, which is struggling with difficulty arising from the assertions of the apostle, which represent the blessings procured by redemption as being co-extensive with the mischiefs introduced by the fall. The evils and blessings in question are in many important respects co-extensive; and in their *highest* sense they are in this way regarded as being suspended on something *which is to be done* on the part of man in order either to suffer the one or to enjoy the other. What hinders, then, that Adam in respect to the evils which he has introduced, should be contrasted (as Paul has contrasted him) with Christ in respect to the blessings which he had introduced?

After all, there are many serious and considerate men, accustomed to a different mode of representing this subject, who probably will not concede to this view. But with the exception of some whose views are excessive on this point, I have an apprehension that the difference consists more in *words and modes of interpretation*, than in opinion as to the *facts* in the case. They take it for granted, at the outset, that in all respects in which our present condition differs from that of Adam before his fall, in those respects it must be *the consequence of sin;* and to this I do not object; excepting that the latitude of the assertion "*all* respects," may possibly be too wide. What is called high orthodoxy maintains, moreover, that the disposition with which we are born is itself not only sin, but a part of the *punishment* of sin; and, as we could not ourselves sin before we had an existence, that Adam's sin is imputed to us, and we are punished for it, by being born with a disposition which is itself sinful, and which is also a part of the *penalty* of Adam's sin imputed to us. The argument is, that inasmuch as we are born heirs of woe and heirs of a disposition to sin, this must be a punishment for guilt which is either our own in a strict sense, or our own by imputation.

Now that men are born with a disposition that will certainly and always lead them to sin, in all their acts of a moral nature, before they are regenerated, I admit as fully as they do. But the fictitious process of accounting for this on the ground of *imputed* sin, which in this way becomes our own, is not what the Bible asserts or seems to maintain. *There is not, in all the Scriptures, an instance in which one man's sin or righteousness is said to be imputed to another.* If there is, let it be produced, and discussion on this point will then cease.

The *natural* state of man I admit to be one that is destitute of any proper disposition to holiness; and therefore, that man in his natural state is exposed to all the terrors of the curse. This is in itself a tremendous evil; it is also the consequence of Adam's fall. The awful turpitude of sin is disclosed by the fact that the consequences fall upon the innocent as well as the guilty. The vicious parent ruins his innocent children; the wicked ruler plunges whole nations into wretchedness. This fact is not illustrated, proved, or accounted for, by saying that his wickedness is *imputed* to these nations? The fact is one which takes place as the natural and regular sequence of wickedness, under the present constitution of things.

So in the case of Adam and his posterity. All are sufferers on his account. The original state of man is lost. A new one is come in, in consequence of his sin, which is fraught with danger and sorrow. It is certain now, that all who come to sufficient maturity to sin, will sin. This certainty has been occasioned by the fall. In this way "all are made sinners by the disobedience of one," *i. e.*, all are placed in a condition in which they will surely be sinners and nothing else, in case of moral development or of ability to commit sin. More than this cannot be made out. More is not even contended for by moderate and sober writers, whenever they lose sight of the doctrine of imputation. In proof of this, we may appeal to the fact, that they have made a broad distinction between *original* and *actual* sin. Why this? Plainly because the human mind revolts at confounding our own personal and voluntary acts as free agents, with the disposition that the God of nature has given us, and in which we had no concurrence. But where does the Bible make *two sorts* of sin, we might well ask; two sorts so immeasurably different as these? The one free, voluntary, of our own choice; the other antecedent to all choice or action?

Then, again, the advocates for imputation do most of them concede the salvation of infants, who die before the commission of *actual* sin. Why? Plainly because they cannot bring their minds to place voluntary sins on a level with involuntary ones. Pictet himself, strenuous as he is in orthodoxy, puts the question, whether final damnation would ensue merely on the ground of *original* sin? And this he answers by the declaration, that he does not believe it would.

Of what use then is it to confound things by giving them one and the same name (sin), which we afterwards separate so widely from each other, and which we cannot help separating, without doing violence to the first laws of our moral consciousness? If I might be permitted to suggest an answer, it would be, that it answers no other purpose but to keep Christians separated from each other, and to perpetuate disputes about *names*, while as to *things* they are essentially agreed. Different modes of explanation they may adopt. In difficult and mysterious matters men will always do this. But why should we refuse to see, that calling certain things by certain names, helps neither to establish nor explain them? A fictitious ground for a resting-place, which is never adopted by the sacred writers, can never add to the peace or harmony, or valuable stores of theologians.

In a word, it does not follow, because men are born heirs of woe and exposed to become *actual* sinners, that this is to be considered as individual and personal *punishment* (in the proper sense of this word); nor that any light is thrown on this mystery by saying, that they are sinners by imputation. *Imputed* sin and *veritable* punishment do not match together. Eternal justice is in no good measure vindicated by coupling them together. The mind remains, after all fictitious efforts of this nature, just where it was before. The facts are seen and confessed; but the mode of accounting for them in this way, the mind is not obligated to receive, while no declarations of such a nature can be pointed out in the Scriptures.

My positions are, that all men are born destitute of a predominant disposition to holiness; that all who come to moral action will sin and always sin before regeneration; that this state of things is brought upon us by Adam's fall; that suffering and personal sin, however, in such a world as this now is, are by no means co-extensive; that the tremendous evil of sin is, that it often affects the innocent (innocent in regard to the particular matter that occasioned the evil) as well as the guilty; and that admitting these facts, we have the substance of the scriptural doctrine respecting the fall and its consequences. The *quo modo, i. e.*, the manner of accounting for such facts as these, I cannot regard as important, excepting that it should not be *anti-scriptural*. A mere *law-fiction* cannot help us here; and here, moreover, the sacred writers have not speculated; why then should we?

It is only when men hold fast to the position, that there can be no evil in the world which is not *penally* in the proper sense—penalty in respect to the particular individual who suffers it—that they need to be embarrassed with the question, why we are heirs of woe, and of a disposition that leads to

EXCURSUS IV. ON ROM. V. 14.

actual sin. Tell us then, all ye who assume such a position, Was Adam in paradise, before his fall, exposed to no evil? Did he suffer none? Positive pains of body or of mind, I grant he did not suffer; but was it no evil to be exposed to the temptations of Satan? Did it prove to be none? Nay, I might well ask, to what greater evil could he have been subjected, unless it was final perdition, than to be thus exposed to the wiles of Satan? Why then should we be so often and so confidently told, that *all* evil is the penalty of sin, and only the penalty of it? It is not so, it has not been so. In a world of *trial*, there is and must be evil of some kind or other, in some degree or other; else trial is but an empty name.

We need not to be over solicitous then to answer the question, How can all the present evils suffered by men, or evils to which they are exposed, be accounted for? That Adam's fall has been concerned with them, or most of them, in their present form, is clearly and abundantly taught by Paul in the chapter before us. But in what way, *i. e.*, how far in all respects, and the *modus operandi*, this chapter does neither assert nor explain. Why need we do what the apostle has left undone? To say that these evils come because of *imputed* sin, is explaining nothing, satisfying in no degree the enquiring mind, helping the case in no respect. It is only changing *res obscura* for *nomen obscurius*. Enough that we believe the *facts*, as simply stated; speculation beyond this has hitherto availed little indeed, and promises but little for the future.

I must make one more remark in this connection. The inquiry has often been made: On the ground that the evils of the present life and physical death stand connected with the fall of Adam, how can it be that the redemption of Christ does not liberate the elect from *all* these evils? In reply to this I would say to the enquirer. Mark well that Paul does not aver, that the blessings procured by Christ do in *all* respects stand *directly opposed* to the evils introduced by Adam, so as to prevent their occurrence in any degree. Not at all. He only avers that blessings *superabound*, and that they are of the like *extent* with the evils. We have seen that this is true; and we have abundant assurance, also, that all the sufferings and sorrows of this life, which the children of God are called on to undergo, will turn to good account at last in respect to their spiritual interests. This does not show indeed that they are not evils in themselves; but only that they may be converted into a blessing, by that infinite power and wisdom and benevolence which have redeemed man. It sets the redemption of Christ in a new and glorious light, that such are the effects of it; and in such a light it was the design of Paul to place it, in the paragraph before us. As I have before said, suffering and sorrow in some degree may be necessary (so infinite wisdom has adjudged) to our discipline in our sinful and fallen state, but they do not substantially detract and they never can detract, from the actual superabounding of the blessings which the gospel has introduced.

(4) The τύπος is not between the *person* of Adam as such, and that of Christ. See commentary, p. 179.

(5) The apostle nowhere declares Adam to be the *federal* head or representative of all his posterity; nor Christ to be the *federal* head of his spirit-

ual children. It would be indispensable, indeed, to the admission of the latter idea, that Christ should be regarded as the federal head of the elect *only* But as we have seen, the representations of the present passage do not admit of such an exegesis. The usual doctrine of the more recent Protestant symbols, in respect to the *federal* and *representative* capacity of Christ and Adam, took its rise in the time and in consequence of the disputes of Augustine; it was variously modified and represented by the schoolmen of after ages. It was, however, more fully developed in its present form at the time of Cocceius, who gave occasion to such a development by his manner of considering the covenants of law and grace. Whatever may be correct or incorrect in the more usual representations about federal head, it does not appear to me to be taught in the chapter before us. It is drawn from it, as all must admit, merely in the way of theological deduction It is a deduction indeed, which in some respects, and in a modified sense, seems to present nothing inconsistent with scriptural doctrine; inasmuch as all men are affected more or less by what Adam their first progenitor did, and also by what Christ has done in order to introduce a dispensation of grace But this particular form of expression casts no new additional light on the difficulties of our subject; and, from the nature of the case, it cannot be justly deemed essential to a full belief in the Christian doctrine of depravity or of redemption.

(6) Calvin points out two other points of dissimilitude between Adam and Christ, which he says the apostle did not think unworthy of notice, but which he omitted to notice merely because the turn of his discourse did not allow him to do it. These are (*a*) "Quod peccato Adae *non per solam im putationem* damnamur, acsi alieni peccati exigeretur a nobis poena; sed *ideo* ejus poenam sustinemus, *quia et culpæ sumus rei, quatenus scilicet natura nostra in ipso vitiata, inuiquitatis reatu obstringitur apud Deum.*

"At per Christi justitiam *alio modo* in salutem restituimur; neque enim id nobis accepta fertur *qui intra nos sit,* sed quod Christum, cum bonis suis omnibus, Patris, largitate nobis donatum possidemus." Calvin then adds (which those should note well who may hold that Christ's righteousness does in any proper sense become our own): "Itaque donum justitiæ *non qualitatem* qua nos Deus imbuat, sed *gratuitam justitiæ imputationem* significat."

(*b*) "Altera [differentia] est, quod *non ad omnes homines* pervenit Christi beneficium, quemadmodum *universum suum genus* damnatione Adam involvit." He then goes on to state that the ground of this is, that "our corruption comes in the course of nature (he means that it is transmitted by natural generation), and so pervades the *whole mass;* but we must possess faith in order to participate in the blessings proffered by Christ. To be depraved, it is necessary only to be a man; to participate in the righteousness of Christ, one must be a believer The infants of believers have by covenant a right of adoption, by which they come into communion with Christ; other infants are not exempt from the common lot Comm on Rom v 17

The *first* point, is that Adam's sin is not imputed to us merely as the sin of another, *i. e.,* one which is put to our account, but that our nature has become vitiated in consequence of it, and the fault thus becomes inherent, and in a proper sense our own. Calvin and Turretin are directly at variance here, and Edwards and Stapfer take sides with the former. But the righteousness of Christ does never become *inherently* our own, for the pardon bestowed on account of it is simply gratuitous.

Into a discussion of this topic my limits do not allow me here to go. Calvin may be in the right or in the wrong, just as one understands and defines his assertions. He denies that *punishment* for another's sins is exacted of us; and here I fully believe him to be in the right, for punishment, in the proper sense of this word, and under a system of law which is strictly just, must ever have relation to one's own offences. But *sufferers* because of Adam's sin we truly are, for how else shall we account for it, that we are born destitute of a disposition to holiness, and possessed of one which (in case of moral development) will certainly lead us to sin? To say that Adam's *vitiosity* is *transmitted* to us by natural generation, or in any simply physical way, helps nothing in the way of explanation. What matters it, whether we have Adam's vitiosity, or another one *de novo*, if after all we actually have such a vitiosity as fact shows that we do possess? The *modus in quo* of obtaining it, is a question of no practical moment; and it is wonderful that so much stress should have been laid upon it. How is the fact in question in any way illustrated, established, or vindicated by such a supposition? The transmission of a *moral* character in the way of natural descent is a problem that (to say the least) must always remain dark and difficult, for in a strict and proper sense every man forms his own moral character. But the fact that all men are so born, since the fall, that they are disposed to evil and not to good, at the first opening of moral development, is a fact which universal experience testifies. With this simple fact we may well rest satisfied. Speculation has not yet helped us to any adequate *eclaircissement*, and, so far as I can see, is not likely to do so.

In regard to the *second* point of discrepancy made by Calvin, it would seem to show that he regarded Christ as here represented to be the federal head of only the elect. See the discussion of this point in commentary, p. 222, and above, p. 449.

EXCURSUS V.

On Rom. v. 16 (p. 188 seq.)

I CANNOT see that the considerations here suggested suffer any abatement of their force, on the supposition that the οἱ πολλοί (on whom the blessings procured by Christ are conferred) comprises only *the elect*; as some strenuously maintain. For the elect are never made partakers of *actual* pardon and justification, without repentance and faith; and these are both acts of their own, for it is not the sanctifying Spirit of God who repents and believes for them. And these are not only their own acts, but they are truly acts which constitute a *conditio sine qua non* of real pardon and justification. But how is it, now, on the other side of the antithesis? According to the views of those who advocate the above sentiment, the very *elect* are partakers of Adam's sin and guilt to the full extent of final and eternal damnation, antecedently to any act or choice of their own. So, at all events, Turretin states this matter; and so others who think with him. But, looked at in this simple light, how are the particulars of the comparison to be made out? Or in what important respect is there any real τύπος left between the one and the other? The simple thing, that the act of one had influence on others, seems to be all that remains: the manner of that influence, the condition of it, its extent, the degree of causality or efficacy which should be attributed to it, are all thrown out of the question; and yet these are the main points of importance and interest. When the question is put: "Whether the influence of the Spirit of God in regeneration is *efficient* as *causa principalis*, or whether it is secondary or subordinate, *i. e.*, whether it operates merely as *causa occasionalis*?" it is rightly thought by most theologians to be a fundamental question in evangelical theology. It is not so much the fact itself, that the spirit of God *does* influence the sinner who is converted, which interests us, as it is the *degree* and *kind* and *extent* and *condition* of his influence. So in the case of the first and second Adam. The mere fact that each had *some kind of influence* is of little interest or importance compared with the degree and kind and condition and extent of influence. But how are these to be at all compared, when things so diverse are brought together, as many bring together in the present case? On the one side, many blessings are *unconditionally* bestowed on all men without exception; yet still higher and eternal happiness is made altogether *conditional*, even after all which Christ has done; for it is suspended on their own voluntary acts of repentance and faith. But on the other, there is not only unconditional and universal temporal evil to a certain extent (for this all candid persons would seem constrained to admit), but there is unconditional and universal sin, guilt, and misery, in their ultimate and eternal measure, before any voluntary act at all of the nascent human being, and before he is in any proper physiological and pneumatical sense capable of any free moral agency whatever. Nor can we, if we keep upon Turretin's ground, draw back from this statement, as some have lately attempted to do. This is and has been the dominant opinion among those who sometimes claim the exclusive right to be called the highly orthodox party in the reformed churches; as every man may satisfy himself who will read Turretin, Van Maestricht, or other writers of the like character. And assuming this statement for our basis, where, I ask again, is the τύπος that remains, in any respect that can be a matter of much interest or importance?

Should it be said, as it has been, that the grand τύπος in this case is *imputation* on both sides—imputation of Adam's sin to his posterity, and of Christ's righteousness to the elect—the simple answer is, that this is not once asserted, nor even hinted (so far as I am able to discover) in the whole passage. Whatever may be elsewhere taught respecting *imputation*, it is not to be found here. And indeed with respect to the other parts of the Bible, it is plain matter of fact that the Scriptures (as has once and again been said) never speak of any man's sin being imputed to *others;* it is the imputation of one's *own* sin or fault to *himself*, which they speak of (as we have already seen, p. 123 above), and not the imputation of the sin of one man to others who did not commit that sin.

Moreover can it be that the train of evils that result from the fall, are no more than suppository, *i. e.*, imputed ones? And are the unspeakable blessings that come to us on account of what Christ has done and suffered, only *imputed, i. e*, supposititious ones, or at least are they only from a supposititious source? Does not the mind spontaneously ask, Can imputed sin be punished otherwise than by imputed damnation, unless the eternal laws of right and wrong — of even-handed justice, are to be overturned and set aside? And must not imputed righteousness correspond with imputed happiness? Else how can we join *par cum pari*? And what is the kind of moral government that we must be led to believe in, by this method of representing the subject? A world, not of *realities*, but of *imputations;* all as it were *factitious*, and nothing real and veritable as to the original ground of punishment or reward! Moreover, according to the scheme in question, while Adam's sin is not only imputed to us, and thus imputed brings upon us the sentence of real and veritable death in its final and eternal power, and while there is besides this an *inherent* original sin (the penalty of imputed sin) which also subjects us to the like condemnation; yet, on the other hand, Christ's righteousness, although said to be *imputed* to us, is acknowledged as never becoming *inherent* (for then we should be absolutely perfect), but is reckoned only as supposititious. Here then is *par cum impari*. The two cases are immeasurably diverse, and the real τύπος seems to be much, if not altogether obscured. Must we not force our way, when we oblige ourselves to move in such a direction as this?

After all, however, it is rather the *language* employed, and the costume put upon this whole matter by such modes of representation, than the real ultimate object in view, at least the object in view as conceived of by sober and judicious men, to which one may reasonably object. The extremes of the *imputation doctrine* do certainly lead to very serious difficulties, some of which are stated above, and many others might be added, if this were the proper place. It is enough to say, once more, that *there is not in all the Bible one assertion, that Adam's sin or Christ's righteousness is imputed to us;* nor one declaration that any man's sin is ever imputed by God or man to another man. If this be not a correct statement, those who discredit it have the obvious means before them of correcting it. But if it does not need correction, then why should we be compelled to admit, as essential truth, the *modus* of stating a doctrine which has no parallel in the Scriptures; which we may therefore regard as not expressly warranted by the word of God; which is so obviously adapted to raise difficulties in the mind on the score of God's justice and impartiality; which seems to resolve the grand features of redemption into mere arbitrary sovereignty, which counts things to be what all confess they are not, which seems also to present the moral governor of the universe as doing with the one hand for the sake of undoing with the other, and doing much — very much that is all-important — in a merely fictitious way, and not as veritable reality; why, I would most respectfully ask, should we be compelled to adopt such a statement, unless the Bible absolutely demands it? Every Protestant, at least, is at liberty to ask this question; and he is at liberty to choose a different mode of stating the subject, until it can be shown that the Bible requires this mode, and this only.

But I speak, of course, only of *ultraism* in these views. It is altogether plain that many, I believe I might say of most sober, judicious, and pious men, who have well studied this subject, and are attached to this mode of representation, use the terms *imputation* and *impute* only as a convenient or rather *compendious* method of expressing their belief, that the posterity of Adam have greatly suffered on account of his sin, and that they receive many blessings on account of what Christ has done and suffered. In the *thing itself*, as thus stated, all men of what is called *evangelical* sentiment must agree and do agree. The objection to *imputation* and *impute*, as employed by ultra-theologians, is, that these words (as they apply them) have no warrant in Scripture; that they are adapted to mislead; and that the doctrine *apparently* inculcated by them is liable to many appalling objections, among which one of the most urgent is, that the sin of Adam and the righteousness of Christ are represented as imputed in the like way, when after all the method is so exceedingly diverse, as we have seen above. At least this latter assertion is most palpably true, when the consequences of imputation which are invariably connected with it by those who strenuously maintain the doctrine, are taken into view. For as they present the matter, the consequence of Adam's *imputed* sin, is to be born an heir of damnation and of *inherent* sin; and the latter is regarded both as the *punishment* of the former and as a new cause for other punishment, and also as the cause of all subsequent actual sin; while, on the other hand, men are not regarded as born holy on account of Christ; not even the *elect* are so born; nor is there ever any *inherent* holiness in them because Christ's righteousness is imputed to them. They are made really and veritably holy in part (not *putatively* so), by the sanctifying influences of the Spirit of God, on account of what Christ has done and suffered; so that their holiness is not in this case factitious, and the Redeemer's holiness is not veritably theirs. If it were so, then *perfect* holiness would be theirs, and they could then present a *claim* of salvation on the ground of meeting the demands of the law. Mere *imputed* holiness, however, never can answer proper legal demands; and therefore it can never entitle sinners to a legal acquittal. Pardon is given altogether of *grace;* not on the ground of either real or factitious, *i e*, imputed obedience. The first of these sinners cannot plead; the second, law (as such) does not in itself admit.

If any one should reply, that Christ is and is called *the Lord our righteousness;* my answer would be, that he is at the same time called *our wisdom and sanctification and redemption*. Now he is by this representation made just as much our imputed wisdom, and our imputed sanctification, and our imputed redemption, as he is our imputed righteousness. But what possible sense could be made from *imputation* as applied to all these? What is our *im-*

puted redemption? The simple meaning, then, of all is, that Christ is the author of the wisdom which the gospel has revealed; he is the procuring cause of the sanctification which believers experience; he is the author of the eternal redemption of which they are made partakers; and he is *the Lord their righteousness* (δικαιοσύνη) in the same way, *i. e*, he is the meritorious cause of their justification or pardon.

EXCURSUS VI.

On Rom. v. 19, διὰ τῆς παρακοῆς τοῦ ἑνὸς ἀνθρώπου ἁμαρτωλοὶ κατεστάθησαν οἱ πολλοί (pp 198, 199).

The meaning of the word κατεστάθησαν has been sufficiently discussed. The general idea in the whole declaration still remains in some measure to be ascertained. Those who are familiar with the idiom of the original Scriptures must know, that *causation* of every degree and kind was usually expressed by the Hebrews in one and the same way. We are accustomed, when we wish for nice distinctions, to speak of *efficient* or *principal* cause, and of *secondary* or *instrumental* or *occasional* cause, etc. But it is not so generally in the Scriptures. 'God moves David to go and number Israel, and Satan moves David to go and number Israel.' The very same verb is applied to both agents in this case. So 'the Lord hardened Pharaoh's heart, and Pharaoh hardened his own heart;' see Exod. vii 13, ix. 12, x. 1, 20, 27, xi. 10, xiv. 8; Rom. ix 18; Deut ii. 30; Isai lxiii. 17; John xii. 40. So evil is ascribed to God, both moral and natural; 2 Sam. xii. 11, xvi. 10; 1 Kings xxii. 22; Josh. xi 20; Ps. cv. 25; 1 Kings xi. 23, xxiv. 1. In like manner God is said to give men a new heart, and they are commanded to 'make to themselves a new heart;' the Spirit of God is said to convince and convert, and regenerate the sinner; and the same thing is often ascribed, for the most part in the like words, to the gospel and to the power of divine truth. Now he who has not carefully noted and weighed these obvious and highly important facts, is in great danger of making out in some way a very partial system of theology, and of contradicting in his exegesis of one part of the Bible, what the sacred writers have affirmed in another.

To apply this to the case before us. *Were constituted sinners* means, that Adam was, in some sense or other, the cause or occasion of his posterity becoming sinners. But whether this was through a degradation of their nature physically propagated down from father to son; or whether it was (as Chrysostom, Œcumenius, Pelagius, Erasmus, and others have with little probability maintained), only by virtue of the example which he set, or whether it was in some other way, is not determined by the language of the text Such expressions, as we have seen above, do not determine of themselves either the *degree* or the *kind* of causality. Principal or subordinate causation in this case may either of them be expressed by the phrase διὰ τῆς — κατεστάθησαν. The strenuous advocate for *imputation* avers, however, that the posterity of Adam were constituted sinners, *by his offence being imputed to them, and their being treated as though they had committed it.*

But when I look at the nature of this case, and ask what language the apostle would most probably have employed, had he designed to convey such a meaning, I am constrained to say, that the case can hardly be supposed with probability, that he would have employed merely such language as that before us, when other modes of expression more explicit and obvious were within his reach. "Ὅτι ἐν αὐτῷ ἁμαρτωλοὶ ἐλογίσθησαν — ὅτι αὐτοῖς ἐλογίσθη ἡ ἁμαρτία αὐτοῦ — or else ὅτι ἦσαν ὑπόδικοι διὰ τῆς ἁμαρτίας αὐτοῦ, or something equivalent to these expressions, might, not to say must, have been added after οἱ πολλοί, so as to prevent all mistake. But as the matter now is, with the necessarily *active* sense of ἁμαρτωλοί, the language itself cannot lead us philologically to the supposition of an *imputation* scheme of sin. See comm. on this verse and the preceding Excursus.

That men should be *constituted* or *made sinners* by the disobedience of Adam, most naturally means, I had almost said, must necessarily mean, that in some way his offence so affected them as that they become actual sinners *in propriâ personâ.* Now is anything more common than this mode of expression? 'A man of vicious character,' we say, 'corrupts his whole family. A profligate of winning exterior corrupts the whole neighborhood of youth around him. One sceptic makes many doubters in revelation. Voltaire made half of literary Europe sceptical.' Now in these and a thousand other like expressions, we do mean to assert an active influence, a real causality in some proper sense, of the evil done or spoken. Yet we never once think, for example, of Voltaire's scepticism being *imputed* to half of literary Europe; nor do we once imagine, that any of the classes above named as being corrupted are corrupted without any voluntary agency of their own The *sin* of corrupt feelings and affections is *entirely their own:* it matters not what the causes were which operated on them, so long as they were after all left to their own choice whether they would yield to the excitement or resist it.

So far then as the force of *language* is concerned, the expression ἁμαρτωλοὶ κατεστάθησαν can never be proved to mean that Adam's posterity were made sinners only by imputation. Indeed it must mean something more than this and different from it. It is *real* and not fictitious and merely putative sin, of which the apostle is here speaking; as we may see by appealing to ver. 12, and to the nature of the case and the meaning of ἁμαρτωλοί.

In what way, then, does Adam's sin operate, in order to produce the effect which the apostle attributes to it? The degree, the extent, and nature of this influence, seem all to be laid open in the text. It amounts to such a degree as to involve us in a ruinous state or condition; it extends to all the posterity of Adam; it is a cause or ground of moral depravation, for it is the cause or occasion of all men's coming into condemnation, and therefore it must be a cause of their becoming sinners But after all, the *modus operandi* is not declared by the apostle. He does not say, whether the operation of

Adam's sin is on our physical or mental constitution; or whether it has influence merely on the condition in which we are placed, as being expelled from paradise and surrounded by peculiar temptations; nor whether it is example merely of Adam which we copy; and therefore a man may believe all that Paul has *here* taught, who refrains from speculations on any of these points, or on any others of the like nature. Better indeed would it have been for the quiet of the churches, if many had entirely refrained from all the particular modes of explanation which they have urged; for the danger is great that we may not only substitute our own individual belief and speculations for essential doctrines of the Scriptures here, but also for a commentary upon the text, and then elevate what we have thus superadded to an eminence far above the text itself.

It is not then from the text or context here that we can explain the *modus operandi* of Adam's sin. But from facts elsewhere disclosed and well known by observation we may learn, that all men are now born destitute of a holy disposition, *i. e.*, a disposition that would lead them to obey the divine law. Our nature then is *degenerate and fallen;* and what can have rendered it so but sin? Then, again, Adam's sin occasioned the expulsion of our race from paradise; the ground was cursed on account of this; we are now born in a state in which we are everywhere surrounded and assailed by temptations; we have no predominant inclination or disposition to resist them, although we have the physiological and psychological power to do so; and for all these reasons (and these are enough to account for the fact without the aid of *imputation*), all men are constituted, or do become sinners. That they are *actual* sinners in the womb, before they are capable of moral knowledge and action, Paul has expressly denied in Rom. ix 11, "The children being not yet born, neither having done any good or evil" Even those who make *two sorts* of sin, viz., *original* and *actual*, would seem virtually to admit the truth which the apostle here affirms, if they admit infants to be guilty of only *putative* sin. But still, that men are born with a disposition that will lead them to sin, or occasion them to sin, is altogether certain from Scripture and from fact. Now this is a state the opposite of that in which Adam was created; for his predominant disposition was that which led to holy action. Such facts as these the apostle plainly refers to in our text. And we may safely admit them; inasmuch as they are confirmed by Scripture, and by every day's experience. But the *modus operandi* by which they are brought about, must still remain, in many respects, entirely hidden from our view. Why should we waste our time and talents, and spoil our benevolent feelings towards others, in pushing our speculations where the sacred writers have not led the way, and where facts will not warrant us in pushing them?

One more remark of a philological nature should be made on the manner in which *causality* is stated in this verse, viz., διὰ τῆς παρακοῆς. That διά may in particular cases stand before a Genitive which denotes *principal* cause, is sufficiently plain from examples in John i 3, iii 17; Rom. xi 36, i 5; 1 Cor i 9; Gal i 1; 2 Thess ii. 2; Heb. i. 3, δι' ἑαυτοῦ. But that such phrases as διὰ παρακοῆς κατεστάθησαν cannot, from the mere form of the language, be made to mean *principal* cause, is not only clear from the fact that διά before the Genitive usually designates instrumental or secondary cause, but from the fact also that cases occur where it would be absurd to construe it as designating *causa principalis*. For example · Paul says in Rom vii. 5, τὰ παθήματα τῶν ἁμαρτιῶν, τὰ δ ι ὰ τοῦ νόμου, *our sinful passions which are by the law.* In ver. 7 he says · "I had not known sin, but διὰ τοῦ νόμου." In ver. 8 he says · " Sin, taking occasion διὰ τῆς ἐντολῆς, wrought in me all manner of concupiscence;" and so in ver. 11. Is the law then the efficient cause of sinful passions and actions ? Yet the law had something to do with these ; and it is therefore (as usual among the sacred writers) reckoned as a cause or ground of them ; but by no means the exclusive or principal or only cause. And so in the case before us; if Adam's sin as imputed to us, if original sin indeed either imputed or inherent (as theologians speak), be the sole and exclusive cause of all our sin, then what was the cause of Adam's *first* sin ? He surely was not influenced by *original* sin, in either sense that is assigned to this word. The truth seems plainly to be, that there was originally a susceptability in our nature of being impressed and excited by allurements to sin ; else how happened it that Adam was moved to sin ? Even the spotless Saviour was *tempted* ; and if there were no sympathies in his nature like to our own, or rather, like to those of Adam in his primitive state, how could he be tempted, and how could the apostle appeal (as he does in Heb. ii. 14—18, iv. 15, 16) to his *sympathy* with us who are tempted, as the peculiar ground of hope and relief for us when we are subjected to temptations ?

The point of *degradation* and *fall*, then, would seem to develop itself peculiarly in this particular, viz., that our sympathies towards sinful objects are now much stronger and higher than those of Adam in his primitive state ; such indeed as to render it certain that our moral acts will all be sinful, until we become regenerated and sanctified. This renders certain the great fact stated by the apostle, that all men *become sinners* through the disobedience of Adam But that they are actual sinners *before* moral action, can be made out when it is shown that sin does not consist in *moral* action ; and that moral action begins before birth, can be made out when the assertion of Paul, that Jacob and Esau (when old enough to struggle together in the womb) "had not done any good or evil."

The reason *why* God made such a constitution of human nature, which would suffer in all its branches by reason of an act of sin in our first parents, he has not given. We leave that to his infinite wisdom and goodness, cheerfully confiding in the great and certain truth that he does all things well. We are concerned only with *facts ;* and the facts are few, plain, and simple, if we receive them as the Scriptures have left them, and content ourselves without addition to them by our own speculations. See further in Bib Repos. for Apr. 1836, p. 241 sq. ; Apr. 1839, p 261 sq , and July 1839, p. 26 sq.

EXCURSUS VII.

On Rom vii. 5 — 25 (pp. 234 — 263).

First, it is the just principle of interpretation, that we should understand every writer, when this can be done in consonance with the laws of language, as speaking to the purpose which he has immediately before him. There are very many truths of the gospel, and many plain and important truths, which are not taught in this or that passage of Scripture. The question concerning chap vii 5 — 25 is not, whether it be true that there is a contest in the breast of Christians, which might, at least for the most part, be well described by the words there found; but, whether such a view of the subject is congruous with the present design and argument of the apostle.

Secondly, no theory of interpretation can, in the present case, be duly and satisfactorily supported, by appealing merely to the form and intensity of particular expressions. If this can be allowed here, then are we certain that two opposite theories may be equally well established, viz , that the individual whose experience is represented is a saint, and is not one. That he is one, may be made out by such expressions as the following : viz., σύμφημι τῷ νόμῳ, ver. 16 ; τὸ γὰρ θέλειν [sc. τὸ καλὸν] παράκειταί μοι, ver 18 ; τῷ θέλοντι ἐμοὶ ποιεῖν τὸ καλόν, ver 21 ; συνήδομαι γὰρ τῷ νόμῳ τοῦ θεοῦ κατὰ τὸν ἔσω ἄνθρωπον, ver. 22 ; and τῷ μὲν νοΐ δουλεύω νόμῳ θεοῦ, ver. 25 ; while with equal certainty and by the same reasoning, we may prove that he is not a saint, from ἐγὼ δὲ σαρκικός εἰμι, πεπραμένος ὑπὸ τὴν ἁμαρτίαν ver 14 ; ὃ μισῶ τοῦτο πράσσω, ver. 15 ; οὐκ οἰκεῖ ἐν ἐμοὶ τοῦτ' ἔστι ἐν τῇ σαρκί μου, ἀγαθόν, ver 18 ; τὸ δὲ κατεργάζεσθαι τὸ καλὸν οὐχ εὑρίσκω, ver. 18 ; ὃ οὐ θέλω κακὸν, τοῦτο πράσσω, ver 19 ; ἐμοὶ τὸ κακὸν, παράκειται, ver. 21 ; βλέπω ἕτερον νόμον ἐν τοῖς μέλεσι . . . . αἰχμαλωτίζοντά με τῷ νόμῳ τῆς ἁμαρτίας, ver 23 ; τῇ δὲ σαρκὶ [δουλεύω] νόμῳ ἁμαρτίας, ver 25. Stronger language than this, viz., " I am σαρκικός, and *sold under sin*," i. e., a bond-slave to sin, and wholly devoted to its service and obedient to its orders, cannot well be found in the New Testament.

Whoever insists, then, that the passage before us must be applied to the Christian, because of some strong expressions in it which seem to indicate true moral good, should also take notice that, by the very same principles of interpretation, he will of course be obliged to concede that a *carnal* state and entire devotedness to the passions and appetites is described. To avoid this conclusion, he considers these last expressions as used in a *qualified* or *moderated* sense, and accounts for them by the fervor of the writer's feelings and the nature of the contrast. But who does not see that the very same rule, when applied to the passages which seem to indicate moral good or holiness, will so modify them as to make the application of them to true Christians altogether unnecessary ? The *reason* and *conscience* of the unsanctified, especially when they are awakened by the terrors of the divine law, present sufficient ground to justify the use of the language here employed, in such a modified sense as that now supposed.

In fact, it appears a very plain case, that neither class of commentators, that is, neither those who apply chap. vii. 7—25 to Christians, nor those who apply it to the unregenerate, can find satisfactory ground for so doing, merely in the *phraseology*, or *modes of expression* employed. Either party who adopts this ground, must deny his opponent the same liberties which he himself takes; or else involve himself in inextricable difficulties, by admitting that the same grounds of explanation may be taken by others, which he takes for himself. But he can do neither of these; not the first, because the common sense of all men would cry out against him; not the last, because this would prove the very contrary of what he holds, or else prove that the apostle has really contradicted himself.

The laws of interpretation demand that a *modified* sense is to be given to such particular forms of expression as seem to stand in the way of the argument and the object of the writer. This we always give in *fairly* construing the language of men, on all occasions, whether it be written or spoken. The *literal* interpretation of all expressions, in an animated contrast, drawn by a man of such powerful feeling as Paul, would hardly be contended for in any case in which polemic theology was not concerned. As well might we insist that such declarations of our Saviour as · "it is easier for a camel to go through the eye of a needle, than for a rich man to enter into the kingdom of God;" or: "if he had not come and spoken to the Jews, they would not have had sin;" will any one insist now that these declarations should be *literally* interpreted. No one will doubt then that the passage in question must be so modified as to agree with the context, and the scope of reasoning which the writer is aiming at, if that can be determined.

If the reader will now look back, he will see that I have not, in any case, laid any particular stress on the form or intensity of expression, in my remarks on vii. 5—25; and the reason of this is evident enough from what has already been said above. At the same time, I have supposed that the expressions σύμφημι τῷ νόμῳ, συνήδομαι τῷ νόμῳ, τῷ νοῖ δουλεύω τῷ νόμῳ, etc , are those which the writer intended should be specially modified by the reader; and this because the *object* of his discourse requires them to be modified. This is the ground on which I rest my interpretation, and not on the form or strength of single words or phrases, on either side of the contrast.

With these remarks in view, I proceed to offer, in a summary way, my reasons for adopting the exegesis which the commentary presents.

1. The object of the apostle in vii. 7 to viii. 17, is to illustrate and confirm what he had said in vii 5, 6; and which he had before intimated in vi 14. Chap vii 7—25 is as plainly a comment on vii. 5, as chap. viii. 1—17 is on vii. 6; and antithesis between vii 7—25 and viii. 1—25, seems to be plain and certain As this is a fundamental point in the interpretation of the whole, the reader will allow me to be full and explicit in the discussion of it.

At the beginning of chap viii., we find a distinction made, and a transition of the discourse marked by ἄ ρ α ν ῦ ν, *now then, i. e* , in our *present* state, in the *present* condition of Christians, viz., as contradistinguished from their

EXCURSUS VII. ON ROM. VII. 5—25.   465

former state. What was this former state? It was a carnal state, ἐν σαρκί, ver. 5; σαρκικός, ver 14; one in which they were subject to the law of sin, ver 23 What makes this transition the more striking is, that in ver. 6 the antithesis between the two conditions there described, is pointed out by the very same word as here, viz, by νυνί.

If now we examine *particulars* in these two discourses (vii. 7—25, and viii 1—17), we shall find them in direct *antithesis* to each other. *E. g*, the complaint in vii 24 of miserable subjection to the influence of carnal desires stands opposed to the thanks in vii 25, uttered in reference to the deliverance which the writer is about to describe In vii 23, the person described is a *captive* to sin, *i. e.*, altogether subject to the influence of sinful passions and desires; in viii 2, he is represented as delivered from the law of sin and death. In vii. 14, an incessant and irreconcilable opposition is represented as existing between the law of God and the person there described, in viii. 4, he is represented as possessing the ability and the disposition to keep, at least in some good measure, the precepts of the law. In vii. 18, the person described is represented as having no good thing ἐν τῇ σαρκί [αὐτοῦ] and as finding no power to effect what is good, even when his mind or conscience approves it or would prefer it; in viii 3, 4, this disability is represented as removed. In vii 5, 14, 18, the person described is represented as being ἐν σαρκί, σαρκικός; in viii. 9 he is declared to be οὐκ ἐν σαρκί. In vii 14 he is represented as the *bond-slave* of sin; (πεπραμένον ὑπὸ τὴν ἁμαρτίαν), *i. e.*, as altogether under the power of sin; in viii 11, 14 he is represented as having the Spirit of God to dwell in him, and as being led, *i. e*, influenced or guided by that Spirit.

In a word, the whole tenor of the two discourses is such as is adapted to make the impression, that they are in antithesis to each other, and that they are designed by the writer to be so It is only the difficulties in regard to *subordinate* parts, that can occasion or sustain any doubts in respect to this subject Indeed, I cannot better express my convictions of the antithetic nature of the two passages, the connection in which they stand, and the design of the writer, than in the words of Tholuck "Truly if one has respect only to the *connection* of the latter part of Rom vii, with what goes before, and what follows after, it is impossible to explain this [the latter part of Rom. vii] of any one, except of him who is still under the law"

2 The object of the writer (which is to show that the law is insufficient for the *sanctification* of sinners) would not be effectually promoted by supposing that he represents the experience of Christians in chap vii For if Christians, who are of course under grace, and are dead to the law (vi 14, vii 6), are actually still in the state here represented, then would it follow that neither grace nor law hinders them from being the servants of sin. But to aver that *grace* does not effect this, is to contradict viii 1—17.

3. The *tout ensemble* of the representation in chap vii. seems to render it certain, that a true Christian cannot be here described What is the result of the whole? It is, that notwithstanding all the opposition which the law of God and the law of the mind make to sin, yet the person in question practises it, and habitually practises it, on all occasions, and under all cir-

cumstances. In every contest here, the sinful carnal mind comes off victorious. Is this "overcoming the world?" Is this to be 'born of God so as not to sin?' Is this 'loving Christ so as to keep his commandments?' Is this 'doing no iniquity?' Is this "walking not after the flesh, but after the Spirit?" In a word, is it possible to make this accord with chap. viii. 1—17?

4. If chap. vii. represents the *Christian* struggle with sin, then what is the state into which the Christian goes, as represented in chap. viii.? The answer must be: One in which there is no more struggle. But when — where — was ever such a state on earth? It has often been imagined and asserted, but not proved. But if now the transition is from a state in which sin was altogether predominant, into one in which grace on the whole reigns and triumphs, then all is easy and intelligible. On any other ground it is inexplicable; at least, it is so to me.

It were easy to add more reasons; but if these are well-grounded, they are sufficient. It is proper, now, briefly to pass in review some of the exegesis and the allegations of those, who maintain that a regenerate person is described in vii 5 — 25.

(1) Their interpretation (viz, that which most of them give) of vii. 9 leads, as may be seen in the commentary on vii. 9, to inextricable difficulty, and contradiction of the context. It is equally opposed to the *usus loquendi*, and to those parts of the discourse which precede and which follow.

(2) It is alleged, that the contest described in Rom. vii 14 —25 is one which accords with the feelings and experience of every Christian; and that he is thus conscious that the interpretation given to it by those who apply it to Christians, must be correct.

This consideration is, in fact, the main dependence of those who support the exegesis just named; I mean, that by such an appeal to feeling, they produce more conviction on the mind of Christians, than is produced by all their other arguments. After all, however, this is far from determining the case. Let us look at the subject in all its bearings.

I concede, in the first place, that Christians have a contest with sin; and that this is as plain and certain as it is that they are not wholly sanctified in the present life. It is developed by almost every page of Scripture, and every day's experience. That this contest is often a vehement one; that the passions rage, yea, that they do sometimes even gain the victory; is equally plain and certain. It follows now, of course, that as the language of Rom. vii. 14 — 25 is intended to describe a contest between the good principle and the bad one in men, and also a contest in which the evil principle comes off victorious; so this language can hardly fail of being appropriate, to describe all those cases in a Christian's experience, in which sin triumphs. Every Christian at once recognizes and feels, that such cases may be described in language like that which the apostle employs.

Here is the advantage which the patrons of this opinion enjoy, and which they have not failed to push even to its utmost extent. After all, however, the ground is unfairly taken, and unfairly maintained. For, first, it is *only a part* of the case. While Christians have many a contest in which they are

EXCURSUS VII. ON ROM. VII. 5—25.

overcome by sin, yet they must be victors in far the greater number of cases, if the whole be collectively taken. If this be not true then it cannot be true that 'he who loveth Christ, keepeth his commandments;' it cannot be true that 'they who love the law of God, do no iniquity;' nor true that "he who is born of God sinneth not;" nor that faith enables him who cherishes it to "overcome the world." As, however, there is no denying the truth of these and the like declarations, and no receding from them, nor explaining them away as meaning less than *habitual victory* over sin; so it follows, that when verses 15 — 25 are applied to Christian experience, they are wrongly applied. The person represented in these verses *succumbs to sin* IN EVERY INSTANCE *of contest.* The Christian must not — cannot — does not, so fight against sin. To assert this would be to contradict the whole tenor of the Scriptures; it would be abrogating, at once, all which is declared in so pointed a manner, in chap. viii 1 — 17.

Secondly, as I have already noted, there stands in the way of this interpretation the fact, that a *great transition* is marked by the commencement of chap. viii ; one of which no satisfactory account can be given, if vii. 14—25 is to be interpreted as belonging to those who are under grace.

Thirdly, I repeat the remark, that the question is not, whether what is here said *might* be applied to Christians, but whether, from the tenor of the context, it appears to be the intention of the writer that it *should* be so applied.

(3) So far as reasoning or argument is concerned, the main allegation of those who apply verses 14 — 25 to Christian experience, remains yet to be considered. It is this, viz , that 'the declarations made in these verses respecting the *internal man*, are such as comport only with the state or condition of a regenerate man ; and if this be not admitted, then we must concede that the unregenerate are subjects of moral good.' But,

First, this allegation takes for granted, that the phrases σύμφημι τῷ νόμῳ, συνήδομαι τῷ νόμῳ, etc., are to be taken in their full strength, without any modification. But in respect to such an interpretation, see commentary on verse 22, and the former part of this Excursus, on the subject of deducing arguments merely from the forms of expression, without a special reference to the context, and the object which the writer has in view. When the whole of this is weighed, I would inquire, whether he who interprets chap. vii 5—25, as having respect to one who is under law, has not just as good a claim to insist that σαρκικός, πεπραμένος ὑπὸ τὴν ἁμαρτίαν, αἰχμαλωτίζοντά με τῷ νόμῳ τῆς ἁμαρτίας, etc , shall be taken without abatement or modification ? And thus it will follow that the writer has described an impossible state, one in which a man is *under law*, and *under grace* at one and the same time; one in which sin has a power predominant in all cases, and grace a power on the whole predominant, at one and the same time. The answer to this question may be found, in the considerations which have been suggested above.

But secondly, the whole of the allegation which I am discussing, appears to me to rest on ground entirely unsafe and unsatisfactory. It will be admitted by those who are conversant with the dispute about the meaning of the passage before us, that Augustine was the first who suggested the idea, that it must be applied to Christian experience. This he did, however, in the heat of dispute with Pelagius. At an earlier period of his life, he held to the common exegesis of the church, as is certain from Prop. XLV. in Epist. ad Rom.; Intelligitur hinc ille homo describi, *qui nondum sub gratia.* So in Confess VII 21, VIII 5, Ad Simplic. 1. But Pelagius, who denied the fallen state of man, urged upon him the declaration above referred to, viz., *delighting in the law of God after the inner man, serving the law of God with the mind*, etc. Augustine felt himself pressed by them, and made his escape by protesting against the exegesis of his antagonist. He recanted his former opinion respecting verses 14—25, and became a strenuous advocate for an interpretation which through him has gained an extensive ground among Christians, and maintains its footing among many down to the present hour.

It is difficult to say how far men, and even good men, will sometimes go in matters of interpretation and criticism, in order to relieve themselves from the straits occasioned by warm dispute. It was, in all probability, the dispute of the church at Rome with the Montanists, which first occasioned it to doubt and then to deny, the Pauline origin of the epistle to the Hebrews. Luther's dispute with the Roman Catholics, on the subject of *justification by faith alone*, led him to discard the epistle of James, and to call it, by way of contempt, *epistola straminea*. And the like have many others done, for similar reasons. Such seems to have been the ground of Augustine's new exegesis.

But when we come, now, seriously and calmly to inquire whether there is any cause of alarm in respect to the doctrine of the natural man's depravity, because Rom 7—25 is interpreted as having respect to him, we can see that this is so far from being the case, that the opposite is true; I mean, that this depravity is rendered much more conspicuous and aggravated by this exegesis. Let us see if this be not palpable and certain.

That men are *moral* beings, does not make them sinners or saints. That they have faculties which can distinguish between good and evil, only shows that they are capable of doing good or evil, or of being righteous or wicked. *Conscience* and *reason* belong to the *pura naturalia* of the human race. Man, in the full and proper sense of this word, cannot exist without them. It is no more an evidence, then, that a man is holy or good in the Scripture sense of the word, because his reason and conscience distinguish good from evil, and testify in behalf of the good, than it is that he is holy because he has a moral nature. Such a distinction and such an approbation are inseparable from the essential nature of reason and conscience.

Consider moreover, that the guilt of a sinner who continues to yield to the solicitations of his carnal desires, is proportioned entirely to the measure of light which he has, and to the inducements set before him to act in a different manner. "Where there is no law, there is no transgression." "To him that knoweth to do good, and doeth it not, to him it is sin." Then of course the sinner, with reason, and conscience, and the law of God all remonstrating against his conduct, is involved in guilt of the deepest dye, while an offender (if I may so call him) without any of these checks, would be no offender at all. "He that knoweth his master's will, and doeth it not, shall be beaten with many stripes." And so it ought to be. What then can render the person's case more aggravated, who is described in verses 14—25, than the fact that he resists so much light and such powerful motives to pursue a different course ?

Is it, then, denying the depravity of the unregenerate, when we assign to them faculties to do good, and light as to their duty, and strong excitement to perform it, and represent them as after all refusing to do good, and uniformly hearkening to the voice of sin ? I appeal to the reason and conscience of all men, whether such an accusation against the exegesis in question, is not in a high degree unjust and unfounded. Nay, I might go farther; I may say, it is the contrary exegesis which is pressed with the very difficulty it urges against the other. For if the sinner is born without reason and conscience, and is without light; or if he is born with reason and conscience that are incapable of distinguishing good from evil, or of giving the preference to the former ; then his depravity and desperate guilt can in no way be made out, consistently with the first principles of a moral sense. Of all the charges then brought against the exegesis which I have defended, that of its diminishing the guilt of unregenerate men is the most unfounded and unjust.

I have discussed the principal arguments, so far as I am acquainted with them, of those who interpret verses 14—25 as having a relation to Christian experience I have already remarked upon the allegation, that Paul here speaks in the first person singular, and must therefore be relating his own experience, p 246, seq. There is no objection to allowing it to be Paul's experience; but *when* had he such experience ? And why does he speak of himself ? These are the questions to be answered ; and I have endeavored to answer them at the close of vii. 12.

I cannot conclude this already protracted Excursus, without adverting for a moment, to the history of the exegesis introduced by Augustine.

As has been already stated, the most ancient Fathers of the Church, without a dissenting voice, so far as we have any means of ascertaining their views, were united in the belief, that an *unregenerate, unsanctified* person is described in vii 5—25. So Origen, Tertullian, Chrysostom, and Theodoret. In this state did the views of the church remain down to the time of Augustine, whose first opinion, and whose change of it, and how unnecessary it was as far as the doctrine of depravity is concerned, have already been described

The exegesis of Augustine, however, found favor in the churches where his sentiments respecting original sin were received ; and prevailed very extensively and for a long time. In like manner with him, have Anselm, Thomas Aquinas, Cornelius a Lapide, Luther, Melancthon, Calvin, Beza, Spener, Buddæus, Koppe, and many others, explained the passage in question ; and most commentators among evangelical Christians in Great Britain and in this country, have followed the same opinion

On the other hand, besides all the ancient Greek and some of the Latin Fathers, there are many distinguished men who have defended the sentiment which has been above exhibited. Such are Erasmus, Raphel, Episcopius, Limborch, Turretin, Le Clerc, Heumann, Bucer, Schomer, Francke, G. Arnold, Bengel, Reinhard, Storr, Flatt, Knapp, Tholuck, and (so far as I know) all the evangelical commentators of the present time on the continent of Europe. Most of the English Episcopal church, also, for many years, and not a few of the Scotch, Dutch, and English Presbyterian and Congregational divines, have adopted the same interpretation. I cannot but believe that the time is not far distant, when there will be but one opinion among intelligent Christians, about the passage in question; as there was but one before the dispute of Augustine with Pelagius. In this respect there is ground of trust, that the ancient and modern churches will yet fully harmonize.

EXCURSUS VIII.

On κτίσις in Rom. viii. 19 (pp. 284—286).

Tholuck argues that κτίσις means *the material creation* here; first, from the connection in which it stands, and the predicates which are assigned to it; and secondly, from both Jewish and Christian belief respecting the renewal of the natural world at a future period.

First he says, that the more usual meaning of κτίσις is the *natural world*. That this is not so in the New Testament, is plain from the examples adduced in the commentary. But still, that the world may very naturally, in itself considered, be thus employed has been freely conceded.

His next argument is, that αὐτὴ ἡ κτίσις in ver. 21, indicates a descent from the noble to the ignoble part of creation; i. e., αὐτὴ ἡ κτίσις indicates, that "Not only the nobler part of creation, but even *this inferior creation*, of which he is now speaking, also longs for a disclosure of the glory which is to be revealed."

The answer to this is, that such an exegesis of αὐτὴ ἡ κτίσις would necessarily imply, that a higher and nobler κτίσις had been already mentioned in the preceding context, with which this inferior one is now compared. The expectation of the *nobler* part of creation is first mentioned in ver. 23, υἱοθεσίαν ἀπεκδεχόμενοι. The force of αὐτὴ ἡ κτίσις must therefore be made out in another way. Paul had just said, ἡ κτίσις *is made subject to a frail and perishing state* (ματαιότητι), *with the hope, i e*, in a condition or in circumstances in which it is permitted to hope, that καὶ αὐτὴ ἡ κτίσις, *even this very same creature may be freed*, etc. Tholuck does not seem to have noted, that the expression is not simply αὐτὴ, but καὶ αὐτὴ; which necessarily refers it to the preceding κτίσις, the frail and perishing κτίσις which had just been described, and precludes any implied comparison with a nobler κτίσις, which indulged the like hopes.

A third reason of Tholuck for the signification which he here assigns for κτίσις is, that in ver. 22, πᾶσα ἡ κτίσις is mentioned.

EXCURSUS VIII. ON ROM VIII. 19.

But why the apostle could not say πᾶσα ἡ κτίσις, if he meant the world of *rational* beings, just as well as he could if he meant the world of *nature*, I am not aware, and more especially so, since in Mark xvi. 15, and Col. i. 23, this very expression is made use of (πάσῃ τῇ κτίσει — ἐν πάσῃ τῇ κτίσει) in order to denote the universality of the rational world.

Finally, Tholuck avers that the predicates ματαιότης and δουλεία τῆς φθορᾶς (verses 20, 21,) more naturally belong to the material creation.

But this I cannot see. Above all, I cannot see it, when the apostle says, that the κτίσις *was made subject* ματαιότητι, οὐχ ἑκοῦσα, *not voluntarily, not of of its own choice*. Does this belong more naturally, then, to the material than the rational creation? Of which is *choice* more naturally predicated? Then again, is not ματαιότης, *a frail and dying state*, as easily and naturally to be predicated of *men*, as it is of the material world? And taken as a whole, is not the latter far less subject to ματαιότης than the race of men? Comp, ματαιότης in Eph iv. 17—19; Rom. i. 21, seq. Once more, is not δουλεία τῆς φθορᾶς, *the bondage of a mortal or perishing condition*, as naturally predicated of men as it is of the material world? Rather, is it not much more naturally applied to human beings, than it is to the world in which they live? So Paul seems to have thought, and so expressed himself, see φθορά in 1 Cor xv. 50. Comp. 2 Pet ii 18, 19; i. 4.

None of the reasons, then, assigned by Tholuck for the exegesis which he defends, that are drawn from the exigency of the passage, seem to be well-grounded. So much is true, viz that the *usus loquendi* in itself considered would admit the sense which he gives to κτίσις. But that the *exigentia loci* renders probable this meaning, does not seem in any good degree to be made out.

We come, next, to the second class of reasons assigned by Tholuck in defence of his interpretation; viz, those derived from the Jewish and Christian belief, respecting the renovation of the *natural* world at a future period.

The passages of Scripture mainly relied on are 2 Pet. iii. 7—12; Rev. xxi. 1; Isai xi. 6, seq., lxv. 17, seq.; Heb. xii. 26, seq. Hints of the same doctrine are supposed to be contained in Matt. xiii. 38, seq; xix 28, and Acts iii 21.

All the force of argument from these and the like passages must rest on a *literal* interpretation of them. But how can passages of this nature be urged as having a literal meaning, after reading Rev. xxi, and xxii 1—5? Or if this does not satisfy the mind, then compare passages of a similar nature, viz, those which have respect to the Messiah's kingdom on earth, his spiritual kingdom *before* the end of time, and during the gathering in of his saints. What immeasurable absurdities and contradictions must be involved in a literal exegesis here? For such examples, see Bib Repos. Vol I. p. 389 seq.

I have a difficulty, also, as to the *logical* commentary of the passage provided we adopt the interpretation defended by Tholuck Let us examine this for a moment. The apostle begins by saying, that present afflictions should not be laid to heart by Christians, because of the future glory which is reserved for them. What now is demanded, in order that this should be believed, and that Christians should regulate their thoughts and conduct by it? Why plainly nothing more is required, than that they should cherish a confirmed belief of it, a steadfast hope that such glory will be bestowed. Such is the conclusion in ver 25. But how is this hope to be animated and supported? Plainly by considerations which add to the assurance, that *future* glory is in prospect. And what are these? They are, that God has enstamped on our very nature the desire of such a state, and that he has placed us in such a frail and dying condition, as that the whole human race naturally and instinctively look to such a state and hope for it. The present is manifestly a state of trial; even Christians, who have the earnest of future glory within themselves, are not exempt from this. But the very fact that we are in a state of trial and probation, naturally points to an end or result of this. And what is such an end, but a state of *future* happiness? for here happiness in a higher sense is not to be attained.

But suppose now that the *material* world is that which sighs after and hopes for deliverance from its present frail and perishable state; has this a direct bearing on the subject in question? The answer must be in the negative; so thought Turretin, as his notes most clearly show. But then it may be said, that it has a bearing upon it by way of implication; because the renovation of the material world is necessarily connected with the future happiness of the saints. In this point of view I acknowledge it would not be irrelevant But is not this less direct, less forcible, less convincing, than the appeal to the wants and desires of which every human breast is conscious? Of two modes of exegesis, either of which is possible, I must prefer that which imparts the most life and energy to the reasoning and argument of the writer.

I have another substantial difficulty with the interpretation under examination. It is this: if κτίσις means the material or natural world, on the one hand, and αὐτοὶ τὴν ἀπαρχὴν τοῦ πνεύματος ἔχοντες means Christians on the other (which Tholuck and Flatt both avow), then here is a *lacuna* which cannot well be imagined or accounted for. Christians are subject to a frail and dying state, but are looking for a better one; and the natural world is in the same circumstances; but the world of men in general, the world of rational beings who are not regenerate, have no concern or interest in all this; they are not even mentioned. Can it be supposed now, that the apostle has made such an important, unspeakably important, omission as this, in such a discourse and in such a connection? The *natural, physical world* brought into the account, but the world of perishing *men* left out! I must have confirmation "strong as proof from holy writ," to make me adopt an interpretation that offers such a manifest incongruity.

Such are my reasons for not regarding as weighty the arguments offered by the advocates of the interpretation I am examining; and such are my positive grounds for rejecting it

I come, at last, to the interpretation which I have supposed above to be the correct and proper, viz, that κτίσις most probably means *men, mankind in general*, as stated above, No 2, *b*. That such an interpretation is agreeable to the *usus loquendi*, is clear from the statement there made. It only remains, then, to inquire, *whether it accords with the nature of the passage in which the word stands, and whether it can be vindicated from the objections made to it* In reference to the former point, see the commentary on this verse, and in reference to the latter, see Bib. Repos. as quoted above.

EXCURSUS IX.

On Rom. viii. 28, τοῖς κατὰ πρόθεσιν κλητοῖς οὖσι. (p. 296.)

THE difficulty arising from this passage, and the temptation to deny or obscure what I must believe to be its plain and inevitable meaning, are both suggested by the following question : *"* How can God have had an *eternal* purpose as to those who are to be saved, and yet men be free agents, free even in the matter of their own repentance and conversion ?" It will not be expected, of course, that I should here discuss at length a metaphysical question, which the disputes and contentions of more than 4000 years have not settled ; for in every age and nation, where religious inquiries have been pursued, the difficulty before us has for substance presented itself to the minds of thinking men. One may say that three parties exist, and perhaps have in every age existed, in respect to it; viz., (1) Those who embrace the doctrine of *fatality*, and therefore deny the proper free agency of man. (2) Those who deny the divine *decrees* or *eternal purposes* of God, and make in effect a kind of independent agency of man. (3) Those who believe both in the divine foreknowledge, purpose, or decree (for the difference between these is in *name* only, not in reality), and also in the entire free agency of man. Among this latter class, I would choose my lot. The Scriptures seem to me plainly to hold forth both of these doctrines. Yea, so far are the sacred writers from apprehending any inconsistency in them, that they bring them both forward (*i. e*. divine agency and purpose, and human agency and purpose) at one and the same time, not seeming even to apprehend that any one will speculate on them so as to make out any contradiction. For example : Acts ii. 23, " Him, being delivered by the *determinate counsel* and *foreknowledge* of God, ye have taken, and by *wicked* hands have crucified and slain ;" *i. e*, the determinate counsel (ὡρισμένη βουλή) and foreknowledge of God did not render the hands of the Jews less wicked, who crucified the Saviour. Of course they must have acted in a *voluntary* manner, *i. e*, as agents altogether free ; for a sin *involuntary*, *i e*, without consent of the will, is a contradiction in terms, so far as moral turpitude is concerned.

Again ; Phil. ii. 12, 13, " *Work out your own salvation* with fear and trembling ; for *it is God who worketh in you both to will and to do* of his good pleasure ;" *i. e.*, the very ground on which I urge diligence in the matter of your Christian duties is, that God helps you *both to will and to do.*

These are a specimen of the philosophy (if I may so speak) with which the Bible is full. The attributes of an *omniscient* God, his designs, his very nature, prove that he must have *purposes;* and such as will not be frustrated. *Prediction* or *prophecy* proves this, and puts it beyond all rational contradiction. Is it *uncertain,* whether what the prophets of God have foretold will come to pass? Yet are not the men by whom the things foretold are brought to pass, free agents in all cases of this nature, just as they were in the crucifixion of the Lord of glory?

But you will ask: '*How* is this?' To which I answer at once: I do not know. The *manner* in which God's purposes are consistent with free agency, I do not pretend to know. The *fact* that they are consistent, I do know; because I am conscious of being a free agent; I am as certain of it as I am of my own existence. I am equally certain that God is omniscient, and has always been so; and therefore he must have always perfectly known every thing that will take place. If he knew it with *certainty* (and if he did not, then he did not *know* it at all), then is it *uncertain* whether it will take place? And if it is certain, then how does this differ from what is said to be *decreed?* The name *decree,* indeed, seems to have carried along with it a kind of terror to many minds; but, so far as I can see, it implies neither more nor less than *divine purpose* or *divine will.* And can it be, that sober-minded Christians will, on reflection, maintain that there is no divine purpose or will?

To all the arguments adduced from such a statement of *facts* to prove the doctrine of *fatalism,* I have only to reply, that fact itself *disproves* this; for we are conscious of being *free* agents. The Scriptures disprove this: for they everywhere treat men as *free* agents. And this is enough; for these are the two highest possible sources of proof, and with these we ought to rest satisfied. As to the question *How* is our free agency made to consist with God's eternal purposes? I have said nothing: for I know nothing. *How* ten thousand thousand other things, which I believe, and which all men believe, can be true or take place, no one in the present world knows, or ever will know, anything; *e. g., How* do heat, moisture, and earth make one plant green and another red, one nutritive and another poisonous, in the very same bed of earth? yet we all believe the fact that they do.

Who can show it to be absurd, now, that God should have had an *eternal* purpose, and yet man be a *free agent?* Does the certain knowledge we now have of a *past* event, destroy the free agency of those who were concerned in bringing about that event? Did any *previous* knowledge of the same necessarily interfere with their free agency? And as to free agency itself; cannot God make a creature *in his own image,* free like himself, rational like himself, the originator of thoughts and volitions like himself? Can this be disproved? The fact that we are *dependent* beings, will not prove that we may not be *free* agents as to the exercise of the powers with which we are endowed, — free in a sense like to that in which God himself, as a rational being, is free. Nor will this establish any *contingency* or *uncertainty* of events, in the universe. Could not God as well foresee what would be the free and voluntary thought of men, in consequence of the powers which he should give them, as he could foresee thoughts and volitions which would proceed from the operation of external causes upon them? Until this can be denied on the ground of reason and argument, the sentiment in question is not justly liable to the charge of introducing the doctrine of casual *contingency* or *uncertainty* into the plans of the divine mind.

I only add, that when we say, 'God has had an *eternal purpose* in respect to those who are called' (and the apostle does say this, Eph. iii. 11; 2 Tim. i. 9), we speak ἀνθρωποπάθως. With God there is no time. 'A thousand years are as one day, and one day as a thousand years.' With him it is an ETERNAL NOW, as it has often and forcibly been expressed. So the expressions, PRE-*destination*, FORE-*ordination*, etc., strictly speaking, are *anthropopathic*. 'Non PRÆ-*videntia*, sed PRO-*videntia* potius dicitur,' says Boethius, De consol. Philos i. 5. prop. 6. If God has any purposes, they are *eternal*. We must, then, either deny that he has any purposes, or else admit their eternal existence; and this being admitted, the κλητοὶ κατὰ πρόθεσιν are truly such as the apostle describes them to be in the sequel of chap. viii.

EXCURSUS X.

On Rom. viii. 28—30. [p. 295, sq.]

ON the disputes which have arisen from the paragraph in verses 28 — 30, I shall not comment at large in this place; but I cannot pass by the subject without making a few remarks.

That man should be entirely *dependent* on God, and yet be a free agent at the same time, presents, it has been often asserted, an impossibility, an absurdity, a contradiction of terms, a scheme of fatalism, etc. After all, however, the mere disciple of Naturalism, who sets *revelation* entirely aside, but allows the natural perfections of the Godhead (among which are omniscience and omnipotence), falls into the very same difficulties inevitably, which he puts solely to the account of Revelation. If there be a God, a Creator, almighty and omniscient, then we are perfectly and entirely dependent on him; from everlasting moreover, he has known all that we are and shall be; he has known this with *absolute certainty;* and if so, then what we are and shall be is not *fortuitous*. This the disciple of nature can no more deny, than the disciple of revelation And this involves at once all the real difficulties which are charged to the account of those who believe in the plain and simple allegations of the passage before us.

Once admit the idea of an omniscient and omnipotent Creator, and the difficulty of reconciling dependence and free agency comes up of course; and it bears equally, moreover, on every system which admits this truth. It is wonderful that this should not be more extensively seen and felt by writers, who are in the habit of charging all difficulties of this nature to the opinions of those who favor the sentiments of Calvin.

After all, if there be any force in the objections made against the doctrine in question, *it arises only from reasoning analogically in respect to the laws and qualities of matter and those of mind*. In a piece of physical machinery, every motion will be in accordance with the laws of motion and mechanical power, and all necessarily according to the contrivance of the mechanist; *i. e.*, the laws of matter and motion remaining the same, the result which is calculated upon is necessary; and it is always the *same*, for there is no volition in the machine, nothing to resist, alter, or modify the influence to which it is subjected.

Not so in the world of immaterial and *spiritual* being. Man is made *in the image of God;* therefore he has a free agency like to that of his Maker. From its very nature, this free agency is incapable of *mechanical* control. Motives, arguments, inducements may move, convince, persuade; but they cannot control by a necessity like that in the world of matter That they cannot, is owing to the very nature itself of a free agent, who is no longer free, if he have no *ultimate* choice and power of his own. The Bible everywhere ascribes such a power to man. He resists light, knowledge, persuasion; he remains unmoved (at least undetermined) by all the motives drawn from earth, heaven, and hell; he resists and grieves the Spirit of God himself Such are the representations of the Scripture. Is this representation truth or fiction? Which is the same as to ask : Are men *in fact* free agents, or only so in *name* and *appearance?*

That they are in fact free, is what I believe. Nor can I be persuaded, that illustrations of free agency drawn from the material world, are in any tolerable measure apposite to our subject. Our souls are *spirit*, not matter. They are like the God who made them; not like the dust on which we tread. All arguments, then, drawn from cause or causation and effect in the *material* world, and applied to the subject of *spiritual* agency and influence, are wrongly applied, and cannot serve to cast anything but darkness on this deeply interesting subject. All the deductions in respect to *fatalism* moreover, which are made out and charged upon those who hold the doctrine of God's foreknowledge and eternal purposes, are made out by a process of reasoning which has its basis in material analogies. A regular, necessitous, mechanical concatenation of cause and effect, altogether like that in the world of nature, is predicated of the doctrine of the divine purposes or decrees; and then the charge of fatalism and absurdity of course follows Let those who would avoid this take good care, then, not to reason about *spirit* in the same way as they do about matter.

Can any one prove, that the Spirit of God may not influence the human mind, in a manner perfectly consistent with its entire free agency—influence it to accept the offers of salvation, and become σύμμορφος τοῦ υἱοῦ τοῦ Θεοῦ? He can no more do this, than he can prove that one man cannot influence another, without impairing his freedom of action; an event which takes place every hour, and in all parts of this lower world. Above all, who can show that truth can influence men while they remain free, and yet that the Spirit, who is the author of all truth, cannot operate as effectually and with as little interference with free agency, as the truth which he has revealed?

EXCURSUS X. ON ROM. VIII. 28—30.

So little foundation is there for the charge of fatalism, against the doctrine of divine influence upon the souls of men!

Those who are saved *freely* repent, *freely* believe, *freely* accept the terms of salvation. Why can they not be as free under the influence of the Spirit, as they are under the influence of the truth which he has revealed? And none but penitents will be saved. There is no room then to say, that a belief in the divine eternal purposes makes it a matter of indifference whether a man lives a virtuous and holy life or not, and that if he is to be saved, he will be saved, let him do what he may. The plain and certain truth is, that he 'is *not* to be saved' unless he become *conformed to the image of Christ*, and that *without holiness no man shall see the Lord*. This is God's everlasting purpose, his eternal decree; and sooner than this can be violated, heaven and earth shall pass away. All accusations of such a nature, then, against the doctrine in question, properly understood, are ungrounded and unjust.

In regard to the dispute whether God προώρισε τοὺς κλητούς, from his *mere good pleasure*, or from a *foresight of their faith and good works;* it is easy to see, that the paragraph of the epistle which is under consideration does not decide on this. So far the question seems to be fully settled, by other texts of Scripture, viz., that the *merit* or *obedience* of the κλητοί was not the ground or reason of their regeneration and sanctification. This would be assuming that holiness existed before it did exist; that it was the *ground* of that which it followed only as a *consequence*.

On the other hand; as to the *decretum absolutum*, as it has been called, viz., the determination that the κλητοί should be saved, irrespectively of their character and actions, one cannot well see how this is to be made out. So much must be true, viz., that they are not regenerated, sanctified, or saved, on account of *merit;* all is of *grace, pure grace*. If this be all that any one means by the *decretum absolutum*, there can be no reasonable objection made to it. But on the other hand; as God is *omniscient*, and therefore must know every part of every man's character, through all stages of his being; as all things, in their fullest extent, must have always been naked and open to his view; so we cannot once imagine, that any decree or purpose in respect to the κλητοί can have been made *irrespectively* of their *whole* character. Such an *irrespection* (if I may use the word) is impossible. God has never determined, and from his holy nature never can determine to save any except such as are *conformed to the image of his Son*. All stands or falls together. A *decretum absolutum, i. e*, a decree which should separate these, or have no regard to these, would be a different one from that which the apostle has stated; and I may add, different from what we can ever imagine to be possible.

To what purpose, then, can disputes on such a question be raised or fostered? Happy would it be for the church, had there been no occasion in times past to mourn over them! It is truly important to distinguish that which is revealed, from that which is not; and to content ourselves with the one, and dismiss the other. "Secret things belong to the Lord our God; but things revealed to us and our children."

I will only add, that the phrase, *God out of his mere good pleasure*, is very liable to be misunderstood and perverted, as it often has been, and it is to be regretted that it was ever introduced into the technology of religion. My own apprehension is, that most of those who employ it, use it merely to signify *without regard to merit, without being induced by considerations of meritorious obedience.* In this sense, as applied to God in respect to his purposes of renewing and sanctifying sinners, it is strictly true. Merit they have not; obedience they exhibit not, while in their unrenewed and unsanctified state. But then the phrase is often understood as conveying the idea, that God, in a way *merely arbitrary, i. e.*, without any good reasons whatever, did choose some to everlasting life. This can never be true at all; no, not in any sense whatever. All that can ever be true is, that *God has done this while the reasons are entirely unknown to us.* He surely never did and never will determine or do any thing, without the *highest* and *best* reasons; although he may not unfold them to us.

'How,' it is asked, 'can God have determined from eternity who are to be saved,' *i e.*, whom he will effectually call, and justify, and sanctify, and bring to glory, and yet men be free to choose or refuse salvation? And the difficulty in all this is, that they suppose a regular concatenation of causes and influence must be arranged in the spiritual world, which will just as mechanically and certainly bring about the end, as that gravitation will make a stone fall to the earth. They join, with all this transfer of *physical* causation and effect over to spiritual things, the idea, that regard to the character or efforts of those who are saved is to be left out of the question; and then they make out in their own minds, the idea of *fatalism,* an undistinguishing fatalism, which acts thus and so, merely because it chooses to do this or that, without any good and sufficient reason whatever. And taking such a view of the doctrine of predestination, of course they think it very reasonable to reject it.

In answer to all this it may be said (1), That it is impossible even to imagine a case in which God can be supposed not to have before him *the whole* of every individual character of those who belong to the κλητοί (2) All that the Scripture teaches in regard to the ground or reason of his purpose of mercy towards these, is, that it is *not* on account of *merit* or *desert* in them; they are regenerated, and sanctified, and saved through *grace,* grace only; "not of works, lest any man should boast." Farther than this *negative* assertion, the Scripture does not go; and who knows any thing more than what is *revealed* concerning it? (3) The Bible, and experience, and reason, all unite in giving testimony of the highest kind which the human mind can receive, that whatever may be the purposes of God, *men in* FACT *are free agents;* free in all their spiritual exercises, as well as any others: and what is thus *in fact* conciliated or harmonized, cannot in its own nature be contradictory or absurd. (4) The *eternal* purpose of God is no more in the way of free agency, than his *present* purpose; for his present purpose is neither more nor less than his eternal one, and his eternal one neither more nor less than his present one. With him there is one *eternal* NOW; and all ideas of causation, and concatenation of causes and influence, drawn from sensible objects that are *temporary* and *successive,* only serve to mislead the mind in regard to God, when they are applied to him. (5) All the difficulties which ever have been or ever can be raised in regard to the *foreordination* or *decree* of God, concentre at last in one single point, viz., How can a creature be perfectly dependent, entirely under the control and within the power of another, and yet be *free?* And all the difficulty here comes at last upon the *how;* it lies not in the *fact;* for the fact that such is the case, is put beyond all doubt by the testimony of Scripture and experience.

Now as this HOW lies equally in the way of all who admit the existence of an *omniscient* and omnipotent Creator — I say *equally* in the way of all such, for this is plainly the case unless they are fatalists — and since, moreover, this question is plainly beyond the boundaries of human knowledge; it does not seem to me reasonable to declaim against those who admit that the doctrine of divine foreknowledge implies of course divine purpose; and that divine purpose must have been *always* the same, inasmuch as God is immutable, "the same yesterday, to-day, and for ever." At any rate, no arguments of an *a priori* nature can serve to set aside the plain, direct, inevitable meaning of the passage in Rom viii 28, *seq* Nor if it presents a difficulty can we free ourselves from this, even if we reject revelation. A God-almighty and omniscient, and a creature frail and entirely dependent, and yet free, always and every where present the same paradox to the human understanding. The Jew, the Mohammedan, and the Theist, are obliged to encounter it, in common with the Christian of strict creed and principles.

EXCURSUS XI.

On Rom ix. 17, εἰς αὐτὸ τοῦτο ἐξήγειρά σε (p. 333).

BUT what is the *meaning* of the entire assertion, the words of which we have thus considered in the commentary? Does it mean that God did *actively* and by his *immediate* influence on the heart or mind of Pharaoh, *excite* him or *rouse* him up to do evil, *i e*, to continue obstinate and rebellious against himself? Or that God had excited or roused him up by the various plagues sent on him and his people, so that his opposition to letting the people of Israel go had become more active and more bitter? The first of these meanings is the one which it is said some writers have ventured to give. *E. g.*, Augustine, (de Gratiâ et lib. Arbit. c. 21): His et talibus testimoniis Scripturarum satis manifestatur operari Deum *in cordibus hominum ad inclinandas eorum voluptates quocumque voluerit, sive ad bona pro suâ misericordiâ sive* AD MALA pro meritis eorum, etc. So Gomar, as represented by Hales "Not unjustly does God condemn the sinner, for he has ordained the means of condemnation [*i. e*, sin]; so that he condemns no one, without having first plunged him into sin." — *Golden Remains*, p. 435, ed 1688. Augustine says, more expressly and fully than above, on the verse before us. Excitavi te ut contumacius resisteres, non tantum permittendo, *sed multa etiam tam* INTUS *quam foris operando.* So Anselm, as quoted by Tholuck. Cum malus esses, prodigiis quasi sopitum excitavi, *ut in malitia persisteres atque deterior fieres.* After quoting this passage, Tholuck exclaims: "Is it God or the devil who speaks thus?" And on the other passages just quoted he says: "Can God speak thus to man [viz can he say what these comments represent him as saying?] then woe to us! for we are mere dwarfs in the hands of an irresistible Cyclops, created and dashed in pieces at his pleasure." And again: "Then have Satan and God exchanged offices. God goeth about as a roaring lion, seeking whom he may devour; and Satan exults that the almighty, from whose hand none can escape, places at his disposal the victims of his vengeance." He then goes on to say, that this is just what pantheism would exult in, viz., that pantheism which abolishes all distinction between good and evil.

These expressions, it must be admitted, bear very hardly on such men as Augustine, Anselm, Calvin, Beza, P. Martyr, Parœus, Gomar, and many others. Yet so much must we concede, viz., that the Scriptures not only teach us God's entire abhorrence of sin, and the freedom of man in sinning, but they do also, in so many words, assert that " God cannot be tempted with evil, neither tempteth he any man; but every man is tempted, when he is drawn away of his own lust and enticed," James i. 13, 14. With this unequivocal assertion of an apostle before our eyes, an assertion bearing directly on the specific point of *internal excitement* to do evil, we ought not to take any position which maintains that *God operated* DIRECTLY *on the heart and mind of Pharaoh*, in order to harden him and make him more desperate.

God does not permit wicked men to say truly that such is the case, in respect to his dealings with them. Thus he says to the Jews: "Will ye steal, murder, and commit adultery, and swear falsely, and burn incense to Baal, and walk after other gods whom ye know not; and come and stand before me in this house ... and say: *We are delivered* [נִצַּלְנוּ, *we are reserved*] to do all these abominations?" Jer. vii. 9, 10 Nay, the Scripture directly decides, that there may be a "determinate counsel and foreknowledge of God" respecting a thing which is exceedingly sinful, and yet that those who are agents in bringing it about may be altogether voluntary and guilty, Acts ii. 23. *Guilty* or *wicked* they could not be, unless they were *voluntary* agents.

But having advanced thus far, we must go still farther in order to obtain satisfaction as to the point in question. This can be obtained only by a considerate and extensive survey of the *usus loquendi* in the Scriptures, with reference to God *as the author of all things* There is a sense, in which he is the author of all things, yea, of all actions. He has created all things. Under his control, and by his direction and power, they come into existence None but atheists will deny this. He continues to hold them all under his control, *i. e*, he governs the universe; and in him "we live, and move, and have our being." He directs all things after the counsel of his own will; *i. e.*, he so guides and controls all things, all events, all creatures and their actions, as finally to accomplish his own blessed and glorious purposes, both of mercy and justice.

The moment we admit him to be an *omniscient* and *omnipotent* God, that moment we admit that he must have *foreseen* from eternity *all* the actions of his creatures, all their thoughts and affections and wishes and desires. We cannot deny that, foreseeing all these with all their consequences, he brought them into being, and placed them (for surely it was *he* who ordered their lot) in circumstances, where he knew they would act as he had foreseen they would. It is impossible to deny this, without denying the *omniscience* of God, and his *immutability*.

Now the Scripture most evidently admits and inculcates all these truths. Such being the fact, there is plainly a sense in which all things and events may be ascribed to God. He *foreknew* them; and his creating and governing and controlling power renders it *certain* that they will come to pass; for how could he *foreknow* what is *uncertain*? Accordingly, the Bible declares that 'we live and move and have our being in God.' Nay it goes farther than this; however we may stumble at the expressions, or revolt at the sentiment. It ascribes *evil*, yea, *moral* evil, to God in some sense or other; an assertion which must not be hazarded without proof, and which shall be supported by an overwhelming mass of examples. Let the reader now turn to the following passages and attentively consider them; viz., 2 Sam. xii. 11, xvi. 10; 1 Kings, xxii. 22; Josh. xi. 20; Ps cv. 25; 1 Kings xi. 23; 2 Sam xxiv. 1. Let him next examine the texts which declare that God hardened the heart of one and another; *e. g.*, of Pharaoh, Exod vii. 13, ix 12, x 1, 20, 27, xi 10, xiv. 8; Rom. ix. 18; of Sihon king of the Amorites, Deut. ii. 30; of the Israelites, Isai. lxiii. 17; John xii. 40. Who can read such texts as these, and so many, and yet aver that the Scripture teaches us, that there is *no* sense in which it is true that God hardens the hearts of men?

But the great question yet remains, Does God do this in such a way, *i. e.*, is he so concerned in it, and only so concerned, that man's free agency is still left entire, and so that all the moral blame of his sins is to be attributed *solely* to him? This question we may answer in the *affirmative*. The Bible does indeed speak of God as hardening the hearts of men, in some sense or other. In what sense, is not specifically said, although it is very plainly implied. That he does this in the way of *direct* influence on the heart or mind, seems to be unequivocally denied in James i. 13, 14. That what we are allowed to attribute to him, in respect to the hardening of the heart, cannot be any thing which takes away the criminality and guilt of men, nor any thing which in any measure abridges the entire freedom of their own actions, is clear from the fact, that *the sacred writers often and everywhere ascribe the hardening of the heart to the wicked themselves*. So, expressly, in respect to Pharaoh, Exod viii 15, 32, ix. 34, 1 Sam. vi 6, in respect to others, 2 Chron. xxxvi. 13; Ps. xcv. 8; Prov. xxviii. 14, Job ix. 4, and so of *hardening the neck*, which for substance has the same meaning, 2 Kings xvii. 14; Jer. vii. 26, xix. 15; Prov xxix. 1; Neh. ix. 16,

17, 29. In other expressions the *passive* voice only is made use of, without designating any agent: *e. g.*, Exod. vii. 22, viii. 19, ix. 7, 35, et alibi.

With these texts may be compared Isai. vi. 10, where the prophet is bid to go *and make the heart of the people stupid*, their ears heavy, and to close up their eyes. Read now the comments on this, in Matt xiii. 15; Mark iv. 12; John xii. 40; Acts xxviii. 26, 27. A comparison of these is replete with instruction; for in Isai vi. 10, the *prophet* is represented as hardening the Jews because he declares to them the divine word, and they, hearing and rejecting it, became more hardened. In John xii 40, *God* is represented as *hardening their heart* (which seems also to be implied in Mark iv. 12); while in Matt. xiii. 15 and Acts xxviii 26, 27, the plain and necessary implication is, that the Jews hardened their own hearts. Here then is one and the same case, which is represented in three different ways. (1) The prophet hardens the Jews. (2) God does the same thing. (3) The Jewish people do it themselves. Is all this true, or is one part contradictory to another? We may safely answer: it is *all* true. The prophet is said *to harden the hearts* of the Jews, merely because he is the instrument of delivering messages to them; while they, in consequence of abusing these, become more hardened and guilty. God hardens their hearts, in that by his providence he sustains them in life, upholds the use of all their powers, causes the prophets to warn and reprove them, and places them in circumstances where they must receive these warnings and reproofs. Under this arrangement of his Providence they become more hardened and wicked.

In this sense, and in this only, do the Scriptures seem to affirm that he is concerned with the hardening of men's hearts.

The Jews hardened their own hearts, inasmuch as they freely and voluntarily abused all the blessings and privileges which the providence and mercy of God had bestowed upon them, and thus became more stupid and corrupt.

Surely no one will say that the prophet (Isai. vi. 10) hardens the hearts of the Jews, by *direct* and *positive* influence upon them. It is *not* necessary, then, when it is declared that *God hardened the heart of Pharaoh*, to draw the conclusion that this was done by *direct* and *positive* influence. That it is not necessary, can be made clear from the following illustration of Scripture usage. In 2 Sam. xxiv. 1, it is said, *The Lord moved* (וַיָּסֶת) *David to go and number Israel*, etc., which, under the circumstances then existing, and with the views that David had, was a great sin in the sight of heaven, and was punished by a signal judgment of God. Here observe, that וַיָּסֶת is applied directly to Jehovah, without any intimation of a *secondary* agent or instrument; and so one might argue (as some do in regard to other expressions of the like nature in the Scriptures), that God is here asserted to be the *direct* exciting cause, which occasioned David to number Israel, etc. Yet in 1 Chron. xxi. 1 the very same thing is ascribed to Satan. *And Satan moved* וַיָּסֶת *David to go and number Israel*, etc. Observe that the *very same verb* is employed in the second case, as in the first. Now as Satan is the *tempter* of men to sin, and as "God *tempted no man*," we must say, Here is a clear case, in which that is ascribed to God, which he permits or suffers to be brought about under his superintendence or government of the universe, by agents of an inferior character. This seems, at least, to be a clear case; and it is one which has a very important bearing on the subject before us.

It is true that God *roused up* Pharaoh, so that he was the occasion of the divine power and glory being displayed in all the land of Egypt. But was this done by *direct* and *immediate* operation in hardening his heart, or was it through the signs and wonders, which the power and providence of God performed before the eyes and in the country of this contumacious monarch? In the latter way, we may safely answer, inasmuch as Pharaoh and others are said, in the Scriptures, *to harden their own hearts*. There was *another agency* here, then, besides that of Jehovah; just as in the case stated above. God in his providence did send Moses and Aaron with a commission to make demands on the king of Egypt in behalf of the oppressed Hebrews; he sent plagues upon Egypt by his miraculous power; and all these things under arrangements of his providence being brought to act upon Pharaoh, he became worse and worse. The Lord hardened his heart, because the Lord was the author of commands and messages and miracles, which were the occasion of Pharaoh's hardening his own heart. In just such a way, Paul says that *our sinful passions are by the law*, τὰ παθήματα τῶν ἁμαρτιῶν τὰ διὰ τοῦ νόμου, Rom. vii. 5, which he afterwards explains by saying ἡ γὰρ ἁμαρτία ἀφορμὴν λαβοῦσα, κ. τ. λ., Rom. vii. 11.

That God was the author of the commands and messages delivered by Moses and Aaron to Pharaoh, is clear; that he was the author of the judgments inflicted on the land of Egypt is clear; that he knew what effect these would produce on the heart of Pharaoh, is equally certain; and that he designed to turn all this into ultimate good, and to glorify himself, the Bible often asserts or implies. There is no difficulty then in saying, with reference to all this, and in the sense stated above, that God hardened Pharaoh's heart, or that he *roused him up*, viz., by his messages and the miracles which he wrought. It is a clear case, that the active and bitter indignation and contumacy of Pharaoh was greatly increased or excited by these doings of Divine Providence; and therefore the sentiment of our text remains true; while, at the same time, God is not the author of Pharaoh's sin (in the common sense of this expression), any more than he is the author of our sin, because he has given us powers and faculties by which we may sin, and, with full knowledge that we should sin, has placed us in a world where we are of course surrounded by temptations and enticements to sin. After all this we are *free agents*, we sin, *voluntarily*, and we are therefore accountable for it; all which was equally true of Pharaoh.

To all that has now been said to illustrate and vindicate the true sense of ἐξήγειρα, it may be added, that the conclusion drawn by the apostle in ver. 18, clearly implies that he gave such a sense to verses 16, 17, as has been given above: "Therefore he hath mercy on whom he will, and *whom he will, he hardeneth*." Now if ἐξήγειρα does not imply some kind of agency, something done on the part of God which has a connection with the hardening of Pharaoh's heart, how can the apostle deduce the conclusion in ver. 18 from the assertion in verses 16, 17 ? This consideration alone seems fully and finally to decide the point, in regard to the exegesis put upon ἐξήγειρα by Tholuck, who follows the διετηρήθης of the Seventy, and construes it of *preserving* Pharaoh i. e., upholding him in life during the continuance of the plagues in Egypt. Six of these had already been inflicted, when the words in ver 17 were spoken. Tholuck says that Pharaoh might have easily been taken off by the plagues, and therefore, ἐξήγειρα relates, as he maintains, to Pharaoh's having been preserved in life. And in the same way many others have construed the word ἐξήγειρα. But this will hardly satisfy the demands of critical exegesis. The six plagues already inflicted were, the turning of the waters of the Nile into blood, Exod. vii. 14, seq.; the sending of the frogs, Exod. viii. 1, seq.; of the lice, Exod. viii. 16, seq.; of the flies, Exod. viii. 20, seq.; the murrain of beasts, Exod. ix. 1, seq.; and the plague of boils and blains, Exod. ix. 8, seq. Now as all these plagues were merely *temporary*, and as we have no intimation in the sacred records that they occasioned the loss of human life among the Egyptians, so there seems to be no special reason for putting this sense on הֶעֱמַדְתִּיךָ, viz. I *have preserved thee*, or *kept thee alive*.

And then, if this be adopted, how does the conclusion of the apostle in ver. 18 follow, viz , ὃν δὲ θέλει σκληρύνει ? Does *preserving in life*, or *making one to keep his standing*, necessarily import a τὸ σκληρύνειν or σκλήρωμα ? I am altogether unable to see how Paul could deduce such a conclusion from such premises.

I must therefore accede to what seems to be the plain and evident meaning of ἐξήγειρα, viz., that God in his providence did so direct things, viz., the warnings to Pharaoh, the commands addressed to him, and the signs and wonders in his land, that he was excited to more vehement resistance and contumely, which ended in his signal overthrow and destruction In all this Pharaoh was entirely voluntary and free. The case differs not, in principle, from what happens every day. As has been before remarked, God creates men: he endows them with powers and faculties which enable them to sin ; and places them in a world surrounded by temptation; and all this, knowing certainly that they will sin. Every one must agree to this. But are not men free agents still ? Do they not sin *voluntarily* ? Does not the blame of this attach entirely to themselves ? Can any part of it be justly charged upon God ? Surely not; and if not, then there is a sense in which he may say, that *he roused up Pharaoh in order that he might show forth his power and glory in all the earth ;* and this without making himself the proper author of sin. In *one* sense, God does all that takes place under his providence and government of the world; for he preserves all creatures and all worlds, and gives them all their powers, faculties, and opportunities of action. In another sense, God is *not* the author of sin ; " God tempteth no man " Man is the proper author of his own sin; "every man is tempted when he is drawn away by his own lust, and enticed to sin." In one sense God hath made all things for himself, yea, " *the wicked for the day of evil,*" Prov xvi 4, and in the like sense he *roused up* Pharaoh. So far as he is concerned with all this, it is in a way that is perfectly consistent with the freedom of men in action;

and all his designs are to bring good out of evil, and thus to promote the glory of his own name; as is intimated in the verse before us.

All the difficulty which is involved in these declarations in their full extent, is involved in the principle (which even Theism admits), that God is *omniscient*, *omnipotent*, and *immutable*. The Deist has, in reality, the very same difficulties to cope with here, so far as free agency and the sinfulness of men are concerned, as the evangelical Christian. The *nodus* of the whole is our ignorance of the *manner* in which free agency and entire dependence, foreknowledge and voluntary action, consist together and are harmonized. But as *fact* only is known to us, viz., the fact that they do coexist; and as the *manner* of their coexistence or consistency is beyond the boundaries of human knowledge; so I do not see how those, who are stumbled at the subject under consideration, can ever satisfy themselves, so long as they insist on first knowing the *manner* of the consistency, before they admit the *fact*.

In the apostle's time, the very same objection was made to his doctrine, which has been made ever since, and is still every day repeated. So the verses in the sequel plainly show us. They show, moreover, that the apostle was understood in the same way by objectors, as his words at first view would seem to mean; for if this were not so, what ground was there for the objection which is raised?

The difficulty of this subject, the manner in which it has so often been misunderstood and abused, and a wish to contribute (if possible) something to remove some of its perplexities from the minds of readers who may peruse these pages, are my apology for dwelling so long upon it. That there are difficulties still which remain unexplained, and which ever must remain so while 'we know in part,' *i. e.*, while we continue in the present world, I do not feel disposed at all to deny. But this is confessedly the case in regard to a multitude of other things, which all admit without hesitation; and admit them, too, even while the *modus* of them remains utterly inexplicable.

EXCURSUS XII.

On the various designations in Rom. xii. 8 (p. 393).

I HAVE, in this commentary, given the reader the *usual* exegesis of the passage in question, viz., ὁ μεταδιδοὺς, ἐν ἁπλότητι· ὁ προϊστάμενος, ἐν σπουδῇ· ὁ ἐλεῶν, ἐν ἱλαρότητι. But an attentive and repeated examination of it has raised many doubts in my mind whether there is not a radical mistake at the foundation of this whole interpretation. I refer not now to the *verbal* criticisms merely; which, it is obvious, are in general well founded and correct. But I refer to the assumption, in this case, that ὁ μεταδιδούς, ὁ προϊστάμενος, and ὁ ἐλεῶν designate *officers* or *offices* in the church; I mean *officers* in the usual and proper sense of the word, viz., men set apart by the special designation and appointment of the church, for the performance of some peculiar and appropriate duties. I have a predominant persuasion, that these words here designate duties which individuals *merely as such* were to perform, and to whom the church looked for such performance because they had ability or opportunity to perform them, or (if it shall be thought more probable) who were specially desired by the church to perform them. In the last case it might be true, for example, that to an individual in the church who was wealthy, the church looked in a peculiar manner with expectation that he would aid the poor; or (to adduce another example) it might happen that some individual had leisure, and also particular qualifications for visiting the sick, consoling mourners, counselling the perplexed, relieving the distressed by various personal attentions, etc., and the church looked to him as a ὁ ἐλεῶν, or they made a special request of him that he would attend to such duties. All this might be, nay, it is all very natural and probable; while, at the same time, this would not prove that there were regularly instituted *officers* in the church, designated by ὁ μεταδιδούς, ὁ προιστάμενος, and ὁ ἐλεῶν.

These hints give the general views which I feel compelled to entertain of the words under examination. But as the whole subject has an important bearing on the polity of the Christian church, I feel obliged to assign reasons for such an opinion.

(1) It is obvious that the apostle does not here confine himself to *extraordinary* and *miraculous* gifts only, although he includes them. The προφήτης was one who spoke under the influence of inspiration; but ὁ διδάσκων and ὁ παρακαλῶν might or might not be inspired; for the office itself was of a permanent or general nature, and not limited to special circumstances. So the διάκονος might or might not be an inspired man; for Stephen (Acts vi. vii.) was "full of the Holy Ghost," while we have no particular reason to believe that all of his brethren in office were endowed with the same gift. The same is true of ὁ μεταδιδούς, ὁ προιστάμενος, and ὁ ἐλεῶν : for the respective individuals who performed the duties designated by these words, might, at times, enjoy special divine assistance and direction. But this belongs not essentially to the nature of the duties themselves, which may in general be performed without miraculous interposition.

(2) It is equally obvious that the apostle, in the whole extent of his exhortation here, includes both public and private, official and unofficial duties. A bare inspection of verses, 6 — 21 sets this question at rest. He means to say, that inasmuch as all Christians are members of one and the same body, all their gifts and talents, of whatever kind or nature, whether adapted to the performance of public or private duties, whether they are aided by the special influence of the Spirit or otherwise — *all* were to be employed in the most efficient and profitable manner. Such is the evident tenor of his whole discourse. Who, for example, would seek in verses 9, 10 seq., for directions only to men in official stations? There is no reasonable question, therefore, respecting the *general principle* which I have here laid down, in regard to the whole paragraph which contains the apostle's exhortation. But *where* does he dismiss the address to the *officers* of the church as such, and

begin with individuals or laymen? This is the very gist of the question; and in order to throw some light on this, I observe,

(3) That the very construction and natural order of verses 6 — 8 favor the supposition, that the last three classes of men named are *private*, not *official* persons.

In respect to the *natural order* of the passage, it would seem to be an obvious dictate of propriety, that the apostle should begin first with the officers of the church; and this he has plainly done; for we have προφήτης, διάκονος, διδάσκαλος, ὁ παρακαλῶν, before he proceeds to the rest. Now if, after παρακαλῶν, he proceeds to *unofficial* men (as I suppose), then it would be perfectly natural to select from among these, those who are particularly distinguished in the church for their usefulness; and so he seems to have done. The reader will not fail to notice, moreover, that here (before ὁ μεταδιδούς) the construction is changed by the apostle, εἴτε being omitted as if purposely to designate a change in classification.

(4) It is difficult, if not impossible, to make out *official* distinctions through the whole of verses 6 — 8. How does ὁ μεταδιδούς, as an *officer* of the church, differ from ὁ διάκονος? And again; how does ὁ ἐλεῶν differ from both, or from either? A question which none of the commentators have answered with any good degree of satisfaction. Indeed most of them pass the difficulty over with entire silence; which is at least the most easy, if not the most instructive, method of commentary. Here then according to them, are two supplementary offices to that of διάκονος; the main and originally the only duty of which was, *to take care of the poor*.

But further, who is ὁ προιστάμενος? He who *presides* over the church? If so, how can he be placed the *sixth* in rank here, and the *seventh* in 1 Cor. xii 28? (See κυβερνήσεις there.) Then again, why should ὁ προιστάμενος not have a place among the *teachers*, instead of being placed where it has, on the right and left hand, an office of mere *charity*? Does the *presiding* officer of the whole church ever rank in this way, in times either ancient or modern? I know of no such example.

I am aware, indeed, that the apostle has not strictly followed the order of office here, as to dignity or rank, inasmuch as he has mentioned the *deacon* before the *teacher* or *exhorter*. But there is an apparent reason for this. In speaking of the *official* classes of the Romish church, the highest and lowest office, viz, that of *prophet* and *deacon*, i e., the *two extremes* of office, occurred first · which is a very natural method of thought. These the apostle wrote down as they occurred. He then supplied the intermediate offices, viz, that of teacher and exhorter, *i e.*, the proper *doctrinal* instructor, whether in public or private, and *exhorter*, or practical and persuasive preacher. This will account very naturally for the order of officers *here*. But in 1 Cor. xii. 28, the apostle *ex-professo* recounts the natural order *seriatim*; which he makes to be, 1. Apostles; 2 Prophets; 3. Teachers; 4. Such as possessed miraculous powers in general (δυνάμεις); 5. Such as possessed the gift of healing the sick, 6. Ἀντιλήψεις; 7. Κυβερνήσεις; 8. Those who spoke various languages; 9 Interpreters (comp. ver. 30).

Here, then, the ὁ μεταδιδούς, ὁ προϊστάμενος, and ὁ ἐλεῶν of our text, are omitted (unless indeed the ὁ προϊστάμενος is found in the κυβερνήσεις, of which more hereafter), and ἀντίληψεις comes in for ὁ διάκονος. So Bretschneider on ἀντίληψις. "haud dubie ad munus diaconorum et diaconissarum respicitur, ut etiam patres eccles. putârunt." That this last declaration is correct, one may see by consulting Suicer's *Thesaurus*, sub. voc. ἀντίληψις. Vitringa thinks that ἀντίληψις means *the interpreters of foreign languages* (comp. 1 Cor. xii 30, διερμενεύουσι); *de Vet. Synag* II. 31; p. 509. But the other exegesis is most natural; for ἀντίληψις means, *help, assistance, care;* and here the *abstract* (as grammarians say) being used for the *concrete*, the sense is *curatores*, i. e, διάκονοι.

It is obvious, now, that in this noted passage in 1 Cor. xii. 28, ὁ μεταδιδούς and ὁ ἐλεῶν are omitted; and this gives very strong reason to suspect that these were not properly *offices* in the church.

But how is it with ὁ προϊστάμενος ? Is he not found in the κυβερνήσεις of 1 Cor. xii. 28 ? This looks probable at first view; but let us examine a little more thoroughly.

First, I remark, that the word προϊστημι and its derivates are by no means confined to designate the idea of presiding over *persons*. It sometimes conveys the idea of being placed over any *thing*, or any kind of *business*, in order to take care of it, see that it is done, etc., *i. e.*, the *undertaker* in anything, the *protector* or *curator* of any person or thing, the Greeks call ὁ προϊστάμενος, ὁ προεστώς, ὁ προϊστάτης, i. q., *patron, helper*. Accordingly the word occurs in the sense of *aiding, assisting*, etc, in Rom xvi. 2, where the brethren of the Roman church are charged by the apostle to *aid*, in any manner she may need, Phebe, who had been a προστάτις of many Christians, *i. e.*, *a helper*, *a curator*, one who had aided them by her personal attention and by her charity. The grammarian Varinus explains προστασία by βοήθεια. In the letter of Athanasius *ad Solitarios*, when speaking of the disposition of Zenobia to Paul of Samosata, he says: προέστη τοῦ Σαμοσάτεως, she *aided him of Samosata*.* So Theophylact, commenting on Rom. xii. 8, says: Προΐστασθαί ἐστι τὸ βοηθεῖν, καὶ διὰ ῥημάτων καὶ διὰ τοῦ σώματος αὐτοῦ τῷ βοηθείας δεομένῳ, i. e , προΐστασθαι means TO AID, *both by words and by personal services, him who is needy.*

That such a meaning then *may be given to* ὁ προϊστάμενος in Rom. xii. 8, seems clear. The *usus loquendi* allows it. What then does the context demand ? Let us see what precedes, and what follows.

What precedes is, ὁ μεταδιδοὺς, ἐν ἁπλότητι; which I now render, *let him who imparts* [charity], *do it with liberality*. So, beyond all doubt, the words may be rendered. That ἁπλότης may mean *liberality*, one may see in 2 Cor. viii 2, ix. 11, 13; James i. 5. So Xenophon. ἁπλούστατον δέ μοι δοκεῖ εἶναι, κ. τ. λ., *it seems to me to be the part of a most liberal man*, etc., Cyrop. VIII. p. 155. So Josephus, speaking of Araunah's liberal offer to David (2 Sam. xxiv 19—24), says · David highly esteemed his ἁπλότητα, *liberality*, etc Antiq. VII. 10. So in Test XII Patriarch, p 624: ὁ θεὸς συνεργεῖ τῇ ἁπλότητί μου, *God helped my liberal disposition*. See other examples in

---

* Reiche has quoted this in the sense of 'he *presided over* Samosata!'

Kypke in loc. As to ὁ μεταδιδούς, which is commonly applied to one who *distributes* charity, and so made for substance synonymous with διάκονος, it is very doubtful, to say the least, whether the word will bear this construction. Bretschneider has indeed given it such a meaning (as others before him have often done), but as Vitringa long ago observed (De Vet Synag. II. 3 p. 501), "the proper Greek word for *distribute* is διαδίδωμι;" as one may see in John vi 11; Luke xviii. 22 (also in xi 22, it has the like sense), Acts iv. 35. The like sense this verb has in the classics. But μεταδίδωμι properly means *to impart among others what belongs to one's self, to give of one's own to others;* which is, or at any rate may be, a very different thing from *distributing* the alms of the church.

If these words be rightly explained, we have in them a command of the apostle, that those who are able μεταδιδόναι, *to give in charity, should do this in a liberal manner.* That all this is congruous and appropriate, I presume no one will venture to deny.

We have seen what *precedes* ὁ προιστάμενος. Let us now see what *follows* it. This is ὁ ἐλεῶν, ἐν ἱλαρότητι, *let him who performs deeds of mercy, do it cheerfully, i. e*, let him go about his task with a willing mind voluntarily, not grudgingly and with a forbidding demeanor. The duty of ὁ ἐλεῶν may differ from that of ὁ μεταδιδούς, in this respect, viz., that the former consisted in personal cares and services bestowed upon the sick and unfortunate, while the latter consisted in donations of money, food, etc. These latter duties devolved especially on the *rich;* the former could be performed by all classes of Christians.

Between these two classes of *benefactors*, then, the apostle places ὁ προιστάμενος. If these classes, now, are *officers* of the church, it would seem probable that ὁ προιστάμενος does not here stand for one. That ὁ ἐλεῶν cannot be made to mean an *officer* of the church, the silence of most commentators concerning it would seem pretty strongly to indicate. Accordingly Vitringa does not hesitate to say Quicquid enim adversæ opinionis auctores statuant, *fieri non potest* ut per τὸν ἐλεοῦντα describantur aliqui ecclesiæ *officiarii* [officers.]

It does seem most probable, therefore, that ὁ προιστάμενος is of the like tenor with ἡ προστάτις in Rom. xvi. 2, which there means, *one who receives and entertains strangers, i. e.*, a helper of Christian brethren coming from abroad; for such a helper (προστάτις) was Phebe And this seems the more probable, inasmuch as the duty of *hospitality*, so often and so urgently insisted on by the apostles, has no specific mention among the special charities here, unless it be included in this word; although it is touched on as it respects the church in general, in ver. 13. But a camparison with Rom. xvi 2, as I must think, renders the sense now given to ὁ προιστάμενος quite probable

But Tholuck and others appeal to κυβερνήσεις in 1 Cor. xii. 28, and say, that as κυβερνήσεις means there a special gift or office bestowed by the influence of the Spirit, so ὁ προιστάμενος must be considered as corresponding with it But what is κυβέρνησις ? A question difficult to be answered, inasmuch as this word in 1 Cor. xii 28 is a ἅπαξ λεγόμενον. In classic Greek it means *guidance, direction, steering;* and is especially (as also the verb κυβερνάω) applied to designate the *steering* or *guiding* of a ship by the pilot. Hence many critics understand it here (1 Cor. xii. 28) as designating the *office* of a ruler in the church. But how can such an office be placed the *seventh* in rank (for the apostle here seems to make an enumeration according to the order of precedence), and have but one or two offices reckoned below it? This seems to be exceedingly incongruous. The *governor* and *guide* of a Christian church would seem, in the order of nature, to stand at its *head*.

I ask, in the next place, how it should happen that κυβερνήσεις stands here in such a position, having in order before it ἀντιλήψεις, *opitulatores, curatores* (i. q., διάκονοι), and after it γένη γλωσσῶν? Why does it not stand next before or after προφήτας or διδασκάλους, where we should almost of necessity expect to find it, if it mean *presidents* or *governors* of the church?

Moved by such difficulties, I feel constrained to seek another than a *classical* meaning for κυβερνήσεις. But as in the New Testament the word is not elsewhere to be found, we must resort to the Septuagint: and here the word is *uniformly* employed as the rendering of the Hebrew תַחְבֻּלוֹת *skilful dexterity, wise foresight, power of prudent* or *skilful management.* In this very sense κυβέρνησις is plainly employed in Prov i. 5, xi. 14, xxiv 6. μετὰ κυβερνήσεως γίνεται πόλεμος; and these are all the instances in which the word occurs in the Septuagint. In accordance with this meaning is the Lex. Cyrilli; κυβέρνησις, φρόνησις. So the Glossæ ineditæ in Prov. Salom.: κυβέρνησις, ἐπιστήμη τῶν πραττομένων. So also Hesychius: κυβερνήσεις, προνοετικαὶ ἐπιστῆμαι καὶ φρονήσεις, *considerate knowledge and understanding.*

In view of all this, we may now venture to translate κυβερνήσεις *skilful discernment* or *insight.* But in what respect? To answer thus, we must let the apostle explain himself. Let us go back, then, to 1 Cor. xii 8—10, and there we shall find nearly if not quite the same reckoning of spiritual gifts as in verses 28—30. But there, before γένη γλωσσῶν, stands διακρίσεις τῶν πνευμάτων; which does not at all appear in verses 28—30, unless it be designated by κυβερνήσεις. That it should not in fact be included in this latter passage, distinguished as such a gift must be, and important as it was in the then state of the church, would be singular. Now as in 1 Cor. xii. 28, γένη γλωσσῶν comes immediately after κυβερνήσεις, and in ver. 10 immediately after διακρίσεις πνευμάτων, so it is natural to conclude, that the apostle means to designate the same thing by κυβερνήσεις as he does by διακρίσεις πνευμάτων For as *peculiar skill* and *insight* would be appropriate and necessary to the *discerning of spirits*, so the qualifications for such a duty may be used to designate the persons who are to perform it. Philology allows this, but above all, the order, concinnity, and consistency of the apostle's discourse here, seem to render it necessary, or at least quite probable. This being conceded, it would follow that no argument from κυβερνήσεις can be adduced in order to show that ὁ προϊστάμενος in Rom xii. 8 means a *ruler* in the Christian church

I am the more satisfied with this view of the subject, as I find it was fully embraced by Lightfoot and Vitringa, " quos [in re critica] facile principes nominarem " See Vitringa, De Vet Synag II. 3. p. 507 seq

EXCURSUS XII. ON ROM. XII. 8. 491

It remains only that I notice one objection more to the meaning which I have assigned to ὁ προϊστάμενος. This is, that in 1 Thess. v. 12 and in Tim. iii. 4, 12, it means *governors, overseers* of the church; and consequently that is the most probable meaning in Rom. xii. 8.

On this allegation I must be very brief, as I have already put the patience of the reader to a trial. In 1 Thess. v. 12 the apostle says to the church: 'Affectionately regard τοὺς κοπιῶντας ἐν ὑμῖν, καὶ προϊσταμένους ὑμῶν ἐν κυρίῳ καὶ νουθετοῦντας ὑμᾶς. The question is, whether he means here *different* classes of officers, or *one* and the *same* class, in the exercise of divers gifts. I know of no way in which this question can be definitely and certainly decided. The insertion of the article before κοπιῶντας (the *first* participial noun in the series), and the omission of it before the other like nouns προϊσταμένους and νουθετοῦντας will not prove, as has sometimes been assumed, that all belong to one class; nor will it prove the contrary; for (1) the article is usually *omitted*, even when the meaning of the nouns employed is plainly diverse, provided they are of the same gender and case; *e. g.*, Mark xv. 1, μετὰ τῶν πρεσβυτέρων καὶ γραμματέων (the latter without τῶν); and so Col. ii. 8, 19, 2 Thess. iii. 2; Rom 1. 20; Phil. ii. 17, et sæpe alibi; see N. Test Gramm. § 89. 9. (2) The article is often *inserted*, where each noun indicates a separate subject; *e. g.*, Mark ii 16, οἱ γραμματεῖς καὶ οἱ φαρισαῖοι; so Luke viii. 24, xi. 39; 1 Thess. iii 11; Phil iii. 10, et alibi sæpe; comp. ut sup. Of course, as usage is both ways, the *omission* of the article here can prove nothing. Nor,

(2) Will the context enable us to decide the point under consideration; as there seems to be nothing in it which has a direct bearing on this point. We are left, therefore, to the simple nature of the case. What can be gathered from this? I answer, (*a*) That τοὺς κοπιῶντας is evidently a *generic*, not a specific term, and may indicate any kind of labor performed in behalf of the church. (*b*) The words προϊσταμένους and νουθετοῦντας appear to be *specific* here, *i. e.*, to designate particular (and probably different) classes of persons. The most probable interpretation, then, is that προϊσταμένους and νουθετοῦντας designate the *specific* classes, comprehended under the genus κοπιῶντας. This being admitted (and certainly no one will say this is an improbable exegesis), it would seem altogether probable, that προϊσταμένους here has the like sense as in Rom. xii. 8, viz, those who applied themselves to the *external* temporal business or concerns of the church, while νουθετοῦντας designates all the various kinds of teachers. The exhortation of the apostle, then, is to regard with kindly feelings those who labored in any respect, whether temporal or spiritual, for the good of the church. This determines nothing, therefore, against our interpretation of ὁ προϊστάμενος in Rom. xii 8

From what has now been said, it is easy to explain 1 Tim. v. 17, "Let the elders καλῶς προεστῶτες *managing well* [the concerns of the church], be accounted worthy of double honor [i. e, of ample maintenance], especially those who labor in word and doctrine." There were then two kinds of elders, or (to speak more accurately) there were two departments in which the πρεσβύτεροι might labor; they might be προεστῶτες, i. e, *standing over, taking care of, serving* the temporal concerns and business, etc., of the church, or they might be specially devoted to preaching and teaching, λόγῳ καὶ διδασκαλίᾳ; or perhaps this latter means, that they might perform the duties of a προεστώς, and also to teach and preach in addition to this. That the government of the church, in the ordinary sense of *presiding over* and *making rules for* the church, is not here meant, at least that it is not necessarily meant, seems to me quite plain, from comparing προΐστημι and its derivates in other places. E. g., in this same epistle, iii. 13, deacons are spoken of who τέκνων καλῶς προϊστάμενοι καὶ τῶν ἰδίων οἴκων, *manage their own children and households, well i. e*, take good care of them; for so ver. 13 explains it οἱ γὰρ καλῶς διακονήσαντες = καλῶς προϊστάμενοι. I cannot refrain from adding, that this last passage throws great light on what has been before said about ὁ προϊστάμενος, and serves very much to confirm it.

So, then, προϊστάμενοι and προεστῶτες may mean the performers of any service or services which pertain to the *external* welfare and management of the church. That the πρεσβύτεροι sometimes did such services, is clear from 1 Tim v. 17. But that others might perform them, is equally clear from Rom xii 8; 1 Cor. xii. 28; Rom xvi 2, etc.

We can now account for it that the apostle says, in Rom. xii 8, 'Let ὁ προϊστάμενος do his duty ἐν σπουδῇ, *with diligence, i. e.*, with active watchful attention and effort' But how ἐν σπουδῇ can be applicable to *ruling*, in the common sense of this word, has been a difficulty which has perplexed not a few, who have undertaken to expound this passage. We might exhort a *ruler* to perform the duties of his office with *impartiality*, with a due regard to *justice* and *equity*, etc.; but to exhort him *to govern ἐν σπουδῇ*, seems hardly congruous.

On the whole, I am brought by a kind of philological necessity to the conclusion, that church *officers*, in the appropriate sense of this word, are not designated by ὁ μεταδιδούς, ὁ προϊστάμενος, and ὁ ἐλεῶν in Rom. xii. 8, but that the apostle refers to individuals in the church, conspicuous for their attention to the duties respectively indicated by these words, which duties were, the giving of money or substance, the management of the external temporal affairs and business and interests of the church, and the succoring of the sick and unfortunate by personal attention and effort.

THE

EPISTLE TO THE ROMANS.

Introduction and Salutation.

1 PAUL, a servant of Jesus Christ, a chosen apostle, set apart
2 for the gospel of God, | which he formerly declared by his
3 prophets in the holy Scriptures, | concerning his Son (born
4 of the seed of David in respect to the flesh, | the decreed Son
of God with power in respect to the spirit of holiness after his
5 resurrection from the dead), Jesus Christ our Lord, | (by
whom we have received grace and apostleship, in order to
promote the obedience of faith among all nations, for his
6 name's sake, | among whom are ye also called of Jesus
7 Christ,) | to all who are at Rome, beloved of God, chosen
saints; grace be unto you, and peace from God our Father
and the Lord Jesus Christ.
8 First, I thank my God, through Jesus Christ, on account
9 of you all, that your faith is spoken of in all the world. For
God is my witness, whom I serve with my spirit in the gospel of his Son, how unceasingly I make remembrance of you,
10 always asking in my prayers, that if possible, at some time
before long, I may (God willing) make a prosperous journey
11 and come to you. For I am desirous to see you, in order to
bestow on you some spiritual favor, so that you may be con-
12 firmed. This also [I desire], to be comforted among you by
the mutual faith both of you and me.
13 Moreover, I would not have you ignorant, brethren, that I
have often purposed to come unto you (but have been hindered until now), that I might have some fruit among you, as
14 also among other Gentiles. I am a debtor both to Greeks
15 and Barbarians, both to the learned and the unlearned: such
being the case, I am ready, according to my ability, to preach
the gospel even to you who are at Rome.

Subjects of consideration proposed

16 For I am not ashamed of the gospel of Christ, since it is

the power of God for salvation to every one that believeth;
17 to the Jew first, and then to the Greek. For by it the justification which is of God is revealed, [justification] by faith for the faithful; as it is written: "The just shall live by
18 faith." For the wrath of God from heaven is revealed against all ungodliness and unrighteousness of men,

Universal depravity and guilt of the Gentiles.

19 Who wickedly hinder the truth; | because that which might be known of God,* is manifest in them, inasmuch as God
20 hath manifested it to them; | (for the invisible things of him, since the creation of the world, are clearly seen by the things which are made, even his eternal power and Godhead); so
21 that they are without excuse; because, when they knew God, they glorified him not as God, neither were thankful, but became foolish in their imaginations, and their inconsiderate
22 mind was darkened. Professing themselves to be wise, they
23 became fools, | and exchanged the glory of the immortal God for an image like to mortal man, and fowls, and four-footed
24 beasts, and reptiles. Wherefore God even gave them up, in the lusts of their hearts, to uncleanness, to dishonor their own
25 bodies among themselves; who exchanged the true God for a false one, and worshipped and served the creature rather than
26 the Creator, who is blessed for ever, Amen! On account of this, God gave them up to base passions; for their women changed their natural use into that which is against nature.
27 And in like manner also the males, leaving the natural use of the female, burned in their lust toward each other, males with males doing that which is shameful, and receiving in them-
28 selves the reward of their error which is due. And inasmuch as they did not like to retain God in their knowledge, God gave them up to a reprobate mind, to do those things which
29 are base: being filled with all iniquity, uncleanness, malice, covetousness, mischief; full of envy, murder, strife, deceit, ma-
30 levolence; | backbiters, open slanderers, haters of God, railers, proud, boasters, inventors of evil things, disobedient to
31 parents, | inconsiderate, covenant-breakers, destitute of natu-
32 ral affection, implacable, unmerciful: who, knowing the ordinance of God that they who do such things are worthy of death, not only do the same things, but even bestow commendation on those who do them.

The Jews equally guilty with the Gentiles.

II. Therefore thou art without excuse, O man, whoever thou

* Or that which is known.

art that judgest; for while thou art passing sentence upon
another, thou condemnest thyself, since thou who judgest doest
2 the same things. For we know that the judgment of God is
3 according to truth, against those who do such things. Dost
thou think, then, O man, who condemnest those that do such
things, and doest the same, that thou shalt escape the judg-
4 ment of God? Or dost thou despise his abounding goodness
and forbearance and long-suffering, not acknowledging that the
5 goodness of God leadeth thee to repentance? According to
thy hard and impenitent heart, however, thou art treasuring
up for thyself wrath in the day of wrath, when the righteous
6 judgment of God shall be revealed; who will render to every
7 man according to his works; to those who by patient continuance in well-doing seek for glory and honor and immortality,
8 eternal life; but to those who are contentious, and disobey the
9 truth and obey unrighteousness, indignation and wrath. Affliction and distress [shall be] upon every soul of man that
10 doeth evil, first of the Jew and then of the Greek; but glory
and honor and peace [shall be] to every one who doeth good,
11 first to the Jew and then to the Greek; (for with God there
12 is no respect of persons; since so many as have sinned without law shall perish without law, and so many as have sinned
13 under the law shall be condemned by the law; for not the hearers of the law are just with God, but the doers of the law will
14 be justified; for when the Gentiles who have no law, do in a
natural state such things as the law requireth, these, being
15 destitute of the law, are a law to themselves; who shew that
the work which the law requireth, is written upon their hearts,
their consciences bearing witness, and their thoughts alter-
16 nately accusing or excusing); in the day when God shall
judge the secret things of men by Jesus Christ, according to
my gospel.
17 If now thou art surnamed *Jew*, and dost lean upon the law,
18 and make thy boast of God; | and art acquainted with [his]
will, and canst distinguish things which differ, being instructed
19 by the law; thou art confident also of being thyself a guide to
20 the blind, a light to those who are in darkness, | an instructor
of the ignorant, a teacher of little children, one having the
representation of true knowledge in the law; dost thou then
21 who teachest another, not instruct thyself? Dost thou who
22 preachest against stealing, thyself steal? Dost thou who for-
23 biddest to commit adultery, thyself commit adultery? Dost
thou who abhorrest idols, thyself commit robbery in holy
24 things? Dost thou who gloriest in the law, thyself dishonor
God by transgressing the law? For as it is written, "the

name of God is on your account blasphemed among the Gentiles."

25 Circumcision indeed is profitable, if thou dost obey the law; but if thou art a transgressor of the law, thy circumcision be-
26 cometh uncircumcision. If, moreover, he who is uncircumcised keep the precepts of the law, shall not his uncircumci-
27 sion be counted for circumcision? Yea, he who keepeth the law in his natural uncircumcised state, will condemn thee, who, in possession of the Scriptures and a partaker of circum-
28 cision, art a transgressor of the law. For he is not a Jew, who is one outwardly; nor is that which is outward, [merely]
29 in the flesh, circumcision. But he is a Jew, who is one inwardly; and circumcision is of the heart, spiritual not literal; whose praise is not of men, but of God.

Answer to some objections   Further confirmation of the depravity and guilt of the Jews   General conclusion from the facts stated.

III. 'WHAT then is the advantage of the Jew? Or what the profit of circumcision?'
2 Much in diverse respects; the most important however is, that they were entrusted with the oracles of God.
3 'What then if some did not believe? Will their unbelief make void the faithfulness of God?'
4 By no means; but let God be [counted] true, and every man false; as it is written: "That thou mightest be justified when thou speakest, and overcome when thou art judged."
5 'But if our unrighteousness commend the righteousness of God, what shall we say? Is God unjust, who inflicteth punisment?'
6 (I speak after the manner of men). By no means; otherwise, how shall God judge the world?
7 'Still, if God's faithfulness to his word has on account of my deceitfulness abounded more unto his glory, why am I any longer condemned as a sinner?'
8 Shall we then [say] (as it is slanderously reported and as some affirm that we do say): Let us do evil that good may come? whose condemnation is just.
9 'What then? Have we any preëminence?' None at a'l; for we have already made good the charge against both Jews
10 and Gentiles, that they are all under sin. As it is written:
11 "There is none righteous, not even one; there is none who
12 understandeth, there is none who seeketh after God; all have gone out of the way, together have they become corrupt;
13 there is none who doeth good, not even one. Their throat is an open sepulchre; with their tongues do they deceive. The

14 poison of asps is under their lips. | Whose mouth is full of
15 cursing and bitterness. Their feet are swift to shed blood;
16/17 destruction and misery attend their steps; | the way of peace
18 they know not. There is no fear of God before their eyes.
19 Now we know whatsoever things the law saith, it speaketh to those who are under the law; so that every mouth must
20 be stopped, and the whole world become guilty before God, | because that by works of law shall no flesh be justified before him, for by the law is the knowledge of sin.

Gratuitous justification by Christ is the only way of salvation.

21 But now, the justification without law which is of God is revealed, to which testimony is given by the law and the
22 prophets; a justification then which is of God by faith in Jesus Christ; [offered] to all, and [bestowed] on all who
23 believe, for there is no distinction. For all have sinned and
24 come short of divine approbation, | being justified freely by his grace through the redemption which is by Christ Jesus;
25 whom God hath set forth as a propitiatory [sacrifice] by faith in his blood, in order to declare his justification through remission, by the forbearance of God, of sins formerly com-
26 mitted; in order to declare his justification at the present time; so that he might be just and yet the justifier of him that believeth in Jesus.
27 Where then is boasting? It is excluded. By what law?
28 Of works? Nay, but by the law of faith; for we have come to the conclusion, that a man is justified by faith without
29 works of law. Is he the God of the Jews only? Is he not
30 also of the Gentiles? Yea, of the Gentiles also; since it is one and the same God, who will justify the circumcised by
31 faith and the uncircumcised by faith. Do we then make void the law through faith? By no means; we confirm the law.

The Scriptures of the Old Testament teach the doctrine of justification by grace only

IV. 'WHAT then shall we say that Abraham our father obtained, in respect to the flesh?'
2 No ground of glorying; for if Abraham was justified by works, he hath ground of glorying; but [this he hath] not
3 before God. For what saith the Scripture? "And Abraham believed God, and it was counted to him for righteous-
4 ness." Now to him that worketh, reward is not counted as a
5 matter of grace, but as a debt; but to him who worketh not, but believeth on him who justifieth the ungodly, his faith is counted for righteousness.

6 In like manner, also, David pronounceth happy the man, to
7 whom God imputeth righteousness without works: "Blessed
are they whose iniquities are forgiven, and whose sins are
8 covered; blessed is the man to whom the Lord imputeth not
iniquity."
9 [Is] this a declaration of blessedness, then, concerning
those who are circumcised [only], or concerning the uncircumcised? [Concerning the uncircumcised also], for we say
10 that faith was counted to Abraham for righteousness. How
then was it counted? While he was in a state of circumcision, or of uncircumcision? Not in a state of circumcision,
11 but of uncircumcision. And he received the sign of circumcision, as a seal of the righteousness by faith which [he
obtained] in a state of uncircumcision; in order that he
might be the father of all the uncircumcised who believe, so
12 that righteousness might also be counted to them; and the
father of the circumcised, who are not only of the circumcision, but walk in the steps of that faith which our father
Abraham had while in a state of circumcision.
13 For the promise was not made by law to Abraham or to his
seed, that he should be heir of the word; but by the right-
14 eousness of faith. If now they who are of the law, are
heirs, faith is rendered of no effect, and the promise is made
void; for the law worketh wrath, because where there is no
16 law there is no transgression. On this account it was of
faith, so that it must be of grace, in order that the promise
might be sure to all the seed, not only to him who is under
17 the law, but to him who is of the faith of Abraham;— who
is the father of us all | (as it is written: "A father of many
nations have I made thee"), in the sight of God in whom he
believed, who giveth life to the dead, and calleth the things
18 which are not, as if they were; | who, against hope, believed
in hope that he should become the father of many nations
(according to what had been said: "So shall thy seed
19 be") | and being not weak in faith, he considered not his
own body already dead (as he was about one hundred years
20 of age), nor yet the deadness of Sarah's womb; neither did he
through unbelief doubt the promise of God, but he was
21 strong in faith, giving glory to God, | and being fully persuaded that what he had promised he was also able to per-
22 form. Wherefore it was verily counted to him for righteous-
23 ness. Yet it was not recorded merely for his sake, that
it was counted to him; but also for our sake, to whom it will
be counted, to us who believe on him who raised up Jesus
24 our Lord from the dead, | who was delivered up on account

of our offences, and was raised for the sake of our justification.

The fruits of justification, as to their certainty and extent.

V. THEREFORE being justified by faith, we have peace with
2 God, through our Lord Jesus Christ; by whom also we have obtained access [to God], through belief in that grace* in which we stand, and rejoice in hope of the glory of God.
3 And not only so, but we rejoice also in our afflictions,
4 knowing that affliction produceth patience, | and patience approbation, and approbation hope, | and hope maketh not
5 ashamed; for the love of God is shed abroad in our hearts
6 by the Holy Spirit which is given to us. For while we were yet without strength, Christ died in due time for the
7 ungodly. Now scarcely for a just man will any one die; although for his benefactor some one, perhaps, might venture
8 even to die. But God commended his love to us, in that
9 while we were yet sinners Christ died for us. Much more
10 then, being now justified by his blood, shall we be saved from wrath by him. For, if, when we were enemies, we were reconciled to God by the death of his Son; much more, being reconciled, shall we be saved by his life.
11 And not only so, but we also rejoice in God through our Lord Jesus Christ, by whom we have now obtained reconciliation.
12 Therefore, as by one man, sin entered into the world, and death by sin; and so death came upon all men, because that
13 all have sinned; (for until the law sin was in the world,
14 although sin is not accounted for where there is no law; yet death reigned from Adam unto Moses, even over those who had not sinned in like manner as Adam; who is a type of him
15 that was to come. But not as the offence, so the free gift also; for if by the offence of one the many died, much more has the grace of God and the gift which is by the grace of
16 one man, Jesus Christ, abounded unto the many. Moreover, not as the [condemnation] by one who sinned, is the free gift; for sentence was by one [offence] unto condemnation, but the free gift is unto justification from many offences.
17 For if by the offence of one death reigned because of that one, much more shall they who receive abundance of grace and of the gift of justification, reign in life by one, Jesus
18 Christ;) therefore, as by one offence [sentence came] upon all men unto condemnation, so by one righteousness [the free

---

* Or, we have obtained access through faith unto that grace, etc

19 gift came] upon all men unto justification of life; for as by the disobedience of one man the many were made sinners, so by the obedience of one the many will be made righteous.
20 The law moreover was introduced, so that offence should
21 abound; but where sin abounded, grace superabounded; so that, as sin reigned by death, in like manner grace also might reign by justification unto eternal life, through Jesus Christ our Lord.

Gratuitous justification does not encourage men to sin, but restrains them from it.

VI. WHAT shall we say then? May we continue in sin, that grace may abound?
2 By no means. How shall we, who are dead to sin, any
3 longer live in it? Know ye not, that so many of us as have been baptized into Christ Jesus, have been baptized into his
4 death? We have then been buried with him by baptism into his death; so that, as Christ was raised from the dead by the glory of the Father, in like manner we also should walk in
5 newness of life. For if we have become kindred with him by a death like unto his, then we shall also be [kindred] by a
6 resurrection: for we know this, that our old man is crucified, as he was, that the body of sin might be destroyed, in order
7 that we should no longer serve sin; for he who is dead, is
8 freed from sin. If now we are dead with Christ, we believe
9 that we shall also live with him; knowing that Christ, being raised from the dead, dieth no more, death hath no longer any
10 dominion over him. For in that he died, he died once for all
11 unto sin; but in that he liveth, he liveth unto God. In like manner you also must account yourselves dead unto sin, but alive unto God through Jesus Christ.
12 Let not sin reign, then, in your mortal body, that ye should
13 obey the lusts thereof; neither proffer your members to sin as instruments of iniquity; but proffer yourselves to God as alive from the dead, and your members to God as instruments
14 of righteousness. For sin shall not have dominion over you; since ye are not under the law, but under grace.
15 'What then? Shall we sin, because we are not under law, but under grace?'
16 By no means. Know ye not, that to whomsoever ye proffer yourselves as servants ready to obey, ye are servants to him whom ye obey, whether of sin unto death, or of obedience
17 unto justification? But thanks be to God, that ye were the servants of sin, but have become obedient from the heart to that model of doctrine in which ye have been instructed.
18 Moreover being freed from sin, ye have become the servants

19 of righteousness. (I speak in language common to men, because of the weakness of your flesh); for as ye have proffered your members* as servants to impurity and iniquity in order to commit iniquity, so now proffer your members* to
20 righteousness in order to be holy. For when ye were the servants of sin, ye were free in respect to righteousness.
21 What fruit had ye then, in those things of which ye are now
22 ashamed? for the end of those things is death. But now, being freed from sin and having become servants to God, ye have your fruit in respect to holiness, and in the end [ye will
23 have] eternal life. For the wages of sin is death; but the gift of God, eternal life, through Jesus Christ our Lord.

Those who are under law cannot be freed from the power and penalty of sin.

VII. Know ye not, brethren, (for I speak to those acquainted with the law,) that the law hath dominion over a man so long
2 as he liveth? For the married woman is bound to her husband so long as he liveth; but if her husband die, she is freed
3 from the law of her husband. Therefore, if she marry another while her husband is living, she shall be called an adulteress; but if her husband die, she is freed from the law, so that she will not become an adulteress by marrying another husband.
4 Thus, my brethren, ye also have become dead to the law by the body of Christ, in order that ye should be joined to another who is risen from the dead; so that we may bring
5 forth fruit unto God. For when we were in the flesh, our sinful passions which were by the law, wrought in our mem-
6 bers to bring forth fruit unto death; but now we are freed from the law by which we were held in bondage, inasmuch as we have become dead to it; so that we serve [God] with a new spirit, and not according to the ancient letter.
7 'What shall we say then? Is the law sin?'
By no means. Still, I had not known sin except by the law; for I had not known inordinate desire unless the law
8 had said, "Thou shalt not desire inordinately." But sin, taking occasion by the commandment, wrought out in me all manner of inordinate desire; for without the law sin is dead.
9/10 Once, moreover, I was alive without the law; but when the commandment came, sin revived, and I died; yea, the commandment which was unto life, the very same was found to
11 be death to me. For sin taking occasion by the command-

* Or yourselves

12 ment deceived me, and by it slew me; so that the law is holy
and the commandment holy and just and good.
13 'Has then that which is good become death unto me?'
By no means; but sin [has become death], in order that it
might manifest itself as causing death to me by that which is
good, so that through the commandment sin might be exceed-
14 ingly sinful. For we know that the law is spiritual; but I
15 am carnal, sold under sin. For that which I practise, I approve not; for not what I approve do I perform, but that
16 which I hate, I do. If then I do that which I approve not, I
17 give consent to the law as good. But now it is no longer I
18 who do this, but sin which dwelleth in me. For I know that
in me, that is, in my flesh, there dwelleth no good thing; for
to approve is easy for me, but to do what is good I find no
19 [readiness]. For the good which I approve, that I do not;
20 but the evil which I condemn, that I do. Now if I do that
which I approve not, it is no longer I who do it, but sin
21 which dwelleth in me. I find, then, that it is a law to me,
22 when desirous to do good, that evil is near me. For I take
23 pleasure in the law of God, as to the inner man; but I perceive another law in my members, warring against the law of
my mind, and making me a captive to the law of sin which is
24 in my members. Wretched man that I am! Who shall de-
25 liver me from the body which causeth this death? I thank
God, through Jesus Christ our Lord! Wherefore I, the same
person, serve with my mind the law of God, but with my
flesh the law of sin.

A state of grace delivers from the bondage and penalty of sin.

VIII. But now, there is no condemnation to those who are in
2 Christ Jesus.* For the law of the Spirit of life in Christ
3 Jesus, hath freed me from the law of sin and death. For
what the law could not accomplish, in that it was weak through
the flesh, God [accomplished], who, sending his own Son in
the likeness of sinful flesh and on account of sin, condemned
4 sin in the flesh; so that the precepts of the law might be fulfilled in us, who walk not according to the flesh but according
5 to the Spirit. For they who live according to the flesh, do
mind the things of the flesh; but they who live according to
6 the Spirit, the things of the Spirit. For the mind of the flesh
7 is death; but the mind of the Spirit is life and peace. Because the mind of the flesh is enmity against God; for it is

* *Who walk not after the flesh, but after the Spirit,* is probably spurious here, and is therefore omitted.

not subject to his law, nor indeed can be. Those then who
8 are in the flesh cannot please God. Ye, however, are not in
9 the flesh but in the Spirit, if so be that the Spirit of God
dwelleth in you. If now any one hath not the Spirit of
10 Christ, he is none of his; but if Christ be in you, the body
indeed is mortified on account of sin, but the Spirit liveth on
11 account of righteousness. But if the Spirit of him who raised
up Jesus from the dead, dwelleth in you, he who raised up
Christ from the dead will also quicken your mortal bodies,
because of his Spirit which dwelleth in you.
12 Therefore, brethren, we are not debtors to the flesh, to live
13 according to the flesh; | for if ye live according to the flesh,
ye shall die; but if through the Spirit ye mortify the deeds
14 of the body, ye shall live. For as many as are led by the
15 Spirit of God, these are the sons of God. For ye have not
received a servile spirit, that ye should again be in fear: but
ye have received a filial Spirit, by which we cry Abba,
16 Father! The same Spirit beareth witness in our spirit, that
17 we are children of God. But if children, then heirs; heirs
of God, and joint heirs with Christ, if so be that we suffer
with him in order that we may be also glorified with him.

Fruits of the grace and sanctification proffered in the gospel

18 Moreover I reckon the sufferings of the present time as not
worthy of regard, when compared with the glory which is to
19 be revealed to us. For the earnest expectation of the crea-
20 ture is waiting for the revelation of the children of God. For
21 the creature was made subject to frailty (not of its own choice
but through him who put it in subjection), in hope that this
same creature may be freed from the bondage of a perishing
state, and [brought] into the glorious liberty of the children
22 of God. For we know that every creature sighs and groans
23 together even to the present time. Yet not only so, but those
who have the first fruits of the Spirit, even we ourselves
groan within ourselves, waiting for our adoption, the redemp-
24 tion of our body. For we are saved in hope. Now hope
which is seen, is not hope: for what a man seeth, how doth
25 he still hope for it? But if we hope for that which we do
not see, we patiently wait for it.
26 In like manner, also, the Spirit helpeth much our infirmities; for we know not what we should pray for as we ought;
the same Spirit, however, maketh earnest intercession for us,
27 in sighs which cannot be uttered; but he who searcheth
hearts knoweth the mind of the Spirit, that he maketh intercession in behalf of the saints according to the will of God.

28 We know, moreover, that all things work together for good
to those who love God, to those who are called according to
29 his purpose. For those whom he foreknew, he also predestinated to be conformed to the image of his Son, in order that
30 he should be the first-born among many brethren. Those also whom he predestinated, the same he likewise called; and those whom he called, the same he also justified; and those whom he justified, the same he also glorified.

31 What shall we say, then, concerning these things? If God
32 be for us, who is against us? Even he who spared not his own Son, but gave him up for us all — how shall he not also
33 with him freely give us all things? | Who shall accuse the
34 elect of God? It is God that justifieth; | who is he that condemneth? It is Christ who died [for us]; yea rather, who has also risen, who moreover is at the right hand of God, and
35 also intercedeth for us. Who shall separate us from the love of Christ? Shall affliction, or anguish, or persecution, or
36 famine, or nakedness, or peril, or sword? (As it is written: "For thy sake are we continually exposed to death, we are
37 counted as sheep for the slaughter.") Nay, in all these things
38 we are more than conquerors through him who loved us. For I am persuaded that neither death nor life, neither angels nor principalities, neither things present nor future, nor powers,
39 | neither height nor depth, nor any other created thing, shall be able to separate us from the love of God which is in Christ Jesus our Lord.

God has a right to make those whom he chooses to be partakers of his favor; and this right he has always exercised.

IX. I SAY the truth in Christ, I speak not falsely (as my con-
2 science testifieth for me in the Holy Spirit), | that I have
3 great sorrow and continual anguish in my heart. For I could wish even myself to be devoted to destruction by Christ, in-
4 stead of my brethren, my kinsmen after the flesh; | who are Israelites; to whom pertaineth the adoption, and the glory, and the covenants, and the giving of the law, and the rites of
5 service, and the promises; | whose are the fathers; and from whom Christ [descended] in respect to the flesh, who is God over all, blessed forever, Amen!

6 However, it is not so that the word of God has been rendered void; for they are not all Israel who are of Israel;
7 | neither are all the seed of Abraham children, | but, "in Isaac
8 shall thy seed be called;" that is, not the children of the flesh are the children of God, but the children of promise, are
9 counted for the seed. For the word of promise was thus:

"According to this time will I come, and Sarah shall have a son."

10 And not only so, but Rebecca also, having conceived by
11 one, our father Isaac, | for [the children] being not yet born, neither having done any thing good or evil, that the purpose of God according to election might stand, not of works but of
12 him that calleth, | it was said to her; "The elder shall serve
13 the younger;" | as it is written: "Jacob have I loved, but Esau have I hated."
14 "What shall we say then? Is there unrighteousness with God?"
15 By no means; for he saith to Moses: "I will have mercy on whomsoever I will have mercy, and I will have compas-
16 sion on whomsoever I will have compassion." Therefore it is not of him that willeth, nor of him that runneth, but of God
17 who showeth mercy. For the Scripture saith to Pharaoh: "For this very purpose have I roused thee up, that I might show forth my power in thee, and declare my name in all the
18 land." Therefore on whom he will he hath mercy, and whom he will he hardeneth.
19 Thou wilt say then to me; Why doth he yet find fault, for
20 who resisteth his will? But rather [I may say], Who art thou, O man, that repliest against God? Shall the thing formed say to him who formed it: Why hast thou made me
21 thus? Hath not the potter power over the clay, to make out of the same lump one vessel to honor and another to dishonor?
22 What now if God, purposing to manifest his indignation and make known his power, endured with much long-suffering the
23 vessels of wrath fitted for destruction; and that he might make known the riches of his glory towards the vessels of
24 mercy which he had before prepared for glory, | [shewed mercy] even to us whom he hath called, not only of the Jews
25 but also of the Gentiles? To the like purpose he saith also in Hosea: "I will call him who was not my people, my peo-
26 ple; and her who was not my beloved, beloved. And it shall come to pass, that in the place where it was said to them: 'Ye are not my people,' there shall they be called the sons of the living God."
27 Isaiah moreover saith concerning Israel: "Although the number of the children of Israel be as the sand of the sea,
28 [only] a remnant shall be saved. For he will execute his word which he hath decreed in righteousness; for the Lord
29 will execute his word decreed concerning the land." Yea, as Isaiah had before said, "Except the Lord of Sabaoth had left

us a remnant, we should have been like Sodom, we should have been made like to Gomorrah."

30 'What shall we say then?' That the Gentiles, who did not seek after justification, have obtained justification, and that
31 justification, which is by faith; but Israel, who sought after a law of justification, have not attained to a law of justification.
32 Why? Because [they sought] not by faith, but by works of law; for they stumbled at the stone of stumbling; | as it is
33 written: "Behold! I lay in Zion a stone of stumbling and a rock of offence; but every one who believeth on him shall not be ashamed."

The unbelief and rejection of the Jews, and the reception of the Gentiles through faith, are truly consistent with the declarations of the ancient Scriptures.

X. BRETHREN, the kind desire of my heart and my prayer to
2 God for them is, that they may be saved. For I bear them witness, that they have a zeal for God, but not according to
3 knowledge. For being ignorant of the justification which is of God, and seeking to establish their own justification, they have not submitted themselves to the justification which is of
4 God. For Christ is the end of the law unto justification, to every one who believeth.
5 For Moses describeth the justification which is of the law, namely, "The man who doeth these things shall live by
6 them." But justification by faith speaketh thus: "Say not in thine heart, Who shall ascend into heaven?" that is, to
7 bring down Christ; or, "Who shall descend into the abyss?" that is, to bring up Christ from the dead. But what saith it?
8 "The word is near to thee, in thy mouth and in thy heart;
9 that is, the word of faith which we preach. For if thou shalt openly confess the Lord Jesus with thy mouth, and believe in thy heart that God raised him from the dead, thou shalt be
10 saved; because with the heart there is belief unto justification, and with the mouth confession is made unto salvation
11 For the Scripture saith: "No one who believeth on him, shall be ashamed."
·12 There is therefore no difference between the Jew and Greek; because there is the same Lord of all, who is rich
13 [in mercy] unto all them that call upon him; for "every one who calleth on the name of the Lord shall be saved."
14 'How then shall they call on him in whom they have not believed? And how shall they believe in him of whom
15 they have not heard? And how shall they hear without a preacher? | And how shall they preach except they be sent?'

As it is written: "How beautiful are the feet of those who publish salvation, who proclaim good tidings!"
16 Yet all have not obeyed the gospel; for Isaiah saith: "Lord, who hath believed our report?"
17 'Faith, then, cometh by hearing; and hearing by the word of God."
18 But I say, Have they not heard? Yea, truly, "their sound hath gone forth into all the earth; their words to the ends of
19 the world." But I say: Doth not Israel know? First Moses saith: "I will move you to jealousy by that which is no nation; I will excite you to indignation by a foolish people."
20 But Isaiah is very bold, and saith: "I was found by those who sought me not; I made myself manifest to those who did
21 not inquire for me." But unto Israel he saith: "All the day long have I stretched out my hand to a disobedient and gainsaying people."

God hath not cast away the Jews entirely and utterly Some are now saved; and all will finally be converted, with the fulness of the Gentiles. God's dealings with them are unsearchable, but wise.

XI. 'I say then, hath God cast away his people?'
2 By no means; for I myself am an Israelite, of the seed of Abraham, of the tribe of Benjamin. God hath not cast away his people whom he foreknew. Know ye not what the Scripture saith in [the history of] Elijah, when he maketh in-
3 tercession to God against Israel? 'Lord, they have killed thy prophets, and digged down thine altars; and I only am left,
4 and they are seeking my life.' But what saith the answer of God to him? "I have reserved for myself seven thousand
5 men, who have not bowed the knee to Baal." In like manner, then, there is even at the present time a remnant accord-
6 ing to the election of grace. But if it be of grace, then it is no more of works; otherwise grace is no more grace. But if it be of works, it is no more of grace; otherwise work is no more work.
7 'What then? that which Israel sought after, he hath not obtained.'
8 But the elect have obtained it; and the rest were blinded; | as it is written: "God hath given them the spirit of slumber, eyes that see not and ears that hear not, even unto this day."
9 David also saith: "Let their table become a snare to catch them, and an occasion of falling and a recompense to them.
10 Let their eyes be darkened so that they cannot see, and their back be always bowed down."
11 'I say then, have they stumbled so as utterly to fall?'

By no means; but by their fall salvation [is come] to the
12 Gentiles to provoke their emulation. If now their fall hath
been the riches of the world, and their degradation the riches of
13 the Gentiles, how much more their fulness? For I say this
to you Gentiles (inasmuch as I am indeed an apostle of the
14 Gentiles I do honor to my office), | if by any means I may
excite to emulation some of my kinsmen after the flesh, and
15 save some of them. For if the casting away of them be the
reconciliation of the world, what shall the reception of them
16 be but life from the dead. If, moreover, the first fruits were
holy, so shall the mass be; and if the root be holy, so will be
17 the branches. But if some of the branches were broken off,
and thou, being a wild olive, wert engrafted in their stead
and made partaker of the root and fatness of the olive, | glory
18 not over the branches: but if thou dost glory, thou dost not
19 support the root but the root thee. Thou wilt say, then:
'The branches were broken off, that I might be grafted in.'
20 Be it so: they were broken off by unbelief, and thou standest
21 by faith; be not high-minded but fear; for if God spared
not the natural branches, then [fear] lest he should not spare
thee.

22 Behold, then, the kindness and severity of God! Severity
toward those who have fallen away; but kindness toward
thee, provided thou dost abide in his kindness, otherwise even
23 thou shalt be cut off. But even they, unless they continue in
unbelief, shall be grafted in; for God is able again to graft
24 them in. For if thou wert cut out from the olive which was
wild by nature and contrary to thy nature, how much more
shall the natural branches be grafted into their own olive!

25 Moreover, I would not have you ignorant, brethren, of this
mystery (lest ye should be wise in your own conceit), that
blindness has come upon Israel in part, until the fulness of
26 the Gentiles shall come in. And thus all Israel shall be
saved; even as it is written: "A deliverer shall come out
27 of Zion, and shall turn away ungodliness from Jacob;" | also:
"This is my covenant with them, when I shall take away
28 their sins." In respect to the gospel [they have become]
enemies on your account; but in respect to the election [they
29 are] beloved for their father's sake. For the gifts and call-
30 ings of God, he will not repent of. For as ye were formerly
disobedient to God, but have now obtained mercy through
31 their unbelief; so they too have now become disobedient,
that they may obtain mercy through the mercy shown to you.
32 For God | concluded all in unbelief, so that he might have
mercy on all.

33 O the boundless riches both of the wisdom and knowledge
of God! How unsearchable are his counsels, and his ways
34 past finding out! For who hath known the mind of the
35 Lord, or who hath been his counsellor? Or who hath first
36 given him any thing, and it will be repaid? For of him, and
by him, and for him, are all things; to him be the glory for
ever, Amen!

Exhortation to piety, humility, diligent improvement of gifts, kind sympathy and benevolent feeling.

XII. I ENTREAT you, therefore, by the tender mercies of God,
to present your bodies a living sacrifice, holy, acceptable to
2 God which is your rational service. And be not conformed
to this world; but be ye transformed by the renewing of your
mind, that ye may learn what the will of God is, even that
which is good and acceptable and perfect.
3 I say, moreover, by the grace given to me, to every one
among you, that he think not of himself more highly than he
ought to think, but that he think modestly, according to the
4 measure of faith which God hath imparted to him. For as
in one body we have many members, but all the members
5 have not the same office, so we, being many, are one body in
Christ, and are members one of another.
6 Having then gifts which differ according to the grace that
is given us, whether prophecy, [let it be] according to the
7 proportion of faith; | whether ministry, [let there be dili-
8 gence] in ministration; whether teaching, in instruction; | or
exhorting, in exhortation. Let the distributer [do his duty]
with simplicity; the superintendent, with diligence; he who
9 performs offices of compassion, with cheerfulness. Let benevolence be sincere; abhor that which is evil; cleave to
that which is good.
10 As to brotherly love, [be] kindly affectionate one toward
11 another; as to honor, give to each other the preference; | as
to diligence, be not slothful; be fervent in spirit; engaged in
12 the Lord's service; | rejoice in hope; be patient in affliction;
13 persevere in prayer; make the wants of the saints your own;
14 practise hospitality. Bless those who curse you; bless, and
15 curse not. Rejoice with those who rejoice; and weep with
16 those who weep. Think mutually the same thing; do not
regard high things, but suffer yourselves to be influenced by
humble ones. Be not wise in your own conceit.
17 Render to no man evil for evil; seek after that which is
18 good in the sight of all. If it be possible, so far as in you
19 lieth, be at peace with all men. Avenge not yourselves, be-

loved, but defer anger; for it is written: "Retribution is
20 mine, I will render it, saith the Lord." Therefore, "if thine
enemy hunger, feed him; if he thirst, give him drink; for in
21 so doing, thou shalt heap coals of fire upon his head." Be
not overcome by evil, but overcome evil with good.

Exhortation to obey civil rulers, and to exhibit a kind and peaceable demeanor
towards all men.

XIII. LET every soul be subject to the supreme magistracies;
for there is no magistracy except of God; and those which
2 be, are ordained of God. So he that resisteth the magistracy,
resisteth the ordinance of God; and they who resist, shall
3 receive for themselves condemnation. For rulers are not a
terror to good works but to evil ones; and wilt thou not stand
4 in awe of the magistracy? Do good, and thou shalt have
praise for it; for [the magistrate] is a servant of God for thy
benefit. But if thou doest evil, fear; for he beareth the sword
not in vain, since he is the minister of God, avenging unto
5 indignation the evil doer. Therefore we ought to yield subjection, not only because of indignation, but for conscience' sake.
6 On this very account also pay tribute; for they are God's
7 ministers who attend to this matter. Therefore render to all
that which is due; tribute, to whom tribute; custom, to whom
8 custom; fear, to whom fear; honor to whom honor. Owe no
man anything, except to love one another; for he who loveth
9 another fulfilleth the law. For this [is the law]: "Thou
shalt not commit adultery; thou shalt not kill; thou shalt not
steal; thou shalt not covet;" and if there be any other command, it is summarily comprehended in this precept, namely:
10 "Thou shalt love thy neighbor as thyself." Love worketh
no ill to its neighbor; love, then, is the fulfilling of the law.
11 And this [do], since ye know the time, that the hour has
already come when we should awake out of sleep; for now
12 is our salvation nearer than when we believed. The night is
far spent, the day is at hand; let us put away then the works
13 of darkness, and put on the armor of light. Let us walk in
a becoming manner, as in the day; not in revelling and
drunkenness, not in chambering and wantonness, not in strife
14 and bitter envy; | but put ye on the Lord Jesus Christ,
and make no provision for the flesh, in respect to its lusts.

Caution against making external rites and observances matters of division and
contention among Christians.

XIV. HIM that is weak in faith receive with kindness, not in
2 order to judge of his opinions. One believeth that he may

3 eat everything; but he who is weak eateth herbs. Let not him who eateth, despise him who eateth not; nor him who eateth not, condemn him who eateth; for God hath accepted him.
4 Who art thou, that condemnest the servant of another? By his own master he standeth or falleth; and he shall stand, for God is able to make him stand.
5 One man esteemeth one day above another; another esteemeth every day [alike]; let each one be fully persuaded in his
6 own mind. He who regardeth the day, regardeth it for [the honoring of] the Lord; and he who regardeth not the day, for [the honoring of] the Lord he doth not regard it. Likewise he who eateth, eateth for [the honoring of] the Lord, for he giveth God thanks; and he who eateth not for [the honoring of] the Lord he eateth not, and giveth God thanks.
7 For no one of us liveth to himself; and no one of us dieth
8 to himself; for whether we live, we live to the Lord, and whether we die, we die to the Lord; whether we live, then,
9 or die, we are the Lord's. For Christ both died and revived for this very purpose, that he might be Lord of the dead and of the living.
10 But thou, why dost thou condemn thy brother? Even thou, why dost thou despise thy brother? For we must
11 all stand before the judgment-seat of Christ. For it is written, "As I live, saith the Lord, every knee shall bow to
12 me, and every tongue shall confess to God." Every one of us, therefore, must give an account of himself to God.
13 Let us then, no longer judge one another; but rather let us decide not to put a stumbling block or a cause of falling in
14 the way of a brother. I know, and am persuaded of the Lord Jesus, that nothing is unclean of itself; but to him who
15 deemeth anything to be unclean, it is unclean. Now if thy brother is grieved because of meat, thou dost not walk as love requireth; destroy not him by thy meat, for whom Christ
16 died. Let not your good, then, be evil spoken of; for the
17 kingdom of God is not meat and drink, but righteousness and peace and joy in the Holy Ghost.
18 Now he who serveth Christ, as to these things, is accepta-
19 ble to God and approved by men. Therefore let us strive
20 after peace and mutual edification. Destroy not the work of God on account of meat. All [meats] are clean; yet they are hurtful to him, who eateth so as to give offence thereby.
21 It is good not to eat flesh, nor to drink wine, nor [to do any thing] whereby thy brother stumbleth, or hath cause of
22 offence, or is made weak. Hast thou faith, keep it to thyself before God. Happy the man, who doth not condemn himself

23 in that which he alloweth! But he who doubteth, is condemned if he eat, because it is not of faith; and every thing which is not of faith, is sin.

Various exhortations to charity and kindness. Expression of the apostle's regard for the church at Rome, of his intention to visit them, and of his desire for an interest in their prayers.

XV. WE, however, who are strong, ought to bear with the in-
2 firmities of the weak, and not to please ourselves. Let each one of us please his neighbor, in respect to that which is
3 good, unto edification. For Christ did not seek his own pleasure; but [with him it was] according to that which is written: "The reproaches of those who reproached thee,
4 have fallen upon me." For whatsoever things were written in ancient times, were written for our instruction; that through patience and the admonition of the Scriptures, we might obtain hope.
5 Now may the God from whom is patience and admonition, give to you mutual unity of sentiment, according to Christ
6 Jesus, that with one mind and with one voice ye may glorify God, even the Father of our Lord Jesus Christ!
7 Wherefore deal kindly with each other, even as Christ hath dealt kindly with you, unto the glory of God.
8 I say, moreover, that Jesus Christ became the minister of the circumcision, on account of the truth of God, in order to
9 confirm the promises made to the fathers; also, that the Gentiles shall glorify God for his mercy; even as it is written: "Therefore will I celebrate thy praise among the Gentiles,
10 and to thy name will I sing." And again he saith: "Rejoice,
11 ye Gentiles, with his people." And again: "Praise the
12 Lord, all ye Gentiles; and laud him, all ye people." And again Isaiah saith: "There shall be a root of Jesse, and one shall rise to be a leader of the Gentiles; upon him shall the Gentiles place their hopes."
13 Now may the God of hope fill you with all joy and peace in believing, that you may abound in hope, through the influence of the Holy Spirit!
14 Moreover, I am myself well persuaded concerning you, my brethren, that ye are full of kindness, abounding in all know-
15 ledge, and able to admonish one another. But I have written to you in part the more boldly, brethren, as one repeating admonitions, because of the grace which is bestowed by God
16 upon me, | that I should be a minister of Jesus Christ to the Gentiles, performing the office of a priest in respect to the gospel of God, that the offering of the Gentiles might be ac-

17 ceptable, being purified by the Holy Spirit. I have then cause of glorying in Christ Jesus, as to those things which per-
18 tain to God; for I will not venture to mention anything which Christ hath not wrought by me, in order to bring the
19 Gentiles to obedience, by word and by deed, | by the power of signs and wonders, by the power of the Holy Spirit; so that from Jerusalem and round about, even to Illyricum, I
20 have fully proclaimed the gospel of Christ, | and I was strongly desirous so to preach the gospel (not where Christ was named, lest I should build on another man's founda-
21 tion, | but) as it is written: "They shall see to whom no declaration was made respecting him, and they who have not heard shall understand."
22 On this account I have been greatly hindered from coming
23 to you. But now, having no longer any place in these regions, and being desirous for many years of making you a
24 visit; whenever I may go into Spain, I hope, as I pass on, to see you, and to be sent on my way thither, when I am in part
25 first satisfied with your company. But at present I am going
26 to Jerusalem, to supply the wants of the saints. For it hath seemed good to Macedonia and Achaia, to make some contri-
27 bution for the saints in poverty at Jerusalem. [I say] it hath seemed good, for verily they are debtors; because if the Gentiles have shared in their spiritual things, they ought surely
28 to assist them in temporal things. Now when this duty shall have been performed, and this fruit secured to them, I shall
29 pass through the midst of you into Spain. I know, also, that when I come to you, I shall come with abundant blessings of the gospel of Christ.
30 Moreover I beseech you, brethren, by our Lord Jesus Christ and by the love of the Spirit, that ye strive together
31 for me, in your prayers to God in my behalf, | that I may be delivered from the unbelieving in Judea, and that my service
32 for Jerusalem may be acceptable to the saints; [also] that I may come to you with joy (if God will), and may be re-
33 freshed among you. The God of peace be with you all, Amen!

Various salutations. Caution against divisions. Conclusion

XVI. Now I commend to you Phebe our sister, who is a dea-
2 coness of the church of Cenchrea, | that ye may receive her in the Lord in a manner worthy of the saints, and give her assistance in any thing wherein she may need it of you; for she herself hath been a helper of many, and especially of me.

3 Salute Priscilla and Aquila, my fellow-laborers in Christ
4 Jesus | (who exposed themselves to great danger in my behalf; to whom not only I myself am grateful, but even all the churches of the Gentiles); | and the church which is at
5 their house. Salute Epenetus, my beloved, who is the first
6 fruit of Asia in Christ   Salute Mary, who labored much for
7 us. Salute Andronicus and Junias, my kinsmen and fellow-prisoners, who are of note among the apostles, and who were
8 before me in Christ. Salute Amplias my beloved in the
9 Lord. Salute Urbanus, our fellow-laborer in Christ. Salute
10 them of the household of Aristobulus. Salute Herodian, my
11 kinsman. Salute them of the household of Narcissus, who
12 are in the Lord. Salute Tryphene and Tryphosa, who labor in the Lord. Salute Persis the beloved, who labored much
13 in the Lord. Salute Rufus, elect in the Lord, and his mother,
14 and mine. Salute Asyncritus, Phlegon, Hermas, Patrobas,
15 Hermes, and the brethren with them. Salute Philologus and Julias, Nereus and his sister, and Olympas, and all the saints
16 with them. Salute each other with a holy kiss. All the churches of Christ salute you.
17 Moreover I beseech you, brethren, to beware of those who occasion divisions and offences, contrary to the doctrines
18 which ye have learned. For such serve not the Lord Jesus Christ, but their own appetite; and by flattery and fair
19 speeches they beguile the minds of the simple. For your obedience is known to all; I rejoice therefore concerning you, and desire you to be wise in respect to that which is good,
20 but simple in respect to that which is evil. May the God of all peace shortly bruise Satan under your feet! The grace of our Lord Jesus Christ be with you!
21 Timothy my fellow-laborer, and Luke and Jason, and Sosi-
22 pater, my kinsmen, salute you. (I Tertius, who wrote this
23 epistle, salute you in the Lord). Gaius saluteth you, who is my host and that of the whole church. Erastus saluteth you,
24 the chamberlain of the city, and Quartus, a brother. The grace of our Lord Jesus Christ be with you all, Amen!
25 Now unto him who is able to establish you, according to my gospel, even the gospel of Jesus Christ; according to the revelation of the mystery which was kept silent in ancient
26 times, | but is now manifested by the prophetic Scriptures, [and] according to the command of the eternal God made
27 known to all nations for the obedience of faith;—to the only wise God, through Jesus Christ, to whom be glory for ever, Amen!

www.ingramcontent.com/pod-product-compliance
Lightning Source LLC
Chambersburg PA
CBHW071218290426
44108CB00013B/1218